ACADEMIC WRITING, REAL WORLD TOPICS

ACADEMIC WRITING, REAL WORLD TOPICS

Michael Rectenwald and Lisa Carl

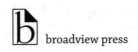

broadview press

LIBRARY AND ARCHIVES CANADA CATALOGUING IN PUBLICATION

Rectenwald, Michael, author
    Academic writing, real world topics / Michael Rectenwald and Lisa Carl.

Includes bibliographical references and index.
ISBN 978-1-55481-246-2 (pbk.)

    1. Academic writing—Handbooks, manuals, etc. I. Carl, Lisa, author II. Title.

LB2369.R43 2015   808.02   C2015-901889-7

BROADVIEW PRESS is an independent, international publishing house, incorporated in 1985. Broadview believes in shared ownership, both with its employees and with the general public; since the year 2000 Broadview shares have traded publicly on the Toronto Venture Exchange under the symbol BDP.

We welcome comments and suggestions regarding any aspect of our publications—please feel free to contact us at the addresses below or at broadview@broadviewpress.com.

NORTH AMERICA
Post Office Box 1243
Peterborough, Ontario
Canada K9J 7H5

555 Riverwalk Parkway
Tonawanda, NY 14150, USA
tel: (705) 743–8990
fax: (705) 743–8353

customerservice@broadviewpress.com

UK, EUROPE, CENTRAL ASIA, MIDDLE EAST, AFRICA, INDIA, AND SOUTHEAST ASIA
Eurospan Group, 3 Henrietta St., London WC2E 8LU, United Kingdom
TEL: 44 (0) 1767 604972 FAX: 44 (0) 1767 601640
eurospan@turpin-distribution.com

AUSTRALIA & NEW ZEALAND
Footprint Books
1/6a Prosperity Parade
Warriewood, NSW 2102, Australia
tel: 61 1300 260090
fax: 61 02 9997 3185
info@footprint.com.au

www.broadviewpress.com

Broadview Press acknowledges the financial support of the Government of Canada through the Canada Book Fund for our publishing activities.

Edited by Martin R. Boyne
Cover design and interior by Em Dash Design

Printed in Canada

CONTENTS

PART I

ACADEMIC WRITING: A GUIDE

PART II

REAL WORLD TOPICS

A PREFACE FOR INSTRUCTORS

Like many textbooks perhaps, this one began in frustration. As members of a committee charged with developing across-the-curriculum writing instruction, we eventually began a search for textbooks. We wanted to introduce first-year writers to instructions and examples based on a broad range of academic and scholarly writing. We also wanted to present academic writing as relevant, exciting, and important. The most likely candidates, we assumed, would be writing across the curriculum (WAC) and writing in the disciplines (WID) textbooks.

We soon found that the books in these categories consisted of lengthy instruction in academic research and writing, along with collections of readings culled almost exclusively from mainstream newspapers and magazines, trade publications, and general-audience nonfiction books. In other words, the existing WAC and WID books contained little if any actual academic writing. Further, most of the topics seemed shop-worn (especially for instructors), and many of the essays seemed dated; none seemed to adequately represent what we took to be the most exciting and important issues of our time. Meanwhile, those few non-WAC/WID textbooks that did represent scholarly prose were confined to the humanities and social sciences. Science and technology fields were virtually absent. And such textbooks were lopsided in more than disciplinary ways: few seemed to explore the incredible diversity of perspectives that we regularly encountered in the academy.

Our students were compelled to take first-year writing—a course supposedly designed to prepare them for writing in future courses, regardless of their chosen major. They thus needed access to a wide array of writing drawn from the entire disciplinary spectrum. They also required immediate access to the different ways of thinking available to them as members of the academic community. But we held another requirement for a book: writers, we knew from experience, are far more likely to be engaged when they are asked to participate in lively conversations about contemporary and complex topics. Nothing stifles writing and discussion more than the sense of working in isolation, or writing about largely settled, dead-end issues. We wanted a text that collected essays clustered around timely, compelling, and intriguing topics.

Having no luck finding such a book, we decided to write it ourselves.

ACADEMIC WRITING, REAL WORLD TOPICS

We endeavored to create a book that provided completely up-to-date rhetorical instruction in conversation with cutting-edge readings divided into several chapters, each chapter focusing on a topic area relevant to student writers both inside and outside the academy. *Academic Writing, Real World Topics* features contemporary readings on major issues of real import to contemporary students: living in a digital culture, learning from games, learning in a digital age, living in a global culture, our post-human future, surviving economic crisis and prospects for the future, and assessing armed global conflict. Students will see how contemporary writers like themselves respond to issues relevant to their lives while maintaining scholarly rigor and incorporating the ideas of others, past and present.

Guide to Academic Writing

Part I of *Academic Writing, Real World Topics* is a Guide to academic writing. This part of the book covers rhetorical strategies and approaches to academic writing within and across the major divisions of the academy: the humanities, the social sciences, and the sciences and technology fields.

Rhetoric that Speaks to Content

In keeping with our belief—based on research and experience—that instruction should be treated in the contexts of reading and writing, we employ extensive cross-referencing between the rhetoric and the reader. For each writing strategy or essay element that we explain in the rhetoric, we provide examples from essays in the reader, or from one of many resources included in each chapter's Suggested Additional Resources. For example, the section on essay conclusions gives three examples of conclusions, each taken from the Real World Topics section and written by a scholar in each of the discipline areas (humanities, social sciences, and physical sciences). Page numbers after each example allow readers to flip to the full essay. The Real World Topics section also refers to the Guide to academic writing in chapter introductions, essay questions, and questions for synthesis and contribution. Rhetorical modes and examples are indexed in the back of the book for quick cross-reference.

Thus, the rhetoric shows student writers how to employ scholarly *writing practices as demonstrated by the readings*, while the readings invite students to engage with scholarly *content in connection with the rhetoric*.

Interdisciplinary Connections

Accompanying its focus on disciplinary distinctions is another important guiding rationale for this book: the making of interdisciplinary connections. Many WAC textbooks (and surely most WID textbooks) divide their readings into disciplinary or broader academic categories. Such an arrangement recommends an insularity that defeats one of the principles guiding writing in and across the disciplines: that the various approaches to knowledge and the world are interconnected and that disciplines as seemingly disparate as biology and history share many features. Furthermore, such disciplines often speak to each other in their writings on the same or closely related topics.

Disciplinary Distinctions

Academic Writing, Real World Topics aims to reveal these connections and shared features, but it also clarifies disciplinary distinctions. In fact, when different disciplinary approaches are juxtaposed, their distinctive features become more apparent. Throughout this book, we highlight the distinguishing features of writing in the various areas of the academy, demonstrating through examples and instruction the crucial role that the writing context and the composition of the reading audience plays in the composition of academic prose.

Focus on Scholarly Writing

Academic Writing, Real World Topics focuses primarily on academic, scholarly writing. It includes timely, often introductory, yet scholarly essays that speak to one another within and across disciplinary boundaries. Most of the essays address topics with scholarly rigor, sourcing, and disciplinary/interdisciplinary commitment. However, in order to demonstrate the distinctions between academic and other writing, we have included a few essays written by academics for general audiences or in trade magazines, as well as the writing of non-academics originally published in mainstream or specialized venues. These inclusions are designed to help students move from more general discourse toward academic reading, research, and writing.

Full-Length Essays

With a few exceptions, *Academic Writing, Real World Topics* uses essays or chapters in their entirety. Full-length essays allow students to see how all the parts of a piece of writing work together. Essay lengths vary from two to twenty-five pages.

Chapter Introductions Put Readings in Context

Each chapter is preceded by an introduction of eight to fifteen pages, which contextualizes the readings as part of broad discourses. The introductions are general and synoptic rather than exhaustive and synthetic. That is, we aim at orienting students to the topics, rather than doing the work of interpretation, summary, synthesis, and contribution for them.

Chapter introductions to this book's topics may be introducing the intricacies of an issue to both students *and* teacher. Armed with these introductions and guiding questions, instructors can confidently apply their own expertise in writing to salient issues in a variety of academic fields.

Instruction in Digital Media Literacy

As teachers of such courses as "writing for digital media," "multi-modal authorship," "writing for television and film," and "writing and the network," we insisted on a book that responds adequately to the explosion of digital media both inside and outside the academy. Two chapters of the reader are devoted to aspects of the digital media—its impact on the world at large and its impact on education.

We also address digital media literacy in the Guide to academic writing. Rather than attempting to suppress or ignore social media and other Web 2.0 technologies as many other writing textbooks are doing, instructional apparatuses throughout the reader call for the use of these technologies as tools for research, communications, interpretation, and composition.

Writing Instruction Designed for the Spectrum of Students

First-year writing is compulsory at virtually every university and college in the United States. Students come to the course often not entirely enthusiastically, but with a common need: to prepare themselves for writing in future courses in every discipline. They need—and instructors need to provide—access to a wide array of writing drawn from the entire disciplinary spectrum. In addition, students and their instructors require immediate access to the variety of ways of thinking available to them as members of the academic community.

This book provides students with that access, and instructors with that resource. Designed for the spectrum of student writers, from reluctant to gung-ho, from the well prepared to the less prepared, it demystifies as much as possible the reading and writing processes of academic writers.

Classroom Success

We have classroom-tested the Guide to academic writing, as well as all of the chapters in Real World Topics, and have found that each works extremely well to encourage and foster student discussion and writing.

Other Features of This Text

- **Combined author/subject headnotes before each reading.** Each reading is prefaced with a short, one- to two-page introduction, including a short biography of the author.
- **Sample student essays.** Students often ask us for samples of how a "real student" would write an assigned essay. In order to help allay student anxieties about how they, as non-experts, could approach a topic, we provide several essays written by college students, which respond to prompts we suggest at the end of each chapter. These annotated essays are one example of how *Academic Writing, Real World Topics* links rhetorical instruction to content.
- **Annotated readings.** We include fully annotated academic essays throughout. Annotations point to various features of the text, important passages, rhetorical moves, cues for careful reading, and notes on possible interpretations.
- **"As You Read" guides to each chapter and reading.** Chapter introductions and author/subject headnotes end with a guide to orient students to the readings. These guides help focus student attention on particular issues in the texts. They also provide handy class discussion-starters for instructors. "As You Read" guides to the chapter introductions encourage readers to locate connections or points of contact among readings, while "As You Read" guides to the essays encourage students to connect readings to their own experience.
- **"What It Says" questions after each reading.** Each essay is followed by at least four reading comprehension questions, which may be used for out-of-class reflection or writing, or for in-class discussion or writing.
- **"How It Says It" questions after each reading.** Each essay is also followed by at least three prompts designed to help students identify, understand, and practice the rhetorical moves employed by the authors. Instructors may use these prompts for classroom discussion or as preliminary writing assignments to move readers beyond content comprehension and toward planning discipline-specific and/or interdisciplinary writing about a given topic.

- **"Write about It" questions after each reading.** Each essay is followed by at least two "Write about It" questions that prompt students to grapple with and offer inventive, sustained responses to the arguments presented.
- **Writing prompts that facilitate synthesis and contribution at the end of each chapter.** Each chapter ends with at least four questions and suggestions for writing. The prompts point to and encourage the characteristic moves made by writers as they converse with others and construct their own arguments. The "**Questions for Synthesis**" are designed to move students toward the synthesis and analysis of texts and topics. Then, based on thoughtful analysis of a group of sources, the "**Questions for Contribution**" are designed to guide students into making their own contributions to the topic area, often in more formal essays that draw on further research.
- **"Suggested Additional Resources" bibliography at the end of each chapter introduction.** In order to facilitate additional research into the topics treated, we also include a Suggested Additional Resources list at the end of each chapter introduction. This material, which includes articles, books, blog posts, websites, films, and short videos, is essential for demonstrating that the essays we include are introductory and that the essays in each chapter merely open up a vast and varied area of inquiry.
- **Index and Glossary.** At the end of the book we include a subject/name index, as well as a glossary containing definitions of key terms used in the humanities, social sciences, and physical sciences and technology fields. The glossary also includes brief definitions of the disciplines and some of the approaches they take.

CONTACT US

We hope your experience teaching with *Academic Writing, Real World Topics* is as rewarding for you and your students as it has been for us and ours. We welcome your comments, questions, critiques, suggestions, and stories of classroom experiences related to this book. Please write to: AcademicWritingRealWorldTopics@gmail.com.

PART I

ACADEMIC WRITING: A GUIDE

INTRODUCTION

The Basics

As a first-year college student, you may or may not have declared a major. But you *have* decided to enter academia for at least two years. You will be asked to read, interpret, summarize, and contribute to academic **discourses**. This guide will introduce you to the **rhetorical strategies** (the strategies you use to get your point across and persuade your audience) common to all academic disciplines, as well as to those specific to each of the major divisions in the academy:

- the humanities,
- the social sciences, and
- science and technology.

Two ideas to keep in mind:

- **Each discipline has its own conventions.** Each major academic grouping has its own writing conventions: styles, methods, and approaches. Sometimes these conventions are specific to broad academic areas; sometimes they are discipline-specific.

BUT ...

- **Good writing is good writing.** You can apply most of what you learn here to everything you write, in any field. Writers in every field use similar means to organize material, address the reader, consider the texts of others, and cite sources.

23

This book gets you started with academic writing. But the skills you learn here you can use throughout life:

- **In undergraduate courses**, to write psychology research papers, science lab reports, literary analyses, and history papers, for example.
- **In job applications**, for application letters and résumés.
- **On the job**, for grant proposals, reports, memos, directions for employees, a new business plan, or a justification for a salary increase.
- **Off the job**, for writing e-mails, texts, and tweets to friends, blogs, letters to the editor, or contemplations on life.
- **In graduate courses** in any field, if you choose to continue.

Formal Writing—What's That?

The writing maneuvers described below represent conscious choices that writers make every time they write formal academic or scholarly papers. The word "formal" brings up images of stiff, haughty people trying to impress each other with obscure words and hard-to-follow arguments. That is not what we mean.

A "formal" paper:

- **acknowledges what others have written** on the subject already, and gives it serious consideration;
- **is written clearly**, allowing others to understand and respond;
- **follows a structure or set of conventions** that scholars within each discipline follow. For example, before submitting it for a grade, for review, or for publication, writers of formal papers usually
  - annotate and summarize relevant texts,
  - synthesize the views of others,
  - carefully plan their approach to the topic, and
  - draft, revise, and edit their work.

"Formal writing," therefore, is not an academic exercise completed just to fulfill an assignment. It's writing that effectively and persuasively enters an important conversation in order to make a significant contribution.

REAL WORLD TOPICS

Part II of this book, Real World Topics, is a compilation of real academic writing. In Part II, you will see how real writers put the strategies you learned about in Part I into action.

The Readings

Reading is one of the best ways to learn how to write; theoretical discussions are less helpful without the context of real-world writing. So as you read this guide, you will be pointed to specific examples from Part II, as well as to pieces of academic writing published elsewhere. We hope the examples will help you understand how a particular writing maneuver operates in real academic writing.

The writing we draw from for Real World Topics includes the kind of writing we imagine you practicing—writing that engages complex, controversial, and exciting topics. Our aim is to introduce you to a variety of academic writing—in the context of lively and relevant conversations, rather than dull, dead areas of research. The articles in this book are written by scholars discussing critical issues that affect, inform, or interest academics and other scholars, as well as the world at large. The readings draw on various disciplines and represent the major groupings of the university: the arts, humanities, social sciences (including economics and business), physical sciences, and technology. These essays are meant to introduce you not only to academic writing, but also to scholarly thought itself.

We hope the readings found here will serve as invitations to their respective fields and to the world of thought and action that they represent. We also hope that the topics we introduce—living in a digital culture, learning from games, learning in a digital age, living in a global culture, our post-human future, surviving economic crisis and the future, and assessing armed global conflict—will interest you as a citizen of the world, now and beyond your academic career.

The topics we have included are designed to provoke spirited responses. Initially, you will read to familiarize yourself with the topics at hand. But we hope you will soon be drawn into the conversation. Ultimately, you will read the articles with a view to writing essays of your own: you will be reading as a writer.

Reading as a Writer

What does it mean to read as a writer? It means that you are reading not only to consume the texts of others, but also to respond to them. It also means that even as you read carefully to understand *what* the writer is saying, you will simultaneously read to understand *how* the writer is saying it and *why* he or she is putting it that way.

After each of the readings in Part II,

- The first set of prompts for discussion and writing ask you to consider **"What It Says"**—the content of an argument.
- The second set of prompts asks you to consider **"How It Says It"**—the kinds of maneuvers the writers use to make their cases.

We often need to see how an argument is constructed in order to understand it. But knowing how something is put together is especially important when you are setting out to put a similar thing together yourself. Thus, when you read, **look for the writer's characteristic maneuvers**. This may take two readings or more to figure out, particularly when a text is dense. But you will find that you get better at identifying the parts of an essay—and the moves made by writers within those parts—as you practice reading and interpreting them, especially when you practice constructing arguments in response to those you've read.

- The third section of prompts gets you started with this task, asking you to **"Write about It"**—to incorporate your own ideas and to respond thoughtfully and creatively to the discussion. The questions for synthesis and contribution at the end of each chapter help you to put the texts into conversation with each other and to contribute to a conversation yourself.

Digital and Visual Literacy

Whether or not you are a **digital native** (see Chapters 1 and 3 in Part II), you are living in a world saturated with digital media. In fact, if you are anything like the authors of this book, **Web 2.0** technologies may very well account for a good deal of your leisure activities. The digital world has profoundly altered the ways in which all of us receive and read "texts." In this book, we use the word "texts" broadly—to refer to messages that may include words, still images, moving images, music, sound effects, visual effects, and other graphics. All of these elements, we believe, require both skills to compose and skills to interpret.

Yet in most secondary educational environments and in much of higher education as well, digital and visual literacy, or the kind of "reading" required in the digital world, is often ignored, or even denigrated as lacking legitimacy or worth. In the United States in particular, where standardized testing prevails in primary and secondary education, digital and visual literacy is even more prone to being

ANNOTATING A TEXT

In general, highlighter pens are of limited use. Your brain often doesn't process the information, so you'll have to come back to it later and put it into your own words to make sure you've got a handle on it.

A more effective method is to **annotate** or **gloss** a text. See the annotated article on pages 121–41 for an example. Annotating or glossing can take several forms, all of which you can use on one article:

- Note important terms and central ideas.
- Note the **topic**, **thesis**, and **evidence**. See the sections below for discussions of these terms. Again, it will be more effective to rewrite these parts of the text in your own words rather than merely underlining or highlighting them.
- Ask questions about the text. There may be something you don't understand that you'll need to look up in another source or read further to clarify.
- Note how one idea connects, or might connect, to another text or another idea in the same text. Linking what you already know to new information is the best way to learn and remember the new information. Once a concept is clear in your own head, you'll find it much easier to respond to.
- Make a short note in the margin that summarizes quotations that are striking or interesting. You might want to come back and quote or paraphrase these when you begin writing your own essay.
- List your own responses to the text as you read. Especially if the article is long and complex, you might have a hard time remembering your responses once you go to write your own essay. Including your responses to the text in the margins will help you to keep track of your own reactions to the reading.
- Once you've read the essay, write a short note of your impressions of it. Compare the article to others you've read. Note ideas you still don't understand. Note possible "holes" in the argument, or interesting ways you could expand upon or rebut the argument.

overlooked. Many students receive little or no training in the skills of analyzing or re-evaluating digital texts.

In this book, we hope to partially redress this situation by

1. valuing digital communications;
2. including readings that deal with the importance of digital communications in the world and in education;
3. asking you to communicate using Web 2.0 technologies;
4. asking you to interpret digital media as part of reading and responding to the compositions of others.

We hope that the value and importance we place on digital media not only will make you feel more comfortable as you enter into academic discourse, but also, and more importantly, will aid you in its composition and interpretation.

ACADEMIC WRITING: CONTRIBUTING TO A CONVERSATION

Imagine walking into a dorm or living room full of people engaged in a lively debate. You catch bits of the discussion. Something about the conversation engages you, but you're not exactly sure what the topic is or what others have said. Now imagine that instead of listening for a while and getting a summary from one or more of the discussants, you jump right in and offer your position on the matter. The others stop the discussion just long enough to stare at you, confused.

Why? Perhaps your point has already been offered and has been refuted and dismissed. Perhaps what you've offered is not exactly on point. Or worse, you may have no idea what the conversation is about and have just said something entirely irrelevant.

While academic discourses are generally written, they are ongoing conversations between people. In fact, in many ways, they resemble conversations you may have through e-mail, on Facebook, instant messaging, Tumblr, or some other blog: participants write in response to others and in anticipation of future responses. Many academic writers have gotten to know what others think about a topic by reading their writing. Others, often students, are new to the conversation and simply have to catch up to get involved.

Every time you approach a discourse that is new to you, that's the position you're in—you need to catch up. In academic conversations, this is done mostly through reading, but it also takes place in conferences or other face-to-face meetings among scholars.

The point is, **academics do not write in a vacuum**. They are contributing to ongoing discussions.

Read the examples below, by authors who

1. recognize that they are contributing to an ongoing conversation, and
2. make clear what they intend to contribute.

Contributing to an Academic Conversation

Humanities: Philosophy

In the passage below, Francis Fukuyama acknowledges a movement known as transhumanism and the aims and claims of this movement. Entering the conversation, he signals his disapproval by using the phrase "a strange liberation movement."

Soon after the passage quoted below, he refers to transhumanists as "some sort of odd cult," but he soon tells the reader why they should be taken seriously.

> For the last several decades, a strange liberation movement has grown within the developed world. Its crusaders aim much higher than civil rights campaigners, feminists, or gay-rights advocates. They want nothing less than to liberate the human race from its biological constraints. As "transhumanists" see it, humans must wrest their biological destiny from evolution's blind process of random variation and adaptation and move to the next stage as a species.
> Source: Francis Fukuyama, "Transhumanism" (see Chapter 5, pp. 447–49).

Social Sciences: Political Science

In the passage below, Eva Kassens-Noor introduces her study on the use of Twitter in higher education by noting the importance that other scholars have placed on such Web 2.0 applications. She makes clear the premium that students place on such technologies, and their growing importance for the workplace, and notes educators in higher education who have taken up the challenge of both using and studying Web 2.0 technologies. She then briefly mentions the findings of several studies on Twitter in order to mark out the territory for her own contribution.

> Hannay and Fretwell (2011) predict that Web 2.0 applications will soon be taken up by universities and suggest these technologies will have implications for the academic workplace; students will demand that faculty members communicate digitally, via instant messaging, Twitter and other technologies. Similarly, companies will expect their recruits, our graduates, to be versed in social media technologies (Wankel, 2009). It is unsurprising, then, that we, as educators, are being encouraged to use Twitter to enable interactivity, excite learners, and foster greater student participation.
>
> Responding to this challenge, educators in higher education have started to experiment with Twitter in the hope students seize the opportunity to interact more frequently, engage more thoughtfully, and foster learning inside and beyond the classroom (Grosseck and Holotescu, 2008; Junco et al., 2011; Perez, 2009; Schroeder et al., 2010). Establishing five social media literacies, namely attention, participation, collaboration, network awareness, and critical consumption, Rheingold (2010) emphasizes the need for Twitter to be a valuable communication tool, in contrast to Twitter's potential pitfall of being a mere distraction (Wankel, 2009). Ultimately, Twitter can be a powerful collaboration tool (Corbeil and Corbeil, 2011; Rheingold, 2010). Summarizing, Reuben (2008) emphasizes the tremendous potential Twitter could play in education, but acknowledges that no one has found the right niche just yet.
> Source: Eva Kassens-Noor, "Twitter as a Teaching Practice to Enhance Active and Informal Learning in Higher Education: The Case of Sustainable Tweets" (see Chapter 3, pp. 291–308).

Physical Sciences: Climatology

In response to Mark Z. Jacobson and Mark A. Delucchi's article "A Path to Sustainable Energy by 2030," included in the companion website devoted to sustaining our global environment (http://sites.broadviewpress.com/realworldtopics), Tom Moriarty, a senior scientist at the US Department of Energy's National Renewable Energy Laboratory, wrote the following in his blog, *Climate Sanity*:

> The cover story of the November issue of *Scientific American*, "A Path to Sustainable Energy by 2030," by Mark Z. Jacobson and Mark A. Delucchi, promises a path to a "sustainable future" for the whole world in just 20 years. They define "sustainable" as a world where all energy sources are derived from water, wind and solar. Nuclear need not apply. The article had a few words about the cost, but much was left out. Jacobson and Delucchi conclude that their grand plan will cost about $100 trillion. I found this ridiculously large sum to be too low. My rough calculations yield a cost of $200 trillion. This post is an attempt to fill in a few blanks.
> Source: T. Moriarty, "*Scientific American*'s 'A Path to Sustainable Energy by 2030': The Cost"
> (see http://sites.broadviewpress.com/realworldtopics, Suggested Additional Resources).

Research: Finding Reliable Sources

Thanks to the explosion of information technologies over the past few decades, chances are you will be able to do a good deal of textual research without even leaving your chair: on the Internet. Your challenge on the Internet will be to cull reliable from unreliable sources. Luckily, many articles and books are now available electronically, making your job much easier. In addition, many databases are probably available in electronic form at the library website at your college or university.

The following are some useful databases:

- ERIC: journals, magazines, other periodicals
- JSTOR: journals, magazines, other periodicals
- MLA Bibliography: journals, magazines, other periodicals
- ProQuest: journals, magazines, other periodicals
- Questia: electronic texts (requires an individual subscription at a monthly fee; available in some libraries)
- WorldCat: comprehensive database of published works
- Google Scholar: published books and peer-reviewed journal articles.

The goal of online database research is to produce sufficient resources to give you an overview of your topic area, but not so numerous that you have to wade through thousands of articles only tangentially related to your topic.

Further research sources include:

- your school's library, for books and journals that are not yet digitized;
- empirical observations made in a lab through studies or experiments; and
- interviews you've conducted with experts in the field or with others who can provide you with evidence or testimonials related to your topic.

Once you have pulled together published research, plus whatever experiments or surveys you have conducted yourself, you are ready to carefully read, annotate, summarize, and synthesize your information. More on that later.

First, here's an overview of how to organize, respond to, and document your research material, based on the academic discipline in which you're conducting research. A few basics:

- **Research needs, methods, and formats vary** by type of writing project, division of the academy, and discipline.
- **Research is also documented differently**, depending on the discipline for which the research is conducted.
  - The **physical sciences**, and to a somewhat lesser degree the social sciences, tend to rely on new experiments or studies that produce data. In the physical sciences, researchers explain the parameters of their study (known as the **research protocol**) and describe their research process in a "Methods and Materials" section of their reports, as discussed on page 87.
  - **Humanities** scholars analyze creative work or respond to the theories and analyses of other humanities scholars with a new theory or analysis.
  - **Social scientists** might analyze data collected by other social scientists and provide an alternative conclusion, or they might conduct their own studies, involving fieldwork and/or synthesizing and analyzing written records.

Research Methods

Humanities: Literary Theory

In the passage below, N. Katherine Hayles reveals a process common to research and writing in the humanities: reading and analyzing the research and opinions of others on the subject at hand.

In her discussion of the Turing test, invented by computer scientist Alan Turing to determine whether computers can think, Hayles graciously introduces Andrew Hodges's biography of Turing. She notes Hodges's characterization of Turing as a nerdy computer scientist, out of touch with "sex, society, politics." Later in her essay, Hayles will express her disagreement with Hodges's interpretation of the Turing test.

In his thoughtful and perceptive intellectual biography of Turing, Andrew Hodges suggests that Turing's predilection was always to deal with the world as if it were a formal puzzle. To a remarkable extent, Hodges says, Turing was blind to the distinction between saying and doing. Turing fundamentally did not understand that "questions involving sex, society, politics or secrets would demonstrate how what it was possible for people to say might be limited not by puzzle-solving intelligence but by the restrictions on what might be done" (pp. 423-24). In a fine insight, Hodges suggests that "the discrete state machine, communicating by teleprinter alone, was like an ideal for [Turing's] own life, in which he would be left alone in a room of his own, to deal with the outside world solely by rational argument. It was the embodiment of a perfect J.S. Mill liberal, concentrating upon the free will and free speech of the individual" (p. 425).

Source: N. Katherine Hayles, "Prologue," *How We Became Posthuman: Virtual Bodies in Cybernetics, Literature, and Informatics* (see Chapter 5, pp. 496–500).

FOCUS

CONDUCTING ONLINE RESEARCH

To use databases most effectively, it helps to have in mind a specific area of inquiry or a question you hope to solve within your topic. With this idea in mind, you can type a search phrase or keywords into the search box in your database. Listed below are some steps for getting started researching your topic.

- Start with the most specific phrase you can think of.
- Limit your search to peer-reviewed journals published within the last few years. This will give you a quick idea of what the current conversations are on your topic.
- One example: type "21st century US hate crime law" in your search box, and limit your search to full-text articles in peer-reviewed journals published between January 2014 and December 2015.

- Did this search produce a reasonably long list of articles? If so, scroll through the titles and click on the ones that look most relevant.
- Read the abstract for each article. This short synopsis will tell you whether the article is relevant to your research.
- Did your search terms yield no or very few results? You'll need to broaden your search. For example, this time you might try "US hate crime law." Don't give up: You might have to come up with several search phrases before you have a workable list of articles.

Social Sciences: Economics

Social-science research may be based on personal observation or on a synthesis of previous claims and studies. To make a reasonable claim, social scientists must have a large sample of subjects on which they base their conclusions or claims. This sample may be the result of either a field study or a synthesis of the previous research, resulting in a new claim.

In the passage below, economist Anne Sibert introduces research regarding gender attitudes toward risk in order to support her argument that the financial crisis of 2008 was partly due to testosterone-driven, risky behavior in a male-dominated banking culture.

> There is a substantial economics literature on the effect of gender on attitudes toward risk and most of it appears to support the idea that men are less risk averse than women in their financial decision making. There is also a sizable literature documenting that men tend to be more overconfident than women. Barber and Odean (2001) find that men are substantially more overconfident than women in financial markets. In general, overconfidence is not found to be related to ability (see Lundeberg et al (1994)) and that success is more likely to increase overconfidence in men than in women (see, for example, Beyer (1990)). Thus, if confidence helps produce successful outcomes, there is more likely to be a strong feedback loop in confidence in men than in women.
> Source: Anne Sibert, "Why Did the Bankers Behave So Badly?" (see Chapter 6, pp. 522–26).

Physical Sciences: Neurology and Psychiatry

In the following excerpt, psychiatrist Gary Smith and writer Mimi Vorgan introduce the method of their study, which aims to show that digital technology changes the neural patterns of the brains in those who use them. They began by finding "naïve" subjects, or people who have rarely if ever used a computer, and a control group of computer-savvy subjects in the same age range. They go on to tell how they used magnetic resonance imaging (MRI) to detect brain activities while the two groups read documents and gazed at static pictures, as compared with searching the Internet. The establishment of a control situation (reading and looking at still photos) allowed them to detect initial differences in brain activity between the naïve and savvy computer users while the users searched the Internet. Subsequent Internet use by the formerly naïve subjects demonstrates, they argue, that repeated digital technology use rapidly alters brain patterns. Note that the article, published in *Scientific American Mind*, is written for a general, scholarly readership.

One of us (Small) enlisted the help of Susan Bookheimer and Teena Moody, U.C.L.A. experts in neuropsychology and neuroimaging. We planned to use functional magnetic resonance imaging to measure the brain's activity during a common Internet computer task: searching Google for accurate information. We first needed to find people who were relatively inexperienced and naive to the computer.

After initial difficulty finding people who had not yet used PCs, we were able to recruit three volunteers in their mid-50s and 60s who were new to the technology yet willing to give it a try. To compare the brain activity of these three naive volunteers, we also recruited three computer-savvy volunteers of comparable age, gender and socioeconomic background. For our experiment, we chose searching on Google for specific and accurate information on a variety of topics, ranging from the health benefits of eating chocolate to planning a trip to the Galápagos.

Next, we had to figure out a way to perform MRIs on the volunteers while they used the Internet. Because the study subjects had to be inside a long, narrow tube of an MRI machine during the experiment, there would be no space for a computer, keyboard or mouse. To re-create the Google-search experience inside the scanner, we had the volunteers wear a pair of special goggles that presented images of website pages. The system allowed the volunteers to navigate the simulated computer screen and make choices to advance their search by pressing one finger on a small keypad, conveniently placed.

Source: Gary Small and Gigi Vorgan, "Meet Your iBrain: How Technology Changes the Way We Think" (see Chapter 1, pp. 143–49).

Here's Where You Come In: Entering the Conversation

Let's say you've done your homework. You've

- read a good deal about your topic;
- read and annotated a number of sources; and
- studied the arguments others have made in the area.

It's time to make a move. It's time to enter the conversation.

You have most likely been writing papers this way for some time, and perhaps have become unconscious of your process. But an essay intended for scholars in a field requires more conscious decisions at each step because its subject matter will be relatively complex.

Before you even start to write, you will make numerous decisions about your paper's purpose, topic, and thesis or argument, even if you do so without recognizing it. You have probably noticed that often you discover what you're trying to say *as* you write, not *before* you write. That's the frustration and the joy of writing: it is a **heuristic** process, an open-ended method of learning with no hard-and-fast formulae, no steps or process guaranteed to produce brilliance. But thoughtful consideration of your purpose, topic, and thesis will help focus your initial draft.

WRITING WITH A PURPOSE

Academic discourse attempts to create some kind of change in the reader, and sometimes even in the field itself. Despite its often stodgy or ivory-tower connotations, academic writing frequently proposes changes in the world at large.

Your purpose as an academic writer is to add something to the conversation that

- changes the reader's mind about an issue;
- teaches the reader something; or
- allows the reader to see an issue from another perspective.

As we've said, to do so you will first need to have a good grasp on what other participants in the conversation have already said. But if all you have done is rehash old arguments, your writing is a series of summaries; it has no purpose as a **contribution**.

Once you have decided on your purpose, you must decide how to get that purpose across. That's where rhetorical strategies come in. And the strategies you use depend on

- your topic;
- your thesis;
- your audience;
- the nature of your evidence; and
- other considerations.

The Topic

The word "topic" is derived from the Greek word *topos* (pl. *topoi*), which means "place." Thus a topic can be thought of as an *area* of discussion.

Your topic is the general subject area of your paper—what your paper is *about*.

A topic differs from an argument in two important ways:

- knowledgeable people may take any number of positions within a topic or area;

- it's *objective*: it is not a stance, but rather a subject upon which your argument and the arguments of others will focus.

In other words, when you decide on a topic, you have yet to take a side; you have simply announced the subject area you will address.

Issues

<table>
<tr>
<td>

PRACTICE SESSION

Think of an eating choice that will have such an impact on others that it becomes an issue. Explain why this topic is an issue.

</td>
<td>

A topic that is fraught with controversy is often called an **issue**. The issue might be the depiction of violence against women in horror films, sustainable energy, or the proper interpretation of a poem. In any case, something is at stake, and people or organizations have something to gain or lose in the resolution of the controversy.

While **all issues are topics, not all topics are issues**. One's preference for Brussels sprouts over cauliflower may be a topic of conversation, but it is generally not an

</td>
</tr>
</table>

issue. But eating choices can become issues when they impact the lives of others. For example, vegans believe that eating animal products is unethical.

Expressions of Purpose and Topic

HUMANITIES: INTERDISCIPLINARY STUDIES

In the excerpt below, Cathy N. Davidson, Distinguished Professor and director of The Futures Initiative at The City University of New York, signals that her topic is a new kind of multitasking that distributes tasks among the several members of a group. Such multitasking, she asserts, "is the ideal mode of the 21st century." She further makes clear that her purpose is to critique and propose changes to "current practices of our educational institutions" based on their mismatch with the digital, hyperconnected age in which we live.

> I want to suggest a different way of seeing, one that's based on multitasking our attention—not by seeing it all alone but by distributing various parts of the task among others dedicated to the same end. For most of us, this is a new pattern of attention. Multitasking is the ideal mode of the 21st century, not just because of information overload but also because our digital age was structured without anything like a central node broadcasting one stream of information that we pay attention to at a given moment. On the Internet, everything links to everything, and all of it is available all the time.
>
> Unfortunately, current practices of our educational institutions— and workplaces—are a mismatch between the age we live in and

the institutions we have built over the last 100-plus years. The 20th century taught us that completing one task before starting another one was the route to success. Everything about 20th-century education, like the 20th-century workplace, has been designed to reinforce our attention to regular, systematic tasks that we take to completion. Attention to task is at the heart of industrial labor management, from the assembly line to the modern office, and of educational philosophy, from grade school to graduate school.

Source: Cathy N. Davidson, "Collaborative Learning for the Digital Age" (see Chapter 3, pp. 282–90).

SOCIAL SCIENCES: POLITICAL SCIENCE

In the passage below, political scientists John F. Freie and Susan M. Behuniak introduce their topic, participatory education in a digital age. They make clear that their purpose is to test the claims made by educators for the liberatory potential of information and communication technologies (ICTs) against Paulo Freire's liberatory educational politics. They signal their doubt with the use of the word "yet" to begin the second sentence.

The concern that students be active participants in their learning has varied roots (e.g., Maria Montessori, John Dewey, Henry Giroux), but it is Paulo Freire's opposition to oppressive pedagogies that is frequently invoked to justify the use of information and communication technologies (ICTs) in higher education. Yet, these overt or implicit references to Freire's groundbreaking theory of liberatory education warrant critical appraisal because they constitute a curious practice.

This is so for two main reasons. First, even within political science (our discipline), Freire is regarded as a "radical" both because he challenged mainstream educational practices and goals, and argued in favor of democratizing the classroom. Given this, why does the ICT literature so enthusiastically embrace him? Second, when Freire wrote his critique of education in the 1970s, he was responding to the practices of the modern milieu; i.e., a textual world in which information was transmitted through publications, the study of textbooks, the giving of lectures, and the taking of notes. But we are clearly in a transformative time; a post-modern world in which the textual is rapidly being replaced by the digital. How, then, to understand Freire's call for liberatory pedagogy in this new age?

These are the questions we address in this article. We begin with a review of the digital technologies and the claims made by the educators who use and study them. Next, we revisit Freire's critique of oppressive pedagogies, the terminologies he employed, and the educational philosophy he advocated. With this as background, we apply Freire to three ICTs to show the extent to which his critique is prescient. We end by suggesting what Freire offers in formulating a liberatory educational theory for the digital age.

Source: John F. Freie and Susan M. Behuniak, "Paulo Freire and ICTs: Liberatory Education Theory in a Digital Age" (see Chapter 3, pp. 337–54).

PHYSICAL SCIENCES: PHYSICS, PHILOSOPHY OF SCIENCE

In the following passage, Matthew B. Crawford's topic is the place of science in a liberal education. Below is the fourth paragraph of his essay, "Science Education and Liberal Education." As is the case here, an article's title often is an excellent distillation of the paper's topic: sometimes the title hints at the thesis as well.

As a component of liberal education, science is both similar to and different from the humanities in spirit and effect. The humanities might be understood simply as a record of the best that has been thought about the human situation. Acquaintance with this record has the effect of freeing us from the present, with its necessarily partial view, and opening us up to the full range of human possibilities. Further, to enter truly into the great works of the past, or of other cultures, requires an *effort* to free oneself from the present and its certainties. A cultivated willingness to make that effort is perhaps the cardinal intellectual virtue. Science makes similar demands, with similarly liberal effects. In studying nature closely, we are confronted with the fallibility of common sense. In fact, heavier things do not fall faster than lighter ones. More radically, the very idea of nature stands as a rebuke to convention altogether.

Source: M.B. Crawford, "Science Education and Liberal Education" (see Chapter 3, Suggested Additional Resources, p. 272).

Narrowing Your Topic

Often writers begin with broad topical areas. They soon find, however, that their chosen topic is just too broad for a short paper, or even for a whole book. (They also may find that their topic is not an issue that people care about.)

For example, in response to a five-page paper assignment, a student writer takes as her topic "the media." She has a lot to say about the media and also notices hundreds of sources that address the media in some way or other. She finds herself overwhelmed.

She then realizes, perhaps with the help of her writing instructor, that her topic is just too broad for a single paper. Media studies is a vast field that treats hundreds if not thousands of concerns. Few *books* would tackle such a massive and amorphous subject as "the media."

The writer decides that violence in the media is her real interest. This subtopic is more plausible than writing about "the media," but is still too broad. In fact, most likely a topic like violence in the media would amount to a survey of some existing literature. How would one measure the effects of media violence in general? Could the writer set up a study on the necessary scale?

Perhaps, instead, she decides that she's interested in the depiction of violence against female characters in horror films.

After an additional conference with her writing instructor, she decides that she might examine the function of violence against women within the plots of a few horror films. This is a manageable topic that surely will yield more satisfying results—in the context of a student paper—than the other two, much broader topics. Now, instead of having to set up an elaborate experiment, with a large sample of viewers studied over a period of time, she can focus on an issue *within* the films, looking in particular at how violence against women functions in the plots.

Whether your broad area of concern is the media or something else, your writing experience will be more rewarding when you **locate a *particular* issue or subtopic within a broader field**.

The Thesis Statement

While a topic is the general subject matter or issue you're writing about—whether violence against women in horror films, the effects of globalization on cultures, or global climate change, for example—the **thesis** is the point you're trying to make about a topic area. It is the *stance* or *position* you are taking.

It's important to understand the difference between a **thesis statement** and a thesis. The former is a short announcement, if you will, of the point your paper will demonstrate. It is a relatively short, general statement of your paper's argument or position. A thesis, however, refers to the argument that runs through the entire essay—to all of the supporting information, data, and references to other scholars' work. Every paragraph in your paper, every fact, illustration, graphic, quotation, and question you use should directly relate to your thesis. Anything that does not relate to your thesis does not belong in your paper.

The general practice across the academic disciplines is to make the thesis statement early in the paper—at the end of the introduction, usually in the first paragraph in a shorter paper. However, a thesis statement need not be a single sentence found in a predictable place. With more complex topics, thesis statements often consist of two or three sentences, placed strategically in the essay.

While the thesis statement usually comes early in the paper, when you write a paper of your own you may have to do a considerable amount of work before you discover just what your main argument is. You may have to go back to the introduction, after writing much of the body of your paper, in order to work your thesis in.

That's fine. The process of writing is **recursive**: that is, it involves repeatedly returning to the beginning after working through the paper several times to revise and restate your position.

In fact, it is very rare for a writer to end up with the same thesis he or she started with. Academic writers begin with a preliminary or **working thesis**—an argument that makes sense to them after they have assessed their topic, read through the literature on that topic, asked some questions about the issue, and found something that has not yet been addressed or a perspective that has not been offered.

Then, once they start writing, reading more, and reconsidering, they will refine their original thesis, substantially revise it, or completely overturn it and come up with another perspective on their topic. This is how the writing process works, and it's why we often say that **writing is in itself a process of discovery**.

Framing a Working Thesis

Finding a thesis requires considerable groundwork. First, you need to find an area of study that is interesting and timely. Often, your professor will have assigned you a general area of inquiry, but you will need to focus it further. Sometimes your professor will give you a specific topic to approach. Either way, your paper will have to establish this as an area of important inquiry.

Next, you will need to read, summarize, and synthesize what other scholars have said on this subject. Again, your professor may have given you a list of articles to read—but these may only be a start, and you may need to read further, especially as you refine your thesis.

You will then have to identify some "problem" in the current scholarship that your paper will "solve." Or you could think of it as a "silence" in the academic conversation.

For example, you may discover that other scholars have

- misunderstood the issue,
- misinterpreted the data,
- failed to consider an issue critical to the topic, or
- incompletely considered the implications of current knowledge on the topic.

Although arriving at a preliminary thesis can be arduous, finding something new to write about is exhilarating.

Remember that you can build up to your thesis in your introduction, where you

- establish that your topic is interesting, relevant, and timely;
- summarize what other scholars have discovered and written on the topic;
- explain your assessment of the "silence" in others' scholarship on the topic, as discussed above.

Once you've set the stage, your thesis statement will seem like the next logical step. Of course, there are as many ways of expressing a thesis confidently and clearly as there are good writers.

Once you have arrived at a working thesis, you have to ask yourself, "How am I going to get the reader to side with me?" To help answer this question, we need to break the thesis into its parts.

The Claim

The first part of a thesis is the **claim**, the stance you are taking or the statement you are making about a particular topic. This is the paper's **main assertion**.

For example, in his essay "Is Google Making Us Stupid?" (Chapter 1, pp. 110–18), Nicholas Carr writes, "And what the Net seems to be doing is chipping away my capacity for concentration and contemplation. My mind now expects to take in information the way the Net distributes it: in a swiftly moving stream of particles. Once I was a scuba diver in the sea of words. Now I zip along the surface like a guy on a Jet Ski."

Here, the claim is, "And what the Net seems to be doing is chipping away my capacity for concentration and contemplation."

Reasons

Merely claiming something is not enough, however. A good thesis consists of more than a statement of your belief. A thesis statement should include an abbreviated expression of why the reader should accept your claim.

Your reasons may include

- **empirical evidence**/logical reasoning (**logos**),
- an emotional appeal (**pathos**), and
- other kinds of support.

In part, in the essay introduced above, Carr goes on to support his claim with anecdotes from his friends whose experience has been similar, but then notes that "anecdotes don't prove much." He follows these up with the findings of a related research study and the views of several experts in psychology and neurology. He might have included an abbreviated statement of his reasons or support for his claim within the thesis statement.

Every essay in Real World Topics contains a thesis—take a look now and see if you can identify some. (Some may be implicit rather than explicitly stated.) Notice that there are many ways to state a thesis, even within each academic division. Below are some examples.

Sample Thesis Statements

HUMANITIES: PHILOSOPHY

In this excerpt from Chapter 7 of his book *Cosmopolitanism: Ethics in a World of Strangers*, included in Chapter 4 of Real World Topics, the philosopher and African Studies scholar Kwame Anthony Appiah introduces the question of cultural **homogenization**, which many theorists believe is one of the negative outcomes of **globalization**. Appiah suggests that rather than strictly causing homogenization, globalization also actually threatens it—by breaking up long-standing homogeneous communities, especially in cities. Appiah later suggests that such "cultural contamination" long predates contemporary globalization or Americanization. An advocate of cosmopolitanism, Appiah celebrates cultural **hybridity**, which he believes has always been a feature of civilization.

> People who complain about the homogeneity produced by globalization often fail to notice that globalization is, equally, a threat to homogeneity. You can see this as clearly in Kumasi as anywhere. The capital of Asante is accessible to you, whoever you are—emotionally, intellectually, and, of course, physically. It is integrated into the global markets. None of this makes it Western, or American, or British. It is still Kumasi. What it isn't, just because it's a city, is homogeneous. English, German, Chinese, Syrian, Lebanese, Burkinabe, Ivorian, Nigerian, Indian: I can find you families of each description.
> Source: Kwame Anthony Appiah, "Cosmopolitan Contamination" (see Chapter 4, pp. 417–25).

SOCIAL SCIENCES: SOCIOLOGY

In this passage, the sociologist George Ritzer assumes that his readers are sufficiently aware of the ubiquity of McDonald's restaurants to claim that this kind of globalization applies to "every other aspect of society." He establishes his topic's significance and timeliness by claiming that "McDonaldization" is "an inexorable process." He promises to demonstrate this thesis in the paper to follow, using the phrase "As you will see." Ritzer's use of the second person includes the reader in the argument, implying that Ritzer is taking the reader along with him as together they discover the global effects of McDonaldization.

> As you will see, McDonaldization affects not only the restaurant business but also education, work, the criminal justice system, health care, travel, leisure, dieting, politics, the family, religion, and virtually every other aspect of society. McDonaldization has shown every sign of being an

inexorable process, sweeping through seemingly impervious institutions and regions of the world.

Source: George Ritzer, "An Introduction to McDonaldization" (see Chapter 4, pp. 372–91).

PHYSICAL SCIENCES: NEUROLOGY AND PSYCHIATRY

In the passage below, Gary Small and Gigi Vorgan stake their claim about the effects of digital technology on the brain. Notice that the thesis is carried over several sentences and makes several claims: the use of digital technologies is changing the way we live and communicate; but it is also changing our brains, impacting how we think, feel, and behave.

> The current explosion of digital technology not only is changing the way we live and communicate but also is rapidly and profoundly altering our brains. Daily exposure to high technology—computers, smart phones, videogames, search engines such as Google and Yahoo—stimulates brain cell alteration and neurotransmitter release, gradually strengthening new neural pathways in our brains while weakening old ones. Because of the current technological revolution, our brains are evolving right now—at a speed like never before.
>
> Besides influencing how we think, digital technology is altering how we feel, how we behave. Seven out of 10 American homes are wired for high-speed Internet. We rely on the Internet and digital technology for entertainment, political discussion, and communication with friends and co-workers. As the brain evolves and shifts its focus toward new technological skills, it drifts away from fundamental social skills, such as reading facial expressions during conversation or grasping the emotional context of a subtle gesture.
>
> Source: Gary Small and Gigi Vorgan, "Meet Your iBrain: How Technology Changes the Way We Think" (see Chapter 1, pp. 143–49).

Qualifying Your Thesis

An overstated thesis—one that claims more than your paper delivers—weakens the paper considerably. Overstated thesis statements can be vast overgeneralizations: "Since the beginning of time, human beings …" Or they may simply be statements that are too strong for the evidence. The following is probably an overstatement: "With this study, we have discovered the unmistakable cause of cancer."

If you find that you've overstated your thesis, you do not necessarily have to junk it and start over. You may simply need to modify it so as to make it more defensible. Such modifications are called **qualifiers**. A qualifier is a word or phrase that limits the generality (but not the viability) of a claim. Following is a list of common qualifiers:

- most
- usually
- generally
- in most cases
- often

- sometimes
- some (followed by a noun)
- in some cases
- it may be the case that

PRACTICE SESSION

Think of a topic of interest to you and find a controversy (issue) within it. Then write a strong thesis statement (a claim about the topic, with the general reasons supporting it). If necessary, qualify your thesis using one of the qualifiers above.

For example, a claim might read: "Many rape victims go through a serious depression immediately after and often for years after the event." This qualifies the thesis so as to avoid overstatement, but it does not weaken it. In order to be valid, of course, this claim must be supported by data that demonstrate the rates and lengths of depression in rape victims.

But a qualified thesis can also be constructed in more subtle ways, for example: "With the rare exception of...." The latter qualifier is called a **reservation**. A reservation holds the thesis to be true, but only when a condition is met or a factor is absent.

A claim that includes a qualifier can protect your argument from **rebuttal** based on a minor exception or an unforeseen condition that may occur to the reader but not to the writer.

The Thesis as a Unifying Thread

Every paragraph of an essay should be informed by the thesis and should support it. The thesis is the unifying thread that runs through the rest of your paper. The body of an essay (see pp. 64–69) is essentially an extended thesis statement, drawn out in all of its complexity and detail. For example, after he makes his thesis statement in his essay "An Introduction to McDonaldization" (see the excerpt above), George Ritzer takes his reader step-by-step through his thesis, using such subheadings as "The Long Arm of McDonaldization," "The Dimensions of McDonaldization," "The Case of Ikea," and "The Advantages of McDonaldization" to support and illustrate his argument.

Refining Your Thesis

Once you have a tentative thesis—a general, relatively short but inclusive statement of your claim and your reasons for it—you should work on focusing it and expressing it with confidence. A thesis statement should make as strong a case as possible without overstatement. You may find that your working thesis is overstated, or that it is slightly off the mark. At this point, it's time to review your sources, and if you have further questions on the topic, or come up against gaps in your own knowledge, read more sources. Each time you read a new source, reconsider your thesis. Does it still work?

If not, modify it in light of what you have just read. Of course you will not be able to read everything on a given topic, but satisfy yourself that you have examined the issue from several possible perspectives. It often helps to look up the sources listed or data cited in primary source material. Do the sources contradict each other? Could the data be interpreted in a different way? Asking these questions, and continually refining your thesis, will lead you to your final or definitive thesis.

An important determining factor regarding your thesis is the specific form that your contribution to current scholarship will take. Each type of assertion requires a different approach. For example, are you saying that other scholars have

- *misunderstood the issue?* The introduction or body of your essay will summarize what other scholars have claimed. Your thesis will directly address the nature of the misunderstanding and explain your position. The body of your essay will enumerate your reasons for making this claim.
- *misinterpreted the data?* The introduction or body of your essay will summarize existing data and how other scholars have interpreted it. Your thesis will state in specific terms an alternative way of interpreting the data. The body of your essay will demonstrate in specific terms why your interpretation is more valid than (or just as valid as) previous interpretations.
- *failed to consider an issue critical to the topic?* The introduction or body of your essay will summarize what others have written on the topic. Your thesis statement will assert that issue X must be considered in relation to this topic. The body of your essay will support your assertion that issue X is critical.
- *incompletely considered the implications of current knowledge on the topic?* The introduction or body of your essay will summarize inferences others have made about the topic. Your thesis will assert that implication X is critical to a complete understanding of the topic. The body of your essay will explain in specific terms why implication X is critical.

Audience

As you work on developing your purpose, topic, and thesis statement, you should also consider the nature of your audience. Writers sometimes make the mistake of writing to the *page* (or the screen) instead of to a human being. In order to get your point across effectively, you need to envision your intended reader.

Critical Theorists Imagine Their Readers

A diverse group of twentieth-century critical theorists focused on the role of the reader in the meaning of a text. As you read these brief explanations of their theories, think about ways in which you might imagine your reader as you write.

WOLFGANG ISER: THE IDEAL READER

The German literary scholar Wolfgang Iser (1926-2007) is known for his "reader-response" theory. For Iser, the reader is an active participant in the text. The reader helps create or complete the text's meaning, based on his or her cultural and social experience, knowledge, and beliefs. A text then becomes, not the writer's unchanging self-expression, but a kind of performance between the writer and the reader.

Iser imagined an "ideal reader" who is not necessarily an expert in the subject he or she is reading, but is

- intelligent,
- engaged, and
- well-read,

and thus "gets" what the writer is saying because the writer and the reader share

- cultural contexts (age, race, socioeconomic status, and level of education) and
- beliefs (political leanings, religious views, relative cynicism or idealism).

STANLEY FISH: THE INFORMED READER

The American critic Stanley Fish (b. 1938) imagines a reader who possesses what he calls "literary competence." This reader has all the knowledge she needs to understand the text, but in reading she adds her own reactions to the text, thus becoming more self-aware as she reads.

Fish suggests that, in some way, the informed reader already understands the piece of writing, or at least is well prepared to understand it.

ERWIN WOLFF: THE INTENDED READER

The German critic Erwin Wolff (1924-2007) posited that writers create an "intended reader" to whom they address their writing, shaping the way they tell their story or construct their argument based on this imagined reader.

By making the reader's response to the text critical to what and how he or she writes, the writer, in a sense, "embeds" the reader in the text.

Similarly, a critic may look for meaning in a text by imagining how the writer's contemporaries might have experienced a text. When and where was the text written? Who was reading it when it was published? What were the readers' socioeconomic status, worldview, religious beliefs, moral code, ethnic affiliations, and gender?

A critic with a complex understanding of a text's intended reader might better comprehend the goals of the writer and thus the meaning of the text.

Constructing Your Own Ideal Reader

Your own notion of your reader might or might not fit well with one of those presented above. However you imagine your reader, think of someone willing to listen to your argument but not already convinced of it.

Write for someone who

- is educated and intelligent,
- has a basic knowledge of your topic,
- does not have unlimited time or patience, and
- can either come up with alternative arguments, or
- will wonder why you have not considered any.

Your ideal reader does not need to already accept your thesis. In fact, a weaker paper will likely result from imagining that you are "preaching to the choir," as if your reader already agrees with you.

As you imagine the readers of your paper, also ask these questions:

- How and why is this topic important to them?
- What are their predispositions or biases?

Writing Style: Adapt It to Your Ideal Reader

Writing style includes the following features:

- the **attitude** or **tone** you take toward your topic (casual, formal or somewhere in between; humorous; sarcastic; somber; angry; serious; neutral);
- **perspective** (first-, second-, or third-person?) (see the section on narrative perspective, pp. 50–52);
- **organization** (what are the structural traditions in this field, and what structure will best carry your argument?);
- **diction** or word choice:

- If your audience is **non-expert yet academic**, you would use words common to all academics, and be sure to define any discipline-specific terms.
- If you are writing for an **intra-disciplinary** audience, or readers with disciplinary concerns, you can use jargon associated with that field without explanation. Intra-disciplinary essays also tend to allow writers to delve more deeply and specifically into a subject.
- **Interdisciplinary** essays tend to be more general and perhaps make references to other fields, so as to allow non-experts to tie their own knowledge to this unfamiliar data or idea.

Addressing Audience

HUMANITIES: PHILOSOPHY

The excerpt below comes from an essay by philosopher John Nolt on global warming, a topic more commonly addressed by physical scientists. Throughout his essay, Nolt uses the first and second person, a narrative perspective that can draw in readers, helping them identify with the subject and see how it might directly affect their lives. This approach could help Nolt promote his argument: that every American is personally responsible for global warming. In his conclusion, below, Nolt discusses the implications of his results. In doing so, he implicates not only the reader ("you,") but also himself ("me," "us"), a rhetorical move that might disarm the reader, making him or her more receptive to Nolt's message.

We estimated above that the average American is responsible for about one two-billionth of current and near-term emissions. Yet even if emissions are reduced to low levels fairly quickly—that is, even under the most optimistic of scenarios—billions of people may ultimately be harmed by them. If over the next millennium as few as four billion people (about 4%) are harmed (that is, suffer and/or die) as a result of current and near-term global emissions, then the average American causes through his/her greenhouse gas emissions the serious suffering and/or deaths of two future people.

... But even though [this figure] is rough and even though there is no such thing as the average American, it gives us, I contend, some sense of the moral significance of our own complicity in a greenhouse-gas-intensive economy. For the amount of harm done by the average American is not very different from the amount of harm done by you or me.

Source: John Nolt, "How Harmful Are the Average American's Greenhouse Gas Emissions?" (see http://sites.broadviewpress.com/realworldtopics).

SOCIAL SCIENCES: INTERNATIONAL RELATIONS

The passage below is from an article originally written for the *Harvard International Review*, which publishes articles aimed at "both academic and lay readers who wish to think seriously about international affairs." Its writers are Harvard faculty and students as well as other experts in international affairs.

Amy Lifland, a Harvard undergraduate student when she wrote this essay, seems to have this audience in mind as she writes. She opens her article by emphasizing the immediate and widespread nature of the threat of cybercrime. While beginning with its effect on America (her audience is largely American), she quickly expands the scope of her message to the international stage—and to the military.

> In the past six months, hackers have infiltrated the websites and internal servers of the United States Senate, the CIA, numerous other state and federal agencies, private corporations, and individuals. The onslaught seems unstoppable, and the FBI and other US law enforcement agencies struggle to identify and arrest the hackers responsible for the attacks. Many hackers are after money, concentrating on identity theft and other frauds that have allowed them to steal tens of millions of dollars, primarily from small businesses in the United States. More ominous, however, is the recent trend of attempted and successful cyber-infiltrations into government agencies, the military, and the email accounts of government officials and other individuals with high security clearances, in the United States as well as other nations.
>
> Source: Amy Lifland, "Cyberwar: The Future of Conflict" (see Chapter 7, pp. 611–13).

PHYSICAL SCIENCES: PHILOSOPHY OF SCIENCE

Matthew B. Crawford's article "Science Education and Liberal Education" was published in the journal *The New Atlantis*, whose editors describe their readers as including "policymakers who know too little about science" and "scientists who often fail to think seriously or deeply about the ethical and social implications of their work." In this article, Crawford seems to focus on those who make education policy, and to persuade them that science education is critical but that policymakers and teachers will inspire future scientists only if they appeal to the intrinsic rewards of studying science. Crawford's tone is conversational, his language simple and direct, and he establishes himself as a reliable source because he has first-hand experience as a science teacher. Notice that

PRACTICE SESSION

Imagine the readers of your thesis statement (from the previous practice session). Write a brief description of your readers, explaining the reasons you might use to convince them that your thesis is correct, or at least that it is worthy of serious consideration.

he avoids accusation or provocation by choosing the passive voice and by qualifying his statement with "generally." Instead of "policymakers always promote science on the ground that ...," he writes, "the learning of science is generally promoted on the ground that...." This rhetorical move is likely to disarm the reader and encourage her or him to be receptive to his argument.

> Teaching is a curious thing. It seems to be effective only when the student is made to feel pleasure in learning. That pleasure is inherently private, yet the learning of science is generally promoted on the ground that it serves some public good. In the era of Sputnik, that public good was clear to all: national defense. Now we hear that scientific literacy is important if America is to maintain its technological edge—not because we are in a race with the Soviets, but because technological innovation drives economic growth. But such fretting in a public-policy mode fails to get at the private experience of individual students. "Why should *I* study physics?" Imagine the question as posed by a truculent sixteen-year-old, staring you down from his desk in the back row. The question is legitimate and compelling, and cannot be evaded with blather about economic growth.
>
> The answer spoken by educators is necessarily a public thing, and education surely serves a public good, but that good must be founded on the private pleasures of the student, not on some abstract desideratum like technological progress. Appealing to self-interest, a teacher might be tempted to say, "Look at how much money techno-geeks have made for themselves in the last decade," but this is sleight of hand, since the new billionaires have been primarily in software, and manipulating the conventions of computer code has little to do with natural science. There are countless ways to make a fortune that are more reliable and less demanding than the study of nature.
>
> Source: M.B. Crawford, "Science Education and Liberal Education" (see Chapter 3, Suggested Additional Resources, p. 272).

Narrative Perspective

As you're writing an academic paper, you also should ask yourself this question: How can I best persuade my reader to trust and respect what I am attempting to communicate? This is where **narrative perspective** enters your composition process.

Third Person: Perceived Objectivity

Many academic papers are written in the third person. This perspective creates some **rhetorical distance** between the writer and his or her argument.

For example, a scientific paper written in the first person might lead readers to believe that the writer or writers have a personal stake in the results that might interfere with "scientific objectivity." Science traditionally relies on a dispassionate statement of fact verified by several observers over the observations or beliefs of a single person. In this situation, first person sometimes seems out of place.

In theory, the third person may lend an argument an aura of **objectivity**, of reasoned, measured thought, unsullied by emotion or personal bias. The third-person perspective, referred to in literature as the **omniscient voice**, focuses the reader's attention on what is being said, rather than on who is saying it.

Some critics and philosophers of science argue that the apparent objectivity of the writer that is created with the third person is a myth. No writer, they say, can be other than subjective (personally invested) or intersubjective (connected to the beliefs of a larger community). Regardless of your position on this philosophical point, it is important to observe that the third-person voice works to distance the writer from his or her argument, making the writing more convincing in some contexts and in some parts of the paper. In other words, the third-person voice of scientific objectivity is an effective rhetorical strategy for making certain kinds of arguments.

First and Second Person: Personal Stake in Narrative

The first person and the second person are most commonly used in editorials, personal essays, fiction, and poetry. These perspectives might create **complicity** between the writer and the reader; the writer is speaking to the reader as if the two are involved in an intimate discussion.

The first person is used in academic writing when the writer acknowledges a personal stake in the issue. This has been a recent trend in the humanities. Writers influenced by **feminism**, **gender studies**, **cultural studies**, and **postmodern theory** are particularly partial to this kind of writing. See for example the article by philosopher John Nolt in the standalone website.

As Anne M. Penrose and Steven B. Katz note in their book *Writing in the Sciences*, the first person is increasingly common in scientific writing as well. They explain this trend by pointing to the fact that the first person is naturally connected with **active voice** (e.g., *I titrated* the solution, *We experimented with*) rather than **passive voice** (e.g., *the solution* was titrated). Writers using the first person can more easily report on research methods; active voice is generally more direct and brief.

NOTE

WHY IS "I" THE FIRST PERSON?
The answer is not as profound as you might expect! This usage derives from the order in which a verb is conjugated. For example, if you were to conjugate the verb "to be," You'd write: I am; you are; he, she, or it is. Since you begin with the "I" form of "to be," "I" is known as the "first person."

The first person is most often used to report on the methods and materials used in scientific research, which is usually presented in a separate section of scientific articles (see the section on research methods in the academic divisions, above).

On the other hand, since the first person has the effect of focusing the attention on the writer rather than on the subject at hand, its use may make the writer seem more personally involved in his or her argument and perhaps less reliable.

The second person, while rarely used in academic writing, can be effective when used sparingly. Directly addressing the reader in an informal way sometimes has the effect of pulling the reader into the argument, encouraging him or her to see the issue as directly affecting his or her life.

On the downside, "you" and "your" are too informal for much academic writing. Also, if overused, the second person can begin to feel intrusive, and even cloying, as if the writer is trying to establish an unearned familiarity with the reader.

TABLE 1: NARRATIVE PERSPECTIVE

NARRATIVE PERSPECTIVE	EXAMPLE
First Person Singular: I, me, my, mine	*I argue, I hold, It is my position that …*
First Person Plural: we, our, ours	*We argue, We believe …*
Second Person Singular/Plural: you, your, yours	*You might think, (You) think about it …*
Third Person Singular: he, him, his; she, her, hers; it, its; one, one's	*He writes, In her opinion, One concludes …*
Third Person Plural: they, them, their, theirs	*They write, According to them …*

Evidence

Evidence can vary in type, depending on the discipline and the purpose of the paper, from lab or study results, to the research and opinions of experts in the field, to personal experience. The purpose of evidence, though, is invariable: it supports your argument or main points.

Presentation of Evidence

HUMANITIES: PHILOSOPHY

In his article "How Harmful Are the Average American's Greenhouse Gas Emissions?," philosopher John Nolt argues that every American creates harmful greenhouse gases. Philosophers often define concepts that others might take for granted. Early in the article, for example, Nolt defines "average American"; in this excerpt he defines "greenhouse gas emissions." Philosophers also consider the moral implications of human action. Here, Nolt cites "obvious moral reasons" for one of his choices. Like many writers in the humanities, he uses the first person ("I will not take ..." and "we will simply take ..."). His oblique reference to flatulence draws in the reader with humor, seeming to parody scientific language ("bodily methane emissions"). These approaches can help a writer get the reader on his side. However, Nolt also backs up his claims with data, indicating that he is a rational being concerned with accuracy (**ethos**).

> To obtain the greenhouse gas emissions of the average American, then, we will simply take the total greenhouse gas emissions for the American nation and divide by the population. But to do that we first need to define "greenhouse gas emissions."
>
> ### Greenhouse Gas Emissions
>
> Greenhouse gas emissions are emissions by humans of gases that contribute significantly to global climate change. These gases are, in order of importance: carbon dioxide, methane, nitrous oxide, and various halocarbons. Yet not all anthropogenic emissions of these gases should count. We ought, in particular, to make an exception for the carbon dioxide we produce in breathing. The contribution of human respiration to total anthropogenic emissions—though perhaps larger than one might expect—is still relatively small: something on the order of 3 or 4%. For obvious moral reasons, I will not count these emissions. I will likewise ignore (though there is no delicate way to say this), the fact that CO_2 is not the only greenhouse gas emitted by the human body. Fortunately, bodily methane emissions are comparatively miniscule.
>
> Source: John Nolt, "How Harmful Are the Average American's Greenhouse Gas Emissions?" (see http://sites.broadviewpress.com/realworldtopics).

SOCIAL SCIENCES: PSYCHOLOGY

In his book *The Better Angels of Our Nature: Why Violence Has Declined*, experimental psychologist Steven Pinker argues that, contrary to what most people believe, the world has become less violent over the millennia. In the excerpt below, Pinker supports his claim with a well-organized summary of how, over the ages, human beings have learned to curb their violent impulses, empathize with others, and employ reason to solve problems.

Social scientists, as well as humanities scholars, and to a lesser degree physical scientists, often call on well-known documents to bolster their cases. Here, Pinker backs up his case with a reference to a "classic book" by the sociologist Norbert Elias.

The many developments that make up the human retreat from violence can be grouped into six major trends. The first, which took place on the scale of millennia, was the transition from the anarchy of the hunting, gathering, and horticultural societies in which our species spent most of its evolutionary history, to the first agricultural civilizations beginning around five thousand years ago. With that change came a reduction in the chronic raiding and feuding that characterized life in a state of nature. According to evidence from forensic archeology and ethnographic vital statistics, the change helped produce a more or less fivefold decrease in rates of violent death.

The second transition spanned more than half a millennium and is best documented in Europe. Between the late Middle Ages and the twentieth century, European countries saw a tenfold-to-fiftyfold decline in their rates of homicide. In his classic book *The Civilizing Process*, the sociologist Norbert Elias attributed this surprising decline to the consolidation of a patchwork of feudal territories into large kingdoms with centralized authority and an infrastructure of commerce.

Source: Steven Pinker, "Why the World Is More Peaceful" (see Chapter 7, pp. 626–35).

PHYSICAL SCIENCES: ENVIRONMENTAL SCIENCE

In her article "The Diplomats Fiddle while Africa Burns," environmental scientist and activist Jessica Wilson argues that 1) "human-induced 'global warming' ... drives climate change," and 2) the actions taken by the world's leaders have been inadequate to alleviate human-caused global warming.

Wilson's article was originally published as a "Commentary" in the *South Africa Journal of Science*. Unlike a traditional scientific article, Wilson's piece does not take an "objective" stance or style. In her opening sentence, Wilson's language is evocative, her tone derisive. She opens with, "All this cloak-and-dagger politics in the corridors of power would be bearable if the negotiations were even close to mirroring what is needed to respond to climate change." However, as her readers are most likely scientists—if not necessarily environmental scientists— she uses standard scientific protocol for persuading her reader: she presents specific data, culled from the research of legitimate scientists. For example, she cites three studies (as evidenced by the superscripted numbers). Then she notes figures that the United Nations Environment Programme "has identified" as a gap between "pledged" and "needed" reductions in greenhouse gas emissions. (In this excerpt, and in the article published on the companion website, we have retained South African spellings [e.g., tonne for ton].)

All this cloak-and-dagger politics in the corridors of power would be bearable if the negotiations were even close to mirroring what is needed to respond to climate change. With current commitments, we are headed for a 3.5°C rise in temperature by the end of the 21st century, and a risk that it could be higher.[4,5] The United Nations Environment Programme has identified a 6 to 12 *billion* tonne gap between pledged emission reductions of carbon dioxide equivalent and what is needed to meet the 2°C target.[6] Built into the UNFCCC process is an agreement to review the adequacy of this target, with both African countries and the Association of Small Island States arguing for it to be 1.5°C. With this tighter target, the gigatonne gap becomes even larger.

Source: Jessica Wilson, "The Diplomats Fiddle while Africa Burns" (see http://sites. broadviewpress.com/realworldtopics).

Appeals

An appeal is a method a writer uses to persuade his or her reader. Aristotle divided these appeals into three types: ethos, pathos, and logos.

Ethos

Ethos convinces the reader by persuading her that the writer is credible because he or she is of sound ethical character, is a sane and reasonable person, and is worthy of respect. The idea is that a reader who finds a *writer* credible will find that writer's *claim* credible. Respectful acknowledgement of opposing viewpoints, along with a reasonable refutation of them, also helps the writer convince the reader that she is an authority of sound mind whose goal is to find the truth using fair and just methods. If the writer can persuade the reader that she is all of the above, the reader is likely to trust the writer, and is therefore more likely to be convinced of her argument.

In the passage below, Bill Joy, co-founder and chief scientist of Sun Microsystems, establishes his ethos in the essay "Why the Future Doesn't Need Us" by telling a story that puts him at the center of the computer-science revolution. Notice how he casually mentions all of the important software that he developed as a college graduate student.

When I went to graduate school at UC Berkeley in the mid-1970s, I started staying up late, often all night, inventing new worlds inside the machines. Solving problems. Writing the code that argued so strongly to be written.... After a few years at Berkeley I started to send out some of the software I had written—an instructional Pascal system, Unix utilities, and a text editor called vi (which is still, to my surprise, widely used more than 20 years later)—to others who had similar small PDP-11 and VAX minicomputers. These adventures in software eventually turned into the Berkeley version of the Unix operating system, which became a personal "success disaster"—so many people wanted it that I never finished my PhD. Instead I got a job working for Darpa putting Berkeley Unix on the Internet and fixing it to be reliable and to run large research applications well. This was all great fun and very rewarding. And, frankly, I saw no robots here, or anywhere near.

Still, by the early 1980s, I was drowning. The Unix releases were very successful, and my little project of one soon had money and some staff, but the problem at Berkeley was always office space rather than money—there wasn't room for the help the project needed, so when the other founders of Sun Microsystems showed up I jumped at the chance to join them. At Sun, the long hours continued into the early days of workstations and personal computers, and I have enjoyed participating in the creation of advanced microprocessor technologies and Internet technologies such as Java and Jini.

Source: Bill Joy, "Why the Future Doesn't Need Us" (see Chapter 5, pp. 476–94).

Pathos

Pathos is an appeal to the reader's emotions. The idea is that a reader who becomes emotionally invested in what she is reading is more likely to be persuaded by the argument.

Appeals to the emotions are not limited to writers in the humanities. A botanist, for example, might describe the unique beauty and grandeur of the giant redwood trees in the American West as part of an argument that laws should protect these trees. An epidemiologist might introduce her study on rugby-related injuries with a narrative about the number of middle-school athletes paralyzed in the last year while playing rugby. She might even present a case study of a particularly promising young rugby player who is now permanently wheelchair-bound as a result of a rugby injury.

The key is to involve the reader on a personal and emotional level without making him feel as if he is being unfairly manipulated or exploited.

However, an argument that overdoes the emotional appeal has resorted to **bathos**—insincere pathos or sentimentality—which could turn the reader *against* the argument.

Logos

Logos is an appeal to logic or sound reasoning. Producing believable data and other factual information goes a long way toward convincing the reader of your position. Your data should be both broad and deep, and if you state your claim or thesis clearly, structure your argument logically, and provide appropriate evidence to back it up, the reader is more likely to side with you.

For example, let's say you're trying to argue that the use of headgear would significantly reduce the incidence of rugby-related injuries. Your data should

1. cover ten years of head-injury data rather than just one; and
2. include several thousand cases, not just a few hundred.

Data that are both broad and deep in this way is known as a **representative sample**, which

1. helps convince the reader that the data are substantive, not merely anecdotal or incidental; and
2. implies that the writer is interested in uncovering the truth, not just in promoting her own agenda regarding headgear.

On the other hand, some appeals do not work or are not fair because they don't make sense for one reason or another. Thus, work to avoid falling into these logical fallacy traps. Table 2 lists, defines, and describes the problems with the most common logical fallacies.

Examples of Faulty Causation Arguments

In 1998 the medical journal *Lancet* published an article by Dr. Andrew Wakefield, which seemed to show that the MMR (measles-mumps-rubella) vaccine caused autism. The Wakefield paper revealed data that showed that children were diagnosed with autism around the same time they received their vaccinations. Therefore, it claimed, the vaccination *caused* autism.

Physicians and other scientists challenged the study's findings, claiming that they could not be reproduced. Wakefield's interpretation of the data employed false logic: *cum hoc ergo propter hoc.* Nevertheless, many parents responded either by refusing to vaccinate their children or by filing suit against vaccine makers for causing autism in their children.

In February 2010, the *Lancet* retracted the paper after it was revealed that Wakefield had been taking money from an attorney who was trying to win a case against companies that make vaccines. Wakefield subsequently lost his license to practice medicine in the United Kingdom.

A second example of a faulty argument can be found in a study reported in the *New York Times* ("Talk Deeply, Be Happy," March 17, 2010), which revealed that people who spend more time having substantive conversations are happier than people who spend more time making small talk.

After reading this study, one might be tempted to believe that merely having more deep discussions will make one happier. But this conclusion may be too hasty. The report notes that the study's principal investigator, Dr. Matthias Mehl, a psychologist at the University of Arizona, recognizes that his small study "doesn't prove a cause-and-effect relationship between the kind of conversations one has and one's happiness."

Mehl's next study involves asking his subjects to consciously "increase the number of substantive conversations they have each day and cut back on small talk" and see what is revealed. In this case, Mehl has wisely avoided concluding that because happier people have substantive conversations, it follows that these conversations cause happiness.

TABLE 2: LOGICAL FALLACIES

FALLACY	DEFINITION	PROBLEM
Ad hominem	This fallacy, which is Latin for "against the man," refers to an argument that attacks the person making the argument, as opposed to the argument he or she is making.	Makes the writer appear to have a personal vendetta against someone who disagrees with him. It tends to destroy the writer's ethos. The argument will be discredited because the attack is personal, not logical.
Fallacy of accident	An argument that uses a generalization that ignores exceptions or strong counterarguments.	If a reader can think of a case in which the writer's statement does not apply, the writer is unlikely to persuade the reader, and the argument will fail.
Slippery slope	The argument that one small step or action inevitably leads to drastic consequences.	Discredited because the writer has not acknowledged the possibility of a middle ground.
Post hoc ergo propter hoc	This false logic contends that because one event happened after another event, the second event must have been caused by the first event. In Latin, the phrase means "after this, therefore because (on account of) this," and is often shortened to "post hoc." It is also known as false cause or coincidental correlation.	An easy fallacy to fall into: if a writer doesn't understand the subtle complexities of a situation, he or she might assume that chronology is linked to causality. Therefore, writers should carefully analyze other causes before claiming that a prior event caused a later event.
Cum hoc ergo propter hoc	This fallacy, similar to *post hoc*, means "correlation does not imply causation." It is a common mistake in the physical sciences but can come up in any field.	Simply because two events or conditions happen together does not mean that one causes the other.

Beginning to Write

When you begin a paper, your instinct might be to start at the beginning. As it turns out, the beginning may be the worst place to start.

As we said when discussing thesis statements, you will often write a great deal before you know exactly what you want to say. If you write your introduction first, you may later find that it is way too general—or that you have found a more interesting and useful focus than the one you started with. Also, it's really hard to write an introduction with a thesis statement when you're not sure where you will end up. So you may find yourself staring at a blank screen or page for way too long.

Here's an alternative—***begin in the middle***:

- First, read over your source material and your notes.
- Then put them aside and just write. This might mean summarizing your research articles, or laying out the main ideas that your paper will address.
- Write freely, without censoring yourself. You can edit later; the important thing is to get the words onto the page or screen.
- You will probably feel much better about the paper once you have written a few pages and have a sense of what shape the paper might take.

FREE WRITING

If you're having a hard time getting started on this step, try a timed, uncensored exercise called free writing. Once you have done one or two free writings, you will at least have something written down that you can shape into something useful for your paper. Here's how to go about it:

- Decide on a limited time period—say, 15 minutes.
- Read over your source material to establish some focus.
- Set your timer and start writing.
- Focus on a continued stream of writing, ignoring those voices in your head that may be telling you, "This is dumb. I can't write." These and other such phrases are self-defeating.
- If you can't rid yourself of these thoughts, write them down, then try to re-focus and get back to the subject at hand. The idea is to try never to allow your pen to stop writing, or your fingers to stop tapping.
- Once your time is up, stop and read over what you have written. You may be surprised at the useful ideas that have come up.
- Underline or highlight the usable parts.
- Put your writing away and take a break.
- Or, if you're feeling inspired, set the timer for another 15 minutes and start again, trying to work from the writing that you have already done.

PARTS OF THE ESSAY

The Introduction

Once you have enough information, data, analysis, commentary, or summary for the body of your paper, read it over. Find your focus. Then start writing.

As we suggested above, you may find that you need to begin with the body of the paper and write at some length before having a clear sense of the topic and your argument about it. In any case, at some point you will need to draft the introduction to the paper. Introductions perform a number of tasks. They

1. introduce the **topic**;
2. give a sense of the **purpose** for writing the essay;
3. present the main **argument** or thesis; and
4. provide a "**map**," or forecast, of the rest of the paper (see pp. 62–64).

Sample Introductions

HUMANITIES: HISTORY

In this essay history professor Timothy D. Snyder argues that when students use laptops in the classroom, their attention is diverted from the most important aspect of their education—interaction with professors and each other. Snyder's introduction takes the reader into his world as he observes his students from the front of the classroom. His first two paragraphs address the subject in a general way, speaking of "professors" and "students." This implies that Snyder's experience is common to many on college campuses. In the third paragraph, Snyder moves to the first person ("I teach at Yale"). This strategy draws readers into the scene with him, possibly encouraging them to side with him. It also gives him ethos: it establishes him as a reliable expert on student use of laptops in the classroom. Notice that Snyder waits until the end of the third paragraph to state his claim, and that he returns to the third person, implying that his argument is widely relevant.

As these first few weeks of the college semester begin, professors look out expectantly into grand lecture halls, where they see, rather than faces of students, the backs of open laptops. The students, for their part, are looking intently at the laptop screens. What are they doing as they stare forward with such apparent focus?

Thanks to wireless Internet access, they are updating their Facebook, Twitter, and Tumblr profiles; they are chatting on Skype, Gchat, or iChat;

they are making travel plans, or reading the newspaper, or following the pennant race. This fall, higher education lost yet another new class of freshmen, as the new students learned that the university classroom is just one more physical place to be on the Internet.

I teach at Yale, where lecturing is taken seriously—and in history, which boasts some of the best teachers. My ratings as a lecturer are consistently high. But even here, I would not have the attention of these very gifted students if I did not ban laptops and smartphones from my classroom. Part of the problem is that students are not paying attention at a given moment; part of the problem is that they often lack the ability to pay attention at all.

Source: Timothy D. Snyder, "Why Laptops in Class Are Distracting America's Future Workforce" (see Chapter 3, pp. 274–76).

SOCIAL SCIENCES: POLITICAL SCIENCE

The introduction below, from a book by Dominic D.P. Johnson and Dominic Tierney entitled *Failing to Win: Perceptions of Victory and Defeat in International Politics*, begins with narration; its style is akin to that of fiction, which woos the reader with vivid, impressionistic description.

Note the liberal use of adjectives (triumphant, fluttering, ferocious, defining, classic), unusual in academic writing but common in literature. This opening quickly resolves to general statements about human behavior and society, a **trope** characteristic of writing in the social sciences.

The writers are also careful to define their terms—what they mean by "observers" and "perceptions," two large and potentially unwieldy terms that benefit from specification. Though this excerpt introduces a book, it could easily introduce a long article. From this opening, the writers turn to specific historical examples of clashes and confluences of perception and reality.

At 10:50 p.m. on 30 April 1945, triumphant Soviet soldiers raised a fluttering hammer and sickle over the Reichstag in Berlin. In a ferocious war, the Red Army had ground the Germans back all the way from the gates of Moscow. Around the world, people celebrated the fall of Berlin as a defining moment in the destruction of the Nazi regime. It was a classic case in which perceptions of victory matched the result on the battlefield.

But people do not always judge victory this way. Observers' perceptions of who won and who lost in a war or crisis often diverge widely from the realities on the ground. Armies can win brilliant triumphs in battle and observers may nevertheless see the outcome as a defeat. Diplomats can make major concessions in crisis negotiations and observers may nevertheless see the outcome as a victory. In this book we dissect the psychological, political and cultural factors that predispose observers to perceive outcomes of international disputes as victories or defeats. By observers we mean anyone paying attention to the event—the public, the media, political elites, leaders themselves, or foreign governments. By perceptions we mean observers' personal interpretations of the world. Sometimes perceptions and reality match, sometimes they do not.

Source: Dominic D.P. Johnson and Dominic Tierney, "Introduction," *Failing to Win: Perceptions of Victory and Defeat in International Politics* (see Chapter 7, Suggested Additional Resources).

PHYSICAL SCIENCES: CLIMATOLOGY

Mark Jacobson and Mark Delucchi begin the introduction to their article, first published in *Scientific American* magazine, by establishing their topic as worthy of consideration by world leaders. They use the first-person plural (*we* think, *our* plan), which creates a conversational tone that is likely to be welcome, given the complexity of their topic. They then make a bold claim: that they have a plan for solving global energy issues in mere decades. Their writing is straightforward, approachable, and—a rarity in climate-change literature—upbeat.

In December [2009] leaders from around the world will meet in Copenhagen to try to agree on cutting back greenhouse gas emissions for decades to come. The most effective step to implement that goal would be a massive shift away from fossil fuels to clean, renewable energy sources. If leaders can have confidence that such a transformation is possible, they might commit to an historic agreement. We think they can.

A year ago former vice president Al Gore threw down a gauntlet: to repower America with 100 percent carbon-free electricity within 10 years. As the two of us started to evaluate the feasibility of such a change, we took on an even larger challenge: to determine how 100 percent of the world's energy, for *all* purposes, could be supplied by wind, water and solar resources, by as early as 2030. Our plan is presented here.

Source: Mark Z. Jacobson and Mark A. Delucchi, "A Path to Sustainable Energy by 2030" (see http://sites.broadviewpress.com/realworldtopics).

Mapping

Mapping, usually part of your introduction, is a survey or forecasting of the points of argument your essay will address. The mapping section outlines (in complete sentences, of course, not in outline form) your discussion of the issue or problem. It lets your readers know how you will make your points, helping them to understand the rest of your paper.

The mapping section should follow shortly after the thesis and should trace, in slightly more detail, the thesis that you just made.

To map your argument, briefly walk through the points you will make and the terrain you will cover to make your argument. This helps your reader see the process of your reasoning. Your mapping section may make clear the positions that others have taken on your problem, and/or introduce what and who you will be discussing. In the body of your essay, you will develop the points outlined in your map.

Examples of Mapping

HUMANITIES: PHILOSOPHY

Here, John Nolt begins his essay by briefly describing a problem within global warming studies, and he then sets up the structure and content of his essay, which will address this problem. He describes not only *what* he will address, but *how* he will address it. This short map is especially useful; because he is a philosopher, Nolt's approach differs from the usual scientific approaches to global warming studies.

> In discussions of global climate change, it is often assumed that the consequences of the choices of a single individual are negligibly small. I am not, however, aware of any serious attempt to justify that assumption.
>
> My aim here is to estimate the degree of harm to human beings done by an average American (resident of the US) through his/her participation in a greenhouse gas-intensive economy. Any such estimate will, of course, incorporate many controversial assumptions. Others attempting to determine the same quantity would almost certainly obtain different results. Nevertheless, I hope to make some progress toward a defensible figure—and, if I fail, at least to contribute to the identification and elucidation of the difficulties in such an attempt.
>
> My method is to refine the meaning of the phrase "the harm done by the average American's greenhouse gas emissions" through a series of stipulative definitions until a rough quantitative estimate of the harm becomes possible.
>
> Source: John Nolt, "How Harmful Are the Average American's Greenhouse Gas Emissions?" (see http://sites.broadviewpress.com/realworldtopics).

SOCIAL SCIENCES: HUMAN-COMPUTER INTERACTION

In the excerpt below, Sarita Yardi maps her article in a single sentence, which occurs at the end of the second paragraph of her paper. This example is proof that a map need not be long or belabored: it just needs to tell the reader what to expect.

This chapter first describes a backchannel chat room that has taken place over multiple years in a large university student community and then explores some unforeseen and exciting opportunities—as well as possible limitations—for redesigning teaching and learning practices in educational environments.

Source: Sarita Yardi, "Whispers in the Classroom" (see Chapter 3, pp. 310–35).

PHYSICAL SCIENCES: COMPUTER SCIENCE

The excerpt below illustrates how mapping is done in the physical sciences: in general, mapping occurs in the Abstract section, which opens science and technology papers, and/or in the Introduction, which follows the Abstract. In this case, the mapping occurs in the Abstract. Here, authors Mark Blythe and Paul Cairns briefly lay out both the content and the structure of their paper. Note the passive voice style ("It is argued"), which is common in scientific papers and lab reports.

This paper offers an example study of the initial reception of the iPhone 3G through YouTube. It begins with a quantitative account of the overall shape of the most frequently viewed returns for an "iPhone 3G" search. A content analysis of the first hundred videos then explores the returns categorized by genre. Comments on the most popular video "Will It Blend" are analyzed using grounded theory. It is argued that social science methods are not sufficient for a rich understanding of such material. The paper concludes with an analysis of "Will it Blend" that draws on cultural and critical theory. It is argued that a multi-methodological approach is necessary to exploit such data and also to address the challenges of next generation HCI.

Source: Mark Blythe and Paul Cairns, "Critical Methods and User Generated Content: The iPhone on YouTube" (see Chapter 1, pp. 151–71).

Essay Body

The body of an essay is its "meat." In the body, a writer supports his or her argument with summary, synthesis, description of research methods and results, narrative, comparison—any combination of rhetorical moves that will persuade the reader of his or her claim.

How you choose to combine those strategies depends on a number of factors, including

- the conventions of your academic division,
- the nature of your essay,

- the kind of evidence you wish to put forth, and
- the potential audience for your essay.

As you read the essays in this book, notice how each author combines modes of discourse and structures. See the essay on pages 120 to 140 for an example of annotations that point to the kinds of modes used to advance an argument. These will give you an idea of the many modes and structures available to you as you begin to put together your own essay.

As we mentioned above, ***it's often easier to begin with the body of your essay and write the introduction and conclusion later***. That's because the body contains the information you want to get across. The introduction leads you to that information, while the conclusion summarizes it or speculates upon new avenues for contemplation suggested in the body of the essay.

One way to begin:

1. list or outline the points you want to make;
2. review your notes for previous research, results, stories, or evidence that supports these points;
3. organize that information beneath each major point;
4. be sure to look for opposing arguments to rebut or at least acknowledge;
5. if you have created a synthesis grid, described below (see pp. 77–79), you have already done much of this work.

The body of a paper lays out, one subtopic at a time, the points you are using to support and elaborate your argument. Each subtopic may be elaborated in more than one paragraph, but a paragraph should not include more than one subtopic. The body is built of a series of linked paragraphs with connected subtopics, moving from point to point logically and linguistically. Linguistic connections include transitional phrases, repetition, synonyms for important concepts, pronouns appropriately and clearly linked to the nouns they refer to, and overall coherence in syntax, or word order.

Connecting the Parts

Often, making connections between sentences and paragraphs is difficult for writers. There are a number of easy methods that help to connect your sentences and paragraphs:

Sentence Continuity: Connect your thoughts from sentence to sentence in order to stay on topic. There are three main ways to do so:

- transitional phrases (e.g., on the other hand, not only ... but also, this concept is also apparent in);

- conjunctions (e.g., as if, but, yet, while, nevertheless, furthermore);
- keywords (repeat words and phrases from the past sentence in the following sentence, or find effective synonyms for these words; use pronouns appropriately, making sure that the noun they refer to is clear).

Paragraph Transitions: Connect your thoughts from paragraph to paragraph by means of your topic sentence. Basically, you use the same tools that you employ for sentence continuity (transitional phrases, conjunctions, keywords), but instead of staying on topic, you are switching to a new topic. However, in changing topics you must also connect the new topic to the previous one.

Topic Sentences: Your topic sentence, generally the first sentence of a new paragraph, helps to connect your new paragraph to the previous one and to advance your thesis based on the way you outlined it in your mapping.

SAMPLES OF STUDENT WRITING

Following are two sample student summaries of Justin Kaplan's essay "Born to Trouble: One Hundred Years of *Huckleberry Finn*." The first generally lacks clear topic sentences and exhibits poor sentence continuity and paragraph transitions. There are other problems as well, but as you will see, they are all easily fixed.

In his essay, "Born to Trouble: One Hundred Years of *Huckleberry Finn*" Justin Kaplan defends and justifies Twain's choice of language and characters by revealing the true nature of the story. People's negative reactions to Huck Finn are due to Twain's intention of presenting a satire. Society has discredited the book and attempted to limit its distribution. Justin Kaplan explains much of the misunderstanding of Mark Twain's book, *The Adventures of Huckleberry Finn*, a novel that has endured criticism and rejection to the point of being banned from schools, libraries, and even a whole state.

Kaplan argues that the main character, Huck, in terms of social etiquette, was definitely not a model adolescent. "Many readers found [the] great novel objectionable because it violated genteel standards of social and literary decorum" (Kaplan 354). Kaplan notes that the book was criticized for allegedly being racist. Some groups found such words as "nigger" as well as the portrayal of Jim, the runaway-slave, to be offensive.

Numerous school councils, libraries, and even the state of Massachusetts banned the novel. Kaplan provides background for his essay by explaining that the main criticism that Twain's book suffered was that it dealt with foul language, poor morality, and basic filth.

It is not merely a story describing the "boyhood high-jinks" (Kaplan 355) of the young "hero," Huck, but rather a satire of the American society of the time that Twain writes about. One sees the raw ugliness and foolishness of people. Critics could only see and be offended by the superficial aspects of the book:

the crude language and blasphemous concepts. Twain's intent was to slander people in such a way that caused an evaluation of one's self and society as a whole. "Offensive as they seemed at the time, these violations of decorum only screened a deeper lever of threat and affront" (354). Twain explains the

> central and constitutive irony [of the book]: "A sound heart and a deformed conscience come in collision and conscience suffers defeat." Huck's "deformed conscience" is the internalized voice of public opinion, of a conventional wisdom that found nothing wrong in the institution of slavery and held as mortal sin any attempt to subvert it... conscience "can be trained to approve any wild thing you want it to approve if you begin its education early and stick to it." (Kaplan 354)

Kaplan's argument is that the book has basically been misunderstood by its critics. Huck learns to overlook the ideas of what he should do in dealing with certain dilemmas that were installed in him through his upbringing (his "conscience") and eventually becomes more comfortable with going by what his heart tells him is right. He "rejects what he considers to be an unjust and immoral law. He also rejects the craving for social approval that, according to Twain, motivate the behavior of most of us" (Kaplan 355). Kaplan's intention is to show that through becoming more of an individual thinker, Huck ultimately becomes a better person. He explains that beyond Twain's "hero's" roughness, there is a good example for the book's readers to follow. Kaplan maintains that the character of Huck, though seen as unkempt, lazy, impolite, and overall a naughty kid, is essentially the most "good" person in the story.

The potentially offensive words such as "nigger" by explaining were essential due to Twain's attempt to be authentic and true to the time in which the story is based. Twain is trying to show the ignorance and foolishness of American people living in the time during which slavery was common practice. Kaplan writes that "One has to be deliberately dense to miss the point Mark Twain is making here and to construe such passages as evidences of his 'racism.'" (357). Twain was known by friends to have a poor opinion of racism and the abuse of basic human rights. Twain's intention was to offend people in such a way that caused them to question their own actions. Kaplan defends Twain's choice of language.

People who were able to read Twain's true meaning were unable to accept it and didn't want to see or admit to having understood it. Kaplan suggests that such reactions to the book as banning it were simply a "way of dealing with [its] profound affront" (355). Perhaps the book is indeed unsuitable for children, as some of its heavy ideas questioning social morals may be hard to understand at their level, but those who attempted to regulate and limit the distribution of the book should have themselves not taken Twain's message lightly. He basically says that those who criticized the novel for being crude and racist simply missed Twain's essential message.

Works Cited

Kaplan, Justin. "Born to Trouble: One Hundred Years of Huckleberry Finn." *Mark Twain's Adventures of Huckleberry Finn: A Case Study in Critical Controversy*. Gerald Graff and James Phelan, eds. New York: St. Martin's Press, 1995. 348-358.

Here is a revision of the same piece of writing. This time the essay has clear topic sentences, indicated with underlining. Phrases for establishing **sentence continuity** (transitional phrases, conjunctions, and keywords) are indicated in bold type. *Paragraph transitions* are indicated in bold italics. As you will see, sometimes these techniques overlap.

In his essay "Born to Trouble: One Hundred Years *of Huckleberry Finn*," Justin Kaplan explains much of society's misunderstanding of Mark Twain's book, *The Adventures of Huckleberry Finn*, a novel that has endured criticism and rejection to the point of being banned from schools, libraries, and even a whole state. The essay defends and justifies Twain's choice of language and characters by revealing the true nature of the story. Kaplan explains that the reasons behind people's negative reactions to Huck Finn have to do with Twain's intention of presenting a satire criticizing society as a whole. Society has dealt with this criticism by discrediting the book and attempting to limit its distribution.

Kaplan provides background for his essay **by *explaining that the main criticism*** that Twain's book suffered was that it dealt with foul language, poor morality, and basic filth. "Many readers found [the] great novel objectionable because it violated genteel standards of social and literary decorum" (Kaplan 354). **Kaplan agrees** that the main character, Huck, in terms of social etiquette, was definitely not a model adolescent. On the superficial side, his crudeness was perhaps a bad example for young readers to follow. **Furthermore**, Kaplan notes that the book was criticized for allegedly being racist. Some groups found **such words as "nigger"** as well as the portrayal of Jim, the runaway slave, to be offensive. **As a result**, numerous school councils, libraries, and even the state of Massachusetts banned the novel.

Kaplan's ***response*** to Huck's critics is that the book has basically been misunderstood by its detractors. It is not merely a story describing the "boyhood high jinks" (Kaplan 355) of the young "hero" Huck, but is rather a satire of the American society of the time that Twain writes about. Through the characters in the story, one sees the **raw ugliness and foolishness** of people. It is unfortunate **that critics could only see** and be offended by the superficial aspects of the book: the crude language and blasphemous concepts. As Kaplan's essay clarifies, Twain's **intent was not to insult** the readers simply with dirty words but rather to slander people in such a way that caused an evaluation of one's self and society as a whole. Kaplan writes: "Offensive as they seemed at the time, **these violations** of decorum only screened a deeper lever of threat and affront" (354). Twain himself explains the

> central and constitutive irony [of the book]: "A sound heart and a deformed conscience come into collision and conscience suffers defeat." Huck's "deformed conscience" is the internalized voice of public opinion, of a conventional wisdom that found nothing wrong in the institution of slavery and held as mortal sin any attempt to subvert it ... conscience "can be trained to approve any wild thing you want it to approve if you begin its education early and stick to it." (Kaplan 354)

Kaplan maintains that ***the character of Huck***, though seen as unkempt, lazy, impolite, and overall a naughty kid, is essentially the "good" character in the story. Defending Huck, he explains that beyond Twain's "hero's" roughness, there is a **good** example for the book's readers to follow: Huck learns to overlook the ideas of what he should do in dealing with certain dilemmas that were installed in him through his upbringing (his "conscience") and eventually becomes more comfortable with going by what his heart tells him is right. **Moreover**, he "rejects what he considers to be an unjust and immoral law. He also rejects the craving for social approval that, according to Twain, motivates the behavior of most of us" (Kaplan 355). Kaplan's **intention** is to show that through becoming more of an individual thinker, **Huck** ultimately becomes a better person.

Kaplan does not limit himself to defending Twain's characterization of Huck. He defends Twain's choice of language **as well** by explaining how potentially offensive words such as "nigger" were essential due to Twain's attempt to be authentic and true to the time in which the story is based. He points out that if anything, **Twain** is trying to show the ignorance and foolishness of American people **living in the time** during which slavery was common practice. **The situation is analogous** to the use of racial slurs such as "gooks" and "chinks" uttered by American soldiers in movies portraying the Vietnam War. Kaplan writes that "One has to be deliberately dense to miss the point Mark Twain is making here and to construe such passages as evidences of his 'racism'" (357). Kaplan adds that Twain was known by friends to have a poor opinion of **racism** and the abuse of basic human rights. **Twain's intention**, as interpreted by Kaplan, was to offend people in such a way that caused them to question their own actions.

Kaplan suggests that *such reactions to the book* as banning it were simply a "way of dealing with [its] profound affront" (355). He basically says that those who **criticized the novel** for being crude and racist simply missed Twain's essential message. People who were able to read Twain's true **meaning** were unable to accept it and didn't want to see or admit to having understood it. Perhaps **the book** is indeed unsuitable for children, as some of its heavy ideas questioning social morals may be hard to understand at their level, but those who attempted to regulate and limit the distribution of the book would best be served by taking Twain's message more seriously themselves.

Works Cited

Kaplan, Justin. "Born to Trouble: One Hundred Years of Huckleberry Finn." *Mark Twain's Adventures of Huckleberry Finn: A Case Study in Critical Controversy*. Gerald Graff and James Phelan, eds. New York: St. Martin's Press, 1995. 348-358.

Notice how the second draft of the essay does the work that the reader had to do in the first essay. In the second draft, the writer connects new topics to previous ones using connecting phrases and the repetition of words or concepts. The writer also connects sentences with transitional phrases and conjunctions. Although the second draft could still be improved with further revision, it provides a much better read than the first draft.

The Conclusion

After you have reviewed and edited the introduction and body of your paper, it will be time to think about the conclusion. You could think of your conclusion as *your last chance to persuade your readers*.

You might want, for example, to

1. leave them with a final thought;
2. suggest an action you want them to take; and/or
3. spark their interest in further study.

You might also think of your conclusion as answering questions that the essay brings up. These questions might suggest implications for the larger public, and for academics beyond your field.

For example:

1. You might consider what your study of the rate of obesity among schoolchildren suggests about the state of public health in America.
2. You might suggest ways in which your study revises previous understandings about the efficacy of air-to-ground missiles used in the Persian Gulf War.
3. You might conclude that your research on early influences on Cubism changes the way art historians should view an artistic genre.

These kinds of conclusions summarize the ways in which your essay adds to the academic conversation. They might even suggest ways in which your essay affects people in general.

Sample Conclusions

HUMANITIES: PHILOSOPHY

In the introduction to his essay "Consciousness," from Chapter 3 of his book *Our Posthuman Future: Consequences of the Biotechnology Revolution*, philosopher Francis Fukuyama claims that despite what some neuroscientists, computer scientists, and proponents of Artificial Intelligence believe, "The fact of the matter is that we are nowhere close to a breakthrough; consciousness remains as stubbornly mysterious as it ever was."

In his conclusion, Fukuyama muses on the possibilities for understanding human consciousness. This conclusion represents something of a softening of his position throughout the essay, in which he expresses deep skepticism—even ridicule—of the claims of some computer scientists that the unraveling of consciousness is

FOCUS

CONCLUSION DOS AND DON'TS

Although there are no hard-and-fast rules for conclusions, these suggestions may prove helpful for writing better conclusions:

- **Do** comment on the implications of your findings to the larger context of the conversation to which you're contributing.
- **Do** consider proposing a plan of action or further research based on the findings of your research or analysis. **Or** summarize the reasons your claim makes sense.
- **Do** end with a question: What remaining mysteries or uncertainties have your findings unearthed? **Or** issue a final persuasive statement.
- **Don't** take your essay in a new direction or raise a point that you should have developed in the body of your paper.
- **Don't** weaken your argument with confessions that you're not an expert in the field. If you've brought in solid evidence to support your thesis in the body of the paper, this kind of statement won't be necessary.
- **Don't** merely reiterate your introduction. Your introduction should indicate where your paper is going. Your conclusion should indicate where it's been. In a longer paper, it's okay to summarize your findings. In a shorter paper, summary will be unnecessary.

close at hand. This softening of rhetoric implies that he is skeptical without being close-minded. It might make a turned-off reader more open to his claim.

> This is not to say that the demystification by science will never happen. Searle himself believes that consciousness is a biological property of the brain much like the firing of neurons or the production of neurotransmitters and that biology will someday be able to explain how organic tissue can produce it. He argues that our present problems in understanding consciousness do not require us to adopt a dualistic ontology or abandon the scientific framework of material causation. The problem of how consciousness arose does not require recourse to the direct intervention of God. It does not, on the other hand, rule it out, either.
>
> Source: Francis Fukuyama, "Consciousness," from *Our Posthuman Future: Consequences of the Biotechnology Revolution* (see Chapter 5, Suggested Additional Resources, p. 444).

SOCIAL SCIENCES: HUMAN-COMPUTER INTERACTION

In her article "Whispers in the Classroom," computer scientist Sarita Yardi presents her research on ways in which online chat rooms could transform classroom learning behaviors and practices. Her conclusion suggests possibilities for the future of education. Notice the transitional words and phrases (*therefore, but, this notion of, once, however, furthermore*) that move her from sentence to sentence and from thought to thought.

The backchannel may therefore enable a type of education that is progressive but meaningful and has long been needed in the American school system. "It means basing instruction on the needs, interests and developmental stage of the child; it means teaching students the skills they need in order to learn any subject, instead of focusing on transmitting a particular subject; it means promoting discovery and self-directed learning by the student through active engagement; it means having students work on projects that express student purposes." This notion of constructivism may be the ticket to avoiding the learning paradox that plagues much of student motivation in the classroom. Once a student knows how to complete a task, he or she is no longer motivated to learn or participate in that task, and performance in that task will not improve. However, the organic, evolving, and everchanging dynamics in the backchannel prevent students from succumbing to this sense of stagnancy in learning. Students may be encouraged to learn through a self-motivated eagerness to explore the opportunities and novelties offered by the backchannel on an ongoing basis. Furthermore, as an online, Web-based medium, it allows youth to continuously refine their existing media practices in parallel to their backchannel use. As digital natives, they can produce, consume, remix, and generate their own learning opportunities. They may truly be creating their own classroom of the future.

Source: Sarita Yardi, "Whispers in the Classroom" (see Chapter 3, pp. 310–35).

PHYSICAL SCIENCES: MATHEMATICS, COMPUTER SCIENCE

In his article "Logistics and Analysis in the Science of War," James A. Harvey III argues that scientific analysis would improve American success in war. In his conclusion, he advocates immediate action on the part of the Army. This article was originally published in *Army Sustainment*, a journal published by the US Army. As Harvey's reading audience consists of US Army decision-makers, his call to action has a good chance of being considered by those who could carry it out.

It is rather easy to demonstrate the need for analysis and the use of science applications in warfare. In particular, given modern advances in technology and the logistics tail needed to support them in an increasingly budget-constrained environment, logistics is an area in which analysis can pay huge dividends. It appears that now is the time to focus more of our analysis capabilities on logistics to preserve combat power in the future Army.

Source: James A. Harvey III, "Logistics and Analysis in the Science of War" (see Chapter 7, Suggested Additional Resources, p. 610).

MAJOR TYPES OF ACADEMIC ESSAY

Academic essays may take any number of forms. Most combine the major "types" discussed below to form a unique structure—ideally, the structure that both writer and reader find makes the clearest, most thorough and effective discussion of a topic or issue.

Summary

Summary is a very important part of academic writing. In the briefest terms, a summary restates and explains other writing (or movies, stage plays, etc.) in more concise and often clearer terms. It's used in all kinds of academic writing as well as in the workplace. In academic settings, summary is often seen merely as a means of restating another writer's words. However, summary also can help you, and then your reader, to understand and interpret the piece of writing being discussed.

Summary is more than repeating someone else's writing in slightly different words.

To summarize a text, you must

- Decide what you think are the most significant parts of the essay by
  - separating the important points from the relatively unimportant, and
  - distinguishing between an example and the point that the example is used to make.
- Understand and explain these crucial points in order to demonstrate how each point fits into the framework of the larger argument.
- Understand what the author is *doing* in order to make the points that he or she makes.

When writing a summary, ask yourself the following:

- What is the thesis of the piece of writing?
- What are the main supporting points?
- How does the author go about making his or her argument?
- What are the author's goals?
- How does a particular point help the author progress toward those goals?
- What key problems does the author discuss?
- To what ends does the author use examples?

- Who or what does the author see as responsible for the problem or problems she or he writes about?
- How does one particular piece of argument fit with another significant piece a few pages back? And so on.

A summary can:

- **Clarify your own understanding of a piece of writing or a set of data.** Most readers skim over what they're reading, missing critical points or nuances of expression. Writing a summary helps you focus on the essential points of a piece of writing. This is a useful **mnemonic** (memory-serving) device. For example, summary helps you study for an essay exam or synthesize the various ideas set out in a series of writings.
- **Clarify your reader's understanding of another author's or researcher's ideas, perspective, or data.** Whether you're writing a long research paper or a short argument, you will need to bring in several perspectives on the issue or topic of controversy, many of which the reader might not be familiar with. You also might want to focus on a single aspect of another author's report or essay. Summaries are essential in either case.

FOCUS

TIPS FOR A GOOD SUMMARY

Use textual evidence: Support your summary with evidence from the text. Use direct quotations and paraphrases to support what you think are the essay's major arguments. Be careful, though, not to let the quotations overtake your own voice. In that case, you might as well hand in a copy of the text itself. Remember, explain the essay or book and support your interpretation; don't copy it.

Write for your audience: Assume your hypothetical audience is composed of people who have either not read the original essay or book, or who read it really quickly and didn't understand it. Your paper is a response to their question, "So tell me, what is the author's point in this essay or book, and how does he or she go about making that point?"

Use summary as a part of a larger argument: Summary does not need to be restricted to a summary paper. Summary is also used within argumentative prose. Summary appears often in published works—of extant research in a field, historical events, movie and book plots, cultural rites, study methods, and so on. If you are writing a scientific paper, for example, you will need to summarize the data of previous researchers as a building block for making your own argument. Once you conduct your experiment or gather your information, you will need to summarize your own data before you can move on to interpret and explain it for yourself and for the reader. Summary rarely stands on its own; writers often go on to critique, refute, or analyze a piece of writing they've summarized. Writing good summaries is therefore a critical skill.

- **Clarify various perspectives on a given issue.** Summary helps to make clear how writers may agree or disagree about major or minor points in a debate. Summarizing a number of pieces of writing helps to show the possible positions that can be taken regarding an issue. Summary helps you to clearly understand the positions of others and thus how your position may differ.
- **Help you to see how a writer has put an argument together.** How do the various parts of the essay fit together? To what end does a writer use a particular illustration? What point is the writer making by bringing up a certain text?

In other words, summary helps the reader to understand *how* an essay works.

Sample Summaries

HUMANITIES: LITERARY THEORY

In the passage below, literary theorist N. Katherine Hayles summarizes Alan Turing's seminal paper in computer science, "Computer Machinery and Intelligence." Hayles ends this short summary of the paper by restating Turing's thesis: If the reader of text cannot tell the difference between the machine and the human based strictly on textual responses to a questioner, then "machines can think."

> You are alone in the room, except for two computer terminals flickering in the dim light. You use the terminals to communicate with two entities in another room, whom you cannot see. Relying solely on their responses to your questions, you must decide which is the man, which the woman. Or, in another version of the famous "imitation game" proposed by Alan Turing in his classic 1950 paper "Computer Machinery and Intelligence," you use the responses to decide which is the human, which the machine. One of the entities wants to help you guess correctly. His/her/its best strategy, Turing suggested, may be to answer your questions truthfully. The other entity wants to mislead you. He/she/it will try to reproduce through the words that appear on your terminal the characteristics of the other entity. Your job is to pose questions that can distinguish verbal performance from embodied reality. If you cannot tell the intelligent machine from the intelligent human, your failure proves, Turing argued, that machines can think.
>
> Source: N. Katherine Hayles, "Prologue," *How We Became Posthuman: Virtual Bodies in Cybernetics, Literature, and Informatics* (see Chapter 5, pp. 496–500).

SOCIAL SCIENCES: POLITICAL SCIENCE

In the excerpt below, David Held et al. summarize three basic positions on globalization. Their overview helps readers get a handle on the prevailing perspectives on this complex issue.

> Contemporary debates have thrown up three broad categories of argument about the nature and impact of cultural globalization.... *Hyperglobalizers* of various kinds describe or predict the homogenization of the world under the auspices of American popular culture or Western consumerism in general. As with other forms of globalization, hyperglobalizers are matched by *skeptics* who point to the thinness and ersatz quality of global cultures by comparison and to the persistent, indeed increasing, importance of cultural differences and conflicts along the geopolitical fault lines of the world's major civilizations. Those taking a *transformationalist* position describe the intermingling of peoples and cultures as generating cultural hybrids and new global cultural networks.
>
> Source: David Held et al., "Globalization, Culture and the Fate of Nations" (see Chapter 4, Suggested Additional Resources, p. 366).

PHYSICAL SCIENCES: MEDICINE

PRACTICE SESSION

Briefly summarize one of the shorter essays in Real World Topics, without omitting any critical points each author makes. Compare your summaries with those of your classmates.

The introduction below, from an article by Azra Ramezankhani et al. on the physical effects of war on children, is a summary of previous research on this topic. Superscripted numbers in the passage refer to previous studies, which are listed under References at the end of the article. The authors end this summary with an explanation of how their research fills a gap in existing knowledge.

Studies on the physical attributes in child and adult populations clearly point to long-term (e.g., secular) changes.[1] Secular changes are due to the interaction of genetic and environmental factors. This interaction is manifested at a specific time as a function of different living conditions in various social groups, as well as on a long-term basis under the influence of gradual changes in living conditions.[1,2] A country's developmental progress and overall changes in socio-economic structure are reflected in the outcome of secular trend studies on physical growth, development and rate of maturation in children.[3] ... Despite some studies about the Iran-Iraq war, there is no research regarding the physical growth of adolescents born during the war years, which is the purpose for conducting this study, e.g., to compare anthropometric and biochemical indices of adolescent boys and girls born during and after this war.

Source: Azra Ramezankhani et al., "Comparison of Anthropometric and Biochemical Indices of Adolescents Born During and After the Iran-Iraq War; Tehran Lipid and Glucose Study" (see Chapter 7, pp. 650–58).

Synthesis

Synthesis can be defined as the combination of important elements of separate materials, abstract elements, or documents. Chemists and other scientists use synthesis to describe the creation of a more complex substance or compound from elements or simpler compounds. Psychologists use synthesis to describe the combination of personal traits, attitudes, and behaviors that create an integrated personality.

As a writing practice, it means to assemble the views, perspectives, or theories from a number of sources in order to clarify each element and to see how each works in concert with or in opposition to the others. It's a way of mapping out the terrain navigated by a group of texts related to a problem or topic. This method is especially useful when you are consulting several complex sources for a research project. Once you have completed a synthesis, you will likely have a much easier time formulating your own thesis and organizing your essay.

Your task in synthesis, then, is to define and characterize the state of the problem.

The Synthesis Grid

One way to manage the process of synthesis when you are working with several sources is to construct a synthesis grid. This process is discussed in detail by David Kaufer et al. in *Arguing from Sources* (1989). The grid is a way of formatting your synthesis as a single unit, so that it's easy to read and refer to as you plan and write your essay. To see how a synthesis grid comes together, study the example below.

To create a synthesis grid:

- Read all your reference articles.
- Create a grid, as in the example below.
- Label your first column "Writers" or "Authors," and list each author in the subsequent rows of the first column.
- In the first row of columns 2 and below, briefly list common points of discussion that *all* the authors discuss regarding the given subject. A common point is a subtopic on which the various authors take a position, not one on which they necessarily agree.

- Within each area of discussion, briefly describe each author's perspective on that point. It's likely that not all authors will comment on all areas, but your grid will be most useful if the common points are discussed by as many authors as possible.
- Write a paper that is organized by common points, noting the stance that various authors take on a subtopic.
- You will likely have to revise this grid several times, as you come up with new areas of discussion, note complexities within them, break them down, and rewrite them to eliminate common points to which only one or two authors refer.

TABLE 3: SYNTHESIS GRID: THE AIMS OF EDUCATION

WRITERS	COMMON POINTS OF DISCUSSION			
	Oppression	The Cultural Legacy	Social Class	Solution
Matthew Arnold	Those denied the full breadth of culture are oppressed, "sacrificed."	Defined properly, the cultural legacy is required by all.	The division between the classes (working class, middle class, etc.) can be narrowed by a thorough all-encompassing education.	"Perfection" can be reached through a thorough widespread education for all that includes and values humanities, arts, and poetry.
Paulo Freire	Banking system of education is oppressive.	Represents historical worldview of the dominant.	Banking system of education maintains the status quo between classes; the educated elite oppresses students in a way that prevents them from reacting against the system.	A problem-posing education will free those formerly oppressed by the banking system.
Adrienne Rich	Oppression comes from patriarchal, false universals/social norms.	Must be critically engaged; deconstruct past conceptions; "re-vise."	Differentiation between classes based on socio-economics should be reconsidered to include divisions created by societies' "gender norms."	One must "unlearn" the patriarchal, false universals by revisiting them through a feminist perspective.
Mark Edmundson	If anything, students are oppressed by the lack of cultural options afforded by the consumer culture.	Required for students to be challenged by "greatness" and "genius." Otherwise students become (or remain) complacent and self-satisfied.	Student populations are mostly middle class because college education is based on consumer model.	The solution has to do with individuals finding passion and facing the challenges that the past offers.

The grid in Table 3 synthesizes readings on a debate about the aims of education, according to various thinkers.

Sample of Student Writing

The introduction below comes from a synthesis paper by a student, Joshua Greenberg, on the patenting of human genetic material. Notice how Greenberg introduces the topic by pointing to its relevance ("Many people still voice surprise upon hearing that other parties have patented roughly one-fifth of their genetic makeup") and by explaining how far the patenting of the human genome has gone. He summarizes relevant court cases and then briefly characterizes the three major positions on gene patenting taken by scholars in the field: "the uphold perspective," "the elimination perspective," and "the compromise perspective."

Greenberg then provides a "map" of the body of his essay, in which he explains what he will do in the rest of the paper (see "Mapping," pp. 62–64). We include the instructor's comments on this draft.

Joshua Greenberg
Writing X, Section Y
Professor _____
November 5, 2007

The Patenting of Genetic Material

Many people still voice surprise upon hearing that other parties have patented roughly one-fifth of their genetic makeup (Crichton). But gene patenting is now firmly entrenched; years have passed since the first gene patent, and the patents have become common intellectual property in the biotechnology industry. Many might point out that gene patenting did not become entrenched only over the past several years. Instead, they might say, the precedent for the practice existed long ago. The case most cited for establishing the legal basis for gene patenting, *Diamond v. Chakrabarty*, comes from 1980 (Andrews). But few know that since as early as 1912, which saw *Parke-Davis & Co. v. H.K. Mulford & Co.*, courts have upheld patents on identified, isolated, and purified products of nature. In *Parke-Davis*, for example, the court upheld a patent on adrenaline, which the patent applicant had identified, isolated, and purified to create an arguably non-naturally occurring substance (Andrews).

> Some general statement about the state of the controversy is needed here or soon.

Even so, the courts have not shown consistency: for in *Cochrane v. Badische Anilin & Soda Fabrik*, the Supreme Court rejected a patent for manufactured alizarine, a dye previously made from natural materials (Andrews). Furthermore, the precedent set in *Diamond v. Chakrabarty* concerned genetically modified bacteria – a new creation – not human genes. Thus, the precedent for gene patenting remains murky; no case has ever directly addressed the issue (Andrews). Likewise, the larger debate over the costs and benefits of gene patenting remains unresolved, with multiple viewpoints scratching and clawing but none walking

> In what sense has no case ever addressed the issue? What distinction does "directly" denote? In other words, what have the courts said about gene patenting?

> OK, good. I take this as the thesis in the context of synthesis (characterization of the debate).

away clearly victorious. These viewpoints generally take on three forms. The first defends gene patenting as acceptable under the patentability standards and as necessary for the progress of the economy; the second criticizes gene patenting as out of line with patentability standards and as detrimental to scientific progress; and the third, while criticizing and supporting gene patenting depending on the circumstances, takes a more hands-off stance on the issue, claiming that more time is necessary to fully understand the impacts of gene patenting.

For convenience, we may term these three perspectives, in order, the uphold perspective, the elimination perspective, and the compromise perspective. Initially, one might be naturally swayed to support "compromises" as the optimal solutions to problems. However, note that these titles pass no judgment upon the advocacies of the perspectives. For example, some scholars may reject the compromise perspective as a compromise only within the narrow context of gene patenting and not within the broader context of intellectual property in general. On the contrary, other scholars may accept the compromise perspective as a reasonable view which fits in well with intellectual property in general.

> OK

Thus, the term "compromise" serves as a mere convenience and does not comment on the quality of the perspective in one direction or another.

> OK, so here is your mapping.

In this essay, I will begin by addressing the arguments in favor of upholding gene patenting. As a contrast, I will then proceed to discuss the arguments in favor of eliminating gene patenting. Lastly, I will explain the compromise perspective, almost as a bridge between the first two perspectives. However, in reality, while the compromise stance shares some aspects of both the elimination and uphold views, its proponents also construct arguments different from those of the other two groups.

Analysis and Contribution

Analysis is a term used often in academia, and it can mean a number of things. You might have a hard time seeing where synthesis leaves off and analysis begins, and, for that matter, where analysis ends and becomes contribution.

That's because the synthesis-analysis-contribution process can be simultaneous: it can happen all at once, during the thinking process and on paper. We separate the terms here to emphasize that they involve different ways of writing and of looking at a piece of writing.

During your academic career, you'll be using analysis in two basic ways:

1. *As a reader*, analyzing the writings of other writers. This involves **assessing both the content and the structure of the essays in question**:

   - how each writer's argument is constructed;
   - the implications of each argument;
   - the conclusions that may be drawn from each argument; and
   - any "holes" in the argument.

2. As a *writer*, to **construct your own argument**. Once you have completed your source synthesis, and perhaps prepared a synthesis grid (see above, pp. 77–79), you will be ready to find within that group of texts an issue or a set of issues that interests you. In your essay, you will

   - analyze the problem or issue itself; and
   - include the observations you have made about how others have approached the problem or issue.

Your analysis will lead to an essay that will represent a contribution to the existing academic conversation on this topic. Your contribution could consist of

- your stance on an issue fraught with controversy;
- a filling-in of a "hole" that you perceive in existing writing on this topic;
- new data that contradict earlier research; or
- new data that confirm earlier research, but in a new context.

Psychologists Sara Prot and her colleagues begin their article "Video Games: Good, Bad, or Other?" with data about the popularity of video games among children and adolescents. "Today, 90% of American children and teens play video games," they write (see Chapter 2, pp. 192–206). This sentence establishes that their topic is relevant to a large number of people. They then cite several contradictory studies about whether video games are "good" or "bad" for young players. This demonstrates that an issue—a controversy, even—exists among academics in the field. The researchers then clearly state the purpose of their study: "The aim of this article is to give an overview of research findings on positive and negative effects of video games, thus providing an empirical answer to the question, 'are video games good or bad?'" They end with a brief map of their article.

Every one of the essays included in Real World Topics, including the sample student papers, is an example of analysis and a contribution to an academic discourse.

Argument

Contrary to the common connotation of the word, when we use the word "argument," we generally do not mean a verbal confrontation between two or more people. In academic contexts especially, argument refers to **a position or stance taken in a piece of writing or a speech**.

Argument is the most common mode of academic writing. But it is usually a compound mode that incorporates the other kinds of writing, discussed above, including summary, synthesis, and analysis. Most if not all argument papers are contributions to ongoing discourses or conversations.

Most arguments include a thesis statement early in the paper. As discussed above, a thesis statement is a short statement that lays out the central argument the writer will use to persuade the reader. A thesis statement includes a claim with reasons. **An argument is thus a sustained elaboration of the thesis statement**. It develops the claim and spends time expressing and defending the reasons for holding it.

The purpose of argument is to persuade the reader to

- accept a particular point of view,
- adopt a certain attitude, or
- take a specific action.

A good argument is usually presented as reasonable and fair-minded. But that doesn't mean that it cannot be vigorously and passionately expressed. Nevertheless, the best arguments make their case clearly. Many topics are complex and include points that are difficult to comprehend. There is no need to make them more complicated. One should never confuse obfuscation with erudition—that is, unnecessary obscurity with scholarly knowledge and sophistication. The better you understand a topic, the easier it will be for you to explain it and make a compelling case for your position. However, clear, straightforward writing is never easy.

An argument should also include a rebuttal of possible counterarguments to the thesis or the ideas behind it. A rebuttal considers counterarguments and refutes them in advance so that the reader doesn't think of them and discount the argument on that basis.

ARGUMENT VERSUS OPINION

As teachers, we are often asked whether a paper can include opinions. Our answer, when we are looking for an argumentative essay, is that an argument is an opinion (a claim), but one that is supported by reasons.

An opinion is a bald assertion made without support. Generally, in formal college-level writing, your teacher is looking for an argument—a claim supported by satisfying reasons.

So in answer to the question, "Can I give my opinion in this paper?" we usually say, "Yes, provided you support it with evidence and reasoning."

Examples of Argument

HUMANITIES: ART HISTORY

In the passage below, artist and Arabic and Islamic studies Professor Safdar Ahmed considers photographs taken at Abu Ghraib Prison in Iraq, in conjunction with the work of the Iraqi painter Ayad Alkadhi. Ahmed begins his essay with vivid descriptions of photographs of prisoners being tortured and humiliated—images that form the basis of Alkadhi's paintings. But Ahmed's *argument* is complex. Once he has drawn in his readers with the horrific facts and images of the Iraq War, he moves to his real concern: the ability of photographs alone to tell the story of war.

> Whilst war photography is an important source for our understanding and memory of modern conflicts, the images from Abu Ghraib tell a partial story. This is because photography cannot complete our understanding of the event depicted in it. To put it another way, photography isolates an event, lifting it out of the time and context in which it arose. As John Berger points out: "the issue of the war which has caused that moment is effectively depoliticised. The picture becomes evidence of the general human condition. It accuses nobody and everybody." For this reason, images of war must exist within an understanding of their contextual importance if they are to have any meaning for the larger issues over which such wars are fought in the first place. If media images of the Vietnam War catalysed a peace movement in the United States during the 1970s, they were only able to do so by fitting within a narrative, and popular sentiment, which was then growing amongst sections of American society. As Susan Sontag observes: "photographs cannot create a moral position, but they can reinforce one—and can help build a nascent one."
> Source: Safdar Ahmed, "'Father of No One's Son': Abu Ghraib and Torture in the Art of Ayad Alkadhi" (see Chapter 7, pp. 637–48).

SOCIAL SCIENCES: ECONOMICS

Economist Irwin Stelzer argues that the Obama administration's $700-billion bail-out of the banking system marks a fundamental shift in the American economic system. "The day has passed," Stelzer writes, "when that engine of capitalism, the financial market, will be allowed to operate more or less unimpeded by government." Anticipating counterarguments that government intervention has always been part of the capitalist system, Stelzer proceeds to acknowledge and then rebut them.

> True, we have long had a Federal Reserve System that sets short term interest rates; true, the institutions that have been nationalized have

always been Government-Sponsored Enterprises (GSEs), privately owned but with a government mission and implicit guarantees to lenders; true, too, the government has long insured depositors at savings institutions against loss. But never before has the government so massively and systematically socialized the risks undertaken by the one-time masters of the universe, Wall Street's investment bankers, who until now more or less controlled the allocation of capital among its several capitalist claimants. Now, the last pure investment banks—Goldman Sachs and Morgan Stanley—have surrendered substantial freedoms by opting to become deposit-taking institutions, subject to federal regulation, in return for access to support of the Fed in times of need. It is not much of an exaggeration to say that capitalism as we have known it is no more, and that a New Capitalism is once again in the process of creation.

Source: Irwin Stelzer, "The New Capitalism" (see Chapter 6, Suggested Additional Resources, p. 520).

PHYSICAL SCIENCES: ENVIRONMENTAL STUDIES

In this passage, Alden Griffith refutes the argument of Michael Crichton, who facetiously announced, in a speech also included on the companion website, that "Aliens Cause Global Warming." Griffith announces that he will comment on two aspects of Crichton's argument: the meaning of "consensus" in the scientific process, and the reliability of climate models.

In the excerpt below, he considers the meaning of consensus using the example of Einstein's theory of relativity. This example points out a flaw in Crichton's assertion that "the claim of consensus has been the first refuge of scoundrels; it is a way to avoid debate by claiming that the matter is already settled." Griffith also claims that Crichton's larger argument is based on a logical fallacy: the straw man argument, which Griffith defines here.

Einstein originally proposed the idea of mass-energy equivalence largely based on theoretical ground and without strong direct empirical evidence. Support grew around the theory, but if you wanted rock-solid "proof," you probably would have had to wait almost three decades until the discovery of the positron (the observed conversion of energy into matter and antimatter). While it currently may seem silly to think of there being a consensus around $E = mc^2$, there was a time when this "fact" needed to build up its own evidence and consensus. And in contrast to climate science, this particular case *does* largely boil down to a relatively straight-forward test that can convincingly support or refute the theory. Crichton's broader implication that all of climate science needs to be 100 percent "solid" is really a strawman argument: an impossible version of reality that is therefore easy to pull apart. Instead of indicating science that's not solid, the consensus on climate change informs us which aspects *are* solid and which are less so.

Source: Alden Griffith, "Crichton's 'Aliens Cause Global Warming'" (see http://sites. broadviewpress.com/realworldtopics).

STRUCTURE AND VISUAL DESIGN: PUTTING IT ALL TOGETHER

Principles of Structure

How writers ultimately organize their essays depends on many variables. The two most important are these:

1. the field in which the writer is writing, and
2. the nature of the particular assignment or project the writer is attempting.

Some principles of structure, discussed in more detail elsewhere in this section, apply across the disciplines:

- Have a clearly stated claim or thesis.
- Include previous research conducted by peers in the field.
- Respond to that research in a way that promotes development within the field.
- Present evidence that supports your claim or thesis (data, examples from the primary source, etc.).
- Be mindful of your audience: Who will be reading the essay, and what are their interests and expertise? Write to those people.
- Present your research or perspective in language and with a structure that best suits your argument. Whether your language is ornate or plain, or your structure linear or non-linear, keep in mind that the purpose of academic writing is to present your case, persuade your reader, and thus contribute to the academic conversation.

Design Basics: How Your Paper Should Look

How should your paper or report look on the page? How should it be structured or organized? As you might imagine, **different disciplines have different formatting traditions** (titles, headings, subheadings, use of white space, margin size, font style, graphics such as charts and graphs, captions, page numbering, etc.). Your professor may specify these elements on the assignment sheet. However, he or she may instead assume that you are aware of the design conventions of the discipline, and won't mention them until your marked first draft or graded paper is returned to you.

Of course, **conventions vary even within disciplines, depending on the purpose of your writing**. A chemistry lab report will differ from a chemistry research paper, for instance. Naturally, each professor will have his or her own format requirements. The suggestions below are merely guidelines.

Humanities

Formatting: Papers written for literature, philosophy, fine arts, history, religion, and foreign languages generally require

- **one-inch margins** on all sides of the paper;
- **your name** and usually the class name and date in the upper corner, perhaps along with the professor's name;
- **a title**, in regular type, not underlined, with no quotation marks unless it includes, for example, the title of a short story;
- **indented paragraphs**: the first lines should be indented half an inch or five spaces;
- **page numbers**: located at the bottom of the page, starting with page 2;
- **subheadings**: humanities papers can include but do not require subheadings; but in papers of 20 pages or more they are standard.

Structure: Introduction, Body, Conclusion

A humanities paper begins with an introduction, which sets out your topic and usually contains the thesis.

The body of the paper presents supporting evidence, usually examples from the primary "text" (e.g., the historical event, philosophical treatise, novel, painting, dance performance, film, or symphony).

The conclusion summarizes the evidence from the body of the paper without reiterating the introduction. There are no "rules" as to the nature of a conclusion to a humanities paper, as long as it presents an original idea and does not merely re-hash the rest of the paper.

A humanities paper's conclusion may

- posit a philosophy or theory of human behavior or community,
- provide ruminations about the author or performer being considered, or
- suggest a proposal for further study.

For examples of humanities structure, see the articles by Nicholas Carr in Chapter 1, Michael Crichton and John Nolt in the companion website, and Francis Fukuyama in Chapter 5.

Social Sciences

The structure of papers written for a sociology, psychology, media studies, political science, economics, or anthropology class varies according to the type of paper required. Social sciences papers could be literature reviews, expository essays, persuasive essays, or case studies.

A social science paper that calls for a study including data will have divisions similar to a physical sciences paper, described below.

A social science paper that calls for a literature overview or that is essentially an essay will have a structure similar to that of a humanities paper, described above.

For examples of social science structure, see the articles by Sarita Yardi in Chapter 3, Anne Sibert in Chapter 6, and Stephen Pinker in Chapter 7.

Physical Sciences

Biology, geology, botany, astronomy, chemistry, geography, computer science, and physics papers will usually be literature reviews, lab reports, or research reports. Literature reviews, a less-common type of scientific paper, summarize significant studies in a research area without presenting new research.

Lab or research reports require several divisions, designated by subheads. They also often include charts, graphs and other data graphics, designated as Figure 1, Figure 2, etc. The lab or research report requires a scientist to present his or her research and place it in the context of other research on the topic. These kinds of papers are expected to present new findings, not merely summarize past research.

Scientific research reports generally use a structure known by the acronym **IMRAD** (Introduction, Materials and Methods, Results, and Discussion/Conclusion). These subgroups are indicated in the paper with subheadings in bold type.

Research reports include, in order:

1. an **abstract**, a one-page (or shorter) summary of the study and its findings;
2. an **introduction**, which includes the hypothesis and a literature review;
3. a **materials and methods** section, which details how the study was conducted;
4. a **results** section, the "meat" of the paper, which contains the data;
5. a **discussion** or **conclusion** section (some have both) which may:
   a. place the research in context,
   b. discuss the implications of the results, and
   c. describe the additional research necessary to explore the issue or further test the validity of the study's hypothesis.

SOURCE CITATION AND DOCUMENTATION

Every source you consult—in other words, every idea or bit of information that you did not think of on your own or is not general knowledge—must be documented. **If you don't document your sources, you will likely be accused of plagiarizing your paper.** The idea is that if you don't credit your sources, you are implying that the information came from you. And that's stealing.

Each academic discipline has specific ways of documenting sources. It's not necessary to memorize all the details of citation styles. However, you should know the basics and the philosophies behind them.

You can get details online from grammar websites such as Citation Machine (http://citationmachine.net/). For information on citation styles not covered in this Guide, consult the following websites:

- **CBE** (Science): Colorado State University Writing Center (http://writing.colostate.edu/guides/researchsources/documentation/cbe_citation/)
- **AP** (Journalism): Missouri State University Writing Center (http://writingcenter.missouristate.edu/24690.htm)
- **AMA** (Medicine): Missouri State University Writing Center (http://writingcenter.missouristate.edu/24690.htm)
- **ASA** (Sociology): Purdue University Online Writing Lab (http://owl.english.purdue.edu/owl/resource/583/01/)
- **BLA** (Law): Cornell University Law School (http://www.law.cornell.edu/citation/)

MLA Style

The humanities (literature, composition, history, religion, art, music, philosophy, drama, foreign languages) use either MLA (Modern Language Association) style or CMS (Chicago) style (for CMS, see below). In brief, MLA style uses **parenthetical notation**. For parenthetical notation, the page number or the author and page number appear in parentheses after a quotation or paraphrase.

More information about MLA style is available at www.mla.org and in *The MLA Handbook for Writers of Research Papers*, which has an accompanying website available to those who purchase the book.

Templates and Examples, MLA Works Cited

Below you'll find templates for three basic types of entries you are likely to make for your Works Cited page. Just plug your book, article, or website information into this template.

Examples come from the articles or suggested readings in this book.

For a Works Cited page entry, the margins are the reverse of a regular paragraph: the first line goes to the margin; subsequent lines are indented five spaces. This format is known as a **hanging paragraph**. To format a hanging paragraph in Word:

1. Go into Paragraph Format.
2. Under "Special," click on "Hanging."
3. Make sure the paragraph is indented .5" (this is the default).

IN TEXT

> Arthur C. Danto clarifies his own argument about art by placing it in opposition to nineteenth-century philosopher Georg Friedrich Hegel's— although earlier he has explored his alliances with Hegel (6).

This citation refers the reader to the entry in the Works Cited listed under Danto's name.

WORKS CITED

Book, print:

> Author last name, Author first name. *Title, with All Major Words Capitalized.* City of publication: Publisher, year of publication.
> Raheja, Michelle H. *Reservation Reelism: Redfacing, Visual Sovereignty, and Representations of Native Americans in Film.* Lincoln: University of Nebraska Press, 2011.

Article in journal or magazine, print:

> Author last name, Author first name. "Article Title, with All Major Words Capitalized." *Journal Title* Volume Number.Issue Number (publication year): page numbers. Print.
> Ahmed, Safdar. "'Father of No One's Son': Abu Ghraib and Torture in the Art of Ayad Alkadhi." *Third Text* 25.3 (May 2011): 325-34. Print.

Online journal or magazine article:

> Author last name, Author first name. *Site Name*. Institution or Sponsor
>   Name, if Applicable, or N.p. if no publisher given, Site Year or
>   Update Year or n.d. if none given. Day Month Year of Access.
> Crichton, Michael. "Aliens Cause Global Warming." *michaelcrichton.net*.
>   Constant C Productions, 1997. Web. 10 Mar. 2010.

Online book:

> Author last name, Author first name. *Title, with All Major Words Capitalized*.
>   City of Publication, Publication Year. *Online Source*. Web. Day
>   Month Year of Access.
> Raheja, Michelle H. *Reservation Reelism: Redfacing, Visual Sovereignty, and
>   Representations of Native Americans in Film*. Lincoln, NE, 2011.
>   <www.thefreelibrary.com> Web. 20 June 2012.

CMS Style

CMS (Chicago Manual of Style) is used in a variety of academic disciplines. The
CMS notes and bibliography style is used in the humanities and the social sciences.
Chicago style is especially popular in history, religious studies, and music. More
information about Chicago style is available at www.chicagomanualofstyle.org.

CMS in Brief

NOTES ENTRIES

- An in-text superscript number [1] refers to a numbered endnote or
  footnote.
- *Endnotes*: a numbered list of sources, located on a separate page at the
  end of the paper, before the Bibliography.
- *Footnotes*: a numbered list of sources, located at the bottom of the page
  where the source is cited. Refer to a specific page or section of the cited
  source. May also include extra information about that source.
- Use the author's first name first.

BIBLIOGRAPHY LIST

- Located on a separate page at the end of the paper.
- Includes all the sources cited in the paper.
- Includes all the sources you consulted but did not specifically cite in the
  text.

CMS Author-Date Style

The CMS author-date style is used in the physical sciences. This style requires an in-text parenthetical notation which includes the author's last name or names and the publication date, as well as a reference list at the end of the paper.

Templates and Examples, CMS References

IN TEXT

The material to be cited is followed by a superscript number that corresponds to a footnote or endnote. This work also will be cited in the bibliography.

Book, print:

> Raheja contends that depictions of Native Americans in film "often either reflected important pressures that Native communities were facing or completely elided Native concerns in ways that demonstrate deep-seated cultural anxieties."[1]

Note:

> 1. First name Last name, *Book Title with All Major Words Capitalized* (City of Publication: Publisher, year), page number.
> 1. Michelle H. Raheja, *Reservation Reelism: Redfacing, Visual Sovereignty, and Representations of Native Americans in Film* (Lincoln: University of Nebraska Press, 2011), 104.

Bibliography:

> Last name, First name. *Book Title with All Major Words Capitalized*. City of Publication: Publisher, year.
> Raheja, Michelle H. *Reservation Reelism: Redfacing, Visual Sovereignty, and Representations of Native Americans in Film*. Lincoln: University of Nebraska Press, 2011.

Journal or magazine article, print

Note:

> 1. First name Last name, "Article Title," *Journal Name* Volume Number (Year): page number.
> 1. Dawn Elizabeth England, Lara Descartes, and Melissa A. Collier-Meek, "Gender Role Portrayal and the Disney Princesses." *Sex Roles* 64 (2011): 555.

Bibliography:

> Last name, First name. "Article Title." *Journal Name* Volume Number (Year):
>   page numbers.
> England, Dawn Elizabeth, Lara Descartes, and Melissa A. Collier-Meek,
>   "Gender Role Portrayal and the Disney Princesses." *Sex Roles* 64
>   (2011): 555-67.

Online journal or magazine article:

Include a DOI (Digital Object Identifier) if the journal lists one. The DOI is a permanent ID; it will take you directly to the source. If no DOI is available, list the URL (Uniform Resource Locater). An access date is only necessary if your professor requires one; ask your professor.

Note:

1.   First name Last name, "Article Title," *Journal Name* number (Year):
      page, DOI or URL.
1.   David Bordwell, "Never the Twain Shall Meet: Why Can't Cinephiles
      and Academics Just Get Along?" *Film Comment* (May/June 2011):
      http://www.filmcomment.com/article/never-the-twain-shall-meet.

Bibliography:

> Last name, First name. "Article Title." Journal Name, Web address
> Bordwell, David. "Never the Twain Shall Meet: Why Can't Cinephiles
>   and Academics Just Get Along?" *Film Comment*,
>   http://www.filmcomment.com/article/never-the-twain-shall-meet.

APA Style

The social sciences (sociology, psychology, anthropology, political science, education, cultural studies, and geography) use APA style, the style designated by the American Psychological Association.

APA style uses parenthetical documentation in the text of the paper, backing it up with a complete entry on the References list at the end of the paper. In general, however, when you summarize or paraphrase a source in APA Style, refer to the source in the sentence by the last name of the author, and in parentheses by the year of publication.

More information on APA style is available at www.APAStyle.org, http://owl.english.purdue.edu, or in the *Publication Manual of the American Psychological Association*.

In-Text Citation, Parenthetical Notation

In "Collaborative Learning for the Digital Age," originally published in the *Chronicle of Higher Education* (Aug. 26, 2011), Davidson summarizes her argument from her most recent book, *Now You See It* (2011), arguing for a model for education based on digital learning and new studies on how the brain works.

This citation refers readers to the entry under Davidson's name for the date specified (2011).

Templates and Examples, APA References

Book, print:

Author last name, First initial. (publication year). *Title, initial word and word after colon capitalized.* City of publication: Publisher.
Davidson, Cathy N. (2011). *Now you see it: How the brain science of attention will transform the way we live, work, and learn.* Cambridge: Cambridge University Press.

Journal or magazine article, print:

Author last name, First initial, & First initial of second author Last name of second author. (publication year). Article title. *Journal Title Volume number* (Issue number), page numbers.
Leiserowitz, A. A. (2006). "Climate change risk perception and policy preferences: the role of affect, imagery and values." *Climate Change 77*, 45-72.

Online Book:

Author Last Name, Author Initials. (Publication Year). *Book title.* Publication City: Publisher. Retrieved Month Day, Year, from www.name. domain (or database.)
Raheja, M. H. (2011). *Reservation Reelism: Redfacing, Visual Sovereignty, and Representations of Native Americans in Film.* Lincoln: University of Nebraska Press. Retrieved June 9, 2012, from www. nebraskapress.unl.edu.

Online journal or magazine article:

Author last name, First initial. (publication year if available, or n.d.). Article title. Retrieved from www.name.domain/full/url.
Bordwell, D. (2011). Never the twain shall meet: Why can't cinephiles and academics just get along? Retrieved from http://www. filmcomment.com/article/never-the-twain-shall-meet.

CSE Style

CSE (Council of Science Editors) style, used primarily in the physical sciences and computer science, has two subsystems: name-year and citation-sequence. The sub-systems vary according to how a source is noted in the text; the reference page style also varies slightly.

In-Text, Name-Year

Indicate your source in parentheses (Author Last Name Publication Year). If you mention the author in the sentence, put just the year in parenthesis. If you are quoting your source directly, provide the page number as well (Author Last Name Publication Year, p. Pages).

In-Text, Citation-Sequence

Indicate your source with a superscript number[1] that corresponds to a number in your reference list. For example:

> Studies on the physical attributes in child and adult populations clearly point to long-term (e.g., secular) changes.[1] Secular changes are due to the interaction of genetic and environmental factors. This interaction is manifested at a specific time as a function of different living conditions in various social groups, as well as on a long-term basis under the influence of gradual changes in living conditions.[1,2]

Or you may indicate your source with a number in parentheses or brackets [1] that corresponds to a number in your reference list. For example:

> The speed of recent technological change has led to almost equally dramatic transformations in the study of HCI. There have been turns to fun and enjoyment [e.g. 5], experience design [e.g. 22], cultural or reflective design [e.g. 1, 3, 25], semiotic design [e.g. 12] and aesthetics [e.g. 6].

Templates and Examples, CSE References

Book, print:

Name-Year:

1. Last Name First Initials, Second Author Last Name First Initials. (Publication Year) *Book Title*. Publisher. City of Publication. number of pages p.
1. De Souza C. (2005) *The Semiotic Engineering of Human-Computer Interaction*. MIT Press. Cambridge, Mass. 312 p.

Citation-Sequence:

1. Last Name First InitialsNoPeriods, Second Author Last Name First Initials. *Book title*. City of Publication: Publisher; Publication Year. number of pages p.
1. De Souza CS. *The semiotic engineering of human-computer interaction*. Cambridge, Mass.: MIT Press; 2005. 312 p.

Journal or magazine article, print

Name-Year:

Last Name InitialsNoPeriods. Publication Year. Title of article. Journal Title Abbrev. Volume:page numbers.
Jacobson MZ and Delucchi MA. 2009. A plan for a sustainable future: How to get all energy from wind, water and solar power by 2030. Sci Am. Nov:58-65.

Citation-Sequence:

Last Name InitialsNoPeriods. Title of article. Journal Title Abbrev. Publication Year; Volume:page numbers.
Jacobson MZ and Delucchi MA. A plan for a sustainable future: How to get all energy from wind, water and solar power by 2030. Sci Am. Nov 2009:58-65.

Online journal or magazine article:

Name-Date:

Last Name InitialsNoPeriods. Publication Year. Article title. *Journal Title* [Internet]. [cited Year Month Day]; Volume(Issue):pages. Available from: webaddress
Capra RG, Lee CA et al. 2008. Selection and context scoping for digital video collections: an investigation of YouTube and blogs. *JCDL 2008* [Internet]. [cited 2010 Jun 21]; 211-220. Available from: http://portal.acm.org/citation.cfm?id=1378889.1378925

Citation-Sequence:

Last name InitialsNoPeriods. Article title. *Journal Title [online journal]* Publication Year: Volume:pages. Available from: webaddress Accessed Year Month Day.
Capra RG, Lee CA et al. Selection and context scoping for digital video collections: an investigation of YouTube and blogs. *JCDL 2008 [online journal]* 2008: 211-220. Available from: http://portal.acm.org/citation.cfm?id=1378889.1378925 Accessed 2010 Jun 21.

PART II REAL WORLD TOPICS

CHAPTER I

LIVING IN A DIGITAL CULTURE

INTRODUCTION

Contexts of Discussion

Over the past four decades, the exponential growth of new media has resulted in what many call the "digital revolution." Surely there is something to be said for this characterization. Never before have so many people been exposed to so much media data, made possible mostly by the digitalization of information of all kinds, including alphanumeric text, still and moving images, and sound.[1] According to a *New York Times* article ("Your Brain on Computers," June 6, 2010), "in 2008, people consumed three times as much information each day as they did in 1960." And now, everyone is involved. Via computers, cell phones, iPods, and numerous other digital media delivery and communications devices, consumers are also producers, adding to the mass of messages relayed instantly across the globe.

Since the spread of the Internet in the 1990s, most aspects of life have felt the effects of digital media and communications. Shopping, news, entertainment, work, education, dating, social networking, and even identity formation have been touched by digital innovations and the **cybersphere**, the realm where digital participants meet. Digitalization is also a major factor in economic, social, and cultural globalization (see Chapter 4).

Any new media "revolution" is inevitably compared to the most important media development of the early modern world: the printing press introduced in fifteenth-century Europe (although a printing press was developed centuries earlier in China). The printing press has been credited with bringing about great changes in social, educational, cultural, and political realms. It has been credited

---

1   In digital media, the production (and reproduction) of texts and other artifacts is no longer a process of printing marks on paper or pressing analog signals onto vinyl or magnetic tape. Rather, digital media is based on exact copies of code—reducible to unique series of zeros and ones.

with increasing literacy rates, instigating the **Protestant Reformation**, and spurring on the **Enlightenment** and the development of democratic nation states. Similarly, some writers and scholars have suggested that the Internet signals the democratization of literacy, the spread of knowledge to the disadvantaged, the decentralization of political power, and a more equitable distribution of wealth. Others have responded with fear or condemnation, seeing instead the downfall of important traditions and institutions, or the changing of brain patterns for the worse. The digital revolution, some claim, promises to bring about such changes as the demise of the book, the reconfiguration if not the "death" of the author, and the break-up of corporate media dominance.

Yet, while digital innovations have wrought many changes, some writers argue that many of the above claims are exaggerations. More recent approaches to digital media have revised the digital media revolution thesis considerably.

As Henry Jenkins suggests in an essay included in this chapter, rather than outmoding earlier forms of media, the new digital media have reused, revamped, and repackaged older media, while delivering a host of new content and genres through old and new delivery systems. According to Jenkins, rather than a single medium overtaking all others, we have witnessed the "convergence" of media forms and the divergence of media delivery systems. Further, just as the printing press did not by itself bring about social, cultural, and political revolutions, the Internet is not a product of technology alone; it involves the conscious and unconscious choices of **social agents** and the intended and unintended consequences of such choices.

The new media landscape has also affected those who study the media and the behaviors associated with them. This chapter looks at both the personal experiences of those who use digital media and some of the varying approaches to this exciting and daunting terrain.

Areas of Research and Conjecture

As we have suggested, the new media affect many areas of life, including work, school, business, and individual behavior. Therefore, numerous fields are involved in their study.

Computer science is the study of computing, including its hardware and software components and their interactions. Computer scientists design computers and computer programs and study their use and improvement. Computer science is a technology field, but programming involves computer languages, which depend on semantics or symbolic meaning-making. Likewise, computer scientists are not only interested in machines. Many are linguists of sorts, involved in creating and understanding languages that can be executed and understood by computers and humans. Computer science shares much with language study, philosophy, logic, and other sciences. This chapter includes a paper by computer scientists Mark Blythe and Paul Cairns.

Human-computer interaction (HCI), as the name suggests, is the study of human beings as they interact with computer technology. The field is an amalgam of disciplines—including anthropology, computer science, psychology, sociology, and even English language studies. HCI researchers undertake quantitative studies of user response to software interfaces. HCI research also includes qualitative or descriptive studies of users' responses to less quantifiable aspects of computing experience, such as the level of enjoyment experienced by computer users. Often delivered via computer interfaces, new media lend themselves to HCI approaches. In their essay, Mark Blythe and Paul Cairns take, in part, an HCI approach to their topic.

As Jay Bolter notes in an essay in *Digital Media Revisited*, included in the Suggested Additional Resources at the end of this introduction, the field of **media studies** originated with the study of mass media, in particular printed media, film, radio, and television. Media productions such as newspapers, movies, radio shows, and television programs are expensive and have generally been undertaken only by organizations or individuals with significant capital. This fact has shaped the kinds of criticism undertaken by media studies scholars.

Most scholarship on mass media has focused on consumers or audiences. The new digital media, by contrast, allow consumers to become producers in their own right. When dealing with digital media, therefore, media scholars have revised their approach to consider how the roles of producers and consumers are reconfigured within a changing and expanding landscape. We include an essay by the well-known digital-media theorist Henry Jenkins in this chapter.

Cultural studies, **literary studies**, **and critical theory** analyze contemporary culture in connection with social, economic, and political life. **Culture** refers to a people's way of life, which includes the arts, literature, leisure activities, mass media, music, popular entertainment, and other forms of shared experience. Cultural studies has been particularly interested in how consumers "resist" and/or reassign meaning to the products of mass media. Likewise, as Bolter argues, the field has been challenged by new media that allow for greater participation by consumers as producers on the web and elsewhere. Mark Blythe and Paul Cairns's essay demonstrates a critical theory or cultural studies approach. Blythe and Cairns show how critical theory can supplement HCI to analyze users' responses to the iPhone on YouTube.

Literary studies and critical theory have responded to digital media by considering the changes that have been wrought for readers and writers. We discuss the implications of digital media for readers and authors in the Issues and Stakeholders section, below. Similarly, historians provide an important perspective on the emergence of digital media and their relationship to and differences from earlier media developments, especially the printing press. We include works from the field of **history** in the Suggested Additional Resources at the end of this introduction.

In the fields of **neurology** and **psychology**, neurologists, along with cognitive scientists and psychologists, study the effects of new media on the brain and behavior. Using brain imaging and behavioral trials, researchers show how digital media are changing individual psychology and even neural patterns in the brain. Some critics of digital culture lament the effects of the Internet, the iPhone, and other devices on "digital natives," as those who have grown up in the digital era are often called. These critics see the new media contributing to an electronic attention deficit disorder of sorts.

In his book *The Shallows: What the Internet Is Doing to Our Brains*, Nicholas Carr develops this position, using findings of neuroscience to argue that digital media are making us into shallow thinkers. The germ of Carr's argument was presented in his *Atlantic* article "Is Google Making Us Stupid?," included in this chapter. We also include "Meet Your iBrain" by Gary Small and Gigi Vorgan, which represents a more optimistic perspective offered by neuroscience and computer science.

Issues and Stakeholders

Convergence versus media revolution: To frame our understanding of new media, we should consider what the changes represent. Does the appearance of digital media signal a revolution, or another kind of shift? That is, are we witnessing and participating in a complete overthrow of existing media conditions, for better or worse? Does it matter?

The stakes involved in the discussion are not merely academic, for if a media revolution *is* underway, some products, practices, and roles should disappear as new ones emerge. For example, some writers have suggested that the printed book or even the printed page will become obsolete. Others suggest that television will converge with or be replaced by Internet technology. If books are gone, then authors will no longer exist, at least as we think of them now. Without books, our means of knowledge storage, dissemination, and access will change. As educational and entertainment content flows "freely" through cyberspace, ownership of and payment for forms of **intellectual property** (the intangible products of creativity) become increasingly difficult to maintain.

As suggested above, the **digital revolution thesis** has been largely dismissed in favor of a more nuanced and complicated position referred to as the **convergence theory**. According to this theory, older media never disappear. Instead, the means of delivering media change, and particular media flow through more than one type of delivery system. Media producers are no longer bound to just one means of delivering their content. For example, entertainment shows and news programs that once were exclusive to television are now available in different forms on the web. CNN has television channels as well as a website that includes written news and streaming video. No longer exclusively communications devices, cell phones now deliver movies and other video as well as music.

Convergence also means that media producers merge. For example, gaming-system makers and movie studios work together to promote each other's products. In a similar way, consumers and producers of new media also converge. Individual videographers produce YouTube videos that become news, while newsreels are streamed on YouTube by individuals wishing to make a point.

Are we witnessing completely new roles, genres, and media, or are the old ones being remade for different purposes and positioned in new ways?

Participatory culture versus corporate domination: The earliest forms of media studies, such as that of the **Frankfurt School of Critical Theory**, primarily attended to the ways in which mass media dominate or attempt to indoctrinate their audiences. This is because the producers of mass media are generally major capital ventures, which supposedly represent dominant interests and ideologies. With the advent of digital media, however, cultural production is no longer limited to major corporate players.

"Not all participants are created equal," as Jenkins asserts, but unprecedented numbers of individuals and groups are able to reach audiences and influence them, and also to have an impact upon the corporate media themselves. Thus the questions we must ask are different: What can we make of this new "participatory culture?" Moreover, how are we to study it? Obviously the older paradigm, wherein media audiences are considered the hapless and passive consumers of corporate **pablum**, no longer applies, if indeed it ever did.

Other new questions emerge to intrigue scholars:

- What does this newfound power signify for the producers of new media?
- What roles can and will they play in the broader social, cultural, economic, and political spheres?
- What will be the relationship between new- and old-style producers?
- How will both relate to their audiences?
- Are the consequences of participatory cultures only beneficial, or are some forms of Internet publicity potentially negative?

Creativity and Property: Digitization changes the means by which creative products are made and reproduced. Digital objects, including texts, images, video, and sound, are reducible to a series of zeros and ones. Because they can be easily copied and distributed, these objects are often subject to piracy, such as through the illegal downloading and sampling of music. **Intellectual property** is the branch of law established for the protection of creative works and inventions. The digital realm has challenged the ability of intellectual property law to protect creative works, including music, videos, photography, books, and computer software.

Some critics suggest that intellectual property law is unsuited for a digital world. John Parry Barlow, whose essay is included in the Suggested Additional Resources, argues that intellectual property, or the ownership of intangible works of creativity, is impossible to maintain. Rather than attempt to patch up the system of legal protections or to stop copying through encryption, Barlow argues that other ways of understanding and rewarding creative production must be developed.

Readers and authors: Because they affect the printed book, digital media innovations usher in a whole host of considerations for literary studies. In his book *Hypertext 3.0*, included in the Suggested Additional Resources, the literary critic George Landow considers a number of implications for the practices of reading and writing brought about by the new media. With the emergence of the web, texts are connected that were once physically isolated. As the borders that once separated texts (and their authors) become more permeable, readers are able to rove from linked text to linked text at the click of a mouse. Given the kind of access to texts that digital hypertext affords, readers are thus accorded larger roles in the creative and interpretive processes.

Readers in fact become co-producers of texts; meaning making is no longer the exclusive province of authors, if it ever was. According to Landow, digital hypertext realizes in practice many of the theoretical claims of **post-structuralism**, including the disappearance (or "death") of the author, the "intertextuality" of all works (that idea that all texts draw from and connect to previously existing ones), and the idea that originality is an insupportable concept, a veritable myth. In the Suggested Additional Resources, we include works that treat the issues of authorship and the intellectual property of authors and other creative producers.

The digital generation: As first-generation "digital natives," the digital generation has a distinct advantage over their parents in terms of new media usage and fluency. Yet parents often have an interest in monitoring and controlling their children's digital media habits. According to media scholars Justine Cassell and Meg Cramer in an essay included in *Digital Youth, Innovation, and the Unexpected*, cited in the Suggested Additional Resources, a digital "moral panic" has ensued, engulfing parents as they try to steer their children's web surfing. The media (typically the old media outlets) warn that Internet and other digital usage endangers children. Many scholars are devoted to addressing the media habits of digital youth in terms of their self-determination, safety, and other issues. At the same time, the digital generation vies for control over its own digital media activities.

The digital generation provides an important experimental group for studying the impact of new media on individual psychology and behavior. The *New York Times* article mentioned above, for example, mostly laments the effects of digital media on the digital generation and beyond. Research suggests, however, that in addition to the problem of "continuous partial attention," users of digital media also have benefited from the kinds of attention training that Internet surfing and searching afford. According to Gary Small and Gigi Vorgan, the ability of the digital generation to make decisions and integrate large amounts of information has improved demonstrably.

The digital divide versus democratization: Despite claims that digital media inevitably result in greater access to information for more people than ever before, a divide between those with access to digital media and those without persists. Furthermore, critics maintain, this divide threatens to exacerbate rather than solve the problem of poverty in developing and developed countries. Rather than granting access to resources, the digital divide keeps the poor continually behind the curve. Do the new digital media really enable democratization and spread its economic benefits, or are media utopians putting too much emphasis on a technological fix? To illustrate the issue, in a 2010 *New York Times* op-ed entitled "Toilets and Cellphones," Roger Cohen noted that there are more cell phones in India than there are toilets. The editorial made clear that access to digital technology is no cure-all for world poverty.

As You Read

The above are just a few of the many issues that scholars have raised about the advent and development of new media. Similarly, the following readings cannot represent all of the possible ways in which to study this complex and vast terrain. Instead, the articles in this chapter argue for particular approaches to the field and for the variety of issues that they address. This wide-open field affords plenty of room for up-and-coming writers.

As you read, consider the approaches as well as the issues involved. You are most likely a digital native yourself. For example,

- How well does a particular approach suit the issue under consideration, as you see it?
- How well do the articles characterize the phenomena?
- How might they do better?

As you read and absorb the articles in this chapter,

1. Consider a subtopic within digital media that you would like to write about.
2. Decide on an approach that you can carry out on your own and without an elaborate research study.
3. Read articles that relate to your topic.
4. Supplement the readings here with the Suggested Additional Resources section below.

Suggested Additional Resources

Advocacy

Molinari, Aleph. *Let's bridge the digital divide!* TED. Filmed Aug. 2011.
    TEDxSanMigueldeAllende. Web.

Business and Economics

Brynjolfsson, Erik, and Andrew McAfee. *Race against the Machine: How the
    Digital Revolution Is Accelerating Innovation, Driving Productivity, and
    Irreversibly Transforming Employment and the Economy.* Lexington, MA:
    Digital Frontier Press, 2012.

De Kare-Silver, M. *E-shock 2020: How the Digital Technology Revolution Is
    Changing Business and All Our Lives.* Basingstoke: Palgrave Macmillan, 2011.

Kurihara, Yutaka. *Information Technology and Economic Development.* Hershey,
    PA: Information Science Reference, 2008. Web.

Levine, Robert. *Free Ride: How Digital Parasites Are Destroying the Culture
    Business, and How the Culture Business Can Fight Back.* New York:
    Doubleday, 2011.

Sharma, Ravi, Margaret Tan, and Francis Pereira. *Understanding the Interactive
    Digital Media Marketplace: Frameworks, Platforms, Communities and Issues.*
    Hershey, PA: Information Science Reference, 2012. Print.

Cultural Studies, Literary Theory

Bolter, Jay D. *Writing Space: Computers, Hypertext, and the Remediation of Print.*
    Mahwah, NJ: Lawrence Erlbaum, 2001.

——, and Diane Gromala. *Windows and Mirrors: Interaction Design, Digital Art,
    and the Myth of Transparency.* Cambridge, MA: MIT Press, 2003. Web.

Braun, Catherine C. *Cultivating Ecologies for Digital Media Work: The Case of
    English Studies.* Carbondale: Southern Illinois UP, 2014.

Campanelli, Vito. *Web Aesthetics: How Digital Media Affect Culture and Society.*
    Rotterdam: NAi Publishers, 2010.

Delany, Paul, and George P. Landow. *Hypermedia and Literary Studies.*
    Cambridge, MA: MIT Press, 1991.

Earhart, Amy E., and Andrew Jewell. *The American Literature Scholar in the
    Digital Age.* Ann Arbor: U of Michigan P and U of Michigan Library, 2011.

Hayles, Katherine. *How We Think: Digital Media and Contemporary Technogenesis.*
    Chicago: U of Chicago P, 2012.

——. *Writing Machines.* Mediawork. Cambridge, MA: MIT Press, 2002.

Landow, George P. *Hypertext 3.0: Critical Theory and New Media in an Era of Globalization*. Baltimore: Johns Hopkins UP, 1992.

Liu, Lydia H. *The Freudian Robot: Digital Media and the Future of the Unconscious*. Chicago: U of Chicago P, 2010.

O'Gorman, Marcel. *E-crit: Digital Media, Critical Theory and the Humanities*. Toronto: U of Toronto P, 2006.

Selber, Stuart A. *Rhetorics and Technologies: New Directions in Writing and Communication*. Columbia: U of South Carolina P, 2010. Web.

Vandendorpe, Christian. *From Papyrus to Hypertext: Toward the Universal Digital Library*. Urbana: U of Illinois P, 2009.

Waes, L., Mariëlle Leijten, and Christine M. Neuwirth. *Writing and Digital Media*. Amsterdam: Elsevier, 2006.

Human-Computer Interaction

Carroll, John M. *HCI Models, Theories, and Frameworks: Toward a Multidisciplinary Science*. Amsterdam: Morgan Kaufmann, 2003.

Coyne, Richard. *The Tuning of Place: Sociable Spaces and Pervasive Digital Media*. Cambridge, MA: MIT Press, 2010. Web.

Erickson, Thomas, and David W. McDonald. *HCI Remixed: Essays on Works That Have Influenced the HCI Community*. Cambridge, MA: MIT Press, 2008.

Winget, Megan A, and William Aspray. *Digital Media: Technological and Social Challenges of the Interactive World*. Lanham, MD: Scarecrow Press, 2011. Web.

Journalism

"Attached to Technology and Paying a Price." *New York Times* 6 June 2010. Web.

Barlow, John P. "The Next Economy of Ideas: Will Copyright Survive the Napster Bomb? Nope, but Creativity Will." *Wired* Aug. 2000. Web.

Bilton, Nick. "The Defense of Computers, the Internet and Our Brains." *New York Times (blog)* 11 June 2010. Web.

Carr, Nicholas G. *The Shallows: What the Internet Is Doing to Our Brains*. New York: W.W. Norton, 2011.

"Digital Society (explained)." YouTube. 2011. Deutsche Bank Group. Web.

Estrin, James. "Embedded on the Front Lines of the Digital Revolution." *New York Times (blog)* 6 May 2012. Web.

"The Internet Is Making You Smarter!" *The Awl*. 8 June 2010. Web.

Pinker, Steven. "Mind Over Mass Media." *New York Times*. 10 June 2010. Web.

Legal and Literary Studies (Intellectual Property Law)

Bently, Lionel, Jennifer Davis, and Jane C. Ginsburg. *Copyright and Piracy: An Interdisciplinary Critique*. Cambridge: Cambridge UP, 2010.

Biagioli, Mario, Peter Jaszi, and Martha Woodmansee. *Making and Unmaking Intellectual Property: Creative Production in Legal and Cultural Perspective*. Chicago: U of Chicago P, 2011.

Coombe, Rosemary. *Dynamic Fair Dealing: Creating Canadian Culture Online*. U of Toronto P, 2014.

Gruner, Richard S. *Intellectual Property and Digital Content*. Cheltenham, UK; Northampton, MA: Edward Elgar Publishing, 2013.

Johns, Adrian. *Piracy: The Intellectual Property Wars from Gutenberg to Gates*. Chicago: U of Chicago P, 2009.

Merges, Robert P. *Justifying Intellectual Property*. Cambridge, MA: Harvard UP, 2011.

Spinello, Richard A., and Herman T. Tavani. *Intellectual Property Rights in a Networked World: Theory and Practice*. Hershey, PA: Information Science Pub, 2005. Web.

Media Studies

Athique, Adrian. *Digital Media and Society: An Introduction*. Cambridge: Polity, 2013.

Baym, Nancy K. *Personal Connections in the Digital Age*. Cambridge: Polity, 2010.

Buckingham, David. *Youth, Identity, and Digital Media*. Cambridge, MA: MIT Press, 2008.

Couldry, Nick. *Media, Society, World: Social Theory and Digital Media Practice*. Cambridge: Polity, 2012.

Hassan, Robert, and Julian Thomas. *The New Media Theory Reader*. Maidenhead: Open University P, 2006.

Howard, Philip N., and Muzammil M. Hussain. *Democracy's Fourth Wave?: Digital Media and the Arab Spring*. Oxford: Oxford University Press, 2013.

Kavoori, Anandam P. *Digital Media Criticism*. New York: Peter Lang, 2010.

Liestol, Gunnar. *Digital Media Revisited*. Cambridge, MA: MIT Press, 2004.

Lister, Martin. *New Media: A Critical Introduction*. Abingdon, UK: Routledge, 2009.

McPherson, Tara. *Digital Youth, Innovation, and the Unexpected*. The John D. and Catherine T. MacArthur Foundation Series on Digital Media and Learning. Cambridge, MA: MIT Press, 2008.

Meikle, Graham, and Sherman Young. *Media Convergence: Networked Digital Media in Everyday Life*. Basingstoke: Palgrave Macmillan, 2012.

Messaris, Paul, and Lee Humphreys. *Digital Media: Transformations in Human Communication*. New York: Peter Lang, 2006.

Metzger, Miriam J., and Andrew J. Flanagin. *Digital Media, Youth, and Credibility*. Cambridge, MA: MIT Press, 2008.

Schlieski, T., and B.D. Johnson. "Entertainment in the Age of Big Data." *Proceedings of the IEEE* 100 (2012): 1404-08.

White, Michele. *The Body and the Screen: Theories of Internet Spectatorship*. Cambridge, MA: MIT Press, 2006.

Social and Political Science

Anduiza, Perea E., Michael J. Jensen, and Laia Jorba. *Digital Media and Political Engagement Worldwide: A Comparative Study*. New York: Cambridge UP, 2012.

Bennett, W.L. *The Logic of Connective Action: Digital Media and the Personalization of Contentious Politics*. Cambridge: Cambridge UP, 2013.

Boler, Megan. *Digital Media and Democracy: Tactics in Hard Times*. Cambridge, MA: MIT Press, 2008. Web.

Cohen, Cathy J., and Joseph Kahne. *Participatory Politics: New Media and Youth Political Action*. Oakland, CA: YPP Research Network, 2012. Web.

Dwyer, Tim. *Media Convergence*. Maidenhead: McGraw Hill/Open University P, 2010.

Healey, Justin. *Social Impacts of Digital Media*. Thirroul, Australia: Spinney, 2011. Web.

Kroker, Arthur, and Marilouise Kroker. *Critical Digital Studies: A Reader*. Toronto: U of Toronto P, 2008.

Yu, Haiqing. *Media and Cultural Transformation in China*. London: Routledge, 2009.

a. Nicholas Carr, "Is Google Making Us Stupid?"

Nicholas Carr is a journalist who writes about technology, culture, and economics. He has been a columnist for the *Guardian*, the *Atlantic*, the *New York Times*, the *Wall Street Journal*, *Wired*, *The Times* of London, the *New Republic*, the *Financial Times*, *Die Zeit*, and other leading periodicals. He also is a member of *Encyclopedia Britannica*'s editorial board of advisors, is on the steering board of the World Economic Forum's cloud computing project, and writes the popular blog *Rough Type*.

Carr has been a writer-in-residence at the University of California, Berkeley, and is a much-sought-after speaker for academic and corporate events. Earlier in his career, he was executive editor of the *Harvard Business Review*. Carr is also the author of several books, including *The Big Switch: Rewiring the World, from Edison to Google* (2008) and *Does IT Matter?* (2004). His most recent book, *The Shallows: What the Internet Is Doing to Our Brains*, is a 2011 Pulitzer Prize nominee and a *New York Times* bestseller. He holds a BA from Dartmouth College and an MA in English and American literature and language from Harvard University.

In this essay, "Is Google Making Us Stupid?," which originally appeared in the highbrow popular magazine the *Atlantic*, Carr introduces his main argument from *The Shallows*. He suggests that the preponderance of digital media in our lives is turning even the most erudite among us into shallow thinkers unable to engage in deep thought or parse complex book-length arguments.

As You Read: Think about your own reading and other media habits. Do you read mostly on- or offline? Have you noticed a difference between reading on the web and reading print? Consider the benefits and potential downsides of digital media in your life:

- Are you able to concentrate on long, abstract articles and books?
- If not, to what extent do you think your digital habits are to blame?

Is Google Making Us Stupid?

"Dave, stop. Stop, will you? Stop, Dave. Will you stop, Dave?" So the supercomputer HAL pleads with the implacable astronaut Dave Bowman in a famous and weirdly poignant scene toward the end of Stanley Kubrick's *2001: A Space Odyssey*. Bowman, having nearly been sent to a deep-space death by the malfunctioning machine, is calmly, coldly disconnecting the memory circuits that control its artificial "brain." "Dave, my mind is going," HAL says, forlornly. "I can feel it. I can feel it."

I can feel it, too. Over the past few years I've had an uncomfortable sense that someone, or something, has been tinkering with my brain, remapping the neural circuitry, reprogramming the memory. My mind isn't going—so far as I can tell—but it's changing. I'm not thinking the way I used to think. I can feel it most strongly when I'm reading. Immersing myself in a book or a lengthy article used to be easy. My mind would get caught up in the narrative or the turns of the argument, and I'd spend hours strolling through long stretches of prose. That's rarely the case anymore. Now my concentration often starts to drift after two or three pages. I get fidgety, lose the thread, begin looking for something else to do. I feel as if I'm always dragging my wayward brain back to the text. The deep reading that used to come naturally has become a struggle.

harder for him to read longer things like novels

I think I know what's going on. For more than a decade now, I've been spending a lot of time online, searching and surfing and sometimes adding to the great databases of the Internet. The Web has been a godsend to me as a writer. Research that once required days in the stacks or periodical rooms of libraries can now be done in minutes. A few Google searches, some quick clicks on hyperlinks, and I've got the telltale fact or pithy quote I was after. Even when I'm not working, I'm as likely as not to be foraging in the Web's info-thickets, reading and writing e-mails, scanning headlines and blog posts, watching videos and listening to podcasts, or just tripping from link to link to link. (Unlike footnotes, to which they're sometimes likened, hyperlinks don't merely point to related works; they propel you toward them.) *— always using internet*

For me, as for others, the Net is becoming a universal medium, the conduit for most of the information that flows through my eyes and ears and into my mind. The advantages of having immediate access to such an incredibly rich store of information are many, and they've been widely described and duly applauded. "The perfect recall of silicon memory," *Wired's* Clive Thompson has written, "can be an enormous boon to thinking." But that boon comes at a price. As the media theorist Marshall McLuhan pointed out in the 1960s, media are not just passive channels of information. They supply the stuff of thought, but they also shape the process of thought. And what the Net seems to be doing is chipping away my capacity for concentration and contemplation. My mind now expects to take in information the way the Net distributes it: in a swiftly moving stream of particles. Once I was a scuba diver in the sea of words. Now I zip along the surface like a guy on a Jet Ski.

thinks the internet changes the way we think and process info

I'm not the only one. When I mention my troubles with reading to friends and acquaintances—literary types, most of them—many say they're having similar experiences. The more they use the Web, the more they have to fight to stay focused on long pieces of writing. Some of the bloggers I follow have also begun mentioning the phenomenon. Scott Karp, who writes a blog about online media, recently confessed that he has stopped reading books altogether. "I was a lit major in college, and used to be [a] voracious book reader," he wrote. "What happened?"

He speculates on the answer: "What if I do all my reading on the web not so much because the way I read has changed, i.e., I'm just seeking convenience, but because the way I THINK has changed?"

Bruce Friedman, who blogs regularly about the use of computers in medicine, also has described how the Internet has altered his mental habits. "I now have almost totally lost the ability to read and absorb a longish article on the web or in print," he wrote earlier this year. A pathologist who has long been on the faculty of the University of Michigan Medical School, Friedman elaborated on his comment in a telephone conversation with me. His thinking, he said, has taken on a "staccato" quality, reflecting the way he quickly scans short passages of text from many sources online. "I can't read *War and Peace* anymore," he admitted. "I've lost the ability to do that. Even a blog post of more than three or four paragraphs is too much to absorb. I skim it."

Anecdotes alone don't prove much. And we still await the long-term neurological and psychological experiments that will provide a definitive picture of how Internet use affects cognition. But a recently published study of online research habits, conducted by scholars from University College London, suggests that we may well be in the midst of a sea change in the way we read and think. As part of the five-year research program, the scholars examined computer logs documenting the behavior of visitors to two popular research sites, one operated by the British Library and one by a UK educational consortium, that provide access to journal articles, e-books, and other sources of written information. They found that people using the sites exhibited "a form of skimming activity," hopping from one source to another and rarely returning to any source they'd already visited. They typically read no more than one or two pages of an article or book before they would "bounce" out to another site. Sometimes they'd save a long article, but there's no evidence that they ever went back and actually read it. The authors of the study report:

> It is clear that users are not reading online in the traditional sense; indeed there are signs that new forms of "reading" are emerging as users "power browse" horizontally through titles, contents pages and abstracts going for quick wins. It almost seems that they go online to avoid reading in the traditional sense.

Thanks to the ubiquity of text on the Internet, not to mention the popularity of text-messaging on cell phones, we may well be reading more today than we did in the 1970s or 1980s, when television was our medium of choice. But it's a different kind of reading, and behind it lies a different kind of thinking—perhaps even a new sense of the self. "We are not only what we read," says Maryanne Wolf, a developmental psychologist at Tufts University and the author of *Proust and the Squid: The Story and Science of the Reading Brain.* "We are how we read." Wolf worries that the style of reading promoted by the Net, a style that puts "efficiency" and "immediacy" above all else, may be weakening our capacity for the kind of deep reading that emerged when an earlier technology, the printing press, made long and complex works of prose commonplace. When we read online, she says, we tend to become "mere decoders of information." Our ability to interpret text, to make the rich mental connections that form when we read deeply and without distraction, remains largely disengaged.

Reading, explains Wolf, is not an instinctive skill for human beings. It's not etched into our genes the way speech is. We have to teach our minds how to translate the symbolic characters we see into the language we understand. And the media or other technologies we use in learning and practicing the craft of reading play an important part in shaping the neural circuits inside our brains. Experiments demonstrate that readers of ideograms, such as the Chinese, develop a mental circuitry for reading that is very different from the circuitry found in those of us whose written language employs an alphabet.

The variations extend across many regions of the brain, including those that govern such essential cognitive functions as memory and the interpretation of visual and auditory stimuli. We can expect as well that the circuits woven by our use of the Net will be different from those woven by our reading of books and other printed works.

Sometime in 1882, Friedrich Nietzsche bought a typewriter—a Malling-Hansen Writing Ball, to be precise. His vision was failing, and keeping his eyes focused on a page had become exhausting and painful, often bringing on crushing headaches. He had been forced to curtail his writing, and he feared that he would soon have to give it up. The typewriter rescued him, at least for a time. Once he had mastered touch-typing, he was able to write with his eyes closed, using only the tips of his fingers.

Words could once again flow from his mind to the page.

But the machine had a subtler effect on his work. One of Nietzsche's friends, a composer, noticed a change in the style of his writing. His already terse prose had become even tighter, more telegraphic. "Perhaps you will through this instrument even take to a new idiom," the friend wrote in a letter, noting that, in his own work, his "'thoughts' in music and language often depend on the quality of pen and paper."

"You are right," Nietzsche replied, "our writing equipment takes part in the forming of our thoughts." Under the sway of the machine, writes the German media scholar Friedrich A. Kittler, Nietzsche's prose "changed from arguments to aphorisms, from thoughts to puns, from rhetoric to telegram style."

The human brain is almost infinitely malleable. People used to think that our mental meshwork, the dense connections formed among the 100 billion or so

> **ALSO SEE**
>
> James Fallows, "Living with a Computer" (*Atlantic*, July 1982)
>
> "The process works this way. When I sit down to write a letter or start the first draft of an article, I simply type on the keyboard and the words appear on the screen...."

neurons inside our skulls, was largely fixed by the time we reached adulthood. But brain researchers have discovered that that's not the case. James Olds, a professor of neuroscience who directs the Krasnow Institute for Advanced Study at George Mason University, says that even the adult mind "is very plastic." Nerve cells routinely break old connections and form new ones. "The brain," according to Olds, "has the ability to reprogram itself on the fly, altering the way it functions."

As we use what the sociologist Daniel Bell has called our "intellectual technologies"—the tools that extend our mental rather than our physical capacities—we inevitably begin to take on the qualities of those technologies. The mechanical clock, which came into common use in the 14th century, provides a compelling example. In *Technics and Civilization*, the historian and cultural critic Lewis Mumford described how the clock "disassociated time from human events and helped create the belief in an independent world of mathematically measurable sequences." The "abstract framework of divided time" became "the point of reference for both action and thought."

The clock's methodical ticking helped bring into being the scientific mind and the scientific man. But it also took something away. As the late MIT computer scientist Joseph Weizenbaum observed in his 1976 book, *Computer Power and Human Reason: From Judgment to Calculation*, the conception of the world that emerged from the widespread use of timekeeping instruments "remains an impoverished version of the older one, for it rests on a rejection of those direct experiences that formed the basis for, and indeed constituted, the old reality." In deciding when to eat, to work, to sleep, to rise, we stopped listening to our senses and started obeying the clock.

The process of adapting to new intellectual technologies is reflected in the changing metaphors we use to explain ourselves to ourselves. When the mechanical clock arrived, people began thinking of their brains as operating "like clockwork." Today, in the age of software, we have come to think of them as operating "like computers." But the changes, neuroscience tells us, go much deeper than metaphor. Thanks to our brain's plasticity, the adaptation occurs also at a biological level.

The Internet promises to have particularly far-reaching effects on cognition. In a paper published in 1936, the British mathematician Alan Turing proved that a digital computer, which at the time existed only as a theoretical machine, could be programmed to perform the function of any other information-processing device. And that's what we're seeing today. The Internet, an immeasurably powerful computing system, is subsuming most of our other intellectual technologies. It's becoming our map and our clock, our printing press and our typewriter, our calculator and our telephone, and our radio and TV.

When the Net absorbs a medium, that medium is re-created in the Net's image. It injects the medium's content with hyperlinks, blinking ads, and other digital gewgaws, and it surrounds the content with the content of all the other media it has absorbed. A new e-mail message, for instance, may announce its arrival as we're glancing over the latest headlines at a newspaper's site. The result is to scatter our attention and diffuse our concentration.

The Net's influence doesn't end at the edges of a computer screen, either. As people's minds become attuned to the crazy quilt of Internet media, traditional media have to adapt to the audience's new expectations. Television programs add text crawls and pop-up ads, and magazines and newspapers shorten their articles, introduce capsule summaries, and crowd their pages with easy-to-browse info-snippets. When, in March of this year, *The New York Times* decided to devote the second and third pages of every edition to article abstracts, its design director, Tom Bodkin, explained that the "shortcuts" would give harried readers a quick "taste" of the day's news, sparing them the "less efficient" method of actually turning the pages and reading the articles. Old media have little choice but to play by the new-media rules.

Never has a communications system played so many roles in our lives—or exerted such broad influence over our thoughts—as the Internet does today. Yet, for all that's been written about the Net, there's been little consideration of how, exactly, it's reprogramming us. The Net's intellectual ethic remains obscure.

About the same time that Nietzsche started using his typewriter, an earnest young man named Frederick Winslow Taylor carried a stopwatch into the Midvale Steel plant in Philadelphia and began a historic series of experiments aimed at improving the efficiency of the plant's machinists. With the approval of Midvale's owners, he recruited a group of factory hands, set them to work on various metal-working machines, and recorded and timed their every movement as well as the operations of the machines. By breaking down every job into a sequence of small, discrete steps and then testing different ways of performing each one, Taylor created a set of precise instructions—an "algorithm," we might say today—for how each worker should work. Midvale's employees grumbled about the strict new regime, claiming that it turned them into little more than automatons, but the factory's productivity soared.

More than a hundred years after the invention of the steam engine, the Industrial Revolution had at last found its philosophy and its philosopher. Taylor's tight industrial choreography—his "system," as he liked to call it—was embraced by manufacturers throughout the country and, in time, around the world. Seeking maximum speed, maximum efficiency, and maximum output, factory owners used time-and-motion studies to organize their work and configure the jobs of their workers. The goal, as Taylor defined it in his celebrated 1911 treatise, *The Principles of Scientific Management*, was to identify and adopt, for every job, the "one best method" of work and thereby to effect "the gradual substitution of science for rule of thumb throughout the mechanic arts." Once his system was applied to all acts of manual labor, Taylor assured his followers, it would bring about a restructuring not only of industry but of society, creating a utopia of perfect efficiency. "In the past the man has been first," he declared; "in the future the system must be first."

Taylor's system is still very much with us; it remains the ethic of industrial manufacturing. And now, thanks to the growing power that computer engineers and software coders wield over our intellectual lives, Taylor's ethic is beginning to govern the realm of the mind as well. The Internet is a machine designed for the efficient and automated collection, transmission, and manipulation of information, and its legions of programmers are intent on finding the "one best method"—the perfect algorithm—to carry out every mental movement of what we've come to describe as "knowledge work."

Google's headquarters, in Mountain View, California—the Googleplex—is the Internet's high church, and the religion practiced inside its walls is Taylorism. Google, says its chief executive, Eric Schmidt, is "a company that's founded around the science of measurement," and it is striving to "systematize every-thing" it does. Drawing on the terabytes of behavioral data it collects through its search engine and other sites, it carries out thousands of experiments a day, according to the *Harvard Business Review*, and it uses the results to refine the algorithms that increasingly control how people find information and extract meaning from it. What Taylor did for the work of the hand, Google is doing for the work of the mind.

The company has declared that its mission is "to organize the world's informa-tion and make it universally accessible and useful." It seeks to develop "the perfect search engine," which it defines as something that "understands exactly what you mean and gives you back exactly what you want." In Google's view, information is a kind of commodity, a utilitarian resource that can be mined and processed with industrial efficiency. The more pieces of information we can "access" and the faster we can extract their gist, the more productive we become as thinkers.

Where does it end? Sergey Brin and Larry Page, the gifted young men who founded Google while pursuing doctoral degrees in computer science at Stanford, speak frequently of their desire to turn their search engine into an artificial intel-ligence, a HAL-like machine that might be connected directly to our brains. "The ultimate search engine is something as smart as people—or smarter," Page said in a speech a few years back. "For us, working on search is a way to work on arti-ficial intelligence." In a 2004 interview with *Newsweek*, Brin said, "Certainly if you had all the world's information directly attached to your brain, or an artifi-cial brain that was smarter than your brain, you'd be better off." Last year, Page told a convention of scientists that Google is "really trying to build artificial intel-ligence and to do it on a large scale."

Such an ambition is a natural one, even an admirable one, for a pair of math whizzes with vast quantities of cash at their disposal and a small army of computer scientists in their employ. A fundamentally scientific enterprise, Google is moti-vated by a desire to use technology, in Eric Schmidt's words, "to solve problems that have never been solved before," and artificial intelligence is the hardest prob-lem out there. Why wouldn't Brin and Page want to be the ones to crack it?

Still, their easy assumption that we'd all "be better off" if our brains were supplemented, or even replaced, by an artificial intelligence is unsettling. It suggests a belief that intelligence is the output of a mechanical process, a series of discrete steps that can be isolated, measured, and optimized. In Google's world, the world we enter when we go online, there's little place for the fuzziness of contemplation. Ambiguity is not an opening for insight but a bug to be fixed. The human brain is just an outdated computer that needs a faster processor and a bigger hard drive.

The idea that our minds should operate as high-speed data-processing machines is not only built into the workings of the Internet, it is the network's reigning business model as well. The faster we surf across the Web—the more links we click and pages we view—the more opportunities Google and other companies gain to collect information about us and to feed us advertisements. Most of the proprietors of the commercial Internet have a financial stake in collecting the crumbs of data we leave behind as we flit from link to link—the more crumbs, the better. The last thing these companies want is to encourage leisurely reading or slow, concentrated thought. It's in their economic interest to drive us to distraction.

Maybe I'm just a worrywart. Just as there's a tendency to glorify technological progress, there's a countertendency to expect the worst of every new tool or machine. In Plato's *Phaedrus*, Socrates bemoaned the development of writing. He feared that, as people came to rely on the written word as a substitute for the knowledge they used to carry inside their heads, they would, in the words of one of the dialogue's characters, "cease to exercise their memory and become forgetful." And because they would be able to "receive a quantity of information without proper instruction," they would "be thought very knowledgeable when they are for the most part quite ignorant." They would be "filled with the conceit of wisdom instead of real wisdom." Socrates wasn't wrong—the new technology did often have the effects he feared—but he was shortsighted. He couldn't foresee the many ways that writing and reading would serve to spread information, spur fresh ideas, and expand human knowledge (if not wisdom).

The arrival of Gutenberg's printing press, in the 15th century, set off another round of teeth gnashing. The Italian humanist Hieronimo Squarciafico worried that the easy availability of books would lead to intellectual laziness, making men "less studious" and weakening their minds. Others argued that cheaply printed books and broadsheets would undermine religious authority, demean the work of scholars and scribes, and spread sedition and debauchery. As New York University professor Clay Shirky notes, "Most of the arguments made against the printing press were correct, even prescient." But, again, the doomsayers were unable to imagine the myriad blessings that the printed word would deliver.

So, yes, you should be skeptical of my skepticism. Perhaps those who dismiss critics of the Internet as Luddites or nostalgists will be proved correct, and from our hyperactive, data-stoked minds will spring a golden age of intellectual discovery and universal wisdom. Then again, the Net isn't the alphabet, and although it may replace the printing press, it produces something altogether different. The kind of deep reading that a sequence of printed pages promotes is valuable not just for the knowledge we acquire from the author's words but for the intellectual vibrations those words set off within our own minds. In the quiet spaces opened up by the sustained, undistracted reading of a book, or by any other act of contemplation, for that matter, we make our own associations, draw our own inferences and analogies, foster our own ideas. Deep reading, as Maryanne Wolf argues, is indistinguishable from deep thinking.

If we lose those quiet spaces, or fill them up with "content," we will sacrifice something important not only in our selves but in our culture. In a recent essay, the playwright Richard Foreman eloquently described what's at stake:

> I come from a tradition of Western culture, in which the ideal (my ideal) was the complex, dense and "cathedral-like" structure of the highly educated and articulate personality—a man or woman who carried inside themselves a personally constructed and unique version of the entire heritage of the West. [But now] I see within us all (myself included) the replacement of complex inner density with a new kind of self—evolving under the pressure of information overload and the technology of the "instantly available."

As we are drained of our "inner repertory of dense cultural inheritance," Foreman concluded, we risk turning into "'pancake people'—spread wide and thin as we connect with that vast network of information accessed by the mere touch of a button."

I'm haunted by that scene in 2001. What makes it so poignant, and so weird, is the computer's emotional response to the disassembly of its mind: its despair as one circuit after another goes dark, its childlike pleading with the astronaut— "I can feel it. I can feel it. I'm afraid"—and its final reversion to what can only be called a state of innocence. HAL's outpouring of feeling contrasts with the emotionlessness that characterizes the human figures in the film, who go about their business with an almost robotic efficiency. Their thoughts and actions feel scripted, as if they're following the steps of an algorithm. In the world of 2001, people have become so machinelike that the most human character turns out to be a machine. That's the essence of Kubrick's dark prophecy: as we come to rely on computers to mediate our understanding of the world, it is our own intelligence that flattens into artificial intelligence.

Source: *The Atlantic* July-Aug. 2008: n.p. Web. http://www.theatlantic.com/magazine/archive/2008/07/is-google-making-us-stupid/306868/.

WHAT IT SAYS

1. What point is Carr making with his reference to Stanley Kubrick's *2001: A Space Odyssey*? Why do you suppose he begins with such a reference?

2. Carr mentions the media theorist Marshall McLuhan. What did McLuhan say about media? What point is Carr making about the Internet and digital media by invoking McLuhan's ideas?

3. Carr mentions that many of his friends report the same problems that he has encountered since becoming an avid Internet user. What is the point of bringing up his friends here? Why is it significant that most are "literary types"?

4. Carr discusses the philosopher Friedrich Nietzsche and his use of a typewriter late in life. What effect did the typewriter have on Nietzsche's writing? What is Carr's point in referring to this philosopher and his use of a typewriter?

5. Carr discusses Frederick Winslow Taylor and his role in improving the efficiency of industry. Carr then draws an analogy between what Taylor did for manufacturing and what Google is doing for the work of the mind. Explain the analogy and what Carr is suggesting by making it.

HOW IT SAYS IT

1. Who is Carr's intended audience? Describe his readers. What cues help identify his readers and their interests?

2. Consider Carr's use of anecdotal evidence. How does anecdote work to advance his argument? Carr acknowledges its limitations. Why? What do you suppose are the limitations of anecdote?

3. Carr uses analogy to make his argument. How do analogies help Carr make his case? Why do you suppose he relies on analogy to such an extent?

WRITE ABOUT IT

1. Write an essay in which you consider your own Internet and other digital media habits and how these affect your abilities to be a good citizen, friend, and student.

2. Carr discusses the changes wrought on the reading, thinking, and information-processing habits of digital users today, especially those of his own generation. Perhaps you do not remember a time when it was different. Write an essay in which you explore the different ways in which the Internet and other digital media affect different generations.

3. Find the thesis statement in Carr's essay and argue against it. In making your counterargument, draw on the same kinds of support that Carr uses to make his case: anecdote, scientific studies, and analogy.

b. Henry Jenkins, "'Worship at the Altar of Convergence': A New Paradigm for Understanding Media Change"

Henry Jenkins is the provost's professor of communication, journalism, and cinematic arts at the University of Southern California. He was previously director of the MIT Comparative Media Studies Program and the Peter de Florez Professor of Humanities. He is the author and/or editor of twelve books on media and popular culture, including *Textual Poachers: Television Fans and Participatory Culture* (1992), *From Barbie to Mortal Kombat: Gender and Computer Games* (1998), and *Hop on Pop: The Politics and Pleasures of Popular Culture* (2002). His newest books include *Convergence Culture: Where Old and New Media Collide* (2006), *Fans, Bloggers and Gamers: Exploring Participatory Culture* (2006), and *The Wow Climax: Tracing the Emotional Impact of Popular Culture* (2007). He also writes a blog: henryjenkins. com. Jenkins has a BA in political science and journalism from Georgia State University, an MA in communication studies from the University of Iowa, and a PhD in communication arts from the University of Wisconsin-Madison.

In this chapter, Jenkins introduces the idea of media convergence and contemplates its implications for media audiences and participatory cultures. He also discusses the struggles of media industries to keep pace with the new convergence culture. He describes his book *Convergence Culture: Where Old and New Media Collide*, from which this essay is taken, as a "public intervention" designed to help media consumers and producers understand the changes in their relationship. Beginning with the bizarre story of how Bert from *Sesame Street* became conflated with Osama Bin Laden thanks to an online photo collage made by an American teenager, Jenkins introduces the reader to the sometimes bizarre ways in which media can converge across the globe.

As You Read: Think about the ways in which you are both a media producer and a media consumer. Consider the ways in which the blurring of the lines between media producers and consumers may be both beneficial and harmful.

"Worship at the Altar of Convergence": A New Paradigm for Understanding Media Change

Worship at the Altar of Convergence
—slogan, the New Orleans Media Experience (2003)

The story circulated in the fall of 2001: Dino Ignacio, a Filipino-American high school student created a Photoshop collage of *Sesame Street*'s Bert interacting with terrorist leader Osama Bin Laden as part of a series of "Bert is Evil" images he posted on his homepage (Figure 1.1). Others depicted Bert as a Klansman, cavorting with Adolf Hitler, dressed as the Unabomber, or having sex with Pamela Anderson. It was all in good fun.

In the wake of September 11, a Bangladesh-based publisher scanned the Web for Bin Laden images to print on anti-American signs, posters, and T-shirts. Sesame Street is available in Pakistan in a localized format; the Arab world, thus, had no exposure to Bert and Ernie. The publisher may not have recognized Bert, but he must have thought the image was a good likeness of the al-Qaeda leader. The image ended up in a collage of similar images that was printed on thousands of posters and distributed across the Middle East.

CNN reporters recorded the unlikely sight of a mob of angry protestors marching through the streets chanting anti-American slogans and waving signs depicting Bert and Bin Laden (Figure 1.2). Representatives from the Children's Television Workshop, creators of the *Sesame Street* series, spotted the CNN footage and threatened to take legal action: "We're outraged that our characters would be used in this unfortunate and distasteful manner. The people responsible for this should

FIGURE 1.1. Dino Ignacio's digital collage of *Sesame Street*'s Bert and Osama Bin Laden.

FIGURE 1.2. Ignacio's collage surprisingly appeared in CNN coverage of anti-American protests following September 11.

be ashamed of themselves. We are exploring all legal options to stop this abuse and any similar abuses in the future." It was not altogether clear who they planned to sic their intellectual property attorneys on—the young man who had initially appropriated their images, or the terrorist supporters who deployed them. Coming full circle, amused fans produced a number of new sites, linking various *Sesame Street* characters with terrorists.

From his bedroom, Ignacio sparked an international controversy. His images crisscrossed the world, sometimes on the backs of commercial media, sometimes via grassroots media. And, in the end, he inspired his own cult following. As the publicity grew, Ignacio became more concerned and ultimately decided to disman-tle his site: "I feel this has gotten too close to reality. ... 'Bert Is Evil' and its following has always been contained and distanced from big media. This issue throws it out in the open."[1] Welcome to convergence culture, where old and new media collide, where grassroots and corporate media intersect, where the power of the media producer and the power of the media consumer inter-act in unpredictable ways.

> This illustration is being used to show the collision of "grassroots and corporate media"—how corporate media was used to generate grassroots imagery and how this then re-emerged in the corporate media.

This book [of which this reading is an extract] is about the relationship be-tween three concepts—media convergence, participatory culture, and collective intelligence.

By convergence, I mean the flow of content across multiple media platforms, the cooperation between multiple media industries, and the migratory behavior of media audiences who will go almost anywhere in search of the kinds of enter-tainment experiences they want. Convergence is a word that manages to describe technological, industrial, cultural, and social changes depending on who's speak-ing and what they think they are talking about. (In this book I will be mixing and matching terms across these various frames of reference. I have added a glossary at the end of the book to help guide readers.)

> Definition of convergence.

In the world of media convergence, every important story gets told, every brand gets sold, and every consumer gets courted across multiple media platforms. Think about the circuits that the "Bert is Evil" images traveled—from *Sesame Street* through Photoshop to the World Wide Web, from Ignacio's bedroom to a print shop in Bangladesh, from the posters held by anti-American protestors that are captured by CNN and into the living rooms of people around the world. Some of its circulation depended on corporate strategies, such as the localization of *Sesame Street* or the global coverage of CNN. Some of its circulation depended on tactics of grassroots appropriation, whether in North America or in the Middle East.

This circulation of media content—across different media systems, compet-ing media economies, and national borders—depends heavily on consumers' active participation. I will argue here against the idea that convergence should be understood primarily as a technological process bringing together multiple media functions within the same devices. Instead, convergence represents a cultural shift

as consumers are encouraged to seek out new information and make connections among dispersed media
content. This book is about the work—and play—spec-
tators perform in the new media system.

> Differs with those who see
> convergence as primarily a matter of
> technology. Convergence involves a
> "cultural shift." (But would this cultural
> shift be possible with the technology?)

The term, participatory culture, contrasts with older notions of passive media
spectatorship. Rather than talking about media producers and consumers as occupying separate roles, we might now see them as participants who interact with
each other according to a new set of rules that none of us fully understands. Not
all participants are created equal. Corporations—and even individuals within
corporate media— still exert greater power than any individual consumer or even
the aggregate of consumers. And some consumers have greater abilities to participate in this emerging culture than others.

Convergence does not occur through media appliances, however sophisticated
they may become. Convergence occurs within the brains of individual consumers and
through their social interactions with others. Each of us constructs our own personal
mythology from bits and fragments of information extracted from the media flow
and transformed into resources through which we make sense of our everyday lives.
Because there is more information on any given topic than anyone can store in their
head, there is an added incentive for us to talk among ourselves about the media we
consume. This conversation creates buzz that is increasingly valued by the media
industry. Consumption has become a collective process—and that's what this book
means by collective intelligence, a term coined by French cybertheorist Pierre Lévy.
None of us can know everything; each of us knows something; and we can put the
pieces together if we pool our resources and combine our skills. Collective intelligence can be seen as an alternative source of media power. We are learning how to
use that power through our day-to-day interactions within convergence culture.
Right now, we are mostly using this collective power through our recreational life,
but soon we will be deploying those skills for more "serious" purposes. In this book, I
explore how collective meaning-making within popular culture is starting to change
the ways religion, education, law, politics, advertising, and even the military operate.

Convergence Talk

Another snapshot of convergence culture at work: In December 2004, a hotly
anticipated Bollywood film, *Rok Sako To Rok Lo* (2004), was screened in its entirety
to movie buffs in Delhi, Bangalore, Hyderabad, Mumbai, and
other parts of India through EDGE-enabled mobile phones
with live video streaming facility. This is believed to be the first
time that a feature film had been fully accessible via mobile

> Example of convergence
> media: new movie first
> released for mobile phones.

phones.[2] It remains to be seen how this kind of distribution fits into people's lives.
Will it substitute for going to the movies or will people simply use it to sample
movies they may want to see at other venues? Who knows?

Over the past several years, many of us have watched as cell phones have become increasingly central to the release strategies of commercial motion pictures around the world, as amateur and professional cell phone movies have competed for prizes in international film festivals, as mobile users have been able to listen into major concerts, as Japanese novelists serialize their work via instant messenger, and as game players have used mobile devices to compete in augmented and alternative reality games. Some functions will take root; others will fail.

Call me old-fashioned. The other week I wanted to buy a cell phone—you know, to make phone calls. I didn't want a video camera, a still camera, a Web access device, an MP3 player, or a game system. I also wasn't interested in something that could show me movie previews, would have customizable ring tones, or would allow me to read novels. I didn't want the electronic equivalent of a Swiss army knife. When the phone rings, I don't want to have to figure out which button to push. I just wanted a phone. The sales clerks sneered at me; they laughed at me behind my back. I was told by company after mobile company that they don't make single-function phones anymore. Nobody wants them. This was a powerful demonstration of how central mobiles have become to the process of media convergence.

What's the point of this personal anecdote?

You've probably been hearing a lot about convergence lately. You are going to be hearing even more.

The media industries are undergoing another paradigm shift. It happens from time to time. In the 1990s, rhetoric about a coming digital revolution contained an implicit and often explicit assumption that new media was going to push aside old media, that the Internet was going to displace broadcasting, and that all of this would enable consumers to more easily access media content that was personally meaningful to them. A best-seller in 1990, Nicholas Negroponte's *Being Digital*, drew a sharp contrast between "passive old media" and "interactive new media," predicting the collapse of broadcast networks in favor of an era of narrowcasting and niche media on demand: "What will happen to broadcast television over the next five years is so phenomenal that it's difficult to comprehend."[3] At one point, he suggests that no government regulation will be necessary to shatter the media conglomerates: "The monolithic empires of mass media are dissolving into an array of cottage industries.... Media barons of today will be grasping to hold onto their centralized empires tomorrow.... The combined forces of technology and human nature will ultimately take a stronger hand in plurality than any laws Congress can invent."[4] Sometimes, the new media companies spoke about convergence, but by this term, they seemed to mean that old media would be absorbed fully and completely into the orbit of the emerging technologies. George Gilder, another digital revolutionary, dismissed such claims: "The computer industry is converging with the television industry in the same sense that the automobile converged with the horse, the TV converged with the nickelodeon, the word-processing program converged with the typewriter, the CAD program converged with the drafting board, and digital desktop publishing converged with the lino-type machine and the letterpress."[5] For Gilder, the computer had come not to transform mass culture but to destroy it.

The popping of the dot-com bubble threw cold water on this talk of a digital revolution. Now, convergence has reemerged as an important reference point as old and new media companies try to imagine the future of the entertainment industry. If the digital revolution paradigm presumed that new media would displace old media, the emerging convergence paradigm assumes that old and new media will interact in ever more complex ways. The digital revolution paradigm claimed that new media was going to change everything. After the dot.com crash, the tendency was to imagine that new media had changed nothing. As with so many things about the current media environment, the truth lay somewhere in between. More and more, industry leaders are returning to convergence as a way of making sense of a moment of disorienting change. Convergence is, in that sense, an old concept taking on new meanings.

> The bursting of the dot.com bubble in the 90s showed that the digital revolution thesis was overstated. After the dot.com bubble burst, people thought that not only was there no digital revolution, but also that nothing had changed. Now, people realize that things have changed, but that the convergence theory best explains the changes. (Is this his thesis?)

There was lots of convergence talk to be heard at the New Orleans Media Experience in October 2003. The New Orleans Media Experience was organized by HSI Productions, Inc., a New York-based company that produces music videos and commercials. HSI has committed to spend $100 million over the next five years, to make New Orleans the mecca for media convergence that Slamdance has become for independent cinema. The New Orleans Media Experience is more than a film festival; it is also a showcase for game releases, a venue for commercials and music videos, an array of concerts and theatrical performances, and a three-day series of panels and discussions with industry leaders.

Inside the auditorium, massive posters featuring images of eyes, ears, mouths, and hands urged attendees to "worship at the Alter of Convergence," but it was far from clear what kind of deity they were genuflecting before. Was it a New Testament God who promised them salvation? An Old Testament God threatening destruction unless they followed His rules? A multifaced deity that spoke like an oracle and demanded blood sacrifices? Perhaps, in keeping with the location, convergence was a voodoo goddess who would give them the power to inflict pain on their competitors?

Like me, the participants had come to New Orleans hoping to glimpse tomorrow before it was too late. Many were nonbelievers who had been burned in the dot-com meltdown and were there to scoff at any new vision. Others were freshly minted from America's top business schools and there to find ways to make their first million. Still others were there because their bosses had sent them, hoping for enlightenment, but willing to settle for one good night in the French Quarter.

The mood was tempered by a sober realization of the dangers of moving too quickly, as embodied by the ghost-town campuses in the Bay Area and the office furniture being sold at bulk prices on eBay; and the dangers of moving too slowly, as represented by the recording industry's desperate flailing as it tries to close the door on file-sharing after the cows have already come stampeding out of the barn. The participants had come to New Orleans in search of the "just right"— the right investments, predictions, and business models. No longer expecting to surf the waves of change, they would be content with staying afloat. The old paradigms were breaking down faster than the new ones were emerging, producing panic among those most invested in the status quo and curiosity in those who saw change as opportunity.

Advertising guys in pinstriped shirts mingled with recording industry flacks with backward baseball caps, Hollywood agents in Hawaiian shirts, pointy-bearded technologists, and shaggy-haired gamers. The only thing they all knew how to do was to exchange business cards.

As represented on the panels at the New Orleans Media Experience, convergence was a "come as you are" party and some of the participants were less ready for what was planned than others. It was also a swap meet where each of the entertainment industries traded problems and solutions, finding through the interplay among media what they can't achieve working in isolation. In every discussion, there emerged different models of convergence followed by the acknowledgment that none of them knew for sure what the outcomes were going to be. Then, everyone adjourned for a quick round of Red Bulls (a conference sponsor) as if funky high-energy drinks were going to blast them over all of those hurdles.

Political economists and business gurus make convergence sound so easy; they look at the charts that show the concentration of media ownership as if they ensure that all of the parts will work together to pursue maximum profits. But from the ground, many of the big media giants look like great big dysfunctional families, whose members aren't speaking with each other and pursue their own short term agendas even at the expense of other divisions of the same companies. In New Orleans, however, the representatives for different industries seemed tentatively ready to lower their guard and speak openly about common visions.

This event was billed as a chance for the general public to learn firsthand about the coming changes in news and entertainment. In accepting an invitation to be on panels, in displaying a willingness to "go public" with their doubts and anxieties, perhaps industry leaders were acknowledging the importance of the role that ordinary consumers can play not just in accepting convergence, but actually in driving the process. If the media industry in recent years has seemed at war with its consumers, in that it is trying to force consumers back into old relationships and into obedience to well-established norms, companies hoped to use this New Orleans event to justify their decisions to consumers and stockholders alike.

Unfortunately, although this was not a closed-door event, it might as well have been. Those few members of the public who did show up were ill-informed. After an intense panel discussion about the challenges of broadening the uses of game consoles, the first member of the audience to raise his hand wanted to know when Grand Theft Auto III was coming out on the Xbox. You can scarcely blame consumers for not knowing how to speak this new language or even what questions to ask when so little previous effort has been made to educate them about convergence thinking.

> This example shows how little people know about convergence thinking, or the most current explanations of media change.

At a panel on game consoles, the big tension was between Sony (a hardware company) and Microsoft (a software company); both had ambitious plans but fundamentally different business models and visions. All agreed that the core challenge was to expand the potential uses of this cheap and readily accessible technology so that it became the "black box," the "Trojan horse" that smuggled convergence culture right into people's living rooms. What was mom going to do with the console when her kids were at school? What would get a family to give a game console to grandpa for Christmas? They had the technology to bring about convergence, but they hadn't figured out why anyone would want it.

Another panel focused on the relationship between video games and traditional media. Increasingly, movie moguls saw games not simply as a means of stamping the franchise logo on some ancillary product but as a means of expanding the storytelling experience. These filmmakers had come of age as gamers and had their own ideas about the creative intersections between the media; they knew who the most creative designers were and they worked the collaboration into their contract. They wanted to use games to explore ideas that couldn't fit within two-hour films.

> These examples show how media interests are working out the details of convergence. It isn't going to happen by itself. Technology doesn't of itself determine how things will go. He's arguing against technological determinism.

Such collaborations meant taking everyone out of their "comfort zones," as one movieland agent explained. These relationships were difficult to sustain, since all parties worried about losing creative control, and since the time spans for development and distribution in the media were radically different. Should the game company try to align its timing to the often unpredictable production cycle of a movie with the hopes of hitting Wal-Mart the same weekend the film opens? Should the movie producers wait for the often equally unpredictable game development cycle to run its course, sitting out the clock while some competitor steals their thunder? Will the game get released weeks or months later, after the buzz of the movie has dried up or, worse yet, after the movie has bombed? Should the game become part of the publicity buildup toward a major release, even though that means starting development before the film project has been "green lighted" by a studio? Working with a television production company is even more nerve wracking, since the turnaround time is much shorter and the risk much higher that the series will never reach the air.

If the game industry folks had the smirking belief that they controlled the future, the record industry types were sweating bullets; their days were numbered unless they figured out how to turn around current trends (such as dwindling audiences, declining sales, and expanding piracy). The panel on "monetizing music" was one of the most heavily attended. Everyone tried to speak at once, yet none of them were sure their "answers" would work. Will the future revenue come from rights management, from billing people for the music they download, or from creating a fee the servers had to pay out to the record industry as a whole? And what about cell phone rings—which some felt represented an unexplored market for new music as well as a grassroots promotional channel? Perhaps the money will lie in the intersection between the various media with new artists promoted via music videos that are paid for by advertisers who want to use their sounds and images for branding, with new artists tracked via the web that allows the public to register its preferences in hours rather than weeks.

> Some media players seem to have more power than others in the arena of convergence.

And so it went, in panel after panel. The New Orleans Media Experience pressed us into the future. Every path forward had roadblocks, most of which felt insurmountable, but somehow, they would either have to be routed around or broken down in the coming decade.

The messages were plain:

1. Convergence is coming and you had better be ready.
2. Convergence is harder than it sounds.
3. Everyone will survive if everyone works together. (Unfortunately, that was the one thing nobody knew how to do.)

The Prophet of Convergence

If *Wired* magazine declared Marshall McLuhan the patron saint of the digital revolution, we might well describe the late MIT political scientist Ithiel de Sola Pool as the prophet of media convergence. Pool's *Technologies of Freedom* (1983) was probably the first book to lay out the concept of convergence as a force of change within the media industries:

> A process called the "convergence of modes" is blurring the lines between media, even between point-to-point communications, such as the post, telephone, and telegraph, and mass communications, such as the press, radio, and television. A single physical means—be it wires, cables or airwaves—may carry services that in the past were provided in separate ways. Conversely, a service that was provided in the past by any one medium—be it broadcasting, the press, or telephony—can now be provided in several different physical ways. So the one-to-one relationship that used to exist between a medium and its use is eroding.[6]

> Cites Pool approvingly. Pool was prescient where convergence was concerned. Likens him to Marshall McLuhan. Why does he compare Pool and McLuhan? McLuhan said that the form of new media is the content of the previous. How does this connect to convergence and Pool?

Some people today talk about divergence rather than convergence, but Pool under-stood that they were two sides of the same phenomenon.

"Once upon a time," Pool explained, "companies that published newspapers, magazines, and books did very little else; their involvement with other media was slight."[7] Each media had its own distinctive functions and markets, and each was regulated under different regimes, depending on whether its character was central-ized or decentralized, marked by scarcity or plentitude, dominated by news or entertainment, and owned by governmental or private interests. Pool felt that these differences were largely the product of political choices and preserved through habit rather than any essential characteristic of the various technologies. But he did see some communications technologies as supporting more diversity and a greater degree of participation than others: "Freedom is fostered when the means of communication are dispersed, decentralized, and easily available, as are print-ing presses or microcomputers. Central control is more likely when the means of communication are concentrated, monopolized, and scarce, as are great networks."[8]

Several forces, however, have begun breaking down the walls separating these different media. New media technologies enabled the same content to flow through many different chan-nels and assume many different forms at the point of reception. Pool was describing what Nicholas Negroponte calls the transfor-mation of "atoms into bytes" or digitization.[9] At the same time, new patterns of cross-media ownership that began in the mid-1980s, during what we can now see as the first phase of a longer process of media concentration, were making it more desirable for companies to distribute content across those various chan-nels rather than within a single media platform. Digitization set the conditions for convergence; corporate conglomerates created its imperative.

> Divergence is the flip side of convergence. That is, as media converge, they also diverge. They deliver their content in divergent forms and formats, through different delivery systems.

> Digitization is one factor that made it possible for the same content to flow through different channels (divergence). But also, "cross-media ownership" helped the process along. Again, he's arguing against a strict technological determinism here. That is, technology does not of itself make convergence or divergence happen.

Much writing about the so-called digital revolution presumed that the outcome of technological change was more or less inev-itable. Pool, on the other hand, predicted a period of prolonged transition, during which the various media systems competed and collaborated, searching for the stability that would always elude them: "Convergence does not mean ultimate stability or unity. It operates as a constant force for unification but always in dynamic tension with change.... There is no immutable law of growing convergence; the process of change is more complicated than that."[10]

As Pool predicted, we are in an age of media transition, one marked by tactical decisions and unintended consequences, mixed signals and competing interests, and most of all, unclear directions and unpredictable outcomes.[11] Two decades later, I find myself reexamining some of the core questions Pool raised—about how we maintain the potential of participatory culture in the wake of growing media concentration, about whether the changes brought about by convergence open

> What will increasing media concentration (ownership of media in fewer hands) do to participatory culture, even in light of convergence?
>
> Jenkins is most interested in the impact of convergence on popular culture, or the cultural expression of the populace.

new opportunities for expression or expand the power of big media. Pool was interested in the impact of convergence on political culture; I am more interested in its impact on popular culture, but the lines between the two have now blurred.

It is beyond my abilities to describe or fully document all of the changes that are occurring. My aim is more modest. I want to describe some of the ways that convergence thinking is reshaping American popular culture and, in particular, the ways it is impacting the relationship between media audiences, producers, and content. Although this chapter will outline the big picture (insofar as any of us can see it clearly yet),

> This is his mapping. It comes late in this essay because this is an introduction to a book.

subsequent chapters [not reprinted here] will examine these changes through a series of case studies focused on specific media franchises and their audiences. My goal is to help ordinary people grasp how convergence is impacting the media they consume and, at the same time, to help industry leaders and poli-

> Expression of purpose.

cymakers understand consumer perspectives on these changes. Writing this book has been challenging because everything seems to be changing at once and there is no vantage point that takes me above the fray. Rather than trying to write from an objective vantage point, I describe in this book what this process looks like from various localized perspectives—advertising executives struggling to reach a changing market, creative artists discovering new ways to tell stories, educators tapping informal learning communities, activists deploying new resources to shape the political future, religious groups contesting the quality of their cultural environs, and, of course, various fan communities who are early adopters and creative users of emerging media.

I can't claim to be a neutral observer in any of this. For one thing, I am not simply a consumer of many of these media products; I am also an active fan. The world of media fandom has been a central theme of my work for almost two decades—an interest that emerges from my own participation within various fan communities as much as it does from my intellectual interests as a media scholar. During that time, I have watched fans move from the invisible margins of popular culture and into the center of current thinking about media production and consumption. For another, through my role as director of the MIT Comparative Media Studies Program, I have been an active participant in discussions among industry insiders and policymakers; I have consulted with some of the companies discussed in this book; my earlier writings on fan communities and participatory culture have been embraced by business schools and are starting to have some modest impact on the way media companies are relating to their consumers; many of the creative artists and media executives I interviewed are people I would

> Significant ethos statements

consider friends. At a time when the roles between producers and consumers are shifting, my job allows me to move among different vantage points. I hope this book allows readers to benefit from my adventures into spaces where few humanists have gone before. Yet, readers should also keep in mind that my engagement with fans and producers alike necessarily colors what I say. My goal here is to document conflicting perspectives on media change rather than to critique them. I don't think we can meaningfully critique convergence until it is more fully understood; yet if the public doesn't get some insights into the discussions that are taking place, they will have little to no input into decisions that will dramatically change their relationship to media.

The Black Box Fallacy

Almost a decade ago, science fiction writer Bruce Sterling established what he calls the Dead Media Project. As his website (http://www.deadmedia.org) explains, "The centralized, dinosaurian one-to-many media that roared and trampled through the twentieth century are poorly adapted to the postmodern technological environment."[12] Anticipating that some of these "dinosaurs" were heading to the tar pits, he constructed a shrine to "the media that have died on the barbed wire of technological change." His collection is astounding, including relics like "the phenakistoscope, the telharmonium, the Edison wax cylinder, the stereopticon ... various species of magic lantern."[13]

Yet, history teaches us that old media never die—and they don't even necessarily fade away. What dies are simply the tools we use to access media content—the 8-track, the Beta tape. These are what media scholars call delivery technologies. Most of what Sterling's project lists falls under this category. Delivery technologies become obsolete and get replaced; media, on the other hand, evolve. Recorded sound is the medium. CDs, MP3 files, and 8-track cassettes are delivery technologies.

> Distinguishes between media and delivery technologies. What's the point of this distinction? To show that media never die? If so, what's the point in telling us that?

To define media, let's turn to historian Lisa Gitelman, who offers a model of media that works on two levels: on the first, a medium is a technology that enables communication; on the second, a medium is a set of associated "protocols" or social and cultural practices that have grown up around that technology.[14] Delivery systems are simply and only technologies; media are also cultural systems. Delivery technologies come and go all the time, but media persist as layers within an ever more complicated information and entertainment stratum.

A medium's content may shift (as occurred when television displaced radio as a storytelling medium, freeing radio to become the primary showcase for rock and roll), its audience may change (as occurs when comics move from a mainstream medium in the 1950s to a niche medium today), and its social status may

> Defines media, drawing on another writer: Media are both technologies and cultural systems.

rise or fall (as occurs when theater moves from a popular form to an elite one), but once a medium establishes itself as satisfying some core human demand, it continues to function within the larger system of communication options.

Once recorded sound becomes a possibility, we have continued to develop new and improved means of recording and playing back sound. Printed words did not kill spoken words. Cinema did not kill theater. Television did not kill radio.[15] Each old medium was forced to coexist with the emerging media. That's why convergence seems more plausible as a way of understanding the past several decades of media change than the old digital revolution paradigm had. Old media are not being displaced. Rather, their functions and status are shifted by the introduction of new technologies.

> Oh, ok. The point is that as media travel through different channels, they may change in content and status, but they will nevertheless continue to exist. This shows how media converge and diverge. An old media converges with a new technology and diverges from an older one. Thus, digital technology changes but does not outmode old media.

The implications of this distinction between media and delivery systems become clearer as Gitelman elaborates on what she means by "protocols." She writes: "Protocols express a huge variety of social, economic, and material relationships. So telephony includes the salutation 'Hello?' (for English speakers, at least) and includes the monthly billing cycle and includes the wires and cables that materially connect our phones.... Cinema includes everything from the sprocket holes that run along the sides of film to the widely shared sense of being able to wait and see 'films' at home on video. And protocols are far from static."[16] This book will have less to say about the technological dimensions of media change than about the shifts in the protocols by which we are producing and consuming media.

> Media are defined by "protocols" or social and economic relationships, not by technology (delivery systems). The book is more about media protocols than technology.

Much contemporary discourse about convergence starts and ends with what I call the Black Box Fallacy. Sooner or later, the argument goes, all media content is going to flow through a single black box into our living rooms (or, in the mobile scenario, through black boxes we carry around with us everywhere we go). If the folks at the New Orleans Media Experience could just figure out which black box will reign supreme, then everyone can make reasonable investments for the future. Part of what makes the black box concept a fallacy is that it reduces media change to technological change and strips aside the cultural levels we are considering here.

I don't know about you, but in my living room, I am seeing more and more black boxes. There are my VCR, my digital cable box, my DVD player, my digital recorder, my sound system, and my two game systems, not to mention a huge mound of videotapes, DVDs and CDs, game cartridges and controllers, sitting atop, laying alongside, toppling over the edge of my television system. (I would definitely qualify as an early adopter, but most American homes now have, or soon will have, their own pile of black boxes.) The perpetual tangle of cords that stands between me and my "home entertainment" center reflects the degree of incompatibility and dysfunction that exist between the various media technologies. And many of my MIT students are lugging around multiple black boxes—their laptops, their cells, their iPods, their Game Boys, their BlackBerrys, you name it.

As Cheskin Research explained in a 2002 report, "The old idea of convergence was that all devices would converge into one central device that did everything for you (à la the universal remote). What we are now seeing is the hardware diverging while the content converges.... Your email needs and expectations are different whether you're at home, work, school, commuting, the airport, etc., and these different devices are designed to suit your needs for accessing content depending on where you are—your situated context."[17] This pull toward more specialized media appliances coexists with a push toward more generic devices. We can see the proliferation of black boxes as symptomatic of a moment of convergence: because no one is sure what kinds of functions should be combined, we are forced to buy a range of specialized and incompatible appliances. On the other end of the spectrum, we may also be forced to deal with an escalation of functions within the same media appliance, functions that decrease the ability of that appliance to serve its original function, and so I can't get a cell phone that is just a phone.

Media convergence is more than simply a technological shift. Convergence alters the relationship between existing technologies, industries, markets, genres, and audiences. Convergence alters the logic by which media industries operate and by which media consumers process news and entertainment. Keep this in mind: convergence refers to a process, not an endpoint. There will be no single black box that controls the flow of media into our homes. Thanks to the proliferation of channels and the portability of new computing and telecommunications technologies, we are entering an era where media will be everywhere. Convergence isn't something that is going to happen one day when we have enough bandwidth or figure out the correct configuration of appliances. Ready or not, we are already living within a convergence culture.

> The Black Box Fallacy is that all media will travel through one black box. But this is mistaken, based as it is on a reduction of media change to technological change. Media convergence also means divergence of media into different channels. No one black box will subsume all the black boxes. Rather, they are multiplying! These black boxes will each carry more media, but no one box will replace all others.

Our cell phones are not simply telecommunications devices; they also allow us to play games, download information from the Internet, and take and send photographs or text messages. Increasingly they allow us to watch previews of new films, download installments of serialized novels, or attend concerts from remote locations. All of this is already happening in northern Europe and Asia. Any of these functions can also be performed using other media appliances. You can listen to the Dixie Chicks through your DVD player, your car radio, your walkman, your iPod, a Web radio station, or a music cable channel.

Fueling this technological convergence is a shift in patterns of media ownership. Whereas old Hollywood focused on cinema, the new media conglomerates have controlling interests across the entire entertainment industry. Warner Bros. produces film, television, popular music, computer games, websites, toys, amusement park rides, books, newspapers, magazines, and comics.

In turn, media convergence impacts the way we consume media. A teenager doing homework may juggle four or five windows, scan the Web, listen to and download MP3 files, chat with friends, word-process a paper, and respond to e-mail, shifting rapidly among tasks. And fans of a popular television series may sample dialogue, summarize episodes, debate subtexts, create original fan fiction, record their own soundtracks, make their own movies—and distribute all of this worldwide via the Internet.

> Convergence involves not only a change in media production, but also consumption. The change ultimately happens in our brains. See the iBrain article!

Convergence is taking place within the same appliances, within the same franchise, within the same company, within the brain of the consumer, and within the same fandom. Convergence involves both a change in the way media is produced and a change in the way media is consumed.

The Cultural Logic of Media Convergence

> This is a reference to Frederic Jameson's book, *Postmodernism, or the Cultural Logic of Late Capitalism*.

Another snapshot of the future: Anthropologist Mizuko Ito has documented the growing place of mobile communications among Japanese youth, describing young couples who remain in constant contact with each other throughout the day, thanks to their access to various mobile technologies.[18] They wake up together, work together, eat together, and go to bed together even though they live miles apart and may have face-to-face contact only a few times a month. We might call it telecocooning.

Convergence doesn't just involve commercially produced materials and services traveling along well-regulated and predictable circuits. It doesn't just involve the mobile companies getting together with the film companies to decide when and where we watch a newly released film. It also occurs when people take media in their own hands. Entertainment content isn't the only thing that flows across multiple media platforms. Our lives, relationships, memories, fantasies, desires also flow across media channels. Being a lover or a mommy or a teacher occurs on multiple platforms.[19] Sometimes we tuck our kids into bed at night and other times we Instant Message them from the other side of the globe.

> Convergence isn't just about entertainment, it's about vital communications, and increased communications.

And yet another snapshot: Intoxicated students at a local high school use their cell phones spontaneously to produce their own soft-core porn movie involving topless cheerleaders making out in the locker room. Within hours, the movie is circulating across the school, being downloaded by students and teachers alike and watched between classes on personal media devices.

> Dangers of media convergence: unwanted "exposure."

When people take media into their own hands, the results can be wonderfully creative; they can also be bad news for all involved.

For the foreseeable future, convergence will be a kind of kludge—a jerry-rigged relationship among different media technologies—rather than a fully integrated system. Right now, the cultural shifts, the legal battles, and the economic consolidations that are fueling media convergence are preceding shifts in the technological infrastructure. How those various transitions unfold will determine the balance of power in the next media era.

> Convergence will be messy for the time being. The future is uncertain.

The American media environment is now being shaped by two seemingly contradictory trends: on the one hand, new media technologies have lowered production and distribution costs, expanded the range of available delivery channels, and enabled consumers to archive, annotate, appropriate, and recirculate media content in powerful new ways. At the same time, there has been an alarming concentration of the ownership of mainstream commercial media, with a small handful of multinational media conglomerates dominating all sectors of the entertainment industry. No one seems capable of describing both sets of changes at the same time, let alone show how they impact each other. Some fear that media is out of control, others that it is too controlled. Some see a world without gatekeepers, others a world where gatekeepers have unprecedented power. Again, the truth lies somewhere in between.

> Two contradictory trends: greater democratization on the one hand, and increased media concentration on the other. No one has been able to account for both and explain their coincidence. Is the net effect cultural anarchy or unprecedented media control? Neither.

Another snapshot: People around the world are affixing stickers showing Yellow Arrows (http://global.yellowarrow.net) alongside public monuments and factories, beneath highway overpasses, onto lamp posts. The arrows provide numbers others can call to access recorded voice messages—personal annotations on our shared urban landscape. They use it to share a beautiful vista or criticize an irresponsible company. And increasingly, companies are co-opting the system to leave their own advertising pitches.

Convergence, as we can see, is both a top-down corporate-driven process and a bottom-up consumer-driven process. Corporate convergence coexists with grassroots convergence. Media companies are learning how to accelerate the flow of media content across delivery channels to expand revenue opportunities, broaden markets, and reinforce viewer commitments. Consumers are learning how to use these different media technologies to bring the flow of media more fully under their control and to interact with other consumers. The promises of this new media environment raise expectations of a freer flow of ideas and content. Inspired by those ideals, consumers are fighting for the right to participate more fully in their culture. Sometimes, corporate and grassroots convergence reinforce each other, creating closer, more rewarding relations between media producers and consumers. Sometimes, these two forces are at war and those struggles will redefine the face of American popular culture.

Convergence requires media companies to rethink old assumptions about what it means to consume media, assumptions that shape both programming and marketing decisions. If old

> Convergence is both a top-down, corporate-driven and a bottom-up, grassroots-driven process. This explains his position that neither possibility—anarchy or complete control—will prevail any time soon, if ever.

consumers were assumed to be passive, the new consumers are active. If old consumers were predictable and stayed where you told them to stay, then new consumers are migratory, showing a declining loyalty to networks or media. If old consumers were isolated individuals, the new consumers are more socially connected. If the work of media consumers was once silent and invisible, the new consumers are now noisy and public.

Media producers are responding to these newly empowered consumers in contradictory ways, sometimes encouraging change, sometimes resisting what they see as renegade behavior. And consumers, in turn, are perplexed by what they see as mixed signals about how much and what kinds of participation they can enjoy.

As they undergo this transition, the media companies are not behaving in a monolithic fashion; often, different divisions of the same company are pursuing radically different strategies, reflecting their uncertainty about how to proceed. On the one hand, convergence represents an expanded opportunity for media conglomerates, since content that succeeds in one sector can spread across other platforms. On the other, convergence represents a risk since most of these media fear a fragmentation or erosion of their markets. Each time they move a viewer from television to the Internet, say, there is a risk that the consumer may not return.

> Media producers and consumers are involved in changing relationships. Neither is sure what exactly to make of the other or how to proceed.

Industry insiders use the term "extension" to refer to their efforts to expand the potential markets by moving content across different delivery systems, "synergy" to refer to the economic opportunities represented by their ability to own and control all of those manifestations, and "franchise" to refer to their coordinated effort to brand and market fictional content under these new conditions. Extension, synergy, and franchising are pushing media industries to embrace convergence. For that reason, the case studies I selected for this book deal with some of the most successful franchises in recent media history. Some (*American Idol*, 2002, and *Survivor*, 2000) originate on television, some (*The Matrix*, 1999, *Star Wars*, 1977) on the big screen, some as books (*Harry Potter*, 1998), and some as games (*The Sims*, 2000), but each extends outward from its originating medium to influence many other sites of cultural production. Each of these franchises offers a different vantage point from which to understand how media convergence is reshaping the relationship between media producers and consumers.

> The terms media insiders use to refer to the processes of convergence from a marketing standpoint: "extension," "synergy," and "franchise." Extending, coordinating, and branding their convergence efforts.

Chapter 1 [not reprinted here], which focuses on *Survivor*, and chapter 2 [not reprinted here], which centers on *American Idol*, look at the phenomenon of reality television. Chapter 1 guides readers through the little known world of *Survivor* spoilers—a group of active consumers who pool their knowledge to try to unearth the series' many secrets before they are revealed on the air. *Survivor* spoiling will be read here as a particularly vivid example of collective intelligence at work. Knowledge communities form around mutual intellectual interests; their members work together to forge new knowledge often in realms where no traditional expertise exists; the pursuit of and assessment of knowledge are at once communal and adversarial. Mapping how these knowledge communities work can help us better understand the social nature of contemporary media consumption. They can also give us insight into how knowledge becomes power in the age of media convergence.

On the other hand, chapter 2 [not reprinted here] examines *American Idol* from the perspective of the media industry, trying to understand how reality television is being shaped by what I call "affective economics." The decreasing value of the thirty-second commercial in an age of TiVos and VCRs is forcing Madison Avenue to rethink its interface with the consuming public. This new "affective economics" encourages companies to transform brands into what one industry insider calls "lovemarks" and to blur the line between entertainment content and brand messages. According to the logic of affective economics, the ideal consumer is active, emotionally engaged, and socially networked. Watching the advert or consuming the product is no longer enough; the company invites the audience inside the brand community. Yet, if such affiliations encourage more active consumption, these same communities can also become protectors of brand integrity and thus critics of the companies that seek to court their allegiance.

Strikingly, in both cases, relations between producers and consumers are breaking down as consumers seek to act upon the invitation to participate in the life of the franchises. In the case of *Survivor*, the spoiler community has become so good at the game that the producers fear they will be unable to protect the rights of other consumers to have a "first time" experience of the unfolding series. In the case of *American Idol*, fans fear that their participation is marginal and that producers still play too active a role in shaping the outcome of the competition. How much participation is too much? When does participation become interference? And conversely, when do producers exert too much power over the entertainment experience?

Chapter 3 [not reprinted here] examines *The Matrix* franchise as an example of what I am calling transmedia storytelling. Transmedia storytelling refers to a new aesthetic that has emerged in response to media convergence—one that places new demands on consumers and depends on the active participation of knowledge communities. Transmedia storytelling is the art of world making. To fully experience any fictional world, consumers must assume the role of hunters and gatherers, chasing down bits of the story across media channels, comparing notes with each other via online discussion groups, and collaborating to ensure that everyone who invests time and effort will come away with a richer entertainment experience. Some would argue that the Wachowski brothers, who wrote and directed the three *Matrix* films, have pushed transmedia storytelling farther than most audience members were prepared to go.

Chapters 4 and 5 [not reprinted here] take us deeper into the realm of participatory culture. Chapter 4 [not reprinted here] deals with *Star Wars* fan filmmakers and gamers, who are actively reshaping George Lucas's mythology to satisfy their own fantasies and desires. Fan cultures will be understood here as a revitalization of the old folk culture process in response to the content of mass culture. Chapter 5 [not reprinted here] deals with young *Harry Potter* fans who are writing their own stories about Hogwarts and its students. In both cases, these grassroots artists are finding themselves in conflict with commercial media producers who want to exert greater control over their intellectual property. We will see in chapter 4 [not reprinted here] that LucasArts has had to continually rethink its relations to *Star Wars* fans throughout the past several decades, trying to strike the right balance between encouraging the enthusiasm of their fans and protecting their investments in the series. Interestingly, as *Star Wars* moves across media channels, different expectations about participation emerge, with the producers of the *Star Wars Galaxies* game encouraging consumers to generate much of the content even as the producers of the *Star Wars* movies issue guidelines enabling and constraining fan participation.

Chapter 5 [not reprinted here] extends this focus on the politics of participation to consider two specific struggles over *Harry Potter*: the conflicting interests between *Harry Potter* fans and Warner Bros., the studio that acquired the film rights to J.K. Rowling's books, and the conflict between conservative Christian critics of the books and teachers who have seen them as a means of encouraging young readers. This chapter maps a range of responses to the withering of traditional gatekeepers and the expansion of fantasy into many different parts of our everyday lives. On the one hand, some conservative Christians are striking back against media convergence and globalization, reasserting traditional authority in the face of profound social and cultural change. On the other hand, some Christians embrace convergence through their own forms of media outreach, fostering a distinctive approach to media literacy education and encouraging the emergence of Christian-inflected fan cultures.

Throughout these five chapters [not reprinted here], I will show how entrenched institutions are taking their models from grassroots fan communities, and reinventing themselves for an era of media convergence and collective intelligence—how the advertising industry has been forced to reconsider consumers' relations to brands, the military is using multiplayer games to rebuild communications between civilians and service members, the legal profession has struggled to understand what "fair use" means in an era where many more people are becoming authors, educators are reassessing the value of informal education, and at least some conservative Christians are making their peace with newer forms of popular culture. In each of these cases, powerful institutions are trying to build stronger connections with their constituencies and consumers are applying skills learned as fans and gamers to work, education, and politics.

Chapter 6 [not reprinted here] will turn from popular culture to public culture, applying my ideas about convergence to offer a perspective on the 2004 American presidential campaign, exploring what it might take to make democracy more participatory. Again and again, citizens were better served by popular culture than they were by news or political discourse; popular culture took on new responsibilities for educating the public about the stakes of this election and inspiring them to participate more fully in the process. In the wake of a divisive campaign, popular media may also model ways we can come together despite our differences. The 2004 elections represent an important transitional moment in the relationship between media and politics as citizens are being encouraged to do much of the dirty work of the campaign and the candidates and parties lost some control over the political process. Here again, all sides are assuming greater participation by citizens and consumers, yet they do not yet agree on the terms of that participation. In my conclusion, I will return to my three key terms—convergence, collective intelligence, and participation. I want to explore some of the implications of the trends I will be discussing in this book for education, media reform, and democratic citizenship. I will be returning there to a core claim: that convergence culture represents a shift in the ways we think about our relations to media, that we are making that shift first through our relations with popular culture, but that the skills we acquire through play may have implications for how we learn, work, participate in the political process, and connect with other people around the world.

I will be focusing throughout this book on the competing and contradictory ideas about participation that are shaping this new media culture. Yet, I must acknowledge that not all consumers have access to the skills and resources needed to be full participants in the cultural practices I am describing.

Mapping of the book, showing how each chapter supports and illustrates his argument about media convergence.

Increasingly, the digital divide is giving way to concern about the participation gap. Throughout the 1990s, the primary question was one of access. Today, most Americans have some limited access to the Internet, say, though for many, that access is through the public library or the local school. Yet many of the activities this book will describe depend on more extended access to those technologies, a greater familiarity with the new kinds of social interactions they enable, a fuller mastery over the conceptual skills that consumers have developed in response to media convergence. As long as the focus remains on access, reform remains focused on technologies; as soon as we begin to talk about participation, the emphasis shifts to cultural protocols and practices.

Most of the people depicted in this book are early adopters. In this country they are disproportionately white, male, middle class, and college educated. These are people who have the greatest access to new media technologies and have mastered the skills needed to fully participate in these new knowledge cultures. I don't assume that these cultural practices will remain the same as we broaden access and participation. In fact, expanding participation necessarily sparks further change. Yet, right now, our best window into convergence culture comes from looking at the experience of these early settlers and first inhabitants. These elite consumers exert a disproportionate influence on media culture in part because advertisers and media producers are so eager to attract and hold their attention. Where they go, the media industry is apt to follow; where the media industry goes, these consumers are apt to be found. Right now, both are chasing their own tails. You are now entering convergence culture. It is not a surprise that we are not yet ready to cope with its complexities and contradictions. We need to find ways to negotiate the changes taking place. No one group can set the terms. No one group can control access and participation.

Don't expect the uncertainties surrounding convergence to be resolved anytime soon. We are entering an era of prolonged transition and transformation in the way media operates. Convergence describes the process by which we will sort through those options. There will be no magical black box that puts everything in order again. Media producers will only find their way through their current problems by renegotiating their relationship with their consumers. Audiences, empowered by these new technologies, occupying a space at the intersection between old and new media, are demanding the right to participate within the culture. Producers who fail to make their peace with this new participatory culture will face declining goodwill and diminished revenues. The resulting struggles and compromises will define the public culture of the future.

> Conclusion: The future is uncertain, but producers who fail to "make their peace" with participatory culture (based on convergence media) will not fare well. The future of convergence will be a result of struggles and compromises between media companies, consumers and participants.

Notes

1. Josh Grossberg, "The Bert-Bin Laden Connection?" E Online, October 10, 2001, http://www.eonline.com/news/42292/the-bert-bin-laden-connection. For a different perspective on Bert and Bin Laden, see Roy Rosenzweig, "Scarcity or Abundance? Preserving the Past in a Digital Era," *American Historical Review* 108 (June 2003).
2. "RSTRL to Premier on Cell Phone," IndiaFM News Bureau, December 6, 2004, http://www.bollywoodhungama.com/news/1174867/RSTRL-to-premiere-on-cell-phone.
3. Nicholas Negroponte, *Being Digital* (New York: Alfred A. Knopf, 1995), p. 54.
4. Ibid., pp. 57-58.
5. George Gilder, "Afterword: The Computer Juggernaut: Life after *Life after Television*," added to the 1994 edition of *Life after Television: The Coming Transformation of Media and American Life* (New York: W.W. Norton), p. 189. The book was originally published in 1990.

6. Ithiel de Sola Pool, *Technologies of Freedom: On Free Speech in an Electronic Age* (Cambridge, MA: Harvard University Press, 1983), p. 23.

7. Ibid.

8. Ibid., p. 5.

9. Negroponte, *Being Digital.*

10. Pool, *Technologies of Freedom*, pp. 53-54.

11. For a fuller discussion of the concept of media in transition, see David Thorburn and Henry Jenkins, "Towards an Aesthetics of Transition," in David Thorburn and Henry Jenkins (eds.), *Rethinking Media Change: The Aesthetics of Transition* (Cambridge, MA: MIT Press, 2003).

12. Bruce Sterling, "The Dead Media Project: A Modest Proposal and a Public Appeal," http://www.deadmedia.org/modest-proposal.html.

13. Ibid.

14. Lisa Gitelman, "Introduction: Media as Historical Subjects," in *Always Already New: Media, History and the Data of Culture* (work in progress).

15. For a useful discussion of the recurring idea that new media kill off old media, see Priscilla Coit Murphy, "Books Are Dead, Long Live Books," in David Thorburn and Henry Jenkins (eds.), *Rethinking Media Change: The Aesthetics of Transition* (Cambridge, MA: MIT Press, 2003).

16. Gitelman, "Introduction."

17. Cheskin Research, "Designing Digital Experiences for Youth," *Market Insights Series*, Fall 2002, pp. 8-9.

18. Mizuko Ito, "Mobile Phones, Japanese Youth and the Re-Placement of the Social Contract," in Rich Ling and Per Petersen (eds.), *Mobile Communications: Re-Negotiation of the Social Sphere* (forthcoming). http://www.itofisher.com/mito/archives/mobileyouth.pdf.

19. For a useful illustration of this point, see Henry Jenkins, "Love Online," in Henry Jenkins (ed.), *Fans, Gamers, and Bloggers* (New York: New York University Press, 2005).

Source: *Convergence Culture: Where Old and New Media Collide*. New York: New York UP, 2006. 1-24.

WHAT IT SAYS

1. What does Jenkins mean by "convergence" in the context of this article?

2. What is "participatory culture"? Explain how "participatory intelligence" creates media power.

3. How does Jenkins contrast the digital revolution paradigm with the convergence paradigm?

4. Jenkins describes the New Orleans Media Experience conference of 2003. What does this description demonstrate? What aspects of convergence culture does it reveal? For example, what issues surfaced at the conference's panel on monetizing music?

5. What specific aspects of the digital revolution did the political scientist Ithiel de Sola Pool accurately predict in 1985? What issues did Pool raise in his 1983 book?

6. What specific distinctions do Jenkins and Gitelman make between media and delivery technologies? What are media protocols and how are they significant?

HOW IT SAYS IT

1. How does Jenkins establish himself as a reliable authority on convergence culture?

2. Explore the ways in which Jenkins uses narrative. Cite examples of narratives he uses and discuss how each works to bolster a specific claim.

3. Who is Jenkins's intended audience? Base your speculation on the ways in which he addresses the reader.

WRITE ABOUT IT

1. Write an essay that discusses the ways in which the Black Box Fallacy has proved more or less true since this essay was written. Give specific examples.

2. Jenkins mentions contradictory trends shaping the American media environment. Write an essay that argues either that "media is out of control," or that it is too controlled.

3. Choose a successful media franchise (Jenkins mentions *American Idol*, *Harry Potter*, and *The Sims*) and discuss how it "extends outward from its originating medium to influence many other sites of cultural production." Explain how your example demonstrates Jenkins's claim that "media convergence is reshaping the relationship between media producers and consumers." Incorporate such ideas as affective communities and transmedia.

c. Gary Small and Gigi Vorgan, "Meet Your iBrain: How Technology Changes the Way We Think"

Gary Small is a professor of psychiatry and biobehavioral sciences at the University of California at Los Angeles, where he also directs the Memory and Aging Research Center. He has developed brain-imaging technology that allows physicians to detect brain aging and Alzheimer's disease years before patients show symptoms. He is the co-author, with Gigi Vorgan, of *The Memory Bible* (2003), *The Memory Prescription* (2005), *The Longevity Bible* (2006), and *iBrain: Surviving the Technological Alteration of the Modern Mind* (2008), which further develops the argument made here. He also has published some 500 scientific papers. He appears frequently on numerous national television shows and writes a blog, "Brain Bootcamp," for *Psychology Today* magazine. He earned his BS degree from UCLA and his MD from the University of Southern California.

Gigi Vorgan, in addition to co-writing books with Gary Small, is a screenwriter, producer, and actress. She writes a blog, "The Simple Life," for *Psychology Today*.

Small and Vorgan's article explores the ways in which our lives and communication styles have changed in response to the extensive use of digital technology. They claim that those who spend a great deal of time on the computer and the cell phone have developed neural pathways that help them process information quickly. At the same time, however, their ability to interact face-to-face with others has weakened. What does this mean for individuals, and for society in general, they ask, and how might we ensure that we retain our ability to interact socially while retaining the advantages of digital technology?

As You Read: Think about your own use of digital technology. How much time do you spend a day listening to music, working or playing on the computer, and talking and texting on your cell phone? Compare that to the time you spend interacting face-to-face with others.

Meet Your iBrain: How Technology Changes the Way We Think

You're on a plane packed with other businesspeople, reading your electronic version of the *Wall Street Journal* on your laptop while downloading files to your BlackBerry and organizing your PowerPoint presentation for your first meeting when you reach New York. You relish the perfect symmetry of your schedule, to-do lists and phone book as you notice a woman in the next row entering little written notes into her leather-bound daily planner. You remember having one of those ... What? Like a zillion years ago? Hey, lady! Wake up and smell the computer age. You're outside the airport now, waiting impatiently for a cab along with dozens of other people. It's finally your turn, and as you reach for the taxi door a large man pushes in front of you, practically knocking you over. Your briefcase goes flying, and your laptop and BlackBerry splatter into pieces on the pavement. As you frantically gather up the remnants of your once perfectly scheduled life, the woman with the daily planner book gracefully steps into a cab and glides away.

The current explosion of digital technology not only is changing the way we live and communicate but also is rapidly and profoundly altering our brains. Daily exposure to high technology—computers, smart phones, videogames, search engines such as Google and Yahoo—stimulates brain cell alteration and neurotransmitter release, gradually strengthening new neural pathways in our brains while weakening old ones. Because of the current technological revolution, our brains are *evolving* right now—at a speed like never before.

Besides influencing how we think, digital technology is altering how we feel, how we behave. Seven out of 10 American homes are wired for high-speed Internet. We rely on the Internet and digital technology for entertainment, political discussion, and communication with friends and co-workers. As the brain evolves and shifts its focus toward new technological skills, it drifts away from fundamental social skills, such as reading facial expressions during conversation or grasping the emotional context of a subtle gesture. A 2002 Stanford University study found that for every hour we spend on our computers, traditional face-to-face interaction time with other people drops by nearly 30 minutes.

Digital Natives

Today's young people in their teens and 20s, who have been dubbed "digital natives," have never known a world without computers, 24-hour TV news, Internet and cell phones—with their video, music, cameras and text messaging. Many of these natives rarely enter a library, let alone look something up in a traditional encyclopedia; they use Google, Yahoo and other online search engines. The neural networks in the brains of these digital natives differ dramatically from those of "digital immigrants," people—including most baby boomers—who came to the digital/computer age as adults but whose basic brain wiring was laid down during a time when direct social interaction was the norm.

Now we are exposing our brains to technology for extensive periods every day, even at very young ages. A 2007 University of Texas at Austin study of more than 1,000 children found that on a typical day, 75 percent of children watch TV, whereas 32 percent of them watch videos or DVDs, with a total daily exposure averaging one hour and 20 minutes. Among those children, five and six-year-olds spend an additional 50 minutes in front of the computer. A 2005 Kaiser Family Foundation study found that young people eight to 18 years of age expose their brains to eight and a half hours of digital and video sensory stimulation a day. The investigators reported that most of the technology exposure is passive, such as watching television and videos (four hours daily) or listening to music (one hour and 45 minutes), whereas other exposure is more active and requires mental participation, such as playing video games (50 minutes daily) or using the computer (one hour).

We know that the brain's neural circuitry responds every moment to whatever sensory input it gets and that the many hours people spend in front of the computer—including trolling the Internet, exchanging e-mail, video conferencing, instant messaging and e-shopping—expose their brains to constant digital stimulation. Our research team at the University of California, Los Angeles, wanted to look at how much impact this extended computer time was having on the brain's neural circuitry, how quickly it could build up new pathways, and whether we could observe and measure these changes as they occurred.

Google in Your Head

One of us (Small) enlisted the help of Susan Bookheimer and Teena Moody, UCLA experts in neuropsychology and neuroimaging. We planned to use functional magnetic resonance imaging to measure the brain's activity during a common Internet computer task: searching Google for accurate information. We first needed to find people who were relatively inexperienced and naive to the computer.

After initial difficulty finding people who had not yet used PCs, we were able to recruit three volunteers in their mid-50s and 60s who were new to the technology yet willing to give it a try. To compare the brain activity of these three naive volunteers, we also recruited three computer-savvy volunteers of comparable age, gender and socioeconomic background. For our experiment, we chose searching on Google for specific and accurate information on a variety of topics, ranging from the health benefits of eating chocolate to planning a trip to the Galápagos.

Next, we had to figure out a way to perform MRIs on the volunteers while they used the Internet. Because the study subjects had to be inside a long, narrow tube of an MRI machine during the experiment, there would be no space for a computer, keyboard or mouse. To re-create the Google-search experience inside the scanner, we had the volunteers wear a pair of special goggles that presented images of website pages. The system allowed the volunteers to navigate the simulated computer screen and make choices to advance their search by pressing one finger on a small keypad, conveniently placed.

To make sure that the fMRI scanner was measuring the neural circuitry that controls Internet searches, we needed to factor out other sources of brain stimulation. To do this, we added a control task in which the study subjects read pages of a book projected through the specialized goggles during the MRI. This task allowed us to subtract from the MRI measurements any nonspecific brain activations that resulted from simply reading text, focusing on a visual image or concentrating.

We wanted to observe and measure only the brain's activity from those mental tasks required for Internet searching, such as scanning for targeted key words, rapidly choosing from among several alternatives going back to a previous page if a particular search choice was not helpful, and so forth. We alternated this control task—simply reading a simulated page of text—with the Internet-searching task. We also controlled for nonspecific brain stimulations caused by the photographs and drawings that are typically displayed on an Internet page.

Finally, to determine whether we could train the brains of Internet-naive volunteers, after the first scanning session we asked each volunteer to search the Internet for an hour every day for five days. We gave the computer-savvy volunteers the same assignment and repeated the fMRI scans on both groups after the five days of search-engine training.

Brain Changes

As we had predicted, the brains of computer-savvy and computer-naive subjects did not show any difference when they were reading the simulated book text; both groups had years of experience in this mental task, and their brains were quite familiar with reading books. In contrast, the two groups showed distinctly different patterns of neural activation when searching on Google. During the baseline scanning session, the computer-savvy subjects used a specific network in the left front part of the brain, known as the dorsolateral prefrontal cortex. The Internet-naive subjects showed minimal, if any, activation in this region.

One of our concerns in designing the study was that five days would not be enough time to observe any changes. But after just five days of practice, the exact same neural circuitry in the front part of the brain became active in the Internet-naive subjects. Five hours on the Internet, and these participants had already rewired their brains. The computer-savvy volunteers activated the same frontal brain region at baseline and had a similar level of activation during their second session, suggesting that for a typical computer-savvy individual, the neural circuit training occurs relatively early and then remains stable.

The dorsolateral prefrontal cortex is involved in our ability to make decisions and integrate complex information. It also is thought to control our mental process of integrating sensations and thoughts, as well as working memory, which is our ability to keep information in mind for a very short time—just long enough to manage an Internet-searching task or to dial a phone number after getting it from directory assistance. In today's digital age, we keep our smart phones at our hip and their earpieces attached to our ears. A laptop is always within reach, and there's no need to fret if we can't find a landline—there's always Wi-Fi (short for wireless fidelity, which supplies a wireless connection to the Internet) to keep us connected.

Our high-tech revolution has plunged us into a state of "continuous partial attention," which software executive Linda Stone, who coined the term in 1998, describes as continually staying busy—keeping tabs on everything while never truly focusing on anything. Continuous partial attention differs from multitasking, wherein we have a purpose for each task and we are trying to improve efficiency and productivity. Instead, when our minds partially attend, and do so continuously, we scan for an opportunity for any type of contact at every given moment.

We virtually chat as our text messages flow, and we keep tabs on active buddy lists (friends and other screen names in an instant message program); everything, everywhere, is connected through our peripheral attention.

Although having all our pals online from moment to moment seems intimate, we risk losing personal touch with our real-life relationships and may experience an artificial sense of intimacy as compared with when we shut down our devices and devote our attention to one individual at a time.

Techno-Brain Burnout

When paying continuous partial attention, people may place their brain in a heightened state of stress. They no longer have time to reflect, contemplate or make thoughtful decisions. Instead they exist in a sense of constant crisis—on alert for a new contact or bit of exciting news or information at any moment. Once people get used to this state, they tend to thrive on the perpetual connectivity. It feeds their ego and sense of self-worth, and it becomes irresistible.

Neuroimaging studies suggest that this sense of self-worth may protect the size of the hippocampus—the horseshoe-shaped brain region in the medial (inward-facing) temporal lobe, which allows us to learn and remember new information. Psychiatry professor Sonia J. Lupien and her associates at McGill University studied hippocampal size in healthy younger and older adult volunteers. Measures of self-esteem correlated significantly with hippocampal size, regardless of age. They also found that the more people felt in control of their lives, the larger the hippocampus.

But at some point, the sense of control and self-worth we feel when we maintain continuous partial attention tends to break down—our brains were not built to sustain such monitoring for extended periods. Eventually the hours of unrelenting digital connectivity can create a unique type of brain strain. Many people who have been working on the Internet for several hours without a break report making frequent errors in their work. On signing off, they notice feeling spaced out, fatigued, irritable and distracted, as if they are in a "digital fog." This new form of mental stress, what Small terms "techno-brain burnout," is threatening to become an epidemic. Under this kind of stress, our brains instinctively signal the adrenal gland to secrete cortisol and adrenaline. In the short run, these stress hormones boost energy levels and augment memory, but over time they actually impair cognition, lead to depression, and alter the neural circuitry in the hippo-campus, amygdala and prefrontal cortex—the brain regions that control mood and thought. Chronic and prolonged techno-brain burnout can even reshape the underlying brain structure.

Research psychologist Sara C. Mednick, then at Harvard University, and her colleagues were able to induce a mild form of techno-brain burnout in volunteers experimentally; they then were able to reduce its impact through power naps and by varying mental assignments. Their study subjects performed a visual task: reporting the direction of three lines in the lower left corner of a computer screen. The volunteers' scores worsened over time, but their performance improved if the scientists alternated the visual task between the lower left and lower right corners of the computer screen. This result suggests that brain burnout may be relieved by varying the location of the mental task.

The investigators also found that the performance of study subjects improved if they took a 20- to 30-minute nap. The neural networks involved in the task were apparently refreshed during rest; however, optimum refreshment and reinvigoration for the task occurred when naps lasted up to 60 minutes—the amount of time it takes for rapid-eye-movement (REM) sleep to kick in.

The New, Improved Brain?

Whether we're digital natives or immigrants, altering our neural networks and synaptic connections through activities such as e-mail, video games, Googling or other technological experiences does sharpen some cognitive abilities. We can learn to react more quickly to visual stimuli and improve many forms of attention, particularly the ability to notice images in our peripheral vision. We develop a better ability to sift through large amounts of information rapidly and decide what's important and what isn't—our mental filters basically learn how to shift into overdrive. In this way, we are able to cope with the massive amounts of data appearing and disappearing on our mental screens from moment to moment. Initially the daily blitz that bombards us can create a form of attention deficit, but our brains are able to adapt in a way that promotes rapid processing.

According to cognitive psychologist Pam Briggs of Northumbria University in England, Web surfers looking for facts on health spend two seconds or less on any particular site before moving on to the next one. She found that when study subjects did stop and focus on a particular site, that site contained data relevant to the search, whereas those they skipped over contained almost nothing relevant to the search. This study indicates that our brains learn to swiftly focus attention, analyze information and almost instantaneously decide on a go or no-go action. Rather than simply catching "digital ADD," many of us are developing neural circuitry that is customized for rapid and incisive spurts of directed concentration.

Digital evolution may well be increasing our intelligence in the way we currently measure and define IQ. Average IQ scores have been steadily rising with the advancing digital culture, and the ability to multi-task without errors is improving. Neuroscientist Paul Kearney of Unitec in New Zealand reported that some computer games can actually improve cognitive ability and multitasking skills. He found that volunteers who played the games eight hours a week improved multitasking skills by two and a half times. Other research at the University of Rochester has shown that playing video games can improve peripheral vision as well. As the modern brain continues to evolve, some attention skills improve, mental response times sharpen and the performance of many brain tasks becomes more efficient.

While the brains of today's digital natives are wiring up for rapid-fire cyber searches, however, the neural circuits that control the more traditional learning methods are neglected and gradually diminished. The pathways for human interaction and communication weaken as customary one-on-one people skills atrophy. Our UCLA research team and other scientists have shown that we can intentionally alter brain wiring and reinvigorate some of these dwindling neural pathways, even while the newly evolved technology circuits bring our brains to extraordinary levels of potential.

All of us, digital natives and immigrants, will master new technologies and take advantage of their efficiencies, but we also need to maintain our people skills and our humanity. Whether in relation to a focused Google search or an empathic listening exercise, our synaptic responses can be measured, shaped and optimized to our advantage, and we can survive the technological adaptation of the modern mind.

Source: *Scientific American Mind* 19 (2008): 42-49.

WHAT IT SAYS

1. What do Small and Vorgan mean when they say that our brains are "evolving right now" as a result of daily exposure to digital technology?

2. What distinction do Small and Vorgan make between "digital natives" and "digital immigrants"? In what specific ways are digital natives' lives different from those of digital immigrants?

3. How does the experiment Small and Vorgan describe help the authors discover the impact of extended time on the computer on the way a person's brain is wired and how quickly it can be re-wired?

4. What is "continuous partial attention" and what are its potential negative results? What do studies suggest may reduce these negative results?

5. What potential positive effects can result from extensive use of digital technology, according to Small and Vorgan? What specific examples do they give to support this claim?

HOW IT SAYS IT

1. Who do Small and Vorgan's intended readers seem to be? What clues in the text lead you to believe this?

2. Discuss the ways in which Small and Vorgan use narrative and description to advance their claims.

3. Compare the structure of this article to the standard essay structure for the sciences, the IMRAD format (see p. 87). In what ways does this article share features with the IMRAD format? In what ways does it differ? Why do you suppose the authors chose this more informal approach?

WRITE ABOUT IT

1. Write a detailed proposal for a business, organization or public policy that would help people integrate technology into their lives without losing valuable face-to-face contact with others.

2. Write an essay that argues *either* that "digital natives" *or* that "digital immigrants" have better, happier, and more fulfilling lives. Give specific examples from your own life and the lives of those around you.

d. Mark Blythe and Paul Cairns, "Critical Methods and User Generated Content: The iPhone on YouTube"

Mark Blythe is a senior research fellow in the department of computer science at the University of York, UK. He is an ethnographer with a background in literary and cultural studies, and is co-editor, with Andrew Monk and Peter Wright, of *Funology: From Usability to Enjoyment* (2003), which considers ways to make human-computer interactions not just usable but also fun. His recent work has focused on theory and method for experience-centered design. He is currently working on a project, "Landscapes for Cross-Generational Engagement," funded by the New Dynamics of Ageing Programme, a multidisciplinary research initiative aimed at improving quality of life for older people.

Paul Cairns is a senior lecturer in human-computer interaction at the University of York. Cairns's research centers on the experience of playing video games, modeling user interactions and mathematical knowledge management. Cairns's book *Research Methods for Human Computer Interaction* (2008), which he wrote with Anna Cox, takes a scientific approach to the design of user interfaces. He also has published numerous articles in professional journals. Cairns received his MA and DPhil degrees from Oxford University.

Blythe and Cairns's study analyzes videos posted to YouTube when the iPhone 3G was released. Their study applies both qualitative content analysis and critical theory to their data, resulting in an unusual melding of physical science, social science, and humanities approaches. (Some of the punctuation has been modified.)

As You Read: Think about your own response to the release of the iPhone 6 or some other technology product. What kind of video might you have made (or did you make) to record your response?

Critical Methods and User Generated Content: The iPhone on YouTube

Abstract

Sites like YouTube offer vast sources of data for studies of Human Computer Interaction (HCI). However, they also present a number of methodological challenges. This paper offers an example study of the initial reception of the iPhone 3G through YouTube. It begins with a quantitative account of the overall shape of the most frequently viewed returns for an "iPhone 3G" search. A content analysis of the first hundred videos then explores the returns categorized by genre. Comments on the most popular video "Will It Blend?" are analyzed using grounded theory. It is argued that social science methods are not sufficient for a rich understanding of such material. The paper concludes with an analysis of "Will It Blend?" that draws on cultural and critical theory. It is argued that a multi-methodological approach is necessary to exploit such data and also to address the challenges of next generation HCI.

ACM Classification Keywords

H5.m. Information interfaces and presentation (e.g., HCI): Miscellaneous.

Author Keywords

Critical Theory, User Experience, User-generated Content, Research Methods, Green HCI, iPhone, YouTube

Introduction: Data Goldmines

User-generated content on sites such as YouTube, Facebook and Myspace offer researchers in many fields unprecedented access to new forms of primary data. YouTube is already being used to critique and review new releases of technology. The launch of new or updated products is followed almost immediately by posts of commentaries and reviews. Often these amateur film makers are engaged in informal usability testing. But there are also less direct responses to new technologies in the form of reflective vlogs or satires. Often these videos receive thousands of comments, providing another source of easily collected data.

Such material could provide a rich resource to inform research and design. However, both the quantity and the quality of this material present challenges for using it in a meaningful way. Because the sites are dynamic and update constantly it is certainly impossible to be exhaustive. To use such material as a research resource requires new and perhaps unfamiliar methods.

The speed of recent technological change has led to almost equally dramatic transformations in the study of HCI. There have been turns to fun and enjoyment [e.g., 5], experience design [e.g., 22], cultural or reflective design [e.g., 1, 3, 25], semiotic design [e.g., 12], and aesthetics [e.g., 6]. Each of these areas has brought HCI into contact with cultural and critical studies. Cultural and critical studies have engaged with the problems now confronting HCI for a very long time. Increasingly, HCI is finding value in these traditions [e.g., 3, 4, 6, 12, 24, 25]. This paper draws on methods from both social science and critical theory to consider YouTube posts following the launch of the iPhone 3G on July 11, 2008.

iPhone Street Preacher

At the Apple store in New York City a queue of people waiting to buy a new iPhone are berated by a street preacher. "You people should use your brain more wisely!" he yells. "And spend money on something important!" [16]. The film is made from within the queue and most of the people seem amused rather than threatened. Someone suggests he can afford it. "You're damn right I can afford it!" the bleach-blond preacher yells. A dog starts barking at him; he tells it to shut up and moves to a different spot to pray and read aloud from the Book of Revelation.

This video is one of the thousands posted to YouTube and returned under a search for "iPhone 3G" in the second week of July 2008. Among just ten comments posted below the clip is one saying that he is proud to be the man who owns the dog. Another writes "Don't spend your money on the new iPhone! Spend it on glowing hair bleach!" Another suggests it would be funnier to "prank people" when the "prankster is believable." It had been viewed only 595 times and was far from representative of the kind of returns following the launch of the iPhone 3G, and for this reason it poses a number of interesting questions about the ways in which YouTube can be used as a resource for research.

As HCI becomes more interested in rich, holistic accounts of user experience, the self-reports available on sites like YouTube offer quick and easy data collection. Yet the very richness of the material opens up a number of potential methodological and theoretical problems. This paper argues that although sites which archive user-generated content provide an invaluable resource to researchers, a multi-methodological approach is necessary to exploit them.

Social Scientific Method in HCI

Since its inception as a discipline, studies in HCI have built on methodological techniques developed in traditions of social science. Quantitative and qualitative techniques have been adopted from psychology, sociology and anthropology in order to study people interacting with technology [e.g., 7, 26]. The designers of early computer interfaces were primarily concerned with measurable outcomes: how long did it take people to complete a task using this or that interface? Such questions could be investigated through the well-established experimental and observational methods of cognitive psychologists. Various questionnaire and experimental protocols, eye tracking and physiological measures have been developed to design and evaluate interaction with increasingly sophisticated interfaces [e.g., 23].

For single users working with a single interface, such methods can be very useful but they cannot provide adequate guidance for design in complex social environments such as the workplace or the home [26]. Here methods from anthropology and sociology were incorporated, in particular detailed observation and in-depth semi-structured interviews. Although these methods did not provide results as easy to interpret as lab-based experimentation, they were nevertheless recognized as essential to the design process: better "quick and dirty" ethnography than no ethnography at all [e.g., 7].

Quantitative and qualitative social science, then, has a long history in HCI. This paper will argue that, alone and in their current form, they are not adequate to making sense of the material available on sites like YouTube or indeed the next generation of human-computer interaction.

Next Generation HCI

The current generation of Interaction Designers draw on a range of sources for inspiration. Lab-based experimentation is no doubt still important but it was clearly not the determining factor in Apple's decision to implement the keyboard on the iPhone. In terms of speed and accuracy, other kinds of keyboards are superior. Clearly there are other concerns at play in the design decisions than efficiency and ease of use. What the criteria are is a matter for speculation. Where Apple do talk about their design philosophy they are not necessarily entirely candid or, indeed, necessarily correct in their interpretation of why something works. In discussions of the iPod, for example, Steve Jobs and other Apple spokespeople frequently discussed its simplicity. Like John Maeda they counseled that the key to success was doing one thing and doing it well [19]. If Apple believed this at the time they clearly changed their minds when they developed the iPod Touch and the iPhone, both of which offer a huge range of functionality above and beyond merely playing music or making calls. Indeed the App Store opens the phone up to third-party developers and an almost infinite range of functionality and widely varying degrees of quality.

Such moves from usability to user experience necessitate an engagement with aesthetics, enjoyment and fun. These are far less tangible and measurable than the dimensions of usability. Neither are they "grossly observable" through ethnographic investigation. The following study of the iPhone will first draw on techniques familiar to the HCI community: quantitative and qualitative data analysis derived from traditions of social science. It will then argue that both of these traditions miss important aspects of cultural artifacts such as YouTube videos and indeed iPhones. The final sections of the paper will be the least familiar to an HCI audience as they will draw on traditions of critical theory.

Profiling YouTube Content

The topic of the iPhone was chosen with some care. Although there are potentially many more interesting lines of inquiry to pursue using YouTube as a data source, the iPhone is particularly appropriate because Apple have explicitly targeted YouTube users in the architecture of the iPhone itself. The iPhone comes with a YouTube application on its first screen; this is more than a simple link to the YouTube site and (unlike other apps) cannot be deleted from the home page. It is not unreasonable then to conclude that Apple's target demographic might also be YouTube users. The videos posted to the site can be taken, broadly, as an indicator of the kinds of responses that "YouTubers" made in the initial excitement of product launch. The sample of videos does not of course represent the iPhone user population. No claims are made here regarding users; rather the sample represents videos posted to YouTube and returned under a search for "iPhone 3G."

A Quantitative Description of the Data

The basic statistics offered by YouTube are the number of hits returned for the search and for each search result the number of views. There are then options to re-order the search results by: relevance, the date the video was added, the number of views and viewer ratings. There are also options to restrict the search results from videos added anytime to those added within the last month, week or day. Our analysis used different combinations of these. Searches were also made at different times in order to confirm previous findings and to observe changes due to the dynamic content of YouTube.

For a search done on August 29, 2008, there were approximately 14,700 search results. For videos uploaded at anytime, the results were sorted by the number of viewings. The first three had more than a million views but only 417 out of the 14,700 had more than 2,500 hits. It was not possible to retrieve search results beyond that point. When this search was repeated two weeks later, there were now 18,000 or so results and four videos with more than a million views. However, only 408 had more than 2,500 hits. Again, it was not possible to view more than the first 426 hits.

Turning to the distribution of viewings, it is common that many social science phenomena follow a Zipf law where the size of objects is in a power law relation to its rank. This is most easily seen by a linear relation in a log-log plot of number views against rank. Figure 1.3 shows such a plot for the ranked search results for "iPhone 3G" made on the August 29 for videos uploaded anytime.

As with the overall distribution of viewings in all of YouTube [9], the overall viewings for iPhone 3G search results initially follow a linear trend but with a sharp drop-off for very low rankings. This suggests that low-ranked videos are harder to find. Indeed, this could be a direct consequence of not being able to access all search results from a single search term.

These straightforward searches and analyses seem to suggest that the numbers returned are rather unreliable because it is not possible to discern exactly what is going on. The fact that search results cannot be viewed beyond a cut-off point first means that the total number of search results is unverifiable and, more importantly for research purposes, there may be relevant videos that simply cannot be found through searching. Of course the very magnitude of YouTube makes archiving a far from trivial problem not just for current research but also future possible research [8].

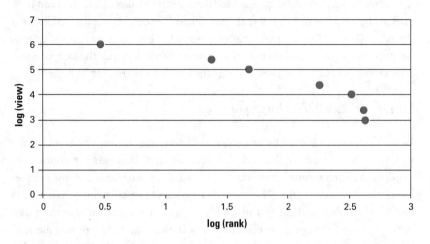

FIGURE 1.3. Log-log plot of views against rank for first 100 videos uploaded anytime

Thus, in order to provide a lasting research contribution when drawing on YouTube, it seems our research methods need to explicitly include an archival element. It may be that the only way to provide data to other researchers is to record the YouTube interactions done at the time through some suitable software such as Morae.

Despite these methodological issues, these searches do convey the kinds of returns that YouTube users would have seen searching the site at this time and it is on this basis that we proceed to a content analysis.

Qualitative Content Analysis

A qualitative content analysis was performed on the first one hundred videos returned for the search "iPhone 3G" on July 14, 2008. Content analysis is a well-known methodological procedure for studying qualitative data and is very frequently used in studies of mass media [21]. It is used for studying textual data, where text is understood to mean any media (e.g., film, newspaper articles, advertisements). Items are coded and counted to indicate patterns and trends in data sets, e.g., sexist images in advertising (Ibid).

A search by relevance for "iPhone 3G" was made on the first Monday after the launch date of Friday, July 11, 2008. At this time the site reported around 2,280 results; the next day there were around 5,880; two months after the launch date there were around 18,100. Four days after this it was down to 12,600. Clearly the time of making a search will determine the kinds of results returned. In the first week of the launch the increase in results for this search was rapid but growth steadied over the following months—as might be predicted as the initial excitement subsides following a product launch. A relevance search was made to gain an impression of the kinds of video being submitted.

The first one hundred videos were categorized and ranked by frequency (see Figure 1.4) as review, reportage, "unboxing," demonstration, satire, advertisement and small number vlog commentaries (e.g., complaints about queues).

By far the most frequent categories of video were reviews and news-style reportage of the launch. Perhaps more surprising was the large number of videos (more than a fifth) showing the moment of "unboxing" when the iPhone was taken out of its packaging for the first time. Less frequent categories were satire, advertisement and vlog commentaries, although view rate searches revealed that the satirical videos were amongst the most popular. The following sections describe in further detail the content of these videos.

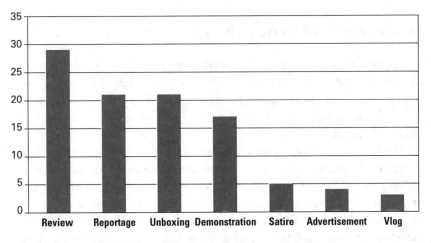

FIGURE 1.4. Categories of "iPhone 3G" video on YouTube

REVIEWS: "FOLK USER EXPERIENCE TESTING"

As might be expected the most frequently occurring returns were reviews. Judging from the comments below these posts, it is clear that one of the main motivations of searching YouTube with the term "iPhone 3G" is to inform decisions about whether to buy one or not. Some of these reviews were "professional" mass media reviews which had been taped from TV news shows and featured expert evaluations. These evaluations were usually filmed in TV studios, although one subjected the iPhone to stress tests on location, showing how it fared when it was dropped from various heights and had drinks spilled on it. The majority of reviews, however, were made by users. Two thirds of these were presented by white males, most in the 20-40 age range although two were children. Five of the videos in this category were almost entirely uncritical celebrations of various features that the users considered to be "cool." The Apps Store was frequently mentioned in this regard. More often the reviews were sober comparisons of the 3G iPhone with its 2G predecessor.

A number of criticisms of the device were made consistently in these reviews. Common complaints were: the low pixel rate and the absence of a flash on the camera; the comparatively poor quality of the material on the back—plastic as opposed to metal in the 2G device; the absence of a copy-paste facility; and the lack of flash support. Interestingly the most frequent complaint two months later was the very poor battery performance, though that did not feature in these early responses, presumably because this would not be noticed until after a longer period of use. It is interesting to note the tone of these reviewers here, which is generally one of world weary expertise; even child reviewers take on this arch manner: "so this is the 3G. It's a little faster."

DEMONSTRATIONS: FUNCTIONALITY AND HACKS

The demonstrations of the iPhone frequently featured the users themselves sitting at a desk and moving the device towards a stationary camera as various functions are explained and illustrated. Frequently these demonstrations merge into review, but here the focus is more on showing what the product can do rather than evaluating it.

Also included in this category are the official launch presentations from Apple events where executives show off various features, to rapturous applause from the crowd. The tone of user-generated demos is remarkably different, and although some are skeptical and ironic featuring introductory songs like "iPhone madness," the tone is generally serious. Clearly the makers of these films intend to inform other potential customers of what they might or might not be letting themselves in for.

Within this category are also videos which Apple might be less happy about: demonstrations of ways to unlock the iPhone and make it available for networks other than the ones Apple have made deals with. Here then are examples of direct resistance to the corporation who makes the device. These users appropriate the technology to their own ends in defiance of the terms by which the device is made available.

Not only are there demonstrations of ways to unlock the software; there are also videos showing the device itself being physically taken apart. With immense care the iPhone is taken to pieces and its separate components are identified and described even to the level of how much each piece would have cost to buy from third parties. There is clearly an ideological if not a directly political agenda in these posts; they are presented as disruptive and mischievous if not outright techno-libertarian.

"UNBOXING"

The word "unboxing" is in the title of many of the videos showing the moment when an iPhone is first removed from its packaging. An astonishing number of videos returned in the first hundred results of this search (twenty one percent) are users simply taking their phones out of the box for the first time. This number has grown considerably, and a search for "iPhone 3G unboxing" conducted two months after the launch date yielded an initially baffling 1,050 results.

This is particularly interesting given the recent focus in HCI on holistic accounts of the user experience. McCarthy and Wright, for example, note that the experience of a product begins long before it is first used [22]. Watching advertisements, discussions with friends, going to the shop, taking it out of its box—these are all a part of the experience of technology. Clearly, Apple understands this very well, and the packaging on the iPod as well as the iPhone has long been praised for its distinctive look and feel. Clearly the amount of videos showing the moment when the box is opened indicates degrees of pride and pleasure in ownership. But there is more going on here.

The moment is dramatic and perhaps lends itself to film better than others. Typically the camera is pointed at a box which is placed on a desk; the user's hands then appear in shot as the product makes its first appearance, literally entering the stage. One video even featured stirring music, added later to enhance the drama of the iPhone's arrival.

Often the video makers here simply narrate what they are doing. Very quickly, however, the commentary becomes review; two remark on the "plasticky feel" as soon as they touch it.

In the moment of unboxing is the pleasure of anticipation. Although they already possess the iPhone they have not yet used it and it is not truly theirs. It remains, while it sits in the box, solely an object of desire. Once it is in the user's hands the experience is no longer one of anticipation but evaluation and, inevitably, disappointment. Boredom and the dismissive tone of the world-weary reviewer can be detected as soon as the moment of unboxing is over.

ADVERTISEMENTS: OFFICIAL AND UNOFFICIAL

Some of the posts in this category were not Apple campaigns: a used car salesman was giving away an iPhone as part of a deal. Most were from the official Apple campaign, however. This featured security guards carrying a locked metal box through stainless-steel corridors. Each inserts a separate key into this box, whereupon it clicks and whirrs as it opens mechanically to, literally, raise the device on a pedestal. Interestingly this echoes the unboxing videos that the users themselves posted. This is a grand high-tech and secure unboxing. At no point is the device touched by human hand, thus prolonging the pleasure of anticipation.

REPORTAGE: LAUNCH DAY QUEUES

Most of the reportage videos had been recorded from TV broadcasts, though some were home-made videos that adopted the format and style of news reports. Typically these reports would begin in a studio setting, where a presenter noted that today was the iPhone launch day, before cutting to location footage and interviews with people queuing up outside stores, buying the device inside and emerging with the box.

A number of these reports focused in particular on the phenomenon of the queue. Interviewers were keen to know how long people had been waiting. The spectacle of the launch and the desire for this device evidenced by willingness to wait were of particular interest here. These videos reported from around the globe and displayed the queues in the UK as well as America and Canada. Most of the Canadian reportage was concerned with the initial pricing of the iPhone, which was far more expensive there than anywhere else in the world. Significantly the YouTube site became a focus for protest, and a number of subscriber lists were formed by Canadians demanding a fairer deal, demands which were eventually met.

SATIRE: PRICE AND iPHONE-MANIA

This category is perhaps the most interesting and certainly the most popular in the "iPhone 3G" search returns. The speed with which these parodies appeared is remarkable, though some referred to the 2G rather than 3G model. One satirical post featured a mock review which focused on the high service costs: "Eviction notices download faster!" Another stages a conversation between a five-year-old phone and an iPhone. The older phone begins by complaining that the comparison is not fair: the iPhone is a different generation of technology, it's sure to have a better camera … uh, no, the iPhone admits, and so on. Two videos mocked people standing in the queue; e.g., a reporter asks a middle-aged man in the queue if he has "ever seen a woman naked?" Another very early post in this category is "Will It Blend?" [28], where a man in a white lab coat wonders if the device will blend and proceeds to test his hypothesis by inserting it into a blender and obliterating it to a fine black dust. Beyond categorizing such videos as comic, this method of analysis has little to add and these posts will be returned to in the final sections of the paper.

Will It Blend?

The remaining sections of this paper will focus on the most popular iPhone 3G return—"Will It Blend?," the most viewed posting returned in the search at the time of writing. "Will It Blend?" is a long-running series of short films in which a middle-aged white male in a lab coat asks, "will it blend?" of various consumer products before putting them into a blender to find out. The series has been phenomenally successful, and according to Wikipedia has now surpassed one hundred million hits.

Each film follows a format which is seldom deviated from. The presenter, Tom Dickson, wearing a white coat and protective goggles, addresses the viewer directly, saying "Will it blend? That is the question" and music reminiscent of a 1960s game show begins as credits roll over clips of previous blendings. After a brief introduction on the item to be blended, Tom tells the viewer which setting he is going to use and the blending begins. He looks up at the camera during this often spectacularly noisy and violent spectacle and flashes a reassuring smile. When he opens the lid, Tom wafts the smoke and warns, "Don't breathe this." He tips the dust onto the desk and a caption appears—"Yes! It Blends!"—the music reaches its climax and the show ends.

Wikipedia describes the series as a "viral ad campaign" and clearly, advertising is one of the motivations for the makers of the films. The "Will It Blend?" website makes all of the videos available but also links to online stores where it is possible to buy the BlendTec blenders. For viral ads to work they must be forwarded on between friends. If this is to happen there must be some other content that will be of interest: few would forward a "Will It Blend?" video because they thought their friends might be interested in purchasing a new blender. Indeed, part of the subtlety of this form of advertising is that it is not often clear that the video is an advertisement at all. The "Will It Blend?" series primarily takes the format of satire; it would be possible to watch the video and have no idea that the makers were trying to sell anything; no caption urges viewers to buy a BlendTec blender; indeed it is only by following several links away from YouTube that viewers may discover that this is possible.

At the time of writing there were 6,888 comments on this video. The following section provides an overview of the kinds of comments made using grounded theory.

GROUNDED THEORY ANALYSIS OF "WILL IT BLEND?" COMMENTS

Qualitative content analysis was an appropriate method for analysing the content of the "iPhone 3G" search returns because genres of media such as review, demonstration, reportage, advertising and satire are well understood and already heavily theorised. The comments made about each video are not so well suited to this kind of analysis. The ability to comment on this kind of video is a relatively new phenomenon and requires a different approach. Grounded theory analysis begins with data, rather than pre-existing categories. Open codes are developed to summarise the data; these are then grouped together and linked in axial coding; the final stage of selective coding involves the selection of typical quotes to illustrate the "theory." Theory here may refer merely to a broad description or set of categories rather than a fully worked predictive schema [10]. Around twenty open codes were grouped into the broad categories of: confusion, dismay and celebration. After the first twenty pages of comments (roughly twelve comments to a page), the coding scheme "saturated"; i.e., new data did not necessitate the creation of new codes (Ibid). Nor did they vary very much over time.

CONFUSION

A number of the comments indicated that the viewers did not understand what was going on: "*I don't get it*". Others raised specific questions about why this was being done and speculated about whether it was sponsored or not. The rest of the comments were split between dismay and celebration.

DISMAY

Although some of the expressions of dismay were comic ("NOOOOOO!") many seemed to indicate sincere outrage, focussing on how much money had been wasted. Occasionally criticism was directed against Blendtec or the persona of Tom Dickson. Several within this category were simple expressions of abuse, a surprising amount of which was homophobic. Many of those dismayed by the destruction commented specifically on wanting an iPhone themselves: "*WTF!!!!???? why! u couldve given it too meeeeeeeee!!!*" Occasionally these were expressed violently "*you know what tom i think you should put your dick in a Blender because i know people who save for years to get something like an i phone. How does that make you feel mike? uh? You should feel ashamed.*" The video then evoked strong responses which polarised between dismay and joy.

CELEBRATION

Unsurprisingly for a comic video, many of the comments were little more than "*Awesome!*" "*HA HA*" or "*LOL*" style indications of laughter. Within these positive responses are a number of jokes ("iphone smoothie, my favorite!") and suggestions for future blendings—a steel bar, a nutcracker at Christmas and "this text comment." Others are appreciative of the power of the blender. A surprising number comment that the girl in the iPhone queue featured briefly is "hot." Some of these comments suggest an anti-iPhone agenda: "you can blend my iPhone if you want its a piece of shit" and "iphone sucks." Occasionally more information is offered: the dust was sold on eBay; Tom lives in the neighbourhood and made smoothies for the kids once. Finally a small number of comments focussed on the aesthetics of the video, saying that slow motion was a good idea or "I love how it just explodes."

Although these comments indicate a wide range of responses from bewilderment to rage to joy, they say little about why the video is powerful and provocative.

For this reason an entirely different methodology and indeed disciplinary tradition is necessary to interpret the video itself.

Limitations of Social Science Based Approaches

The preceding sections have indicated something of the general shape of these data. It is clear that the most common classes of videos are demonstrations and reviews. Yet the most viewed videos on the other hand are comic or satirical takes on the iPhone. The qualitative analysis suggests an ambivalent relationship between iPhone users and their device. The sheer number of videos recording for posterity the moment when the iPhone is removed from its packaging indicates a strong degree of pride and excitement at the moment of purchase. However, the merging of this kind of video with demonstration and review also indicates the development of a burgeoning critical community. Within the reviews are a range of insights which Apple would be foolish to ignore.

But there is a further category of rather more puzzling videos which, though categorizable, are not necessarily easy to explain. These videos indicate the surplus of meaning which is present in these rich data sets and also indicates the limits of this type of inquiry. What are we to make of the video of the preacher telling the New York launch queue that they are going to burn in hell? What is going on when a man puts a brand new iPhone into a blender?

These questions can be asked sociologically but they can also be asked hermeneutically. Sociological approaches are primarily concerned with classification; hermeneutic approaches are concerned with meaning and interpretation. So far "Will It Blend?" has been considered within the broad traditions of sociology. The analysis has been concerned with who is making the video for whom. There has also been a focus on how popular the videos are and a codification of the kinds of comments given. An analysis of the comments indicated that some found the video funny and engaging while others were angered by the waste. And yet these are not the only readings of that video.

ALTERNATIVE INTERPRETIVE STRATEGIES

Although physical scientists might dispute the methods and findings of social scientists, they have broadly similar ambitions: to objectively describe the worlds they are studying. Social science takes on as much of the scientific method as messy social relationships will allow (which is often, of course, not very much). However social science methodologies are not the only ways of taking a structured approach to the study of a cultural artefact. Literary and critical theory offers a range of analytical and interpretive approaches.

New readings of literature and film are constantly being produced. There could never be a correct or final reading of a poem or a film or a YouTube video. In this sense, the meaning of a cultural artefact can never be pinned down. This is not to adopt an anti-scientific epistemology, but rather to say that cultural artefacts allow for other forms of knowing. The kinds of interpretation which critical theory generates do not result in scientific knowledge but rather "imagined hermeneutic understanding" [29] or provocative interpretation. Critical interpretations are often surprising and entirely counter intuitive.

Slavoj Žižek is one of the most celebrated cultural commentators alive today. His critical insights do not attempt to define how most people would view cultural artefacts but rather to convey provocative interpretations that might never have occurred to anyone else. For instance, he interprets the films of Steven Spielberg as being primarily concerned with fatherhood. ET, for example, is befriended by a child whose parents are divorced; ET does not leave until the mother has begun a relationship with one of the good scientists at the end of the film. Similarly, Žižek claims that the dinosaurs are not the real threat in *Jurassic Park*; it is rather the problem of the bad father. Only when Sam Neill has protected the children from danger and kept them safe overnight in a tree do we see one of the benign herbivorous dinosaurs. And for Žižek, the same theme is present in *Schindler's List*. Schindler begins as the bad father, rejecting his responsibilities to the Jews; he ends by becoming the good father and protecting them. For Žižek the film completely infantilizes the Jews and is for this reason reprehensible [29].

Whether Spielberg intends this or not is precisely not the point. The novelist Milan Kundera was once asked if a particular interpretation of his novel was correct or not; he replied that the meaning may be there but he did not put it there [18]. Authorial intent is generally dismissed as a fallacy in cultural studies; often it can never be known (what did Shakespeare mean by *Hamlet*?) and even if it could be known, the meaning goes beyond the intentions of its author. Žižek then is not identifying what Spielberg was "really saying" with these films. Neither is he making claims about how most people interpret them. Rather he provides a counter-intuitive and deliberately provocative "reading" of the films.

As the study of HCI becomes ever more entwined with the study of human culture, these kinds of radical interpretive moves may offer insight into human computer interaction. It may be that this kind of analysis, though not replicable or falsifiable, may nevertheless contain insights into user experience.

Critical Theory

Žižek's critical theory is based in Lacanian psychoanalysis. This is just one thread of critical theory which is a rich and diverse field. Critical theory incorporates a number of theoretical perspectives such as structuralism, post-structuralism, feminism, Marxism, and psychoanalysis [14]. This pluralistic approach to cultural analysis has grown from several sources. In the early 1950s, the Chicago school theorists such as Theodor Adorno developed a mixture of Marxism and phenomenology which sought to analyze and moreover change mass culture. In the early 1960s French theorists such as Roland Barthes and Umberto Eco also turned their attention from "high" to popular culture. Barthes had studied literature and used techniques of close and detailed reading to analyze not poems and novels but other "texts" like films and commercials. In the 1970s, the Birmingham Centre for Contemporary Cultural Studies (BCCCS) was founded by Stuart Hall. There had been a long history of studying sub-cultures in anthropology but this work was primarily a colonial encounter where (typically) western field workers studied non-western cultures, usually with a view to governing them more effectively. In the BCCCS, analytical tools that the West had developed to understand distant countries were turned back onto itself [14].

There is a small but growing literature in HCI which has sought to adopt the practices of critical theory to interaction criticism [e.g., 3, 4, 6, 12, 22, 24, 25]. What, if anything, could critical theory tell us about the iPhone and its representation on YouTube? The following sections apply Žižek's style of analysis to "Will It Blend?" and other videos where the launch of the iPhone 3G provoked acts of destruction.

"LET'S DO SOME THEORY"

The "Will It Blend?" films parody a number of genres from other media. The Tom Dickson persona is a parody of the objective lab-based scientist. With unwavering simplicity he asks an apparently objective empirical question: will it blend? Here then is scientific method: a hypothesis is posed and tested, results are published. Comic effects result from incongruous juxtapositions: *Halo 3*, for instance, in a blender. The scientific method is invoked through the lab setting and the white coat and then undercut by the ridiculous questions and pointless experiments. But science and scientists are not the only subjects being parodied. The music evokes game shows and sitcoms from the 1950s and 60s. Tom Dickson's smiling, avuncular manner also connotes television personalities of previous decades, Tom Boswell in *Happy Days* for example: the benign patriarch. Again this is undercut in the stories of his grandchildren. They beat him at *Halo 3* so he blends their game. Their copy of *Guitar Hero 3* does not feature the Beach Boys so he blends it. But these elements of parody refer to the form rather than the content of the films. The event which distinguishes the highly formulaic shows from each other is the blending of a particular object: often a piece of digital technology. Why?

RESISTANCE AND ECO-CRITICISM

In the introduction to the iPhone 3G episode of "Will It Blend?" the format of the shows is deviated from considerably. As in the other launch-day reportage videos,

Dickson is pictured on location at the AT&T store in front of a queue of people waiting to buy an iPhone. In a piece to camera, he tells the viewer that he is here to *"keep up with the latest technology."* After noting that he is *"not the only one,"* the camera pans to the people in the queue who cheer and clap. A young woman walks past with her new phone, Tom asks if he can see it and she replies *"No! You're going to blend it!"* *"Not me!"* he says and the film cuts to the studio. Here he announces that he has his new iPhone and will not need the old one *"so I'm going to blend it."* A slow motion close-up on the blender shows the iPhone being smashed into smithereens. There is clearly something very satisfying about this spectacle; the close-up and slow motion indicate that we are to enjoy this moment. The next shot shows the blender full of black dust, Dickson takes the top off and realizes that he is smelling the wrong kind of smoke *"this isn't iSmoke, it's 3G smoke!"* At least as far as the narrative of the film is concerned, Dickson has just bought and destroyed a brand new state of the art iPhone.

"Will It Blend?" is not the only video on YouTube to respond to the launch of the iPhone 3G with an act of destruction. *"Is it a Good Idea to Microwave This?"* [17] belongs to a series of films made by *JPizzle1122* that parody "Will It Blend?" He begins microwaving an iPod by saying it is his way of celebrating the release of the iPhone 3G. There is a direct satire on the ultimately commercial nature of "Will It Blend?" in a eulogy of the microwave being used: *"Lacey: the new love of my life, it's everything I ever wanted."* When the iPods are placed into the microwave the person behind the camera says: *"I'm not going to lie. This is like a wet dream for me. To watch Steve Jobs' precious creations melt away in my microwave."* The iPods spark and smoke until they explode and burst open the microwave door. There is an instant replay of this for our viewing pleasure. As they clear up the debris the presenter asks *"Is it a good idea to microwave an iPod?"* and the cameraman answers *"I would say it is."* The presenter explains *"If you can't get it repaired you might as well blow it up in a microwave you bought on Craig's list, am I right?"*

A number of the comic or satirical iPod videos on YouTube take as their subject the problem of what to do with a dead iPod. The *"Dead iPod Song"* [13] by RhettandLink lists the things that might be done with a dead iPod once the "doom seed" has germinated after eighteen months of use. They suggest burying it, using it as a weapon, putting it on a hoagie and calling it an "iPodwich," or putting it into a drawer for your grandchildren to find many years from now as relics of a bygone technological era before music was uploaded directly into our brains.

Like the iPhone street preacher these videos may appear comic, ridiculous and exaggerated but at their heart is a serious concern with what the production and consumption of these devices is doing to us. Similarly the demonstrations of ways to unlock and take apart the iPhone could be read as critical interventions in corporate commodity production cycles.

It would be possible to read these "iDestruction" videos as expressions of resistance to current cycles of commodity production and consumption. Over our lifetime each one of us will throw away enough electronic goods to make a waste sculpture like the WEEE man, which is seven metres tall and weighs 3.3 tonnes (see www.weeeman.org). One of the biggest challenges facing consumer electronics is the high turnover of goods with products moving from shelf to landfill within two years [2]. There is a particularly large annual turnover in computing technologies because, following Moore's Law, they double in power and speed every eighteen months making things like MP3 players into disposable fashion objects. Technological obsolescence, economic obsolescence and perceived obsolescence [11] result in a market where journalists can speculate that even if an MP3 player could be "built like a rock and last ten years" we probably wouldn't want it [15]. After eighteen months to two years the device is going to be obsolete: either it will not work or there will be a much better one available. These videos then are forms of eco-criticism.

For Žižek, a thesis such as this would have to be rejected immediately and countered with its antithesis. The next section then will dismiss the notion that these videos express protest or resistance.

COMMODITY FETISHISM AND THE MYSTIQUE OF THE OBJECT

A first reading of these films suggests an obvious interpretation, one which is partly the film maker's own view of what they are doing: expressing resistance to corporate commodity cycles. But this is a superficial reading. As previously noted, the hidden, or "latent" content of the "Will It Blend?" videos is an injunction to consume: buy blenders. At the level of explicit, or "manifest" content, the videos depict the obliteration of the devices. In the "Dead iPod Song," iJustine opens a drawer and finds it filled with dead iPods. The problem here is: what to do with the body. The answer in all cases is to derive a final moment of pleasure from it, in staging its destruction, whether actual (in the microwave, or the blender) or symbolic (in the imagined iPodless future of the song).

The problem here then is not that the iPhone must die but what to do with it afterwards. There are myriad videos where iPods and iPhones are broken in amusing ways occasionally featuring devices which are presented as still fully working. Like the unboxing videos, these destruction posts celebrate consumption. Buddhist philosophy as well as Lacanian psychoanalysis claim that what we desire is desire itself. Once we have bought an iPhone we can no longer want it. We might want to keep it but this is not the same and this desire too will fade. As the device is utterly destroyed the desire for the next model is properly ignited.

The films are not expressions of protest then but rather a celebration of consumption at its purest. But this antithetical reading must also be rejected in a final synthesis.

THE MEDIUM IS THE WHAT NOW?

"The medium is the message" is Marshall McLuhan's most famous quotation and also perhaps his most enigmatic and annoying. Žižek illustrates its meaning precisely in a discussion of the first Hannibal Lecter film *Manhunter*. Here a detective must watch the home videos of families who have been brutally murdered by a serial killer. He looks for similarities in the layout of the houses, the shape of the gardens, the makeup of the families themselves. Finally he realizes that what they all have in common is home videos. He then narrows the hunt to an employee of the film processing lab that the families all used. It was not the content of the videos then but the fact that they had all made videos that mattered [29]. The medium was the message.

What happens then if we consider not the content of these videos but their medium: posts on YouTube? Whether the films are read as protests against unsustainable commodity production or celebrations of the same is, in a sense, not the point. The films are commentaries on the iPhone, if not entirely ironic then at least removed and distanced.

Žižek argues that the lesson of psychoanalysis at its most basic is this: the purpose of fantasy is not to give us what we want but to tell us what it is that we want. Even the most critical of these videos (the iPod in the microwave) does not seek a world without these devices. Rather it allows the film makers to say—look, we understand this problem, we can comment on it ironically, now let us get on with buying the next generation of devices.

In other words, rather than take some form of direct action in an engagement with, say the environmental movement, posting and watching these videos allows consumers to express their fears and concerns over the rampant cycles of consumption they are engaged in without ever seriously challenging their own complicity in it. They are then "Reflective Consumers," aware of the problems they face and able to articulate an ironic response that positions them somewhere above the dilemma while still allowing them to continue consuming.

Not only the existence but also the popularity of these videos suggests that our relationship with this kind of technology is increasingly ambivalent. The urgency of recent calls for sustainable design and green HCI (e.g., 20) is clear not only in terms of the environment but also user experience. Here then is a critical reading of the iPhone on YouTube; it is by no means final. Other perspectives from critical theory, feminism for example, would offer entirely different and no less provocative or stimulating readings.

Discussion

This paper has argued that user-generated content provides an invaluable resource for researchers interested in human computer interaction. Not just in reviews where users engage in folk usability analyses of their new devices but also in the social and cultural commentaries that surround the launch of new products.

The speed of technological development is increasingly difficult to keep up with. The App Store on the iPhone alone presents almost daily developments. Artists such as Brian Eno are already using it to distribute innovative forms of musical interaction such as *Bloom*. Fortunately for researchers in HCI, users of Web 2.0 sites provide responses to new interactive devices like this, or to take another example, the Wii Fit, as soon as they are released. However, HCI must widen its methodological practice to make full use of these resources.

Web 2.0 sites offer a resource for investigating both sides of human computer interaction: the users and the technologies. There may be a tension in such studies between investigating the topic (here the iPhone) and the medium through which it is discussed (here YouTube). It is therefore vital not only to employ multi-methodological approaches but to understand the limitations of each one. The ready availability of different kinds of data (numbers, videos, text) makes the possible applications and limitations of different methods very clear. Quantitative accounts will show the frequency with which usability problems are reported with this or that device. Qualitative approaches may uncover further insights into how technologies could be improved. However user-generated content is as likely to consist of song and satire as review and demonstration. These kinds of response are far more difficult to analyze and the perspectives available in critical theory may help further understanding of our increasingly complex relationship with technology.

Critical theory has a reputation for jargon and pretension and this reputation is sometimes justified. The physicist Alan Sokal famously hoaxed a cultural studies journal into publishing a "postmodern" physics paper which was "liberally salted with nonsense" [27]. Misgivings about critical theory are understandable because all too often critical theory is not understandable at all. Indeed making critical theory accessible to HCI may make some contribution to clarifying critical theory itself.

The readings offered here drew on traditions of psychoanalytic critical theory. A wide range of other perspectives exist within critical theory including: structuralism, deconstruction, Marxism, feminism, and reception theory. Each of these would have offered quite different readings and insights. Methods which draw on such fractious and diverse traditions must almost by definition be multi-perspectival.

Although HCI has a long history of incorporating methodologies from different disciplines most have been concerned with social science. Critical theory's roots are in the arts and humanities and their theoretical and methodological practices may seem quite alien. As HCI becomes more interested in problems such as aesthetics, interpretation and appropriation it must at least engage with disciplines which have studied these topics for many years. Although this kind of endeavor is not without risk it is increasingly necessary if we are to provide rich understandings of next generation HCI.

References

1. Agre P. (1997) Toward a Critical Technical Practice: Lessons Learned in Trying to Reform AI. Bowker G., Star S., Turner W., and Gasser L., eds, *Social Science, Technical Systems and Cooperative Work*, Erlbaum.

2. Alakeson V., Aldrich T., Goodman J., Jorgensen B., Miller P. (2003) Social Responsibility in the Information Society. Final Report Digital Europe: e-business and sustainable development.

3. Bell G., Blythe M., Gaver W., Sengers P., Wright P. (2003) Designing Culturally Situated Products for the Home, *Ext. Abstracts ACM CHI 2003*, ACM Press, 1062-1063.

4. Blythe M., Bardzell J., Bardzell S., Blackwell A. (2008) Critical Issues in Interaction Design. *Proc. of HCI 2008, vol. 2*, BCS, 183-184.

5. Blythe M.A., Overbeeke K., Monk A.F. and Wright P.C. (2003) *Funology: from usability to enjoyment*. Kluwer, Dordrecht.

6. Bertelsen O., Pold S. (2004) Criticism as an Approach to Interface Aesthetics. *NordiCHI 04*, ACM Press, 23-32.

7. Cairns P., Cox A. (2008) *Research Methods for Human-Computer Interaction*. Cambridge University Press, Cambridge, UK.

8. Capra R.G., Lee C.A. et al. (2008) Selection and context scoping for digital video collections: an investigation of YouTube and Blogs. *JCDL 2008*, 211-220.

9. Cha M., Kwak H. et al. (2007) I Tube, You Tube, Everybody Tubes: analyzing the world's largest user generated content video-system. *IMC '07*, ACM Press, 1-13.

10. Charmaz K. (2006) *Constructing Grounded Theory*. Sage, London.

11. Cooper T. (2004) Inadequate Life? Evidence of Consumer Attitudes to Product Obsolescence. *Journal of Comsumer Policy*, 27(4), 421-449.

12. De Souza C. (2005) *The Semiotic Engineering of Human-Computer Interaction*. MIT Press, Cambridge, MA.

13. *Dead iPod Song (featuring iJustine)* YouTube http://www.youtube.com/watch?v=TYqoA8zsrCk

14. Easthope A., McGowan K., Eds. (1992) *A Critical and Cultural Theory Reader*. OU Press, Milton Keynes.

15. Hickman L. (2006) Is It OK to Use an MP3 Player. *The Guardian*.

16. *iPhone Preacher* YouTube http://www.youtube.com/watch?v=F8Ajy18zOhI

17. *Is it a Good Idea to Microwave an iPod*. YouTube. http://www.youtube.com/watch?v=TYqoA8zsrCk

18. Kundera M. (2005) *The Art of the Novel*. Faber and Faber, London.

19. Maeda J. (2006) *The Laws of Simplicity*. MIT Press, Cambridge, MA.

20. Mankoff J., Blevis E., Borning A., Friedman B., Fussell S., Hasbrouck J., Woodruff A., Sengers P. (2007) Environmental Sustainability and Interaction. CHI 2007 San Jose, CA. pp 2121-2124.

21. Mayring P. (2004) Qualitative Content Analysis in Flickr. In Kardorff U., Steinke E. eds. *A Companion to Qualitative Research*. Sage, London.

22. McCarthy J., Wright P. (2004) *Technology as Experience*. MIT Press, Cambridge, MA.

23. Moggridge B., (2007) *Designing Interactions*. MIT Press, Cambridge, MA.

24. Satchell C. (2008) *Cultural Theory and Real World Design: Dystopian and Utopian Outcomes*. CHI 2008 Florence, Italy. pp 1593-1602.

25. Sengers P., Boehner K., Shay D., Kaye J. (2005) *Critical Computing*. Aarhus, Denmark pp 49-58

26. Sharp H., Rogers Y., Preece J., (2007) *Interaction Design: Beyond Human Computer Interaction*. John Wiley and Sons, Chichester, UK.

27. *Sokal Affair*. Wikipedia. http://en.wikipedia.org/wiki/Sokal_affair

28. *Will It Blend? iPhone 3G* YouTube http://uk.youtube.com/watch?v=DLxq9oxmYUs

29. Žižek S. (2008) *In Defence of Lost Causes*. Verso, London.

Source: *Proceedings of the 27th International Conference on Human Factors in Computing Systems* (2009): 1467-76.

WHAT IT SAYS

1. What has integrating psychology, sociology, and anthropology added to the academic study of computer interfaces?

2. Briefly describe the data-gathering methodology of Blythe and Cairns's study. What issues arose in the collection of this data, according to Blythe and Cairns?

3. What is a "qualitative content analysis"? How specifically did Blythe and Cairns use this type of analysis in their study? For example, describe the categories into which Blythe and Cairns group the videos they analyzed.

4. What is "grounded theory analysis"? How do Blythe and Cairns apply this type of analysis to the "Will It Blend?" video comments?

5. What can critical theory add to a study of human-computer interaction, according to Blythe and Cairns? What specific conclusions result from their application of critical theory to the YouTube videos about the iPhone 3G?

6. What conclusions about the nature and meaning of YouTube videos about the iPhone 3G do Blythe and Cairns draw from their study? What conclusions do the authors draw about human-computer interactions in general?

7. What do Blythe and Cairns say about their own methodologies? What do they say are the benefits and drawbacks of the analytical strategies they used?

HOW IT SAYS IT

1. What method of organization does the article employ? Consider how closely it resembles the IMRAD format. What are the differences between this article's method of organization and the IMRAD format?

2. Consider the sections of the article. What is the function of this sectioning? What does each section contribute to the whole? How do the parts combine to make the argument that Blythe and Cairns want to advance?

3. How does Blythe and Cairns's visual presentation contribute to their study? Examine Figs. 1.3 and 1.4 as well as their subheadings.

WRITE ABOUT IT

1. Create your own study of videos responding to a newly released technology product. Apply analysis strategies characteristic of physical science, social science, the humanities, or a combination of these disciplines. Write up your findings.

2. Write a meta-analysis of Blythe and Cairns's study. In other words, write a study that analyzes the positive and negative aspects of the study itself—its methodologies, the writing style, the ways in which the authors address their readers.

e. Ariela Garvett, "Tweets and Transitions: How the Arab Spring Reaffirms the Internet's Democratizing Potential"

Ariela Garvett is a senior at New York University, majoring in global liberal studies, with politics and Middle Eastern studies minors. She has lived in New York, Johannesburg, and Seattle. Garvett is the career and academic chair of the NYU International Relations Society, and recently returned from two semesters abroad at NYU's campus in Tel Aviv-Jaffa, where she studied Arabic and Hebrew language. She is concurrently pursuing a Master's in international relations as part of an accelerated degree program.

Tweets and Transitions: How the Arab Spring Reaffirms the Internet's Democratizing Potential

Though the Net neither encourages extreme surveillance, nor of its own accord produces governmental change, Internet access tends to promote a more egalitarian society in which users decide what this technology will accomplish, virtually and in reality. Proponents of democracy view the Internet as the ideal forum, hearkening to the classical Athenian model of citizen participation (Saco). Online, surveillance coexists alongside free expression (Winokur), yet the Web's decentralized and open format tends toward democracy.

As an ensemble of Information and Communication Technologies (ICTs), the Internet can inspire democratic reform and horizontal participation on local, regional, national, and global levels. Theoretically, Web 2.0 technologies like Facebook and Twitter lack central authority, providing everyone with access equal opportunities to participate. Only when overarching governmental bodies distort these tools are the Internet's possibilities undermined. Challenging the Net's ideal and ultimately overwhelming form, hegemonic bodies can temporarily obscure the democratic process and instead control the demos, but the general trend inspired by the events of 2011 demonstrate overwhelming citizen activism to reclaim the global network and its extensive power, thereby asserting the basic human rights of self-expression and association.

Instruments for citizen unity and expression, Web 2.0 technologies are shaping the modern era. They empower underrepresented civilians, propelling revolutions, as evidenced by this past year's multiple swift and powerful political changes. Beginning with mass protests in Tunisia, and quickly spreading across much of the Middle East, previously powerless citizens seized a novel form of authority. Utilizing Web 2.0 technologies, activists swiftly organized people on virtual and actual planes to combat decades of hegemonic rule. The effects of such uncontrollable mass collaboration alerted foreigners to ordinarily distant political plight as Arabs garnered legitimate political support at home and abroad. Many nations successfully removed their unpopular dictators by uniting the disenfranchised across forums such as Facebook and Twitter. With the deregulated format of Web 2.0 technologies favoring the causes of protesters, the voices of millions were and are continuously being expressed on a global platform, a feat not possible at such a large scale prior to the emergence of these mechanisms for change. In this essay, I argue that as reflected in the recent political upheavals in North Africa and the Middle East, the Internet is a potentially egalitarian and boundary-less structure that encourages transnational participation for the betterment of humanity.

Davit Chokoshvili, conducting an empirical study during 2011 entitled "The Role of the Internet in Democratic Transition: Case Study of the Arab Spring," insists on the Internet's benefits for the world, specifically analyzing the preconditions and effects of the Arab Spring. He notes that where network access is possible, even on a small scale, exposure to discussions abroad enlighten and inspire users to eventually push for democratic change. This occurs as citizens identify and desire rights and privileges denied to them within their own nations, as expressed by foreigners across the Web. He also proposed that nations that deny their people full Internet access disadvantage themselves in an age driven by technological progress, as participation in the ever-increasing global economy is an aspiration of people and governments alike. The Internet demonstrates the possibilities of change and advancement, and so people aim to transfer their growing virtual freedom into the public sphere. Michael Margolis and Gerson Moreno-Riaño similarly contend in their book, *The Prospect of Internet Democracy*, that the Net is a neutral medium, but when used broadly by citizens for their own interests, it manifests a democratizing effect stemming from its inherent horizontal structure of mass inclusivity.

Echoing Chokoshvili's emphasis on cyberspace's inclusive (and elusive) character, in her essay "The Politics of Invisibility," Diane Saco lauds the Internet's potential for replicating the demos. Though she notes possible flaws in the system, the ultimate effect of transmitting diminished voices outweighs the possibilities for the emergence of enhanced surveillance through an increasingly symmetrical network of one billion active and expressive minds.

However, not all communications scholars are so optimistic about the prospects for the Internet. In his essay, "The Ambiguous Panopticon: Foucault and the Codes of Cyberspace," Mark Winokur describes the Internet as an asymmetrical space that reflects varying levels of control throughout. Charging the system with a panoptic or all-seeing character, Winokur posits that "the Internet construct[s] space with a special attention to the subject's internalizing a particular model of space, and a particular notion of how people are distributed throughout space in relation to one another" (Winokur 1). Winokur is suggesting that the user is always aware of her relationship to others on the web. Because she may indeed be under surveillance at any time, she polices herself. By positioning herself under the gaze cyberspace where everyone is potentially observed by government bodies in collusion with Internet service providers and websites, the Internet user becomes the means of her own subjection, as Michel Foucault claimed regarding the Panopticon in his groundbreaking book, *Discipline and Punish* (1977).[1]

Though compelling, Winokur's characterization falsely inserts boundaries among Internet users, thereby disregarding the existence of multifarious connections within the global platform. Unlike the subject in the Panopticon as described by Foucault, in associating through channels such as social media, blogs, and online news sites, the Internet user constructs the self in relation to technologically constructed communities, built from multiple threads that inextricably intertwine in seemingly infinite paths, free from forced insulation. Users are uninhibited by surveillance and retain their unique identities, because unlimited connections enable mass participation, expression, and interactivity that no single power can entirely enclose or observe. Collectivist in nature, the Web transmits a plethora of opinions that garner importance, and potentially contrast to normally dominating institutions. The Internet does not meet the criteria of the Panopticon, because unhindered, the user joins, expresses, and receives feedback over multiple networks.

The broad aim of social media Web 2.0 technologies is to transmit and multiply user input, to amplify societal foundations through a generated realm that allows for the expression of both personal prerogatives and communal action. As witnessed throughout the Arab Spring, the harnessing of group power enabled "netizens" (network citizens) to broadcast their unfavorable political realities and ask for support in their popular rebellions. Internet access naturally enhances the speed and reproduction of users' messages, therefore social media effectively communicated the virtual public's wants and needs, culminating in a fast and forceful revolution. Thus, as a fulcrum for social power, the Internet galvanized people to challenge authority by simplifying significantly the revolutionary process. Though it allows for panoptic control through its manipulation, the Internet opposes vertical structures of power, founded instead on the equitable

---

1   Foucault's architectural Panopticon houses inmates in a manner that constricts their ability to communicate with one another, while an anonymous figure has the ability to survey any prisoner at any time, completely undetected. Prisoners are stripped of their identities, thereby relinquishing their freedoms to an overarching body, only knowing that there is a constant possibility that they are being observed. This unpredictable, methodical form of discipline, known as panopticism, has been applied to the Internet, a space that supposedly separates, equalizes and surveys all prisoners (i.e., network citizens), who may be observed by a central authority (i.e., government, Big Brother) at any time.

model of relatively horizontal participation in regions that dispense this technology, evidenced by the profound political changes of 2011.

For unpopular regimes to succeed in such a flat structure, the dispensers of power—namely governments—must distribute ICTs in a distorted format, which is an explicit disadvantage to that regime's people in a highly connected world. Global citizens can infiltrate such a debased system by fighting against this disruption of freedom, because the free world recognizes the Internet as a universal liberating device, transcending national borders to deliver unimpeded information and reflecting the popular current. In its unhampered form, the global network inspires limitless and completely open interactions that increase democratic participation wherever it may reach.

Chokoshvili outlines the repercussions of inhibiting citizen participation in the online community, specifically arguing that exclusion interrupts a country's participation in the global economy. He also notes that because the Internet "promotes [a] 'many-to-many' type of interaction [via] technologies like forums, blogs, discussion boards and chat rooms, large number[s] of people engage in the process of exchanging information" (Chokoshvili 7) and those left out effectively stagnate.

The Internet's inclusivity applies only to those offered opportunities to express themselves through the best form of mass communication to date. All others face relative decline—economically, technologically, and politically. By restricting network access, authoritarian regimes impair their citizens' ability to interact and grow as part of the international community. Some states like China censor search engines to the extent that citizens and visitors purchase illegal tools to connect to their favorite sites and engage the global public. Attempting to balance intrusion and inclusion, the PRC is approaching a vital crossroads in their authoritarian system. In other states, even slight exposure to ICTs inspires people's resistance to government control as they become aware of special freedoms abroad, thus prompting the toppling of unpopular and illegitimate regimes, as observed throughout the Arab Spring.

Chokoshvili asserts, "Access to the Internet, no matter how severely limited, still enhances social capital and public spheres" (Chokoshvili 17). Accordingly, even limited exposure to outside forces, whether Western bloggers or news reports concealed by the government, empowers citizens to demand increased liberty based on the models of democratic states. Exposure to the World Wide Web has demonstrably inspired netizens to push for freedom against various forms of unjust domination.

Theorists of the Internet's impact prior to the events of 2011 based their arguments on trends of online consumption and the recording of consumer behaviors, rather than optimism for reviving the demos. Though technology users have yet to realize effective direct democracy, populations are now claiming their rights of free speech and representation in government via online expression. Margolis and Moreno-Riaño contend that, "The Internet has become the most accessible forum ever through which people can express the variety of views, opinions and emotions that exist in modern mass society ... [and it], like other ICTs, is an ideologically neutral medium" (Margolis and Moreno-Riaño 28). Although not *inherently* democratic (or panoptic)—ultimately its effects depend on who controls its tools—the Internet's predominantly decentralized character disadvantages dictatorial regulators and advantages democratic impulses. "Even though the Internet will hardly revolutionize politics, it will increase the leverage of those citizens who actively participate" (Margolis and Moreno-Riaño 32). Their assertion proves partly correct; during the Arab Spring, netizens equipped with ICTs recruited compatriots as well as the international community to their cause. Arab Spring, a compilation of many revolutions, undermined traditional state domination for the potential establishment of liberty. Through solidarity and global communication, protestors garnered support in the face of absolute authority, weakened and toppled decades-old regimes.

Cyberspace's structure provides for the dissolution of authority and the growth of power for its users. According to Chokoshvili,

> The Internet is a complex network of networks, which links hundreds of millions of computing devices operating on various programs. The complexity of those communications clearly indicates that it is virtually impossible for states to control or regulate the Net. (Chokoshvili 6-7)

User-generated content embodies the voices of collective activists, who without a centralized authority evade the invasive policies of oppressive regimes.

Against suspicions of enhanced surveillance, Chokoshvili stresses that Internet access orients itself to the good of cyber-democracy by constructing a potent digital civil society, fairly free from authority's reign. Despite the inescapability of some governmental observation, Saco builds upon this notion of *productive visibility* claiming, "People are disempowered by being excluded from certain spaces, such as cyberspace ... [because] the technology still retains ... a certain emancipatory promise, which is why it needs ... to be democratized, made accessible to others" (Saco 17-18). Rather than face marginalization, Saco argues that users seek online participation in a new version of the ancient agora. Whether participating individually, or enacting democracy within teeming demonstrations, the Internet contributes immensely to the empowerment of users everywhere. Connecting on an international scale affords members of the World Wide Web awareness, influence, and recognition.

Works Cited

Bean, Meredith, and Aaron Norgrove. "Face(book)ing the Future: Identity, Control, and the Formation of the 'Digital Dividual.'" TASA & SAANZ Joint Conference 2007. 4-7 December 2007, Auckland, New Zealand.

Chokoshvili, Davit. "The Role of the Internet in Democratic Transition: Case Study of the Arab Spring." Thesis. Central European University, 2011. Web. <http://www.etd.ceu.hu/2011/chokoshvili_davit.pdf>.

Foucault, Michel. *Discipline and Punish: The Birth of the Prison.* New York: Pantheon Books, 1977. Print.

Margolis, Michael, and Gerson Moreno-Riaño. "The Internet and the Prospect of Democracy." *The Prospect of Internet Democracy.* Farnham: Ashgate, 2009. 14-33. eBook.

Saco, Diane. "The Politics of Visibility." *Cybering Democracy: Public Space and the Internet.* Minneapolis: University of Minnesota Press, 2002. *Electronic Mediations.* Vol. 7. Web.

Winokur, Mark. "The Ambiguous Panopticon: Foucault and the Codes of Cyberspace." Ed. Arthur and Marilouise Kroker. (2003). *CTheory.net.* Web. 18 May 2007. <http://www.ctheory.net/articles.aspx?id=371>.

Questions for Synthesis

1. Write an essay that discusses one of the issues in the Issues and Stakeholders section of this chapter's introduction.

   - Where might each of the authors you have read in the chapter stand on the issue?
   - How have digital media served (or disserved) human beings in consideration of this issue?
   - Do the authors believe that digital technology has affected people positively, negatively, or both? Explain.

   Be sure to include any alternatives these authors offer to the current state of affairs. Remember that your goal here is to pull together the various viewpoints of this chapter's writers on this issue, without making an argument of your own. You may wish to construct a synthesis grid (see pp. 77–79) before you begin to write.

2. Write an essay that explores the various perspectives on *the future* of digital technology taken by the authors in this chapter. Pay attention to how the academic discipline and expertise of each writer affects his or her general claims, predictions, and attitudes regarding digital technology.

   As this is a synthesis essay, not a contribution, your goal is to faithfully represent the positions of these writers, not to express your agreement or disagreement with them. You may wish to construct a synthesis grid (see pp. 77–79) before you begin to write.

Questions for Contribution

1. Argue for or against the current state of digital media. What impact does digital technology have on individuals and global societies right now? How do you propose to

   a. promote the continuation of digital media interaction as it is,
   b. change it completely, or
   c. propose some changes while maintaining aspects of digital media interaction that you view as positive?

   Draw on the sources included in this chapter and consult the Suggested Additional Resources to support your arguments.

2. Write an essay that contemplates ways in which the humanities, social sciences, and physical sciences can benefit most from digital technology in the future.

   Think about the protocols, assumptions, and manners of addressing a problem or idea that characterizes each broad discipline, and think about how each could use digital technology to expand its ability to conduct research, organize information, create useful and interesting images, and communicate with experts and non-experts across the globe. Draw on the sources in this chapter as well as the Suggested Additional Resources to bolster your argument.

CHAPTER 2 LEARNING FROM GAMES

INTRODUCTION

Contexts of Discussion

For most people, computer and video games are pure entertainment—a way to relax after class, something to do with friends, a chance to dream that you're a mystical warrior, a rock legend, or a tennis star.

Today, people can start playing computer games as infants and never stop—there are games designed for every age and interest niche. Video and computer games have become mega-business since the first video games appeared in the 1970s. In 2011, consumers worldwide spent more than $25 billion on computer and video games and gaming hardware. The average American household owns at least one device that plays video games—which isn't surprising, considering that virtually every device with a screen plays games.

Who plays video games? The answer might surprise you. According to a 2012 report published by the Entertainment Software Association (ESA), the average age of game players is 30, with the largest group (37 per cent) aged 36 or older. Also, the gender of game players is almost evenly split between men (53 per cent) and women (47 per cent).

Who buys these games? The average age of buyers is 35; again, buyers are almost evenly split between men and women.

Think most gamers are loners? Not so. The ESA report says that 62 per cent play with someone else, either in person or online. And a majority of this group plays with people they know.

What do gamers look for in a game? According to the ESA report, among the top reasons gamers buy a particular game are the quality of game graphics, an interesting storyline, a sequel to a favorite game, and word of mouth. In 2011, the top five video games were, in order of popularity, *Call of Duty: Modern Warfare 3*, *Just Dance 3*, *Madden NFL 12*, *Elder Scrolls V: Skyrim*, and *Battlefield 3*. Three of these games were rated "mature" by the Entertainment Software Rating Board

(ESRB), as were about 26 per cent of all games sold in 2011 (the largest group, 39 per cent, were rated "Everyone"). (See the Suggested Additional Resources at the end of this introduction.)

But for some scholars, video games are not just about entertainment and profit—they are the subject of serious study. **Game studies**—also known as **gaming theory**—involves such varied fields as behavioral psychology, neurology, computer science, economics, business, sociology, philosophy, media and communication studies, and literary theory. As you might expect, each field draws on the methods, tools, and focus of its discipline. Data—and research funding—exist to back up just about every theory about the link between games and cognition and behavior.

What interests scholars about this "mindless" pastime? Many scholars believe that, far from being mindless, playing games *changes* people's minds. But they don't agree on how. Some researchers, for example, say that playing computer games can speed up brain development in the young; some say it can slow brain degeneration in older people. Others say video games create no lasting effects on players at all.

A large body of research in public health deals with the epidemic of obesity; many blame sedentary activities like video games and are studying the effects of reducing children's screen time as an anti-obesity measure. Meanwhile, other public health advocates and exercise scientists have done research demonstrating the positive effect of active video games, or exergames, such as *Wii* tennis. Medical and social science researchers are also studying the causes and effects of pathological video game use, or video game "addiction."

Some behavioral psychologists and neurologists argue that violent games stimulate aggressive behavior, particularly in boys and young men. These studies have led to efforts to restrict or even ban teenagers from buying violent video games. Others say that playing violent games does not translate to violent behavior. In fact, some researchers claim that these games allow players to "play out" violent tendencies, leaving them *less* violent in their everyday lives. Still others claim that all of these studies on violence and video games are invalidated by methodological flaws, and that further studies are needed.

Another kind of debate that engages game studies scholars is the question of academic "turf wars"—who "owns" game studies? This is perhaps an unanswerable question; the variety of game-related questions and studies emphasize not only the interdisciplinary nature of game studies, but also the near impossibility of assigning game studies to a specific field. In fact, universities with designated programs in game studies are often composed of academics from several fields. Georgia Tech and MIT house game studies within their media and communications or digital media departments; Iowa State University's Media Research Lab is part of its department of psychology. Although game studies are published in a variety of journals, the field has its own web-based journal: *Game Studies: The International Journal of Computer Game Research* (gamestudies.org).

This chapter focuses on the critical study of games, including game design, the role of games in society, and the effects of game-playing on players. We will introduce the "players" in the gaming debates, and discuss what the stakes are for the people and groups involved.

Areas of Research and Conjecture

Neurology is the science of the nerves and the nervous system; **neurobiology** is concerned with the anatomy and physiology of the nervous system. Brain scientists approach video and computer games mostly through the study of the brain. Neurologists, neurobiologists, and other brain scientists conduct research on the ways in which playing games causes changes in the brain's structure and chemistry. These changes often affect the individual's ability to perceive, understand, learn, reason, judge, and imagine—abilities often referred to collectively as **cognition**. Their research might investigate the processes that cause neurological change, the structures in the brain that control such changes, and the extent to which the changes are permanent.

A 2012 study in the *Journal of Cognitive Neuroscience* investigated the effect of playing a violent video game on the structure of the brain. Blogger RebeccG92 responded with a critical evaluation of the investigators' methodology and evidence. Her post, "Playing a First-Person Shooter Video Game Induces Neuroplastic Change: A Critical Evaluation," along with the original article, are included in the Suggested Additional Resources for this chapter.

Psychology is the study of the mental processes and behaviors of individuals. Like neurologists and neurobiologists, **behavioral** and **developmental psychologists** are interested in the ways in which playing video games can affect players' cognitive skills. But psychologists also look at the effects of games on other aspects of behavior, including sociality, violence, and self-esteem. Recent research has considered how the "interactive reward" structure of such games as *Angry Birds*, *Tetris*, *Farmville*, and others conditions players to expect similar rewards in their day-to-day lives. Another question that intrigues psychologists: Does the antisocial behavior (i.e., fighting, killing, stealing) that some video games reward cause the player to behave similarly in real-life situations?

Douglas A. Gentile is a developmental psychologist who directs the Media Lab at Iowa State University, a community of professors and graduate and undergraduate students who conduct research on media's effects on children and adults. Gentile is a co-author of "Video Games: Good, Bad, or Other?," which is included in this chapter. Also included is an article by Stephen Burgess, Steven Paul Stermer, and Melinda C.R. Burgess, whose study of 691 college students found some negative results associated with playing video games.

Philosophy is a field that considers questions of being (**ontology**), proper behavior (**ethics**), and knowledge (**epistemology**). Philosophers interested in game studies have examined the motivations and morality behind cheating on video games and what makes a video game "good" in the moral sense. Can a game be morally reprehensible yet still be considered good by other standards? In their book *Philosophy through Video Games* (2009), for example, philosophers Jon Cogburn and Mark Silcox examine individual video games as philosophical "texts." (See the Suggested Additional Resources at the end of this introduction.)

Literary theory is a field encompassing a large body of ideas and methods used to reveal possible meanings of literature. Literary scholars might study video games to analyze aspects of their story lines, or **narratives**. They are concerned with the structure of games, how stories are told in games, and the meanings created in these games. For instance, a recent article by linguist and literature professor James Paul Gee reflects on the ways in which narrative video games both tell stories and allow the player to participate in storytelling while playing the game. Gee claims that these games train the mind to make sense of the world and even to be empathetic toward other people's situations and perspectives. His article, "Stories, Probes, and Games," as well as several YouTube videos of Gee's lectures on video games, are included in the Suggested Additional Resources at the end of this introduction.

Media and communications studies is the study of mass media, in particular print media, film, radio and television, social media, and other information networks. The media and communications field also considers the ownership structures of media organizations. Media and communications scholars study videogames as they do other mass media artifacts—in terms of how these "texts" are both produced and received. Influential games theorists in media and communications include Jesper Juul at New York University Games Center, Ian Bogost at Georgia Tech, and Espen Aarseth at the University of Oslo in Norway. (See the Suggested Additional Resources.)

Human-Computer Interaction (HCI) is the study of human beings as they interact with computer technology. The field draws upon anthropology, computer science, psychology, sociology, and even English studies. Computer scientists and HCI scholars in game studies may both design video games and construct theories about the games and their structure. Such research has included technical studies on game design, guidelines for better video games, and comparative studies designed to discover common qualities and interactive possibilities among video games and the player experience. *Computer Games and New Media Cultures* (2012) is a useful general book on the subject; the article "General Heuristic Approach to General Game Playing" proposes a mathematic formula for evaluating video games. (See the Suggested Additional Resources.)

Business and marketing as an academic field concerns itself with designing and evaluating processes and practices by which businesses can be organized, including those for creating and maintaining markets for their goods. Business and marketing scholars might study the gaming industry as a relatively young, multi-billion-dollar industry. They might investigate methods for stimulating the purchase of certain games, or methods for targeting specific demographics with particular games, among other sales and marketing issues.

Economics is the study of the distribution and use of valued resources, as well as the stimulants to their creation. Gaming, especially massively multi-player online games (MMOs), provides a huge sample of interactive players, which economists may use to study human economic behavior. Economics and industry analysts also study economic activity in games in order to discover how "real" economies work. For example, academic economist Yanis Varoufakis works as the "economist in residence" for Valve, a large video game company. He writes in his blog that among his goals are to "forge narratives and empirical knowledge that (a) transcend the border separating the 'real' from the digital economies, and (b) bring together lessons from the political economy of our gamers' economies" (http://blogs.valvesoftware.com/economics).

Exercise physiology is the study of the body's responses to a wide range of physical exercise conditions. Exercise physiologists sometimes study the ways in which exercise can reduce or reverse disease. **Physical therapy** is a practice concerned with helping injured and disabled people improve their bodies' mobility and reduce their pain through evaluation and physical intervention. Exercise physiologists, physical therapists, and other public health scientists have studied the potential of active video games, or exergames, such as virtual tennis, golf, baseball, or dance, to improve players' physical condition. A recent study by exercise scientists Lee E.F. Graves et al., for instance, compared the physiological effects of playing Wii Fit with working out on a treadmill or playing **sedentary** video games. (See the Suggested Additional Resources.)

Legal studies is an interdisciplinary field that examines the meanings, values, practices and institutions of law and legality. Lawyers, policymakers, and legal scholars have recently engaged the question of whether sales of violent video games to minors should be restricted by law. An article by Ryan C.W. Hall et al., which considers the legal implications of restricting the sale of violent video games to minors, is included in this chapter. A response to this article, by Christopher J. Ferguson, is also included.

Educational technology is a relatively new interdisciplinary field that involves the study of learning with the use of appropriate technologies. The field incorporates theories of learning and thus is not strictly the study of technological devices. Recently, educational technology scholars have studied ways to develop and improve learning games for all levels of learners. A recent book, which considers a "game canon," a list of games deemed culturally and historically significant enough to be preserved by the Library of Congress, for game studies education, is listed in the Suggested Additional Resources at the end of this chapter introduction.

Issues and Stakeholders

Intelligence: Some scholars contend that games enhance overall brain function, boosting creativity, perception, and cognition. This ability to apply skills learned in a specific activity, such as playing video games, to general activities, such as taking tests or remembering people's names, is known as **broad transfer**.

Walter R. Boot, a psychologist and well-known games scholar, along with fellow psychologists Daniel P. Blakely and Daniel J. Simons, surveyed recent studies linking game playing to improved cognition. They conclude with suggestions for a set of "clinical best practices" for conducting more definitive tests of the link between game playing and cognition. (See the Suggested Additional Resources.) Sara Prot et al., in their article "Video Games: Good, Bad, or Other?," suggest that the effects of video game-playing are multi-dimensional, and that the good-bad dichotomy created by scientists is simplistic and counter-productive. This article is included in this chapter.

Violence: Some scholars apply **social learning theory** to game theory and argue that watching violent video games stimulates or encourages violent behavior. Game theorists applying social learning theory suggest that game players are particularly prone to suggestion because they participate more actively in the action than those who watch violent movies and television shows. These studies have received much media coverage and have raised concerns among lawmakers. One group contends that these data should result in laws banning or seriously restricting violent games. This position is well represented in scholarly journals and the mass media. We include several such sources in the Suggested Additional Resources at the end of this introduction.

On the other hand, some scholars argue that human beings can distinguish "real" from "artificial" situations, and that broad transfer of aggressive behavior does not occur just because someone plays violent computer games. Furthermore, according to **catharsis theory**, some argue that far from producing aggressive behavior in the larger world, violent video games offer gamers a way to act out socially unacceptable behavior in an artificial setting, making them *less* prone to aggressive behaviors in real life.

In this chapter, we include a scholarly conversation on the question of video games and violence. In "A Plea for Caution: Violent Video Games, the Supreme Court, and the Role of Science," published in the *Mayo Clinic Proceedings*, Ryan C.W. Hall, a physician, and his colleagues, a legal scholar and another physician, consider the 2010 US Supreme Court case *Schwarzenegger v. Entertainment Merchants Association*, which considered whether limiting the sale of violent video games to minors violates the Constitution. As studies show both that violent video games cause violent behavior, and that they do not, the authors urge caution in relying on "unsettled science" when making legal decisions.

In response, Christopher J. Ferguson, a clinical psychologist, wrote a letter to the editor of the same journal on the occasion of the Supreme Court's striking down the earlier ruling in *Schwarzenegger v. Entertainment Merchants Association*. Ferguson writes in support of Hall, Day, and Hall, but he takes the issue in a different direction. He urges the medical scientists to let go of "spurious claims" about the dangers of video games. These claims, he writes, are ideological, not data-based, and they harm the integrity of the scientific community. Together, the essay and letter to the editor provide a good example of the ways in which scholars respond to, support, and dispute each other's arguments—sometimes all at the same time.

Exercise: Exercise scientists claim that video games promote health by encouraging exercise. A recent study by exercise scientists Lee E.F. Graves et al. compared the physiological effects of playing *Wii Fit* with working out on a treadmill or playing sedentary video games. They found that, although a treadmill workout provides more benefits, *Wii Fit* is a fun way to get light-to-moderate exercise—and a good alternative to sedentary gaming. Their article, "The Physiological Cost and Enjoyment of *Wii Fit* in Adolescents, Young Adults, and Older Adults," is listed in the Suggested Additional Resources at the end of this introduction.

Gender equity: Although many people still think of video games as a "male sport," girls and women play video games nearly as much as boys and men. Recent studies have speculated on the causes of this phenomenon, and suggested ways to involve girls and women even more, especially as an educational tool for the young and a cognition-improvement tool for the elderly. "Getting (More) Girls into (More) Games," a blog entry by Sarah M. Grimes, a professor of children's literature and new media, reports on the 2010 3G Summit: The Future of Girls, Games and Gender, which focused on ways to encourage girls to become game designers. In "Are Girls Game? How School Libraries Can Provide Gender Equity in E-gaming," Lesley S.J. Farmer, a professor of library science, acknowledges that although e-games can distract students from learning, they also have the potential to provide the kinds of educational and emotional support that particularly benefit girls. Both articles are included in this chapter.

Ludology vs. narratology: Do games represent a new type of media experience entirely, or can they be understood in terms of earlier media studies theories, in particular, in terms of meaning making provided by narratives? This debate is referred to in the field as the ludology/narratology debate. **Ludology** is a term recently proposed by game theorist Gonzalo Frasca to refer to the academic study of game and play activities. The word comes from *ludus*, the Latin word for "game." **Narratology** is the academic study of the structure of a narrative, or story, in comparison with other narratives. Narratology has long been used by literary theorists in the study of literature.

Ludologists approach games as a structure and system unto themselves, radically different in the way they are experienced and understood. These scholars argue that game studies should focus on analyzing a game's form and rules, not on what the game might "represent" in the larger world. According to this camp, game studies must create new means of analysis, rather than relying on traditional modes—such as the study of narrative structure, an analytical perspective used in literary and film studies.

For example, ludologists might research and work on developing "ludic interfaces." These are tools (e.g., a mouse or joystick) that are used to help a game player interact with a game with a focus on "fun" or "play," so that the interface itself is not just an instrumental tool but rather an interesting and entertaining part of the game. A pioneer in this field is Mathias Fuchs, a German computer scientist whose work includes music and video installations and theoretical studies. Fuchs initiated the first master's program in "creative games" at the University of Salford in Greater Manchester, England. Articles by Fuchs, as well as links to the creative games program and videos demonstrating ludic interfaces, are listed in the Suggested Additional Resources. A related article on "turf" wars in game studies—i.e., the debate over to which discipline or disciplines this new field "belongs"—is also included in the Suggested Additional Resources (see "Ludology—Who Gets to Play?").

On the other side of the ludology/narratology debate, narratologists argue that games contain a new kind of narrative, or story, but a story just the same, and thus they may be studied using existing theories of narrative. In his article "Narrative, Games, and Theory: What Bay to Play?," media studies scholar Jan Simon lays out the premise of narratology and suggests that the two approaches (ludology and narratology) should work together to discover new ways of looking at games instead of considering themselves rivals. (See the Suggested Additional Resources.) Similarly, Gonzalo Frasca, mentioned above, has recently argued that these differences in perspective should not lead to a university turf war, as they are compatible forms of inquiry. Frasca maintains a website and blog at www.ludology.org. (See the Suggested Additional Resources.)

As You Read

Consider your own video gaming habits. What kinds of games are you drawn to? Why? In what ways do you think playing video games has changed your behavior, moods, or attitudes? In what ways do games research findings reflect or contradict your own experience?

Suggested Additional Resources

General

Chesher, Chris. "Navigating Sociotechnical Spaces: Comparing Computer Games and Sat Navs as Digital Spatial Media." *Convergence*. August 2012. Web.

Cogburn, Jon, and Mark Silcox. *Philosophy through Video Games*. New York: Routledge, 2009.

Corliss, Jonathan. "Introduction: The Social Science Study of Video Games." *Games and Culture* 6.1 (2010): 3-16. Web.

Entertainment Software Association. "Essential Facts about the Video and Computer Game Industry." Theesa.com. Web.

Frommes, Johan, and Alexander Unger, eds. *Computer Games and New Media Cultures: A Handbook of Digital Games Studies*. New York: Springer, 2012.

Mäyrä, Frans. *An Introduction to Game Studies: Games in Culture*. New York: Sage, 2008. Print and web.

Cognition and Personality

Bijvank, Marije Nije, Elly A. Konijn, and Brad J. Bushman. "'We Don't Need No Education': Video Game Preferences, Video Game Motivations, and Aggressiveness among Adolescent Boys of Different Educational Ability Levels." *Journal of Adolescence* 35.1 (February 2012): 153-62. Web.

Boot, Walter R., Daniel P. Blakely, and Daniel J. Simons. "Do Action Video Games Improve Perception and Cognition?" *Frontiers in Psychology* 2.226 (2011). Web.

Dill-Shackleford, Karen E. "Seeing Is Believing: Toward a Theory of Media Imagery and Social Learning." *The Psychology of Entertainment Media: Blurring the Lines between Entertainment and Persuasion*. Ed. L.J. Shrum. New York: Routledge, 2012. Web.

Gee, James Paul. "Stories, Probes and Games." *Narrative Inquiry* 21.2 (2011): 353-57. Web.

——. "Part 1: Dr. James Gee." International Conference on Technology, Knowledge and Society. YouTube. 2009.

Gentile, Douglas A. "The Multiple Dimensions of Video Game Effects." *Child Development Perspectives* 5.2 (2011): 75-81.

Hotz, Robert Lee. "When Gaming Is Good for You." *Wall Street Journal* March 5, 2012. Web.

Lee, Chiawen, Kirk Damon Aiken, and Huang Chia Hung. "Effects of College Students' Video Gaming Behavior on Self-Concept Clarity and Flow." *Social Behavior and Personality* 40.4 (2012): 673-80. Web.

Masson, Michael E.J., Daniel N. Bub, and Christopher E. Lalonde. "Video-Game Training and Naive Reasoning about Object Motion." *Applied Cognitive Psychology* 25 (October 2009): 166-73. Web.

McGonigal, Jane. *Reality Is Broken: Why Video Games Make Us Better and How They Can Change the World*. New York: Penguin, 2011.

Educational Technology

Adams, Deanne M., Richard E. Mayer, Andrew MacNamara, Alan Koenig, and Richard Wainess. "Narrative Games for Learning: Testing the Discovery and Narrative Hypotheses." *Journal of Educational Psychology* 104.1 (February 2012): 235-49. Web.

Bogost, Ian. *How to Do Things with Videogames*. Minneapolis: U of Minnesota P, 2011.

Juul, Jesper. *A Casual Revolution: Reinventing Video Games and Their Players*. Cambridge, MA: MIT Press, 2009.

Exercise Physiology

Graves, Lee E.F., Nicola D. Ridgers, Karen Williams, Gareth Stratton, Greg Atkinson, and Nigel T. Cable. "The Physiological Cost and Enjoyment of Wii Fit in Adolescents, Young Adults, and Older Adults." *Journal of Physical Activity and Health* 7 (2010): 393-401.

Gender Studies

Burgess, Melinda C.R., Steven Paul Stermer, and Stephen R. Burgess. "Sex, Lies, and Video Games: The Portrayal of Male and Female Characters on Video Game Covers." *Sex Roles* 57 (2011): 419-33. Web.

Stermer, S. Paul, and Melissa Burkley. "SeX-Box: Exposure to Sexist Video Games Predicts Benevolent Sexism." *Psychology of Popular Media Culture* (2012). Web.

Ludology

Frasca, Gonzalo. "Ludologists Love Stories, Too: Notes from a Debate that Never Took Place." Ludology.org. Web.

Fuchs, Mathias. "Ludic Interfaces: Driver and Product of Gamification." *GAME: The Italian Journal of Game Studies* 1 (2012). Web.

——. "Mouseology—Ludic Interfaces—Zero Interfaces." *Coded Cultures: Creative Practices out of Diversity*. Ed. Georg Russegger, Matthias Tarasiewicz, Michal Wlodkowski. New York: Springer, 2011.

Juul, Jesper. *A Casual Revolution: Reinventing Videogames and Their Players*. Cambridge, MA: MIT Press, 2012.

———. "The Ludologists." jesperjuul.com. Web.

Whalen, Jack. "Ludology—Who Gets to Play?" *M/C: A Journal of Media and Culture* 7:2 (March 2004). Web

Violence

Anderson, Craig A., Douglas A. Gentile, and Katherine E. Buckley. *Violent Video Game Effects on Children and Adolescents: Theory, Research, and Public Policy*. New York: Oxford UP, 2007.

Beck, V.S., S. Boys, C. Rose, and E. Beck. "Violence against Women in Video Games: A Prequel or Sequel to Rape Myth Acceptance?" *Journal of Interpersonal Violence* 30 (April 2012). Web.

Gentile, D.A., ed. *Media Violence and Children*. (In series *Advances in Applied Developmental Psychology*, I. Sigel, series ed.) Westport, CT: Praeger, 2003.

Saleem, M., C.A. Anderson, and D.A. Gentile. "Effects of Prosocial, Neutral, and Violent Video Games on Children's Helpful and Hurtful Behaviors." *Aggressive Behavior* 38 (2012): 281-87. Web.

van Vught, Jasper, Gareth Schott, and Raphaël Marczak. "Age-Restriction: Re-Examining the Interactive Experience of 'Harmful' Game Content." *Proceedings of DiGRA Nordic 2012 Conference: Local and Global—Games in Culture and Society*. Authors & Digital Games Research Association (DiGRA). 2012. Web.

a. Sara Prot, Katelyn A. McDonald, Craig A. Anderson, and Douglas A. Gentile, "Video Games: Good, Bad, or Other?"

Sara Prot is a graduate student in social psychology at Iowa State University, where she teaches research methods in psychology and introductory psychology and conducts research at the Self and Social Perception Laboratory.

Katelyn A. McDonald is a medical illustrator in Nenana, Alaska. She holds a BA from the University of Alaska at Fairbanks, and an MA in biological and premedical illustration from Iowa State University.

Craig A. Anderson is distinguished professor of psychology and director of the Center for the Study of Violence at Iowa State University. He is co-author of the book *Violent Video Game Effects on Children and Adolescents: Theory, Research, and Public Policy* (with Douglas A. Gentile and K.E. Buckley, 2007). He has authored or co-authored numerous book chapters and articles, including recent work in *Behavior* and *Psychology of Violence*. Anderson holds a BA from Butler University, and MA and PhD degrees from Stanford University, all in psychology.

Douglas A. Gentile is an associate professor of psychology and director of the Media Research Lab at Iowa State University, where he investigates the effects of media on children and adults, including media violence, video games, advertising, educational media, news/propaganda, virtual reality, and music. He is the author or co-author of numerous journal articles, editor of the book *Media Violence and Children* (2003), and co-author (with Craig A. Anderson and K.E. Buckley) of the book *Violent Video Game Effects on Children and Adolescents: Theory, Research, and Public Policy* (2007). Gentile holds a BA in psychology from State University of New York at Buffalo, and MA and PhD degrees in child psychology from the Institute of Child Development at the University of Minnesota.

In this article, Prot et al. review and analyze current contradictory studies on the effects of video games on players. Their essay provides a useful overview of some of the major debates in game studies today.

As You Read: Consider the varying results of video game studies. Which of the studies make the most sense to you, based on your own experience with video games?

Video Games: Good, Bad, or Other?

Keywords

Media effects, video games, aggression, prosocial behavior

Key Points

- The growing popularity of video games has instigated a debate among parents, researchers, video game producers and policymakers concerning their harmful and helpful effects.
- Video games are very effective teachers that affect players in multiple domains.
- Some of these effects can be harmful (e.g., effects of violent video games on aggression).
- Other video game effects can be beneficial (e.g., effects of action games on visual-spatial skills).
- Video game effects are complex and would be better understood as multiple dimensions rather than a simplistic "good-bad" dichotomy.

Video games are an extremely popular pastime among children and adolescents. Today, 90% of American children and teens play video games.[1,2] On a typical day, youth play video games for an average of two hours.[3] Time spent playing is even higher among some segments of the population, with 25% of young males reporting playing video games for four hours a day or more.[4]

The rising popularity of video games has instigated a debate among parents, researchers, video game producers, and policymakers concerning potential harmful and helpful effects of video games on children. Views expressed in this debate have often been extreme, either idealizing or vilifying video games.[5-7] The critics and the proponents tend to ignore research evidence supporting the views of the opposing camps and label video games as clearly "good" or "bad."

Are video games good or bad? Several relevant findings on the effects of video games are displayed in Table 2.1. The explosion in research on video games in the past ten years has helped increase our understanding of how video games affect players. It is clear that video games are powerful teachers that have significant effects in several domains, some of which could be considered beneficial and some of which could be considered harmful.[19,20]

The aim of this article is to give an overview of research findings on positive and negative effects of video games, thus providing an empirical answer to the question, "are video games good or bad?" Several negative effects of video games

TABLE 2.1. Summary of main research findings on positive and negative effects of video games on players

Positive Effects	Negative Effects

Action games improve a range of visual-spatial skills[8]
Educational games successfully teach specific knowledge and skills[9]
Exergames can improve physical activity levels[10]
Prosocial games
  Increase empathy and helping[11]
  May decrease aggression[12]
	Violent games
	  Increase aggressive thoughts, feelings and behaviors[13]
	  Desensitize players to violence, decrease empathy and helping[14-16]
	Video game play is negatively related to school performance[17]
	Video games may exacerbate attention problems[18]
	It seems that some players can become addicted to video games[1]

are reviewed first, including effects of violent video games on aggression-related variables as well as effects on attention deficits, school performance, and gaming addiction. Next, positive effects of video games are described, including effects of action games on visual-spatial skills, and effects of educational video games, exergames, and prosocial video games. Finally, some conclusions and guidelines are offered with the goal of helping pediatricians, parents, and other caregivers protect children from negative effects while maximizing the positive effects of video games.

Five Dimensions of the Effects of Video Games

BOX 2.1. Five Dimensions of the Effects of Video Games

1. Amount of game play
2. Content of play
3. Context of the game
4. Structure of the game
5. Mechanics of game play

Gentile and colleagues[21-23] have proposed that video games can affect players on at least five dimensions (Box 2.1).

Games are multidimensional and have complex effects on players. Each dimension is likely to be associated with different effects. The amount of game play has been linked to poorer academic performance and increased risk of obesity.[24,25] Violent game content is a significant risk factor for aggression, whereas prosocial game content can increase empathy and helping, and educational games can improve specific skills.[9,11,13] The context in which games are played may alter or create new effects. For example, playing in virtual teams can encourage collaboration.[26] Research on effects of game structure shows that fast-paced action games can increase visual/spatial skills (sometimes misinterpreted as "improved attention").[27-29] Innovative game mechanics such as the interactive *Wii* controller have been successfully used to promote physical activity and have even been used for physical therapy.[10,30]

A great strength of this approach is that it offers a different way of thinking about the effects of video games that surpasses a simplistic good-versus-bad dichotomy. Video games are complex and may influence players in different ways through different learning mechanisms. Even a single video game, such as *Grand Theft Auto*, might simultaneously have positive effects on players (improved visual processing) and negative effects (increased aggressive thoughts and feelings).

Negative Effects of Video Games

VIOLENT VIDEO GAME EFFECTS

By far the largest and best understood research domain concerns the effects of violent video games on aggression. Findings of experimental, correlational, and longitudinal studies confirm that video game violence can significantly increase aggressive thoughts, emotions, and behavior over both the short term and the long term.[13,17]

Although there are differing opinions about the strength of the data, a recent comprehensive meta-analytical review examined effects of violent video games on 6 relevant outcomes (aggressive behavior, aggressive cognition, aggressive affect, physiological arousal, empathy, and prosocial behavior).[13] The meta-analysis included 136 research articles with 381 effect-size estimates involving more than 130,000 participants. This large sample included both published and unpublished studies from Eastern and Western cultures. The main findings of the meta-analysis are shown in Figure 2.1. Video game play had significant effects on all 6 outcomes. Exposure to violent video games can be seen as a causal risk factor for increased aggressive behavior, cognition, and affect, with reduced empathy and prosocial behavior.

Are the effect sizes large enough to be considered important? Even small effect sizes can have large practical consequences. Because such a high percentage of children and adolescents spend large amounts of time playing violent games, small effects can accumulate and significantly influence individuals and society. In fact, the obtained effect sizes of violent video games on aggression-related variables are comparable in size with the effect of second-hand smoke on lung cancer and the effect of calcium intake on bone mass (see Figure 2.1).[31]

AGGRESSIVE COGNITION, AFFECT, AND BEHAVIOR

Findings from experimental, correlational, and longitudinal studies generally show that violent video game play is a significant risk factor for aggression (Box 2.2). This effect has been demonstrated in both short-term and long-term contexts, and in diverse populations.

Studies suggest that violent video games increase aggression by increasing aggressive thoughts and emotions, even when their physiologic arousal properties have been controlled. Playing violent video games can prime aggressive thoughts,

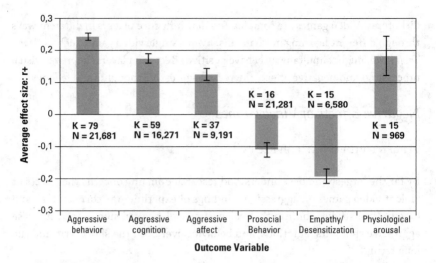

FIGURE 2.1. Effects of violent video games on aggression and related variables (results from the "Best raw" sample). K, number of effects; N, total sample size. Vertical capped bars are the upper and lower 95% confidence intervals. (From Anderson CA, Shibuya A, Ihori N, et al. Violent video game effects on aggression, empathy, and prosocial behavior in Eastern and Western countries. Psychol Bull 2010;136:162–6; with permission.)

increase positive attitudes toward violence, and help create a hostile attribution bias: a tendency to perceive other people's behaviors as malevolent.[33-35] In the short term, exposure to video game violence produces feelings of anger and hostility in players.[36] Even the critics of violent game research support the findings on aggressive thoughts, arousal, and decreased prosocial behavior.[37] Over longer periods of time, such changes can lead to the development of an aggressive personality.[15]

Empathy, Desensitization, and Helping

Another line of research has found that video game violence produces desensitization to violence and decreases in empathy and helping. Desensitization can be defined as reduction in physiological and emotional reactivity to violence.[14] Short-term exposure to violent media has been shown to produce physiological desensitization in only 20 minutes, whereas habitual video game playing has been linked to chronic desensitization.[14,38,39]

A related line of research examined links between violent video games and empathy, the degree to which a person identifies and commiserates with a victim.[13] Empathy has been shown to significantly mediate the link between violent video game play and aggressive behavior.[15] It seems that this emotional numbing can also lead to a reduction in helping behavior. For example, students who had just played a violent video game were less likely to perceive a fight they witnessed as serious or to help the injured victim.[16]

BOX 2.2. Effects of Violent Video Games on Aggressive Behavior

- Experimental studies have been used to show causal effects of video game violence on immediate increases in aggression. For example, in a laboratory experiment, children and adolescents were more likely to blast a supposed opponent with loud noise through headphones after playing a violent video game compared with a nonviolent game.[17]

- Correlational studies enabled researchers to explore associations between violent video game play and real-life instances of aggression. For example, adolescents who had consumed greater amounts of video game violence were more likely to be involved in a physical fight.[32]

- Longitudinal studies have shown relationships between video game violence and increases of aggression over time. For example, children who played more violent games early in the school year were found to display more physical and verbal aggression five months later.[17]

- Meta-analyses combine results of multiple studies and provide the strongest evidence that video game violence increases the risk of aggression. The most recent meta-analysis in this area showed a significant effect of video game violence on aggressive behaviors across different types of research designs.[13]

ATTENTION DEFICITS AND COGNITIVE CONTROL

Findings of positive effects of gaming experience on visuospatial skills are sometimes misinterpreted to mean that video games benefit attention in general. However, a growing body of evidence suggests that video games may actually exacerbate attention problems and have harmful effects on some aspects of cognitive control.

- Several studies have found correlations between attention problems in childhood and video game play.[16,40,41] High excitement and rapid changes of focus that occur in many video games may weaken children's abilities to maintain focus on less exciting tasks (e.g., schoolwork) and shorten their attention spans.

- In a longitudinal study on video game use and attention problems, video game play predicted children's attention problems 13 months later, even while controlling for other relevant variables (earlier attention problems, television viewing, and gender).[18] A three-year longitudinal study of more than 3,000 children found evidence of a bidirectional relation between attention problems and video game playing, and found a stronger relation between the amount of gaming and later attention problems than for the content of gaming.[42]

- Several studies have also shown negative relations between video game play and cognitive control.[43-45] It seems that video games have specific effects on different types of cognitive processing: they can increase visuospatial processing skills and can also harm proactive cognitive control.[27,45]

VIDEO GAME ADDICTION

There are now scores of studies looking at what is being called pathological gaming or video game "addiction." Many researchers define pathologic use of video games in the same way as pathological gambling, focusing on damage to family, social, school, occupational, and psychological functioning.[19] Like gambling, playing video games starts as a form of entertainment. It becomes pathological for some people when video games start producing negative life consequences.[21] Overall, studies examining pathological video gaming show good reliability and validity. For example, a study conducted in the United States with a national sample of 1100 youth found that 8.5% of youth gamers could be classified as pathological,[21] and similar percentages are being found in other countries.[46-51] At present, video game addiction is not classified as a formal disorder in the *Diagnostic and Statistical Manual of Mental Disorders* (DSM). The American Psychiatric Association has proposed a new category for the DSM-V of addiction-like behavioral disorders. Gambling has been moved into this category, but more research is needed before video game and Internet addictions should be included.[52]

VIDEO GAMES AND SCHOOL PERFORMANCE

Several studies have found a significant negative relation between the amount of screen time (television viewing and video game play) and school performance of children, adolescents, and college students.[3,17,25,33,53,54] That is, high amounts of time on screen media are associated with poorer school performance. One explanation is the displacement hypothesis, which states that video games (and other screen media) may displace time that would otherwise be spent on activities such as reading, homework, or other enrichment activities.[32] There has been some evidence to support the displacement hypothesis. In one study of a large nationally represented sample of youth aged 10 to 19 years, gamers spent 30% less time reading and 34% less time doing homework in comparison with nongamers.[55]

Positive Effects of Video Games

VISUAL-SPATIAL SKILLS

Several studies show that video game play can improve a wide range of visual and spatial skills.[27-29,56]

- Correlational studies have found positive associations between gaming experience and performance in numerous visual tasks, such as target localization[29] and faster visual reaction times.[8]

- Experimental studies have demonstrated that even as little as ten hours of video game play can improve spatial attention and mental rotation.[27,57]

These beneficial effects may have a range of practical applications. For example, an early experimental study showed that Israeli Air Force cadets trained using the game *Space Fortress 2* had better subsequent flight performance.[58] As a result, the game became a part of the training program of the Israeli Air Force. The largest enhancements to visuospatial processing have been shown for fast-paced action games, which also often contain violence.[8] This fact illustrates the point that the effects of video games are not simple, and a game can simultaneously have positive effects (increased visuospatial skills) and negative effects (increased aggressive emotions, thoughts, and behaviors).

EDUCATIONAL VIDEO GAMES

Video games are highly effective teachers. Well-designed video games are attention-grabbing, set clear objectives, provide feedback and reinforcement, actively involve the player, offer adaptable levels of difficulty, and use many other powerful teaching techniques.[20] A wide range of educational games have been developed, taking advantage of these features of video games and using them to teach specific knowledge and skills.

- Schools: Video games have been successfully used to teach children and adolescents a variety of topics, such as reading skills, mathematics, and biology.[9,59]
- Business: Video games are often used to teach job skills to employees. For example, Canon USA uses a video game to train copier technicians, Volvo uses an online game to teach car sales employees, and the US military uses video games to train combat skills and increase recruitment.[60,61]
- Health-related outcomes: Games have been developed to teach youth about smoking, diabetes, and cancer.[62-64] These games have been shown to be highly effective. For example, asthmatic children who played the game *Bronkie the Bronchiasaurus* showed significant improvements in their knowledge about asthma and self-care behaviors.[62]

EXERGAMES

Video games have traditionally been a sedentary activity. However, in recent years a new type of video game has emerged that requires interactive physical activity. Exercise games, or exergames, combine video games and exercise.[65]

- Active games, such as *Dance Dance Revolution* and *Wii Fit* can increase energy expenditure, prolong time spent in physical activity, and increase preference for physical activity among players.[66-68]
- Exergames have been shown to increase engagement and enjoyment. For example, a six-week-long training study demonstrated that interactive videobikes increase adherence to a training program and attitudes toward exercise compared with traditional bikes.[10]
- Particularly positive attitudes toward exergaming are found among sedentary individuals, indicating that this may be an effective way of increasing physical activity in this group.[65]

It is a worrying fact that American children tend to spend more than six hours per day watching television and playing video games, yet almost half of preschool children do not meet recommended levels of physical activity of at least one hour per day prescribed by the American Academy of Pediatrics.[3,69] Given the tremendous popularity of video games among youth, combining gaming and physical activity may be a good strategy to increase physical activity among children and adolescents.

PROSOCIAL VIDEO GAMES

Prosocial video games are those in which the primary purpose of the player is to help other game characters. Although the literature on the effects of prosocial games is much smaller than that on effects of violent video games, there is growing support for the idea that prosocial video games can promote prosocial tendencies.[11,70] It must be noted that games with violent content are not considered truly prosocial, even if the player's character is helping other players by killing mutual enemies.

Playing a nonviolent prosocial video game in the laboratory has actually been shown to decrease aggressive thoughts, feelings, and behaviors.[12,71] Prosocial video game play can also increase prosocial thoughts, enhance empathy, and promote helping behavior.[70,72-74] For example, in a series of experimental studies, playing a prosocial video game made participants more predisposed to help the researcher pick up fallen pencils, agree to participate in further experiments, and come to the aid of a female experimenter who was being harassed by a supposed ex-boyfriend (actually a confederate).[11]

These findings are not limited to laboratory experiments. For example, a large-sample correlational study showed significant associations between prosocial video game play and prosocial behaviors in real life (e.g., spending money to help those who are in need).[71] In a follow-up longitudinal study, prosocial game play predicted increases in prosocial behavior among children over a period of three to four months, confirming that prosocial games can have a long-term impact on helping.[12]

Guidelines for Parents, Pediatricians, and Other Caregivers

The research on positive and negative effects of video games clearly shows that video games are effective teachers that can affect players in multiple ways simultaneously. Therefore, the original question asked about whether games were "good" or "bad" is demonstrated to be a false dichotomy. Some effects are harmful (such as effects of violent video games on aggression and the effect of screen time on poorer school performance), whereas others are beneficial (e.g., effects of action games on visual-spatial skills).

Suggestions are made in Box 2.3 as to what can be done to maximize the positive effects of video game use and minimize harm.

BOX 2.3. Advice for Pediatricians, Parents, and Other Caregivers on Choosing and Using Video Games

- Ask about games and other media use at well-child checkups. Pediatricians and general practitioners are in the unique role of helping parents to understand that they need to take their children's media use seriously. Parents setting limits on the amount and content of children's media is a powerful protective factor for children.[2,17,32]
- Do not rely solely on ratings. Even games rated E for Everyone often contain depictions of violence.[75] Instead, try playing the game yourself, ask someone to demonstrate it for you, or look for descriptions or video clips of the game on the Internet.
- Choose well. Select nonviolent games that have been shown to have positive effects, such as educational games, prosocial games, and exergames. Do not allow access to violent video games, defined as games in which you must harm other characters to advance.
- Set limits on both the amount and content of games. Create clear rules about amount of time and the kind of content that is allowed. Even positive games can be played too much. The American Academy of Pediatrics recommends no more than one to two hours of total screen time (video games, TV, DVDs, computer, and so forth, all summed together) per day.
- Keep game devices in public space. When gaming devices are in private space (child's bedroom), it is very difficult to control either content or time. Move them to public space (e.g., living room, kitchen).
- Stay involved. Explain to your children why playing violent games or playing games for an excessive amount of time may be harmful to them. Discuss your family's values concerning violence and aggression. Help them learn to make good choices.
- Spread the word. Help educate others in your community (parents, youth, public officials). Although almost 100% of pediatricians have been convinced by the data that the media have significant effects,[76] the public do not know this. The mainstream media often sensationalize and polarize discussion on this topic; it is important that people understand that there are both potential benefits and harms to be derived from game play.

References

1. Gentile DA. Pathological video-game use among youth ages 8-18: a national study. Psychol Sci 2009;20(5):594-602.

2. Gentile DA, Walsh DA. A normative study of family media habits. J Appl Dev Psychol 2002;23:157-78.

3. Rideout VJ, Foehr UG, Roberts DF. Generation M^2—media in the lives of 8- to 18-year olds. Menlo Park (CA): Kaiser Family Foundation; 2010.

4. Bailey K, West R, Anderson CA. The influence of video games on social, cognitive, and affective information processing. In: Decety J, Cacioppo J, editors. Handbook of social neuroscience. New York: Oxford University Press; 2011. p. 1001-11.

5. Cavalli E. Jack Thompson reaches out to Take-Two exec's mother. Wired; 2008. Available at: http://www.wired.com/gamelife/2008/04/jack-thompson-p/. Accessed January 2, 2012.

6. Entertainment Software Association. The transformation of the video game industry. ESA; 2011. Available at: http://www.theesa.com/games-improving-what-matters/ESA_FS_Transformation_2011.pdf. Accessed January 2, 2012.

7. Entertainment Software Association. Essential facts about games and violence. ESA; 2011. Available at: http://www.theesa.com/facts/pdfs/ESA_EF_About_Games_and_Violence.pdf. Accessed January 2, 2012.

8. Achtman RL, Green CS, Bavelier D. Video games as a tool to train visual skills. Restor Neurol Neurosci 2008;26(4-5):435-46.

9. Murphy R, Penuel W, Means B, et al. E-DESK: a review of recent evidence on the effectiveness of discrete educational software. Menlo Park (CA): SRI International; 2001.

10. Rhodes RE, Warburton DE, Bredin SS. Predicting the effect of interactive video bikes on exercise adherence: an efficacy trial. Psychol Health Med 2009;14(6): 631-40.

11. Greitemeyer T, Osswald S. Effects of prosocial video games on prosocial behavior. J Pers Soc Psychol 2010;98(2):211-21.

12. Sestir MA, Bartholow BD. Violent and nonviolent video games produce opposing effects on aggressive and prosocial outcomes. J Exp Soc Psychol 2010;46:934-42.

13. Anderson CA, Shibuya A, Ihori N, et al. Violent video game effects on aggression, empathy, and prosocial behavior in Eastern and Western countries. Psychol Bull 2010;136:151-73.

14. Carnagey NL, Anderson CA, Bushman BJ. The effect of video game violence on physiological desensitization to real-life violence. J Exp Soc Psychol 2007;43:489-96.

15. Bartholow BD, Sestir MA, Davis E. Correlates and consequences of exposure to video game violence: hostile personality, empathy, and aggressive behavior. Psychol Bull 2005;31:1573-86.

16. Bushman BJ, Anderson CA. Comfortably numb: desensitizing effects of violent media on helping others. Psychol Sci 2009;20:273-7.

17. Anderson CA, Gentile DA, Buckley KE. Violent video game effects on children and adolescents: theory, research, and public policy. New York: Oxford University Press; 2007.

18. Swing EL, Gentile DA, Anderson CA, et al. Television and video game exposure and the development of attention problems. Pediatrics 2010;126:214-21.

19. Anderson CA, Gentile DA, Dill KE. Prosocial, antisocial and other effects of recreational video games. In: Singer DG, Singer JL, editors. Handbook of children and the media. 2nd edition. Thousand Oaks (CA): Sage; 2012. p. 231-72.

20. Gentile DA, Gentile JR. Violent video games as exemplary teachers: a conceptual analysis. J Youth Adolesc 2008;9:127-41.

21. Gentile DA. The multiple dimensions of video game effects. Child Dev Perspect 2011;5:75-81.

22. Gentile DA, Stone W. Violent video game effects on children and adolescents: a review of the literature. Minerva Pediatr 2005;57:337-58.

23. Khoo A, Gentile DA. Problem based learning in the world of games. In: Tan OS, Hung D, editors. Problem-based learning and e-learning breakthroughs. Singapore: Thomson Publishing; 2007. p. 97-129.

24. Berkey CS, Rockett HRH, Field AE, et al. Activity, dietary intake, and weight changes in a longitudinal study of preadolescent and adolescent boys and girls. Pediatrics 2000;105:e56.

25. Cordes C, Miller E. Fool's gold: a critical look at computers in childhood. College Park (MD): Alliance for Childhood; 2000.

26. Hamalainen R. Designing and evaluating collaboration in a virtual game environment for vocational learning. Comput Educ 2008;50:98-109.

27. Green CS, Bavelier D. Action video game modifies visual selective attention. Nature 2003;423(6939):534-7.

28. Green CS, Bavelier D. Effect of action video games on the spatial distribution of visuospatial attention. J Exp Psychol Hum Percept Perform 2006;32(6):1465-78.

29. Green CS, Bavelier D. Action video game experience alters the spatial resolution of attention. Psychol Sci 2007;18(1):88-94.

30. Deutsch JE, Borbely M, Filler J, et al. Use of a low-cost, commercially available gaming console (Wii) for rehabilitation of an adolescent with cerebral palsy. Phys Ther 2008;8:1196-207.

31. Bushman BJ, Huesmann LR. Effects of televised violence on aggression. In: Singer D, Singer J, editors. Handbook of children and the media. Thousand Oaks (CA): Sage Publications; 2001. p. 223-54.

32. Gentile DA, Lynch PJ, Linder JR, et al. The effects of violent video game habits on adolescent hostility, aggressive behaviors, and school performance. J Adolesc 2004;27(1):5-22.

33. Anderson CA, Dill KE. Video games and aggressive thoughts, feelings, and behavior in the laboratory and in life. J Pers Soc Psychol 2000;78:772-90.

34. Funk JB, Baldacci HB, Pasold T, et al. Violence exposure in real-life, video games, television, movies, and the Internet: is there desensitization? J Adolesc 2004;27(1):23-39.

35. Kirsh SJ. Seeing the world through "Mortal Kombat" colored glasses: violent video games and the development of a short-term hostile attribution bias. Childhood 1998;5:177-84. Available at: http://chd.sagepub.com/content/5/2/177.abstract. Accessed March 16, 2012.

36. Carnagey NL, Anderson CA. The effects of reward and punishment in violent video games on aggressive affect, cognition, and behavior. Psychol Sci 2005; 16:882-9.

37. Ferguson CJ. Evidence for publication bias in video game violence effects literature: a meta-analytic review. Aggression and Violent Behaviour 2007;12:470-82.

38. Bailey K, West R, Anderson CA. The association between chronic exposure to video game violence and affective picture processing: an ERP study. Cogn Affect Behav Neurosci 2011;11:259-76.

39. Bartholow BD, Bushman BJ, Sestir MA. Chronic violent video game exposure and desensitization to violence: behavioral and event-related brain potential data. J Exp Soc Psychol 2005;42(2):283-90.

40. Bioulac S, Arfi L, Bouvard MP. Attention deficit/hyperactivity disorder and video games: a comparative study of hyperactive and control children. Eur Psychiatry 2008;23(2):134-41.

41. Mistry KB, Minkovitz CS, Strobino DM, et al. Children's television exposure and behavioral and social outcomes at 5.5 years: does timing of exposure matter? Pediatrics 2007;120:762-9.

42. Gentile DA, Swing EL, Lim CG, et al. Video game playing, attention problems, and impulsiveness: evidence of bidirectional causality. Psychology of Popular Media Culture 2012;1:62-70.

43. Bailey K, West R, Anderson CA. A negative association between video game experience and proactive cognitive control. Psychophysiology 2010;47:34-42.

44. Kronenberger WG, Mathews VP, Dunn DW, et al. Media violence exposure and executive functioning in aggressive and control adolescents. J Clin Psychol 2005;61(6):725-37.

45. Mathews VP, Kronenberger WG, Wang Y, et al. Media violence exposure and frontal lobe activation measured by functional magnetic resonance imaging in aggressive and nonaggressive adolescents. J Comput Assist Tomogr 2005;29:287-92.

46. Choo H, Gentile DA, Sim T, et al. Pathological video-gaming among Singaporean youth. Ann Acad Med Singapore 2010;39:822-9.

47. Gentile DA, Choo H, Liau A, et al. Pathological video game use among youth: a two-year longitudinal study. Pediatrics 2011;127:e319-29.

48. Peng LH, Li X. A survey of Chinese college students addicted to video games. China Education Innovation Herald 2009;28:111-2.

49. Porter G, Starcevic V, Berle D, et al. Recognizing problem video game use. Aust N Z J Psychiatry 2010;44:120-8.

50. Grüsser SM, Thalemann R, Griffiths MD. Excessive computer game playing: evidence for addiction and aggression? Cyberpsychol Behav 2007;10(2):290-2.

51. Ko CH, Yen JY, Yen CF, et al. Factors predictive for incidence and remission of Internet addiction in young adolescents: a prospective study. Cyberpsychol Behav 2007;10(4):545-51.

52. APA. DSM-V development. American Psychiatric Association; 2012. Available at: http://www.dsm5.org/Pages/Default.aspx. Accessed January 2, 2012.

53. Chan PA, Rabinowitz T. A cross-sectional analysis of video games and attention deficit hyperactivity disorder symptoms in adolescents. Ann Gen Psychiatr 2006;5:16.

54. Sharif I, Sargent JD. Association between television, movie, and video game exposure and school performance. Pediatrics 2006;118(4):1061-70.

55. Cummings HMM, Vandewater EAP. Relation of adolescent video game play to time spent in other activities. Arch Pediatr Adolesc Med 2007;161(7):684-9.

56. Dye MW, Green CS, Bavelier D. The development of attention skills in action video game players. Neuropsychologia 2009;47(8-9):1780-9.

57. Feng J, Spence I, Pratt J. Playing an action video game reduces gender differences in spatial cognition. Psychol Sci 2007;18(10):850-5.

58. Gopher D, Weil M, Bareket T. Transfer of skill from a computer game trainer to flight. Hum Factors 1994;36:1-19.

59. Corbett AT, Koedinger KR, Hadley W. Cognitive tutors: from the research classroom to all classrooms. In: Goodman PS, editor. Technology enhanced learning. Mahwah (NJ): Lawrence Erlbaum; 2001. p. 235-63.

60. Entertainment Software Association. Games: improving education. Available at: http://www.theesa.com/games-improving-what-matters/ESA_FS_Education_2011.pdf. Accessed January 2, 2012.

61. Flood S. All play and more work. In: Computing. 2006. Available at: http://www.computing.co.uk/computing/analysis/2152597/play-work. Accessed January 2, 2012.

62. Lieberman DA. Management of chronic pediatric diseases with interactive health games: Theory and research findings. J Ambul Care Manage 2001;24(1):26-38.

63. Brown SJ, Lieberman DA, Gemeny BA, et al. Educational video game for juvenile diabetes: results of a controlled trial. Med Inform 1997;22(1):77-89.

64. Kato PM, Cole SW, Bradlyn AS, et al. A video game improves behavioral outcomes in adolescents and young adults with cancer: a randomized trial. Pediatrics 2008;122:e305-17.

65. Klein MJ, Simmers CS. Exergaming: virtual inspiration, real perspiration. Young Consumers 2009;10:35-45.

66. Biddiss E, Irwin J. Active video games to promote physical activity in children and youth. Arch Pediatr Adolesc Med 2010;164(7):664-72.

67. Graf DL, Pratt LV, Hester CN, et al. Playing active video games increases energy expenditure in children. Pediatrics 2009;124(2):534-40.

68. Mellecker RR, McManus AM. Energy expenditure and cardiovascular responses to seated and active gaming in children. Arch Pediatr Adolesc Med 2008;162(9):886-91.

69. Tucker P. The physical activity levels of preschool-aged children: a systematic review. Early Child Res Q 2008;3(4):547-58.

70. Gentile DA, Anderson CA, Yukawa S, et al. The effects of prosocial video games on prosocial behaviors: international evidence from correlational, longitudinal, and experimental studies. Pers Soc Psychol Bull 2009;35(6):752-63.

71. Narvaez D, Mattan B, MacMichael C, et al. Kill bandits, collect gold or save the dying: the effects of playing a prosocial video game. Media Psychology Review 2008;1(1). Available at: http://mprcenter.org/mpr/index.php?option=com_content&view=article&id=35&Itemid=121.

72. Greitemeyer T, Osswald S. Prosocial video games reduce aggressive cognitions. J Exp Soc Psychol 2009;4:896-900.

73. Greitemeyer T, Osswald S. Playing prosocial video games increases the accessibility of prosocial thoughts. J Soc Psychol 2011;151(2):121-8.

74. Greitemeyer T, Osswald S, Brauer M. Playing prosocial video games increases empathy and decreases schadenfreude. Emotion 2010;10(6):796-802.

75. Gentile DA. The rating systems for media products. In: Calvert S, Wilson B, editors. Handbook of children, media, and development. Oxford (United Kingdom): Blackwell Publishing; 2008. p. 527-51.

76. Gentile DA, Oberg C, Sherwood NE, et al. Well-child exams in the video age: pediatricians and the AAP guidelines for children's media use. Pediatrics 2004; 114:1235-41.

Source: *Children, Adolescents, and the Media* 59.3 (2012): 647-58.

WHAT IT SAYS

1. What information does the third paragraph of this article give about the study to follow? How is this information helpful?

2. Drawing on the list in Box 2.1, briefly explain the negative and/or the positive effects of each dimension of video game playing, according to studies.

3. According to Prot et al., in what ways are the small effect sizes shown in Figure 2.1 important?

4. In what ways do violent video games increase the risk for aggressive behavior, according to some scholars? Prot et al. distinguish among experimental, correlational, and longitudinal studies. What do these terms mean?

5. Explain "chronic desensitization" and a "lack of helping behavior." What is meant by these phrases?

6. Explain how video games can lead to the negative effects discussed in the article. What is the "displacement hypothesis" as it relates to gaming?

7. Explain how video games can lead to the positive effects discussed in the article.

8. Prot et al. admit that they began their article with a "false dichotomy." What does this term mean, and what was their false dichotomy? According to the authors, what is another way of understanding video games, other than in terms of this false dichotomy?

HOW IT SAYS IT

1. How do the graphics in this article help to advance the overall argument? What purpose is served by a *variety* of graphic structures?

2. Who is the intended audience for this article? How can you tell?

3. How does Prot et al.'s admission that they began with a "false dichotomy" work to advance their argument?

WRITE ABOUT IT

1. Based on the findings in this study, write a public-health policy paper designed to protect children from the negative effects of playing video games, while maximizing the benefits.

2. Form a writing team and write a grant proposal for a follow-up study designed to test the results of at least one study mentioned by Prot et al. Imagine that the study's subjects will be your classmates (those other than the writing team). Before you begin, look for similar grant proposals for an idea about how to structure the proposal. Also, find at least three private or public institutions that might fund your study and direct your proposal to one of them.

3. Write and produce a short documentary on the effects of playing video games on public health in general, or on the health of young people in particular. Use existing video footage and photographs, and/or add your own images, interviews, etc., to existing footage.

b. Sara M. Grimes, "Getting (More) Girls into (More) Games"

Sara M. Grimes is an assistant professor of children's literature and new media at the University of Toronto, and visiting professor at the University of St. Michael's College. Her research and teaching focus on children's digital media cultures, child-generated content in digital games, play studies, and critical theories of technology in digital games. Grimes has published numerous articles in such journals as *New Media & Society*, *The Information Society*, the *International Journal of Media & Cultural Politics*, and *Communication, Culture & Critique*. She maintains her own research blog, *Gamine Expedition*, and contributes to such online forums as the *Escapist* magazine and *Shaping Youth*.

Grimes is associate director of the University of Toronto's Inclusive Design Institute, Mobile and Pervasive Computing Cluster, and is on the advisory boards of the Media Awareness Network's Young Canadians in a Wired World Phase 3, and Atmosphere Industries' "Privacy: The Game!" She holds a BA degree from the University of Ottawa, and MA and PhD degrees from Simon Fraser University, all in communication.

In this article, in light of a recent summit on girls, games, and gender, Grimes reflects on efforts in the 1980s and early 1990s to close the gender gap between male and female game players and game designers.

As You Read: Who among your friends and acquaintances plays video games? Do the females play games? Do the male and female gamers you know play different games? If so, how are they different? Do the males spend more time gaming than the females, or vice versa? In what ways might the gaming industry find your observations interesting or useful?

Getting (More) Girls into (More) Games

Years ago, when the idea of "games for learning" was still a relatively new concept, a small but important movement emerged around issues of gender in gaming. Led by scholars, designers and members of the game community, the primary objective was to address a gaming gender gap that had formed in the 80s and early 90s. Then as now, boys were generally gaming more (and more often) than girls, male characters appeared far more often than female characters within games, and there were far fewer women than men in the game industry. The "Girls Games Movement" articulated a growing concern about the hidden yet systematic ways in which girls were being deterred from entering into technology design, as well as other IT and engineering professions. By the mid-1990s, the movement had crystallized around a push for "female friendly" games and an emphasis on bringing more women into the industry.

With some important exceptions (see also That Game Company, Tale of Tales and Her Interactive), both missions fell markedly short of expectations. Ambiguous, often highly presumptuous, ideas about what constitutes "female-friendly" gave birth to a new genre of "pink games"—games that rely on (and reproduce) stereotypes about girls' likes and play preferences. Meanwhile, the mainstream game industry remains heavily male dominated.

While the issue of "girls and gaming" has resurfaced several times over the years, there has been a noticeable shift in approach. During the past decade, girls and women have continued to *play* digital games in greater and greater numbers. They have done this in various ways, from embracing mainstream games, to contributing to the massive success of gender-inclusive games like *Mario Kart* and *Dance Dance Revolution*, to sustaining a small but enduring "pink games" market. Much of the discussion has now shifted onto the importance of paying better attention to the games girls *do* play, and finding out more about how and why. The conversation has also broadened to include boys and men, through a more inclusive consideration of the issues that *all* players face when it comes to games and gender.

In other respects the gender gap first observed in the 1990s remains as wide as ever. Girls and women are more likely to play free, online and "casual" games, as opposed to the console, computer or subscription games considered as "core" within game culture. They are less likely to own, select or purchase their own game technologies. There is still a notable lack of women working as designers and programmers—a disparity found across the IT industries, where female participation has actually decreased since the 1980s.

These were some of the issues addressed at the 3G Summit: The Future of Girls, Games and Gender, held this past summer at Columbia College in Chicago. The event brought together 50 teenage girls from local schools with five leading female game designers and scholars (Mary Flanagan, Susan Ruiz, Jennifer Jensen, Erin Robinson and Tracy Fullerton) for four days of dialogue, design workshops and gaming. A key theme of the event was breaking down barriers that keep girls out of game design, thereby disrupting the cycle of self-perpetuating *status quo* that has developed within mainstream game culture.

The 3G participants had some great ideas about how this might be done. Highlighting the immense flexibility of the growing independent games market, they encouraged girls and boys to start carving out their own niches, and not to be afraid of redefining and realizing their own visions of what a "game" can be. I think that this time, the call to action has come at a uniquely opportune moment. Not only are we now seeing entire schools built around game design (i.e., Katie Salen's Quest to Learn), but entry into game creation has become more accessible (and fun) than ever. Just look at the recent outcrop of "user-generated content" tools found in games such as *Little Big Planet* and *Kodu*. Not to mention the emergence of easy-to-use design platforms like *Scratch*.

I'm hopeful that these tools will open up game design to girls and young women, as well as boys who might not otherwise feel drawn to (or even welcome in) design and programming. The focus that these games and tools place on creativity, fun and community-building (i.e., sharing your creations with other players) also provides an alternative entry point into STEM—one that enables kids to merge technical skill development with their own interests, creativity and storytelling practices. I can't wait to see what games girls will produce when given the tools and encouragement to let their imaginations run wild. After all, kids are the consummate experts when it comes to finding new and innovative ways to play.

Source: Blog post. *The Joan Ganz Cooney Center at Sesame Workshop: Advancing Children's Learning in a Digital Age.* Oct.-Nov. 2010. Web. http://www.joanganzcooneycenter. org/2010/10/22/getting-more-girls-into-more-games/.

WHAT IT SAYS

1. What is the Girls Games Movement, and what circumstances caused its formation?
2. What resulted from the Girls Games Movement in the 1990s? What are "pink games"?
3. What has happened to the Girls Games Movement since the 1990s?
4. What was the 3G Summit? What were its goals?
5. What does Grimes think of the state of girls in gaming today?
6. What does Grimes foresee happening to the way games are played, and who plays them?

HOW IT SAYS IT

1. What effect does Grimes's use of the first-person perspective have on the success of her argument?
2. Who does Grimes seem to be writing to in this blog? How can you tell?
3. What effect does the structure of Grimes's article (the way in which she organizes her information) have on the success of her argument?

WRITE ABOUT IT

1. Conduct an online search of articles on the 3G Summit. Write a comparison paper that analyzes the various ways in which the reports discuss the summit.
2. Write and produce a short documentary on gender issues in contemporary gaming. Use existing video footage and photographs and/or add your own images, interviews, etc., to existing footage.

c. Lesley S.J. Farmer, "Are Girls Game? How School Libraries Can Provide Gender Equity in E-Gaming"

Lesley S.J. Farmer is a professor of librarianship at California State University, Long Beach. Her more than 20 books include *Instructional Design for Librarians and Information Professionals* (2011), *The Neal-Schuman Technology Management Handbook for School Library Media Centers* (with Marc E. McPhee, 2010), and *Teen Girls and Technology: What's the Problem, What's the Solution?* (2008).

She is the recipient of the American Library Association's 2011 Beta Phi Mu Award, donated by the Beta Phi Mu International Library Honorary Society for distinguished service to education in librarianship.

Farmer holds an MS in library science from the University of North Carolina at Chapel Hill, and a PhD in adult education from Temple University.

In this article, Farmer discusses ways for school librarians to encourage more girls to engage in computer games, and makes a case for the role of e-gaming in enhancing learning.

As You Read: Consider ways in which playing video games has enhanced—or detracted from—your ability to learn. Has Farmer's article changed your mind about the positive role of e-gaming in education? What kinds of gender differences have you noticed among your peers in regards to e-gaming?

Are Girls Game? How School Libraries Can Provide Gender Equity in E-Gaming

Gaming has come to the library. School librarians are increasingly incorporating gaming into their program of resources and services. Besides addressing the natural interest that youth have in games, school librarians recognize the educational benefits of games, particularly in terms of information and digital literacies. While board games have been around for centuries, e-gaming (that is, playing video, console, and computer games) is a relatively new phenomenon. And, unlike board games that have interested both sexes, e-games seem to engage boys more than girls. How can school librarians address this apparent inequity and provide positive e-gaming experiences for all students?

The Youthful World of E-Gaming

E-games have come a long way from the early days of Pong. In 2010 the US video game industry, encompassing almost nine thousand companies, posted $40.7 billion in revenues and $2-3 billion in profits. Two-thirds of the market segment consisted of games and software; another quarter consisted of consoles and accessories, and online subscriptions accounted for the rest (Thormahlen 2011). Two-thirds of US homes own either a console or PC used to run e-games, and almost half of household heads play e-games on cell phones or PDAs (Entertainment Software Association 2011).

Even a decade ago, nearly all children played e-games or knew someone who did. By 2008, 97 percent of teens played video games, with three-quarters playing weekly, and a third playing daily; most played socially, with only a quarter usually playing alone (Kahne, Middaugh, and Evans 2008).

Gender Differences in E-Gaming

The face of e-gamers has changed recently. It is no longer a male domain; females now comprise forty percent of the e-gaming population, largely due to Nintendo's Wii and cell-phone casual e-games (Thormahlen 2011). Nevertheless, male youth tend to play e-games more frequently and for a longer time than do girls; the difference being most glaring between younger boys and older girls—the latter accounting for only 4 percent of the total video-game audience (Nielsen 2007).

More importantly, gaming practices differ along gender lines during teenage years. As girls enter puberty, their e-gaming activity drops significantly, largely because of continuing gendered perceptions about e-gaming. As teens explore their sexual identity, they are more sensitive to sexual stereotypes, and girls tend to distance themselves from the mechanical and violent nature of some e-games (Agosto 2004). Girls also have difficulty identifying themselves with the characters, which tend to be male or non-human; moreover, the default female characters represent stereotypical sexualized images (Graner Ray 2004). In addition, girls are more likely to give up on a complicated game than are boys, and if girls have negative first experiences, they are less likely to become long-term gamers (Forssell 2008). Even seasoned girl gamers do not fit a simple boy-girl dichotomy because they tend to particularize their gaming behavior. Nonetheless, gendered differences fade with experience and age (Beavis and Charles 2007). These gendered differences can impact girls' futures. For instance, girls may generalize their negative e-gaming experiences, and avoid technology courses in college or as part of professional development.

As more courses incorporate e-gaming activities, girls may find themselves disadvantaged in such learning environments. Furthermore, since 85 percent of jobs now involve technology, girls who shy away from technology because of e-gaming failure may self-limit their professional options. Their avoidance of technology results in lost contributions to society.

Why E-Games?

E-gaming can be so engaging that it can detract from academics, but it can also foster 21st-century skills of information literacy, problem solving, communication, and collaboration. In terms of learning theory, e-gaming is usually associated with activity theory, which relates a subject and an object with mediational means; tools also mediate between the player and the larger culture. The characteristics of activity-theory-based gaming inform teaching and learning in several ways, according to Brian Myers: use of fixed, equitable structure and rules; clear goals within a rich context that provide meaning and relevance; opportunities to explore identities; cognitive and affective engagement; specific and timely feedback; and sense of control and personal investment (2008). These elements all resonate with girls, so the key to success for learning through e-games is gender-sensitive implementation.

E-games per se will not guarantee effective learning. Like other learning activities, they need to address academic content and concepts, and build skills and knowledge as players evaluate circumstances and solve problems successfully within the time frame available. Additionally, intentional instructional design to incorporate e-gaming is required; merely assigning an e-game without context and rationale will turn off girls in particular. On the other hand, when incorporated thoughtfully, e-games can introduce technology through motivating activities, improve problem-solving and collaboration skills, enhance spatial skills, and increase self-efficacy, all of which especially benefit girls (Brosnan 1998, Cooper and Weaver 2003). In short, when e-games are introduced in gender-inclusive ways, all students can succeed academically and psychologically.

E-Games in School Libraries

As school library programs support the academic and personal needs of students, these programs are trying to reach out to their population more proactively, meeting them on youth's territory. In terms of e-gaming, that can include gaming books, physical access and online links to educationally appropriate e-games, and incorporation of e-gaming in instruction. In the process, school librarians should consider the interests of girls in their game selection so that both sexes can enjoy e-gaming experiences.

Works Cited

Agosto, Denise E. 2004. "Girls and Gaming: A Summary of the Research with Implications for Practice." *Teacher Librarian* 31, no. 3 (February), 8-14.

Beavis, Catherine, and Claire Charles. 2007. "Would the 'Real' Girl Gamer Please Stand Up? Gender, LAN Cafés, and The Reformulation of the 'Girl' Gamer." *Gender & Education* 19, No. 6 (November), 691-705.

Brosnan, Mark J. 1998. "The Impact of Psychological Gender, Gender-Related Perceptions, Significant Others, and the Introduction of Technology upon Computer Anxiety in Students." *Journal of Educational Computing Research* 18, no. 1, 63-78.

Cooper, Joel, and Kimberlee D. Weaver. 2003. *Gender and Computers: Understanding the Digital Divide*. Mahwah, NJ: Erlbaum.

Entertainment Software Association. 2011. "Game Player Data." www.theesa. com/facts/gameplayer/asp.

Forssell, Karen S. 2008. "Girls, Games, and Getting Interested in Technology." *Proceedings of Society for Information Technology and Teacher Education International Conference 2008*. K. McFerrin, et al., eds. Chesapeake, VA: American Association of Computer Education, 991-96.

Graner Ray, Sheri. 2004. *Gender-Inclusive Game Design: Expanding the Market*. Hingham, MA: Charles River Media.

Kahne, Joseph, Ellen Middough, and Chris Evans. 2008. *The Civic Potential of Video Games*. Boston: MacArthur Foundation.

Myers, Brian. 2008. "Minds at Play: Using Computer Game Design to Promote Media Literacy." *American Libraries* 39, no. 5 (May), 54-57.

Nielsen Company. 2008. *The State of the Console*. Chicago: Nielsen.

Thormahlen, C. 2001. "Video Games in the U.S." IBISWorld Industry Report. Los Angeles: IBISWorld.

Source: *Knowledge Quest* 40.1 (2011): 16-17.

WHAT IT SAYS

1. What issue in e-gaming does Farmer's article address?

2. What claim does Farmer make in the section, "The Youthful World of E-Gaming"? What evidence does she use to support this claim?

3. What claims does Farmer make about gender differences in e-gaming? What reasons does she give in support of this claim?

4. How do these gender differences in youthful gaming affect girls as they mature? What is the social impact of these effects, according to Farmer?

5. E-gaming can foster information literacy, problem solving, communication, and collaboration, according to Farmer. In what specific ways do games foster these skills? Look up and explain any terms you do not understand.

6. Why does Farmer recommend "gender-sensitive implementation" of e-gaming in school? What kinds of e-gaming programs does she recommend?

HOW IT SAYS IT

1. How do the subtitled section divisions in this article work to help Farmer make her argument?

2. Who is the intended audience for this article? How can you tell?

3. How does Farmer use ethos to promote her argument? Consider both the author introduction and the article itself.

WRITE ABOUT IT

1. Write a proposal to your city's public school board or to your state board of education that is designed to implement Farmer's recommendations for e-gaming as an educational asset, and her suggestions for addressing gender differences in e-gaming. Before you begin, research the content and structure of these kinds of proposals.

2. Form a writing team and write a grant proposal to provide funds for e-gaming programs in your town's public libraries or public schools. Be sure to make a strong case for these programs as promoting youth education and narrowing gender gaps. Before you begin, look for similar grant proposals for an idea about how to structure the proposal. Also, find at least three private or public institutions that might fund your study and direct your proposal to one of them.

3. Write and produce a short documentary on the effects of the gender gap in e-gaming on girls and women. Use existing video footage and photographs, and/or add your own images, interviews, etc., to existing footage.

d. Kristin McCombs, Bryan Raudenbush, Andrea Bova, and Mark Sappington, "Effects of Peppermint Scent Administration on Cognitive Video Game Performance"

Kristin McCombs is a PhD student in educational psychology at Kent State University, where she teaches psychology and works at the Center for Educational Technologies. She also teaches dance to youth. McCombs holds a BA in psychology and history from Wheeling Jesuit University in Wheeling, West Virginia, and an MA in educational psychology research methodology from the University of Pittsburgh.

Bryan Raudenbush is an associate professor of psychology, department chair, and director of undergraduate research at Wheeling Jesuit University. He is the author of *The Psychology of Food and Eating* (1995) and *Statistics for the Behavioral Sciences* (2004), as well as numerous book chapters and journal articles. Raudenbush holds a BS in psychology from Pennsylvania State University, an MS in experimental psychology from Shippensburg University, and a PhD in physiological psychology from the University of Cincinnati.

Andrea Bova is an undergraduate psychology major at Wheeling Jesuit University. She graduated from Baldwin High School in Pittsburgh.

Mark Sappington is an undergraduate psychology major at Wheeling Jesuit University. He graduated from University High School in Morgantown, West Virginia.

In this article, McCombs et al. report on their testing of previous studies, which showed that video gamers performed better when they sniffed peppermint while gaming. In this study, the researchers tracked both video game performance and changes in pulse and blood pressure in participants who inhaled peppermint while playing video games. The study follows the IMRAD (introduction, methods, results, and discussion) structure common in social and physical science writing.

As You Read: Think about the factors that seem to make you play video games better—or worse. Have you noticed that certain smells, noises, room temperature, or locations affect your performance? Do you play better when relaxed, or when excited?

Effects of Peppermint Scent Administration on Cognitive Video Game Performance

Past research suggests the positive effects of both video game play and the benefits of peppermint scent administration. The present study assessed the combination of video game play and peppermint scent administration on physiology, mood, game performance, and task load. Participants completed a control condition with no scent administration to serve as a baseline, and were then assigned to either repeat the control condition or to complete an experimental condition in which peppermint scent was delivered via nasal cannula at 3 LPM. Participants played 3 Nintendo *Wii Fit Plus* games requiring cognitive and hand/eye reactions (*Perfect 10*, *Snowball Fight*, and *Obstacle Course*). Participants in the peppermint scent condition showed greater improvements, such as completing significantly more levels, more hits, more stars, and distance completed. Further, participants in the peppermint condition reported less mental demand, perceived effort, and anxiety. Control group participants had a significantly lower pulse change and diastolic blood pressure change, whereas, participants in the peppermint scent condition experienced no significant difference in pulse suggesting that the scent administration promoted greater physiological arousal, thus keeping them engaged in the testing process. Implications include the combination of video games and a physiologically arousing scent (specifically, peppermint) to further promote cognitive performance.

A struggle within the realm of video game research involves the games' so-called "bad reputation." As many video games involve violence, aggression, addiction, and gender bias (Selfton-Green, 2005; Schrader & McCreery, 2007), many critics dismiss them as learning tools entirely, despite the widespread appeal and educational value they may possess. This "bad reputation" stems from the violence and illegality portrayed in games such as *Grand Theft Auto* and from the demeaning sexuality illustrated in games such as *Dead or Alive* (Gee, 2003). Other games, such as the violent African zombie game *Resident Evil 5*, create controversy for their racial stereotyping. Because, in part, of the huge popularity of such games, other more socially or educationally appropriate games have been overshadowed. However, the Nintendo *Wii* game system is changing the way video games are considered; many of that system's games involve an active and family-friendly approach to video game play.

Despite the occasionally questionable outlook on video games, research and real world findings note their benefits and applicability. The games themselves can provide goals for the player, positive reinforcement, and increasing challenge as he or she progresses through different levels (Gee, 2003). Games can support intrinsic motivation, since many require the player to be actively engaged through observing the environment, discover new aspects to a particular level or challenge, and solve problems (Dickey, 2005).

A subcategory of educational gaming is "edutainment." Games in this category include Nintendo's *Brain Age* and *Big Brain Academy* which aim to improve logic, memory, and mathematical skill, amongst other cognitive challenges, and Playstation 2's *Konami Kid Playground*, which is a game that teaches numbers, letters, colors, and shapes to preschoolers. Such games are targeted towards a mass market, i.e. not aimed for classroom use exclusively, and are intended to teach the user a skill or content while he or she has fun progressing through the levels of the game.

Thus, it becomes important to describe a context when such learning is of importance. Educational implications of gaming are diverse. The current study hopes to quantify the cognitive benefits of video game use in a non-formal learning environment. Although it is still fairly new to the market, the majority of the use of the Nintendo *Wii* game system is for entertainment purposes and, more seriously but less frequently, for rehabilitation purposes (Peltier, 2007). However, new games are being developed that tie into the Nintendo brand's broader goals of reaching a wide range of ages and engaging them in a wide variety of activities. While some research on the *Wii*'s rehabilitation abilities suggests that it can be effectively used to help rehabilitate stroke victims and cardiac patients as well as help physical therapy patients to improve their range of motion (Peltier, 2007), the *Wii* has not yet been used to study cognition.

Shin and Rosenbaum (2002) examined the ways in which cognitive and perceptual motor processes coordinate in a video arithmetic task. In their study, participants completed a video game task that involved arithmetic, aiming, or both. Results indicate that aiming occurred faster in the non-combined tasks. This suggests that a distraction of an additional task may hinder performance. Likewise, the current study hopes to examine how cognitive function can be enhanced through scent and gaming. Further, Barlett, Vowels, Shanteau, Crow, and Miller (2009) studied the impact of computer games on cognitive performance and found that participants who did not play a game showed no cognitive change while participants that played either a violent or non-violent game showed an increase in cognitive performance. Lee and LaRose (2007) assessed various mechanisms of video game consumption behaviors. Results indicate that those who had low amounts of experience had less self-regulation and habit strength than regular players.

Essentially, this means that regular gamers handle input from video games more efficiently than do novice gamers. Additionally, several studies suggest the benefit scents can have on performance and mood. Zoladz and Raudenbush (2005) examined the effects of scents on cognition and found a task-dependent relationship between scent and the enhancement of cognitive processing. Specifically, cinnamon scent improved participants' scores on tasks related to attentional processes, virtual recognition memory, working memory, and visual-motor response speed. This research suggests that certain scents have the ability to increase cognitive performance. Similarly, Moss, Hewitt, Moss, and Wesnes (2008) examined scent-influenced cognitive performance and showed that peppermint scent enhanced memory whereas ylang-ylang both impaired it and lengthened processing speed.

Diego, Jones, Field, Hernandez-Reif, Schanberg, Kuhn, McAdam, Galamaga, and Galamaga (1998) studied the effects of lavender and rosemary scent administration on alertness, math computations, and mood. The lavender group showed increased alertness and performed the math computations faster and more accurately, while also indicating a more relaxed and less depressed mood. Those participants in the rosemary group showed increased cognition; however, only the speed of their math computations increased following scent administration, not their accuracy. Participants in this group reported that they felt more alert and relaxed as well as lower levels of anxiety.

Finally, Moss, Cook, Wesnes, and Duckett (2003) researched the olfactory impact of lavender and rosemary oils on memory tasks and attention. Lavender was found to impair both memory and attention. Rosemary showed a significant increase in performance for memory; however, rosemary negatively impacted the speed of memory. The lavender and control groups were significantly less alert than the rosemary group. Combined results of this study show that olfactory properties can produce objective effects on performance.

Thus, a foundation of previous research supports the current need for an examination of the effects of scent administration on cognition during video game play. Potential implications for positive findings from this research include using scent to enhance cognitive performance in other settings, such as a classroom, with the goal of raising test performance. The present study examines the effects of peppermint scent on video game performance using the Nintendo *Wii Fit Plus* game system, specifically for three games related to cognition and judgment. It is hypothesized that peppermint scent administration will promote greater performance during game play than an unscented control condition.

Method

PARTICIPANTS

The participants consisted of 32 students who were enrolled in a university psychology class. Students received course credit for their participation if they needed it. Participants ranged in age from 17 to 22 years of age. Those who had not yet turned 18 had parent or guardian consent to participate in the study. All participants were Caucasian.

GAMING

The participants played three games on the Nintendo *Wii Fit Plus* game:

Perfect 10: On the television screen, balls containing numbers are displayed. Participants must shift their weight to highlight the appropriate balls to add up to 20 while standing on the balance board. Both positive and negative numbers are displayed as difficulty increases through rounds of the game. All participants played on the expert difficulty level, which has 20 rounds.

Snowball Fight: During this game, the participant's avatar is placed behind a shield, and the participant must shift weight on the *Wii* balance board to see other characters in the snowball fight to throw snowballs at them with the *Wii* remote. The players' life levels are affected if they are hit with snowballs in quick succession. It is possible for the players' avatar to be knocked unconscious in this game, which ends the 90 seconds allotted for the game.

Obstacle Course: In this game, participants run in place on the balance board. They must consider the timing of their steps as they are faced with obstacles, such as slippery ice, rolling logs, and swinging bombs, in the multi-level course. The game was played on the hard level.

INSTRUMENTS

An Omron Automatic Blood Pressure Monitor (Model HEM 705CP) was used to measure participants' blood pressure and pulse readings.

To assess mood, participants completed the *Profile of Mood States* (POMS; McNair, Lorr, & Droppleman, 1971). The POMS consists of a list of 65 adjectives concerning mood. Participants indicate the extent to which each adjective describes them at a particular moment using a 5-point scale. In addition to being able to assess each of the 65 adjectives, the POMS also contains summative subscales related to depression, fatigue, tension, anxiety, and vigor. The POMS is a widely-used scale that has adequate reliability and validity (McNair, Lorr, & Droppleman, 1971).

Participants also completed the *NASA Task Load Index* (NASA-TLX; Hart & Staveland, 1998). The NASA-TLX is a multidimensional scale which measures both overall workload as well as specific components of workload in a given task along with three dimensions (mental, physical, and temporal demand) related to the demands imposed upon the participant by the task, and the three dimensions (effort, frustration, and performance) related to the interaction of the participant and the task. For this scale, participants are asked to make a mark on a 120cm line with ends marked low to high. If participants place their mark near the left side of the line, it is considered to be a low rating, whereas if the mark is near the right side of the line, it is considered to be a high rating. The left and right sides of the line are labeled as low or high, respectively. The scale has been shown to have adequate reliability and validity based on data from 3,461 participants from two population databases (Hart & Staveland, 1988).

Finally, participants completed a general video game questionnaire asking game play preferences and the number of hours each week video games are played. Video game experience information was collected for use as possible covariates in data analysis.

PROCEDURE

Participation required two visits, with each visit lasting approximately 40 minutes. During the first visit, participants were taken to a separate testing room to play the *Wii*. Participants rested for 5 minutes before baseline physiological measures were taken. All participants completed a control session first, to serve as a baseline. During this session, participants wore a nasal cannula delivering oxygen at 3LMP. The participant was instructed to play 3 games on the Wii Fit Plus game for the Nintendo *Wii* game system: *Perfect 10*, *Snowball Fight*, and *Obstacle Course*. Upon completion of the *Wii* session, participants completed the POMS (McNair, Lorr, & Droppleman, 1971) and NASA-TLX (Hart & Staveland, 1998) was administered along with the gaming questionnaire.

For the second visit, participants were randomly assigned to one of two conditions: a control condition that was exactly like their first visit, or an experimental condition during which peppermint-scented oxygen was delivered through the cannula at 3 LPM. The experimental session was otherwise similar to the control session. The division of the second visit into two groups was done to have comparison groups.

Results

Data were analyzed using paired sample *t*-tests using the control and peppermint scent conditions as two separate groups. See Table 2.2 for means, standard deviations, and statistical outcomes.

For those in the peppermint condition, a statistically significant difference was found as the number of levels completed increased for the second visit for *Perfect 10*. Statistical significance was also found in the number of hits during *Snowball Fight*, as well as the number of stars participants earned, which indicate a higher level of success. The third game, *Obstacle Course*, showed significant differences in the number of levels completed and distance completed on the course, again with the peppermint group showing an increase for both.

Analysis of the NASA-TLX showed participants in the peppermint condition indicated more mental demand, more perceived effort, and more anxiety. This suggests peppermint kept them more engaged in the gaming process.

In terms of physiological data, participants in the control group had a significantly lower pre/post pulse change and a trend for a lower pre/post diastolic blood pressure change at the end of their session; whereas, participants in the peppermint scent condition experienced no significant difference in pulse from pre to post, suggesting that the scent administration promoted greater physiological arousal, thus keeping them engaged in the testing process. No statistical significance was found for any of the subscales of the POMS.

TABLE 2.2. Means, SDs, and Statistical Analyses for the Control and Peppermint Conditions among the Assessment Measures

	CONTROL				
	Pre	Post	t	df	p
Measure	$M\ (SD)$	$M\ (SD)$			
Perfect 10 levels completed	18.0 (5.4)	21.5 (5.0)	-4.0	16	.001
Snowball hits	11.5 (7.8)	19.2 (10.3)			
-4.0	16	.001			
Snowball stars	1.1 (.05)	1.8 (0.8)	-3.4	16	.003
Obstacle levels	1.2 (1.1)	1.1 (1.1)	.4	16	.67
Obstacle distance	180.3 (144)	144.7 (163)	1.2	12	.26
Mental demand	58.0 (30.2)	49.9 (27.2)	1.5	16	.16
Effort	55.2 (32.8)	55.6 (27.8)			
-0.5	16	.96			
Anxiety	8.1 (4.0)	8.5 (6.2)	-0.3	16	.76
Systolic BP	-2.9 (13.6)	0.3 (17.4)	-0.6	15	.538
Diastolic BP	-1.4 (6.6)	5.8 (11.8)	3.1	15	.008
Pulse	4.5 (8.1)	-3.2 (15.0)	2.1	15	.058
	PEPPERMINT				
	Pre	Post	t	df	p
Measure	$M\ (SD)$	$M\ (SD)$			
Perfect 10 levels completed	19.6 (5.8)	22.4 (4.4)	-3.0	14	.01
Snowball hits	16.7 (9.1)	24.3 (9.0)	-4.0	14	.001
Snowball stars	1.5 (.05)	2.0 (0.7)	-4.0	14	.001
Obstacle levels	0.6 (.80)	1.3 (0.9)	-2.9	14	.012
Obstacle distance	83.9 (70)	140.3 (94.1)	-2.0	9	.08
Mental demand	62.5 (29.7)	53.4 (22.3)	2.0	14	.07
Effort	77.9 (19.0)	68.7 (23.4)	2.4	14	.039
Anxiety	12.5 (7.3)	9.8 (5.5)	2.4	14	.031
Systolic BP	-1.2 (15.3)	-5.7 (19.7)	0.9	14	.376
Diastolic BP	1.2 (13.2)	0.1 (14.3)	0.4	14	.699
Pulse	-1.0 (14.5)	5.2 (16.7)	-1.7	14	.118

Discussion

As previous research suggests, peppermint scent administration can be an effective adjunct to learning and attention. The results of the current study support the benefits of peppermint scent administration in several ways, such as performance and perceived task load. In terms of performance, participants' improvement in the experimental condition (peppermint scent administration) was significantly higher than participants' improvement in the control condition (no scent administration). Participants in the peppermint scent administration condition rated their perceived mental demand lower than the mental demand perceived by participants in the control group. Also, effort ratings for those in the peppermint scent administration condition improved over time. Zoladz and Raudenbush (2005) reported that peppermint scent administration enhanced performance on tasks related to attention, memory, and response speed and Raudenbush, Grayhem, Sears, and Wilson (2009) found that scent improved alertness, mood, and workload during simulated driving tasks. With individuals feeling less fatigued on tasks when peppermint scent is administered, it may be advantageous to present the scent when facing a grueling task. Further, when individuals are exposed to a pleasant scent, cognitive functioning improves in terms of speed, accuracy, and memory (Wilmes, Harrington, Kohler-Evans, & Sumpter, 2008).

As the study by Barker, Grayhem, Koon, Perkins, Whalen, and Raudenbush (2003) suggested, peppermint scent can improve performance on tasks related to speed and accuracy. While the Barker et al. (2003) study focused on clerical skills and the present study assessed video game play performance, future research could apply these findings to an ecologically valid classroom learning experience.

References

Barker, S., Grayhem, P., Perkins, J., Whalen, A., & Raudenbush, B. (2003). Improved performance on clerical tasks associated with administration of peppermint odor. *Perceptual and Motor Skills, 97*, 1007-1010.

Barlett, C., Vowels, C., Shanteau, J., Crow, J., & Miller, T. (2009). The effect of violent and non-violent computer games on cognitive performance. *Computers in Human Behavior, 25*(1), 96-102.

Dickey, M. (2005). Engaging by design: How engagement strategies in popular computer and video games can inform instructional design. *Educational Technology Research & Development, 53*(2), 67-83.

Diego, M., Jones, N., Field, T., Hernandez-Reif, M., Scanberg, S., Kuhn, C., McAdam, V., & Galamaga, M. (1998). Aromatherapy positively effects mood, EEG patterns of alertness and math computations. *The International Journal of Neuroscience, 96*(3-4), 217-224.

Gee, J. (2003). *What video games have to teach us about learning and literacy*. New York: Palgrave Macmillan.

Hart, S., & Staveland, L. (1998). Development of a multi-dimensional workload rating scale: Results of empirical and theoretical research. In P.A. Hancock and N. Meshkati (Eds), *Human Mental Workload*. Amsterdam: Elsevier.

Lee, D., & LaRose, R. (2007). A socio-cognitive model of video game usage. *Journal of Broadcasting & Electronic Media, 51*(4), 632-650.

McNair, D., Lorr, M., & Droppleman, L. (1971). *Profile of Mood States*. San Diego, CA: Educational and Industrial Testing Service.

Moss, M., Cook, J., Wesnes, K., & Duckett, P. (2003). Aromas of rosemary and lavender essential oils differentially affect cognition and mood in healthy adults. *International Journal of Neuroscience, 113*(1), 15.

Moss, M., Hewitt, S., Moss, L., & Wesnes, K. (2008). Modulation of cognitive performance and mood by aromas of peppermint and ylang-ylang. *International Journal of Neuroscience, 118*(1), 59-77.

Peltier, M. (2007). Wii can work it out. *Nursing Homes: Long Care Management, 56*(9), 72-73.

Raudenbush, B., Grayhem, R., Sears, T., & Wilson, I. (2009). Effects of peppermint and cinnamon odor administration on simulated driving alertness, mood, and workload. *North American Journal of Psychology, 11*(2), 245-256.

Schrader, P., & McCreery, M. (2007). The acquisition of skill and expertise in massively multiplayer online games. *Educational Technology Research and Development, 56*(5-6), 557-574.

Sefton-Green, J. (2005). Changing the rules? Computer games, theory, learning and play. *Discourse: studies in the cultural politics of education, 26*(3), 411-419.

Shin, J., & Rosenbaum, D. (2002). Reaching while calculating: Scheduling of cognitive and perceptual-motor processes. *Journal of Experimental Psychology: General, 131*(2), 206-219.

Simpson, E. (2005). What teachers need to know about the video game generation. *Tech Trends: Linking research and practice to improve learning, 49*(5), 17-22.

Wilmes, B., Harrington, L., Kohler-Evans, P., & Sumpter, D. (2008). Coming to our senses: Incorporating brain research findings into classroom instruction. *Education, 128*(4), 659-666.

Zoladz, P., & Raudenbush, B. (2005). Cognitive enhancement through stimulation of the chemical senses. *North American Journal of Psychology, 7*(1), 125-138.

Source: *North American Journal of Psychology* 13.3 (2011): 383-90.

WHAT IT SAYS

1. What issues in video game research does this study address?

2. What is the goal or purpose of this study?

3. How does this study differ from similar studies? What results have these earlier studies revealed? You may wish to answer this with a chart or list.

4. Why is this study important, according to McCombs et al.?

5. What is the hypothesis of this study?

6. Why did participation in this study require two visits, or testing periods? In what ways was the second visit different from the first?

7. In general, what were the results of the test? What did these results suggest, according to McCombs et al.?

HOW IT SAYS IT

1. How does Table 2.2 work to promote the study's conclusion?

2. Who is the intended audience for this article? How can you tell?

3. How do the numerous citations of previous studies, both in the text and in the reference list, work to promote this study's argument?

WRITE ABOUT IT

1. Create a synthesis grid that includes all the studies mentioned in McCombs et al. Before you begin, review the section on synthesis grids in the Guide to academic writing (pp. 77–79).

2. Working as a group, design, carry out, and write a report on a brief study intended to reproduce the results of McCombs et al. Use your classmates as study participants.

3. Write a proposal addressed to an administrator or administrative committee at your university that uses McCombs et al.'s results to recommend the use of peppermint to improve cognitive functioning on campus. Propose practical ways for the program to be implemented, including ways to administer peppermint to students. Address the moral and legal implications of this program. Before you begin, look for similar grant proposals for ideas about how to structure the proposal.

e. Stephen R. Burgess, Steven Paul Stermer, and Melinda C.R. Burgess, "Video Game Playing and Academic Performance in College Students"

Stephen R. Burgess is an associate professor of psychology at Southwestern Oklahoma State University, where his research focuses on literacy and comprehension development, influence of attitudes and prior knowledge on decision making and critical-thinking ability, and stereotype development and use in decision making. His many articles have been published in *Reading and Writing: An Interdisciplinary Journal*, *Early Child Development and Care*, and *Journal of Educational Psychology*, among other publications. Burgess holds a BA from Wake Forest University, an MA from Hollins College, and a PhD degree from Florida State University, all in psychology.

Steven Paul Stermer is a graduate student in the PhD program in psychology at Oklahoma State University, where his research focuses on the influence of video games on aggressive and sexist attitudes and behaviors, and on alcohol use. He has co-published articles on these topics in such journals as *Social Cognition*, *Psychology of Popular Media Culture*, and *Social and Personality Psychology Compass*. Stermer holds a BS from Southwestern Oklahoma State University and an MS in psychology from Oklahoma State University.

Melinda C.R. Burgess is an associate professor of psychology at Southwestern Oklahoma State University. She is author of the book *The Cross Race Effect in Facial Recognition: A Function of Expertise?* (1997) and a chapter on media imagery and social learning in *The Psychology of Entertainment Media* (with Karen E. Dill, 2012), and has co-published numerous journal articles on sexual and racial stereotypes in video games, and on experienced players' desensitization to violence.

In this article, Burgess, Stermer, and Burgess investigate the ways in which playing video games during college affects students' grades, and contemplate the reasons for these effects.

As You Read: Think about your own video gaming habits. Has gaming affected your performance in school? If so, how? If not, why not? What effect has gaming had on the attitudes and school performance of your fellow students?

Video Game Playing and Academic Performance in College Students

Introduction

The relations between media consumption, especially TV viewing, and school performance have been extensively examined. However, even though video game playing may have replaced TV viewing as the most frequent form of media usage, relatively little research has examined its relations to school performance, especially in older students. We surveyed 671 college students concerning their history of video game usage and school performance. In general, video game players had lower GPAs, but this finding varied by gender. Video game players also reported a greater likelihood of playing video games to avoid doing homework. There were consistent negative associations between liking to play violent video games and school performance.

The popularity of video games has grown tremendously over the past 20 years. Video games now rival television and film as entertainment media for leisure time use. Contemporary youth report watching between 2 and 3 hours of TV per day and playing video games between 23 and 60 minutes per day (Marshall, Gorely, & Biddle, 2006). Eighty-one percent of American youth report playing at least once per month and about 9% of 8-18 year olds can be considered pathological users (Gentile, 2009). Fewer studies have addressed adult playing time, but 49% of gamers are between 18-49 years old and the average game player age is 34 (Entertainment Software Association [ESA], 2010). Overall, approximately 81% of 18-29-year-olds play video games (Lenhart, Jones, & MacGill, 2008).

Video game research has primarily focused on the relations between aggression and video game use. Video game playing has been associated with increases in aggressive behavior and decreases in prosocial behavior (Anderson, 2004; Gentile & Anderson, 2003). Relatively little research has examined the relationship between video game use and other behaviors like school performance. Before TV viewing and other forms of media became mainstream forms of entertainment, educators and parents expressed concern that this entertainment might begin to compete for academic time and eventually decrease school performance (Gentile & Anderson, 2003; Shin, 2004). As video games become more prevalent, concerns are also being expressed about potential detrimental relationships between video game play and school performance.

This concern is proving to be particularly interesting due to the attributes of video games that make them unique. For example, the effects of video game playing could be greater than for other types of media because of the interactive demands of playing the video game. Students may report being able to study while watching TV, whereas playing a video game may require more focused attention. Video games also incorporate basic learning principles and instructional techniques such as actively reinforcing behaviors and an adaptable level of difficulty that make them more appealing (Swing, Gentile, & Anderson, 2009).

The relation between media consumption and school performance is complex. There are many different types of media, (e.g., television, music, video games, internet, magazines) with some having demonstrated educational value (Din & Calao, 2001). TV has received the most research attention. Children that view programs that focus on educational content, such as Sesame Street, typically display more advanced language skills than then-peers (Wright, Huston, Murphy, St. Peters, Pinon, Scantlin, & Kotler, 2001). This is especially true of children from disadvantaged homes. However, TV viewing in general is associated with lower levels of doing homework, studying, and leisure reading (Shin, 2004). Studies examining the effects of video games have also yielded mixed outcomes. For example, video game playing and computer use have been associated with higher levels of spatial skills, (Reisenhuber, 2004; Terlecki & Newcombe, 2005) but overall poorer performance in school (Roberts, Foehr, Rideout, & Brodie, 1999).

Theoretical accounts of the effects of video game playing have focused on two major issues: time spent playing and level of violent content. The time-displacement hypothesis proposes that time spent engaged in one activity prevents the tie from being spent in another, more fruitful activity. Many children and adolescents have a certain amount of discretionary or free time. The majority of free time is spent on nonproductive pursuits such as TV viewing and video game playing (Larson & Verma, 1999) which become problematic when they consume too much time. For example, the time-displacement hypothesis proposes time spent watching TV displaces time that would or could be spent engaging in other activities that may be more educational in nature (e.g., reading, studying) that may then decrease educational achievement. (Beentjes & Van der Voort, 1989; Shin, 2004). Partial support for the time-displacement hypothesis comes from several studies examining the relations between TV viewing and academic and behavioral outcomes. In general, more than 10 hours per week of TV viewing has been associated with decreased school performance (Shann, 2001) and increased sedentary behavior (Nelson, Gordan-Larsen, Adair, & Popkin, 2005; Van de Bulck & Van Mierlo, 2004). Similar results may be expected for video game playing as their interactive and engrossing nature makes them more appealing than less interesting activities such as homework. Results have been mixed with most studies finding negative correlations between time spent playing video games and school performance (Anand, 2007; Ogletree & Drake, 2007), and others finding no significant relations (Wack & Tantleff-Dunn, 2009).

The violent content of video games may be especially troublesome. There is a negative relation between exposure to violent media and academic performance

(Huesmann, 1986; Huesmann & Miller, 1994). Increased exposure to violent video game playing may disrupt school performance by increasing aggressive behavior (Anderson & Dill, 2000). For example, there is a negative correlation between average high school grades and violent video game exposure (Gentile, Lynch, Linder, & Walsh 2004). One possibility is that exposure to violence in video games increases aggressive thoughts, aggressive behavior, and angry feelings among players who may become more likely to engage in hostile interactions with peers and authority figures such as teachers (Gentile et al., 2004; Swing et al., 2009). These interactions could result in lower school attendance, increased suspensions, and poorer interactions with peers and teachers. Interestingly, violent video games are among the most popular for both males and females (Funk, Buchman, &, Germann, 2000), but a greater percentage of males prefer violent games (Hartmann & Klimmt, 2006).

One of the oversights in video game research is the paucity of studies examining college age students and academic variables. Many current college age students grew up playing video games, whereas twenty years ago this would not have been the norm. Thus the relation between video game play and school performance may have changed as video games have become more mainstream. Educational level is associated with video game play. Current students who are at least 18 are more likely to play video games than non-students. Approximately 82% of full-time and 69% of part-time students report playing video games compared to 49% of non-students (Gentile, 2009). Video games may also now be experienced as part of a social interaction. Video games may serve as social facilitators or group activities either in person or via online play (Wack & Tantleff-Dunn, 2009). Many video game players and non-players spend time watching others play video games (Entertainment Software Association [ESA], 2010; Stermer et al., 2006).

The Present Study

In the present study, we surveyed college students to examine the relations between video game playing and school performance. College and high school GPA were used as measures of school performance. Video game exposure was measured via self-reported time spent playing video games per week. Passive video game exposure, watching other people play, was examined in order to create a more complete picture of time spent in video-game related activities. Participants also completed questions designed to assess their interest in and exposure to violent video games. We predicted video game playing would be significantly negatively correlated with school performance. In addition, we expected a stronger relation for males than for females. We expected that video game watching would be significantly negatively correlated with school performance. We predicted that high frequency video game players would have poorer attitudes towards homework than lower frequency users. Finally, we predicted that violent video game enjoyment would be significantly negatively correlated with school performance.

Method

PARTICIPANTS

Six hundred seventy one participants (391 females and 280 males) completed the survey materials. All participants were between the ages of 18 and 31 years old (M = 21.6, SD = 2.5). Participants were primarily recruited from general psychology classes at a regional university in the Midwestern United States and received course credit for their participation. Participants were 80.5% Caucasian, 7.8% Black / African American, 4% Latino/a, and 7.7% Multiethnic or other.

MATERIALS

To increase sample size, the materials were provided in either an online survey format or a paper survey. Approximately half of the participants were given the survey in a paper form and the others completed the survey through a website designed explicitly for this survey. The questions were identical in both formats. There were no significant differences between the groups that used the paper versus the online format (all p's > .05).

The survey was designed to assess general demographic information, school performance, and experience playing video games. Demographic information requested included age, sex, and school classification (e.g., year in school and highest year of schooling completed). Self-reported high school GPA, college GPA, and ACT score were used as measures of school performance. Current video game experience was assessed by asking the number of hours per week video games were played and the number of hours per week spent watching others play video games. Prior video game experience was assessed by asking at what age the participant first played video games. Participants were also asked how often they play video games instead of doing homework (six point likert scale from strongly disagree to strongly agree).

A subset of 282 participants (174 females, 108 males) completed a longer questionnaire containing additional questions about violent video games. There were no significant differences between those asked the violent video game questions and those not asked (all p's > .05). For example, the participants rated how likely they were to use the most violent way to play a video game, how much they liked to play video games because they are violent and how angry they get when they lose when playing a video game using a six point likert scale from not likely to very likely.

PROCEDURE

Participants completed the survey after giving informed consent. They were asked to complete either the paper copy or the online version of the survey. For the

TABLE 2.3. Descriptives for Demographics and Video Game Experience

Variable	OVERALL (N = 671)			MALES (N = 280)			FEMALES (N = 391)		
	Mean	D	Range	Mean	SD	Range	Mean	SD	Range
Age	21.56	2.53	18–30	21.94	2.58	.18–30	21.29	2.47	18–30
ACT score	23	3.89	13–35	23.16	4.06	15–35	22.87	3.76	13–35
High school GPA	3.59	0.43	1.6–4.0	3.49	0.45	2.0–4.0	3.66	0.4	1.6–4.0
College GPA	3.24	0.54	0.5–4.0	3.16	0.56	1.0–4.0	3.3	0.52	0.5–4.0
Homework[a]	2.25	1.62	1–6	2.96	1.75	1–6	1.76	1.31	1–6
Video games played week (hours)	3.93	8.23	0.0–100	7.10	9.52	0–75	1.67	6.25	0–100
Video games watched week (hours)	2.04	4.94	0.0–87	2.10	3.67	0–35	2.00	5.67	3.0–22
Age first played video games	9.26	3.85	2–24	9.18	3.89	2–24	9.34	3.83	3–22

a: I often play video games instead of doing homework: Rating on scale of 1 (strongly disagree) to 6 (strongly agree)

paper version of the survey, participants were asked to read and sign an informed consent form if they agreed to participate. For the online version of the survey, the first page consisted of the identical consent form and consent was indicated by proceeding to the end and submitting the survey.

Results

Descriptive statistics for the demographic and video game experience variables are presented in Table 2.3. Participants reported a wide range of prior video game playing experience and current use. Overall, 58.9% reported playing video games at some time. The average hours played per week was 3.9 (SD = 8.2). There was considerable variability in the hours played per week (range = 0 to 100). Of those that had played video games, the average age of first playing was 9.3 (SD = 3.9) years. Participants also reported watching others playing video games an average of 2.0 (SD = 4.9) hours per week. There were differences in the video game experience variables by sex. Approximately 40% of the females reported playing versus 89% of the males. Approximately 47% of the females and 56% of the males reported watching others play.

More males than females played at least 10 hours per week (28.2% versus 4.6%). Approximately 5% of males and females reported watching others play at least 10 hours per week. Due to the differences in distribution of video game playing between females and males, we conducted and reported separate regression analyses for males, females, and the overall sample.

MULTIPLE REGRESSION ANALYSES

Multiple regression analyses were conducted to determine the amount of variance in college GPA explained by the measured variables (see Table 2.4). For the

TABLE 2.4. Multiple Regression Analyses Predicting College GPA

Predictor Variable	OVERALL (N = 671) Beta	Males (N = 280) Beta	FEMALES (N = 391) Beta
Age	.04	−.04	.12*
ACT score	.29*	.28*	.32*
High school GPA	.31*	.34*	.21*
Sex	−.05	NA	NA
Video games played week (hours)	−.13*	−.14*	−.12
Age first played video games	.04	.15*	.09
Video games watched per week (hours)	.02	−.21	.07
Play and watch interaction	.07	.26	.05
Overall model F	23.6***	17.9***	10.0
Full model variance explained	27.7	34.3	22.0

* = p < .05, ** = p < .01, *** = p < .001

overall group analysis, age, ACT score, sex of participant, and high school GPA were entered as control variables. The measures of VG playing (i.e., age regularly first played video games, hours played per week, hours watched others play per week, and the interaction of hours played and watched per week) were entered to examine the relations of video game playing experience to school performance. All variables were entered simultaneously. When the entire sample was examined, the combination of variables explained 27.7% of the variance in college GPA (p < .001) with high school GPA, ACT score, and hours of video games played per week the only significant unique predictors. The video game variables contributed approximately 1 percent unique variance to the prediction of college GPA.

Since patterns of video game playing differed significantly between males and females, we conducted additional regression analyses with males and females separately. For females, the combination of variables (i.e., age, ACT score, high school GPA, age regularly first played video games, hours played per week, hours watched others play per week, and the interaction of hours played and watched per week) explained 22.0% of the variance in college GPA (p < .001), with age, high school GPA, and ACT score the only significant unique predictors. For females, the video game measures did not add significant unique variance to the prediction of college GPA. For males, a different pattern of results emerged. The combination of variables explained 34.3% of the variance in college GPA (p < .001) with high school GPA, ACT score, age first started playing video games, hours per week play video games, and the interaction of hours per week play and hours per week watch video games played the significant unique predictors. Hours of video games watched per week was not significant (p = .052). For males, the combination of video game measures added 4.7% unique variance to the prediction of college GPA.

HOMEWORK ANALYSES

It is possible that students who spend more time playing video games will spend less time completing homework and studying. We examined the relations between video game playing and homework (i.e., level of agreement with statement, "I often play video games instead of doing homework"). Overall, those who agreed more strongly with the homework statement tended to play video games more hours per week (r = .38, p <.001), watch others play more hours per week (r = .13, p <.01), and to have begun playing video games regularly at an earlier age (r =-. 14, p <.01). For males, those who agreed more strongly with the homework statement tended to play video games more hours per week (r = .31, p <.001), watch others play more hours per week (r = .13, p <.05), and to have begun playing video games regularly at an earlier age (r = -.13, p <.05). For females, those who agreed more strongly with the homework statement tended to play video games more hours per week (r = .27, p <.001), watch others play more hours per week (r = .15, p <.05), and to have begun playing video games regularly at an earlier age (r = -.16, p <.05). The same pattern of results was observed for males and females suggesting that females who played video games were also more likely to spend less time on homework. Therefore, in the present study, there was some evidence that those who spend more time with video games also spend less time involved in academic activities. Future research needs to be conducted examining class attendance and more diverse measures of study time.

TABLE 2.5. Correlations between Questions about Violence in Video Games and College GPA

	Overall	Males	Females
I am likely to use the most violent way to play a video game	.13*	.15	.07
I like to play video games because they are violent	−.29***	−.33**	−.15*
I get angry when I lose a video game	−.12*	-.22*	.09
I use video games as an opportunity to vent my anger	−.17*	−.17	−.07
I yell at the TV when I lose a video game	−.11	−.11	−.03
I would rather not play a video game that contains violence	.13*	.32***	−.04
I think violent video games make people violent	.09	.28**	−.08
I break things when I lose a video game	−.18**	−.19*	−.08
There are not enough non-violent video games	.20**	.27**	.14
I think video games are too violent	.22***	.37***	.05

All video game questions on scale of 1 (strongly disagree) to 6 (strongly agree)
Significant group differences in percent use at least weekly noted by: * < .05, ** < .01, *** <.001
Overall N = 282

VIOLENCE AND VIDEO GAMES ANALYSES

Previous researchers have suggested violent video game playing is associated with school performance because of increases in aggression and decreases in prosocial skills (Anderson & Dill, 2000). We examined the relations of college GPA and violent video game playing in the subset of 282 participants described in the methods section (see Table 2.5). Eight of the ten questions pertaining to violence and video games were significant in the overall sample. However, this was mainly due to the males. When the females were examined separately, only one correlation was significant. In contrast, seven of the ten questions yielded significant correlations for the males. In general, males that expressed a greater preference for playing violent video games or using violent solutions within the video games had lower college GPAs. The directionality of these findings should be interpreted with caution given their correlational nature.

Discussion

Large numbers of children, teens, and adults spend significant portions of their leisure time playing video games. The effects of exposure to the violent content of many of these games has been widely examined and documented. Just as they did with TV viewing, parents, teachers, and policy makers have expressed concern over the potential detrimental effects of video game playing on time spent in educational activities and school performance. Previous studies have found inconsistent relations between video game playing and school performance (Anderson & Dill, 2000; Creasey & Myers, 1986). However, today's young adults have had the opportunity to grow up with video games as part of the mainstream culture. The potential effects of video game playing may be changing as more people are playing at younger ages and continuing to play into adulthood.

This study extended the current research examining video game playing and school performance in two major ways. First, we focused on college students. Most previous research has examined the relations of video game playing and school performance in younger players, but today's college students grew up in a world where video games were readily available and are now part of the mainstream culture. Second, we included measures of video game playing and watching others play. Video games have become a central part of the social world for many youth and adults. Therefore, it is important to develop a more complete understanding of the potential effects of direct video game exposure as well as the time spent with others around video games.

We found that video game playing was significantly negatively correlated with college GPA, but the results differed by sex. The negative associations with video playing were consistently more evident for the male players. Although females currently make up a significant percentage of those who play video games, males in our sample played more often, started playing at a younger age, and played different types of games. For example, males were significantly more likely to play violent video games.

We examined the time spent playing as well as time spent watching others playing video games. As video games become more social in nature, it is important to consider the time that is spent in passive as well as active exposure to game content. We found students that spent more time watching others play video games tended to have lower college GPAs. This is an important finding since video games are no longer the solitary endeavor that stereotypically defined the early game systems. Video game playing has now become a central social activity for many players (Stermer, Burgess, Burgess, Davis, McCarter, Jones, & Johnson, 2006; Wack & Tantleff-Dunn, 2009).

Why might video game playing be associated with lower college performance? There are several possibilities. Shin (2004) examined four groups of hypotheses regarding how television viewing might stimulate or reduce academic achievement in children. The hypothesis most obviously relevant to video game use was the time-displacement hypothesis. It holds that media consumption displaces or takes away from intellectually demanding activities such as homework and studying (Beentjes & Van der Voort, 1989). Media consumption is thought to be more entertaining than school-related activities. Video games are considered the most engaging and potentially addicting of the various forms of media (Anderson, 2004; Swing et al., 2009). It is possible that frequent video game players spend less time on homework and studying than lower frequency players and non-players, but the relations between amount of time spent playing video games and homework have been shown to be low (Schie & Wiegman, 1997). In the present study, those that agreed more strongly with a question about doing homework ("I often play video games instead of doing homework") tended to have significantly more video game playing experience. The same pattern of results was evident for males and females. Therefore, in the present study, there is some evidence that those who spend more time with video games also spend less time involved in academic activities. Future research needs to examine more diverse measures of academic involvement such as class attendance.

It should be noted that one major problem with the displacement hypothesis is the assumption that if the targeted behavior were removed (e.g., TV viewing, video game playing), it would be replaced by studying or another relevant academic behavior. For example, if a student spends 10 hours per week playing video games, then this is time that is not available for more educationally relevant activities. However, video games may merely be the most attractive option available to those that would not engage or those that are less likely to engage in academic behaviors. There are many competitors for students' attention. The decision to play a video game or to study may operate differently with younger students versus older youth and adults. On one hand, older students should possess more highly developed reasoning systems and better self-regulation abilities. However, older students, especially college students, are also much less likely to have an outside figure, such as a parent, to help place appropriate guidelines on time spent playing and may have to navigate the gauntlet of peer pressure alone. This may place lower level students and more immature students at greater risk.

Another possible explanation for the relations between video game playing and school performance focuses on the violent nature of many video games. Playing violent games has been shown to decrease prosocial behavior and to increase aggressive thoughts and behaviors (Anderson & Dill, 2000; Gentile et al., 2004). The increase in violent behavior may lead to lower school performance by decreasing education time available to students (Gentile et al., 2004; Huesmann, 1986). For example, more violent students may get into more fights at school or be more antagonistic in their interactions with teachers. Anderson and Dill (2000) noted that this type of students is less likely to be represented in a college population compared to a sample including younger students. A subset of 282 participants from the current study were also asked questions concerning how much they liked violent video games. For males, 7 of the 10 measures of violent video game questions were significantly correlated with college GPA whereas only one measure was significantly correlated for females. Additional research is needed to examine the potential role of violent video game playing in school performance.

There are several important limitations to the current study. The use of one time self-report measures is an area of concern because of the difficulty of estimating time spent on an activity over time. One-shot self-report measures of weekly video game playing estimates have been shown to moderately correlate with diary assessments (Burgess & Jones, 2010). Our primary measure of school performance was a global measure of GPA. The validity of the findings could be increased with more measures of academic performance and functioning. The findings are also limited by the nature of the correlational design. Longitudinal examinations would be needed to more completely examine the role of video game playing in school performance in older students. Longitudinal studies would also permit a lifespan perspective to be used in determining how video game, especially violent video game, playing may factor into social functioning and aggressive behavior in the academic setting.

In summary, the current study adds to the existing literature examining the relations between video game playing and school performance. We found a pattern of significant negative relations between time spent playing and watching video games and academic performance in college students. The pattern was more pronounced for males and those with high levels of video game exposure demonstrated the lowest GPAs. Future research is needed that explores the mechanisms of these relations. The landscape of video games is in a state of flux. More and more students, both male and female, are playing and observing others playing video games. Games are now readily available in various portable media devices and systems such as the *Wii* are now marketed directly towards the non-traditional gamer. An answer to how video game playing relates to school performance will require researchers to continue to expand how they define the question.

References

Anand, V. (2007). A study of time management: The correlation between video game usage and academic performance markers. *Cyber Psychology & Behavior*, 10, 552-559.

Anderson, C.A., & Dill, K.E. (2000). Video games and aggressive thoughts, feelings, and behavior in the laboratory and in life. *Journal of Personality & Social Psychology*, 78, 722-790.

Anderson, C.A. (2004). An update on the effects of playing video games. *Journal of Adolescence*, 27, 113-122.

Beentjes, J.W.J., & van der Voort, T.H.A. (1989). Television and young people's reading behavior: A review of research. *European Journal of Communication*, 4, 51-77.

Burgess S.R., & Jones, K. (2010). Reading and media habits of college students by sex and remedial status. *College Student Journal*, 44, 492-508.

Creasey, G.L., & Myers, B.J. (1986). Video games and children: Effects on leisure activities, schoolwork, and peer involvement. *Merrill-Palmer Quarterly*, 32, 251-262.

Din, F.S., & Calao, J. (2001). The effects of playing educational video games on kindergarten achievement. *Child Study Journal*, 31, 95-102.

Entertainment Software Association (2010). 2010 sales, demographic, and usage data. http://www.theesa.com/facts/pdfs/ESA%5FEssential%5FFacts%5F2010.PDF.

Funk, J.B., Buchman, D.D., & Germann, J.N. (2000). Preference for violent electronic games, self-concept and gender differences in young children. *American Journal of Orthopsychiatry*, 70, 233-241.

Gentile, D.A., & Anderson, C.A. (2003). Violent video games: The newest media violence hazard. In: Gentile, D.A., ed. *Media Violence and Children: A complete guide for parents and professionals*. Westport, CT: Praeger, pp. 131-152.

Gentile, D.A., Lynch, P.J., Under, J.R., & Walsh, D.A. The effects of violent video game habits on adolescent hostility, aggressive behaviors, and school performance. *Journal of Adolescence*, 27, 5-22.

Gentile, D.A. (2009). Pathological video game use among youth 8 to 18: A national study. *Psychological Science*, 20, 594-602.

Hartmann, T., & Klimmt, C. (2006). Gender and computer games: Exploring females' dislikes. *Journal of Computer-Mediated Communication*, 77, 910-931.

Huesmann, L.R., & Miller, L.S. (1994). Long-term effects of repeated exposure to media violence in childhood. In: Huesmann, L.R, ed. *Aggressive behavior: current perspectives*. New York, NY: Plenum Press, pp. 153-186.

Huesmann, L.R. (1986), Psychological processes promoting the relation between exposure to media violence and aggressive behavior by the viewer. *Journal of Social Issues*, 42, 125-140.

Larson, R.W., Verma, S. (1999). How children and adolescents spend their time across the world: Work, play, and developmental opportunities. *Psychological Bulletin*, 125, 701-736.

Lenhart, A., Jones, S., MacGill, A.R. (2008). Pew Internet Project Memo 2008. *Pew Internet & American Life Project*. http://www.pewinternet.Org/?/media//Files/Reports/2008/PIP%5FAdult%5Fgaming%5Fmemo.pdf.pdf

Marshall, S.J., Gorely, T., Biddle, S.J.H. (2006). A descriptive epidemiology of screen based media use in youth: A review and critique. *Journal of Adolescence*, 29, 333-349.

Nelson, M.C., Gordan-Larsen, P., Adair, L.S., & Popkin, B.M. (2005). Adolescent physical activity and sedentary behavior: Patterning and long-term maintenance. *American Journal of Preventive Medicine*, 28, 259-266.

Ogletree, S.M., & Drake, R. (2007). College students' video game participation and perceptions: Gender differences and implications. *Sex Roles*, 56, 537-542.

Reisenhuber, M. (2004). An action video game modifies visual processing. *Trends in Neurosciences*, 27, 72-4.

Roberts, D.F., Foehr, U.G., Rideout, V.J., & Brodie, M. (1999). *Kids and media @ the new millennium*. Menlo Park, CA: Kaiser Family Foundation.

Schie, E.G., & Wiegman, O. (1997). Child and videogames: Leisure activities, aggression, social integration, and school performance. *Journal of Applied Social Psychology*, 27, 1175-1194.

Shann, M.H. (2001). Students' use of time outside of school: a case for after school programs for urban middle school youth. *The Urban Review*, 33, 339-356.

Shin, N. (2004). Exploring pathways from television viewing to academic achievement in school age children. *The Journal of Genetic Psychology*, 165, 367-381.

Stermer, P., Burgess, M., & Burgess, S. (2006). Are experienced video game players desensitized to violence? Poster presented at the annual meeting of the Association for Psychological Science, New York, NY.

Stermer, P., Burgess, S., Burgess, M., Davis, C, McCarter, S., Jones, K., Johnson, M. (2006). Video game playing experience and preferences in males and females. Poster presented at the annual meeting of the Southwestern Psychological Society, Austin, TX.

Swing, E.L., Gentile, D.A., & Anderson, C.A. (2009). Learning processes and violent video games. (2009). In: Ferdig, R.E. ed. *Handbook of research on effective electronic gaming in education* (Volume 2). Hershey, PA: Information Science Reference, pp. 876-892.

Terlecki, M.S., & Newcombe, N.S. (2005). How important is the digital divide? The relation of computer and videogame usage to gender differences in mental rotation ability. *Sex Roles*, 53 433-441.

Van den Bulck, J., & Van Mierlo J. (2004). Energy intake associated with television viewing in adolescents, a cross sectional study. *Appetite*, 43, 181-184.

Wack, E., & Tantleff-Dunn, S. (2009). Relationships between electronic game play, obesity, and psychosocial functioning in young men. *Cyber Psychology & Behavior*, 241-244.

Wright, J.C., Huston, A.C., Murphy, K.C., St. Peters, M., Pinon, M., Scantlin, R., & Kotler, J. (2001). The relations of early television viewing to school readiness and vocabulary of children from low-income families: The early window project. *Child Development*, 72, 1347-1366.

Source: *College Student Journal* 46.2 (2012): 376-87.

WHAT IT SAYS

1. What characteristics of video games and video game playing might make gaming more harmful than watching television, according to Burgess, Stermer, and Burgess?

2. Why is the relationship between media consumption and school performance difficult to assess? How is the relationship between video game playing and school performance uniquely complex?

3. What is the "time-consumption hypothesis" as it relates to media use? What have studies of this hypothesis revealed?

4. What gap have Burgess, Stermer, and Burgess found in previous video game research? How do they propose to fill this gap? In other words, how will this study differ from similar studies?

5. What are the hypotheses of this study? What is an "informed consent" form, and why is its use important to this study? What is a "regression analysis," especially as it relates to this study?

6. Summarize the results of this study. In what ways do they support or invalidate the hypotheses? In what ways are these results significant?

7. What implications might this study have for video game players? What implications might it have for educators?

HOW IT SAYS IT

1. In what ways does the structure of this report differ from traditional IMRAD structure? How does this variation work as a rhetorical device?

2. Who is the intended audience for this article? How can you tell?

3. How do Tables 2.3, 2.4, and 2.5 work to promote this study's argument?

WRITE ABOUT IT

1. Create a synthesis grid that includes all the studies mentioned in the article. Before you begin, review the section on synthesis grids in the Guide to academic writing (pp. 77–79).

2. Working as a group, design, carry out, and report on a brief study intended to reproduce the results of Burgess, Stermer, and Burgess. Use your classmates as study participants.

3. Write an essay in which you imagine that you are a professor, residential life director, or college administrator. Based on this study's findings, propose a gaming policy designed to promote academic achievement while encouraging recreational pursuit and respecting individual rights at your college or university. Address the social, moral, intellectual, and legal implications of this program. Before you begin, research your institution's current policies regarding student recreational pursuits, and consider how your proposal will work within existing policies. This relationship should inform the ways in which you present your argument.

f. Ryan C.W. Hall, Terri Day, and Richard C.W. Hall, "A Plea for Caution: Violent Video Games, the Supreme Court, and the Role of Science"

Ryan C.W. Hall is an assistant professor of psychiatry at the University of Central Florida College of Medicine and affiliate instructor at the University of South Florida in Tampa. He is the author of 30 research articles. Hall holds a BA in biology and psychology from Johns Hopkins University, and an MD from Georgetown University.

Terri Day is a professor of law at Barry University Dwayne O. Andreas School of Law in Orlando, Florida, where she teaches in the areas of torts, professional responsibility, First Amendment, and Constitutional law. Prior to becoming a lawyer, she worked in social work and as a documentarian. She is the author of numerous scholarly articles.

Day received a BA from the University of Wisconsin, an MSSA from Case Western Reserve University, a JD from the University of Florida, and an LLM degree from Yale University.

Richard C.W. Hall is courtesy clinical psychiatrist at the University of Florida in Gainesville and maintains a private psychiatry practice in Maitland, Florida. In addition to having published numerous research articles, he is deputy editor of the journal *Psychosomatics*, co-author of *Handbook of Psychiatric Diagnostic Procedures* (with Thomas P. Beresford, 1987), and author of *Psychiatry in Crisis* (1982). Hall received a BS from Johns Hopkins University and an MD from the University of Florida College of Medicine.

This article, which first appeared in *Mayo Clinic Proceedings*, discusses the role of the Supreme Court in making rulings about violent video games. It provides a useful example of scholars from different fields—in this case, medicine and law—working together to create interdisciplinary scholarship.

As You Read: Does it make sense to restrict certain populations from playing certain types of video games? Why or why not?

A Plea for Caution: Violent Video Games, the Supreme Court, and the Role of Science

Abstract

On November 2, 2010, the US Supreme Court heard arguments in the case of *Schwarzenegger v. Entertainment Merchants Association*, with a ruling expected in 2011. This case addressed whether states have the right to restrict freedom of speech by limiting the sale of violent video games to minors. To date, eight states have tried to pass legislation to this effect, with all attempts being found unconstitutional by lower courts; in large part, the Supreme Court's decision will be determined by its review and interpretation of the medical and social science literature addressing the effects of violent video games on children. Those on both sides of the violent video game debate claim that the scientific literature supports their opinions. Some involved in the debate have proclaimed that the debate is scientifically settled and that only people holding personal interests and biases oppose these "established truths." We review the historical similarities found in the 1950s comic book debate and studies identified from a PubMed search of the term *violent video games* showing both the harmful and beneficial effects of these video games. We define factors that physicians need to consider when reading and stating opinions about this literature. Opinions from past court rulings are discussed to provide insight into how judges may approach the application of these social science studies to the current legal issue. Although on the surface the case of *Schwarzenegger v. Entertainment Merchants Association* pertains only to the restriction of violent video games, it may establish principles about how medical and public health testimony can affect fundamental constitutional rights and how much and on what basis the courts will defer to legislators' reliance on unsettled science.

On November 2, 2010, the US Supreme Court heard oral arguments for *Schwarzenegger v. Entertainment Merchants Association*[1] (oral arguments available at http://www.oyez.org), a case involving whether states can place statutory restrictions and labeling requirements on the sale or rental of "violent video games" to minors without violating constitutional principles of free speech guaranteed by the First and Fourteenth Amendments.[1,2] Laws that restrict minors' access to sexual materials otherwise legal for adults (the "sliding scale" notion of restriction on free speech, with more restrictions for minors but fewer for adults) are constitutional because such material is deemed a less valued or protected form of speech. Proponents of violent video game restrictions argue that the sliding scale standard applied to minors' access to sexual materials should apply to violent video games as well. However, "violent material" has always been seen as protected speech because of its potential political and societal impact (e.g., photos and combat footage from the Vietnam War that changed public perception of the war). One of the crucial questions the Supreme Court justices will address in *Schwarzenegger v. Entertainment Merchants Association* is whether violent speech can be restricted under certain circumstances and, if so, whether a causal link is needed between the violent media and harm to satisfy First Amendment principles.[3] This determination will require the justices to focus on whether the evidence available in the scientific literature is sufficient to support such a link.

Scientifically, two competing social theories have been formulated about the potential effects of video game violence. The first is that video games increase violence because they teach players how to be violent and reinforce violent tendencies. The second theory is that video games have a neutral or possibly beneficial effect because they provide a socially acceptable, physically nondestructive outlet for the release of aggression and thereby promote better mental health.

Legally, the ruling in *Schwarzenegger v. Entertainment Merchants Association* may have implications for how scientific evidence is viewed and weighed by the Court, especially when it comes to the question of restricting constitutional rights. For example, what deference should a court give legislative findings or what level of persuasion or proof would be required before scientific evidence is seen as conclusive enough to limit constitutionally protected liberties? Is it sufficient for such evidence to be clear and convincing or does a higher standard apply, such as beyond a reasonable doubt, for courts to determine that a government restriction on First Amendment protected speech satisfies strict scrutiny analysis (the standard of review applied to government restrictions on protected speech)? Past cases such as *Daubert, Joiner,* and *Kumho Tire* primarily focused on how to keep junk science out of the court room and who is qualified to provide an expert opinion.[4-6] *Daubert* provided judges with principles to guide them in performing a "gatekeeping function," including the following: (1) Can or has the theory or technique in question been tested? (2) Has it been subjected to peer review and publication? (3) Is there a known or potential error rate? (4) Is there a maintenance of standards regarding its operation? and (5) Has it gained widespread acceptance within a relevant scientific community?[4] The *Daubert* trilogy, as the 3 previous cases are known, was never intended to instruct legislators about how to determine which side of a scientific debate should be endorsed to justify First Amendment restrictions. In turn, the *Daubert* trilogy does not provide guidance to judges in determining how much deference to give legislative findings grounded on unsettled science. The *Schwarzenegger* decision may allow the Court to elucidate principles guiding judges on how much deference to give to scientific evidence and theories, especially when a conflict exists in the scientific community.

This article will review the 1950s comic book debate to highlight common elements in debates pertaining to media, children, and harm; the current state of the conflicted scientific literature concerning video game violence and the potential bias in that literature; and the opinions thus far of lower courts on the debate.

TABLE 2.6. Common Arguments Made about Comic Books in the 1950s and Violent Video Games

Children learn to be violent from reading comic books or playing violent video games	Children have increased aggression from exposure to comic books or violent video games
Comic books and violent video games lead to actual aggressive behavior	Comic books and violent video games have a pernicious negative effect on society
The negative effect of comic books and violent video games reaches the level of a public health concern	To protect society and children, minors must be denied access to the material
The scientific literature concerning long-term negative effects of comic books and violent video games has been conclusively determined	Anyone who does not acknowledge the scientifically proven harm of comic books and violent video games does so out of a personal bias and/or financial concerns

The 1950s Comic Book Debate

The comic book debate of the 1950s is eerily similar to the current debate about the effects of video games on children. In 1954, the US Senate Subcommittee on Juvenile Delinquency held hearings on the effects of comic books on America's youth.[3,7,8] The primary focus of the Senate hearings was "crime and horror" comic books, some of which graphically showed horrific images such as dismembered bodies. Concerns were voiced that these comics would lead to a decline in public morals, an increase in violence and aggression, an increase in general lawlessness, and societal disrespect and deterioration.[8] Medical and social science experts became involved in the debate, writing articles such as "The Problem of the Comic Books" and "The Psychopathology of Comic Books," which were published in reputable journals.[9,10] A leading proponent to limit, if not ban, the sale of "horror and crime comics," as he defined them, was Dr. Fredric Wertham, a forensic psychiatrist.[7] Many of the concerns that dominate the current video game debate were also expressed by Dr. Wertham in his testimony to the Senate subcommittee (Table 2.6 summarizes these similarities):

> I would like to point out to you one other crime comic book which we have found to be particularly injurious to the ethical development of children and those are the Superman comic books. They arose in children's fantasies of sadistic joy in seeing other people punished over and over again, while you yourself remain immune. We have called it the "Superman complex."

In these comic books, the crime is always real and Superman's triumph over [evil] is unreal. Moreover, these books like any other, teach complete contempt of the police ... may say here on this subject *there is practically no controversy* ... as long as the crime comic books industry exists in its present form, *there are no secure homes*.... crime comic books, as I define them, are the overwhelming majority of all comic books ... There is an endless stream of brutality ... I can only say that, in my opinion, *this is a public-health problem*.... I think it ought to be possible to keep the children under 15 from seeing them displayed to them and preventing these being sold directly to children.... The children don't say that this does them any harm, and that is an interesting thing because it has been so misrepresented by the comic book industry and their spokesmen in all the *biased opinions* that they peddle and that they hand out to unsuspecting newspaper editors (Italics added by author for emphasis).[8]

In large part because of these hearings, the comic book industry voluntarily adopted the Comics Code Authority standards.[3,7] Considering that Dr. Wertham's testimony in Canada led to a ban on the import and sale of certain comic book titles, this seemed to be a reasonable step for the American comic book industry to take.[8]

The concern about comic books persists to this day, as evidenced by mental health "authorities" focusing on the negative male stereotype that boys learn from comic book characters. However, the "destructive" comic books of the 1950s are currently being lauded for the positive societal values they taught. Sharon Lamb, PhD, was quoted in a 2010 press release as saying: "[The comic book heroes of the past did fight criminals], but [they] were heroes boys could look up to and learn from because, outside of their costumes, they were real people with real problems and many vulnerabilities."[11]

Sixty years in the future, will social scientists be espousing the positive benefits of today's video games as they currently are doing with yesterday's comic books?

Review of the Literature on Violent Video Games

As already noted, the scientific community remains divided on the effect of violent video games on youth. Some investigators argue that the effect is negative, whereas others see a neutral to a beneficial effect. A review of the literature supporting each theory follows, as well as a specific case in point of such conflicting opinions. A critical stance toward current findings is advised given that the science on this issue remains unsettled.

THEORY 1: VIOLENT VIDEO GAMES HAVE A NEGATIVE EFFECT ON YOUTH

Articles reviewing the effects of video game content on general populations have found links between playing violent video games and changes in behavior, self-concept, and/or thought process. Barlett and Rodeheffer[12] found that persons who played realistic violent games for 45 minutes had a greater increase in arousal and aggressive feelings than persons who played unrealistic violent video games or nonviolent video games for the same period.

A study by Bushman and Anderson[13] (frequently quoted experts in the current debate) tried to address whether playing violent video games would lead to changes in behavior. In their study, participants played either a violent or nonviolent video game and were then exposed to a staged confrontation. Bushman and Anderson found many variations between the groups. First, the players of violent video games were less likely to help those involved in the staged confrontation than the players of the nonviolent games (21% vs 25%). Second, players of the violent video game rated the fight as less serious (mean score, 5.91 vs 6.44 on a scale of 1-10, with 1 being the least serious and 10 being the most serious). Third, players of violent video games took longer to help if they did help (73.3 seconds vs 16.2 seconds). Fourth, players of the violent video game were less likely to "hear" the confrontation taking place (94% vs 99%).[13] Bushman and Anderson thought that this study demonstrated a definable change in behavior that was specifically related to playing violent video games.

In a different experiment by Bushman and Anderson,[13] a similar definable behavioral change was found after viewing violent movies. Those who had just seen a violent movie took 26% longer to offer assistance to a person with an injury (a person on crutches) than did people who were about to see the violent movie or were about to see or had just seen a nonviolent movie (6.89 seconds vs 5.46 seconds).[13] Findings that exposure to violent media may negatively affect health (e.g., increased risk of substance use, sexual activity, obesity, or poor body image) and behavior have also been reported for other media, such as television and music.[14-17] The American Academy of Pediatrics started issuing official policy statements as early as 2001 that violent media (e.g., television, movies, music, and video games) "represent a significant risk to the health of children and adolescents."[15,16] This raises the question of whether the reported change in behavior is specific to any particular form of media or is caused by the violent content itself, regardless of the way it is experienced. Unfortunately, it is sometimes difficult to directly compare the varying studies to determine which media, if any, have the most profound effect on behavior because different measures and study designs are used. Even when comparing the two studies done by Bushman and Anderson, the methods vary; one measured the time helping an injured person, whereas the second measured the time to help a person after a physical altercation, a situation in which rendering assistance may have exposed the study participant to more risk. Although both studies reported measured time to a response after exposure to violent media, the risks are not comparable.

Many published studies suggest that certain populations are more at risk and/or are more likely to play violent video games than others.[3] Studies suggest that at-risk individuals are usually male, have preexisting personality disorders or traits (e.g., conduct disorder), have preexisting mental health conditions (e.g., attention deficit disorder), have had difficult or traumatic upbringings, and are insecure (with poor self-esteem).[18,19] A review of the literature by Frölich et al.[19] showed that children with attention deficit disorder were at a higher risk of showing "addictive" behavior to violent video games and that violent video games "might be a significant risk variable for aggressive behavior" in persons who already have aggressive personality traits.

Many studies have found a correlation or association between the amount of time a game is played and subsequent changes in behavior.[3] A study by Hastings et al.,[20] which relied on parents' self-report of their children's video game-playing behaviors, suggested that spending a large amount of time playing violent video games was correlated with troublesome behavior and poor academic achievement. The same study also indicated that children who played more educational games had more positive outcomes.

Although not as frequently studied, the effects of playing positive "prosocial" video games have been examined.[21-23] In a study by Greitemeyer and Osswald,[21] players of a prosocial video game were more likely to help after a mishap, more willing to assist in further experiments, and more likely to intervene in a harassment situation, the opposite of what was found in the Bushman and Anderson study of violent video game players.[13] Their findings supported the notion that video games affect individuals, as would be hypothesized from "general learning theories."[22] Specifically, a person's behavior is reinforced and/or encouraged by either prosocial or violent tactics that were rewarded by advancing in or winning the game.

THEORY 2: VIOLENT VIDEO GAMES HAVE A MINIMAL, UNDETERMINED, OR BENEFICIAL EFFECT ON YOUTH

Although many articles have suggested a connection between violent video games and aggression, several have found no such relationship.[24] In 2007, a meta-analysis by Ferguson[25] found that, once "publication bias" was corrected, no significant correlation existed between violent video games and aggressive behavior. A study from Iran by Allahverdipour et al.[26] found that "nongamers" and "excessive gamers" both had lower self-reported mental health wellness scores than "low to moderate gamers." This finding suggests that excessive playing may be detrimental, but that there is some protective or, at least, nondeleterious effect to playing in moderation.[26] This finding is in line with social theory, which suggests that video games, like sports, may provide an outlet for individuals to work through aggression and, therefore, have better mental functioning and overall lower levels of aggression. Other studies have pointed to the positive attributes of violent video game playing, such as improved visual-spatial coordination, increased peripheral attention, and increased reactive decision-making capabilities.[25]

In a study by Ferguson et al.[27] examining the multivariate risk factors for youth violence, the most salient positive predictors of youth violence were delinquent peer influences, antisocial personality traits, depression, and parents or guardians who use psychological abuse in intimate relationships. The factors that were not found to be predictive of youth violence included neighborhood quality, parental use of domestic violence in intimate relationships, and exposure to violent television or video games.

In a study that may be directly applicable to the question before the Supreme Court in the *Schwarzenegger* case, Regenbogen et al.[28] used functional magnetic resonance imaging (fMRI) studies of the brain to determine whether there was a change in brain imaging that suggested a loss of distinction between virtual and actual violence in players of violent video games compared with controls. What they found is that "the ability to differentiate automatically between real and virtual violence has not been diminished by a long-term history of violent video game play, nor have gamers' neural responses to real violence, in particular, been subject to desensitization processes." This would indicate that, at least on a population basis, video games do not cause people to lose their grip on what is real vs. what is fantasy.

A review of the literature published in 2009 by Mitrofan et al.,[29] which tried to assess the association between watching violent television and playing violent video games and the emergence of behavioral problems in children with emotional difficulties, found the literature to be confused and contradictory. The overall conclusion of the authors was that the literature consisted of "insufficient, contradictory and methodologically flawed evidence on the association between television viewing and video game playing and aggression in children and young people with behavioral and emotional difficulties." The authors warned that better studies were needed before any true evidence-based public health policy could be formulated.

A CASE IN POINT: THE CONFLICTING RESPONSE TO THE META-ANALYSIS BY C.A. ANDERSON

The reactions to a meta-analysis performed by C.A. Anderson et al.[30] illustrate the two sides of the debate. The first was written by Huesmann,[31] who has authored more than 30 articles about violence and aggression. The second is a commentary written by Ferguson and Kilburn,[32] who together have published more than 40 articles on the subject of violence.

Huesmann,[31] in his commentary "[n]ailing the coffin shut on doubts that violent video games stimulate aggression," wrote:

Observational learning theory has evolved into social-cognitive information processing models that explain that what a child observes in any venue has both short-term and long-term influences on the child's behaviors and cognitions. C.A. Anderson et al.'s (2010) extensive meta-analysis of the effects of violent video games confirms what these theories predict and what prior research about other violent mass media has found [an association].... Contrary to some critics' assertions, the meta-analysis of C.A. Anderson et al. is methodologically sound and comprehensive. Yet the results of meta-analyses are unlikely to change the critics' views or the public's perception that the issue is undecided because some studies have yielded null effects, because many people are concerned that the implications of the research threaten freedom of expression, and because many people have their identities or self-interests closely tied to violent video games.

Dr. Huesmann's commentary is strikingly similar in tone to the testimony provided by Dr. Wertham regarding comic books in the 1950s.

In their commentary casting doubt on the link between the viewing of violent video games and aggression, Ferguson and Kilburn[32] wrote:

The issue of violent video game influences on youth violence and aggression remains intensely debated in the scholarly literature and among the general public. Several recent meta-analyses, examining outcome measures most closely related to serious aggressive acts, found little evidence for a relationship between violent video games and aggression or violence. In a new meta-analysis, C.A. Anderson et al. (2010) questioned these findings. However, their analysis has several methodological issues ... includ[ing] many studies that do not relate well to serious aggression, an apparently biased sample of unpublished studies, and a "best practices" analysis that appears unreliable and does not consider the impact of unstandardized aggression measures on the inflation of effect size estimates.

THE NEED FOR CRITICAL REVIEW OF THE LITERATURE

Many questions are raised by the split nature of the scientific literature regarding violence and video games. Do these articles represent "good science"? Are the results applicable to the real world? Were the results influenced by intentional (e.g., researchers' personal beliefs) or unintentional (e.g., sampling errors) bias?[29,32-34] In an attempt to answer these questions, we searched the PubMed database in 2010 using the search term *violent video game* with no limit on time frame, identifying 92 relevant publications. The findings of the identified articles are depicted in Table 2.7. After reviewing the available publications in this one database, we realized that physicians should be mindful of several very important concerns when reading this or similar literature defining the risk of violence.

The study of the long-term effects of video games is "new," and the conflicting findings have not yet been fully vetted.[35] Home video game consoles did not become common household items until the late 1970s and early 1980s and did not develop enough processing power to render realistic depictions of violence until the late 1990s.[3] Video games of the type being targeted by legislation did not enter the market in large numbers until after industry rating labels went into effect in 1994.[3]

It should be remembered that a correlation does not prove a causation.[33] For example, in the past, a correlation was reported between coffee consumption and lung and pancreatic cancer. However, is the real culprit the coffee the person is drinking or the proverbial cigarette he or she smokes with the coffee?[3,36] Do children with less parental involvement and supervision play more violent video games? If that is the case, then is the correlation with violence due not to the games per se but rather to a lack of parental supervision and interaction? The game time played would be then an accurate marker but not the real causative variable. If parents are asked to complete a survey about their children, are they likely or able to identify their own failings as parents?

One must also determine if a finding in the literature is "clinically" or practically relevant.[37,38] For example, many studies indicate that self-reported levels of aggression increase while playing video games.[33,38] Do these findings then translate into these players becoming more aggressive later or being more likely to engage in real violence?[33,37,38] The simple conclusion is that they probably do become more aggressive later, and, as previously mentioned, some academic studies support this hypothesis. However, studies also indicate that people who engage in or watch sports such as football, hockey, or martial arts (e.g., judo) also show increased aggression while playing in or watching the event.[39-44] Are they at the same risk of future violence as the people who play video games? If multiple routine daily activities, such as watching or playing sports, driving a car, watching TV, reading a comic book, or playing video games, increase aggression and alter behavior, is the effect so common that it loses its significance as a specific public health concern?[38,45]

When assessing the validity of data, we should remember that data are often processed by people with "theories" about how the mind learns and works.[46] Often, these theories change over time and drift in and out of academic, social, and political favor, as did the theory of the *schizophrenogenic mother*. At one time, the schizophrenogenic mother was a well-accepted theory to explain how environmental stressors, namely maternal interactions with children, could cause the child to become schizophrenic.[47] However, with a better understanding of central neurochemistry and the development of effective medications and new research techniques (e.g., functional positron emission tomography, magnetic resonance imaging, and

TABLE 2.7. Findings of 92 Articles Addressing Violent Video Games[a,b]

Finding	No. of articles
Provided data supporting some association between video games and behavior	37
Involved video games but did not directly assess only violent video games (looked at other factors as well, such as television viewing)	36
Reviewed past studies on violent video games	13
Opinion article making recommendations to clinicians or parents	10
Reviewed the physiological effects caused by playing video games, such as heart rate changes or changes on functional imaging studies	7
Showed effects for specific populations, such as those with preexisting personality trait disturbance and mental illnesses	7
Showed potential positive and negative effects from video games	4
Found no evidence for a relationship between video game viewing and behavior	1

[a] Articles were identified by searching PubMed in 2010 for the search term *violent video game* without limiting date parameters.
[b] Some articles fell into multiple categories and were counted more than once.

genetic studies), the schizophrenogenic mother is no longer seen as the prime cause of schizophrenia. If the Court had ruled on the validity of the scientific evidence defining the cause of schizophrenia in the 1950s (i.e., the schizophrenogenic mother) compared with the information available in 2010 (i.e., genetics), such a ruling today would be seen as "good law" based on unfounded, premature, or bad science.

How the Courts Have Reacted

Previous court cases addressing states' attempts to restrict access to video games are summarized in Table 2.8. The federal district court case of *Entertainment Software Association v. Rod Blagojevich* is particularly instructive to the issues before the Supreme Court because of its analysis of the scientific literature regarding violent video games.[48] The court in that case found that the conclusions of the scientific proponents testifying in favor of limiting video games were overstated:

> Dr. Anderson [PhD] testified that "it seems clear that exposure to violent video games increases aggressive behavior, aggressive thinking, physiological arousal, aggressive feelings, and is also associated with a decrease in prosocial behavior." ... The research underlying Dr. Anderson's testimony, however, does not support such a stark and sweeping conclusion ... [Defense experts] noted that Dr. Anderson not only had failed to cite any peer-reviewed studies that had shown a definitive causal link between violent video game play and aggression, but had also ignored research that reached conflicting conclusions.... They also cited studies concluding that in certain instances, there was a *negative* relationship

between violent video game play and aggressive thoughts and behavior (e.g., initial increases in aggression wore off if the individual was allowed to play violent video game for longer period) ... Dr. Anderson also has not provided evidence to show that the purported relationship between violent video game exposure and aggressive thoughts or behavior is any greater than with other types of media violence ... or other factors that contribute to aggression, such as poverty. In fact, several of the studies he uses to support his conclusions examine media violence generally and do not disaggregate the effect of video game violence or compare the effects of video game violence to these or other forms of media violence.[48]

TABLE 2.8. Synopsis of Previous Court Cases Regarding the Sale, Rental, or Distribution of Violent Video Games to Minors

---

Court of Appeals cases

Software Dealers Association v. Schwarzenegger, 556 F3d 950 (9th Cir 2009)
   Restrictions on the sale and rental of video games violate the First Amendment and the "variable obscenity" standard applicable to minors is not applicable. This case led to *Schwarzenegger v. Entertainment Merchants Association*, 130 SCt 2398 (2010)

Interactive Digital Software Association v. St Louis County, 329 F3d 954 (8th Cir 2003)
   The county ordinance making it unlawful for any person to knowingly sell, rent, or make available violent video games to minors without a parent or guardian's consent violates the First Amendment

American Amusement Machine Association v. Kendrick, 224 F3d 572 (7th Cir 2001)
   Legislation restricting access to violent video games is unconstitutional

Video Software Dealers Association v. Webster, 968 F2d 684 (8th Cir 1992)
   Imposing a penalty on those who sell or rent violent video games to minors is unconstitutional

---

Federal District Court cases

Entertainment Merchant Association v. Henry, No. CIV-060675-C, 2007 WL 2743097 (WD Okla Sept 17, 2007)
   Provision of criminal statute imposing penalties to anyone who knowingly sells, rents, furnishes, distributes, or disseminates material harmful to minors, including material depicting inappropriate violence, is unconstitutional

Entertainment Software Association v. Foti, 451 F Supp 2d 823 (MD La 2006)
   Statute criminalizing the distribution of video or computer games "appealing to minors' morbid interest in violence" violates the First Amendment

Entertainment Software Association v. Hatch, 443 F Supp 2d 1065 (D Minn 2006)
   Imposing fines on minors who buy or rent violent video games and requiring merchants to post signs warning of such penalties violate the First Amendment

Entertainment Software Association v. Granholm, 426 F Supp 2d 646 (ED Mich 2006)
   Invalidated state statute criminalizing "knowingly disseminating to a minor an ultra-violent explicit video game that is harmful to minors"

Entertainment Software Association v. Blagojevich, 404 F Supp 2d 1051 (ND Ill 2005)
   The state did not meet its burden to show that such restriction is necessary to satisfy the government's interest in preventing violent and aggressive behavior in minors

Video Software Dealers Association v. Maleng, 325 F Supp 2d 1180 (WD Wash 2004)
   The relationship between the violence in video games and antisocial behavior in minors is not sufficiently substantial to support restrictions on violent video games

Implications for Physicians

The current debate about whether violence is caused by video games will not be the last time that groups of social scientists on both sides will feel compelled to weigh in with "hard data and opinions" to advance their political or social agenda. As scientists, if we remember our history, we will be less likely to put forth theories, such as the Superman complex and the schizophrenogenic mother, as uncontested facts. It is hard to prove a direct causal relationship between violence and media to the average judge and/or juror considering the fact that millions if not billions of people have watched violence on television and in movies, listened to rap music, and played violent video games and have not engaged in violent acts.

Physicians only need to look at the current video game debate to understand how "scientific literature" may be applied, appropriately or inappropriately, to influence social policy. Misuse can have a profound effect on how medicine and physicians are viewed by the public and the courts. The *Schwarzenegger* decision may further change the standard by which medical testimony is accepted by the Court, as did the *Daubert* trilogy. To date, the lower courts have taken a very strict view in determining that science needs to show *definitive* causation. If the Supreme Court agrees with the lower courts, the future implications of its decision may be difficult to predict. It could result in a judicial free-for-all, leaving it up to each judge to make up his or her own mind about whether an issue has been conclusively decided scientifically. Alternatively, it could result in such strict guidelines on when scientific information can be used to justify a statutory restriction on constitutional rights that it severely limits scientific usefulness. It is important that we, as physicians, accurately report our scientific literature, its implications, and limitations; otherwise, we will see our testimony discounted, as was the testimony of Dr. Anderson, by the US District Court for the Northern District of Illinois.[48]

References

1. Arnold Schwarzenegger, Governor of California, et al, v. Entertainment Merchants Association, et al. No. 08-1448. 130 SCt 2398 (2010).

2. US Supreme Court Media. *Schwarzenegger v. Entertainment Merchants Association*. Oyez website. http://www.oyez.org/cases/2010-2019/2010/2010_08_1448. Accessed February 16, 2011.

3. Day T, Hall R. Déjà vu: from comic books to video games: legislative reliance on "soft science" to protect against uncertain societal harm linked to violence v. the First Amendment. *Oregon Law Rev.* 2010;89(2):415-504.

4. *Daubert v. Merrell Dow Pharm, Inc.* 509 US 579, 589-98 (1993).

5. *General Electric Co v. Joiner.* 522 US 136 (1997).

6. *Kumho Tire Co v. Carmichael*, 526 US 137 (1999).

7. Menand L. *The Horror: Congress Investigates the Comics* [book review]. *New Yorker Magazine*, March 31, 2008. http://www.newyorker.com/arts/critics/books/2008/03/31/080331crbo_books_menand. Accessed February 16, 2011.

8. TheComicBooks.com. United States Senate Subcommittee on juvenile delinquency testimony of Dr. Fredric Wertham, April 21, 1954. http://www.thecomicbooks.com/1954senatetranscripts.html. Accessed February 16, 2011.

9. The problem of the comic books. *Am J Psychiatry*. 1956;112(10):854.

10. Wertham F, Legman G. The psychopathology of comic books. *Am J Psychother*. 1948;2(3):472-490.

11. American Psychological Association. Today's superheroes send wrong image to boys, say researchers: 'macho' masculine stereotype not healthy for relationships. Published August 15, 2010. http://www.apa.org/news/press/releases/2010/08/macho-stereotype-unhealthy.aspx. Accessed February 16, 2011.

12. Barlett CP, Rodeheffer C. Effects of realism on extended violent and nonviolent video game play on aggressive thoughts, feelings, and physiological arousal. *Aggress Behav*. 2009;35(3):213-224.

13. Bushman BJ, Anderson CA. Comfortably numb: desensitizing effects of violent media on helping others. *Psychol Sci*. 2009;20(2):273-277.

14. Council on Communications and Media. From the American Academy of Pediatrics: Policy statement-impact of music, music lyrics, and music videos on children and youth. *Pediatrics*. 2009;124(5):1488-1494.

15. Council on Communications and Media. From the American Academy of Pediatrics: policy statement—media violence. *Pediatrics*. 2009;124(5):1495-1503.

16. Committee on Public Education. American Academy of Pediatrics: media violence. *Pediatrics*. 2001;108(5):1222-1226.

17. Committee on Public Education. American Academy of Pediatrics: Children, adolescents, and television. *Pediatrics*. 2001;107(2):423-426.

18. Tisseron S. Videogames risks: diagnosis and management. *Arch Pediatr*. 2009;16(1):73-76.

19. Frölich J, Lehmkuhl G, Döpfner M. Computer games in childhood and adolescence: relations to addictive behavior, ADHD, and aggression. *Z Kinder Jugendpsychiatr Psychother*. 2009;37(5):393-402.

20. Hastings EC, Karas TL, Winsler A, et al. Young children's video/computer game use: relations with school performance and behavior. *Issues Ment Health Nurs*. 2009;30(10):638-649.

21. Greitemeyer T, Osswald S. Effects of prosocial video games on prosocial behavior. *J Pers Soc Psychol*. 2010;98(2):211-221.

22. Gentile DA, Anderson CA, Yukawa S, et al. The effects of prosocial video games on prosocial behaviors: international evidence from correlational, longitudinal, and experimental studies. *Pers Soc Psychol Bull*. 2009;35(6):752-763.

23. Greitemeyer T, Osswald S, Brauer M. Playing prosocial video games increases empathy and decreases schadenfreude. *Emotion*. 2010;10(6):796-802.

24. Ferguson CJ, Kilburn J. The public health risks of media violence: a meta-analytic review. *J Pediatr*. 2009;154(5):759-763.

25. Ferguson CJ. The good, the bad and the ugly: a meta-analytic review of positive and negative effects of violent video games, *Psychiatr Q*. 2007;78(4):309-316.

26. Allahverdipour H, Bazargan M, Farhadinasab A, et al. Correlates of video games playing among adolescents in an Islamic country. *BMC Public Health*. 2010;10:286.

27. Ferguson CJ, San Miguel C, Hartley RD. A multivariate analysis of youth violence and aggression: the influence of family, peers, depression, and media violence. *J Pediatr*. 2009;155(6):904-908.

28. Regenbogen C, Herrmann M, Fehr T. The neural processing of voluntary completed, real and virtual violent and nonviolent computer game scenarios displaying predefined actions in gamers and nongamers. *Soc Neurosci*. 2010;5(2):221-240.

29. Mitrofan O, Paul M, Spencer N. Is aggression in children with behavioral and emotional difficulties associated with television viewing and video game playing? A systematic review. *Child Care Health Dev*. 2009;35(1):5-15.

30. Anderson CA, Shibuya A, Ihori N, et al. Violent video game effects on aggression, empathy, and prosocial behavior in eastern and western countries: a meta-analytic review. *Psychol Bull*. 2010;136(2):151-173.

31. Huesmann LR. Nailing the coffin shut on doubts that violent video games stimulate aggression: comment on Anderson et al. (2010). *Psychol Bull*. 2010;136(2):179-181.

32. Ferguson CJ, Kilburn J. Much ado about nothing: the misestimation and overinterpretation of violent video game effects in eastern and western nations: comment on Anderson et al. (2010). *Psychol Bull*. 2010;136:174-178.

33. Browne KD, Hamilton-Giachritsis C. The influence of violent media on children and adolescents: a public-health approach. *Lancet*. 2005;365(9460):702-710.

34. Anderson CA. An update on the effects of playing violent video games. *J Adolesc*. 2004;27(1):113-122.

35. Villani VS, Olson CK, Jellinek MS. Media literacy for clinicians and parents. *Child Adolesc Psychiatr Clin N Am*. 2005;14(3):523-553.

36. Tang N, Wu Y, Ma J, et al. Coffee consumption and risk of lung cancer: a meta-analysis. *Lung Cancer*. 2010;67(1):117-22.

37. Funk JB. Children's exposure to violent video games and desensitization to violence. *Child Adolesc Psychiatr Clin N Am*. 2005;14(3):387-404.

38. Olson CK. Media violence research and youth violence data: why do they conflict? *Acad Psychiatry*. 2004;28(2):144-150.

39. Warden KB, Grasso SC, Luyben PD. Comparisons of rates and forms of aggression among members of men's and women's collegiate recreational flag football teams. *J Prev Interv Community*. 2009;37(3):209-215.

40. Thomas S, Reeves C, Smith A. English soccer teams' aggressive behavior when playing away from home. *Percept Mot Skills*. 2006;102(2):317-320.

41. Moore SC, Shepherd JP, Eden S, et al. The effect of rugby match outcome on spectator aggression and intention to drink alcohol. *Crim Behav Ment Health*. 2007;17(2):118-127.

42. Reynes E, Lorant J. Effect of traditional judo training on aggressiveness among young boys. *Percept Mot Skills*. 2002;94(1):21-25.

43. Begg DJ, Langley JD, Moffitt T, et al. Sport and delinquency: an examination of the deterrence hypothesis in a longitudinal study. *Br J Sports Med*. 1996;30(4):335-341.

44. Frank MG, Gilovich T. The dark side of self- and social perception: black uniforms and aggression in professional sports. *J Pers Soc Psychol*. 1988;54(1):74-85.

45. Deffenbacher JL, Richards TL, Filetti LB, et al. Angry drivers: a test of state-trait theory. *Violence Vict*. 2005;20(4):455-469.

46. Huesmann LR. The impact of electronic media violence: scientific theory and research. *J Adolesc Health*. 2007;41(6)(suppl 1):S6-S13.

47. Nuffield EJ. The schizogenic mother. *Med J Aust*. 1954;2(8):283-286.

48. *Entertainment Software Ass'n v. Blagojevich*, 404 F Supp 2d 1051 (ND Ill 2005).

Source: *Mayo Clinic Proceedings* 86.4 (2011): 315-21.

WHAT IT SAYS

1. What is the "sliding scale argument," as it relates to the First Amendment to the US Constitution? How is it relevant in *Schwarzenegger v. Entertainment Merchants Association*?

2. What competing theories in game studies apply to this case? Briefly summarize Theory 1 and Theory 2.

3. In what ways is the *Daubert* trilogy not applicable to *Schwarzenegger v. Entertainment Merchants Association*, according to Hall, Day, and Hall?

4. What is the 1950s comic book debate? What is the "Superman complex"? How is it relevant to the present case?

5. What is a "meta-analysis"? What is the gist of Huesmann's and Wertham's testimony?

6. What is meant by the phrase, "a correlation does not prove a causation"? What logical fallacy does this sentence express? (See p. 58 in the Guide to academic writing.) How does it apply to Hall, Day, and Hall's argument?

7. In what ways is *Entertainment Software Association v. Rod Blagojevich* relevant to *Schwarzenegger v. Entertainment Merchants Association*?

8. What are the possible implications of the outcome of *Schwarzenegger v. Entertainment Merchants Association*?

HOW IT SAYS IT

1. How does Table 2.7 serve to advance the argument of the article?

2. How do the long excerpts from Dr. Fredric Wertham's and Dr. L.R. Huesmann's testimony serve to promote the argument?

3. How do the numerous citations of previous studies, both in the text and in the reference list, work to promote this study's argument?

WRITE ABOUT IT

1. Create a synthesis grid that includes all the evidence (studies, testimony, etc.) mentioned in this article. Before you begin, review the section on synthesis grids in the Guide to academic writing (see pp. 77–79).

2. Imagine that you are a member of the Supreme Court. Write a response that takes a stance for or against *Schwarzenegger v. Entertainment Merchants Association*. Support your arguments using Hall, Day, and Hall, as well as your assessment of the constitutionality of this case, based on your reading of the US Constitution and previous cases. If you wish, discuss this case as a group and write both a majority and a minority ruling.

3. Imagine that you are a member of the California senate. Write a speech to deliver to your fellow senators in which you argue for or against legislation to restrict the sale or rental of violent video games to minors. Use Hall, Day, and Hall and other studies to back up your argument. Propose practical ways for your version of the law to be implemented. Address the moral and legal implications of this program. If you wish, videotape the speech and post it online.

g. Christopher J. Ferguson, "A Further Plea for Caution against Medical Professionals Overstating Video Game Violence Effects"

Christopher J. Ferguson is an associate professor of psychology and criminal justice at Texas A&M International University in Laredo. His research involves the impact of genetics, family environment, personality, mental health, and media violence on violent behavior. His most recent studies have questioned the common belief among psychologists that violent media violence contributes to aggression. His publications include numerous scientific articles, a book, *Violent Crime: Clinical and Social Implications* (2009), and a novel, *The Suicide Kings* (2012).

Ferguson holds a BA from Stetson University, an MS from Florida International University, and a PhD from the University of Central Florida, all in psychology.

The letter below is a response to Hall, Day, and Hall's article on overstating the effects of violent video games. In line with his research, Ferguson adds to Hall, Day, and Hall's argument, strengthening it. The letter also updates the status of the US Supreme Court case *Schwarzenegger v. Entertainment Merchants Association*.

As You Read: Think about your own reaction to the Hall, Day, and Hall article. In what ways is your response similar to Ferguson's? In what ways do you disagree?

A Further Plea for Caution against Medical Professionals Overstating Video Game Violence Effects

To the Editor: On the day I write this, the US Supreme Court has struck down California's attempt to ban violent video games to minors. The State of California, while acknowledging that existing research could not determine that video games cause harm to minors, nonetheless relied on a biased and misleading representation of the research in this field to support *their contention* that video games "harm" minors. Writing for the US Supreme Court majority, Justice Antonin Scalia noted that the research is in fact "not compelling" and "most of the studies suffer from significant, admitted flaws in methodology." The only "harm" by video games in this case is not to minors but to the scientific community itself because it has insisted on an ideological position that increasingly has come at odds with the data.

In generations past, medical scholars warned society about the purported harms of various media ranging from dime novels through jazz music, comic books, rock and roll music, and Dungeons and Dragons (a role-playing game).[1] None of these fears materialized, and the scientific community expended significant capital in pursuing these beliefs long past the time in which data could support them. In their article, Hall et al.[2] caution us that medical science may be repeating the errors of the past, ratcheting up claims of harmful video game violence effects even as data increasingly contradict such claims. As one of the leading video game researchers in the United States, I read this well-researched and timely article with great interest. To the warning by Hall et al., I add my own: Previous claims of "harm" due to video games were a mistake, and the medical community will only expend further political and scientific capital by insisting on the existence of harmful effects despite increasing evidence to the contrary.

Careful review of the scientific evidence reveals that not only are data increasingly pointing away from harmful effects but also that such data were never consistent even when some scholars attempted to claim they were.[3] Methodological problems abound in this field, including lack of valid aggression measures, failure to adequately control for other important variables, and a tendency to interpret weak and inconsistent results as if supportive of causal theories. However, although small in number, a few studies have corrected these issues. When aggression is measured using valid tools and other variables are carefully controlled, little evidence emerges for harmful video game violence effects.[4-6] Interestingly, these results are achieved regardless of the position in the debates the authors have taken in the past, although some scholars attempt to deemphasize their own results.[5] Prospective analyses have found little evidence for long-term harm,[6] and some suggest violent game exposure may be associated with reduced aggression.[7] Of three groups to have conducted meta-analyses on the topic, two replicated each other in concluding that no evidence exists for harmful effects.[8,9] Both these groups have been critical of the third group[10] for, among other issues, exaggerating the importance of the weak effects observed in their own research and failing to include studies that conflicted with their views. Add to these societal data in which the introduction of violent games into our society has been met with a precipitous decline in youth violence to 40-year lows, and we see that the data from various sources converge to oppose the belief that violent games are harmful.

These conclusions are not merely my own but are also based on a review of the literature by the Australian government,[11] to date the only independent review on the topic. (Policy statements by professional groups were compromised by committees of antigame scholars reviewing their own work and declaring it beyond further debate. Such statements should not be considered independent reviews.) The US Supreme Court now appears to concur in this assessment as well. Thus, comments by Hall et al. and other scholars increasingly warn us of the damage done by the insistence on a rigid scientific ideology in the face of contrasting evidence. I have little doubt that the reasonable cautionary statements by Hall et al. will be met by angry calls from some scholars for an insistence on doctrinal purity. In past media moral panics, medical scholars expended significant prestige and capital insisting media effects *must be true* even as evidence rolled in to contradict those claims. We have reached this point once again. I call on medical science to begin the process of self-correction and cease making spurious claims for harmful effects that increasingly conflict with the available data. The time for scientific correction has arrived.

Christopher J. Ferguson, PhD
Texas A&M International University
Laredo

References

1. Ferguson CJ. Blazing angels or resident evil? Can violent video games be a force for good? *Rev Gen Psychol.* 2010;14(2):68-81.

2. Hall RCW, Day T, Hall RCW. A plea for caution: violent video games, the Supreme Court, and the role of science. *Mayo Clin Proc.* 2011;86(4):315-321.

3. Olson C. Children's motivations for video game play in the context of normal development. *Rev Gen Psychol.* 2010;14(2):180-187.

4. Desai RA, Krishnan-Sarin S, Cavallo D, Potenza MN. Video-gaming among high school students: health correlates, gender differences, and problematic gaming. *Pediatrics.* 2010;126(6):e1414-e1424.

5. Ybarra ML, Diener-West M, Markow D, Leaf PJ, Hamburger M, Boxer P. Linkages between internet and other media violence with seriously violent behavior by youth. *Pediatrics.* 2008;122(5):929-937.

6. Ferguson CJ. Video games and youth violence: a prospective analysis in adolescents. *J Youth Adolesc.* 2011;40(4):377-391.

7. Shibuya A, Sakamoto A, Ihori N, Yukawa S. The effects of the presence and contexts of video game violence on children: a longitudinal study in Japan. *Simul Gaming.* 2008;39(4):528-539.

8. Sherry J. Violent video games and aggression: Why can't we find effects? In: Preiss RW, Gayle BM, Burrell N, Allen M, Bruant J, eds. *Mass Media Effects Research: Advances Through Meta-analysis.* Mahwah, NJ: Lawrence Erlbaum Associates; 2007:245-262.

9. Ferguson CJ, Kilburn J. The public health risks of media violence: a meta-analytic review. *J Pediatr.* 2009;154(5):759-763.

10. Anderson CA, Shibuya A, Ihori N, et al. Violent video game effects on aggression, empathy, and prosocial behavior in Eastern and Western countries: a meta-analytic review. *Psychol Bull.* 2010; 136(2): 151-173.

11. Australian Government, Attorney General's Department. *Literature Review on the Impact of Playing Violent Video Games on Aggression.* Published September 2010. Commonwealth of Australia. http://www.ag.gov.au/www/ agd/rwpattach.nsf/VAP/%283A6790B96C927794AF1031D9395C5C20%29~ Literature+Review+-+VVGs+and+Aggression+-+November+2010.PDF/$file/ Literature+Review+-+VVGs+and+Aggression+-+November+2010.PDF. Accessed July 7, 2011.

Source: *Mayo Clinic Proceedings* 86.8 (2011): 820-21.

WHAT IT SAYS

1. What factors caused the US Supreme Court to strike down *Schwarzenegger v. Entertainment Merchants Association?*

2. In what ways does Ferguson's argument extend the argument of Hall, Day, and Hall? What specific evidence supports these additional claims?

3. What "methodological problems" does Ferguson cite regarding video game research? What is the effect of these problems, according to Ferguson?

4. What methodological improvements have provided for more reliable data, according to Ferguson?

5. What do the more reliable studies show about violent video games, according to Ferguson? What other evidence backs up the results of these studies?

6. What response to the Supreme Court does Ferguson predict? What response does he recommend?

HOW IT SAYS IT

1. How does Ferguson use ethos to support his argument?

2. How does Ferguson use the study of Hall, Day, and Hall to promote his own argument?

3. What effect does putting quotation marks around the word "harm" have in this letter?

WRITE ABOUT IT

1. If you created a synthesis grid for the evidence (studies, testimony, etc.) presented by Hall, Day, and Hall, add evidence from Ferguson. Then write a short reflection on the ways in which Ferguson strengthens or weakens the argument of Hall, Day, and Hall.

2. Read the majority and the minority opinion on *Schwarzenegger v. Entertainment Merchants Association*. Then write an analysis of both opinions, and reflect on the implications of this decision for further regulation, or de-regulation, of video game design, sales, and rentals. Part of your reflection could include actual changes in video game design, sales, and rentals since this decision.

3. Create a short documentary that reflects on the Supreme Court decision in *Schwarzenegger v. Entertainment Merchants Association*, and its implications for the future of video games and the gaming industry. Use existing footage and/or new interviews and other images to illustrate your documentary. Post your video online and enable comments.

Questions for Synthesis

1. Write an essay that explores the views expressed by the authors in this chapter on the effects of video and electronic gaming on players. Be especially aware of contradictions and confluences among the various arguments.

   - How do the various authors interpret the effects of playing violent video games on behavior?
   - How do the various authors interpret the effects of playing video games on cognition?
   - What actions should be taken in light of these effects, according to the authors?
   - On what specific points do the authors agree and disagree?

   Remember that this is a synthesis essay, not a contribution. Your goal is to faithfully represent the positions of these writers, not to argue your position. You may wish to construct a synthesis grid (see pp. 77–79) to begin writing.

2. Write an essay that explores proposals the authors in this chapter make for responding to the effects of playing video games. What outcomes do the authors predict to the recommendations that they provide? Write this essay as a synthesis of the authors' views, not as a contribution.

Questions for Contribution

1. Keeping in mind all the articles and points of view in this chapter, write an essay that argues *for* or *against* <u>one</u> of these aspects of gaming:

   - the negative effects of violent video games on the behavior of players, particularly younger players;
   - the positive effects of video games on cognition and learning among players;
   - the need to regulate the content of video games, for all players or exclusively for young players;
   - the need to incorporate video and e-gaming into the classroom at all levels, in order to encourage brain development and learning.

2. Write a detailed set of guidelines for responding to the behavioral and cognitive effects of playing video games. Consider the legal, moral, and practical implications of these guidelines on all groups involved (game designers and producers, players, parents, educators, etc.). Include in your guidelines a plan for persuading these groups both to agree to and to follow your guidelines.

   You may wish to present your plan as a videotaped presentation that is posted online, or as a speech delivered live before your class.

   Illustrate your points with slides, photographs, and video and audio clips, so that your presentation involves more than just a "talking head." For support and examples, draw on the sources included in this chapter, the Suggested Additional Resources, and recent news events and statistics. Be sure to acknowledge and address views contrary to your own.

3. Write an educational plan for an elementary, secondary, or university policy on the use of video and e-games to promote cognition and learning. Make a strong case for the positive effects of game playing on learning. Include practical instructions for implementing your plan. Structure your essay or presentation so that a non-expert can easily follow it. For support, draw on the sources in this chapter, the Suggested Additional Resources, and, if applicable, your own experience.

CHAPTER 3

LEARNING IN A DIGITAL AGE

INTRODUCTION

Contexts of Discussion

Here you are, in college. You've decided to enroll in a program of higher education for a reason: to educate yourself. But what does it mean to be educated? What is an educated person? More importantly, how should you go about becoming educated? If you're not sure of the answers to these questions, you are not alone. Education has been a subject of controversy for some time. And the controversy has never been more heated than it is right now.

You've enrolled in a college or university as higher education grapples with the digital revolution, or, as some prefer, digital **convergence** (see the essay by Henry Jenkins in Chapter 1). Colleges and universities struggle to keep pace with the digital age; meanwhile, digital media throw a new light on learning, teaching, and what it means to know.

This chapter explores many of the important issues involved with learning and education in a digital age.

As a college student today, you are most likely deeply immersed in **Web 2.0** and other digital technologies, far more so than most of your teachers. Perhaps you are a **digital native**. If so, the relatively new Web 2.0 technologies are likely second nature to you. You likely have used them to meet, play, date, and learn. They are an integral part of your social life. They have likely played an important part in shaping your identity. Likewise, you may expect that this technology will play a part in your formal education. Whether that expectation will be met depends both on the attitudes and the policies of your institution and instructors, and on your own ability to integrate these technologies into your formal education.

As you may have guessed, not all educators agree about the role of digital technologies in the classroom and beyond. Some see the digital explosion as an unnecessary invasion of the curriculum, or as a set of onerous requirements imposed by administrators. Many others seek to maximize the potential that new technologies offer and to discover the best uses for them. Still others encourage critical evaluation and engagement as opposed to unqualified enthusiasm and acceptance.

Scholars in many fields are involved in the study of learning in a digital age. Below, we discuss some of these fields and their interests in the study of digital technology and learning.

Areas of Research and Conjecture

Pedagogy is the study of theories, beliefs, policies, and discourses related to education and teaching. All the essays in this chapter are arguments about pedagogy.

One of the most relevant selections that we include in the Suggested Additional Resources is *Pedagogy of the Oppressed*, a pioneering work by the Brazilian educational theorist Paolo Freire, first published in Portuguese in 1968. Freire argued that conventional education serves to produce students who, as passive recipients of knowledge, become docile subjects who accept the status quo. In place of this "banking" concept of education, Freire proposed a participatory pedagogy of liberation from oppressive socio-economic conditions. In Freire's "problem-posing" model, students and teachers become co-creators of knowledge in a world that is being remade through the process of the educational situation itself.

Many educators have been directly or indirectly influenced by Freire's work; the question of participatory education figures prominently in the readings in this chapter. See in particular Sarita Yardi's "Whispers in the Classroom," and "Paulo Freire and ICTs: Liberatory Education Theory in a Digital Age," by John Freie and Susan M. Behuniak.

Educational technology is a relatively new interdisciplinary field that involves the study of learning with the use of appropriate technologies. The field incorporates theories of learning and thus is not strictly the study of technological devices. It is generally distinguished from **instructional technology** in that the latter is understood to be the study of the uses of various technological devices for learning, whereas educational technology is a study of learning itself, with technology as one component. Most of the essays in this chapter can be considered contributions to the field of educational technology.

The digital humanities is an interdisciplinary humanities field aimed at developing publishing, teaching, and research methodologies derived from computing. Digitization has made possible an array of computational tools with the potential to radically change reading, publishing, and research. These include data mining of vast data sets (for example, periodicals from the nineteenth century), textual analysis and text classification, and the curating of online publications. Scholars involved in the digital humanities focus on implementing technologies that enhance their research with quantitative analysis. We include the writings of several practitioners and proponents, as well as critics, of the digital humanities in the Suggested Additional Resources.

The field of **media studies** originated with the study of mass media: print media, film, radio, and television. Of course, current media studies scholars are also interested in the study of digital media and the role of digital technologies in the classroom and beyond. For example, media studies scholar Henry Jenkins, whose essay is included in Chapter 1, studies the role of digital technologies in developing a participatory culture in education. A white paper Jenkins co-authored with Ravi Purushotma, entitled "Confronting the Challenges of Participatory Culture: Media Education for the 21st Century," is included in the Suggested Additional Resources at the end of this introduction.

As we suggested above, digital technology has impacted nearly every discipline in higher education. Experimentation and regular practices are underway in the humanities, social sciences, sciences, and technology. Some uses are considered in this chapter. For a discussion of others, see the paper by John Seely Brown, "Learning in the Digital Age," included in Suggested Additional Resources.

Issues and Stakeholders

Information and Knowledge: Our era has been called the **Information Age**, and for good reason: we are awash in information. For example, a January 2012 issue of the *Economist* reported that more than 300 billion e-mails, 200 million tweets, and 2.5 billion text messages circulate through our digital networks every day. As of December 2011, there were more than 366 million Internet websites. Google Books aims to put the world's collective publications online, creating a virtual utopia of literary access.

Does all this information make us smarter, or, as some have suggested, dumber? Educational theorists like to remind us that knowledge and information are not identical: information exists independently of any knower—it exists "out there" in the infospheres that we have created; knowledge, on the other hand, requires a knower, or, some argue, a knowledge community. In a sense, knowledge cannot be isolated or pinpointed in discrete units. Rather, it is intimately intertwined with the people who know, and is generally only demonstrable in practice.

Knowledge consists of both "know-how" and "know-what." It requires knowers to assimilate conventions or ways of being in the world. Knowing how to write an essay, for example, involves understanding conventions and methods that are based in communities and not strictly in any one person's mind. Likewise, the Information Age presents challenges and opportunities for knowledge communities.

The articles in this chapter address such questions as these:

- With all the information available in the world, what does it mean to be knowledgeable?
- Can Internet technologies facilitate the learning processes necessary for acquiring knowledge?
- Do **information and communication technologies (ICTs)** merely propagate information that passes for knowledge?
- Might ICTs *interfere* with learning?

Teachers and students: The emergence of the digital world in education, many scholars suggest, means that the relationship between students and teachers has changed, as has the relationship of students to knowledge itself.

Sarita Yardi argues in her essay "Whispers in the Classroom," included in this chapter, that as information becomes more democratically distributed through the Internet, the roles of students and teachers also change. According to Yardi, the relationship of teacher to student is no longer one of the teapot to the teacup, or, in Paolo Freire's famous analogy, of the depositor to the bank account. In the digital age, because information is so readily available on the Internet, the teacher's role shifts from knowledge-bearer to facilitator; students become producers of their own knowledge, rather than receptacles of the teacher's knowledge. Given the ready access to knowledge acquisition and production, students become empowered at the expense of their teachers' power—or so the theory goes. No longer the sole possessors of knowledge, teachers will have to reconstruct their roles in education.

Not everyone celebrates such changes in power dynamics. Some teachers, presumably, may resent and argue against ceding their authority. Others welcome the ways in which digital technology can be further integrated into the classroom, potentially allowing students to become more active in their own educations. Cathy N. Davidson is one such theorist and educator. Her essay, "Collaborative Learning for the Digital Age," is included in this chapter.

Others suggest that the issue is more complicated than a simple opposition between progressive pedagogues on one side and anti-technology educational conservatives on the other. In this chapter, John F. Freie and Susan M. Behuniak argue that the new technologies only superficially resemble the kinds of participatory culture imagined by Freire. Instead, ICTs might even be agents of banking education, or the depositing of information into students, which Freire deemed to be so oppressive.

New and old literacies: Literacy theorists have long maintained that book learning constitutes only one of many kinds of literacy. Further, literacy is always context-dependent; it requires not only (or sometimes not even) study, but also participation in an area of knowledge. Today, competence extends beyond print-based textual literacy to visual literacies, including new kinds of textual and image communications and interpretation. The ability to "write," "read," and interpret multimedia texts is crucial in a digital world.

Digital natives and savvy Internet participants have developed their own semantics, syntax, and composition conventions as part of online communications in a digital culture. These include not only textual abbreviations on Twitter, Facebook, and other social media sites but also an ability to communicate volumes through static and moving images, music, and other media. Equally important, digital natives are accustomed to sifting through and synthesizing masses of information, a skill that is key to literacy today.

The readings in this chapter address such questions as these:

- Will these new literacies become essential to higher education, or will they be relegated to the margins?
- Will laptops or electronic tablets replace books, or will they be banished from the classroom? (See the essay by Timothy Snyder, "Why Laptops in Class Are Distracting America's Future Workforce," included in this chapter.)
- Will the new literacies become mandatory?
- How will the new literacies be incorporated and assessed?

Online-only education: Another major issue involves the availability and viability of online-only education. Related to the use of ICTs in and around the face-to-face classroom, online-only education has arisen as an alternative to higher education. Piloted by such institutions as the University of Phoenix, online education has been taken up for course offerings by numerous colleges and universities. Recently, elite institutions such as Stanford and Princeton began offering online courses to students beyond those enrolled at brick-and-mortar campuses. See the essay by Thomas Friedman, entitled "Come the Revolution," in this chapter.

Advocates point to the cost savings and increased availability of online education for a much broader population segment who otherwise could not afford the increasingly prohibitive costs of higher education. They commend the interactive qualities of online education as students create virtual communities of participatory learners. Yet others suggest that online-only education misses a critical component of a university education: embodied learning communities. Information delivery does not equal knowledge, these critics assert. Knowledge involves the interaction of participants in knowledge communities. This kind of experiential learning cannot be distributed through online networks alone. It must be encountered in direct, in-person contact with other knowledge practitioners. This is the view asserted by Freie and Behuniak in this chapter, and by John Seely Brown in "Learning in the Digital Age," included in the Suggested Additional Resources at the end of this introduction.

New careers: The new digital knowledge economy has opened up a host of new career opportunities, including positions in archives and preservation management, human computer interaction (HCI), information analysis and retrieval, information management, information policy, library and information services, records management, and social computing. But these new careers (and almost all careers) will require individuals who are at least minimally trained in the digital arts and sciences. On this topic, see *The New Information Professional: Your Guide to Careers in the Digital Age* by Judy Lawson, Joanna Kroll, and Kelly Kowatch. For an overview of the skills needed in a knowledge economy, see "What You (Really) Need to Know," by Lawrence H. Summers. Both sources are included in the Suggested Additional Resources.

As You Read

Consider how readings in this chapter connect with your own uses of digital technologies and your experiences in formal education:

- How well do the writers address the issues, as you see them?
- Do they characterize your own uses of digital technologies, especially Web 2.0 applications?
- What do you make of the changes underway in higher education?

Suggested Additional Resources

Communications and Media Studies

Bennett, W.L. *Civic Life Online: Learning How Digital Media Can Engage Youth.* The John D. and Catherine T. MacArthur Foundation Series on Digital Media and Learning. Cambridge, MA: MIT Press, 2008.

Daley, Elizabeth. "Expanding the Concept of Literacy." *Educause Review* 38.2 (2003): 32-40.

Flew, Terry, and Richard Keith Smith. *New Media: An Introduction.* South Melbourne, Vic.: Oxford University Press, 2014.

Itō, Mizuko. *Living and Learning with New Media: Summary of Findings from the Digital Youth Project.* Chicago: John D. and Catherine T. MacArthur Foundation, 2008. Web.

——, and Judd Antin. *Hanging Out, Messing Around, and Geeking Out: Kids Living and Learning with New Media.* Cambridge, MA: MIT Press, 2010. Web.

Jenkins, Henry, and Ravi Purushotma. *Confronting the Challenges of Participatory Culture: Media Education for the 21st Century.* Chicago: MacArthur Foundation, 2009. Web.

Squire, Kurt, and Henry Jenkins. *Video Games and Learning: Teaching and Participatory Culture in the Digital Age.* New York: Teachers College Press, 2011.

Computer Science

Wong, Yue-Ling. *Digital Media Primer*. Indianapolis: Prentice Hall, 2008.

Digital Humanities

Aiden, Erez, and Jean-Baptiste Michel. *Uncharted: Big Data as a Lens on Human Culture*. New York: Riverhead, 2013.

Berry, David M. *Understanding Digital Humanities*. Houndmills, UK: Palgrave Macmillan, 2012.

Borgman, Christine L. *Scholarship in the Digital Age: Information, Infrastructure, and the Internet*. Cambridge, MA: MIT Press, 2007.

Bryson, Tim. *Digital Humanities*. Washington, DC: Association of Research Libraries, 2011. Web.

Bugeja, Michael J., and Daniela V. Dimitrova. *Vanishing Act: The Erosion of Online Footnotes and Implications for Scholarship in the Digital Age*. Duluth, MN: Litwin Books, 2010.

Burdick, Anne. *Digital Humanities*. Cambridge, MA: MIT Press, 2012. Web.

Deegan, Marilyn, and Willard McCarty. *Collaborative Research in the Digital Humanities*. Farnham, UK: Ashgate, 2011. Web.

Deyrup, Marta M. *Digital Scholarship*. New York: Routledge, 2009. Web.

Earhart, Amy E., and Andrew Jewell. *The American Literature Scholar in the Digital Age*. Ann Arbor: University of Michigan Press and University of Michigan Library, 2011.

Fitzpatrick, Kathleen. *Planned Obsolescence: Publishing, Technology, and the Future of the Academy*. New York: New York UP, 2011. Web.

Gold, Matthew K. *Debates in the Digital Humanities*. Minneapolis: U of Minnesota P, 2012.

Jockers, Matthew L. *Macroanalysis: Digital Methods and Literary History*. Champaign: U of Illinois P, 2013.

McGann, Jerome J. *A New Republic of Letters: Memory and Scholarship in the Age of Digital Reproduction*. Cambridge, MA: Harvard UP, 2014.

Moretti, Franco. *Distant Reading*. London: Verso, 2013.

Schreibman, Susan, Ray Siemens, and John Unsworth. *A Companion to Digital Humanities*. Oxford: Blackwell Publishing, 2007. Web.

Terras, Melissa M., Julianne Nyhan, and Edward Vanhoutte. *Defining Digital Humanities: A Reader*. Farnham, UK: Ashgate, 2013.

Wardrip-Fruin, Noah, and Michael Mateus. "Media Systems—Envisioning the Future of Digital Humanities." *Journal of Digital Humanities* 3.1 (2014). Web.

Warwick, Claire, Melissa M. Terras, and Julianne Nyhan. *Digital Humanities in Practice*. London: Facet Publishing in association with UCL Centre for Digital Humanities, 2012.

Weinberger, David. *Everything Is Miscellaneous: The Power of the New Digital Disorder*. New York: Times Books, 2007.

Weller, Toni. *History in the Digital Age*. London: Routledge, 2013.

Whitson, Roger, and Jason Whittaker. *William Blake and the Digital Humanities: Collaboration, Participation, and Social Media*. New York: Routledge, 2013.

Education

Alvermann, Donna E. *Adolescents' Online Literacies: Connecting Classrooms, Digital Media, and Popular Culture*. New York: Peter Lang, 2010.

Brown, John Seely. "Learning in the Digital Age." *The Internet and the University: Forum 2001*. Ed. Maureen Devlin, Richard C. Larson, and Joel W. Meyerson. Boulder, CO: EDUCAUSE, 2002. 65-86.

Coley, Toby F. *Teaching with Digital Media in Writing Studies: An Exploration of Ethical Responsibilities*. New York: Peter Lang, 2012.

Crawford, Matthew B. "Science Education and Liberal Education." *The New Atlantis* (Spring 2005): 49-60.

Davidson, Cathy N., and David T. Goldberg. *The Future of Thinking: Learning Institutions in a Digital Age*. Cambridge, MA: MIT Press, 2010. Web.

DePietro, Peter. "Transforming Education with New Media: Participatory Pedagogy, Interactive Learning and Web 2.0." *International Journal of Technology, Knowledge & Society* 8.5 (2012): 1-11.

Drotner, Kirsten, Hans S. Jensen, and Kim Schrøder. *Informal Learning and Digital Media*. Newcastle, UK: Cambridge Scholars, 2008.

Everett, Anna. *Learning Race and Ethnicity: Youth and Digital Media*. The John D. and Catherine T. MacArthur Foundation Series on Digital Media and Learning. Cambridge, MA: MIT Press, 2008.

Flanagin, Andrew J., Miriam J. Metzger, and Ethan Hartsell. *Kids and Credibility: An Empirical Examination of Youth, Digital Media Use, and Information Credibility*. Cambridge, MA: MIT Press, 2010.

Freire, Paulo. *Pedagogy of the Oppressed*. New York: Continuum, 2004.

Gee, James P. *New Digital Media and Learning as an Emerging Area and "Worked Examples" as One Way Forward*. Cambridge, MA: MIT Press, 2010. Web.

Itō, Mizuko. *Connected Learning: An Agenda for Research and Design*. Digital Media and Learning Research Hub, 2013. Archival material.

James, Carrie. *Young People, Ethics, and the New Digital Media: A Synthesis from the Goodplay Project*. Cambridge, MA: MIT Press, 2009. Web.

King, Kathleen P., and Thomas D. Cox. *The Professor's Guide to Taming Technology: Leveraging Digital Media, Web 2.0, and More for Learning*. Charlotte, NC: Information Age, 2011.

Lawson, Judy, Joanna Kroll, and Kelly Kowatch. *The New Information Professional: Your Guide to Careers in the Digital Age*. New York: Neal-Schuman, 2010. Web.

Luke, Timothy W., and Jeremy Hunsinger. *Putting Knowledge to Work and Letting Information Play: The Center for Digital Discourse and Culture*. Blacksburg, VA: Center for Digital Discourse and Culture, Virginia Tech, 2009. Web.

McClure, Randall, and James P. Purdy, eds. *The New Digital Scholar: Exploring and Enriching the Research and Writing Practices of Nextgen Students*. Medford, NJ: Information Today, 2013.

McPherson, Tara. *Digital Youth, Innovation, and the Unexpected*. Cambridge, MA: MIT Press, 2008. Web.

Pfeffer, Thomas. *Virtualization of Universities: Digital Media and the Organization of Higher Education Institutions*. New York: Springer, 2012. Web.

Potter, John. *Digital Media and Learner Identity: The New Curatorship*. New York: Palgrave Macmillan, 2012.

Schwartz, Daniel L., and Dylan Arena. *Measuring What Matters Most: Choice-based Assessments for the Digital Age*. Cambridge, MA: MIT Press, 2013.

Weller, Martin. *The Digital Scholar: How Technology Is Transforming Scholarly Practice*. London: Bloomsbury Academic, 2011. Web.

Williamson, Ben. *The Future of the Curriculum: School Knowledge in the Digital Age*. Cambridge, MA: MIT Press, 2013.

Journalism

Digital Media—New Learners of the 21st Century. PBS Home Video, 2011. Web.

Fish, Stanley. "The Digital Humanities and the Transcending of Mortality." Editorial. *New York Times* 9 Jan. 2012. Web.

Kirsch, Adam. "Technology Is Taking Over English Departments: The False Promise of the Digital Humanities." *New Republic* 2 May 2014. Web.

Lawrence, Summers H. "What You (Really) Need to Know." *New York Times* 20 Jan. 2012. Web.

Self, Will. "The Novel Is Dead (this Time It's for Real)." *Guardian* 3 May 2014. Web.

Talbert, Robert. "Flipped Learning Skepticism: Can Students Really Learn on Their Own?" Blog post. *Casting Out Nines*. 1 April 2014. Web.

——. "Flipped Learning Skepticism: Is Flipped Learning Just Self-Teaching?" Blog post. *Casting Out Nines*. 28 April 2014. Web.

——. "Toward a Common Definition of 'Flipped Learning.'" Blog post. *Casting Out Nines*. 30 April 2014. Web.

"Top Universities Test the Online Appeal of Free." *New York Times* 17 July 2012. Web.

a. Timothy D. Snyder, "Why Laptops in Class Are Distracting America's Future Workforce"

Timothy D. Snyder is Bird White Housum Professor of History at Yale University. He has written five award-winning books, including *Nationalism, Marxism, and Modern Central Europe: A Biography of Kazimierz Kelles-Krauz* (1998), *The Reconstruction of Nations: Poland, Ukraine, Lithuania, Belarus, 1569-1999* (2003), *Sketches from a Secret War: A Polish Artist's Mission to Liberate Soviet Ukraine* (2005), and *The Red Prince: The Secret Lives of A Habsburg Archduke* (2008). He also is co-editor of *Wall around the West: State Power and Immigration Controls in Europe and North America* (2001).

In 2010 Snyder published *Bloodlands: Europe Between Hitler and Stalin*, a history of Nazi and Soviet mass killing on the lands between Berlin and Moscow. It has received a number of honors, including the Leipzig Prize for European Understanding and the Ralph Waldo Emerson Award in the Humanities. It was named a book of the year by some dozen publications, has been translated into more than 20 languages, and was a bestseller in four countries. Recently he helped Tony Judt compose a thematic history of political ideas and intellectuals in politics, *Thinking the Twentieth Century* (2012).

A graduate of Brown University, Snyder earned his PhD in 1995 at the University of Oxford as a Marshall Scholar. He was an Academy Scholar at Harvard University from 1998 to 2001 and has also studied at the Institut für die Wissenschaften vom Menschen in Vienna.

In this essay, "Why Laptops in Class Are Distracting America's Future Workforce," published in the *Christian Science Monitor*, Snyder argues against student laptop use in the classroom, suggesting that in-class screen time diverts student attention from the most important aspect of their educations—interaction with professors and each other. Technology-focused college students, he argues, are missing out on the best part of American life. He also asserts that the digital habits that students are developing in and outside the classroom will spill over into the workplace.

As You Read: What are your thoughts about the use of laptops (or any device connected to the Internet) in the classroom? Are digital media distracting you and your peers? Does the Internet have a place in the classroom? If so, what is it?

Why Laptops in Class Are Distracting America's Future Workforce

As these first few weeks of the college semester begin, professors look out expectantly into grand lecture halls, where they see, rather than faces of students, the backs of open laptops. The students, for their part, are looking intently at the laptop screens. What are they doing as they stare forward with such apparent focus?

Thanks to wireless Internet access, they are updating their Facebook, Twitter, and Tumblr profiles; they are chatting on Skype, Gchat, or iChat; they are making travel plans, or reading the newspaper, or following the pennant race. This fall, higher education lost yet another new class of freshmen, as the new students learned that the university classroom is just one more physical place to be on the Internet.

I teach at Yale, where lecturing is taken seriously—and in history, which boasts some of the best teachers. My ratings as a lecturer are consistently high. But even here, I would not have the attention of these very gifted students if I did not ban laptops and smartphones from my classroom. Part of the problem is that students are not paying attention at a given moment; part of the problem is that they often lack the ability to pay attention at all.

Of course, some of them think they are paying attention: The well-intentioned are checking the professor's facts by googling. This is not a good use of that powerful tool, because what they learn in the class comes only from the class, and has a richness and precision they won't get online. Once the search happens, the students miss the next minute of lecture, or even more, as they then follow the next appealing link. It doesn't take long to get from googling Habermas to reading about Lady Gaga.

The Scale of the Problem

Almost none of my colleagues have any sense of the scale of the problem. To most professors over 50, the computer is an educational tool. If a student asked a professor for permission to bring a television set to class, the professor would be shocked. But a laptop connected to the Internet is, among other things, a television set. During lectures, students at our very best schools watch TV shows, video clips, and movies on YouTube, Hulu, or Vimeo. The forest of laptops may look much better than a television set on every desk, but in fact, it's far worse.

In the beginning, about 15 years ago, students really did just use their laptops to take notes. But step by step, and so imperceptibly, we have moved to a situation where even the students who want to take notes are distracted by their own screens and those of their neighbors. The one devoted student using pen and paper is also distracted by the glow and flash, and the noise of fingers on keypads. It's hard, as a student at another Ivy League school told me, to keep the focus after forty-five minutes of hard work when one neighbor has a music video going and the other is checking his stocks on line.

What We're Losing

Meanwhile, we are losing the long tradition of people learning from other people. The lecture course, in one form or another, has been around for more than 2,000 years. The ability of one human being to reach another by speech is an irreplaceable part of what it means to be human. In seminars, laptops are still more harmful, serving as physical barriers that prevent a group of students from becoming a class.

Even more concerning, after university, students who could not concentrate in the classroom will become workers who cannot concentrate in the workplace. It is possible that the American economy will never out-compete others because we have the most easily distracted workforce.

How to Reconnect with Our Humanity

Removing laptops from the classroom gives students a chance to focus, and a chance to learn to focus. Without the flash of screens and the sound of typing, they find themselves ... learning. In most courses, much is lost and nothing is gained by the use of the Internet. If the students need to use the Internet, they have the remaining 23 hours of the day, and indeed the rest of their lives, to do their screen-staring.

College students who spend their time online are missing out not only on education, but on experience. The four years of university are probably the best part of American life. It seems a shame to spend that time doing something that can be done anywhere and at any time. By allowing students to spend class time on the Internet, we professors are sending the message that college is just one more backdrop for googling.

And what do the students think? Almost all of them, judging from the student evaluations of my previous courses, saw the logic of the laptop ban, and liked the atmosphere of calm and concentration that it permitted. If, at some future point, the tide of student opinion turns against me, I have one final argument: Ever since the laptop ban was inaugurated, my students have been earning far better grades.

Source: *The Christian Science Monitor* 7 Oct. 2010. Web. http://www.csmonitor.com/Commentary/Opinion/2010/1007/Why-laptops-in-class-are-distracting-America-s-future-workforce.

WHAT IT SAYS

1. In paragraph four of the essay, Snyder suggests that students who search for information about their professors' lectures during class time may think that they are paying attention, but they are not. What are they missing out on by googling such information, according to Snyder? What is the difference between what students might find on the Internet and what they might experience otherwise?

2. In the same paragraph, Snyder states: "It doesn't take long to get from googling Habermas to reading about Lady Gaga." What is Snyder getting at with this remark? Who is Habermas and why is Habermas being contrasted with Lady Gaga? Further, what does the connection Snyder draws between the two say about the Internet?

3. Snyder notes that the classroom lecture has a history of more than 2,000 years. Why does he mention this historical fact?

4. Snyder seems to suggest that the ubiquity of the Internet comes at a great cost. What is this cost?

5. Why does Snyder mention his students' grades at the end of the essay?

HOW IT SAYS IT

1. Snyder mentions that he teaches at Yale and that his teaching ratings are consistently high. Why do you suppose he mentions his institutional affiliation and his teaching ratings? How do these ethos statements help to advance his argument?

2. Who is Snyder trying to convince? What hints does he give about his intended audience?

3. Describe the tone and diction of the essay. How are these features related to Snyder's argument and audience?

WRITE ABOUT IT

1. Write an essay in which you consider your own Internet and other digital media habits and how these impact your ability to be a good student.

2. Write an essay in which you argue against Snyder's thesis. What might be your claim? What kinds of reasons (evidence, logical reasoning, appeals) might you give to support your case? For example, what advantages might there be for Internet use in the classroom? How might a technologically interactive classroom improve the educational experience?

3. Write an essay in which you examine Snyder's philosophy of teaching or pedagogy. Describe what he sees as the role of the teacher and the student in the educational situation. What is the object of education, as Snyder might put it?

b. Thomas L. Friedman, "Come the Revolution"

Thomas L. Friedman is an internationally renowned author, reporter, and columnist and the recipient of three Pulitzer Prizes, most recently in 2002. Friedman joined *The New York Times* in 1981 and was appointed Beirut bureau chief in 1982. In 1984 he was transferred to Jerusalem, where he served as Israel bureau chief until 1988. He became the paper's foreign-affairs op-ed columnist in 1995. Previously, he served as chief economic correspondent in the Washington bureau and before that he was the paper's chief White House correspondent. In 2005, Mr. Friedman was elected to the Pulitzer Prize Board.

Friedman is the author of six bestselling and award-winning books, including *From Beirut to Jerusalem* (1989), *The Lexus and the Olive Tree* (2000), *Longitudes and Attitudes: Exploring the World After September 11* (2003), *The World Is Flat: A Brief History of the Twenty-First Century* (first published 2005), *Hot, Flat, and Crowded* (2008), and, with Michael Mandelbaum, *That Used to Be Us: How America Fell Behind in the World We Invented and How We Can Come Back* (2011).

Friedman received a BA degree in Mediterranean studies from Brandeis University in 1975 and a Master of Philosophy degree in Modern Middle East studies from Oxford in 1978.

In this article, "Come the Revolution," published in *The New York Times*, Friedman welcomes online-only higher education as both timely and necessary.

As You Read: Consider the possibility of an online-only college education. Do you feel as confident as Friedman that online-only education is the solution to the problems of rising tuition and the increased importance of education in a "knowledge economy"?

Come the Revolution

Andrew Ng is an associate professor of computer science at Stanford, and he has a rather charming way of explaining how the new interactive online education company that he cofounded, Coursera, hopes to revolutionize higher education by allowing students from all over the world to not only hear his lectures, but to do homework assignments, be graded, receive a certificate for completing the course and use that to get a better job or gain admission to a better school.

"I normally teach 400 students," Ng explained, but last semester he taught 100,000 in an online course on machine learning. "To reach that many students before," he said, "I would have had to teach my normal Stanford class for 250 years."

Welcome to the college education revolution. Big breakthroughs happen when what is suddenly possible meets what is desperately necessary. The costs of getting a college degree have been rising faster than those of health care, so the need to provide low-cost, quality higher education is more acute than ever. At the same time, in a knowledge economy, getting a higher-education degree is more vital than ever. And thanks to the spread of high-speed wireless technology, high-speed Internet, smartphones, Facebook, the cloud and tablet computers, the world has gone from connected to hyperconnected in just seven years. Finally, a generation that has grown up on these technologies is increasingly comfortable learning and interacting with professors through online platforms.

The combination of all these factors gave birth to Coursera.org, which launched on April 18, with the backing of Silicon Valley venture funds, as my colleague John Markoff first reported.

Private companies, like Phoenix, have been offering online degrees for a fee for years. And schools like MIT and Stanford have been offering lectures for free online. Coursera is the next step: building an interactive platform that will allow the best schools in the world to not only offer a wide range of free course lectures online, but also a system of testing, grading, student-to-student help and awarding certificates of completion of a course for under $100. (Sounds like a good deal. Tuition at the real-life Stanford is over $40,000 a year.) Coursera is starting with 40 courses online—from computing to the humanities—offered by professors from Stanford, Princeton, Michigan and the University of Pennsylvania.

"The universities produce and own the content, and we are the platform that hosts and streams it," explained Daphne Koller, a Stanford computer science professor who founded Coursera with Ng after seeing tens of thousands of students following their free Stanford lectures online. "We will also be working with employers to connect students—only with their consent—with job opportunities that are appropriate to their newly acquired skills. So, for instance, a biomedical company looking for someone with programming and computational biology skills might ask us for students who did well in our courses on cloud computing and genomics. It is great for employers and employees—and it enables someone with a less traditional education to get the credentials to open up these opportunities."

MIT, Harvard and private companies, like Udacity, are creating similar platforms. In five years this will be a huge industry.

While the lectures are in English, students have been forming study groups in their own countries to help one another. The biggest enrollments are from the United States, Britain, Russia, India and Brazil. "One Iranian student e-mailed to say he found a way to download the class videos and was burning them onto CDs and circulating them," Ng said last Thursday. "We just broke a million enrollments."

To make learning easier, Coursera chops up its lectures into short segments and offers online quizzes, which can be auto-graded, to cover each new idea. It operates on the honor system but is building tools to reduce cheating.

In each course, students post questions in an online forum for all to see and then vote questions and answers up and down. "So the most helpful questions bubble to the top and the bad ones get voted down," Ng said. "With 100,000 students, you can log every single question. It is a huge data mine." Also, if a student has a question about that day's lecture and it's morning in Cairo but 3 a.m. at Stanford, no problem. "There is always someone up somewhere to answer your question" after you post it, he said. The median response time is 22 minutes.

These top-quality learning platforms could enable budget-strained community colleges in America to "flip" their classrooms. That is, download the world's best lecturers on any subject and let their own professors concentrate on working face-to-face with students. Says Koller: "It will allow people who lack access to world-class learning—because of financial, geographic or time constraints—to have an opportunity to make a better life for themselves and their families."

When you consider how many problems around the world are attributable to the lack of education, that is very good news. Let the revolution begin.

Source: *The New York Times* 15 May 2012. Web. http://www.nytimes.com/2012/05/16/opinion/friedman-come-the-revolution.html.

WHAT IT SAYS

1. What are the advantages of online-only higher education, according to Friedman?

2. What is the significance of schools such as Stanford, Princeton, Michigan, and the University of Pennsylvania offering online-only classes?

3. How do students enrolled in online-only classes interact with each other and their professors, according to Friedman?

4. Who do you think might be opposed to online-only education, and why?

5. Friedman calls the online-only movement a "revolution." What are the implications of this characterization?

HOW IT SAYS IT

1. What kind of evidence does Friedman use to support his case that online-only education is the next best thing for education?

2. Friedman's main source for the article is Stanford associate professor of computer science Andrew Ng. How does Friedman's reference to Ng help or hurt his argument for online-only education?

3. Who is the audience for Friedman's article? What interests might they have in this point of view?

WRITE ABOUT IT

1. Review your decision to attend your current college or university. Why did you finally make the choice for either brick-and-mortar higher education, or online-only?

2. Write an essay against online education. Consider the argument put forth by Friedman. Is online-only inappropriate for some fields of study? Which ones, and why? What kinds of experiences and interactions may be missing from online-only education? Why are these experiences and interactions important?

3. Write an essay in which you examine Friedman's views on education. What are the aims of education for Friedman? What are its main goals and how can they be reached?

c. Cathy N. Davidson, "Collaborative Learning for the Digital Age"

Cathy N. Davidson is John Hope Franklin Humanities Institute Professor of Interdisciplinary Studies and Ruth F. Devarney Professor of English at Duke University. She was vice provost for interdisciplinary studies at Duke University from 1998 until 2006.

She is co-founder of Humanities, Arts, Science, and Technology Advanced Collaboratory, HASTAC ("haystack"), a network of innovators dedicated to new forms of learning for the digital age. She is also co-director of the $2-million annual HASTAC/John D. and Catherine T. MacArthur Foundation Digital Media and Learning Competition. She was appointed to the National Council on the Humanities by President Obama in 2011.

Davidson is the author of more than twenty books, including (with photographer Bill Bamberger) *Closing: The Life and Death of an American Factory* (1999), (with HASTAC co-founder David Theo Goldberg) *The Future of Thinking: Learning Institutions in a Digital Age* (2010), and *Now You See It: How the Brain Science of Attention Will Transform the Way We Live, Work, and Learn* (2011). She maintains a blog on learning in a digital age at www.cathydavidson.com.

In "Collaborative Learning for the Digital Age," originally published in the *Chronicle of Higher Education*, Davidson summarizes her argument from her most recent book, *Now You See It*, arguing for a model of education based on digital learning and new studies on how the brain works.

As You Read: Consider your own educational experiences and how they compare to what Davidson describes. What do you think of her approach to higher education in the digital age?

Collaborative Learning for the Digital Age

Five or six years ago, I attended a lecture on the science of attention. A philosopher who conducts research over in the medical school was talking about attention blindness, the basic feature of the human brain that, when we concentrate intensely on one task, causes us to miss just about everything else. Because we can't see what we can't see, our lecturer was determined to catch us in the act. He had us watch a video of six people tossing basketballs back and forth, three in white shirts and three in black, and our task was to keep track only of the tosses among the people in white. I hadn't seen the video back then, although it's now a classic, featured on punk-style TV shows or YouTube versions enacted at frat houses under less than lucid conditions. The tape rolled, and everyone began counting.

Everyone except me. I'm dyslexic, and the moment I saw that grainy tape with the confusing basketball tossers, I knew I wouldn't be able to keep track of their movements, so I let my mind wander. My curiosity was piqued, though, when about 30 seconds into the tape, a gorilla sauntered in among the players. She (we later learned a female student was in the gorilla suit) stared at the camera, thumped her chest, and then strode away while they continued passing the balls.

When the tape stopped, the philosopher asked how many people had counted at least a dozen basketball tosses. Hands went up all over. He then asked who had counted 13, 14, and congratulated those who'd scored the perfect 15. Then he asked, "And who saw the gorilla?"

I raised my hand and was surprised to discover I was the only person at my table and one of only three or four in the large room to do so. He'd set us up, trapping us in our own attention blindness.

Yes, there had been a trick, but he wasn't the one who had played it on us. By concentrating so hard on counting, we had managed to miss the gorilla in the midst.

Attention blindness is the fundamental structuring principle of the brain, and I believe that it presents us with a tremendous opportunity. My take is different from that of many neuroscientists: Where they perceive the shortcomings of the individual, I sense an opportunity for collaboration. Fortunately, given the interactive nature of most of our lives in the digital age, we have the tools to harness our different forms of attention and take advantage of them.

It's not easy to acknowledge that everything we've learned about how to pay attention means that we've been missing everything else. It's not easy for us rational, competent, confident types to admit that the very key to our success—our ability to pinpoint a problem and solve it, an achievement honed in all those years in school and beyond—may be exactly what limits us. For more than a hundred years, we've been training people to see in a particularly individual, deliberative way. No one ever told us that our way of seeing excluded everything else.

I want to suggest a different way of seeing, one that's based on multitasking our attention—not by seeing it all alone but by distributing various parts of the task among others dedicated to the same end. For most of us, this is a new pattern of attention.

Multitasking is the ideal mode of the 21st century, not just because of information overload but also because our digital age was structured without anything like a central node broadcasting one stream of information that we pay attention to at a given moment. On the Internet, everything links to everything, and all of it is available all the time.

Unfortunately, current practices of our educational institutions—and workplaces—are a mismatch between the age we live in and the institutions we have built over the last 100-plus years. The 20th century taught us that completing one task before starting another one was the route to success. Everything about 20th-century education, like the 20th-century workplace, has been designed to reinforce our attention to regular, systematic tasks that we take to completion. Attention to task is at the heart of industrial labor management, from the assembly line to the modern office, and of educational philosophy, from grade school to graduate school.

The *Newsweek* cover story proclaimed, "iPod, Therefore I Am." On MTV News, it was "Dude, I just got a free iPod!"

Peter Jennings smirked at the ABC-TV news audience, "Shakespeare on the iPod? Calculus on the iPod?"

And the staff of the Duke *Chronicle* was apoplectic: "The University seems intent on transforming the iPod into an academic device, when the simple fact of the matter is that iPods are made to listen to music. It is an unnecessarily expensive toy that does not become an academic tool simply because it is thrown into a classroom."

What had those pundits so riled up? In 2003, we at Duke were approached by Apple about becoming one of six Apple Digital Campuses. Each college would choose a technology that Apple was developing and propose a campus use for it. It would be a partnership of business and education, exploratory in all ways. We chose a flashy new music-listening gadget that young people loved but that baffled most adults.

When we gave a free iPod to every member of the entering first-year class, there were no conditions. We simply asked students to dream up learning applications for this cool little white device with the adorable earbuds, and we invited them to pitch their ideas to the faculty. If one of their professors decided to use iPods in a course, the professor, too, would receive a free Duke-branded iPod, and so would all the students in the class (whether they were first-years or not).

This was an educational experiment without a syllabus. No lesson plan. No assessment matrix rigged to show that our investment had been a wise one. No assignment to count the basketballs. After all, as we knew from the science of attention, to direct attention in one way precluded all the other ways. If it were a reality show, we might have called it *Project Classroom Makeover*.

At the time, I was vice provost for interdisciplinary studies at Duke, a position equivalent to what in industry would be the R&D person, and I was among those responsible for cooking up the iPod experiment. In the world of technology, "crowdsourcing" means inviting a group to collaborate on a solution to a problem, but that term didn't yet exist in 2003. It was coined by Jeff Howe of *Wired* magazine in 2006 to refer to the widespread Internet practice of posting an open call requesting help in completing some task, whether writing code (that's how much of the open-source code that powers the Mozilla browser was written) or creating a winning logo (like the "Birdie" design of Twitter, which cost a total of six bucks).

In the iPod experiment, we were crowdsourcing educational innovation for a digital age. Crowdsourced thinking is very different from "credentialing," or relying on top-down expertise. If anything, crowdsourcing is suspicious of expertise, because the more expert we are, the more likely we are to be limited in what we conceive to be the problem, let alone the answer.

Once the pieces were in place, we decided to take our educational experiment one step further. By giving the iPods to first-year students, we ended up with a lot of angry sophomores, juniors, and seniors. They'd paid hefty private-university tuition, too! So we relented and said any student could have a free iPod—just so long as she persuaded a professor to require one for a course and came up with a learning app in that course. Does that sound sneaky? Far be it from me to say that we planned it.

The real treasure trove was to be found in the students' innovations. Working together, and often alongside their professors, they came up with far more learning apps for their iPods than anyone—even at Apple—had dreamed possible. Most predictable were uses whereby students downloaded audio archives relevant to their courses—Nobel Prize acceptance speeches by physicists and poets, the McCarthy hearings, famous trials. Almost instantly, students figured out that they could record lectures on their iPods and listen at their leisure.

Interconnection was the part the students grasped before any of us did. Students who had grown up connected digitally gravitated to ways that the iPod could be used for collective learning. They turned iPods into social media and networked their learning in ways we did not anticipate. In the School of the Environment, one class interviewed families in a North Carolina community concerned with lead paint in their homes and schools, commented on one another's interviews, and together created an audio documentary that aired on local and regional radio stations and all over the Web. In the music department, students uploaded their own compositions to their iPods so their fellow students could listen and critique.

After eight years in Duke's central administration, I was excited to take the methods we had gleaned from the iPod experiment back into the classroom. I decided to offer a new course called "This Is Your Brain on the Internet," a title that pays homage to Daniel J. Levitin's inspiring book *This Is Your Brain on Music* (Dutton, 2006), a kind of music-lover's guide to the brain. Levitin argues that music makes complex circuits throughout the brain, requiring different kinds of brain function for listening, processing, and producing, and thus makes us think differently. Substitute the word "Internet" for "music," and you've got the gist of my course.

I advertised the class widely, and I was delighted to look over the roster of the 18 students in the seminar and find more than 18 majors, minors, and certificates represented. I created a bare-bones suggested reading list that included, for example, articles in specialized journals like *Cognition* and *Developmental Neuropsychology*, pieces in popular magazines like *Wired* and *Science*, novels, and memoirs. There were lots of websites, too, of course, but I left the rest loose. This class was structured to be peer-led, with student interest and student research driving the design. "Participatory learning" is one term used to describe how we can learn together from one another's skills. "Cognitive surplus" is another used in the digital world for that "more than the sum of the parts" form of collaborative thinking that happens when groups think together online.

We used a method that I call "collaboration by difference." Collaboration by difference is an antidote to attention blindness. It signifies that the complex and interconnected problems of our time cannot be solved by anyone alone, and that those who think they can act in an entirely focused, solitary fashion are undoubtedly missing the main point that is right there in front of them, thumping its chest and staring them in the face. Collaboration by difference respects and rewards different forms and levels of expertise, perspective, culture, age, ability, and insight, treating difference not as a deficit but as a point of distinction. It always seems more cumbersome in the short run to seek out divergent and even quirky opinions, but it turns out to be efficient in the end and necessary for success if one seeks an outcome that is unexpected and sustainable. That's what I was aiming for.

I had the students each contribute a new entry or amend an existing entry on Wikipedia, or find another public forum where they could contribute to public discourse. There was still a lot of criticism about the lack of peer review in Wikipedia entries, and some professors were banning Wikipedia use in the classroom. I didn't understand that. Wikipedia is an educator's fantasy, all the world's knowledge shared voluntarily and free in a format theoretically available to all, and which anyone can edit. Instead of banning it, I challenged my students to use their knowledge to make Wikipedia better. All conceded that it had turned out to be much harder to get their work to "stick" on Wikipedia than it was to write a traditional term paper.

Given that I was teaching a class based on learning and the Internet, having my students blog was a no-brainer. I supplemented that with more traditionally structured academic writing, a term paper. When I had both samples in front of me, I discovered something curious. Their writing online, at least in their blogs, was incomparably better than in the traditional papers. In fact, given all the tripe one hears from pundits about how the Internet dumbs our kids down, I was shocked that elegant bloggers often turned out to be the clunkiest and most pretentious of research-paper writers. Term papers rolled in that were shot through with jargon, stilted diction, poor word choice, rambling thoughts, and even pretentious grammatical errors (such as the ungrammatical but proper-sounding use of "I" instead of "me" as an object of a preposition).

But it got me thinking: What if bad writing is a product of the form of writing required in college—the term paper—and not necessarily intrinsic to a student's natural writing style or thought process? I hadn't thought of that until I read my students' lengthy, weekly blogs and saw the difference in quality. If students are trying to figure out what kind of writing we want in order to get a good grade, communication is secondary. What if "research paper" is a category that invites, even requires, linguistic and syntactic gobbledygook?

Research indicates that, at every age level, people take their writing more seriously when it will be evaluated by peers than when it is to be judged by teachers. Online blogs directed at peers exhibit fewer typographical and factual errors, less plagiarism, and generally better, more elegant and persuasive prose than classroom assignments by the same writers. Longitudinal studies of student writers conducted by Stanford University's Andrea Lunsford, a professor of English, assessed student writing at Stanford year after year. Lunsford surprised everyone with her findings that students were becoming more literate, rhetorically dexterous, and fluent—not less, as many feared. The Internet, she discovered, had allowed them to develop their writing.

The semester flew by, and we went wherever it took us. The objective was to get rid of a lot of the truisms about "the dumbest generation" and actually look at how new theories of the brain and of attention might help us understand how forms of thinking and collaborating online maximize brain activity. We spent a good deal of time thinking about how accident, disruption, distraction, and difference increase the motivation to learn and to solve problems, both individually and collectively. To find examples, we spent time with a dance ensemble rehearsing a new piece, a jazz band improvising together, and teams of surgeons and computer programmers performing robotic surgery. We walked inside a monkey's brain in a virtual-reality cave. In another virtual-reality environment, we found ourselves trembling, unable to step off what we knew was a two-inch drop, because it looked as if we were on a ledge over a deep canyon.

One of our readings was *On Intelligence* (Times Books, 2004), a unified theory of the brain written by Jeff Hawkins (the neuroscientist who invented the Palm Pilot) with Sandra Blakeslee. I agree with many of Hawkins's ideas about the brain's "memory-prediction framework." My own interest is in how memories— reinforced behaviors from the past—predict future learning, and in how we can intentionally disrupt that pattern to spark innovation and creativity. Hawkins is interested in how we can use the pattern to create next-generation artificial intelligence that will enhance the performance, and profitability, of computerized gadgets like the Palm Pilot. The students and I had been having a heated debate about his theories when a student discovered that Hawkins happened to be in our area to give a lecture. I was away at a meeting, when suddenly my BlackBerry was vibrating with e-mails and IM's from my students, who had convened the class without me to present a special guest on a special topic: Jeff Hawkins debating the ideas of Jeff Hawkins. It felt a bit like the gag in the classic Woody Allen movie *Annie Hall*, when someone in the line to purchase movie tickets is expounding pompously on the ideas of Marshall McLuhan and then McLuhan himself steps into the conversation.

It was that kind of class.

"Jeff Hawkins thought it was odd that we decided to hold class when you weren't there," one student texted me. "Why wouldn't we? That's how it works in 'This Is Your Brain on the Internet.'"

Project Classroom Makeover. I heard the pride. "Step aside, Prof. Davidson: This is a university!"

"Nonsense!" "Absurd!"

"A wacko holding forth on a soapbox. If Prof. Davidson just wants to yammer and lead discussions, she should resign her position and head for a park or subway platform, and pass a hat for donations."

Some days, it's not easy being Prof. Davidson.

What caused the ruckus in the blogosphere this time was a blog I posted on the Hastac, an online network, which I co-founded in 2002, dedicated to new forms of learning for a digital age. The post, "How to Crowdsource Grading," proposed a form of assessment that I planned to use the next time I taught "This Is Your Brain on the Internet."

It was my students' fault, really. By the end of the course, I felt confident. I settled in with their evaluations, waiting for the accolades to flow, a pedagogical shower of appreciation. And mostly that's what I read, thankfully. But there was one group of students who had some candid feedback, and it took me by surprise. They said everything about the course had been bold, new, and exciting.

Everything, that is, except the grading.

They pointed out that I had used entirely conventional methods for testing and evaluating their work. We had talked as a class about the new modes of assessment on the Internet—like public commenting on products and services and leaderboards (peer evaluations adapted from sports sites)—where the consumer of content could also evaluate that content. These students said they loved the class but were perplexed that my assessment method had been so 20th century: Midterm. Final. Research paper. Graded A, B, C, D. The students were right. You couldn't get more 20th century than that.

The students signed their names to the course evaluations. It turned out the critics were A+ students. That stopped me in my tracks. If you're a teacher worth your salt, you pay attention when the A+ students say something is wrong.

I was embarrassed that I had overlooked such a crucial part of our brain on the Internet. I contacted my students and said they'd made me rethink some very old habits. Unlearning. I promised I would rectify my mistake the next time I taught the course. I thought about my promise, came up with what seemed like a good system, then wrote about it in my blog.

My new grading method, which set off such waves of vitriol, combined old-fashioned contract grading with peer review. Contract grading goes back at least to the 1960s. In it, the requirements of a course are laid out in advance, and students contract to do all of the assignments or only some of them. A student with a heavy course or workload who doesn't need an A, for example, might contract to do everything but the final project and then, according to the contract, she might earn a B. It's all very adult.

But I also wanted some quality control. So I added the crowdsourcing component based on the way I had already structured the course. I thought that since pairs of students were leading each class session and also responding to their peers' required weekly reading blogs, why not have them determine whether the blogs were good enough to count as fulfilling the terms of the contract? If a blog didn't pass muster, it would be the task of the student leaders that week to tell the blogger and offer feedback on what would be required for it to count. Student leaders for a class period would have to do that carefully, for next week a classmate would be evaluating their work.

I also liked the idea of students' each having a turn at being the one giving the grades. That's not a role most students experience, even though every study of learning shows that you learn best by teaching someone else. Besides, if constant public self-presentation and constant public feedback are characteristics of a digital age, why aren't we rethinking how we evaluate, measure, test, assess, and create standards? Isn't that another aspect of our brain on the Internet?

There are many ways of crowdsourcing, and mine was simply to extend the concept of peer leadership to grading. The blogosphere was convinced that either I or my students would be pulling a fast one if the grading were crowdsourced and students had a role in it. That says to me that we don't believe people can learn unless they are forced to, unless they know it will "count on the test." As an educator, I find that very depressing. As a student of the Internet, I also find it implausible. If you give people the means to self-publish—whether it's a photo from their iPhone or a blog—they do so. They seem to love learning and sharing what they know with others. But much of our emphasis on grading is based on the assumption that learning is like cod-liver oil: It is good for you, even though it tastes horrible going down. And much of our educational emphasis is on getting one answer right on one test—as if that says something about the quality of what you have learned or the likelihood that you will remember it after the test is over.

Grading, in a curious way, exemplifies our deepest convictions about excellence and authority, and specifically about the right of those with authority to define what constitutes excellence. If we crowdsource grading, we are suggesting that young people without credentials are fit to judge quality and value. Welcome to the Internet, where everyone's a critic and anyone can express a view about the new iPhone, restaurant, or quarterback. That democratizing of who can pass judgment is digital thinking. As I found out, it is quite unsettling to people stuck in top-down models of formal education and authority.

Learn. Unlearn. Relearn. In addition to the content of our course—which ranged across cognitive psychology, neuroscience, management theory, literature and the arts, and the various fields that compose science-and-technology studies—"This Is Your Brain on the Internet" was intended to model a different way of knowing the world, one that encompasses new and different forms of collaboration and attention. More than anything, it courted failure. Unlearning.

"I smell a reality TV show," one critic sniffed.

That's not such a bad idea, actually. Maybe I'll try that next time I teach "This Is Your Brain on the Internet." They can air it right after Project Classroom Makeover.

Source: *The Chronicle of Higher Education* 26 Aug. 2011. Web. http://chronicle.com/article/Collaborative-Learning-for-the/128789/.

WHAT IT SAYS

1. What does Davidson mean by the term "multi-tasking" in this essay? How does her definition differ from the usual meaning of the term?

2. Davidson writes that "current practices of our education institutions—and our workplaces—are a mismatch between the age we live in and the institutions we have built over the last 100-plus years." What does she mean by this? How are our current educational and workplace practices incompatible with the age we live in? What about the digital age makes it different from the industrial age?

3. What does Davidson mean by the terms "crowdsourcing" and "collaboration by difference"? How do these concepts apply to education?

4. Davidson describes her class "This Is Your Brain on the Internet" in some detail. What lessons for educational practice does she intend to convey with this discussion?

5. What new grading process did Davidson adopt the second time she taught the course "This Is Your Brain on the Internet"? How did she involve her students in the grading process?

HOW IT SAYS IT

1. Davidson tells us early on that she is dyslexic. What is the effect of this revelation? How is it connected to what she has to say about learning in the digital age?

2. Describe the tone and diction of Davidson's essay. How do these relate to her argument?

3. Davidson's essay was first published in the *Chronicle Review* of the *Chronicle of Higher Education*. Who is the audience for Davidson's essay? What interest might they have in her recommendations?

WRITE ABOUT IT

1. Consider your own educational experience and compare and contrast it to the educational situations described by Davidson in this essay.

2. Write an essay in which you examine Davidson's philosophy of education or pedagogy. What are her views about education? What are the aims of education and how can they be reached? What are the roles of the teacher and students, according to Davidson?

3. Write an essay in which you argue against Davidson's approach to teaching in higher education. What flaws do you find in her methods?

d. Eva Kassens-Noor, "Twitter as a Teaching Practice to Enhance Active and Informal Learning in Higher Education: The Case of Sustainable Tweets"

Eva Kassens-Noor is an assistant professor of urban and transport planning in the School of Planning, Design and Construction at Michigan State University. She holds a joint appointment with the global urban studies program and is adjunct assistant professor in the department of geography. Kassens-Noor has consulted with various organizations for large-scale events, including the Athens Airport Authority for the 2004 Summer Olympics, the Vancouver Airport Authority for the 2010 Winter Olympics, and the Holy Mecca for 2009 Pilgrimage planning. She is the author of several articles as well as a book, *Planning Olympic Legacies: Transport Dreams and Urban Realities* (2012).

Born in Germany, she received her Diplom-Ingenieur (equivalent to a BA and 1-year MS) in business engineering at the Universität Karlsruhe in Germany, her MST (Master of Science in Transportation) from the civil and engineering department at MIT, and her PhD from the department of urban studies and planning at MIT.

In this essay, Kassens-Noor reviews the literature on the use of Twitter in higher education and reports her study on the use of Twitter in an urban planning and sustainability course.

As You Read: Consider the use of Twitter in the class that Kassens-Noor describes. How might you use Twitter in your own education?

Twitter as a Teaching Practice to Enhance Active and Informal Learning in Higher Education: The Case of Sustainable Tweets

Abstract

With the rise of Web 2.0, a multitude of new possibilities on how to use these online technologies for active learning has intrigued researchers. While most instructors have used Twitter for in-class discussions, this study explores the teaching practice of Twitter as an active, informal, outside-of-class learning tool. Through a comparative experiment in a small classroom setting, this study asks whether the use of Twitter aids students in learning of a particular subject matter. And if so, in which learning contexts Twitter offers advantages over more traditional teaching methods. This exploratory study showed potential opportunities and pitfalls that Twitter could bring to the e-learning community in higher education.

Keywords

active learning, informal learning, sustainability, teaching practice, Twitter, Web 2.0

Twitter as a Teaching Practice

THE ROLE OF INFORMAL AND ACTIVE LEARNING IN HIGHER EDUCATION

As a pioneer in education, Dewey (1938) posited that students' experiences are a key factor in their learning process. Since then, remarkable educators have sought to invent, improve and implement teaching practices that engage students and connect classroom information with real-life experiences. In particular during the past two decades, instructors have applied active and informal learning methods to enhance students' interactions in peer-to-peer discussions in and outside of class (Chickering and Gamson, 1991; Conlon, 2004).

Active learning is one of the key principles highlighted in Chickering and Gamson's (1991) hallmark study on good practices in undergraduate education. Active learning involves a multitude of teaching practices, such as lively debates between instructor and students, peer-to-peer discussions, reflective writing and team work, all of which enable students to discover, process, and apply knowledge through engagement (Bonwell and Eison, 1991; McKinney and Heyl, 2008; Meyers and Jones, 1993). While students actively participate in multiple learning contexts, their learning evolves within formal and informal settings (Greenhow et al., 2009). Informal learning is a course-related activity outside the classroom that centers around students' self-directed and independent learning activities including peer-to-peer interactions (Aspden and Thorpe, 2009; Jamieson, 2009). In particular, networking is considered an informal learning strategy (Marsick and Watkins, 1990). Based on empirical evidence from MBA students, Yang and Lu (2001) suggest that informal learning ought to be an essential component in education, because it enhances academic performance. As "non-classroom, disciplinary-based facilities" (Jamieson, 2009: 20) for informal student learning activities continue to decrease, Jamieson (2009) highlights the need to create outside-of-class options for students to interact.

With the advent of Web 2.0 applications, cyberspace has offered new communication spaces for informal and active learning activities and also altered how information is transmitted among students. Hicks and Graber (2010: 627) hypothesize that Web 2.0 might have created a different "learning and information reality"compared with the traditional reflective and collaborative discourse. Therefore, they encourage research into these technologies in order to inform higher education teaching practices about how instructors can design and use these new web tools.

A BRIEF INTRODUCTION TO TWITTER, MICROBLOGS AND WEB 2.0

Web 2.0 refers to a variety of web-enabled applications built on open source and driven by user-generated and user-manipulated content. The most frequently used Web 2.0 applications include wikis (Wikipedia.org), podcasts (YouTube.com), blogs (blogspot.com), and social networking sites (facebook.com, Twitter.com). Especially in recent years, social networking sites have seen an explosive growth as a way of communication (Fox et al., 2009). At the end of 2009, about 19% of Internet users logged into social networking sites to bring their friends up to date or to keep informed about their friends' lives. Also in 2009, the number of users on social networking sites tripled (Fox et al., 2009). This explosive growth trend continued throughout 2010 (Borasky, 2010). As a free Web 2.0 application, Twitter has become a popular microblogging tool and social networking website among younger generations (Java et al., 2007; McFedries, 2007). Since Twitter's inauguration in 2006, this online community has seen a steep rise in users, especially those under 34 years old (Fox et al., 2009). Through Twitter, people communicate by exchanging quick, frequent, and short messages of up to 140 characters in length. These are called tweets and belong to the group of microblogs (Stevens, 2008). Twitter community members can post their tweets directly on their own Twitter website via mobile phone, email, and instant messaging. At the end of 2009, 65 million people used Twitter around the globe, a 14-fold increase since early in 2008 (ComScore, 2010). Most tweeters reside in North America, Europe, and Asia (Java et al., 2007). Usually, tweeters provide updates on their current status, as Twitter was designed to briefly answer the question: "What are you doing?" (Twitter, 2010). Users can also post links to pictures, more expansive blogs, and other websites (Java et al., 2007).

TWITTER IN HIGHER EDUCATION

Hannay and Fretwell (2011) predict that Web 2.0 applications will soon be taken up by universities and suggest these technologies will have implications for the academic workplace; students will demand that faculty members communicate digitally, via instant messaging, Twitter and other technologies. Similarly, companies will expect their recruits, our graduates, to be versed in social media technologies (Wankel, 2009). It is unsurprising, then, that we, as educators, are being encouraged to use Twitter to enable interactivity, excite learners, and foster greater student participation.

Responding to this challenge, educators in higher education have started to experiment with Twitter in the hope students seize the opportunity to interact more frequently, engage more thoughtfully, and foster learning inside and beyond the classroom (Grosseck and Holotescu, 2008; Junco et al., 2011; Perez, 2009; Schroeder et al., 2010). Establishing five social media literacies, namely attention, participation, collaboration, network awareness, and critical consumption, Rheingold (2010) emphasizes the need for Twitter to be a valuable communication tool, in contrast to Twitter's potential pitfall of being a mere distraction (Wankel, 2009). Ultimately, Twitter can be a powerful collaboration tool (Corbeil and Corbeil, 2011; Rheingold, 2010). Summarizing, Reuben (2008) emphasizes the tremendous potential Twitter could play in education, but acknowledges that no one has found the right niche just yet.

TWITTER AS AN INSTANT FEEDBACK TOOL DURING CLASS

Microblogging as a way to enhance student learning has a substantial impact within class settings (Ebner, 2009; Ebner et al., 2010); accordingly faculty have primarily experimented with Twitter in classrooms (Young, 2009). Most of these experiments have focused on Twitter as an in-class instant feedback tool between teachers and students. For example, Dunlap and Lowenthal (2009) analyzed the use of Twitter in online courses; DeCosta et al. (2010) looked at Twitter as a tool for student-teacher communication; Parry (2008) identified 13 ways in which Twitter can be used during class; and Croxall (2010) found that Twitter enables frequent class discussions. This "live-tweeting" encourages careful listening, paying close attention, gathering information, and multi-tasking (Wankel, 2009).

Another form of using Twitter is for student-student communication outside the classroom yet within a formal class-setting. Twibes, entire classes that form Twitter groups, spread information in real time; one example is field trips, during which participants tweeted classmates who remained at the university (Richardson,

2009; Rogers-Estable, 2009). Within classroom settings, Twitter has been primar-ily used as an instant feedback tool for student-teacher communication and is in the early stages of exploration for student-student interaction.

TWITTER AS A LEARNING TOOL

The e-learning community increasingly has looked to social networks as tools for creating and sharing knowledge (Grosseck and Holotescu, 2008; Huberman et al., 2008). In particular, micro-blogging is a new form of communication that can support informal learning beyond classrooms (Ebner et al., 2010). Twitter can support students' informal learning activities (Aspden and Thorpe, 2009). It can also be an active learning tool (Cherney, 2008) that promotes connections with real-life learning, thereby encouraging critical reflection and fostering enhanced understanding (Bonwell and Eison, 1991).

One of the few empirical studies exploring the effects of Twitter on college students was conducted by Junco et al. (2011) with 125 pre-health majors. Splitting the students into two sections, the researchers found that Twitter had a positive impact on both student engagement and grades. Owing to the use of Twitter, class conversations were extended beyond sessions, students more easily and more readily displayed openness about feelings and their own shortcomings, more cross-communication took place, and unlikely interpersonal relationships were forged based on shared values and interests. In short, Twitter catalyzed connec-tions more quickly than classroom discussions. Furthermore, instructor-student communication was improved when Twitter provided a comfortable platform for asking deeply probing questions.

PURPOSE OF THE STUDY AND RESEARCH QUESTIONS

This evolving stream of literature supports three conclusions about Twitter. First, all instructors who have experimented with Twitter agree that it can have a posi-tive impact on engagement. Second, studies have focused almost exclusively on Twitter used as an instant feedback tool inside the classroom. Third, scholars suggest Twitter holds potential as a powerful learning tool that can readily transmit knowl-edge, inform learners, and extend beyond individuals to their social networks.

Despite a multitude of websites suggesting the use of Twitter in academic settings and advising on how to use the Web 2.0 tool (Parry, 2008; Perez, 2009; Reuben, 2008), there are very few empirical studies that actually support this advice. In particular, studies have yet to examine qualitatively the effect of using Twitter beyond the classroom as an active and informal learning tool focused on peer-to-peer interactions.

Therefore, the goal of this study is to stimulate scholarly discussion about Twitter as an active, informal, outside of class, peer-to-peer interaction tool that aids the in-class learning process. This study is an exploration of ways in which today's students apply, create, and retain knowledge when using Twitter compared with more traditional approaches to learning. In this study, traditional approaches are defined as individual homework assignments and in-class discussion. The research questions that ultimately drive this study are "Does the use of Twitter aid students in learning a particular subject matter? And, if so, in which learning contexts does Twitter offer advantages over more traditional teaching methods?"

Methodology

This methodology section is divided into three sections. The first introduces the study participants. The second explains the study's design and implementation procedure. The third elaborates on measures and analysis.

PARTICIPANTS

The Twitter experiment ran in a Midwestern research tier I university class, in which students grapple with how urban planners can create sustainable and climate-resilient cities. Between 25 March 2010 and 22 April 2010 (Earth Day, a day during which people worldwide inspire awareness and learn to protect the natural environment), 15 students participated in the study; eight were upper-level undergraduates and seven were graduate students. The students' grade point average (GPA) was 3.58 and their age averaged at 23.65 years. As a cross-disciplinary class, the students majored in urban planning, construction management, and environmental studies.

Prior to the class, five students had used Twitter, three of them rarely and two on a weekly basis. Their reasons for using Twitter were primarily to receive news updates, to stay in touch with friends, and to gather information about jobs. Furthermore, two students indicated their interest in celebrities.

Prior to the start of the study, the experiment was deemed as expedited via the instructor's institutional review board (IRB). The IRB is an appointed committee acting independently and ethically to protect the rights and welfare of human research subjects. Fourteen students provided informed consent to release the findings of this study. The student who did not want to participate in the study was excluded from the evaluation, and this student's contributions to the study have been destroyed. In the course of the study, two students did not turn in their assignments. Hence both were deemed as non-active participants and excluded from the evaluation of the study. To ensure confidentiality, the students who took part were asked to adopt code names for the exercise, such as "Captain Planet", or "Earthability", and keep their diaries and new Twitter accounts exclusively under these code names. Thereby, the collected data could not be associated with any one student and any potential teacher-student power relationship bias was eliminated.

TABLE 3.1. Group Characteristics

Student characteristics	Twitter	Traditional (diary and discussion)
Active participants/Total	6/7	6/8
Undergraduates/Graduates	4/2	4/2
Average GPA	3.57	3.59
Age	23.3	24
Time spent on exercise	2 hours	1 hour 40 min + 30 min discussion

As part of the course, students were asked to identify unsustainable practices in cities and suggest remedies. Divided in groups, one group would use Twitter to create and exchange information, while the other group would keep a personal diary and discuss their entries once among the group members towards the end of the course (a third option, to write an individual essay, was not selected by any of the students). In the end, a quiz would indicate which group had retained more knowledge.

DESIGN AND PROCEDURE

Students were offered three choices to complete their sustainability assignment: (1) the "Twitter group" would use Twitter as their only communication mechanism, (2) the "traditional group" would have one in-class discussion and keep individual diaries, (3) the 'essay group' would write 5,000 words on unsustainable practices and their remedies. No student chose the third option. The assignment was a for-credit exercise. To avoid the potential bias of a student-teacher power relationship, the students received full credit for the exercise if either the Twitter assignment or the traditional assignment was completed on time.

The Twitter group and the traditional group show comparable group characteristics (Table 3.1). Active participants provided informed consent to make the results of this study public and regularly produced Twitter or diary entries. After the exclusion of the two non-active participants, each group had an equal number of students: four undergraduate and two graduate students. The average GPAs in the two groups were almost identical, and there was only a slight difference in their average ages. Data from five sources were collected during the experiment: surveys, tweets, diaries, a group discussion, and a pop-quiz. The surveys were given to all students in-class before the study exercise began (14 January 2010), asking them to report whether they had used Twitter and, if so, for what purpose. After the study (22 April 2010), the Twitter group was required to hand in printouts of all their tweets and re-tweets (answers to tweets) made during the study. On the same day, the traditional group had to hand in their diaries and hold a team discussion about their diaries in class. This discussion was audio-recorded

TABLE 3.2. Extract from Diary Instruction Sheet

Date	Unsustainable practice	Remedy

and the tape was transcribed by a third person, who did not know the students. The 30-minute quiz was given to students on 27 April 2010. The in-class quiz first asked students about their demographics: which group they belonged to, their current under-graduate or graduate year, the time they had spent on the exercise, their GPA, and their age. The second part of the quiz asked students to recall an unsustainable practice and potential remedies they had explored *in their respective groups*. To avoid potential bias in this knowledge-retention exercise, students were not informed about the quiz beforehand.

The sustainability assignment was introduced to all students during an in-class presentation on 18 March 2010; handouts further clarified instructions for the assignment to the two groups. One email reminder to continue their diaries and to keep posting tweets was sent (1 April 2010) a week after the exercise started.

Starting on 25 March 2010, the Twitter group was instructed to post a tweet whenever they found an unsustainable practice in daily life (for example, buying a paper cup) and suggest a remedy (for example, bringing their own reusable cup to buy coffee).

TWITTER RULES

- Each *new tweet* has to briefly describe an unsustainable practice and suggest a remedy.
- Each *answer to a tweet* has to either add an additional remedy or refute that the previous tweet contains an unsustainable practice.
- Tweet daily (if possible multiple times—as soon as you identify a practice/remedy).

The Twitter group members were not allowed to discuss their tweets outside the online forum. For communication and evaluation purposes, each of the Twitter group participants joined the course leader's Twitter list called "the sustainable city" under their code names. Prior to the start of the project, the students were informed that the instructor would not interfere or add to the knowledge application and creation exercise unless the students were posting inappropriate tweets.

Also starting on 25 March 2010, the traditional group members were instructed to keep a daily diary according to Table 3.2.

The students discussed their diary entries within their "traditional group" during class time on 22 April 2010. A time slot of 30 minutes was allotted for discussion while the Twitter group left the classroom.

MEASURES AND ANALYSIS

All collected material was tracked, examined, and evaluated. Knowledge application and creation were qualitatively assessed through content analysis of four sources: tweets, diaries, surveys, and the transcript of the team discussion among the diary-keeping students. Knowledge retention was qualitatively assessed through content analysis of the in-class pop quiz.

Scoring and coding were conducted after the end of the study with various cross-checks. First, the course leader coded the tweets by key words, pairing the unsustainable practices with their remedies. Then, the instructor identified all students who noted the same unsustainable practice and the same remedies. The identical coding procedure was applied to the diary entries. Thereafter, the transcript was coded and cross-compared with the diary entries, marking similar and different unsustainable practices and their remedies. Finally, the quiz was coded according to the same procedure. A second coder independently applied the same methodology; discrepancies were discussed and mutually agreed upon.

TABLE 3.3. Traditional and Twitter participation

	Expected Baseline	Total Entries	Average		
			per day	per person	per person per day
Diary entries	174	131	4.5	21.8	0.75
Tweets	174	88	3	14.7	0.5

Results

The results are split in two sections: the first reports on knowledge creation, the second reports on knowledge retention. The distinction between the two is important, because they measure different outcomes of the learning process. Whereas the former focuses on the communicative advantages Twitter may offer as an instant tool and readily available database, the latter shows which teaching practice has the potential for long-term recollection of the created and shared ideas. Before launching into the results sections, a brief comparison between the two groups is necessary in regards to participation and knowledge comprehension.

Both groups showed a good understanding of the content taught in class: the unsustainable practices and their remedies. Throughout the exercise, the students applied the knowledge they had learned during class and applied it faultlessly via Twitter, diaries, and in the team discussion.

Both groups frequently tweeted or kept their diaries, but both groups participated less than expected (Table 3.3). The baseline of 174 entries represents the minimum number of expected entries (29 days × 6 student entries) per group, in which all students had followed the instructions by tweeting at least daily or making at least one diary entry per day.

Even though the traditional students made more entries than the Twitter students (Table 3.3), the Twitter students reported a higher amount of time spent on their entries than the traditional students; while students reported to have spent two hours on average on the Twitter exercise, the traditional group reported 10 minutes more: 1 hour 40 minutes for their diary entries and the 30-minute discussion.

KNOWLEDGE CREATION

The Twitter group found more unsustainable practices and found more remedies per *identified* practice. Overall, the Twitter students identified 64 unsustainable practices with 65 remedies through their tweets. In contrast, the traditional group found 10 fewer unsustainable practices, but gave a variety of remedies per *identified* practice, totaling 70 remedies. For example, the Twitter group identified as an unsustainable practice that individuals drove cars, and suggested one remedy: riding a bike. In contrast, the traditional group found the same unsustainable practice (an individual driving a car), but identified seven remedies to the *identified* unsustainable practice: car-sharing, transit (using public transport), using hybrid cars, collating trips by car, cycling, walking, and using more energy-efficient air travel.

For the traditional group, the venue to share their individual work and discuss their diaries was the in-class meeting on 22 April 2010. During the discussion, the traditional group managed to analyze 28 unsustainable practices (~55% of all unsustainable practices created by the entire group) including various remedies.

KNOWLEDGE RETENTION

The traditional group reported on average 10 unsustainable practices including remedies during the pop quiz. On average, 70% of these practices were those created by themselves, which means the students had either reported those unsustainable practices and remedies in their own diaries or invented new ones during the quiz. The other 30% of reported unsustainable practices and remedies were those discussed during the 30-minute in-class meeting.

The Twitter students reported fewer unsustainable practices and remedies than the traditional group. On average, they reported 7.6 unsustainable practices with remedies during the quiz. In contrast with the traditional group, the Twitter students remembered over 60% of the unsustainable practices and remedies that others had created on Twitter, while only 40% were from their own source of ideas.

Discussion of Twitter and Traditional Group Activity

KNOWLEDGE CREATION

The following interpretations might explain why (1) the Twitter group found more unsustainable practices with matching remedies than the traditional group and (2) why the traditional group reported a variety of remedies per *identified* practice, but found overall fewer unsustainable practices than the Twitter group.

(1) The traditional group found fewer unsustainable practices, because no communication among the students took place during the collection of ideas. Consecutively, the same unsustainable practice was identified multiple times by different members of the traditional group; in their diaries, they reported 18 unsustainable practices at least twice. In contrast, the Twitter group only mentioned the same unsustainable practice eight times. This interpretation supports the findings of Rheingold (2010) and Richardson (2009) that Twitter is a powerful collaboration tool between students. Additionally, the comparative nature of the study suggests that Twitter is better suited for creating and sharing large amounts of information compared with traditional teaching methods. A further advantage Twitter provides is tracking the tweets by time and date automatically; it ensured continuous participation throughout the entire month, which may also have contributed to the greater number of unsustainable practices identified. In contrast, the traditional students could have completed their diaries the day before their assignment was due or might have thought about the exercise only on a weekly basis. Because both groups presented information equivalent in quality, this suggests Twitter is also useful for informal out-of-classroom assignments, just like other microblogging tools (Ebner et al., 2010).

(2) The traditional group created more remedies per identified practice, because there was no character limit for diary entries. In contrast, the Twitter group had to adhere to the 140 characters per tweet (Figure 3.1). For multiple remedies, students would have had to start a new tweet.

Starting new tweets might have been a barrier for reflective thinking (no student tweeted twice within a short time frame or even within the same day). The multitude of remedies created by the diary-keeping students suggests that traditional teaching practices allowed for more in-depth thinking and self-reflective learning because diaries did not create artificial writing barriers. While Twitter can be an active learning tool (Cherney, 2008), tweets seem to defeat an essential attribute for active learning, because tweeters do not have "space to think".

earthability commuting via airplane between major metro areas weekly is unsustainable-we need to invest more in high-speed rail sooner than later
9:46 AM Apr 22nd via web   ↰ **Reply**

CaptainPlanet76 Happy Earth Day! Get out side and be active in your community! In support of your environment!
8:02 AM Apr 22nd via web

EconEnviEqui building a walmart on a wetland in a fringe city is unsustainable, should build in one of the many vacent lots in lansing.
6:13 PM Apr 21st via web

MSUGreenMachine Extension cords are not meant to be plugged in permanently. Either find a power cord on call your electrician
5:09 PM Apr 21st via UberTwitter

CaptainPlanet76 try to eat only certified sustainable fish! Our fisheries are becoming greatly depleted we have to act!
7:20 Apr 21st via web

MSUGreenMachine Don't be so fast to turn on that air conditioner. Open up a window
8:19 PM Apr 20th via UberTwitter

EconEnviEqui when eating fast food, consume less, dont grab more napkins then needed.
4:29 PM Apr 20th via web

Photovoltaicell Current use of fossil fuels cannot be supported by our fossil fuel supply, alternative energy much be researched and implemented.
3:27 PM Apr 20th via web

FIGURE 3.1. Extract from the Sustainable City Twitter Site (Source: http://Twitter.com/#/list/ekassens/the-sustainable-city).

Twitter showed another pitfall in comparison with interactive face-to-face discussions. During the traditional group meeting, students offered knowledge that was not part of the exercise per se. The student conversation shown in Table 3.4 exemplifies this finding. As this extract of the transcribed discussion meeting shows, because one student explained the reason for packaged food (sanitary purposes), all students in the traditional group knew about that reason after the discussion. While the same discussion came up in the Twitter group (fast food packaging) with the same remedies (do not eat at all, or minimum packaging), none of the students explained why packaging was necessary.

TABLE 3.4. Extract from Traditional Group Discussion

Participant A:	Another thing that really upsets me, if you ever go get fast food, everything is packaged. It comes in a bag. The food is wrapped.
Participant B:	Yes.
Participant A:	The plastic straw is wrapped, the plastic fork is wrapped. It's like it's ridiculous. So, my remedy was to stop eating fast food, because it's bad for you anyway.
Participant C:	But then, if we like...., I'll just ask them for stuff without the bag.
Participant B:	Will they give you that?
Participant A:	Yeah, well I kinda force them to. They're like "are you sure?" [laughter]
Participant D:	Yeah, I do the same thing in other food stores.
Participant E:	The one thing about the, sorry, real quick, about the fast food is like, I think they have to do that for sanitary purposes.

TABLE 3.5. Extracts from James Bond's diary

Date	Unsustainable practice	Remedy
25 Mar	I drove my car to school today.	Ride the bus or ride my bike.
3 Apr	I went to Cirque du Soleil today and there were hundreds of recyclable cups just getting thrown in the trash or left on the ground.	Provide obvious recycle bins at the Breslin center.
12 Apr	My roommate left the light on in the hallway all day while nobody was home.	Turn off the light when one leaves.

KNOWLEDGE RETENTION

The Twitter students reported a much higher percentage of team-created solutions than the traditional group in the pop quiz. There are multiple explanations for the discrepancy in outcomes.

First, continuous tweeting fosters team communication and prolonged interactive engagement in the learning process. This combination enhances the understanding of the team-created unsustainable practices and remedies. Therefore, the tweeters remembered more solutions that were jointly created on Twitter. This interpretation would support the findings of Aspen and Thorpe (2009), who posit that Twitter can be a powerful active learning tool.

Second, the diary format, as individual work, is intrinsically self-reflective (Table 3.5). Therefore, traditional students might have primarily recalled their own ideas. This interpretation would support the idea that self-reflection is encouraged more strongly in diaries than on Twitter. This outcome supports evidence found during the knowledge creation exercise of this study: Twitter may be superior in gathering the amount of information, but is less powerful at fostering self-reflective thinking.

Third, because only half of the overall unsustainable practices identified were discussed during the traditional group meeting, the traditional students were more likely to report from their diaries. In contrast, through Twitter, gathering of information was more easily facilitated, as also suggested by Wankel (2009).

These three reasons, however, do not explain why traditional students seemed to have retained overall more knowledge about sustainable lifestyles than Twitter students (10 vs 7.6 unsustainable practices including remedies identified in the test), especially given that the Twitter group could draw from a larger pool of existing ideas. This result, collapsed to a single assignment, is in contrast to Junco et al.'s (2011) findings of Twitter's positive impact on grades. One possible explanation is that the traditional group had the chance to share their knowledge shortly before the test during their scheduled discussion session, whereas the Twitter group probably did not reread all tweets shortly before the quiz.

Conclusions

This exploratory study filled some knowledge gaps in the largely unexplored Twitter territory. Twitter as an active, informal learning tool has some distinct advantages and disadvantages over traditional team work. The advantages lie in that Twitter can foster the combined knowledge creation of a group better than individuals' diaries and discussion, because Twitter facilitates sharing of ideas beyond the classroom via an online platform that allows readily available access at random times to continue such discussion. The disadvantages of Twitter lie in constraining critical thinking and self-reflection because of the tweets' character limit. As in previous studies (DeCosta et al., 2010; Dunlap and Lowenthal, 2009), Twitter had a positive impact on student learning, because instantaneous peer-to-peer communication via Twitter enhanced understanding of unsustainable practices and remedies. Twitter, like other microblogging tools (Ebner et al., 2010), also supports informal learning. In contrast to Junco et al. (2011), this study contradicts the finding that students using Twitter more easily and more readily displayed openness about feelings and their own shortcomings. This study instead suggests that the diary-keeping students showed a stronger display of self-reflection: more students identified their own flaws, whereas Twitter students only identified faults of others.

This study has several limitations. First, the small sample size limits the generalizability of results. Having six students in each of the groups only allowed for a glimpse into the advantages and disadvantages Twitter could provide to the learning community. Second, the ways in which this study measured knowledge application, creation, and retention are clearly limited. All assessment methods contain obvious biases, because knowledge application, creation and retention are not equivalent to writing in diaries or on Twitter nor to recalling facts in a quiz. As proxies though, the five sources combined offer important lessons on the value of using Twitter as a new teaching practice. Third, the study stretched only over one month. Given these limitations, future research should sample a larger study group, observe the students' knowledge creation and application over longer periods of time, and comparatively apply both teaching practices to a variety of topics in order to provide further insights into the benefits and pitfalls of Twitter.

While most researchers have argued that Twitter can encourage creativity and stimulate conversation and collaboration, research is still in its infant stages in exploring the "different approaches to teaching and learning … in order to take advantage of the potential of digital media and Web applications" that Hicks and Graber (2010: 627) suggest exist. Despite the small sample size, this work offers valuable insights into the applicability and usability of Twitter as a teaching practice. As an informal, active, outside the classroom tool, Twitter can be a powerful teaching practice to relate theoretical concepts to practical applications in everyday life.

As a first step, this study showed that the use of Twitter can display both sides of the coin as it depends on the course content, the assignment task, and the instructor's intent whether or not Twitter is the right tool for learning aspects of the subject matter. So, in some contexts Twitter will better aid students in learning a particular subject matter compared with more traditional teaching methods, but in other contexts it would hinder them. If instructors intend to engage students on a particular subject matter, bridging theory and practice while including real-world examples (linear applicative learning), Twitter provides distinct advantages over the traditional individual home-work assignments and in-class discussions. Offering a 24/7 available communication platform, Twitter is a powerful tool in applying and creating ideas. In contrast, if the instructor intends to foster critical, in-depth and self-reflective thinking among the students and their peers, this study suggests Twitter is likely to be an unsuitable teaching practice for the class.

Assuming continuous growth of the social network, Twitter may become a phenomenon that captures our millennial student generation. If wisely introduced by educators this tool could become a powerful medium that extends beyond classrooms.

References

Aspden EJ and Thorpe LP (2009) Where do you learn? Tweeting to inform learning space development. *Educause Quarterly* 32(1). Available at: http://www.educause.edu/EDUCAUSE+Quarterly/EDUCAUSE QuarterlyMagazineVolum/WhereDoYouLearnTweetingtoInfor/163852

Bonwell CC and Eison JA (1991) *Active Learning: Creating Excitement in the Classroom. ASHE-ERIC Higher Education Report No. 1.* Washington, DC: George Washington University, School of Education and Human Development.

Borasky ME (2010) A visual history of Twitter's growth. Available at: http://borasky-research.net (accessed 10 December 2010).

Cherney ID (2008) The effects of active learning on students' memories for course content. *Active Learning in Higher Education* 9(2): 152-71.

Chickering AW and Gamson ZF, eds (1991) *Applying the Seven Principles for Good Practice in Under-graduate Education.* San Francisco, CA: Jossey-Bass.

ComScore (2010) Data passport—first half of 2010. Measuring the digital world. Available at: http://www.slideshare.net/StephaneHuy/comscore-2010-rapport-premier-semestre (accessed 15 December 2010).

Conlon TJ (2004) A review of informal learning literature, theory and implications for practice in developing global professional competence. *Journal of European Industrial Training* 28(2-4): 283-95.

Corbeil JR and Corbeil ME (2011) The birth of a social networking phenomenon. In: Wankel C (ed.) *Educating Educators with Social Media (Cutting-edge Technologies in Higher Education, Volume 1).* Bingley: Emerald Group, pp. 13-32.

Croxall B (2010) Reflections on teaching with social media. "ProfHacker," *Chronicle of Higher Education,* 7 June 2010. Available at: http://chronicle.com/blogPost/Reflections-on-Teaching-with/24556/ (accessed 5 September 2010).

DeCosta M, Clifton J and Roen D (2010) Collaboration and social interaction in English classrooms. *English Journal (High school edition)* 99(5): 14.

Dewey J (1938) *Experience and Education.* New York, NY: Collier Books.

Dunlap JC and Lowenthal PR (2009) Tweeting the night away: Using Twitter to enhance social presence. *Journal of Information Systems Education* 20(2): 129.

Ebner M (2009) Introducing live microblogging: How single presentations can be enhanced by the mass. *Journal of Research in Innovative Teaching* 2(1): 108-19.

Ebner M, Lienhardt C, Rohs M and Meyer I (2010) Microblogs in Higher Education—A chance to facilitate informal and process-oriented learning? *Computers and Education* 55: 92-100.

Fox S, Zickuhr K and Smith A (2009) Twitter and status updating, fall 2009—Report: Social Networking, Web 2.0. Available at: www.pewinternet.org/~/media//Files/.../PIP_Twitter_Fall_2009web.pdf (accessed 10 January 2011).

Greenhow C, Robelia B and Hughes J (2009) Learning, teaching, and scholarship in a digital age. Web 2.0 and classroom research: What path should we take now? *Educational Researcher* 38(4): 246-59.

Grosseck G and Holotescu C (2008) Can we use Twitter for educational activities? Paper presented at the 4th International Scientific Conference eLSE: eLearning and Software for Education, Bucharest, Rumania, 17-18 April.

Hannay M and Fretwell C (2011) The higher education workplace: Meeting the needs of multiple generations. *Research in Higher Education Journal* 10(March): 1-12.

Hicks A and Graber A (2010) Shifting paradigms: Teaching, learning and Web 2.0. *Reference Services Review* 38(4): 621-33.

Huberman B, Romero DM and Wu F (2008) Social networks that matter: Twitter under the microscope (updated 1 September 2010). Available at: http://www.hpl.hp.com/research/scl/papers/twitter/ (accessed 5 January 2011).

Jamieson P (2009) The serious matter of informal learning. *Planning for Higher Education* 37(2): 18-25.

Java A, Song X, Finin T and Tseng B (2007) Why we Twitter: Understanding microblogging usage and communities. In: *Proceedings of the Joint 9th WEBKBB and 1st SNA-KBB Workshop 2007*, August 2007. Available at: http://ebiquity.umbc.edu/get/a/publication/369.pdf (accessed 16 September 2010).

Junco R, Heibergert G and Loken E (2011) The effect of Twitter on college student engagement and grades. *Journal of Computer Assisted Learning* 27: 119-32.

Marsick V and Watkins K (1990) *Informal and Incidental Learning in the Workplace*. New York: Routledge and Kegan Paul.

McFedries P (2007) Technically speaking: All a-Twitter. *IEEE Spectrum* 44(10): 84.

McKinney K and Heyl B, eds (2008) *Sociology Through Active Learning*. Thousand Oaks, CA: SAGE/Pine Forge Press.

Meyers C and Jones TB (1993) *Promoting Active Learning: Strategies for the College Classroom*. San Francisco, CA: Jossey-Bass.

Parry B (2008) Twitter for academia. Available at: http://academhack.outside-thetext.com/home/2008/twitter-for-academia/ (accessed 10 September 2010).

Perez E (2009) Professors experiment with Twitter as teaching tool. *The Milwaukee Journal Sentinel* 27. Available at: http://www.jsonline.com/news/education/43747152.html (accessed 2 February 2011).

Reuben R (2008) The use of social media in higher education for marketing and communications: A guide for professionals in higher education. Available at: http://doteduguru.com/id423-social-media-uses-higher-education-marketing-communication.html (accessed 10 September 2010).

Rheingold H (2010) Attention and other 21st-century social media literacies. *Educause Review (1527-6619)* 45(5): 14.

Richardson W (2009) *Blogs, Wikis, Podcasts, and Other Powerful Web Tools for Classrooms*. Thousand Oaks, CA: Corwin Press.

Rogers-Estable M (2009) Web 2.0 and distance education: Tools and techniques. *Distance Learning* 6(4): 55-60.

Schroeder A, Minocha S and Schneider C (2010) The strengths, weaknesses, and threats of using social software in higher and further education teaching and learning. *Journal of Computer Assisted Learning* 26: 159-74.

Stevens V (2008) Trial by Twitter: The rise and slide of the year's most viral micro-blogging platform. *TESLEJ: Teaching English as a Second or Foreign Language* 12(1). Available at: http://tesl-ej.org/ej45/int.html (accessed 15 September 2010).

Twitter (2010) Twitter: www.twitter.com (accessed 20 December 2010).

Wankel C (2009) Management education using social media. *Organization Management Journal* 6(4): 251-63.

Yang B and Lu D (2001) Predicting academic performance in management education: An empirical investigation of MBA success. *Journal of Education for Business* 77(1): 15-20.

Young J (2009) Teaching with Twitter: Not for the faint of heart. *Chronicle of Higher Education*. Available at: http://chronicle.com/article/Teaching-With-Twitter-Not-for/49230/ (accessed 10 September 2010).

Source: *Active Learning in Higher Education* 13.1 (2012): 9-21.

WHAT IT SAYS

1. According to Kassens-Noor, how has Twitter been used in the classroom?

2. What was the goal of Kassens-Noor's own study?

3. Briefly describe the methodology of the study and what question(s) it was designed to answer.

4. Briefly describe the results of the study in terms of both knowledge creation and knowledge retention.

5. What does Kassens-Noor conclude about the use of Twitter in higher education? What is Twitter good for? What weaknesses does it have? How might it be best applied to the educational process?

HOW IT SAYS IT

1. Describe the intended audience for Kassens-Noor's essay. Who are her intended readers and how can you tell?

2. Kassens-Noor's study follows the IMRAD format (see p. 87). Why do you suppose she chose this form of presentation? How does it work to advance her argument?

3. Consider the use of tables in Kassen-Noor's essay. What does each of the tables help to illustrate? How do these tables help to advance her point?

WRITE ABOUT IT

1. Consider your use of Web 2.0 technologies. Write a short essay in which you explore how Web 2.0 technologies have contributed to and/or detracted from your educational experiences.

2. Write an essay in which you examine Kassens-Noor's pedagogical values. According to Kassens-Noor, what kinds of experiences should education provide? What are the roles of the teacher and student? What should students be able to do as a result of higher education? What should they take away from the classroom?

3. Write an essay in which you argue for or against the use of Twitter in higher education. What bad student habits might Twitter reinforce? Alternatively, how might Twitter aid in the learning process?

4. Use your Twitter account, or establish one if you don't have one, and write a series of tweets in which you address the three preceding questions. Direct your tweets to your professor for this class. Make sure you learn your professor's Twitter name (if she or he has one). Work to condense your writing without using abbreviations such as "u r" for "you are." Capture the discussions in a screen shot or series of screen shots and bring the tweets to class for discussion.

e. Sarita Yardi, "Whispers in the Classroom"

Sarita Yardi is an assistant professor at the University of Michigan's School of Information. Her research involves the design, measurement, and analysis of social computing applications toward positive social outcomes, and spans the areas of social computing, HCI, and social network analysis. Her dissertation explores parents and parenting strategies with respect to their children's Internet use.

Yardi is a PhD candidate in the College of Computing at Georgia Tech University. She received her MS from the School of Information at the University of California at Berkeley in 2006 and her BS in computer engineering at Dartmouth College in 2002.

The essay below was published in *Hanging Out, Messing Around, and Geeking Out: Kids Living and Learning with New Media* (MIT Press, 2009), which examines young people's everyday new-media practices, including video game playing, text-messaging, digital media production, and social media use. The book was written by members of the Digital Youth Project, funded by the John D. and Catherine T. MacArthur Foundation as part of its series Foundation Reports on Digital Media and Learning. Yardi's essay proposes that student chat rooms could transform classroom learning behaviors and practices by changing the ways in which students interact with each other and with their professors to create and disseminate knowledge. She suggests that chat rooms present one alternative to the "banking concept" of education disparaged by Paulo Freire.

As You Read: Think about the ways in which you interact with your professors and with other students in your classes. In what ways does your experience compare with those that Yardi describes?

Whispers in the Classroom

Introduction

"Let's face it—our school doesn't have a book for everything." —Autumn[1]

Online chat rooms are a novel communication medium that provide an opportunity to transform classroom learning in unexpected and powerful ways. Youth are a demographic of highly engaged, core members of the "always on" crowd—active

---

1   Digital Media Essay Contest (DMEC), Global Kids' Digital Media Initiative 2006, supported by the John D. and Catherine T. MacArthur Foundation, http://globalkids.org/olp/dmec/.

users of the internet, instant messaging, video games, and social networking sites. Numerous studies have documented how young people use instant messaging and online chat rooms in their personal lives. Some youth today perceive technologies to be entirely new and in the position of setting unprecedented opportunities for interactions online. One high school student stated that, "I can't see how people in the past survived without digital media." Similarly, another asserts that, "My generation, those born in the early '90s, are the first humans to be so profoundly impacted by today's new technology."[2] Their familiarity with and enthusiasm for these tools suggests a valuable opportunity to examine how such communication media can be transferred into more formal educational settings to enable both formal and informal learning through student discussions and interactions online. Students can learn from one another through collaborative knowledge sharing, while educators can use the tool to gain more insight into what and how their students are learning. Kyle, a high school teenager from Wyoming, captures many of the most important factors in chat room use when he says:

> Chat rooms can be a way to experience intelligent conversation and try out new ways of saying things, often without having to deal with the fear of being wrong or being laughed at. Kids are using this great tool to enhance personal relationships based on simple dialogue. I'm not going to encourage such behavior, but it is better than what could be going on. Chat rooms and other forms of online communication provide a launching pad for the great thinking minds of America's youth, with little or no consequence for failure.[3]

As wireless networks have been introduced in conference halls, hotels, university auditoriums, and in particular, the classroom, laptop users have realized that they do not have to sit idly during a lecture or presentation. Behavior can range from surfing the Web and checking e-mail while blatantly disregarding the frontchannel speaker to actively engaging in the frontchannel discussion through concurrent related discussions, debates, fact checking, resource sharing, and collaboration. The recent surge in interest has generated a number of conference-based case studies that look to describe the implications of backchannel chats.

Participants in these conferences have expressed a wide range of opinions about the usefulness of the backchannel in context of the frontchannel discussion. Similarly, a number of educators have considered the effects of unrestricted wireless access in the classroom, and some have attempted to incorporate these

---

2   Ibid.

3   Ibid.

technologies into their lectures and lesson plans.[4] However, little research has been conducted on how chat rooms affect learning experiences and environments. Chat rooms could transform how course material, learning behaviors and practices, and interactions between students and teachers, fundamentally change the ways in which teachers and students create and disseminate ideas, knowledge, and understanding. This chapter first describes a backchannel chat room that has taken place over multiple years in a large university student community and then explores some unforeseen and exciting opportunities—as well as possible limitations—for redesigning teaching and learning practices in educational environments.

Background: What Is a Backchannel?

Chat rooms can be accessed through any Web-based chat sites or by downloading a chat client to one's computer and then connecting to an online server through this local client. Internet Relay Chat is a client-based chat environment that enables groups of people to collaborate and chat from any physical location. It was first used in the 1980s and has since grown into one of the most popular real-time chat systems around the world. It is a multiuser system where people meet on channels to talk in groups or privately. There are no restrictions on the number of people who can participate in a given discussion or the number of channels that can be formed. Chat room conversations tend to be thought of as ephemeral and impermanent due to their synchronous nature. The interaction is rarely thought out in advance, and conversations occur spontaneously. Similar to face-to-face conversation, there is little archiving of chat conversations. Although chat logs may be maintained, they are rarely referred to after the chat has occurred.

The central function of the backchannel chat room is its use as a secondary or background complement to an existing frontchannel. The frontchannel may consist of a professor, teacher, speaker, lecturer, conference panel, or other similar environment containing a centralized discussion leader who is usually colocated in the same physical space as the participants. The frontchannel usually implies a single focus of attention. The backchannel can function to enhance the frontchannel discussion by encouraging user participation and interaction, changing the dynamics of the room from a strictly one-to-many interaction to a many-to-many interaction. Activities in the backchannel may include establishing guidelines, inviting participants, excluding outsiders, posing questions, providing answers,

---

4   A.B. Campbell and R.P. Pargas, Laptops in the Classroom, in *SIGCSE Bulletin* 35 (2003): 98-102; D. Franklin and K. Hammond, The Intelligent Classroom: Providing Competent Assistance, in *Proceedings of Autonomous Agents* (Montreal, Canada, May, 2001), (ACM Press, 2001), 161-168; M. Ratto, R.B. Shapiro, T.M. Truong, and W.G. Griswold, The Activeclass Project: Experiments in Encouraging Classroom Participation, in *Computer Support for Collaborative Learning* 2003; H. Hembrooke and G. Gay, The Laptop and the Lecture: The Effects of Multitasking in Learning Environments, *Journal of Computing in Higher Education* 15, no. 1 (2003).

critiquing what is being said in physical or digital communication channels, or sharing information and resources.[5]

With a thorough understanding of the opportunities and limitations of the backchannel, educators and instructional designers could transform the classroom experience from a passive lecture model to one of active, collaborative, and engaged knowledge production. Students can learn through a different communication medium, while educators can use the tool to gain more insight into what and how their students are learning. Some questions addressed in this chapter include:

- In what ways does chat augment class discussion and how can this information be used by educators?
- What can chat data say about classroom interactions?
- What types of interactions occur in this backchannel and how do they contribute to the academic learning space?
- How does this communication medium change techniques for information and knowledge sharing?
- Is there a compelling story to be told or is it simply noise—wasted bandwidth that distracts participants from their face-to-face environment?

A Case Study in a University Backchannel

The notion of "the academy" as an institution of modern higher education has been transformed from a tradition of an intellectual quest for truth, philosophy, and the arts, with an often stark and disciplined rigor into a socially-oriented, student-empowered learning space. The sense of entitlement in the modern undergraduate student is significant. They want to be able to select which courses they are taking, participate in fully-funded sports teams, have access to clean and often luxurious living standards, and complain if an academic setting has a dearth of social options, food selection, or entertainment opportunities. Such is the environment at the university described in this case study. It is an internationally renowned academic institution, highly sought after by undergraduate, graduate, and faculty scholars.

A student set up a designated Internet Relay Chat channel at this university in which fellow students could easily chat together in an online social environment. No specific purpose or use was attached to the chat room, and an automated login welcome message simply declared that it was to be used by university community members and guests. The chat room experienced an enormous surge in traffic within a matter of weeks. Activity then maintained an overall steady state,

---

5   J.F. McCarthy and d.m. boyd, Digital Backchannels in Shared Physical Spaces: Experiences at an Academic Conference, in *CHI '05 Extended Abstracts on Human Factors in Computing Systems* (*Portland, OR, April 2-7, 2005*), 1641-1644 (New York: ACM Press, 2005).

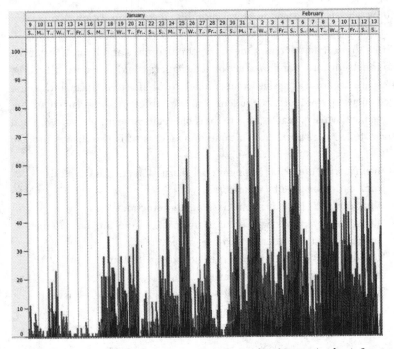

FIGURE 3.2. Number of Chat Entries Over First Six Weeks of Spring Academic Semester

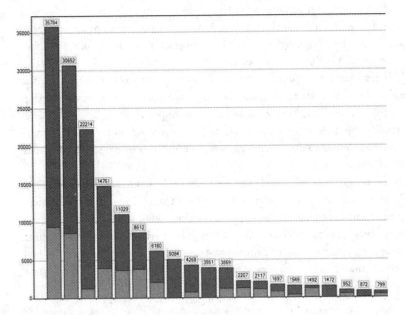

FIGURE 3.3. Total Chat Entries by User Over One Year

amassing a few hundred postings on any given day, and generating a total log of over 300,000 user entries within the first year. In the following year, the new incoming class quickly assimilated into the existing virtual community, integrating into and redefining its culture and social dynamics.

Students login throughout the day, during class, outside of class, and in the evening. With the goal of better understanding patterns of behavior, chat log users and time stamps were plotted in information visualization software to highlight trends in adoption and usage within the classroom. In Figure 3.2, user count is plotted versus the first six weeks of the spring academic semester, showing a general increase in user participation. This suggests that students become more engaged in the chat room community over time. Figure 3.3 shows total entries by user. The curve shows a power log trend in behavior, indicating that a few users participate most often.

While these tools help to measure quantitative trends over time, they do not help to shed light into the constantly evolving, organic, and unstructured social dynamics of the chat room. In this environment, there is no sense of ownership, nor is there a moderator or leader within the virtual community. It is a self-generated, self-sustained, and thriving online community. Nobody anticipated that from this community would emerge a powerful new genre of computer-mediated learning. As students became comfortable with the affordances offered by the chat room, while simultaneously developing a growing sense of community through their physical social interactions, the channel was unintentionally appropriated into a space for self-directed learning. It provided an open and unrestricted bandwidth through which to engage in a professor's lecture. They had created an environment that was rich for collaborative learning and knowledge production, a communication medium through which to engage in active, creative, discovery-based learning. Students who may have been too shy and inhibited in the physical classroom had an opportunity to express themselves in the backchannel. The chat room transitioned from a simple tool for social communication to a tightly knit community. This conversion was both unanticipated and unexpected and elicited a wide variety of reactions from students and teachers. They were surprised, confused, curious, excited, eager, and intrigued. Regardless of their perceptions, there was a clear lack of understanding about the future of the backchannel in classrooms, but nonetheless, a sense of enthusiasm about its potential for change.

The backchannel presents a unique toolkit through which people can create, identify, and filter new modes of interaction. Young people adopt and appropriate new forms of communication technologies and digital media in order to experiment with their self-identity, develop their social networks, and nurture their personal friendship and relationships. This suggests a powerful opportunity for engaging them by incorporating these practices into new classroom teaching and learning paradigms. The emerging experiences offered by this digital backchannel offer an exciting space in which to explore new directions in collaborative learning. In light of the increasing role of new media technologies and computer-mediated communication as ubiquitous tools in our everyday lives, researchers need to address the need for a better understanding of how these tools can be incorporated into the classroom environment to facilitate enhanced teaching and learning.

Historical Background: Conflicts and Context

Conflicts in backchannel use have their theoretical underpinnings in historical and ongoing power struggles over who maintains ownership and control within the classroom. Should teachers run the classroom or should students direct their own learning environment? Can the two pedagogical models coexist? Educational pedagogy has evolved over time in parallel with the cultural, societal, and governmental influences in which it is embedded. For example, Pink Floyd's famous and controversial song, "Another Brick in the Wall" reflects the counterculture sentiment of its time with a chorus line: "We don't need no education. We don't need no thought control.... Teacher! Leave the kids alone. Hey! Teacher! Leave the kids alone!" As the lyrics suggest, the traditional educational classroom setting has historically been perceived by some as an environment of oppression. Freire describes such oppression as banking, in which students are the depositories and the teacher is the depositor.[6] In this model, students are given agency only so far as to receive, file, and store the deposits, rather than to engage in creative, transformative, and knowledge construction processes. Students are force-fed facts and information, required to regurgitate the teacher's personal mantra. Unmotivated students fail the system and uninspired students may despise the system. Students who learn to work within the system align themselves on the fast track to success.

More recently, teachers, educators, parents, and policy makers are paying increasing attention to the implications of enabling online access in classrooms. In the wake of recent legislative acts, such as the No Child Left Behind Act[7] and the Deleting Online Predators Act,[8] the question of ownership and regulation in schools is revisited in this context of internet use. These acts seek to protect youth in their online environments and to enable more equal access of these environments to all students. Yet, by demonizing the negative effects of youths' online activities, these laws may have inadvertently caused a culture of fear and moral panic surrounding online environments that limit the potential for designing powerful and novel learning opportunities that take advantage of Web-based opportunities, such as chat rooms and backchannels. Despite the negative perceptions that are frequently perpetuated by mainstream media, the large majority of youth are not looking to engage in unsafe behaviors online, but instead want

---

6   P. Freire, *Pedagogy of the Oppressed* (Harmondsworth, UK: Penguin, 1992).

7   http://www.ed.gov/nclb/landing.jhtml.

8   http://thomas.loc.gov/cgi-bin/query/z?c109:H.R.5319.

ownership over their online activities. In particular, recent studies show that teenagers are often more aware of the implications of their online activities in terms of safety, learning, and privacy than they may be given credit for.[9] Amber, a teenager from Wyoming, suggests that "technology is changing things so rapidly that the control procedures need to change with it.... The only real answers would be the ones worked out by students and adults alike."[10] Dahye, a teenager from Brooklyn, asserts that "we own these new digital medias, we shouldn't be slaves to them."[11] Teens are looking to use the internet to socialize with their peers, for entertainment, and to search for information.

The students who use the backchannel may simply be looking to engage in an environment in the classroom that is not forced, regardless of the actual interactions that play out within this space. Ironically, because regulation in schools prevents free access to the Web, those youth who may be the most in need of free access to information are cut off from the ability to utilize these resources. Furthermore, schools are well equipped to serve students at the most crucial points in their stages of technology adoption, during introductory and educational phases of adoption and when a high quality, reliable connection is otherwise unavailable. Educators are in, perhaps, the best position to be a watchdog for youth's online activities. Educators can teach youth about empowerment and professionalism and the necessary means for articulating and understanding credibility and assessment in their online worlds. A good educational environment requires teachers who motivate their students, facilitate knowledge building, engage participation, and foster a passion for lifelong learning. To deny students this right is to deny them their fundamental right to learn. Such deprivation would be to deconstruct the very premise upon which our economic and cultural existence rests. Thus, the role of chat rooms in the classroom and the contradictory notions of ownership that are suggested uproot the very premise upon which traditional classroom learning has been constructed. The polarization of opinion in who *should* have control in this learning environment can lead to embittered debates that may be motivated by personal agendas and politically and historically rooted beliefs. This chapter, therefore, discusses the role of a backchannel chat room in context of such political divisions, seeking to overcome these challenges to harness the potential of the backchannel as a communication medium for enabling new forms of learning.

The following sections examine some of the potential affordances and struggles surrounding the use of a backchannel in a school setting. These include its role in establishing social trust and individual identity, its ability to create a sustained sense of space, its function as a site of power negotiations, and its capacity to improve learning using strategies for situated pedagogy and knowledge creation.

---

9   A. Lenhart and M. Madden, *Social Networking Websites and Teens: An Overview* (Washington, DC: Pew Internet & American Life Project, 2007), http://www.pewinternet.org/PPF/r/198/report display.asp.

10 Digital Media Essay Contest, 2006.

11 Ibid.

The section below highlights some of the potential benefits of the backchannel, and is followed by a description of its primary disadvantages that are drawn from the case study environment. These dynamics are then used to explore ways in which the backchannel could be used in the classroom and to dissect the conflicts and challenges in doing so. The final section suggests rules and methods for designing a productive backchannel environment with recommendations for changes in educational pedagogy and teaching and learning styles.

Benefits: Innovations in Learning

As the emerging participatory culture on the internet has clearly demonstrated, new technologies can help to enable equal participation across domains that have previously been restricted to authorities within a particular field. How might this change the classroom learning environment? "People with expertise contributed answers, tidbits, essays, pages of software code, lore of astonishing variety," Howard Rheingold writes in *Smart Mobs*.[12] People want to establish themselves as an authority on a subject by becoming both producers and authors in digital media. If students can participate in a lecture, how they make sense of the transmitted information will not be the same as if they were simply listening. On one hand, their shared social construction may create a homogenizing of opinions as they share their perspectives with one another. On the other hand, students are empowered to argue, debate, and discuss with one another, creating an environment in which they can take on as much power as they want.[13] Johnson states that "To understand how these new media experiences work, you have to analyze the message, the medium and the rules. What's interesting here is not just the medium, but rather the rules that govern what gets selected and what doesn't."[14] However, without a common ground upon which to understand its power to engage students, enable new modes of learning, and facilitate teaching, the power of the backchannel may be lost as yet another poorly understood medium that is unsuccessful in school environments.

The potential success of peer-to-peer learning in a chat room is rooted in the theory of constructivist learning. According to this theory, learning is an active process in which learners construct new ideas or concepts based upon their current and past knowledge. The learner selects and transforms information, constructs hypotheses, and makes decisions, relying on a cognitive structure to do so.[15] Classes in which students participate in discussions encourage them to go beyond

---

12 H. Rheingold, *Smart Mobs: The Next Social Revolution* (Cambridge, MA: Perseus Books, 2002).

13 Jack Vinson, More Backchannel Via CSCW, *Knowledge Jolt with Jack* 2004, http://blog.jackvinson.com/archives/2004/12/02/more_backchannel_via_cscw.html.

14 Steven Johnson, *Emergence: The Connected Lives of Ants, Brains, Cities, and Software* (New York: Scribner, 2001).

15 J. Bruner, *Toward a Theory of Instruction* (Cambridge, MA: Harvard University Press, 1966).

merely plugging numbers into formulas or memorizing terms.[16] Similarly, Brown, Collins and Duguid argue that students learn best when given the opportunity to learn skills and theories in the context in which they are used, then construct their interpretations of a subject, and communicate those understandings to others.[17] In the backchannel, students can create their own knowledge by having the freedom to direct the discussion in ways that are relevant, contextual, and instructional for their own learning purposes. The ways in which students use chat rooms emulate their culture of learning, communicating, and interacting. Peer-to-peer interactions support flexible, learner-centered designs in which learning is active and organic rather than static.

The backchannel offers students the opportunity to interact with the teacher, the presentation, and one another in a relatively unrestricted, open environment. Far from the traditional presentation environment where they are at the mercy of whoever is standing in front of the classroom, chat offers the possibility for engagement through multiple modes of transmission. Students can experience a positive engagement with the backchannel, suggesting that they can conduct backchannel discussions that are on-topic, and can even lead to a more involved audience and better interaction with the presenter.[18] Giving students access to a public ubiquitous backchannel also broadens the scope of discourse within the shared physical space. Students are able to ask questions, receive answers, and solicit information without having to interrupt the frontchannel presentation. The signal-to-noise ratio in the frontchannel classroom discussion is improved because only the most important and salient questions are posted verbally, while more peripheral or irrelevant questions can be filtered through the backchannel discussion. Students can ask their peers questions, such as:[19]

> *10:48:10 Student1:* so whats [sic] constructionism?
> *10:48:21 Student1:* same as constructivism?
> *10:48:39 Student2:* no, it is more about making things in learning, like learning by building artifacts

Similarly, they can help explain or link relevant material to the discussion topic.

> *10:51:08 Student1:* Did [lecturer] show us where he got his dataset?
> *10:51:30 Student2:* I don't think he did

16 National Research Council, *Science Teaching Reconsidered: A Handbook* (Washington, DC: National Academy Press, 1997).

17 J. Brown, A. Collins, and P. Duguid, Situated Cognition and the Culture of Learning, *Educational Researcher* 18, no. 1 (1989): 18-42.

18 T. Kennedy, E. Golub, B. Stroope, K. Kee, A. Powell, and S. Zehnder, Wireless Communication in the Classroom: A "Back Channel" to the Learning Process? paper presented at Internet Research 6.0: Internet Generations (Chicago: 2005).

19 All names and direction quotations are changed to maintain anonymity.

> *10:52:17 Student3:* but you can find it in [source]
> *10:52:47 Student2:* Actually, I think this is the link
> *10:52:48 Student2:* [URL]

The backchannel provides a means through which to challenge and verify the authority of the teacher without actually challenging him or her explicitly. Students may be more willing to brainstorm over chat when it is considered a backchannel and the social cost of failure or being wrong is low, or at least, is perceived to be low. They also ask questions about material the teacher already covered in class that they may not feel comfortable asking about again.

> *14:25:10 Student13:* what is microformats again? sorry
> *14:25:59 Student66:* http://microformats.org/about/
> *11:25:29 Student44:* what does participatory design mean? I know he explained it but I forgot.
> *11:25:33 Teaching Assistant:* it's a type of design that brings the users into the process

Students frequently shared resources based on their own expertise. In this way, the backchannel can enhance the professor's lecture, without interrupting the flow of the in-class discussion. The backchannel also enables people who have not had a voice, whether because of educational, economic, social, or cultural barriers, to build an equitable reputation in the classroom by participating in the dialogue.

Disadvantages: Distracted Youth or Engaged Students?

Many opponents to using backchannels in the classroom highlight its potential for distraction. Although students have always been subject to distractions during class, in a modern wireless-enabled physical space, the possibilities for distractions increase exponentially. Some participants have suggested the term "continuous partial attention" to describe an audience member's cognitive ability to pay attention to the speaker's presentation when simultaneously engaged in the backchannel. Others, somewhat cynically, suggest that "continuous partial inattention" is a more appropriate description.[20] Regardless of how well intentioned a student may be, a backchannel is going to elicit reactions and engagement from the group that will be asynchronous and off-topic to the frontchannel presentation. This can cause confusion and disruption for the students as well as the teacher. For example, in the two admissions below, the students acknowledge that they missed part of the lecture because they were not paying attention.

---

20 McCarthy and boyd, "Digital backchannels in shared physical spaces."

10:51:22 *Student4:* Yeah, I missed that, was reading the news headlines
10:51:28 *Student4:* what's that about usability?
18:42:31 *Student6:* Wait, what did she say? I wasn't paying attention. Oooh,
a birdy ...

Similarly, the discussion below took place in class but was unrelated to the
professor's lecture:

17:31:28 *Student12:* yeah. I had a roommate who went running with friends
and ran like 14 miles. He came home and was eating honey directly out of
the jar. It was funny.
17:32:01 *Student12:* I never saw an adult eat honey directly out of the jar
before.
17:32:10 *Student31:* i eat jelly straight from the jar sometimes

Furthermore, discussions can become improper and disrespectful. For example:

13:27:32 *Student4:* i think we should have a goal this semester
13:27:53 *Student18:* to get [Student3] a girlfriend?

It could be argued that these students would be distracted even if they were
not in the chat room. Weighing the costs and benefits of the backchannel in this
case may reveal that the chat room is beneficial for the student because he or she
is able to ask a classmate about what was missed, rather than simply conceding it
as a lost opportunity. At the same time, students recognize that the backchannel
does offer an opportunity for distraction that is more exciting and stimulating
than traditional forms of distraction, such as staring out the window or doodling
on paper. In an unmoderated classroom environment, multitasking online may
easily deteriorate into a range of activities that are unrelated to the professor's
lecture. One student revealed this perspective:

I do occasionally feel kind of guilty about it, I should be paying attention
to the class. Especially when things "get out of hand" people start
laughing, I think, "we shouldn't be doing this...." I try not to let it overtake
my attention. I don't feel like it's a problem. If I can concentrate, it's
helpful. If not, I probably wouldn't be paying attention anyway.

In their study of undergraduate students, Kinzie et al. found that students in
the open laptop condition suffered decrements on traditional measures of memory
for lecture content even though the students felt they were capable of engaging
in on-task discussions and of expressing opinions and exploring instructionally

relevant topics.[21] Although students routinely multitasked in classrooms as they attended to lectures, processed the material, and took notes, both students and the instructors expressed some discomfort with discussion occurring synchronously with classroom lectures. Furthermore, students' experience with and ability to use forms of technology will affect their levels of distraction while using it.

For those youth who are advanced chat room users, the backchannel may enable them to intuitively appropriate the technology to maximize their learning experience. Others who have not interacted in chat rooms may expend significant energy trying to overcome the learning curve of the technology before being able to actually engage in the actual classroom discussion. What may be an innovation in technology and practice to one student is familiar, and perhaps even antiquated, to another. Therefore, the use of backchannels may be helpful for some students while others are better off not using it, depending on the personal experiences of each individual student.

Power Plays: Who Rules the Classroom?

In the midst of the pervasive culture of fear that surrounds many forms of popular new media, the backchannel may be perceived to be a medium that encourages transgression. Those who oppose it may argue that to participate in the backchannel is to purposefully upstage the teacher's role in the classroom. Their claims highlight the politically charged pedagogical implications associated with the backchannel. Cohen states that "passing notes in the classroom is probably as old as formal education itself, but the advent of cell phones and other sophisticated handheld devices has elevated this communication to a digital art form."[22] McCarthy et al. similarly suggest that "the term 'backchannel' is a political term, implying not only the existence of a primary 'frontchannel,' but also carrying implications of an unofficial, unwanted, illicit quality. In the lecture-oriented classroom, backchannels have always had a rich life, enabled by the technology of the day—from whispering, hand signals, and note passing, to today's e-mail, instant messaging, and mobile phone-based SMS."[23] The meaning of the term backchannel thus varies with context and usage. To some it suggests an intangible, clandestine community. To others it suggests an empowering toolkit for participation, collaboration, and informal interactions.

---

21 M.B. Kinzie, S.D. Whitaker, and M.J. Hofer, Instructional Uses of Instant Messaging (IM) During Classroom Lectures, *Educational Technology & Society* 8, no. 2 (2005): 150-160.

22 D. Cohen, Digital Note-Passing Gains Respect Among Adults, *USA Today*, 2005, http://www.usatoday.com/tech/products/services/2004-11-26-im-gains-cred x.htm.

23 J.F. McCarthy, d. boyd, E.F. Churchill, W.G. Griswold, E. Lawley, and M. Zaner. Digital backchannels in Shared Physical Spaces: Attention, Intention and Contention, in *Proceedings of the 2004 ACM Conference on Computer Supported Cooperative Work* (Chicago, November 6-10, 2004), 550-553 (New York: ACM Press, 2004).

There are a number of ways in which the backchannel could be rude or disrespectful to the teacher. First, if the teacher is not aware of the existence of the backchannel, he is placed in a compromisingly uninformed position about the dynamics of the classroom environment. Second, the context of the backchannel discussion could very likely contain negative or disrespectful comments about either the lecture content or personal characteristics of the teacher. Third, as has been described already, students' presence in the backchannel suggests a partial or complete lack of attention to the teacher.

Interviews with professors, teachers, and students revealed a challenging disconnect in perceptions of ownership within the backchannel. There is an ongoing power struggle between teachers and students, both explicit and implicit, which creates a division in approaches to adapting the backchannel in the classroom. This struggle is not new, as educators have always been challenged to maintain a balance of control and power in the classroom. David Labaree, a professor at Stanford's School of Education, declares that "one reason that teaching is such a difficult profession is that its aim is to change the behavior of the client, and . . . its success depends on the willingness of the client to cooperate...."[24] Teachers can succeed only if they can convince or motivate students to cooperate with them. Given that student attendance is mandatory, many develop an inherent resistance to following classroom instruction. However, existing norms do not necessarily apply to new technologies, and must be reconsidered in context of the affordances of the new technology. Is there a possibility for rethinking and reconstructing teaching paradigms using the backchannel that is satisfactory, even embraced, by educators and students alike?

For example, the introduction of computers in the classroom creates a shift in dynamics from one-to-many to many-to-many between the teacher and the students. In a many-to-many interaction, such as that enabled by a backchannel, student culture dominates over the traditional teacher-generated ecology. Therefore, a self-policing model may be needed to facilitate a productive learning culture. Whether in a lecture or a seminar, students have acknowledged the instructor as the moderator of the discussion and rely on the instructor to provide structure and to manage the discussion.[25] Nonetheless, professors have lamented the use of wireless technologies in the classroom, resorting to banning classroom usage or attempting to turn off access. "Some have banned the technology from classes, some turn off the Internet during instruction, while others struggle through lectures knowing that students are instant messaging, looking at photos, writing

24 David Labaree, Progressivism, Schools and Schools of Education: An American Romance, *Paedagogica Historica* 41, nos. 1, 2 (2005): 275-288.

25 R. West and J.C. Pearson, Antecedent and Consequent Conditions of Student Questioning: An Analysis of Classroom Discourse Across the University, *Communication Education* 43 (1994): 299-311.

papers, and playing games instead of focusing on teacher-relayed information."[26] At the University of Virginia, a law professor decided to turn off wireless access during class times. At the University of Texas, a law professor climbed a ladder and disconnected the wireless transmitter due to his frustration with students' inattention. "Laptops are a real problem," says Charles M. Grisham, a professor at the University of Virginia. "You can stand at the door and see students surfing the web, e-mailing to each other.... We wanted to bring this knowledge [technology] into the classroom, but it may be crippling in other ways."[27]

Professors at the university in this study expressed varied opinions about the university backchannel and its use during their lectures. One professor felt that he now had to teach in shorter bursts in the hopes of holding students' attention better. He was not happy about this, since he felt that his subject material required a lot of concentration on complex topics. Another professor, who had not been previously aware of the chat room, expressed discontent at having no awareness of it. This professor asked, somewhat cynically, if she could also be given access to this chat room. She did not appreciate that students might be talking about her without her knowledge. This latter reaction was expressed by a number of professors, lecturers, and teachers. In Golub's study, the lecturer's initial reaction was one of anger and apprehension that students were talking about her behind her back.[28] However, when she realized that the participants in the chat room had been talking about topics related to her presentation, she became more enthusiastic about the idea.

Another university professor confided that the university backchannel was disconcerting for him because he did not know what was being said. "When a whole bunch of people start smiling broadly or snickering, you sometimes go, wait, did I say something weird or what?" He emphasized that he experienced a feeling of disconnection when he did not know what was going on and what people were doing on it. He felt that it could play an interesting role if it were incorporated into the classroom through professor endorsement or a frontchannel display. It would provide an interesting dynamic for teachers and students to combine lecture and debate at the same time. If it were incorporated into the classroom, this professor asked, would it change the entire content of the discussion? "Would it poison the well?" Another professor in the university program expressed a contrasting perspective on the backchannel. He knew that students were chatting online during class because he could easily perceive their engagement with the computers as such. However, he stated that it did not bother him as it did many of the other professors. Although this particular professor did not feel that the possibility that students were chatting about him was a challenge to

---

26 K. Phalen, Taking a Minus and Making It a Plus, *Information Technology & Communication* 7, no. 1 (2003).

27 Ibid.

28 Kennedy et al., "Wireless Communication in the Classroom."

his authority or self-esteem, many university students we interviewed felt that insecurity could explain a professor's opposition to the backchannel:

> Some professors think, "if you don't have anything else to do, then you'll pay attention." I feel like it's almost insecurity, that professors are worried that people aren't paying attention, they get a little pissy about it.

Although it may be partially attributed to their unfamiliarity with technologies, there is also a greater sense of loss of power that could occur. If students are able to direct their own learning styles and materials, the power structure in the classroom could easily transfer from the teacher to the student. While the transition away from a teacher-centric classroom may simply take time to evolve, it could also be argued that it may be time to reinvent teaching. "Faculty may argue that computers are distracting and so should be eliminated from or controlled in the classroom," says John G. Bryan at the University of Cincinnati. "The problem isn't that computers are distracting. The problem is that many faculty work against the computers or in spite of the computers instead of really using the computers to accomplish their instructional goals."[29]

A better understanding of the social dynamics around the technology is essential to improving its use in the classroom. "We must learn from social trends, capture the power of student-technology interactions, and consider how such relationships engender students' motivation for learning. The stipulation is that we as educators must be willing to reshape our traditional norms of communication, as well as be open to drawing upon skills students bring to the classroom."[30] The backchannel offers a relatively moderated environment in which students can assert some ownership and control over their own learning environment. Given the flux in educational goals and teaching theories, teachers are often uncertain about what skills they are ultimately seeking to enable in students. Is the goal of the backchannel to enable students to be more engaged? To seek out their own fields of expertise? To teach the new forms of media literacy? To take advantage of the opportunity to learn from their peers? The use of the backchannel in the classroom could foreshadow a revolution in the classroom in ways that are as yet undetermined but that harbor real potential.

Building Community Identity

Establishing identity and reputation in a virtual community has long been understood to be one of the most important characteristics to increasing participation

---

29 Phalen, "Taking a Minus."

30 D. DeGennaro, Should We Ban Instant Messaging in School?, in *Learning and Leading with Technology* 32, no. 7 (2005).

and engagement within that community.[31] Social recognition was one of the biggest motivators for participants in the university chat room. The most common form of identity recognition is a participant's username. Core community members rarely change usernames, and when they do it is usually because of server or connection problems with their preferred nickname, and they will choose a similar alternative name. Because of the synchronous nature of the university channel and its very strong sense of community, trust is a crucial dynamic of the backchannel environment. Chat's real-time synchronous affordances make it difficult for people to mask their identity within the community. "Rapid responsiveness in communication begets trust. [Chat] forces rapid response, a basis for trust, which if backed up by short message quality provides deeper context for an initial relationship."[32] For both regular community members and new participants, a sense of trust within the channel is mandated at all times. The auto-message upon login explains the chat room community: "[Chat room name] is the [university name]. If you are looking for discussion of [similar sounding name], you are in the wrong place. Unidentified lurkers will be kicked." This is primarily maintained by requesting all users to reveal their true identity. In fact, all regular users on the backchannel know the real identity of any other user at any given time. If a username is present that is not recognized by the backchannel core community, users will immediately query the unidentified user to reveal his or her true identity.

> 17:54:30 Student23: hello Student4
> 17:54:33 Student12: who is Student4?
> 17:54:35 Student4: hi
> 17:54:42 Student4: [Student4 name]
> 17:54:55 Student7: Hey!
> 17:55:02 Student9: hi Student7
> 17:55:10 Student2: welcome to chat room [names]
> 17:55:10 Student4: hello everybody

In a separate episode, two recent alumni of the university who had graduated the previous year entered the chat room to check it out. The current class members knew the identity of the alumni, but the incoming class did not. They immediately questioned the identity of the new participants, but were ultimately willing to trust that they were welcome members of the channel as long as the current members could vouch for their identity.

---

31 S. Turkle, *Life on the Screen: Identity in the Age of the Internet* (New York: Simon & Schuster, 1995); B. Wellman and M. Gulia, Virtual Communities as Communities: Net Surfers Don't Ride Alone, in *Communities in Cyberspace*, eds. M. Smith and P. Kollock (New York: Routledge, 1999), 167–189; Etienne Wenger, *Communities of Practice: Learning, Meaning, and Identity* (Cambridge, UK: Cambridge University Press, 1998).

32 Ross Mayfield, Social Networks, Jobs & the Third Place, *Ross Mayfield's Weblog*, 2003, http://ross.typepad.com/blog/2003/08/socialnetworks.html.

21:37:58 → Student17 has joined
21:38:06 Student54: [Student17 name]?
21:39:11 Student17: yes, [student name]
21:40:22 Student54: how's it going [student name]?
21:40:44 Student17: good, just checking out the [class] topic of the day
21:41:37 Student14: who is [Student17]?
21:41:47 Student17: [Student17 full name]
21:42:01 Student24: incomings meet the alumni
21:42:09 Student14: ... heh. i don't know who that is, but okay - so long as someone does :P

Other key contributors to increasing trust include rules, personal disposition, history, shared category membership, and roles.[33] In particular, establishing a shared context between users is essential to maintaining trust online. For the university community, the sense of a shared context is easily increased through the daily personal interactions that users experience in their face-to-face environment. By chatting informally in the classroom hallways, during lunch, or in outside social settings, users establish a sense of trust that is quickly transferred to their interactions in the online environment. The sense of shared context facilitates discussions and conversations online. The more shared context participants have, the easier it is for them to negotiate their sense of interpersonal trust and reputation.

> You hear an idea, make a joke of it, you've just used something you've just got. Some professors might not like something going on outside of their ideas. Being able to form a joke means you've got it. Some people think it's funny, some don't, it fuels the social network.

There should be a reciprocal relationship between group members and the environment that the chat room provides that will fulfill the social desires of its members for sustained participation. Social presence is high in the university backchannel. Participants acquire instant gratification, approval, and acceptance upon entering the chat room. For example, a student entered the chat room for the first time over a year after matriculating in the program:

11:09:04 → Student18 has joined
11:09:34 Student12: wow, guest appearance by Student18!
11:09:40 Student18: ;D

---

33 J. Pyysiainen, Building Trust in Global Inter-organizational Software Development Projects: Problems and Practices, in *Proceedings of the International Workshop on Global Software Development* (ICSE, 2003).

A chat room that is devoid of social affordances will likely lose participants and isolate the remaining members from one another. Regardless of whether this motivation is selfish or altruistic, participants often go to extreme lengths to enhance their social capital with the community, which serves to then build their reputation in the community, inserting them into a cycle of increased participation and acceptance. People tend to categorize themselves as part of the group if the salience of perceived differences among these individuals is minor, relative to the perceived differences to other individuals. Thus, perceived similarities between different university community members concerning attitudes, beliefs, norms, and values, a common task, or a shared history are significant contributors to social identification and group cohesion. Because participants share a physical space on a regular basis, their ability to build a community and recognize other people with whom they are conversing virtually is significant.

Community as a Third Place

Participants in the university chat room were driven by a desire for a sense of community. They may be "searching for a feeling of community that's been lost as many 'third places' which are neither work nor home, but a third place where people congregate and interact, have closed down."[34] Oldenburg describes how many parents and community members have lamented youth's declining participation in community activities, such as Boy Scouts, local park and recreation teams, and hobby-inspired clubs, which have instead been replaced with participation in online communities, such as MySpace, Friendster, Doom, Neopets, and countless others. Similarly, adults are participating in online card games, chat rooms, and other virtual communities in place of knitting clubs, poker gatherings, or Tupperware parties, as may have been the norm thirty years ago. For this reason, many chat room participants are using their virtual community as a replacement for the camaraderie and support system previously offered by membership in community organizations. The virtual community offers a home away from home.

In the same way, the university backchannel provided a place for students to develop their third place. Participant usage increased during class time, but also in the evenings. For example, participants often reveal their physical location with other participants, creating a sense of shared physical space, even when participants are not actually colocated. Research suggests that digital technology can improve communication in many ways, such as by providing the "virtual hallways" for students and instructors to meet."[35] Subjects who participate in the backchannel

---

34 R. Oldenburg, *The Great Good Place: Cafés, Coffee Shops, Community Centers, Beauty Parlors, General Stores, Bars, Hangouts and How They Get You Through the Day* (New York: Marlowe & Company, 1989).

35 D. Abrahamson, What's a Situation in Situated Cognition? A Constructionist Critique of Authentic Inquiry, in *Proceedings of the Seventh International Conference of the Learning Sciences* (ICLS), eds. S. Barab, K. Hay, and D. Hickey (Bloomington, IN: ICLS, 2006).

stated that they first heard about the channel directly through a social contact. In these cases, they were approached and specifically told about the channel's existence and how to access it. One participant stated that he originally viewed the channel as a way to meet people when he first started school and did not know anyone in the area. In this case, he used the channel as a way to actively seek out friends. He perceived the channel as open to any university community member:

> I don't think there's anyone that's unaware that it exists. Some people think they'd have trouble concentrating or whatever. I feel like not that it's excluding people, but *including* people. I don't know if that makes sense. People who are on [chat] are more of a group. It's building group cohesion where there wouldn't be one otherwise, but I don't think it's an exclusion.

In contrast, those who do not participate said that they had heard about the channel in public spaces, but did not know much about it. Nonparticipants also stated that their social circle did not use the channel or did not use laptops in class at all. This suggests the possibility of a relationship between *existing* social networks and chat participation. It is not necessarily the case that chat participation mirrors social networks within the school, but they may generate strong ties that reinforce existing dynamics. The sense of community also exists outside of the classroom environment. Participants like to share their evening activities, especially regular daily events like cooking, visits to local eateries, and sleeping. In particular, university students who were single would choose to share their common daily activities:

> 22:21:18 *Student9:* I think I might sleep soon
> 22:21:22 *Student9:* I know it sounds lame
> ...
> 22:29:11 *Student9:* I think I am going to crash
> 22:29:14 *Student23:* nite Student9
> 22:29:14 *Student9:* see you all tomorrow

This behavior is usually seen in the evenings and outside of class settings when there is a smaller group of core users logged into the chat room. Because the core users are often the same participants every evening, there is a distinct subculture within the university chat room that encourages this sharing of personal lifestyle activities. The offline interactions thus reinforce online interactions as a third place.

Pedagogy of Hope: Designing the Backchannel

How might a backchannel be designed to maximize its potential as a learning environment and tool for both students and teachers? The complex interplay between teacher and student, teaching and learning, and pedagogy and practice creates a challenging but potentially rich learning ecology. Is it possible to design a sustainable backchannel? Can productive backchannel discourse be fostered without being forced? What are the ideal conditions under which a backchannel will thrive given varied classroom sizes, student ages, subject material, and teaching styles? Abrahamson suggests that designing for emergent situativity can help to merge learning pedagogy and scientific inquiry, creating a potential for an engaging, personally meaningful, and authentic exploration into content.[36] Rick and Guzdial similarly highlight the importance of situating a new medium within its sociocultural context, grounding it in the culture of its users and their practices.[37]

However, the inherently clandestine nature of the backchannel is problematic, implying that there is the possibility that it simply cannot be designed for. One might argue that, by definition, a backchannel is only a backchannel if it has evolved organically through its user community and contextual behaviors. Therefore, in one sense, designing a backchannel is not possible—it is a contradiction in terms. Can a chat room framework be documented or does it have to be learned through experience? Is its emergence and evolution so ingrained in each instance that the only possible form of documentation is through indoctrination? Returning to Friere's antibanking theory of education, it may be that "The important thing ... is for men [students] to come to feel like masters of their thinking by discussing the thinking and views of the world explicitly or implicitly manifest in their own suggestions and those of their comrades [classmates]."[38] The backchannel characteristics could be designed by suggesting certain norms, roles, signals, and behaviors, with the intention of encouraging the backchannel community to adopt such practices. The sections below highlight how such characteristics might be designed and implemented.

Rules of Participation

Craig Smith suggests the development of a protocol for virtual classroom etiquette, "chatiquette," which he bases on research on classroom discourse and conversational turn-taking.[39] While this protocol does reduce the free-flowing interaction characteristic of most chat sessions, it does not constrain the interaction to the

36 Ibid.

37 Jochen Rick and Mark Guzdial, Situating CoWeb: A Scholarship of Application, *International Journal of Computer-Supported Collaborative Learning* 1, no. 1 (2006): 89.

38 Freire, *Pedagogy of the Oppressed*.

39 Craig Smith, Synchronous Discussion in Online Courses: A Pedagogical Strategy for Taming the Chat Beast. http://www.innovateonline.info/index.php?view=article&id=246&action=article.

extent that often occurs with a designated moderator controlling the chat session.[40] Instead, it allows all participants to monitor themselves and others in contributing to the discussion. The socialized conventions that structure and organize face-to-face conversation are lacking in the online environment of synchronous communication. Without the nonverbal and verbal cues that indicate a request to speak, such as a raised hand, synchronous discussions can become disjointed. In a learning context in which the exchange of complicated or sophisticated concepts and principles is being attempted, a lack of coherence and flow can quickly degrade into worthless chatter or confusion.[41] The university chat room differs from many other chat rooms in that it is highly unmoderated. The original channel creator purposely set it up with few rules or regulations, empowering the chat room participants to develop their own ecological community. The underlying purpose of rules is often about establishing control. Who governs the roles that participants play, how they interact with others, and any sense of ownership within the community?

The rules of participation are defined by a number of characteristics, ranging from the technology itself, such as rules that are built into the software, to rules defined by the host. Although the university community has no established moderators or community members who are appointed to moderate the discussion flow, a set of rules has evolved, of which participants maintain a general knowledge and awareness. For example, some of the rules were more explicit, such as the automatic message that is sent each time a user joins the chat room. On the other hand, other rules are learned over time, such as identifying oneself if the username does not clearly indicate real life identity, or not repeating certain discussions outside of the users who were present in the chat room during the specific conversation. Over time, the community can rely on the protocol that has evolved through the sense of flow in the chat room environment. Nonverbal cues are constructed online when participants know one another and learn one another's styles of interactions such that the same type of cue becomes equally transparent. An explicit set of rules and protocol can help to build these intuitive practices. This protocol provides a way to make apparent to all participants the usual nonverbal cues used in turn-taking, and in giving and relinquishing the discussion floor. Once the students become familiar with the protocol, they become self-monitoring and self-regulating. Their ability to facilitate this structure and sustain it emphasizes the importance of building community to create a constructive learning environment.

40 G. Motteram, The Role of Synchronous Communication in Fully Distance Education, *Australian Journal of Educational Technology* 17, no. 2 (2001): 131-149.

41 M. Pimentel, H. Fuks, and C.J.P. Lucena, Mediated Chat Development Process: Avoiding Chat Confusion on Educational Debates, in *Proceedings of Computer Supported Collaborative Learning (CSCL) 2005*, eds. G. Stahl and D. Suthers (Mahwah, NJ: Lawrence Erlbaum Associates, 2005), 499-503.

Guiding the Discussion

Failed exploratory peer-to-peer discussions may occur when ideas are accepted unchallenged or because continuous disputation leads to a breakdown of communication within the group. Exploratory peer discussions rarely broke down in this manner in the university community. As a graduate student community, the learning dynamics are more advanced than those in elementary, high school, or undergraduate classrooms. Failed peer discussions might occur far more frequently in younger learning environments where students are more susceptible to competition or immature group behaviors. In these environments, it would be important to have rules to minimize breakdowns during group communication. These might include guidelines that describe the information, assumptions, tasks, and evaluative criteria for constructive collaborative group work. This could be implemented through the presence of a teacher or teaching assistant within the chat room or a postmortem review of the chat logs on a regular basis in which the dynamics of the group could be studied and improved for future classes. Similarly, the ways in which the backchannel is used in the classroom would influence the types of discussions that took place. One option is to publicly project the chat rooms using one or more screens, where they are separated by comments and questions. In the latter chat room, students could post questions for the teacher. A second option is to use a chat room robot to monitor a channel and provide basic information as well as perform a heuristic analysis of events for postanalysis. For example, entering the command "Define: copernicus" would automatically return a definition from a dictionary lookup robot. A third option is to display the backchannel discussion on the screen in front of the classroom so that students would be less inclined to contribute off-topic postings and would instead focus on the academic discussion. Similarly, a teaching assistant could participate in the backchannel and help facilitate interactions by guiding the discussion and providing scaffolding for the learners.

Assigning Roles

One type of protocol to encourage the development of such rules might be the assigning of roles within the backchannel. Howard Rheingold is designing an innovative new participatory media syllabus (described elsewhere in this series [not reprinted here]) in which he suggests that assigning roles in a chat room backchannel may help to facilitate order and constructive interactions among students. In an unmoderated chat, students must decide to prioritize a single voice and follow it; in an ideal learning environment, however, all voices would be heard, and none would be disposable, spoken over. Rheingold suggests that students have assigned roles, on a rotated basis, such as "google jockey," "wikipedian," "expert," and "cybrarian." In addition to role assignment, structure in the backchannel may be increased through an informed design of curriculum and uses based on its affordances to minimize disruption and unproductive behavior.

Constructing Culture

A successful learning backchannel must be designed based on the classroom culture in which it is being used. For example, the ways in which a backchannel could be used in a fifth grade classroom will differ significantly from its use in a third-year law class. Teachers may need to implement a more controlled and disciplined environment in younger grades, whereas law professors could assume that a Socratic teaching method will effectively command their students' full attention and that the backchannel will therefore be used strictly as a knowledge resource, not as a source of distraction. In smaller groups and seminars, the instructor may choose to explicitly relinquish some of his or her control in order to facilitate a more open discussion, although in these cases students must accept the burden of making sure that the discussions are meaningful and productive. In a small seminar, the backchannel will generally be unnecessary because students are supposed to interact in the physical classroom environment. In a large lecture hall, with hundreds of students, a backchannel could become swamped with too many simultaneous users and conversation threads to be of any use. An ideal class size might be between twenty and forty students, where most know each other and are able to develop a community and sense of trust in their channel, but where there are not so many participants as to weigh it down beyond any academic value.

Teaching Teachers

Education researchers have long emphasized the fact that technology in itself cannot improve instruction.[42] However, technology can enhance the effectiveness of a good instructional design.[43] Many teachers will be more likely to adopt chat room technology in their classrooms if they are first provided support and instruction on how to use the technology.[44] Teachers may need to teach in shorter cycles to hold students' attention. They should adjust their curriculum and teaching styles to provide different and improved environments for scaffolding than the standard lecture format. As students become more accustomed to multitasking in their everyday activities, teachers may find that they need to redesign their teaching styles in order to keep their students engaged. For example, they

---

42 D. Hestenes, M. Wells, and G. Swackhamer, Force Concept Inventory, *The Physics Teacher* 30 (1992): 141-158.

43 C. Hoadley and N. Enyedy, Between Information and Communication: Middle Spaces in Computer Media for Learning, in *Proceedings of the Third International Conference on Computer Support for Collaborative Learning*, eds. C. Hoadley and J. Roschelle (1999), 242-251.

44 L. Cuban, *Teachers & Machines: The Classroom Use of Technology Since 1920* (New York: Teachers College Press, 1988).

could intersperse lectures with group activities and individual activities, allotting shorter time spans to each section. A tighter integration of the backchannel may require their lectures to be more permeable, and the right level of focus and formality will need to be determined. As students' learning styles evolve over time and with changes in technology, teachers can adjust their skill sets in order to facilitate ongoing engagement.

Conclusion: The Backchannel, Up Front

The backchannel in the classroom offers an exciting innovative space for a new learning paradigm. There are a number of salient factors that can be taken advantage of to construct a positive learning environment in the classroom. However, as has been shown, it is not a panacea in itself, but must instead be understood within the greater context of its use for it to offer an improved learning experience for youth. This includes the cultural influences within this technology-mediated learning environment, such as ethnicity, gender, access, experience using technology, and individual student personalities and learning styles. Lessons learned through repeated histories of technological determinism remind us that technology does not have inherent preexisting manifestations, but that meaning and implications emerge as computers and social actors come together in different communities. Innovations in its use are only enabled through a complex interplay of multiple requisite behaviors, practices, and external factors. If we can tease out the variable uses of the medium and understand how they influence its construction as an artifact, then can we encourage innovative and unexpected uses? And for that matter, do we want to? Are youths' innovations with digital media a naturally evolving learning opportunity with an embedded unpredictable and exploratory nature that we should encourage? The institutional contexts of the backchannel are multilayered and complex—from teacher to student to school to parent to district to national standards.

Will Richardson, a teacher, author, and educational researcher, suggests that "shouldn't we hear what [students] are saying, that in a world where the answers to the test are easily accessible that *the test becomes irrelevant*?"[45] Students need to learn how to share ideas and knowledge ethically and appropriately. They need to take ideas that they are taught and make them their own, by exploring and massaging them into their own experiences, as the university students often did on the university backchannel. Richardson continues that, "we need to say to kids 'here is what is important to know, but to learn from it, you need to take it and make it your own, *not just tell it back to me*. Find your own meaning, your own relevance. Make connections outside of these four walls, *because you can and you should and*

---

45 Will Richardson, Weblogg-ed. What Do We Do About That? 2005,
    http://www.weblogg-ed.com/2005/10/25#a4126.

you will.'"[46] The balance of power in the classroom can be mutually constructed by the student and teacher if both parties are able to facilitate constructive discourse about rules and roles of the backchannel in the classroom. Younger students may not have the experience online through which to develop their own learning environment, although their varied levels of engagement and learning within these environments can be used as a metric for designing the most productive educational experience. As students develop the ability for metacognitive self-reflection on their own experiences, they are better equipped to design and coconstruct their ideal personal learning activities by taking advantage of the varied opportunities that the backchannel can facilitate.

The backchannel may therefore enable a type of education that is progressive but meaningful and has long been needed in the American school system. "It means basing instruction on the needs, interests and developmental stage of the child; it means teaching students the skills they need in order to learn any subject, instead of focusing on transmitting a particular subject; it means promoting discovery and self-directed learning by the student through active engagement; it means having students work on projects that express student purposes."[47] This notion of constructivism may be the ticket to avoiding the learning paradox that plagues much of student motivation in the classroom. Once a student knows how to complete a task, he or she is no longer motivated to learn or participate in that task, and performance in that task will not improve. However, the organic, evolving, and ever-changing dynamics in the backchannel prevent students from succumbing to this sense of stagnancy in learning. Students may be encouraged to learn through a self-motivated eagerness to explore the opportunities and novelties offered by the backchannel on an ongoing basis. Furthermore, as an online, Web-based medium, it allows youth to continuously refine their existing media practices in parallel to their backchannel use. As digital natives, they can produce, consume, remix, and generate their own learning opportunities. They may truly be creating their own classroom of the future.

Source: *Digital Youth, Innovation, and the Unexpected.* Cambridge, MA: MIT, 2008. 143-64.

WHAT IT SAYS

1. What does Yardi mean by "frontchannel speaker" and "backchannel chats"? What kinds of activities characterize each?

2. What do the data Yardi presents in Figures 3.2 and 3.3 reveal? What aspects of this data were unanticipated?

46 Ibid.

47 Labaree, "Progressivism, Schools and Schools of Education," 275.

3. Yardi claims that the No Child Left Behind Act and the Deleting Online Predators Act may have created some negative effects on learning. What are these effects, according to Yardi?

4. What are the potential disadvantages of backchannel chats, according to Yardi? What changes does Yardi propose to help ensure that backchannel chats promote rather than detract from learning?

5. What rules govern successful university chat rooms? What kinds of protocols does Yardi recommend to ensure the continued success of university chat rooms?

6. What does Yardi propose that teachers do to foster learning in a classroom influenced by new technology such as chat rooms?

HOW IT SAYS IT

1. Yardi uses graphics to present her data. How do the data work to help Yardi make her claim?

2. Yardi uses excerpts from chat-room discussions to illustrate some of her points. How do these excerpts work to help Yardi make her claim?

3. Consider how Yardi acknowledges the potential disadvantages of backchannel chat rooms in the classroom. What is the point of bringing up objections to her argument?

WRITE ABOUT IT

1. Write an essay that examines your experiences with chat rooms and other technology in the classroom (high school or college). Speculate on the positive and/or negative aspects that this technology has had on your education. If you wish, interview classmates and friends to compare your experience to theirs.

2. Write an essay from the perspective of a high school or college teacher confronted with new technology in the classroom. As an educator, what changes would you make in your teaching style, policies, and strategies to incorporate or eliminate technology in the classroom in order to foster learning?

3. Write an essay in which you argue for or against the use of a chat room in your writing classroom. Draw on personal experience and Yardi's essay to make your claims.

f. John F. Freie and Susan M. Behuniak, "Paulo Freire and ICTs: Liberatory Education Theory in a Digital Age"

John F. Freie is a professor and the chair of political science at Le Moyne College in Syracuse, New York. He is the founder of the department's service learning program and initiated a focus on citizenship education as the department's mission.

Freie is the author of *Counterfeit Community: The Exploitation of Our Longings for Connectedness* (1998) and numerous articles on teaching pedagogies that introduce democratic practices into the classroom. He received his BA from the University of Northern Iowa, his MA from Miami University in Ohio, and his PhD in political science from the University of Missouri.

Susan M. Behuniak is Francis J. Fallon, S.J. Professor of Political Science at Le Moyne College in Syracuse. Her research, teaching, and community service all focus on promoting the rights and "voice" of people who are often marginalized. With John F. Freie, she has taught a course on the politics of cyberspace, and she has studied the impact of techno-digital communication devices on students and on citizens.

Behuniak is the author of *A Caring Jurisprudence: Listening to Patients at the Supreme Court* (1999) and co-author with Arthur Svenson of *Physician-Assisted Suicide: The Anatomy of a Constitutional Law Issue* (2003). She received her BA in mass communications from St. Bonaventure University, and her MA and PhD in political science from SUNY at Albany.

In this essay Freie and Behuniak examine the claims made for digital technologies as supposedly embodying the emancipatory education demanded by Paulo Freire in his groundbreaking book *Pedagogy of the Oppressed* (first published in Portuguese in 1968).

As You Read: Consider this essay and the others you have read about digital technology and education. How does this argument differ from those of the other authors you've read?

Paulo Freire and ICTs: Liberatory Education Theory in a Digital Age

Abstract

In what ways have information and communication technologies (ICTs) in the college classroom transformed the educational experiences of students? We approach this question theoretically by exploring examples of how computers in the classroom can promote the liberation of or further the oppression of students. Drawing on principles from Paulo Freire's classic work, *Pedagogy of the Oppressed* (1970), we argue that contrary to what other commentators have claimed, the dominant tendency of computers employed in college courses is the reinforcement of what Freire criticized over 35 years ago as the "banking system" of education. Too often, instructors who use computer-based pedagogies assume that the core of education is content rather than process; overlook how information becomes knowledge; and substitute shallow forms of participation for true praxis.

Keywords

Paulo Freire, ICTs, Education Theory, Liberatory Education, Computers in the Classroom, Pedagogy

Introduction

The concern that students be active participants in their learning has varied roots (e.g., Maria Montessori, John Dewey, Henry Giroux), but it is Paulo Freire's opposition to oppressive pedagogies that is frequently invoked to justify the use of information and communication technologies (ICTs) in higher education. Yet, these overt or implicit references to Freire's groundbreaking theory of liberatory education warrant critical appraisal because they constitute a curious practice. This is so for two main reasons. First, even within political science (our discipline), Freire is regarded as a "radical" both because he challenged mainstream educational practices and goals, and argued in favor of democratizing the classroom. Given this, why does the ICT literature so enthusiastically embrace him? Second, when Freire wrote his critique of education in the 1970s, he was responding to the practices of the modern milieu; i.e., a textual world in which information was transmitted through publications, the study of textbooks, the giving of lectures, and the taking of notes. But we are clearly in a transformative time, a post-modern world in which the textual is rapidly being replaced by the digital.

How, then, to understand Freire's call for liberatory pedagogy in this new age?

These are the questions we address in this article. We begin with a review of the digital technologies and the claims made by the educators who use and study them. Next, we revisit Freire's critique of oppressive pedagogies, the terminologies he employed, and the educational philosophy he advocated. With this as background, we apply Freire to three ICTs to show the extent to which his critique is prescient.

We end by suggesting what Freire offers in formulating a liberatory educational theory for the digital age.

Digital Technologies in the College Classroom

In a meta-analysis of over 500 studies of the use of computer-based instruction (CBI) in college classrooms, Kulik (1994) reports that students generally test at higher levels, learn quicker, and report more positive attitudes about their courses than students in the controlled conditions without computers. Focusing on particular types of CBIs, research indicates that PowerPoint (probably the most frequently used CBI) provides a predictably paced, easy to understand structure to lectures (Mason and Hlynka 1998; Lowry 1999) and students report more positive attitudes about the course when used (Harknett and Cobane 1997; Atkins-Sayre et al. 1998; Daniels 1999; Lowry 1999; Mantei 2000; Frey and Birnbaum 2002; Susskind 2005). Not only do students enjoy PowerPoint presentations, they also report enhanced self-efficacy (Susskind 2005). But results about academic performance itself are mixed, with some studies reporting enhanced academic performance (Lowry 1999; Mantei 2000; Szabo and Hastings 2000), others showing no apparent effect (Daniels 1999; Rankin and Hoaas 2001), and yet others concluding that effectiveness relies on either the teaching methodologies used to supplement the technology (Bartsch and Cobern 2003; Susskind 2005) or different student learning styles (Levasseur and Sawyer 2006).

Research on the effectiveness of Internet-based instruction, both synchronous and asynchronous, is sparser. Still, the studies conducted so far have shown that achievement is either equal to, or slightly better than, traditional face-to-face courses (Schutte 1997; LaRose et al. 1998; Johnson et al. 2000; Young et al. 2001; Neuhauser 2002; Meyer 2002). Yet, students in traditional classes hold more positive views about the instructor and their relationships with the instructor (Johnson et al. 2000), pointing to some of the limits of online education. For example, where efforts have been made to build online learning communities, they have been met by failure (Parr and Ward 2006).

Many of these studies speak to Sutherland's point: "There is a tendency to think that ICT is so 'new' that its use will be accompanied by 'new' pedagogies that will somehow transform teaching and learning" (2004: 413). Whatever questions have been raised by critics concerning the use of digital technologies in education, they have failed to slow what appears to be the inevitable introduction of almost every type of new technology imaginable. Students today are encouraged to use: Blackboard to access syllabi, course readings, and to discuss the class with other students; Web-based simulations to experience the real world; online tutorials if they need academic help; "clickers" to provide the professor with instantaneous feedback; and even previously banned cell phones are used to access Cellphedia, a cell-phone version of Wikipedia. Although few serious academic studies of the effectiveness of many of these specific technologies yet exist, the claims of advocates intone similar themes. Digital technologies, it is asserted, engage student interests (Hatch et al. 2005), activate previously passive students (Steele 1998;

Newman and Scurry 2001; Trotter 2005; Vonderwell and Turner 2005), provide immediate feedback (Carnevale 2005), create student enthusiasm (Menon et al. 2004), expand the way of communicating complex and abstract ideas (Kennedy 2006), improve student satisfaction with courses (Johnson et al. 2000), increase the participation of introverted students (Strauss 1996), connect learning with real life (Newman and Scurry 2001), and shift education from a teaching focus to a learning focus (Berge and Collins 1995; Schuyler 1997). In sum, the arguments in favor of the use of digital technologies are that they help to develop a participatory learning culture, an environment where the barriers to participation have been lowered, where one's ideas can easily be shared and are appreciated, where students feel a sense of social connection with each other, and where critical thinking is enhanced.

These studies and critics raise a challenging question: Can digital technologies create an educational culture of active participation where students are intensively engaged in the creation of knowledge through interaction with others? Applying the work of Paulo Freire it is our finding that such assertions are usually based on a superficial understanding of concepts such as participation, engagement, active learning, and even knowledge.

Freire's Liberatory Pedagogy

In his best-known book, *Pedagogy of the Oppressed*, Paulo Freire (1970) argues that traditional education (derisively referred to as "banking education") is aligned with the oppressors. Banking education is characterized by the idea that teachers know everything while students know nothing—the teacher selects what material will be studied, creates and enforces the rules and the students obey. The teacher's authority, which stems from his or her knowledge of the material, becomes confused with professional authority, resulting in a dictatorial classroom environment. In such classrooms the teacher is the focal point—the teacher talks and the students listen; the teacher thinks and the students are thought about; the teacher knows everything and the students know nothing. In the traditional classroom the students are objects—empty jugs to be filled with knowledge by the teacher (Freire 1970).

While banking education is dehumanizing for the students, perhaps even more significant, it serves the interests of the oppressors: "the dominant elites utilize the banking concept to encourage passivity in the oppressed, corresponding to the latter's 'submerged' state of consciousness, and take advantage of that passivity to 'fill' that consciousness with slogans which create even more fear of freedom" (Freire 1970: 84). This is referred to by John Gaventa (1980) as the third face of power, a "hidden" form of control of the citizenry that is difficult to overcome even through political movements. Ultimately, it is inconsistent with democratic governance which requires an active citizenry to think critically and to act to transform the community.

Banking education is inherently dehumanizing as it reduces students to mere objects and presents the world as static and external. By presenting the concepts of the oppressors teachers disempower students and reduce the possibilities for liberatory action: "The more completely they accept the passive role imposed on them, the more they tend simply to adapt to the world as it is and to the fragmented view of reality deposited in them" (Freire 1970: 60). Yet, while traditional education is a part of the system of dehumanization and oppression, it is through educational reform that people may become liberated. The solution is to transform the educational structure so that it becomes a mechanism for liberation. This can be done when students "become critically conscious of themselves as the very sorts of creatures that produce (and are produced by) their culture and history" (Glass 2001: 18). When this consciousness occurs, students can challenge the limits of the situations they find themselves in and act to transform themselves and their culture.

Liberatory education relies upon praxis: the interaction of reflection and action upon one's world in order to transform it. To educate does not mean to transmit information, but instead it consists of acts of cognition. Referred to by Freire as "problem-posing education," it relies on dialogical relations between the teacher and the students as they work together in a process of learning. "Through dialogue, the teacher-of-the-students and the students-of-the-teacher cease to exist and a new term emerges: teacher-student with students-teachers" (Freire 1970: 67). Relying on critical thinking, problem-posing education stimulates reflection on one's environment in order to understand it and to recreate it to serve student purposes. Through this education as praxis, people "create history and become historical-social beings" (Freire 1970: 91).

This form of liberatory education requires that students be active participants, not in the terms of activity often asserted in classrooms today (i.e., attentive listeners and questioners), but active as dialogical participants who help define and shape the topic of study, pose questions to be examined, participate with the teacher in a joint process of critical thinking, and who, in the process, redefine their world. Similarly, the teacher must reject the idea that learning is the transfer of information, and, instead, must "create the possibilities for the production or construction of knowledge" (Freire 1998a: 30). Students must be free, but freedom in the classroom has limits; limits defined by the legitimate authority of the class itself.

Given his emphasis on transforming our understanding of knowledge, participation, and community, it is not surprising that advocates of ICTs employ the language and theory of Freire. But are these conscious endorsements of Freire's educational approach or merely cooptations of his language?

Liberatory Theory and ICTs

It is beyond the scope of this paper to develop a comprehensive critique of digital technologies as used in education; thus, we restrict our analysis to the model of education advocated by Freire. Instead, in order to explore our central question of what liberatory pedagogy means in a digital age, we use three concepts central to Freire's philosophy of education—knowledge, participation, and community—to examine three digital technologies—PowerPoint, audience response systems, and the Internet.

PowerPoint and Knowledge

PowerPoint is pervasive. It is now found on over 250 million computers worldwide and it is estimated that 1.25 million presentations take place every hour (Mahin 2004). Originally intended for use in business, it has taken academe by storm, becoming the new standard presentation technique at academic conferences and one of "the most prevalent types of technology being used in the classroom" (Atkins-Sayre et al. 1998: 3).

One of the advantages of PowerPoint "is that it provides structure to a presentation" (Susskind 2005) and allows the presenter to express his or her message unambiguously. For teachers, it helps to focus the presentation on the meaning the information has to the students (Doumont 2005). For students, the imagery of PowerPoint presentations arouses the senses and, according to arousal theory, students pay more attention to the presentations because visual messages dominate other forms of information communication (Grabe et al. 2000). What's more, students enjoy PowerPoint presentations, and when they enjoy their classes they are more likely to learn.

Even accepting the veracity of the claims made by PowerPoint proponents, we maintain that the nature of the technology and its use fall within the banking vision of education. The underlying purpose of PowerPoint is to efficiently convey information (claimed to be synonymous with knowledge) from the presenter to the audience. Even where it is used "appropriately," the technology focuses attention on the presenter by emphasizing the importance of skillfully outlining one's argument, coordinating the topics and subtopics, using color effectively, being conscious of the importance of fonts, and employing appropriate graphics (Mahin 2004). Yet, critics have claimed that PowerPoint encourages generic, superficial, and simplistic thinking (Tufte 2003).

More significant for our argument, however, is that PowerPoint locates control in the hands of the teacher: "What is gained in the use of PowerPoint is power, control over the audience through quality transparencies, and an unwavering sequenced flow" (Hlynka and Mason 1998: 45). In the process, opportunities for creating a dialogical environment between and among the students and the teacher are lost as the focus of the darkened classroom is on the slides. As Pauw

(2002) argues, it creates a "disembodied learning environment that constrains interpersonal engagement" (2).

For users of PowerPoint, knowledge is an object; information is something to be conveyed. But for Freire, "Liberating education consists in acts of cognition, not transferals of information" (Freire 1970: 67). The focus of such education is not the teacher, but the interactive relationships that form between the teacher and the students who are jointly responsible for learning. Far from liberating students, PowerPoint subtly imposes a gossamer image over what is, at base, oppressive control.

Rather than supportive of the use of PowerPoint, then, Freire's critique exposes that ICTs, despite all their newness, amplify the oppressive banking method of education. In fact, given its purpose to transfer information from one powerful knower (the teacher) to passive receivers (the students), Power-Point is a deterministic technology designed to support banking education.

Clickers and Participation

While nearly all of the forms of digital technology claim to transform students from passive to active participants in the classroom, one of the most recent is the audience response system, more commonly referred to as "clickers." Clickers are remote-control hand-held devices that are used by students to register answers to questions posed by the teacher during lectures. They are touted as a way of getting students engaged in class: "clickers help involve every student in a lesson and give teachers immediate feedback about what students are learning" (Trotter 2005: 8). Professors like them because they can obtain instant feedback about how well students are learning the material, and students enjoy them because they feel as if they are playing an electronic game. What's more, their perceived anonymity encourages participation from even the most introverted students.

Student participation is crucial for liberatory education to occur. "Liberation is a praxis: the action and reflection of men upon their world in order to transform it" (Freire 1970: 66). Yet, while one might be able to make a case for clickers being interactive, they fall short of Freire's vision of the meaning of participation for liberation. Instead, they represent a form of faux-participation, giving the appearance of participation, but covering up the fact that the teacher controls the subject matter, the questions, and how the polling information will be used. Rather than truly engaging students in a learning-by-doing atmosphere as is claimed (Menon et al. 2004), clicker technology forces students to accept the world of the teacher-controlled classroom and help structure the class by merely pressing a button from time to time—a poor substitute for participation that transforms one's world. Rather than shifting the subject to student misconceptions as is claimed (Hatch et al. 2005), clickers are supportive of the undemocratic ideology that permeates the classroom by presenting the illusion of participation.

This time it is Freire's language of participation that has been co-opted—stripped of its radicalism to support an ICT that enables only the most superficial form of student involvement. But for Freire, participation is a far more meaningful concept than an opportunity to raise one's hand, push a button, or offer simplistic feedback. Freire ties participation to change and to agency inspired by intellectual struggle, not to knee-jerk reactions to materials that are presented to a captive audience.

The Internet and Community

Online courses that involve various combinations of email, websites, digital recordings, and bulletin boards, have become increasingly popular—this is due in large part because they are pushed by college administrators who value them as cost efficient mechanisms that enable fewer faculty to teach a greater number of students. At their worst, online courses use technology to reinstitute the banking system of education: students are instructed through digitally recorded lectures, are provided with the instructor's PowerPoint notes, are graded by computerized standardized tests, and are only casually invited to "participate" by leaving comments on Blackboard. Such courses often appropriate the language of "student-centered" education by emphasizing the flexibility in scheduling that they offer students as consumers (Clegg et al. 2003: 49).

In contrast, there are other online courses that are "constructivist" because they attempt to transform the educational process from classes that are teacher-oriented to those constructed by all participants. Operating from this perspective, teachers become guides who facilitate the development of student interactions with each other and with prior knowledge to create participatory cultures. These new participatory cultures offer "opportunities for youth to engage in civic debates, to participate in community life, to become political leaders" (Jenkins 2006: 10). Problem solving of real-world problems takes place through group collaboration.

More specifically, it is argued that constructivist online courses can create rich learning environments where the democratic disposition of tolerance of diversity is valued, where the democratic skills of self-regulation and self-assessment are developed, where students learn the art of collaboration, and where self-motivation is fostered (Harasim 1990; Palloff and Pratt 1999; Wagner 1997). When used appropriately, online education becomes "a collective effort to develop critical thinking and mastery of the process of understanding and applying new knowledge" (Hardwick 2000: 127), objectives apparently consistent with Freire's problem-posing educational alternative. Not surprisingly, advocates of online courses have claimed that these courses are examples of Freire's liberation approach to education (Hardwick 2000).

It is here, in the application of ICTs that we believe that Freire's critique is most difficult to discern. On the face of it, online courses employing the constructivist approach appear to be consistent with Freire's problem-posing alternative. That is, they are clearly not examples of banking education. Yet in our judgment, neither are they examples of his alternative liberatory approach to education. This is because Freire's model assumes things that ICTs reject, and in fact, are designed to overcome: a shared physical space (the classroom), face-to-face interactions, and mutual real-time experiences. In addition, ICTs violate these assumptions in the name of liberation. What is missing from their evaluation is another concern of Freire—that of politics.

Although it is a contested point, we agree with Langdon Winner's assertion that all technologies have political qualities (1986; see also Bowers 1988). That is, in their design, their employment, and their impact, technologies and their users shape the world. Some, like PowerPoint and clickers, appear to be deterministic devices because they inherently give control to the instructor and not to the students, and so result in an authoritarian classroom. Others, like online courses, although not deterministic, still affect who is empowered and cultural expectations and values regarding education. The overarching point is that technologies affect the politics of the classroom, and for Freire, the classroom is a concrete and important political space.

On-line courses affect the politics of the classroom in two specific ways. First, although they offer elements of discourse and degrees of student control, they are not grounded in the real. Separated by hours and miles, and insulated from the consequences that come from physical contact with others, student learning in cyberspace is disconnected from the world. The digitalized world is a world of the hyper-real. Images of things that never existed—simulacra—dominate (Jameson 1984; Baudrillard 1994). Because there is no reality upon which simulacra are based, there is no basis upon which to assess their validity: "It no longer needs to be rational, because it no longer measures itself against either an ideal or negative instance" (Baudrillard 1994: 2).

Second, online courses contribute to the flattening of emotion's role in education and in politics. True, they can generate individual excitement and student interest, but it is the role "social emotions" play that intrigues democratic theorists. As all teachers know, emotions in the classroom—especially "social emotions"— are complex, often spontaneous, sometimes volatile, and can have the effect of either improving or undermining the learning environment. Teachers must be skilled at reading and understanding the expression (both verbal and non-verbal) of emotions and in responding in such a way as to enhance the classroom experience. Contrary to common wisdom, emotion and rationality are not opposites but instead complement each other and, in fact, often facilitate learning and political engagement (Damasio 1994; Marcus 2002).

Emotion, of course, is also present among students in online courses, but the differences are dramatic. Emotions are often not expressed to others in the class; when they are they tend to be simplified through the use of a simple emoticon; and they must be reflected upon and "identified" by the students who dare to express them to others. At the same time, the teacher is confronted with the impossible task of trying to interpret the emotion and read how other students are reacting and might react to possible responses from the teacher. In sum, while emotions are important influences on the classroom social relations, advocates of ICTs have not adequately addressed how the complexity of their expressions and the effects they have on learning can be integrated in a positive fashion.

For Freire, then, education must be grounded in the reality of the lives of the students, and this reality is a result of a critical consciousness that emerges through the dialogical process of the group. Although online courses can approximate some of these qualities, they are a thin version of what can be accomplished when members of a class regularly meet, discuss things informally, learn about each other, work together to identify key issues that are central to their lives, and actively join forces to change their environment.

Toward a Theory of Liberatory ICT Pedagogy

Henry Giroux (1981) notes that many illegitimate forms of pedagogical practice often pass themselves off as radical pedagogies in the mode of Freire. This occurs, he believes, because educators either become enchanted with process-based interpersonal activities that provide momentary collective warmth but no critical pedagogy, or because educators ignore the importance of classroom social relations. In either case, the problem is that there is a lack a perspective that allows for "a critical understanding of the complex interplay that exists between pedagogy, ideology, and social change" (Giroux 1981: 128). Liberatory pedagogy helps students generate their own meanings, but that is not enough. A genuine form of liberation education goes further. Liberatory pedagogy must also help students reflect upon the process of thinking *itself* and only then will students "be able to use knowledge as part of a self-determining process that helps them to distinguish false from true knowledge claims" (Giroux 1981: 132). In this, the ICTs are in need of an educational philosophy that will lead toward this active vision of liberation rather than mere cooptation of its language.

With this goal in mind, Freire's liberatory theory suggests five aspects of ICT education that need to be questioned and analyzed in developing an educational philosophy that justifies their use. These include: cognition, non-sequential learning, epistemology, consciousness, and the educator.

1. Cognition. The ICT culture is a culture of visual images rather than words. As has been noted, arousal theory has demonstrated that images tend to drive out other forms of information. Indeed, ICTs have created a postmodern world similar to that envisioned by Fredric Jameson (1984) where surface images take precedence over depth,

where simulation is valued over the "real," and where play dominates over the serious. Yet, liberatory education requires rigor, depth of analysis, and a seriousness of purpose. But instead of rigorous thinking, the visual culture encourages "reflexive thinking," requiring only attention and reaction, not historical perspective or analysis (Miller 2005). The kind of student Freire wishes to create is a student who has a keen sense of the world he or she lives in and develops a perspective that allows for the creation and expression of the self. But, as Sherry Turkle (1995) notes, cyberworld denies any singular sense of the self: "What most characterizes the model of a flexible self is that the lines of communication between its various aspects are open. The open communication encourages an attitude of respect for the many within us and the many within others" (261).

2. Non-sequential learning. The "digital generation" approaches information horizontally. Rather than reading through a book or article from the beginning to the end, those who use ICTs tend to plunge into material at places that strike their interest and then experiment by almost randomly investigating ideas. There is, in effect, no beginning, no middle, and no end; there are merely bundles of information to be delved into in any fashion that suits the student. This ahistoricity runs counter to Freire's belief in the ability of humans to transform their world. One of the distinguishing characteristics of human beings is that they have a past and, by reflecting upon that past, they are able to transform the future. Humans are situated in an historical time and space. By recognizing that space and reflecting upon it they are able to humanize their environment. "Men, as beings 'in a situation,' find themselves rooted in temporal-spatial conditions which mark them and which they also mark. They will tend to reflect on their own 'situationality' to the extent that they are challenged by it to act upon it. Men *are* because they *are in* a situation. And they *will be more* the more they not only critically reflect upon their existence but critically act upon it" (Freire 1970: 100) [emphasis in original]. Interestingly, Freire's description of how animals behave—reflexively, in the moment—seems all too similar to descriptions of the digital generation.

3. Epistemology. Over hundreds of years the modern world has established agreed upon standards to assess truth assertions. In academic circles these standards followed the established disciplines and the quality of one's research could be determined by the reputation of the publication in which the findings were reported. In non-academic circles the test of common sense and reality could be applied. But in the digital age those commonly accepted standards are challenged. The idea of believing what you see can no longer be trusted, and today virtually anything can find publication

on the Web. There is such an overload of information that we no longer have the capacity to consume all that is produced (Goldhaber in Lankshear 2003: 180). But for Freire, the search for truth, and the assumption that an individual can recognize it, are keys to his politics of liberation. Truth is not a fixed reality, an object to be discovered, rather it is an act of cognition and action that occurs through reflection on the world and praxis. The discovery of truth, or more accurately the creation of truth, occurs as people participate in critical dialogue with each other about the world they inhabit.

4. Consciousness. By their very nature, ICTs lead to pedagogies that students enjoy, and in some cases, even insist upon. This appears to be true even when the technology reinforces the banking method of education. As much as Freire struggled back in the 1970s to convince students to reject oppressive forms of learning, the challenge is even stronger today because the ICTs are not only in the classroom but throughout the culture, and they are more appealing than even the most thrilling of lectures ever was. Another challenge is that even though Freire recognized that the pedagogies of the literate age were oppressive, he believed that they still allowed room for thinking when redirected. For example, students could be pointed toward the text and their own writing in order to liberate themselves. Can the same be said of ICTs, especially those that we have argued are deterministic?

5. The Educator. Some of the ICTs require new skills of educators while others actually change their roles. Using PowerPoint and clickers, faculty are now entertainers and artists, searching for creative ways to engage their visually oriented students. Learning as fun and fast is a new challenge for those who were themselves mostly schooled by the methods of lecture and recitation. In addition, some of the technologies call for the "sage on the stage" to become the facilitator in a classroom composed of active learners. What then is the role of the educator in the digital age? Indeed, what does it mean to "educate?" According to Freire, the role of the instructor is complex and multifaceted. Initially, teachers must know and understand the world in which their students live. To facilitate this, teachers must create open, democratic classrooms. This does not mean that authority is relinquished by the teacher, but that instead, authority that has a democratic legitimacy must replace authoritarianism. Having established the democratic character of the class, the teacher then participates in a process of critical dialogue with the students as they, together, search to generate new meanings. But the role of the teacher is not merely to convey information; it is instead, to transform society by transforming students: "The point of departure for this comprehensive practice is knowing, is being convinced, that education is a political practice. Let's repeat, then, that the educator is a politician" (Freire 1998b: 72).

Conclusion

If we are to use digital technologies to liberate students rather than oppress them, we must be more sensitive to the political nature of the technologies themselves. This is true more so today than when Freire first wrote because today's world is not only post-modern but also digital—a challenging combination of unsettling uncertainties and rapid changes in communications (see Lankshear 2003). As we have discussed, these changes alter knowledge, participation, and community, but they also affect our concepts of time, space, truth, identity, and even reality. The development of an educational philosophy to undergird and guide ICTs in the classroom is a political necessity, and this is especially so for those, who like Freire, envision education as liberatory.

References

Atkins-Sayre, Wendy, Sonya Hopkins, Sarah Mohundro, and Ward Sayre. 1998. "Rewards and Liabilities of Presentation Software as an Ancillary Tool: Prison or Paradise?" Paper presented at the annual meeting of the National Communications Association, New York. (ERIC Document Reproduction Service No. ED430260).

Bartsch, Robert and Kristi M. Cobern. 2003. "Effectiveness of PowerPoint Presentations in Lectures," *Computers and Education* 41: 77-86.

Baudrillard, Jean. 1994. *Simulcra and Simulation*. Translated by Sheila Faria Glaser. Ann Arbor: The University of Michigan Press.

Berge, Zane L. and Mauri P. Collins. 1995. *Computer-Mediated Communication and the Online Classroom: Overview and Perspectives*. Cresskill, NJ: Hampton Press.

Bowers, Chet A. 1988. *The Cultural Dimensions of Educational Technology*. New York: Teacher's College Press.

Carnevale, Dan. 2005. "Run a Class Like a Game Show: 'Clickers' Keep Students Involved," *Chronicle of Higher Education* 51 (42): B3.

Clegg, Sue, Alison Hudson, and John Steel. 2003. "The Emperor's New Clothes: Globilization and E-Learning in Higher Education," *British Journal of Sociology of Education* 24 (1): 39-53.

Damasio, Antonio R. 1994. *Descartes' Error: Emotion, Reason, and the Human Brain.* New York: Putnam.

Daniels, Lisa. 1999. "Introducing Technology in the Classroom: PowerPoint as a First Step," *Journal of Computing in Higher Education* 10 (2): 42-56.

DeVoogd, Glenn L., Arvil Loveless, and Nicola Yelland. 2000. "In Search of the Revolutionary Power of Critical Pedagogy: Issues of Ideology, Power, and Culture in Technology Teacher Education," *Society for Information Technology and Teacher Training International Conference: Proceedings* 3: 2419-2424.

Doumont, Jean-Luc. 2005. "The Cognitive Style of PowerPoint: Slides Are Not All Evil," *Technical Communication* 52 (1): 64-70.

Freire, Paulo. 1970. *Pedagogy of the Oppressed.* New York: Continuum.

——. 1973. *Education for Critical Consciousness.* New York: Seabury Press.

——. 1978. *Pedagogy in Process: The Letters to Guinea-Bissau.* New York: Seabury Press.

——. 1998a. *Pedagogy of Freedom.* Lanham, MD: Rowman & Littlefield Publishers.

——. 1998b. *Teachers as Cultural Workers: Letters to Those Who Dare Teach.* Translated by Donald Macedo, Dale Koike, and Alexandre Oliveira. Boulder: Westview Press.

Frey, Barbara A. and David J. Birnbaum. 2002. *Learners' Perceptions of the Value of PowerPoint in Lectures.* Pittsburgh, PA: Center for Instructional Development and Distance Education. (ERIC Document Reproduction Service No. ED467192).

Gaventa, John. 1980. *Power and Powerlessness: Quiescence and Rebellion in an Appalachian Valley.* Urbana: University of Illinois Press.

Giroux, Henry A. 1981. *Ideology, Culture, and the Process of Schooling.* Philadelphia: Temple University Press.

Glass, Ronald David. 2001. "On Paulo Freire's Philosophy of Praxis and the Foundations of Liberation Education," *Educational Researcher* 30 (2): 15-25.

Grabe, Maria Elizabeth, Shuhua Zhou, Annie Lang, and Paul David Bolls. 2000. "Packaging Television News: The Effects of Tabloid on Information Processing and Evaluative Responses," *Journal of Broadcasting and Electronic Media* 44: 581-598.

Harasim, Linda M. 1990. "Online Education: An Environment for Collaboration and Intellectual Amplification," in Linda M. Harasim (ed.) *Online Education: Perspectives on a New Environment*. New York: Prager, pp. 36-67.

Hardwick, Susan W. 2000. "Humanising the Technology Landscape through a Collaborative Pedagogy," *Journal of Geography in Higher Education* 24 (1): 123-129.

Harknett, Richard J. and Craig T. Cobane. 1997. "Introducing Instructional Technology to International Relations," *Political Science and Politics* 30: 496-500.

Hatch, Jay, Murray Jensen, and Randy Moore. 2005. "Manna from Heaven or 'Clickers' from Hell," *Journal of College Science Teaching* 34 (7): 36-39.

Hlynka, Denis and Ralph Mason. 1998. "'PowerPoint' in the Classroom: What Is the Point?" *Educational Technology* 38: 45-48.

Jameson, Fredric. 1984. "Postmodernism, or the Cultural Logic of Late Capitalism," *New Left Review* 146: 53-92.

Jenkins, Henry. 2006. "Confronting the Challenges of Participatory Culture: Media Education for the 21st Century," an Occasional Paper. The John D. and Catherine T. MacArthur Foundation.

Johnson, Scott D., Steven R. Aragon, Najmuddin Shank, and Nilda Palma-Rivas. 2000. "Comparative Analysis of Learner Satisfaction and Learning Outcomes in Online and Face-to-Face Learning Environments," *Journal of Interactive Research* 11: 29-49.

Kennedy, Robert J. 2006. "Learning Technologies: Re-Imagining Schooling," *Education Canada* 46 (2): 45-48.

Kulik, James A. 1994. "Meta-Analytic Studies of Findings on Computer-Based Instruction." In *Technology Assessment in Education and Training*, eds. Eva L. Baker and Harold F. O'Neil, Jr. Hillsdale, NJ: Lawrence Erlbaum.

Lankshear, Colin. 2003. "The Challenge of Digital Epistemologies." *Education, Communication & Information* 3 (2): 167-186.

LaRose, Robert, Jennifer Gregg, and Matt Eastin. 1998. "Audiographic Telecourses for the Web: An Experiment," *Journal of Computer-Mediated Communication [Online]* 4 (2). Available: http://jcmc.indiana.edu/vol4/issue2/larose.html.

Levasseur, David G. and J. Kanan Sawyer. 2006. "Pedagogy Meets PowerPoint: A Research Review of the Effects of Computer-Generated Slides in the Classroom," *The Review of Communication* 6 (1/2): 101-123.

Lowry, Roy B. 1999. "Electronic Presentation of Lectures—Effect Upon Student Performance," *University Chemistry Education* 3 (1): 18-21.

Mahin, Linda. 2004. "PowerPoint Pedagogy," *Business Communication Quarterly* 67: 219-222.

Mantei, Erwin J. 2000. "Using Internet Class Notes and PowerPoint in the Physical Geology Lecture," *Journal of College Science Teaching* 29: 301-305.

Marcus, George E. 2002. *The Sentimental Citizen: Emotion in Democratic Politics.* University Park, PA: The Pennsylvania State University Press.

Mason, Ralph and Denis Hlynka. 1998. "'PowerPoint' in the Classroom: Where Is the Power?" *Educational Technology* 38: 42-45.

Menon, Anil S., Shannon Moffett, Melissa Enriquez, Miriam M. Martinez, Parvati Dev, and Todd Grappone. 2004. "Audience Response Made Easy: Using Personal Digital Assistants as a Classroom Polling Tool," *Journal of the American Medical Informatics Association* 11 (3): 217-220.

Meyer, Katrina A. 2002. *Quality in Distance Education: Focus on On-Line Learning.* ASHE-ERIC Higher Education Report 29. San Francisco: Jossey-Bass.

Miller, M. Rex. 2005. "The Digital Dynamic: How Communications Media Shape Our World," *The Futurist*: 31-36.

Neuhauser, Charlotte. 2002. "Learning Style and Effectiveness of Online and Face-to-Face Instruction," *The American Journal of Distance Education* 16 (2): 99-113.

Newman, Frank and Jamie Scurry. 2001. "Online Technology Pushes Pedagogy to the Forefront," *Chronicle of Higher Education* 47 (44): B7.

Palloff, Rena M. and Keith Pratt. 1999. *Building Learning Communities in Cyberspace: Effective Strategies for the Online Classroom.* San Francisco: Jossey-Bass.

Parr, Judy and Lorrae Ward. 2006. "Building on Foundations: Creating an Online Community," *Journal of Technology and Teacher Education* 14 (4): 775-793.

Pauw, Amy Plantinga. 2002. "Discoveries and Dangers in Teaching Theology with PowerPoint," *Teaching Theology and Religion* 5 (1): 39-41.

Pearson, Matthew and Bridget Somekh. 2006. "Learning Transformation with Technology: A Question of Sociocultural Contexts?" *International Journal of Qualitative Studies in Education* 19 (4): 519-539.

Rankin, Elizabeth L. and David J. Hoass. 2001. "The Use of PowerPoint and Student Performance," *Atlantic Economic Journal* 29 (1): 113.

Schutte, James G. 1997. "Virtual Teaching in Higher Education: The New Intellectual Superhighway or Just Another Traffic Jam?" Available: http://www.csun.edu/sociology/virexp.htm.

Schuyler, Gwyer. 1997. "A Paradigm Shift from Instruction to Learning," ERIC Digest ED414961: 1-6.

Steele, Ray. 1998. "Response System Technology Steps Up to the Plate," *Media & Methods* 34 (3): 10.

Strauss, Susan G. 1996. "Getting a Clue: Communication Media and Information Distribution Effects on Group Process and Performance," *Small Group Research* 27 (1): 115-142.

Susskind, Joshua E. 2005. "PowerPoint's Power in the Classroom: Enhancing Students' Self-efficacy and Attitudes," *Computers and Education* 45: 203-215.

Sutherland, R., V. Armstrong, S. Barnes, R. Brawn, N. Breeze, M. Gall, S. Matthewman, F. Olivero, A. Taylor, P. Triggs, J. Wishart, and P. John. 2004. "Transforming Teaching and Learning: Embedding ICT into Everyday Classroom Practices," *Journal of Computer Assisted Learning* 20: 413-425.

Szabo, Attila and Nigel Hastings. 2000. "Using IT in the Undergraduate Classroom: Should We Replace the Blackboard with PowerPoint?" *Computers and Education* 35: 175-187.

Trotter, Andrew. 2005. "Technology Turns Test-Prep into Clicking Experience," *Education Week* 24 (36): 8.

Tufte, Edward R. 2003. *The Cognitive Style of PowerPoint*. Cheshire, CN: Graphics Press.

Turkle, Sherry. 1995. *Life on the Screen: Identity in the Age of the Internet*. New York: Simon & Schuster.

Vonderwell, Selma and Sandra Turner. 2005. "Active Learning and Preservice Teachers' Experiences in an Online Course: A Case Study," *Journal of Technology and Teacher Education* 13 (1): 65-84.

Wagner, Ellen D. 1997. "Interactivity: From Agents to Outcomes," in Thomas E. Cyrs (ed.) *Teaching and Learning at a Distance: New Directions for Teaching and Learning*. San Francisco: Jossey-Bass, pp. 19-26.

Winner, Langdon. 1986. *The Whale and the Reactor: A Search for Limits in an Age of High Technology*. Chicago: The University of Chicago Press.

Young, Suzanne, Pamela P. Cantrell and Dale G. Shaw. 2001. "Online Instruction: New Roles for Teachers and Students," *Academic Exchange Quarterly* 5 (4): 11-16.

Source: *The International Journal of Technology, Knowledge and Society* 3.4 (2007): 53-61.

WHAT IT SAYS

1. What claims do advocates make for the use of digital technology in higher education? What are these claims based on, according to Freie and Behuniak?

2. What is Paolo Freire's main argument about traditional education in his book *Pedagogy of the Oppressed*, as Freie and Behuniak relate it? What does Freire recommend in place of traditional education? How is Freire's pedagogy thought to be liberating or "liberatory"?

3. What is wrong with the use of PowerPoint presentations in education, according to the authors? What kind of education does it foster and how? How does this form of teaching differ from what Paolo Freire had in mind, according to the authors?

4. What do the authors think of online courses? Do online courses promote participatory culture, or the opposite, banking education? What do Internet information communication technologies (ICTs) lack, according to Freie and Behuniak?

5. According to the essay, how do online courses affect the politics of the classroom? What two aspects of the classroom do they affect most?

6. What conclusion do the authors draw for the uses of digital technologies in higher education?

HOW IT SAYS IT

1. Describe the organization of Freie and Behuniak's essay. What are the parts of the essay and how do they work together to make their case?

2. How do the authors work to convince you that they have faithfully rendered Paulo Freire's argument?

3. Describe Freie and Behuniak's intended audience. What role and stakes do the intended readers most likely have in the educational process?

WRITE ABOUT IT

1. Write a brief summary of Freire's pedagogy as you understand it from the essay you've read.

2. Assume the role of a college administrator and write an e-mail to the faculty that argues for an increase in online course offerings at your college or university. Consider that your audience may have different interests and motives than you have and may be either for or against online courses. Appeal to their interests as educators and employees of the institution.

3. Write a rebuttal to Freie and Behuniak from the perspective of an advocate for ICTs in higher education.

4. Find a blog about online learning or education and write a response to the blogger's post. Invite your classmates and teacher to respond by sharing a link to the blog using Twitter.

Questions for Synthesis

1. Write an essay that discusses the uses of Web 2.0 technologies in higher education.

   - Where do the authors you have read in the chapter stand on the issue?
   - Should Web 2.0 technologies be integrated in the classroom and beyond?
     - If so, how, according to these authors?
     - If not, why not, according to these authors?
   - Consider how each of your authors would change (or retain) contemporary educational practices.

   Remember that your goal here is to pull together the various viewpoints of this chapter's writers on this issue, without making an argument of your own. You may wish to construct a synthesis grid (see pp. 77–79) before you begin to write.

2. Write an essay in which you explore the pedagogy—or philosophy of education—of the various authors.

   - What is the role of the teacher for each of the authors?
   - What is the role of the student?
   - What is the relationship of the student and teacher to knowledge?

   This is a synthesis essay, not a contribution; your goal is to faithfully represent the positions of these writers, not to express your agreement or disagreement with them. You may wish to construct a synthesis grid (see pp. 77–79) before you begin to write.

Questions for Contribution

1. Take a stance regarding the incorporation of digital media in higher education. What role should such media play, if any?

   Include a discussion of your own pedagogy, and make sure that your proposal for digital media in higher education is consistent with your pedagogy. Should higher education

   a. remain as is with regards to digital media use?
   b. incorporate more digital media use?
   c. critically engage with digital media such that its use becomes a topic of inquiry in the curriculum?

   Include a discussion of your rationale for the inclusion, exclusion, and/or critical engagement with digital media. Draw on the sources included in this chapter and consult the Suggested Additional Resources to support your arguments.

2. Using Twitter and at least two other digital media technologies, work in groups to construct a proposal to your college or university administration about the place of digital media technologies in education. Pay specific attention to your educational institution and how it might be changed.

   Use Twitter to tweet pieces of your argument to all the members in your group. Use other digital technologies for incorporating sound, images, and other digital elements. Use links to essays or other texts to support your argument with sourcing.

   When all of the elements of the argument have been tweeted, assemble as a team to translate it into a multimedia proposal.

CHAPTER 4

LIVING IN A GLOBAL CULTURE

INTRODUCTION

Contexts of Discussion

We live in a global village. We've all heard this hundreds of times. But what does it mean? **Globalization**—or the increasingly interconnected and interdependent nature of communication systems, economies, cultures, and politics of contemporary societies—has been a topic of controversy at least since the early 1990s.

This chapter addresses the issue of globalization, in particular as it affects cultures throughout the world. The term **global culture** is used to describe this phenomenon.[1] With the end of the Cold War in the late 1980s, the great ideological divide that separated the West and East finally closed. According to supporters of globalization, the Western system of the free market combined with representative government had won a resounding victory. Some claimed that the great ideological struggles of the past had finally come to an end. The philosopher Francis Fukuyama, whose excerpt is included in Chapter 5, even declared "the end of history," or the end of large-scale struggles between opposing worldviews or major groups. (Fukuyama later revised his thesis significantly, especially in light of the events of September 11, 2001, and the wars that followed.)

According to globalization supporters, an expanding global marketplace promised a seemingly endless extension of wealth. More products would become available to more people, allowing for improved living standards and new lifestyle choices. Globalization, supporters have suggested, could also create possibilities for shared values worldwide, and a greater likelihood that national and ethnic conflicts could be handled peacefully. International non-governmental organizations (NGOs) would lead the effort to spread common values for the benefit of humanity.

---

1 For readings on other aspects of globalization, including job relocation, wages, environmental impacts, and other issues, see the Suggested Additional Resources at the end of this introduction.

Critics of globalization and global culture, on the other hand, argue that globalization represents the Westernization of the rest of the world. The cultural products of globalization—movies, cable TV, music, software, cell phones, sports, fashion, fast food, etc.—flow mostly in one direction: from the United States to the rest of the world. The net effect of this process of global transmission may be **homogenization,** or global sameness.

In an essay in this chapter, George Ritzer uses the term "McDonaldization" to describe the production of a generic global consumer society based on a model perfected by the fast-food chain. The terms "Coca-colonization" and "Coca-globalization" have also been used to describe this process. Given the worldwide reach of Starbucks, some argue that "Starbuckization" best describes the homogenization of global culture today.

Another camp in this debate includes scholars who do not deny the potential for homogenization but who are more optimistic about its effects. These scholars contend that global culture does not strictly or necessarily result in the exclusive predominance of the West. According to this view, McDonaldization is never complete, even in the United States, where it originated. While some areas of culture may become homogenized, others become more heterogeneous. For example, fast food has spread to nearly all parts of the globe, including China, Europe, India, and the former Soviet Union. But thanks to global commerce, international cuisines are now on menus in suburban shopping centers in the United States and elsewhere.

Likewise, globalization makes various places more alike, but it also provides more diversity within cultures. On the one hand, the networks of communication established by global systems—including increased trade and travel, satellite broadcasting, and the Internet—promote the cultural products of dominant corporations. On the other hand, they also allow for the spread of art, food, music, and fashion from non-Western cultures. Further, without the raw materials and cultural influences of the West, some practices would be impossible. For example, the totem poles of the Pacific Northwest would not have been possible without the metal carving knife derived from contact with the islanders with the West. Therefore, according to this view, rather than being diminished, heterogeneity increases with globalization. The economist Tyler Cowen takes this view and points both to it and to other examples in his essay "Trade between Cultures," in this chapter.

Along the same lines, some scholars criticize the homogenization theory on the grounds that it discounts the consumption side of globalization and fails to account for how people actually *use* American and other Western cultural goods. Renowned philosopher, cultural critic, and African Studies scholar Kwame Anthony Appiah represents this view in "Cosmopolitan Contamination," a chapter drawn from his 2006 book *Cosmopolitanism: Ethics in a World of Strangers,* and included in this chapter.

Similarly, some scholars argue that globalization is always complemented by a push-back from the local. As global franchises like Starbucks spread around the world, locals respond by demanding and supplying local counterparts to the global cultural and business giants. Historian and American studies professor Bryant Simon develops this view in his blog essay "Global Brands Contend with Appreciation for the Local," included in this chapter.

Anthropologists have used the terms **hybridization** and **creolization** to refer to the ways in which cultures blend and mix rather than one fully overtaking another. In his book *Coca-Globalization: Following Soft Drinks from New York to New Guinea*, listed in the Suggested Additional Resources, the anthropologist Robert John Foster acknowledges the strengths of the creolization theory while noting the significant changes that have been wrought on **indigenous** cultures as a consequence of global commerce. According to Foster, the recognition of both trends—creolization and the domination of global culture—means that we shouldn't be either overly optimistic or overly pessimistic about the survival of cultural diversity worldwide.

Another perspective on globalization is that its effects on culture remain uncertain and unstable. Scholars in this camp point to the difficulty of determining the impact of Western products on the people and places where they are received. While Western economic and cultural products may extend across the globe, the net effect of this extensive dissemination cannot be easily determined. The reach of culture may be easier to trace than its intensity or durability, for example. The political scientist David Held takes this position in *Global Transformations: Politics, Economics and Culture*, listed in the Suggested Additional Resources.

Yet others see the issues as more complicated and more dangerous than any of these perspectives suggest. Rather than simply producing homogeneity, globalization also fosters tendencies that oppose it. For instance, opposing groups are often hostile to the effects of the economic and cultural dominance of the West. Rather than subscribing to global values, national, ethnic, and religious groups become fiercely attached to traditional beliefs and practices. Some even resort to violence to maintain their integrity. In a selection included in this chapter, Benjamin Barber refers to the struggle between these forces against McDonaldizaton as "Jihad vs. McWorld," or the militant resistance to globalization.

Areas of Research and Conjecture

Globalization and global culture have become important topics of study, touching nearly every discipline in the humanities and social sciences. The natural sciences have also gotten involved (see Michael E. Hochberg, "A Theory of Modern Cultural Shifts and Meltdowns," in the Suggested Additional Resources). The following is a brief discussion of the fields most important to the understanding of global culture.

Anthropology is the study of human origins (physical anthropology) and human diversity (cultural anthropology). Cultural anthropologists conduct field studies of cultures and their interactions. We include a number of works by cultural anthropologists in the Suggested Additional Resources at the end of this introduction.

American studies is an interdisciplinary field dealing with the study of the United States and including scholarship in history, literature, the arts, contemporary and urban life, media, and other aspects of US culture and society. Given that global culture is generally considered at least partially rooted in the US, some American studies scholars are interested in the impact of US cultural and economic products on the rest of the world. American studies is represented in this chapter by Bryant Simon and his article on Starbucks, "Global Brands Contend with Appreciation for the Local."

Cultural studies analyzes contemporary culture in connection with social, economic, and political life. Culture is defined as a people's way of life, which includes the arts, literature, leisure activities, mass media, music, popular entertainment, and other forms of shared experience. Because cultural studies regards culture as consisting of values and representations of people, and as embodying ideology, globalization is an extremely important phenomenon for the field. Cultural studies examines globalization and the resistance to it. Furthermore, cultural studies scholars do not pretend to be "objective." They generally champion those groups subject to domination or cultural erasure.

While the cultural studies approach is not directly represented here, the perspective has influenced many disciplines. Several essays from scholars in the field are listed in the Suggested Additional Resources section at the end of this introduction.

Economics is the study of the distribution and use of valued resources, as well as the stimulants to their creation. Most scholars agree that globalization is motivated primarily by economic gain. Thus, economics is an essential field to consult when considering globalization and global culture. The field is represented in this chapter by Tyler Cowen's essay "Trade between Cultures."

Global studies is a relatively new interdisciplinary field that incorporates sociology, political science, international relations, environmental science, economics, and others to address the issues associated with globalization. Many of the readings included in this chapter and Suggested Additional Resources may be considered contributions to this new field.

Philosophy is a field that considers questions of being (ontology), proper behavior (ethics), and knowledge (epistemology). Given that globalization poses questions regarding individual and group identity, ethics, and even the validity of knowledge claims, it is an important area for philosophers and philosophically minded writers. This chapter includes a selection from the writing of world-renowned philosopher, cultural critic, and African Studies scholar Kwame Anthony Appiah.

Political science is the study of governmental systems and practices, political processes and parties, and the relations between citizens and their governments. Since globalization has a great impact on relations between nations and other political groups, political scientists are especially interested in the process. An essay by political scientist Benjamin Barber is included in this chapter.

Sociology is the study of human behavior within groups and within society at large. Sociologists study social organization and trends and develop theories for understanding them. Since globalization involves changing relations and activities among groups of people, the phenomenon is important for sociology. This chapter includes an essay by sociologist George Ritzer.

Issues and Stakeholders

Trade: Globalization is based on ease of travel, and on international trade and communications. International trade is the exchange of goods across national borders, which results in new and expanded markets for goods produced in one place and sold in another. While, in 1995, cultural exports accounted for only 3 per cent of US exports, there is no doubt that the United States dominates cultural markets worldwide. Visit almost any country in the world and you are sure to find the cultural products of the United States, including movies, television, videos, newspapers, magazines, and books. Fashion, fast food, and theme parks originating from the United States can also be found around the globe. Because they influence behavior and identity, these may also be considered cultural products.

Multinational corporations have a tremendous stake in globalization because it provides ever-expanding markets for their goods. Advocates of free trade argue that globalization (and thus global cultural dissemination) provides new resources, job opportunities, and lifestyle possibilities to more and more people.

Homogenization: In terms of globalization, homogenization means that the cultures in diverse places become more and more like each other. Proponents of the homogenization theory argue that homogenization is a consequence of globalization, which is mostly dominated by Western cultures, especially the United States. Others see the process as far more complex. For example, Tyler Cowen (in this chapter) argues that homogenization and **heterogenization** (the creation of difference) are not mutually exclusive but rather tend to occur together. While the differences among cultures may be reduced, the differences within them are increased.

Cultural imperialism: A major concern of some critics of global culture is that it may result in cultural imperialism or the cultural domination of one group over others. Cultural imperialism is a particular kind of domination; it is not the same as political imperialism, which manifests in political empires such as the Roman and British empires. Rather, cultural imperialism, its theorists contend, works more subtly and insidiously to undermine the cultures into which the dominant culture is imported. To introduce the concept, John Tomlinson, in his critical introduction to the study of the phenomenon (listed in the Suggested Additional Resources), describes a photograph of an aboriginal family in Australia watching television outdoors in the Tanami desert:

It [the photograph] ... suggests that the family is under threat from what they are doing, and notes that the community has set up its own broadcasting organization—the Walpiri Media Association—"to try to defend its unique culture from western culture." Knowing this, we will probably read the picture in a certain way, inferring a domination from the image. The picture can thus quickly be grasped as representing cultural imperialism. (1)

As this passage suggests, not only does cultural imperialism work subtly, but it also requires the participation of those being dominated.

The illustration shows how one culture works to insert itself into another culture—by providing attractive cultural goods that displace and ultimately may erase the subordinated culture. The result is a form of control over the habits, attitudes, and views of those affected. Cultural imperialism is thus a dramatic form of homogenization. Indeed, some critics of globalization and global culture contend that it is an inevitable result of globalization and global culture.

As You Read

Globalization and global culture are controversial and complicated, but the readings in this chapter should provide a good introduction to the topics, and the Suggested Additional Resources section that follows will help to fill out the contours of the debates.

Nevertheless, it will be very difficult to characterize the entirety of the topic without breaking it down a bit. As you read, identify subtopics or issues within the debate. The issues and stakeholders section above can get you started.

- Use a synthesis grid (see pp. 77–79) to visualize the points of agreement and disagreement among the writers included in this chapter.
- Add columns for two other relevant writers you may find in Suggested Additional Resources.
- Also add a column for your own positions.
- Briefly characterize the view of each writer on the subtopic.
- After carefully considering the views of others on these points, begin to formulate your own positions.
- Add your views on the subtopics to the grid.
- Then see how your points on various subtopics fit together.

When you have completed your grid, you will be well on your way to writing a synthesis and a contribution paper.

Suggested Additional Resources

Advocacy

Afro Global Alliance. Afroglobal.org. 2007. Web.

Al-Mayassa, Sheikha. Globalizing the Local, Localizing the Global. TED. Dec. 2010. Web.

Business and Economics

Gabrielsson, Mika, and Vishnu H. Kirpalani. *Handbook of Research on Born Globals*. Cheltenham, UK: Edward Elgar Publishing. 2012. Web.

Gannon, Martin J. *Paradoxes of Culture and Globalization*. Los Angeles: Sage, 2007.

MacRae, Hamish. *The World in 2020: Power, Culture and Prosperity*. Boston: Harvard Business School Press, 1994.

Powell, Benjamin. *Out of Poverty: Sweatshops in the Global Economy*. Cambridge: Cambridge UP, 2014.

Communications/Cultural Studies/Critical Theory

Cheneval, Francis. "Mind the Gap: Introductory Thoughts on Globalization and Cosmopolitanism." *Journal of Philosophical Research* 37 (2012): 263-67. Web.

Jameson, Fredric. *Postmodernism, or, The Cultural Logic of Late Capitalism*. Durham, NC: Duke UP, 1991.

——, and Masao Miyoshi. *The Cultures of Globalization*. Durham, NC: Duke UP, 1998.

Kraidy, Marwan M. *Hybridity, or the Cultural Logic of Globalization*. Philadelphia: Temple UP, 2005.

Landow, George P. *Hypertext 3.0: Critical Theory and New Media in an Era of Globalization*. Baltimore: Johns Hopkins UP, 2006.

Said, Edward W. *Culture and Imperialism*. New York: Vintage Books, 1993.

——, and David Barsamian. *Culture and Resistance: Conversations with Edward W. Said*. Cambridge, MA: South End Press, 2003.

Tomlinson, John. *Cultural Imperialism: A Critical Introduction*. London: Continuum, 2001.

Torelli, Carlos, and Shirley Chang. "Cultural Meanings of Brands and Consumption: A Window into the Cultural Psychology of Globalization." *Social & Personality Psychology Compass* 5.5 (May 2011): 251-62. Web.

Cultural Anthropology

Appadurai, Arjun. *Modernity at Large: Cultural Dimensions of Globalization*.
    Minneapolis: U of Minnesota P, 1996.
Condry, Ian. *Hip-Hop Japan: Rap and the Paths of Cultural Globalization*. Durham,
    NC: Duke UP, 2006.
Geschiere, Peter, and Birgit Meyer. *Globalization and Identity: Dialectics of Flow
    and Closure*. Oxford: Blackwell, 2003.
Howes, David. *Cross-Cultural Consumption: Global Markets, Local Realities*.
    London: Routledge, 1996.
Inda, Jonathan Xavier, and Renato Rosaldo. *The Anthropology of Globalization:
    A Reader*. Malden, MA: Blackwell, 2001.
Lewellen, Ted C. *The Anthropology of Globalization: Cultural Anthropology Enters
    the 21st Century*. Westport, CT: Bergin & Garvey, 2002.
United Nations Educational, Scientific and Cultural Organization. "Culture for
    Sustainable Development." Unesco.org. 2014. Web.

Political Science

Featherstone, Mike. *Global Culture: Nationalism, Globalization, and Modernity:
    A Theory, Culture & Society Special Issue*. London: Sage Publications, 1990.
Held, David. *Global Transformations: Politics, Economics and Culture*. Stanford,
    CA: Stanford UP, 1999.
Scholte, Jan Aart. *Globalization: A Critical Introduction*. Basingstoke, UK:
    Palgrave, 2000.

Sociology

Berger, Peter L., and Samuel P. Huntington. *Many Globalizations: Cultural
    Diversity in the Contemporary World*. New York: Oxford UP, 2004.
Boli, John, and Frank Lechner. *The Globalization Reader*. Malden, MA:
    Blackwell, 2004.
Lash, Scott, and Celia Lury. *Global Culture Industry*. Cambridge: Polity, 2006.
Peiterse, Jan Nederveen. *Globalization and Culture: Global Melange*. Lanham,
    MD: Rowman & Littlefield, 2009.
Ritzer, George. *Enchanting a Disenchanted World: Revolutionizing the Means of
    Consumption*. Thousand Oaks, CA: Pine Forge, 2005.
——. *The Globalization of Nothing 2*. Thousand Oaks, CA: Pine Forge, 2007.
Roberts, J. Timmons. *The Globalization and Development Reader: Perspectives on
    Development and Social Change*. Malden, MA: Blackwell, 2007.
Robertson, Roland. *Globalization: Social Theory and Global Culture*. London:
    Sage, 1992.

a. Bryant Simon, "Global Brands Contend with Appreciation for the Local"

Bryant Simon is a professor of history and director of American studies at Temple University. His recent research focuses on race and class and the creation and destruction of urban spaces. This includes the study of Starbucks and the molding of public culture in the United States and across the globe in the twenty-first century. Simon's many awards include a Senior Fulbright Scholarship, the Richard McCormick Prize for best book on New Jersey history, and the Best Article in Urban History Award from the Urban History Association.

Simon is the author of several books, including *A Fabric of Defeat: The Politics of South Carolina Millhands, 1910-1948* (1998), *Boardwalk of Dreams: Atlantic City and the Fate of Urban America* (2004), and *Everything but the Coffee: Learning about America from Starbucks* (2009).

Simon received BA and PhD degrees from the University of North Carolina at Chapel Hill, and MA degrees from both Yale University and the University of Warwick.

The essay below was published on the *Yale Global Online Magazine*, a publication of the Yale Center for the Study of Globalization. Here we reproduce the original format as closely as possible. Simon argues that the global spread of American cultural products like Starbucks is countered by a drive to preserve local culture and create new local brands.

As You Read: Think about your own patterns of consumption. Are you mostly a customer of national and international chains like Starbucks and McDonald's, or are you more likely to patronize locally owned businesses? What effects of large-scale chains have you noticed on the local culture where you live?

Global Brands Contend with Appreciation for the Local

STRATFORD-UPON-AVON: Shakespeare's birthplace is not immune from a common complaint. When Jim Hyssop saw a Starbucks open up several years ago in downtown Stratford-upon-Avon, near the McDonald's and Pizza Hut already there, he grimly forecast: "If someone blindfolded you, put you in a helicopter and set you down in a town somewhere in England, you wouldn't be able to tell where you are anymore."

FIGURE 4.1. A New Day: India's Café Coffee Day Challenges Starbucks

Like many scholars and residents of places with a past, Hyssop fears that global brands will erode national, regional and neighborhood distinctiveness. As chains deliver the same products, designs and exteriors everywhere, they could, Hyssop worries, create a soulless Generica, "a land where all the high streets look identical."

Although McDonald's serves 47 million customers each day in 119 countries around the world and Starbucks serves about the same number each week in 51 countries, that one-world Generica has not taken control. Instead, the spread of these branded symbols of globalization raises the value of the local. Everywhere multinationals go, they generate a grassroots pushback, an assertion of the enduring value of particular places, tastes and traditions.

Yet this nearly universal assertion of the local is much less widely noted than the fears of the global.

Opened in Seattle in 1971, Starbucks initially seemed more local than global. In its early years, it sold whole bean, freshly roasted coffee out of one store with the owners often standing behind the counter. Even after the company opened a second, then a third store, it retained a small mom-and-pop kind of feel.

As much as those first Starbucks looked and acted local, they were enmeshed in the global. The original logo with a bare-breasted siren imitated an old-world Norse woodcut. And the beans came from far-off places like Guatemala, Sumatra and Ethiopia.

> Everywhere multinationals go, they generate grassroots pushback, an assertion of enduring values of particular places.

Indeed, this remaking of coffee from everyday commodity into an imported, slightly exotic affordable luxury gave Starbucks products their cultural value.

When Howard Schultz took over Starbucks in 1987, he thickened its global networks—opening the company's first international outlet in Vancouver in 1987, then in Tokyo in 1996, Qatar in 2000, Paris in 2004 and Buenos Aires in 2008. By 2009, Starbucks had 16,120 stores on five continents.

> Despite Starbucks' message of high-end universalism, its global expansion did not go uncontested.

As he tells it, Schultz experienced a coffee epiphany in a Milan espresso bar in 1983. Hearing the melodious clanking of saucers and hiss of steaming milk, he decided Americans would pay a premium for a facsimile of the Italian coffee bar.

Schultz did more than just introduce Americans to espressos and cappuccinos. Seeking to enhance brand value by associating it with Europe—the center of coffee culture and knowledge in the minds of most Americans—he and his colleagues sold grande and venti mistos and macchiatos prepared by baristas.

Continental references were just one part of Starbucks's global posture. The company strived to create a transnational setting, distinct from any one locale or nation that was nonetheless still everywhere, everywhere globetrotters, creative types and the upper-middle-class convened. Whereas McDonald's sells an idealized, consumer version of America as a fun, efficient place, Starbucks sold itself as a predictable destination on an increasingly flat global landscape.

Starbucks is the same everywhere, everywhere erasing differences and suggesting that we—those who can afford pricey drinks—are well-informed, sophisticated customers who appreciate quality, yet still care about the environment and the least fortunate. Thus, it became the brand for a new global middle class of the 21st century.

Despite Starbucks' message of high-end universalism, its global expansion did not go uncontested. When the World Trade Organization met in Seattle in 1999, protestors vandalized a Starbucks, accusing the company and other multinationals of polluting the environment and exploiting cheap labor in the developing world.

In 2003, Singapore's Chua Chin Hon wrote, "I'm no anti-globalization protestor," but admitted a change of heart, triggered by a Starbucks opening in Beijing's Forbidden City. He wrote about understanding "the rage against the global capitalist machinery's relentless and oft-times, senseless drive to sell a few more cups of coffee, burgers, or T-shirts."

Four years later, Rui Chenggang, an anchor for Chinese Central Television, demanded that Starbucks leave the nearly 600-hundred-year-old former royal residence. Accusing the company of tainting "China's national culture," he organized a boycott. Eventually Starbucks vacated the location, and a Chinese company took its place—selling lattes and cappuccinos in white cups with green logos.

> Besides street and internet protests, consumers rebelled against sameness with their feet and pocketbooks.

Besides street and internet protests, consumers rebelled against sameness with their feet and pocketbooks. As the branded world of Starbucks, McDonald's, The Gap and Disney spread from North America to Europe to Asia, from cities to the suburbs, the value of traditional, neighborhood venues increased.

Some teenaged Singaporean Malays have responded to the spread of Starbucks and other Western culture markers in their country by embracing Islam, eating and drinking only Malay products including traditional coffee instead of lattes and frappuccinos. Starbucks failed to establish footholds in Australia and Israel, places that already had well-established and locally controlled European style

> The global had generated so much demand for the local that a global chain needed to look local to survive globally.

coffeehouses. Despite Starbucks' presence in New Delhi and Mumbai, most Indian coffee drinkers prefer lattes from Indian-owned companies Coffee Day and Barista.

Starbucks takeover of street corners in Hong Kong triggered a kind of consumer dissent. One-of-a-kind, owner-operated coffeehouses—tiny and unadvertised— sprang up in second- or third-floor apartment living rooms all over the city. "When it comes to café culture," wrote a *Financial Times* reporter, "above ground is the new underground."

Perhaps the strongest resistance to Starbucks and its globalizing impact took place close to the brand's home base. Weary of the lack of choice posed by Starbucks, latte drinkers from Portland, Maine, to Portland, Oregon, search for the local. Even as the economy tanked, they, like those Hong Kong hipsters, go out of their way and pay a little extra for one-of-a-kind items and local settings. Independent coffeehouses, like farmers' markets or bring-your-own-bottle restaurants, have new appeal in the US emerging economy of the small.

While Starbucks has struggled during the New Recession, closing 600 stores in the US and halting expansion abroad, sales at independents, according to industry sources, remain robust.

In 2009, Starbucks responded to the shift towards the small by redesigning and retrofitting several Seattle stores and, later, several London stores. The new cafes didn't carry the Starbucks name or familiar green logo. One was named 15th Avenue Coffee and Tea, another Roy Street Tea and Coffee. In other words, the company opened stealth Starbucks meant to look and sound like independent coffee shops.

The message? The global had generated so much demand for the local that a global chain needed to look local to survive globally, at least in some markets.

This marks a change in the appeal of the big versus the small. What's constant in the age of globalization is that the local and global co-exist, always in conversation and tension with each other. You can't have one without the other.

Source: *YaleGlobal*. 6 July 2010. Web. http://yaleglobal.yale.edu/content/ global-brands-contend-appreciation-local.

WHAT IT SAYS

1. Simon begins by discussing the spread of global culture to a landmark city: Stratford-upon-Avon in the UK, the birthplace of the most celebrated writer in history, William Shakespeare. What is Simon's point in opening with such an example? What is the problem with having Starbucks located in such a place as Shakespeare's birthplace?

2. Simon uses the term "Generica," a word he apparently coined. How did he arrive at such a coinage (what is it a combination of?) and what phenomenon does it refer to?

3. Identify the thesis statement in Simon's essay. Identify the claim. What reasons support the claim?

4. Examine the photograph in Simon's essay. How can you tell that India's Café Coffee Day is competing with Starbucks?

5. What is the appeal of Starbucks and what is its customer base, according to Simon?

6. In addition to protests, what reactions has the spread of Starbucks triggered around the world? How has Starbucks responded?

7. What does Simon conclude about the relationship between the local and the global?

HOW IT SAYS IT

1. What kind of an article is this? Is it a formal academic essay, an informal blog, or something in-between?

2. Who is Simon's intended audience? How can you tell?

3. How does the photograph of India's Café Coffee Day help Simon to advance his argument?

4. Examine the captions that appear beside the essay. What is their function? How do these captions help Simon make his point? How do they relate to the structure of the essay?

WRITE ABOUT IT

1. Write a short essay in which you explore the relationship between local and global stores where you grew up or where you currently reside. What impact does the composition of local and global businesses have on the local culture, individual behaviors, and the formation of communities? Do global chain stores foster a sense of community as well as local stores do?

2. Write an essay in which you argue against Simon's thesis. Draw on examples to support your claims. If possible, use photographs to support your argument.

3. Imagine that you are a resident of Stratford-upon-Avon before the introduction of Starbucks in the community. The city leadership is considering issuing a building permit for Starbucks. Write an email or letter to the city managers in which you either support or oppose the opening of a Starbucks in your town. Research the city's history online, and explore contemporary Stratford on the city's official website: http://www.visitstratforduponavon.co.uk/. If you are for the building of a Starbucks, it's not enough to say that you enjoy the coffee. Whether writing for or against, you need to appeal to the interests of the community that the city leaders represent. Make sure you find out where to send the email or letter.

b. George Ritzer, "An Introduction to McDonaldization"

George Ritzer is distinguished university professor at the University of Maryland, College Park. He is most widely known in academic circles for his important contributions to the study of consumption and globalization. His book *The McDonaldization of Society* (5th edition 2008; first published in 1993), from which this chapter's essay is drawn, is among the best-selling books of sociology ever written. Ritzer has expanded and developed his highly critical analysis of contemporary social life in such books as *Enchanting a Disenchanted World* (2005) and *The Globalization of Nothing* (2007). He is founding editor of the *Journal of Consumer Culture* and has edited several professional volumes, as well as three encyclopedias (including the massive, 11-volume *Blackwell Encyclopedia of Sociology*). He has also published roughly one hundred articles in scholarly journals. Ritzer holds a BA from City College of New York, an MBA from the University of Michigan, and a PhD from Cornell University.

In "An Introduction to McDonaldization," Ritzer presents McDonald's restaurants as both part of, and a model for, the standardization of contemporary culture. McDonald's, an early and successful fast-food restaurant chain, has spread to nearly all parts of the globe. The success of McDonald's, based on a business model of product and service reproducibility, provides certain benefits to both producers and consumers. This model has been copied by other fast-food and casual-dining chains (e.g., Wendy's, Taco Bell, Appleby's), but it has also influenced many other areas of industry and culture, including home renovations and furnishings (e.g., Home Depot and Ikea), fashion and clothing (Gap), news delivery (USA Today), dating (match.com), and even religion (Assembly of God). As Ritzer sees it, McDonaldization represents a broad process of homogenization affecting nearly all areas of contemporary society. Ritzer critiques McDonaldization, but not from a standpoint of nostalgia. Rather, he suggests that the benefits of McDonaldization can be retained while also allowing for a greater use of human creative potential.

As You Read: Consider the process that Ritzer describes. What, if any, are some of the areas of your life that have been affected by McDonaldization?

An Introduction to McDonaldization

Ray Kroc (1902-1984), the genius behind the franchising of McDonald's restaurants, was a man with big ideas and grand ambitions. But even Kroc could not have anticipated the astounding impact of his creation. McDonald's is the basis of one of the most influential developments in contemporary society. Its reverberations extend far beyond its point of origin in the United States and in the fast-food business. It has influenced a wide range of undertakings, indeed the way of life, of a significant portion of the world. And in spite of McDonald's recent and well-publicized economic difficulties, that impact is likely to expand at an accelerating rate.

However, this is *not* a book about McDonald's, or even about the fast-food business, although both will be discussed frequently throughout these pages. I devote all this attention to McDonald's (as well as the industry of which it is part and that it played such a key role in spawning) because it serves here as the major example of, and the paradigm for, a wide-ranging process I call *McDonaldization*—that is,

> the process by which the principles of the fast-food restaurant are coming to dominate more and more sectors of American society as well as of the rest of the world.

As you will see, McDonaldization affects not only the restaurant business but also education, work, the criminal justice system, health care, travel, leisure, dieting, politics, the family, religion, and virtually every other aspect of society. McDonaldization has shown every sign of being an inexorable process, sweeping through seemingly impervious institutions and regions of the world.

The success of McDonald's (in spite of recent troubles; see the closing section of this chapter) itself is apparent: In 2002, its total sales was over $41 billion, with operating income of $2.1 billion. McDonald's, which first began operations in 1955, had 31,172 restaurants throughout the world as of early 2003. Martin Plimmer, a British commentator, archly notes: "There are McDonald's everywhere. There's one near you, and there's one being built right now even nearer to you. Soon, if McDonald's goes on expanding at its present rate, there might even be one in your house. You could find Ronald McDonald's boots under your bed. And maybe his red wig, too."

McDonald's and McDonaldization have had their most obvious influence on the restaurant industry and, more generally, on franchises of all types:

1. According to the International Franchise Association, there were 320,000 small franchised businesses in the United States in 2000 and they did about $1 trillion in annual sales. Although accounting for less than 10% of retail businesses, over 40% of all retail sales come from franchises and they employ more than 8 million people. Franchises are growing rapidly with a new one opening every 8 minutes in the United States. Over 57% of McDonald's restaurants are franchises.

2. In the restaurant industry, the McDonald's model has been adopted not only by other budget-minded hamburger franchises, such as Burger King and Wendy's, but also by a wide array of other low-priced fast-food

businesses. Yum! Brands, Inc. operates nearly 33,000 restaurants in 100 countries under the Pizza Hut, Kentucky Fried Chicken, Taco Bell, A&W Root Beer, and Long John Silver's franchises and has more outlets than McDonald's, although its total sales ($24 billion in 2002) are not nearly as high. Subway (with almost 19,000 outlets in 72 countries) is one of the fastest-growing fast-food businesses and claims to be—and may actually be—the largest restaurant chain in the United States.

3. Starbucks, a relative newcomer to the fast-food industry, has achieved dramatic success of its own. A local Seattle business as late as 1987, Starbucks had over 6,000 company-owned shops (there are no franchises) by 2003, more than ten times the number of shops in 1994. Starbucks has been growing rapidly internationally and is now a presence in Latin America, Europe (it is particularly omnipresent in London), the Middle East, and the Pacific Rim.

4. Perhaps we should not be surprised that the McDonald's model has been extended to casual dining—that is, more upscale, higher-priced restaurants with fuller menus (for example, Outback Steakhouse, Chili's, Olive Garden, and Red Lobster). Morton's is an even more upscale, high-priced chain of steakhouses that has overtly modeled itself after McDonald's: "Despite the fawning service and the huge wine list, a meal at Morton's conforms to the same dictates of uniformity, cost control and portion regulation that have enabled American fast-food chains to rule the world." In fact, the chief executive of Morton's was an owner of a number of Wendy's outlets and admits: "My experience with Wendy's has helped in Morton's venues." To achieve uniformity, employees go "by the book"; "an ingredient-by-ingredient illustrated binder describing the exact specifications of 500 Morton's kitchen items, sauces, and garnishes. A row of color pictures in every Morton's kitchen displays the presentation for each dish."

5. Other types of business are increasingly adapting the principles of the fast-food industry to their needs. Said the vice chairman of Toys 'R Us, "We want to be thought of as a sort of McDonald's of toys." The founder of Kidsports Fun and Fitness Club echoed this desire: "I want to be the McDonald's of the kids' fun and fitness business." Other chains with similar ambitions include Gap, Jiffy Lube, AAMCO Transmissions, Midas Muffler & Brake Shops, Great Clips, H&R Block, Pearle Vision, Bally's, Kampgrounds of America (KOA), KinderCare (dubbed "Kentucky Fried Children"), Jenny Craig, Home Depot, Barnes & Noble, PETsMART.

6. McDonald's has been a resounding success in the international arena. Over half of McDonald's restaurants are outside the United States (in the mid-1980s, only 25% of McDonald's were outside the United States).

The majority (982) of the 1,366 new restaurants opened in 2002 were over-seas (in the United States, the number of restaurants increased by less than four hundred). Well over half of McDonald's revenue comes from its over-seas operations. McDonald's restaurants are now found in 118 nations around the world, serving 46 million customers a day. The leader, by far, is Japan with almost 4,000 restaurants, followed by Canada with over 1,300, and Germany with over 1,200. As of 2002, there were 95 McDonald's in Russia, and the company plans to open many more restaurants in the former Soviet Union and in the vast new territory in Eastern Europe that has been laid bare to the invasion of fast-food restaurants. Great Britain has become the "fast-food capital of Europe," and Israel is described as "McDonaldized," with its shopping malls populated by "Ace Hardware, Toys 'R Us, Office Depot, and TCBY."

7. Many highly McDonaldized firms outside of the fast-food industry have also had success globally. Although most of Blockbuster's 8,500 sites are in the United States, more than 2,000 of them are to be found in twenty-eight other countries. Wal-Mart is the world's largest retailer with 1.3 million employees and $218 billion in sales. Over three thousand of its stores are in the United States (as of 2002). It opened its first international store (in Mexico) in 1991, but it now has more than one thousand units in Mexico, Puerto Rico, Canada, Argentina, Brazil, China, Korea, Germany, and the United Kingdom. In any week, more than 100 million customers visit Wal-Mart stores worldwide.

8. Other nations have developed their own variants of this American institution. Canada has a chain of coffee shops, Tim Hortons (merged with Wendy's not long ago), with 2,200 outlets (160 in the United States). Paris, a city whose love for fine cuisine might lead you to think it would prove immune to fast food, has a large number of fast-food croissanteries; the revered French bread has also been McDonaldized. India has a chain of fast-food restaurants, Nirula's, that sells mutton burgers (about 80% of Indians are Hindus, who eat no beef) as well as local Indian cuisine. Mos Burger is a Japanese chain with over fifteen hundred restaurants that, in addition to the usual fare, sells Teriyaki chicken burgers, rice burgers, and "Oshiruko with brown rice cake." Perhaps the most unlikely spot for an indigenous fast-food restaurant, war-ravaged Beirut of 1984, witnessed the opening of Juicy Burger, with a rainbow instead of golden arches and J.B. the Clown standing in for Ronald McDonald. Its owners hoped that it would become the "McDonald's of the Arab world." Most recently, in the immediate wake of the 2003 war with Iraq, clones of McDonald's (sporting names like "MaDonal" and "Matbax") opened in that country complete with hamburgers, french fries, and even golden arches.

9. And now McDonaldization is coming full circle. Other countries with their own McDonaldized institutions have begun to export them to the United States. The Body Shop, an ecologically sensitive British cosmetics chain had, as of early 2003, over nineteen hundred shops in fifty nations, of which three hundred were in the United States. Furthermore, American firms are now opening copies of this British chain, such as Bath & Body Works. Pret A Manger, a chain of sandwich shops that also originated in Great Britain (interestingly, McDonald's purchased a 33% minority share of the company in 2001), has over 130 company-owned and -run restaurants, mostly in the United Kingdom but now also in New York, Hong Kong, and Tokyo.

10. Ikea, a Swedish-based (but Dutch-owned) home furnishings company, did about 12 billion euros in business in 2002 derived from the over 286 million people (equal to about the entire population of the United States) visiting their 150-plus stores in 29 countries. Purchases were also made from the 118 million copies of their catalog printed in over 45 languages. In fact, that catalog is reputed to be the second largest publication in the world, just after the Bible. An international chain to watch in the coming years is H&M clothing, founded in 1947 and now operating over 900 stores in 17 countries with plans to open another 110 stores by the end of 2003. It currently employs over 39,000 people and sells more than 500 million items a year.

McDonald's as a Global Icon

McDonald's has come to occupy a central place in American popular culture, not just the business world. A new McDonald's opening in a small town can be an important social event. Said one Maryland high school student at such an opening, "Nothing this exciting ever happens in Dale City." Even big-city newspapers avidly cover developments in the fast-food business.

Fast-food restaurants also play symbolic roles on television programs and in the movies. A skit on the legendary television show *Saturday Night Live* satirized specialty chains by detailing the hardships of a franchise that sells nothing but Scotch tape. In the movie *Coming to America* (1988), Eddie Murphy plays an African prince whose introduction to America includes a job at "McDowell's," a thinly disguised McDonald's. In *Falling Down* (1993), Michael Douglas vents his rage against the modern world in a fast-food restaurant dominated by mindless rules designed to frustrate customers. *Moscow on the Hudson* (1984) has Robin Williams, newly arrived from Russia, obtain a job at McDonald's. H.G. Wells, a central character in the movie *Time After Time* (1979), finds himself transported to the modern world of a McDonald's, where he tries to order the tea he was accustomed to drinking in Victorian England. In *Sleeper* (1973), Woody Allen awakens in the future only to encounter a McDonald's. *Tin Men* (1987) ends with the early 1960s heroes driving off into a future represented by a huge golden arch looming in the distance. *Scotland, PA* (2001) brings *Macbeth* to the Pennsylvania of the 1970s. The famous murder scene from the Shakespeare play involves, in this case, plunging a doughnut king's head into the boiling oil of a deep fat fryer. The McBeths then use their ill-gotten gains to transform the king's greasy spoon café into a fast-food restaurant featuring McBeth burgers.

Further proof that McDonald's has become a symbol of American culture is to be found in what happened when plans were made to raze Ray Kroc's first McDonald's restaurant. Hundreds of letters poured into McDonald's headquarters, including the following:

> Please don't tear it down! ... Your company's name is a household word, not only in the United States of America, but all over the world. To destroy this major artifact of contemporary culture would, indeed, destroy part of the faith the people of the world have in your company.

In the end, the restaurant was rebuilt according to the original blueprints and turned into a museum. A McDonald's executive explained the move: "McDonald's ... is really a part of Americana."

Americans aren't the only ones who feel this way. At the opening of the McDonald's in Moscow, one journalist described the franchise as the "ultimate icon of Americana." When Pizza Hut opened in Moscow in 1990, a Russian student said, "It's a piece of America." Reflecting on the growth of fast-food restaurants in Brazil, an executive associated with Pizza Hut of Brazil said that his nation "is experiencing a passion for things American." On the popularity of Kentucky Fried Chicken in Malaysia, the local owner said, "Anything Western, especially American, people here love.... They want to be associated with America."

One could go further and argue that in at least some ways McDonald's has become *more important* than the United States itself. Take the following story about a former US ambassador to Israel officiating at the opening of the first McDonald's in Jerusalem wearing a baseball hat with the McDonald's golden arches logo:

> An Israeli teen-ager walked up to him, carrying his own McDonald's hat, which he handed to Ambassador Indyk with a pen and asked: "Are you the Ambassador? Can I have your autograph?" Somewhat sheepishly, Ambassador Indyk replied: "Sure, I've never been asked for my autograph before."
>
> As the Ambassador prepared to sign his name, the Israeli teen-ager said to him, "Wow, what's it like to be the ambassador from McDonald's, going around the world opening McDonald's restaurants everywhere?" Ambassador Indyk looked at the Israeli youth and said, "No, no. I'm the American ambassador—not the ambassador from McDonald's!"

Ambassador Indyk described what happened next: "I said to him, 'Does this mean you don't want my autograph?' And the kid said, 'No, I don't want your autograph,' and he took his hat back and walked away."

Two other indices of the significance of McDonald's (and, implicitly, McDonaldization) are worth mentioning. The first is the annual "Big Mac Index" (part of "burgernomics") published by a prestigious magazine, *The Economist*. It indicates the purchasing power of various currencies around the world based on the local price (in dollars) of the Big Mac. The Big Mac is used because it is a uniform commodity sold in many different nations. In the 2003 survey, a Big Mac in the United States cost an average of $2.71; in China it was $1.20; in Switzerland it cost $4.52. This measure indicates, at least roughly, where the cost of living is high or low, as well as which currencies are undervalued (China) and which are overvalued (Switzerland). Although *The Economist* is calculating the Big Mac Index tongue-in-cheek, at least in part, the index represents the ubiquity and importance of McDonald's around the world.

The second indicator of McDonald's global significance is the idea developed by Thomas Friedman that "no two countries that both have a McDonald's have ever fought a war since they each got McDonald's." Friedman calls this the "Golden Arches Theory of Conflict Prevention." Another half-serious idea, it implies that the path to world peace lies through the continued international expansion of McDonald's. Unfortunately, it was proved wrong by the NATO bombing of Yugoslavia in 1999, which had sixteen McDonald's as of 2002.

To many people throughout the world, McDonald's has become a sacred institution. At that opening of the McDonald's in Moscow, a worker spoke of it "as if it were the Cathedral in Chartres ... a place to experience 'celestial joy.'" Kowinski argues that indoor shopping malls, which almost always encompass fast-food restaurants, are the modern "cathedrals of consumption" to which people go to practice their "consumer religion." Similarly, a visit to another central element of McDonaldized society, Walt Disney World, has been described as "the middle-class hajj, the compulsory visit to the sunbaked holy city."

McDonald's has achieved its exalted position because virtually all Americans, and many others, have passed through its golden arches on innumerable occasions. Furthermore, most of us have been bombarded by commercials extolling McDonald's virtues, commercials tailored to a variety of audiences and that change as the chain introduces new foods, new contests, and new product tie-ins. These ever-present commercials, combined with the fact that people cannot drive very far without having a McDonald's pop into view, have embedded McDonald's deeply in popular consciousness. A poll of school-age children showed that 96% of them could identify Ronald McDonald, second only to Santa Claus in name recognition.

Over the years, McDonald's has appealed to people in many ways. The restaurants themselves are depicted as spick-and-span, the food is said to be fresh and nutritious, the employees are shown to be young and eager, the managers appear gentle and caring, and the dining experience itself seems fun-filled. People are even led to believe that they contribute through their purchases, at least indirectly, to charities such as the Ronald McDonald Houses for sick children.

The Long-Arm of McDonaldization

McDonald's strives to continually extend its reach within American society and beyond. As the company's chairman said, "Our goal: to totally dominate the quick service restaurant industry worldwide.... I want McDonald's to be more than a leader. I want McDonald's to dominate."

McDonald's began as a phenomenon of suburbs and medium-sized towns, but in more recent years, it has moved into smaller towns that supposedly could not support such a restaurant and into many big cities that are supposedly too sophisticated. You can now find fast-food outlets in New York's Times Square as well as on the Champs-Elysées in Paris. Soon after it opened in 1992, the McDonald's in Moscow sold almost thirty thousand hamburgers a day and employed a staff of twelve hundred young people working two to a cash register. (Today McDonald's controls an astounding 83% of the fast-food market in Russia.) In early 1992, Beijing witnessed the opening of the world's largest McDonald's, with seven hundred seats, twenty-nine cash registers, and nearly one thousand employees. On its first day of business, it set a new one-day record for McDonald's by serving about forty thousand customers.

Small satellite, express, or remote outlets, opened in areas that cannot support full-scale fast-food restaurants, are also expanding rapidly. They are found in small storefronts in large cities and in nontraditional settings such as department stores, service stations, and even schools. These satellites typically offer only limited menus and may rely on larger outlets for food storage and preparation. McDonald's is considering opening express outlets in museums, office buildings, and corporate cafeterias. A flap occurred not long ago over the placement of a McDonald's in the new federal courthouse in Boston. Among the more striking sites for a McDonald's restaurant are the Grand Canyon, the world's tallest building (Petronas Towers in Malaysia), a ski-through on a slope in Sweden, and in a structure in Shrewsbury, England, that dates back to the 13th century.

No longer content to dominate the strips that surround many college campuses, fast-food restaurants have moved onto many of those campuses. The first campus fast-food restaurant opened at the University of Cincinnati in 1973. Today, college cafeterias often look like shopping-mall food courts (and it's no wonder, given that campus food service is a $9.5 billion-a-year business). In conjunction with a variety of "branded partners" (for example, Pizza Hut and Subway), Marriott now supplies food to many colleges and universities. The apparent approval of college administrations puts fast-food restaurants in a position to further influence the younger generation.

We no longer need to leave many highways to obtain fast food quickly and easily. Fast food is now available at many, and in some cases all, convenient rest stops along the road. After "refueling," we can proceed with our trip, which is likely to end in another community that has about the same density and mix of fast-food restaurants as the locale we left behind. Fast food is also increasingly available in hotels, railway stations, and airports.

In other sectors of society, the influence of fast-food restaurants has been subtler but no less profound. Food produced by McDonald's and other fast-food restaurants has begun to appear in high schools and trade schools; over 20% of school cafeterias offer popular brand-name fast foods such as Pizza Hut or Taco Bell at least once a week. Said the director of nutrition for the American School Food Service Association, "Kids today live in a world where fast food has become a way of life. For us to get kids to eat, period, we have to provide some familiar items." Few lower-grade schools as yet have in-house fast-food restaurants. However, many have had to alter school cafeteria menus and procedures to make fast food readily available. Apples, yogurt, and milk may go straight into the trash can, but hamburgers, fries, and shakes are devoured. The attempt to hook school-age children on fast food reached something of a peak in Illinois, where McDonald's operated a program called, "A for Cheeseburger." Students who received As on their report cards received a free cheeseburger, thereby linking success in school with rewards from McDonald's.

The military has also been pressed to offer fast food on both bases and ships. Despite the criticisms by physicians and nutritionists, fast-food outlets increasingly turn up inside hospitals. Although no homes yet have a McDonald's of their own, meals at home often resemble those available in fast-food restaurants. Frozen, microwavable, and prepared foods, which bear a striking resemblance to meals available at fast-food restaurants, often find their way to the dinner table. There are even cookbooks—for example, *Secret Fast Food Recipes: The Fast Food Cookbook*—that allow one to prepare "genuine" fast food at home. Then there is also home delivery of fast foods, especially pizza, as revolutionized by Domino's.

Another type of expansion involves what could be termed "vertical McDonaldization." That is, the demands of the fast-food industry, as is well documented in Eric Schlosser's *Fast Food Nation*, have forced industries that service it to McDonaldize in order to satisfy its insatiable demands. Thus, potato growing and processing, cattle ranching, chicken raising, and meat slaughtering and processing have all had to McDonaldize their operations, and this has led to dramatic increases in production. However, that growth has not come without costs. Meat and poultry are more likely to be disease-ridden, small (often non-McDonaldized) producers and ranchers have been driven out of business, and millions of people have been forced to work in low-paying, demeaning, demanding, and sometimes outright dangerous jobs. For example, in the meatpacking industry, relatively safe, unionized, secure, manageable, and relatively high-paying jobs in firms with once-household names like Swift and Armour have been replaced by unsafe, nonunionized, insecure, unmanageable, and relatively low-paying positions with largely anonymous corporations. While some (largely owners, managers, and stockholders) have profited enormously from vertical McDonaldization, far more have been forced into a marginal economic existence.

McDonald's is such a powerful model that many businesses have acquired nicknames beginning with Mc. Examples include "McDentists" and "McDoctors," meaning drive-in clinics designed to deal quickly and efficiently with minor dental and medical problems; "McChild" care centers, meaning child care centers such as KinderCare; "McStables," designating the nationwide racehorse-training operation of Wayne Lucas; and "McPaper," describing the newspaper USA TODAY.

McDonald's is not always enamored of this proliferation. Take the case of We Be Sushi, a San Francisco chain with a half dozen outlets. A note appears on the back of the menu explaining why the chain was not named "McSushi":

> The original name was *McSushi*. Our sign was up and we were ready to go. But before we could open our doors we received a very formal letter from the lawyers of, you guessed it, McDonald's. It seems that McDonald's has cornered the market on every McFood name possible from McBagle [sic] to McTaco. They explained that the use of the name McSushi would dilute the image of McDonald's.

So powerful is McDonaldization that the derivatives of McDonald's in turn exert their own influence. For example, the success of USA TODAY has led many newspapers across the nation to adopt, for example, shorter stories and colorful weather maps. As one USA TODAY editor said, "The same newspaper editors who call us McPaper have been stealing our McNuggets." Even serious journalistic enterprises such as the New York Times and Washington Post have undergone changes (for example, the use of color) as a result of the success of USA TODAY. The influence of USA TODAY is blatantly manifested in The Boca Raton News, which has been described as "a sort of smorgasbord of snippets, a newspaper that slices and dices the news into even smaller portions than does USA TODAY, spicing it with color graphics and fun facts and cute features like 'Today's Hero' and 'Critter Watch.'" As in USA TODAY, stories in The Boca Raton News usually start and finish on the same page. Many important details, much of a story's context, and much of what the principals have to say is cut back severely or omitted entirely. With its emphasis on light news and color graphics, the main function of the newspaper seems to be entertainment.

Like virtually every other sector of society, sex has undergone McDonaldization. In the movie Sleeper, Woody Allen not only created a futuristic world in which McDonald's was an important and highly visible element, but he also envisioned a society in which people could enter a machine called an "orgasmatron," to experience an orgasm without going through the muss and fuss of sexual intercourse.

Similarly, real-life "dial-a-porn" allows people to have intimate, sexually explicit, even obscene conversations with people they have never met and probably never will meet. There is great specialization here: Dialing numbers such as 555-FOXX will lead to a very different phone message than dialing 555-SEXY. Those who answer the phones mindlessly and repetitively follow "scripts" that have them say such things as, "Sorry, tiger, but your Dream Girl has to go.... Call right back and ask for me." Less scripted are phone sex systems (or Internet chat rooms) that permit erotic conversations between total strangers. The advent of the webcam now permits people even to see (though still not touch) the person with whom they are having virtual sex. As Woody Allen anticipated with his orgasmatron, "Participants can experience an orgasm without ever meeting or touching one another." "In a world where convenience is king, disembodied sex has its allure. You don't have to stir from your comfortable home. You pick up the phone, or log onto the computer and, if you're plugged in, a world of unheard of sexual splendor rolls out before your eyes." In New York City, an official called a three-story pornographic center "the McDonald's of sex" because of its "cookie-cutter cleanliness and compliance with the law." These examples suggest that no aspect of people's lives is immune to McDonaldization.

The Dimensions of McDonaldization

Why has the McDonald's model proven so irresistible? Eating fast food at McDonald's has certainly become a "sign" that, among other things, one is in tune with the contemporary lifestyle. There is also a kind of magic or enchantment associated with such food and its settings. However, the focus here is the four alluring dimensions that lie at the heart of the success of this model and, more generally, of McDonaldization. In short, McDonald's has succeeded because it offers consumers, workers, and managers efficiency, calculability, predictability, and control.

EFFICIENCY

One important element of McDonald's success is *efficiency*, or the optimum method for getting from one point to another. For consumers, McDonald's offers the best available way to get from being hungry to being full. In a society where both parents are likely to work or where a single parent is struggling to keep up, efficiently satisfying hunger is very attractive. In a society where people rush from one spot to another, usually by car, the efficiency of a fast-food meal, perhaps even a drive-through meal, often proves impossible to resist.

The fast-food model offers, or at least appears to offer, an efficient method for satisfying many other needs as well. Woody Allen's orgasmatron offered an efficient method for getting people from quiescence to sexual gratification. Other institutions fashioned on the McDonald's model offer similar efficiency in losing weight, lubricating cars, getting new glasses or contacts, or completing income tax forms.

Like their customers, workers in McDonaldized systems function efficiently following the steps in a predesigned process. They are trained to work this way by managers who watch over them closely to make sure that they do. Organizational rules and regulations also help ensure highly efficient work.

CALCULABILITY

Calculability is an emphasis on the quantitative aspects of products sold (portion size, cost) and services offered (the time it takes to get the product). In McDonaldized systems, quantity has become equivalent to quality; a lot of something, or the quick delivery of it, means it must be good. As two observers of contemporary American culture put it, "As a culture, we tend to believe deeply that in general 'bigger is better.'" Thus, people order the Quarter Pounder, the Big Mac, the large fries. More recent lures are the "double" this (for instance, Burger King's "Double Whopper with Cheese") and the "super-size" that. People can quantify these things and feel that they are getting a lot of food for what appears to be a nominal sum of money (best exemplified by McDonald's current "dollar menu"). This calculation does not take into account an important point, however: The high profit margin of fast-food chains indicates that the owners, not the consumers, get the best deal.

People also tend to calculate how much time it will take to drive to McDonald's, be served the food, eat it, and return home; then, they compare that interval to the time required to prepare food at home. They often conclude, rightly or wrongly, that a trip to the fast-food restaurant will take less time than eating at home. This sort of calculation particularly supports home delivery franchises such as Domino's, as well as other chains that emphasize time saving. A notable example of time saving in another sort of chain is LensCrafters, which promises people "Glasses fast, glasses in one hour."

Some McDonaldized institutions combine the emphases on time and money. Domino's promises pizza delivery in half an hour, or the pizza is free. Pizza Hut will serve a personal pan pizza in five minutes, or it, too, will be free. Workers in McDonaldized systems also tend to emphasize the quantitative rather than the qualitative aspects of their work. Since the quality of the work is allowed to vary little, workers focus on things such as how quickly tasks can be accomplished. In a situation analogous to that of the customer, workers are expected to do a lot of work, very quickly, for low pay.

PREDICTABILITY

McDonald's also offers *predictability*, the assurance that products and services will be the same over time and in all locales. The Egg McMuffin in New York will be, for all intents and purposes, identical to those in Chicago and Los Angeles.

Also, those eaten next week or next year will be identical to those eaten today. Customers take great comfort in knowing that McDonald's offers no surprises. People know that the next Egg McMuffin they eat will not be awful, although it will not be exceptionally delicious, either. The success of the McDonald's model suggests that many people have come to prefer a world in which there are few surprises. "This is strange," notes a British observer, "considering [McDonald's is] the product of a culture which honours individualism above all."

The workers in McDonaldized systems also behave in predictable ways. They follow corporate rules as well as the dictates of third managers. In many cases, what they do, and even what they say, is highly predictable. McDonaldized organizations often have scripts (perhaps the best-known is McDonald's, "Do you want fries with that?") that employees are supposed to memorize and follow whenever the occasion arises. This scripted behavior helps create highly predictable interactions between workers and customers. While customers do not follow scripts, they tend to develop simple recipes for dealing with the employees of McDonaldized systems. As Robin Leidner argues,

> McDonald's pioneered the reutilization of interactive service work and remains an exemplar of extreme standardization. Innovation is not discouraged ... at least among managers and franchisees. Ironically, though, "the object is to look for new, innovative ways to create an experience that is exactly the same no matter what McDonald's you walk into, no matter where it is in the world."

CONTROL THROUGH NONHUMAN TECHNOLOGY

The fourth element in McDonald's success, *control*, is exerted over the people who enter the world of McDonald's. Lines, limited menus, few options, and uncomfortable seats all lead diners to do what management wishes them to do—eat quickly and leave. Furthermore, the drive-through (in some cases, walk-through) window leads diners to leave before they eat. In the Domino's model, customers never enter in the first place.

The people who work in McDonaldized organizations are also controlled to a high degree, usually more blatantly and directly than customers. They are trained to do a limited number of things in precisely the way they are told to do them. The technologies used and the way the organization is set up reinforce this control. Managers and inspectors make sure that workers toe the line.

McDonald's also controls employees by threatening to use, and ultimately using, technology to replace human workers. No matter how well they are programmed and controlled, workers can foul up the system's operation. A slow worker can make the preparation and delivery of a Big Mac inefficient. A worker who refuses to follow the rules might leave the pickles or special sauce off a hamburger, thereby making for unpredictability. And a distracted worker can put too few fries in the box, making an order of large fries seem skimpy. For these and other reasons, McDonald's and other fast-food restaurants have felt compelled to steadily replace human beings with machines. Technology that increases control over workers helps McDonaldized systems assure customers that their products and service will be consistent.

The Advantages of McDonaldization

This discussion of four fundamental characteristics of McDonaldization makes it clear that McDonald's has succeeded so phenomenally for good, solid reasons. Many knowledgeable people such as the economic columnist, Robert Samuelson, strongly support McDonald's business model. Samuelson confesses to "openly worship[ing] McDonald's," and he thinks of it as "the greatest restaurant chain in history." In addition, McDonald's offers many praiseworthy programs that benefit society, such as its Ronald McDonald Houses, which permit parents to stay with children undergoing treatment for serious medical problems; job-training programs for teenagers; programs to help keep its employees in school; efforts to hire and train the handicapped; the McMasters program, aimed at hiring senior citizens; an enviable record of hiring and promoting minorities; and a social responsibility program with social goals improving the environment and animal welfare.

The process of McDonaldization also moved ahead dramatically undoubtedly because it has led to positive changes. Here are a few specific examples:

- A wider range of goods and services is available to a much larger portion of the population than ever before.
- Availability of goods and services depends far less than before on time or geographic location; people can do things, such as obtain money at the grocery store or a bank balance in the middle of the night, that were impossible before.
- People are able to get what they want or need almost instantaneously and get it far more conveniently.
- Goods and services are of a far more uniform quality; at least some people even get better quality goods and services than before McDonaldization.
- Far more economical alternatives to high-priced, customized goods and services are widely available; therefore, people can afford things they could not previously afford.
- Fast, efficient goods and services are available to a population that is working longer hours and has fewer hours to spare.
- In a rapidly changing, unfamiliar, and seemingly hostile world, the comparatively stable, familiar, and safe environment of a McDonaldized system offers comfort.

- Because of quantification, consumers can more easily compare competing products.
- Certain products (for example, diet programs) are safer in a carefully regulated and controlled system.
- People are more likely to be treated similarly, no matter what their race, gender, or social class.
- Organizational and technological innovations are more quickly and easily diffused through networks of identical operators.
- The most popular products of one culture are more easily diffused to others.

A Critique of McDonaldization: The Irrationality of Rationality

Although McDonaldization offers powerful advantages, it has a downside. Efficiency, predictability, calculability, and control through nonhuman technology can be thought of as the basic components of a rational system. However, rational systems inevitably spawn irrationalities. Another way of saying this is that rational systems serve to deny human reason; rational systems are often unreasonable. The downside of McDonaldization will be dealt with most systematically under the heading of the irrationality of rationality; in fact, paradoxically, the irrationality of rationality can be thought of as the fifth dimension of McDonaldization.

For example, McDonaldization has produced a wide array of adverse effects on the environment. One is a side effect of the need to grow uniform potatoes from which to create predictable french fries. The huge farms of the Pacific Northwest that now produce such potatoes rely on the extensive use of chemicals. In addition, the need to produce a perfect fry means that much of the potato is wasted, with the remnants either fed to cattle or used for fertilizer. The underground water supply in the area is now showing high levels of nitrates, which may be traceable to the fertilizer and animal wastes. Many other ecological problems are associated with the McDonaldization of the fast-food industry: the forests felled to produce paper wrappings, the damage caused by packaging materials, the enormous amount of food needed to produce feed cattle, and so on.

Another unreasonable effect is that fast-food restaurants are often dehumanizing settings in which to eat or work. Customers lining up for a burger or waiting in the drive-through line and workers preparing the food often feel as though they are part of an assembly line. Hardly amenable to eating, assembly lines have been shown to be inhuman settings in which to work.

Such criticisms can be extended to all facets of the McDonaldizing world. For example, at the opening of Euro Disney, a French politician said that it will "bombard France with uprooted creations that are to culture what fast food is to gastronomy."

As you have seen, McDonaldization offers many advantages. However, this book will focus on the great costs, and enormous risks of McDonaldization. McDonald's and other purveyors of the fast-food model spend billions of dollars each year outlining the benefits of their system. However, critics of the system have few outlets for their ideas. For example, no one is offering commercials between Saturday-morning cartoons warning children of the dangers associated with fast-food restaurants.

Nonetheless, a legitimate question may be raised about this critique of McDonaldization: Is it animated by a romanticization of the past and an impossible desire to return to a world that no longer exists? Some critics do base their critiques on nostalgia for a time when life was slower and offered more surprises, when people were freer, and when one was more likely to deal with a human being than a robot or a computer. Although they have a point, these critics have undoubtedly exaggerated the positive aspects of a world without McDonald's, and they have certainly tended to forget the liabilities associated with earlier eras. As an example of the latter, take the following anecdote about a visit to a pizzeria in Havana, Cuba, which in many respects is decades behind the United States:

The pizza's not much to rave about—they scrimp on tomato sauce, and the dough is mushy.

It was about 7:30 P.M., and as usual the place was standing-room-only, with people two deep jostling for a stool to come open and a waiting line spilling out onto the sidewalk.

The menu is similarly Spartan.... To drink, there is tap water. That's it—no toppings, no soda, no beer, no coffee, no salt, no pepper. And no special orders.

A very few people are eating. Most are waiting.... Fingers are drumming, flies are buzzing, the clock is ticking. The waiter wears a watch around his belt loop, but he hardly needs it; time is evidently not his chief concern. After a while, tempers begin to fray.

But right now, it's 8:45 P.M. at the pizzeria, I've been waiting an hour and a quarter for two small pies.

Few would prefer such a restaurant to the fast, friendly, diverse offerings of, say, Pizza Hut. More important, however, critics who revere the past do not seem to realize that we are not returning to such a world. In fact, fast-food restaurants have begun to appear even in Havana. The increase in the number of people crowding the planet, the acceleration of technological change, the increasing pace of life—all this and more make it impossible to go back to the world, if it ever existed, of home-cooked meals, traditional restaurant dinners, high-quality foods, meals loaded with surprises, and restaurants run by chefs free to express their creativity.

It is more valid to critique McDonaldization from the perspective of the future. Unfettered by the constraints of McDonaldized systems, but using the technological advances made possible by them, people would have the potential to be far more thoughtful, skillful, creative, and well-rounded than they are now. In short, if the world were less McDonaldized, people would be better able to live up to their human potential.

We must look at McDonaldization as both "enabling" and "constraining." McDonaldized systems enable us to do many things that we were not able to do in the past. However, these systems also keep us from doing things we otherwise would not do. McDonaldization is a "double-edged" phenomenon. We must not lose sight of that fact, even though this book will focus on the constraints associated with McDonaldization—its "dark side."

What Isn't McDonaldized?

This chapter should give you a sense not only of the advantages and disadvantages of McDonaldization but also of the range of phenomena discussed throughout this book. In fact, such a wide range of phenomena can be linked to McDonaldization that you may be led to wonder what isn't McDonaldized. Is McDonaldization the equivalent of modernity? Is everything contemporary McDonaldized?

Although much of the world has been McDonaldized, at least three aspects of contemporary society have largely escaped the process:

- Those aspects traceable to an earlier, "premodern" age. A good example is the mom-and-pop grocery store.
- New businesses that have sprung up or expanded, at least in part, as a reaction against McDonaldization. For instance, people fed up with McDonaldized motel rooms in Holiday Inns or Motel 6s can instead stay in a bed-and-breakfast, which offers a room in a private home with personalized attention and a homemade breakfast from the proprietor.
- Those aspects suggesting a move toward a new, "postmodern" age. For example, in a postmodern society, "modern" high-rise housing projects would make way for smaller, more livable communities.

Thus, although McDonaldization is ubiquitous, there is more to the contemporary world than McDonaldization. It is a very important social process, but it is far from the only process transforming contemporary society.

Furthermore, McDonaldization is not an all-or-nothing process. There are degrees of McDonaldization. Fast-food restaurants, for example, have been heavily McDonaldized, universities moderately McDonaldized, and mom-and-pop groceries only slightly McDonaldized. It is difficult to think of social phenomena that have escaped McDonaldization totally, but some local enterprise in Fiji may yet be untouched by this process.

McDonald's Troubles: Implications for McDonaldization

McDonald's has been much in the news in the early 21st century, and most of the time, the news has been bad (at least for McDonald's)—bombings (some involving fatalities) and protests at restaurants overseas, lawsuits claiming that its food made people obese and that it mislabeled some food as vegetarian, declining stock prices, and its first-ever quarterly loss. McDonald's has responded by withdrawing from several nations, settling lawsuits, closing restaurants, reducing staff, cutting planned expansions, replacing top officials, and remodeling restaurants.

It is hard to predict whether the current situation is merely a short-term downturn to be followed by renewed expansion or the beginning of the end of McDonald's (after all, even the Roman Empire, to say nothing of A&P and Woolworth's, among many others, eventually declined and disappeared).

For the sake of discussion, let's take the worst-case scenario—McDonald's imminently turning off the griddles in the last of its restaurants.

This would clearly be a disastrous event as far as stockholders, franchisees, employees, and devotees of Big Macs and Chicken McNuggets are concerned, but what of its broader implications for the McDonaldization of society? The hypothetical demise of McDonald's would spell the end of the model for this process, but it would be of *no consequence* to the process itself. We might need to find a new model and label—"Starbuckization" suggests itself at the moment because of Starbucks' great current success and its dramatic expansion around the globe— but whatever we call it, the process itself will not only continue but grow more powerful. Can we really envision an alternative future of increasing inefficiency, unpredictability, incalculability, and *less* reliance on new technology?

In the restaurant industry, the decline and eventual disappearance of McDonald's would simply mean greater possibilities for its competitors (Subway, Wendy's) and open the way for more innovative chains (In-N-Out Burger). However, which fast-food chains dominate would be of little consequence to the process of McDonaldization since *all of them* are highly McDonaldized and all are based on the model pioneered by McDonald's. What would be of consequence would be a major revival of old-fashioned, non-McDonaldized alternatives like cafes, "greasy spoons," diners, cafeterias, and the like. However, these are not likely to undergo significant expansion unless some organization finds a way to successfully McDonaldize them. And if they do, it would simply be the McDonaldization of yet another domain.

What is certainly *not* going to happen is a return to the pre-McDonald's era dominated by the kinds of alternatives mentioned above. Can we really envision the approximately 13,000 sites currently occupied by McDonald's restaurants in the United States being filled by a like number of independently owned and operated cafes and diners? The problem of finding skilled short-order cooks to staff them pales in comparison to the difficulty in finding people who will frequent them. It's been nearly fifty years since the franchise revolutionized the fast-food industry with the opening of the first of the McDonald's chain. The vast majority of Americans have known little other than the McDonaldized world of fast food, and for those born before 1955, the alternatives are increasingly dim memories. Thus, McDonaldized systems for the delivery of fast food (e.g., drive-through lanes, home-delivered pizzas), and the McDonaldized food itself (Whoppers, Taco Bell's watered-down version of the taco), have become the standards for many people. A hamburger made on the grill at a diner or a taco from an authentic taco stand are likely to be judged inferior to the more McDonaldized versions. Furthermore, those who are accustomed to the enormous efficiency of the fast-food restaurant are unlikely to put up with the relative inefficiencies of diners or taco stands. Those who have grown used to great predictability are not likely to be comfortable with food served in wildly different quantities and shapes. The greater human involvement in preparing and serving food in non-McDonaldized alternatives is likely to be off-putting to most consumers who have grown acclimated to the dehumanization associated with the nonhuman technologies and scripted counter people found throughout today's fast-food industry. The key point is that McDonald's current difficulties do not auger a return to earlier non-McDonaldized alternatives or even to the widespread creation (if one could even envision such a thing) of some new non-McDonaldized form.

McDonald's is doing better outside the United States, and it is there that we are likely to see a continued expansion of it, and other American fast-food chains, for the foreseeable future (by all accounts, the American market for fast-food restaurants is saturated, and this is a big source of McDonald's problems). More important, as pointed out earlier, many other nations have witnessed the emergence of their own fast-food chains modeled, naturally, after McDonald's. Not only are they expanding within their own borders, but they are also increasingly interested in global expansion (Britain's Pizza Express is expanding into Eastern European countries as San Marzano restaurants), even into the American market. Interesting recent examples include the opening in Manhattan of a number of Pret A Manger (the British chain that, as we have seen, is partly owned by McDonald's) shops offering higher-quality, prewrapped sandwiches, and Polio Capero (from Guatemala) fried-chicken restaurants in Los Angeles and Houston (with plans for big expansion in the United States). In fact, the center of McDonaldization, as was previously the case with many forms of factory production, is increasingly shifting outside the United States. Whether it occurs under the name of Mos Burger (Japan) or Nirula's (India), it is still McDonaldization.

If the principles have proven successful and have proliferated so widely, why is McDonald's in trouble? There are obviously a number of reasons, including many bungled opportunities and initiatives such as efforts to be more attractive to adults, to create new menu items, and to restructure restaurants as well as the chain as a whole. While McDonald's could have done better, the fact is that in the end it has been undercut by its own success. Many competitors have adopted its principles and entered the niche created by McDonald's for fast food. Like many other innovators, McDonald's now finds itself with many rivals who learned not only from McDonald's successes but also from its failures. (One could say that these competitors are "eating McDonald's lunch.") McDonald's, too, may now be better able to overcome its problems and learn from the hot new companies in the fast-food industry. However, whether or not it does, fast-food restaurants and, more generally, the process of McDonaldization are with us for the foreseeable future.

Source: *The McDonaldization of Society 5*. Los Angeles, London, New Delhi: Pine Forge, 2008. 1-24.

WHAT IT SAYS

1. What does Ritzer mean by the term "McDonaldization of society"?

2. Why does Ritzer use McDonald's as the model for a process of standardization that has spread to other restaurants and businesses sectors?

3. What are the global implications of Ritzer's argument about McDonaldization?

4. What are the advantages and what are the disadvantages of McDonaldization, according to Ritzer? What criticism of McDonaldization does Ritzer reject? What criticism does he accept?

5. In what ways can the positive aspects of McDonaldization be retained while its negative aspects are eliminated, according to Ritzer?

HOW IT SAYS IT

1. Ritzer claims that McDonald's and other franchises have rapidly expanded across the globe in recent decades. What evidence does he use to support this claim?

2. What is the effect of Ritzer's use of a numbered format for presenting his case about the McDonaldization of society?

3. Ritzer makes sweeping claims describing a global phenomenon that he calls McDonaldization. Characterize the language choices Ritzer makes to carry his argument.

WRITE ABOUT IT

1. Write an **autoethnography** in which you explore the impact of McDonaldization on your life. What aspects of your experience have been affected by McDonaldization? What areas of your life have not been touched by its reach? What has been your personal response to the standardization of culture and society that Ritzer describes?

2. Write an essay that describes a future in which McDonaldization has either disappeared or expanded exponentially.

3. Critique Ritzer's essay as an example of the McDonaldization of writing.

c. Benjamin Barber, "Jihad vs. McWorld"

Benjamin Barber is Gershon and Carol Kekst Professor of Civil Society and Distinguished University Professor at the University of Maryland, and a principal of the Democracy Collaborative. He is the author of numerous books, including *Fear's Empire: War, Terrorism, and Democracy in an Age of Interdependence* (2003), *Strong Democracy: Participatory Politics for a New Age* (Twentieth Anniversary Revision 2004), and *Consumed: How Markets Corrupt Children, Infantilize Adults, and Swallow Citizens Whole* (2007). Barber received a certificate from the London School of Economics and MA and PhD degrees from Harvard University.

The following essay is the introduction to Barber's book *Jihad vs. McWorld: How Globalism and Tribalism Are Reshaping the World*, published in 1996. Barber sees two opposing and mutually dependent forces shaping global cultures and affecting political life. By "Jihad" he means the provincial, tribal, and often religious beliefs and ways of life that resist, sometimes violently, the expansion of Western cultural and economic hegemony. By "McWorld" he means the processes of global capitalism that threaten to overwhelm indigenous cultures. Both of these forces threaten the national sovereignty of nation-states, which Barber sees as indispensible for democracy. Barber's book, written before 9/11, has proven to be a prescient analysis of contemporary global issues.

As You Read: Barber notes many cases of the interplay of "Jihad" and "McWorld." Many of these historical events and developments may be unfamiliar to you, yet others surely are not. Look up at least one unfamiliar scenario and consider whether Barber's explanation makes sense with reference to it.

Jihad vs. McWorld

History is not over. Nor are we arrived in the wondrous land of techné promised by the futurologists. The collapse of state communism has not delivered people to a safe democratic haven, and the past, fratricide and civil discord perduring, still clouds the horizon just behind us. Those who look back see all of the horrors of the ancient slaughterbench reenacted in disintegral nations like Bosnia, Sri Lanka, Ossetia, and Rwanda and they declare that nothing has changed. Those who look forward prophesize commercial and technological interdependence—a virtual paradise made possible by spreading markets and global technology—and they proclaim that everything is or soon will be different. The rival observers seem to consult different almanacs drawn from the libraries of contrarian planets.

Yet anyone who reads the daily papers carefully, taking in the front page accounts of civil carnage as well as the business page stories on the mechanics of the information superhighway and the economics of communication mergers, anyone who turns deliberately to take in the whole 360 degree horizon, knows that our world and our lives are caught between what William Butler Yeats called the two eternities of race and soul: that of race reflecting the tribal past, that of soul anticipating the cosmopolitan future. Our secular eternities are corrupted, however, race reduced to an insignia of resentment, and soul sized down to fit the demanding body by which it now measures its needs. Neither race nor soul offers us a future that is other than bleak, neither promises a polity that is remotely democratic.

The first scenario rooted in race holds out the grim prospect of a retribalization of large swaths of humankind by war and bloodshed: a threatened balkanization of nationstates in which culture is pitted against culture, people against people, tribe against tribe, a Jihad in the name of a hundred narrowly conceived faiths against every kind of interdependence, every kind of artificial social cooperation and mutuality: against technology, against pop culture, and against integrated markets; against modernity itself as well as the future in which modernity issues. The second paints that future in shimmering pastels, a busy portrait of onrushing economic, technological, and ecological forces that demand integration and uniformity and that mesmerize peoples everywhere with fast music, fast computers, and fast food—MTV, Macintosh, and McDonald's—pressing nations into one homogenous global theme park, one McWorld tied together by communications, information, entertainment, and commerce. Caught between Babel and Disneyland, the planet is falling precipitously apart and coming reluctantly together at the very same moment.

Some stunned observers notice only Babel, complaining about the thousand newly sundered "peoples" who prefer to address their neighbors with sniper rifles and mortars; others—zealots in Disneyland—seize on futurological platitudes and the promise of virtuality, exclaiming "It's a small world after all!" Both are right, but how can that be?

We are compelled to choose between what passes as "the twilight of sovereignty" and an entropic end of all history; or a return to the past's most fractious and demoralizing discord; to "the menace of global anarchy," to Milton's capital of hell, Pandaemonium; to a world totally "out of control."

The apparent truth, which speaks to the paradox at the core of this book, is that the tendencies of both Jihad *and* McWorld are at work, both visible sometimes in the same country at the very same instant. Iranian zealots keep one ear tuned to the mullahs urging holy war and the other cocked to Rupert Murdoch's Star television beaming in *Dynasty*, *Donahue*, and *The Simpsons* from hovering satellites. Chinese entrepreneurs vie for the attention of party cadres in Beijing and simultaneously pursue KFC franchises in cities like Nanjing, Hangzhou, and Xian where twenty-eight outlets serve over 100,000 customers a day. The Russian

Orthodox church, even as it struggles to renew the ancient faith, has entered a joint venture with California businessmen to bottle and sell natural waters under the rubric Saint Springs Water Company. Serbian assassins wear Adidas sneakers and listen to Madonna on Walkman headphones as they take aim through their gunscopes at scurrying Sarajevo civilians looking to fill family watercans. Orthodox Hasids and brooding neo-Nazis have both turned to rock music to get their traditional messages out to the new generation, while fundamentalists plot virtual conspiracies on the Internet.

Now neither Jihad nor McWorld is in itself novel. History ending in the triumph of science and reason or some monstrous perversion thereof (Mary Shelley's Doctor Frankenstein) has been the leitmotiv of every philosopher and poet who has regretted the Age of Reason since the Enlightenment. Yeats lamented "the center will not hold, mere anarchy is loosed upon the world," and observers of Jihad today have little but historical detail to add. The Christian parable of the Fall and of the possibilities of redemption that it makes possible captures the eighteenth-century ambivalence—and our own—about past and future. I want, however, to do more than dress up the central paradox of human history in modern clothes. It is not Jihad and McWorld but the relationship between them that most interests me. For, squeezed between their opposing forces, the world has been sent spinning out of control. Can it be that what Jihad and McWorld have in common is anarchy: the absence of common will and that conscious and collective human control under the guidance of law we call democracy?

Progress moves in steps that sometimes lurch backwards; in history's twisting maze, Jihad not only revolts against but abets McWorld, while McWorld not only imperils but recreates and reinforces Jihad. They produce their contraries and need one another. My object here then is not simply to offer sequential portraits of McWorld and Jihad, but while examining McWorld, to keep Jihad in my field of vision, and while dissecting Jihad, never to forget the context of McWorld. Call it a dialectic of McWorld: a study in the cunning of reason that does honor to the radical differences that distinguish Jihad and McWorld yet that acknowledges their powerful and paradoxical interdependence.

There is a crucial difference, however, between my modest attempt at dialectic and that of the masters of the nineteenth century. Still seduced by the Enlightenment's faith in progress, both Hegel and Marx believed reason's cunning was on the side of progress. But it is harder to believe that the clash of Jihad and McWorld will issue in some overriding good. The outcome seems more likely to pervert than to nurture human liberty. The two may, in opposing each other, work to the same ends, work in apparent tension yet in covert harmony, but democracy is not their beneficiary. In East Berlin, tribal communism has yielded to capitalism. In Marx-Engelsplatz, the stolid, overbearing statues of Marx and Engels face east, as if seeking distant solace from Moscow: but now, circling them along the streets that surround the park that is their prison are chain eateries like TGI Friday's, international hotels like the Radisson, and a circle of neon billboards mocking them with brand names like Panasonic, Coke, and GoldStar. New gods, yes, but more liberty?

What then does it mean in concrete terms to view Jihad and McWorld dialectically when the tendencies of the two sets of forces initially appear so intractably antithetical? After all, Jihad and McWorld operate with equal strength in opposite directions, the one driven by parochial hatreds, the other by universalizing markets, the one recreating ancient subnational and ethnic borders from within, the other making national borders porous from without. Yet Jihad and McWorld have this in common: they both make war on the sovereign nationstate and thus undermine the nation-state's democratic institutions. Each eschews civil society and belittles democratic citizenship, neither seeks alternative democratic institutions. Their common thread is indifference to civil liberty. Jihad forges communities of blood rooted in exclusion and hatred, communities that slight democracy in favor of tyrannical paternalism or consensual tribalism. McWorld forges global markets rooted in consumption and profit, leaving to an untrustworthy, if not altogether fictitious, invisible hand issues of public interest and common good that once might have been nurtured by democratic citizenries and their watchful governments. Such governments, intimidated by market ideology, are actually pulling back at the very moment they ought to be aggressively intervening. What was once understood as protecting the public interest is now excoriated as heavyhanded regulatory browbeating. Justice yields to markets, even though, as Felix Rohatyn has bluntly confessed, "there is a brutal Darwinian logic to these markets. They are nervous and greedy. They look for stability and transparency, but what they reward is not always our preferred form of democracy." If the traditional conservators of freedom were democratic constitutions and Bills of Rights, "the new temples to liberty," George Steiner suggests, "will be McDonald's and Kentucky Fried Chicken."

In being reduced to a choice between the market's universal church and a retribalizing politics of particularist identities, peoples around the globe are threatened with an atavistic return to medieval politics where local tribes and ambitious emperors together ruled the world entire, women and men united by the universal abstraction of Christianity even as they lived out isolated lives in warring fiefdoms defined by involuntary (ascriptive) forms of identity. This was a world in which princes and kings had little real power until they conceived the ideology of nationalism. Nationalism established government on a scale greater than the tribe yet less cosmopolitan than the universal church and in time gave birth to those intermediate, gradually more democratic institutions that would come to constitute the nationstate. Today, at the far end of this history, we seem intent on recreating a world in which our only choices are the secular universalism of the cosmopolitan market and the everyday particularism of the fractious tribe.

In the tumult of the confrontation between global commerce and parochial ethnicity, the virtues of the democratic nation are lost and the instrumentalities by which it permitted peoples to transform themselves into nations and seize sovereign power in the name of liberty and the commonweal are put at risk. Neither Jihad nor McWorld aspires to resecure the civic virtues undermined by its denationalizing practices; neither global markets nor blood communities service public goods or pursue equality and justice. Impartial judiciaries and deliberative assemblies play no role in the roving killer bands that speak on behalf of newly liberated "peoples," and such democratic institutions have at best only marginal influence on the roving multinational corporations that speak on behalf of newly liberated markets. Jihad pursues a bloody politics of identity, McWorld a bloodless economics of profit. Belonging by default to McWorld, everyone is a consumer; seeking a repository for identity, everyone belongs to some tribe. But no one is a citizen. Without citizens, how can there be democracy? [...]

Jihad is, I recognize, a strong term. In its mildest form, it betokens religious struggle on behalf of faith, a kind of Islamic zeal. In its strongest political manifestation, it means bloody holy war on behalf of partisan identity that is metaphysically defined and fanatically defended. Thus, while for many Muslims it may signify only ardor in the name of a religion that can properly be regarded as universalizing (if not quite ecumenical), I borrow its meaning from those militants who make the slaughter of the "other" a higher duty. I use the term in its militant construction to suggest dogmatic and violent particularism of a kind known to Christians no less than Muslims, to Germans and Hindis as well as to Arabs. The phenomena to which I apply the phrase have innocent enough beginnings: identity politics and multicultural diversity can represent strategies of a free society trying to give expression to its diversity. What ends as Jihad may begin as a simple search for a local identity, some set of common personal attributes to hold out against the numbing and neutering uniformities of industrial modernization and the colonizing culture of McWorld.

America is often taken as the model for this kind of benign multiculturalism, although we too have our critics like Arthur Schlesinger, Jr., for whom multiculturalism is never benign and for whom it signals the inaugural logic of a long-term disintegration. Indeed, I will have occasion below to write about an "American Jihad" being waged by the radical Right. The startling fact is that less than 10 percent (about twenty) of the modern world's states are truly homogenous and thus, like Denmark or the Netherlands, can't get smaller unless they fracture into tribes or clans. In only half is there a single ethnic group that comprises even 75 percent of the population. As in the United States, multiculturalism is the rule, homogeneity the exception. Nations like Japan or Spain that appear to the outside world as integral turn out to be remarkably multicultural. And even if language alone, the nation's essential attribute, is made the condition for self-determination, a count of the number of languages spoken around the world suggests the community of nations could grow to over six thousand members.

The modern nation-state has actually acted as a cultural integrator and has adapted well to pluralist ideals: civic ideologies and constitutional faiths around which their many clans and tribes can rally. It has not been too difficult to contrive a civil religion for Americans or French or Swiss, since these "peoples" actually contain multitudes of subnational factions and ethnic tribes earnestly seeking common ground. But for Basques and Normans? What need have they for anything but blood and memory? And what of Alsatians, Bavarians, and East Prussians? Kurds, Ossetians, East Timorese, Quebecois, Abkhazians, Catalonians, Tamils, Inkatha Zulus, Kurile Islander Japanese—peoples without countries inhabiting nations they cannot call their own? Peoples trying to seal themselves off not just from others but from modernity? These are frightened tribes running not to but from civic faith in search of something more palpable and electrifying. How will peoples who define themselves by the slaughter of tribal neighbors be persuaded to subscribe to some flimsy artificial faith organized around abstract civic ideals or commercial markets? Can advertising divert warriors of blood from the genocide required by their ancient grievances? [...]

McWorld is a product of popular culture driven by expansionist commerce. Its template is American, its form style. Its goods are as much images as matériel, an aesthetic as well as a product line. It is about culture as commodity, apparel as ideology. Its symbols are Harley-Davidson motorcycles and Cadillac motorcars hoisted from the roadways, where they once represented a mode of transportation, to the marquees of global market cafés like Harley-Davidson's and the Hard Rock where they become icons of lifestyle. You don't drive them, you feel their vibes and rock to the images they conjure up from old movies and new celebrities, whose personal appearances are the key to the wildly popular international café chain Planet Hollywood. Music, video, theater, books, and theme parks—the new churches of a commercial civilization in which malls are the public squares and suburbs the neighborless neighborhoods—are all constructed as image exports creating a common world taste around common logos, advertising slogans, stars, songs, brand names, jingles, and trademarks. Hard power yields to soft, while ideology is transmuted into a kind of videology that works through sound bites and film clips. Videology is fuzzier and less dogmatic than traditional political ideology: it may as a consequence be far more successful in instilling the novel values required for global markets to succeed.

McWorld's videology remains Jihad's most formidable rival, and in the long run it may attenuate the force of Jihad's recidivist tribalisms. Yet the information revolution's instrumentalities are also Jihad's favored weapons. Hutu or Bosnian Serb identity was less a matter of real historical memory than of media propaganda by a leadership set on liquidating rival clans. In both Rwanda and Bosnia, radio broadcasts whipped listeners into a killing frenzy. As *New York Times* rock critic Jon Pareles has noticed, "regionalism in pop music has become as trendy as microbrewery beer and narrowcasting cable channels, and for the same reasons."

The global culture is what gives the local culture its medium, its audience, and its aspirations. Fascist pop and Hasid rock are not oxymorons; rather they manifest the dialectics of McWorld in particularly dramatic ways. Belgrade's radio includes stations that broadcast Western pop music as a rebuke to hardliner Milosevic's supernationalist government and stations that broadcast native folk tunes laced with anti-foreign and anti-Semitic sentiments. Even the Internet has its neo-Nazi bulletin boards and Turk-trashing Armenian "flamers" (who assail every use of the word *turkey*, fair and fowl alike, so to speak), so that the abstractions of cyberspace too are infected with a peculiar and rabid cultural territoriality all their own.

The dynamics of the Jihad-McWorld linkage are deeply dialectical. Japan has, for example, become more culturally insistent on its own traditions in recent years even as its people seek an ever greater purchase on McWorld. In 1992, the number one restaurant in Japan measured by volume of customers was McDonald's, followed in the number-two spot by the Colonel's Kentucky Fried Chicken. In France, where cultural purists complain bitterly of a looming Sixième République ("la République Américaine"), the government attacks "franglais" even as it funds EuroDisney park just outside of Paris. In the same spirit, the cinema industry makes war on American film imports while it bestows upon Sylvester Stallone one of France's highest honors, the Chevalier des arts et des lettres. Ambivalence also stalks India. just outside of Bombay, cheek by jowl with villages still immersed in poverty and notorious for the informal execution of unwanted female babies or, even, wives, can be found a new town known as SCEEPZ—the Santa Cruz Electronic Export Processing Zone—where Hindi, Tamil, and Mahrarti-speaking computer programmers write software for Swissair, AT&T, and other labor-cost-conscious multinationals. India is thus at once a major exemplar of ancient ethnic and religious tensions and "an emerging power in the international software industry." To go to work at SCEEPZ, says an employee, is "like crossing an international border." Not into another country, but into the virtual nowhereland of McWorld.

More dramatic even than in India, is the strange interplay of Jihad and McWorld in the remnants of Yugoslavia. In an affecting *New Republic* report, Slavenka Drakulic told the brief tragic love story of Admira and Bosko, two young star-crossed lovers from Sarajevo: "They were born in the late 1960s," she writes. "They watched Spielberg movies; they listened to Iggy Pop; they read John le Carré; they went to a disco every Saturday night and fantasized about traveling to Paris or London." Longing for safety, it seems they finally negotiated with all sides for safe passage, and readied their departure from Sarajevo. Before they could cross the magical border that separates their impoverished lane from the seeming sanctuary of McWorld, Jihad caught up to them. Their bodies lay along the riverbank, riddled with bullets from anonymous snipers for whom safe passage signaled an invitation to target practice. The murdered young lovers, as befits émigrés to McWorld, were clothed in jeans and sneakers. So too, one imagines, were their murderers.

Further east, tourists seeking a piece of old Russia that does not take them too far from MTV can find traditional Matryoshka nesting dolls (that fit one inside the other) featuring the nontraditional visages of (from largest to smallest) Bruce Springsteen, Madonna, Boy George, Dave Stewart, and Annie Lennox.

In Russia, in India, in Bosnia, in Japan, and in France too, modem history then leans both ways: toward the meretricious inevitability of McWorld, but also into Jihad's stiff winds, heaving to and fro and giving heart both to the Panglossians and the Pandoras, sometimes for the very same reasons. The Panglossians bank on EuroDisney and Microsoft, while the Pandoras await nihilism and a world in Pandaemonium. Yet McWorld and Jihad do not really force a choice between such polarized scenarios. Together, they are likely to produce some stifling amalgam of the two suspended in chaos. Antithetical in every detail, Jihad and McWorld nonetheless conspire to undermine our hardwon (if only halfwon) civil liberties and the possibility of a global democratic future. In the short run the forces of Jihad, noisier and more obviously nihilistic than those of McWorld, are likely to dominate the near future, etching small stories of local tragedy and regional genocide on the face of our times and creating a climate of instability marked by multimicrowars inimical to global integration. But in the long run, the forces of McWorld are the forces underlying the slow certain thrust of Western civilization and as such may be unstoppable. Jihad's microwars will hold the headlines well into the next century, making predictions of the end of history look terminally dumb. But McWorld's homogenization is likely to establish a macropeace that favors the triumph of commerce and its markets and to give to those who control information, communication, and entertainment ultimate (if inadvert) control over human destiny. Unless we can offer an alternative to the struggle between Jihad and McWorld, the epoch on whose threshold we stand—postcommunist, postindustrial, postriational, yet sectarian, fearful, and bigoted—is likely also to be terminally postdemocratic.

Source: *The Globalization Reader*. Malden, MA: Blackwell, 2004. 29-35.

WHAT IT SAYS

1. What does Barber mean by Jihad? What does he mean by McWorld?

2. In what ways are Jihad and McWorld different, and what do they have in common?

3. What is the relationship between Jihad and McWorld? How does Barber characterize the outcome of this relationship?

4. Barber pits futurologists against those who say history is dead, Babel against Disneyland, and the Panglossians against the Pandoras. Explain each opposition.

5. What are the *global* implications of the opposition of Jihad and McWorld?

HOW IT SAYS IT

1. How does Barber's use of the oppositions outlined in question 4 above work to advance his argument?

2. Point to Barber's uses of description to illustrate the intimate relationship between Jihad and McWorld.

3. Point to Barber's use of metaphor and other figurative language. What is the effect of such language?

WRITE ABOUT IT

1. Write an essay in which you explain why McWorld is objectionable to the advocates of Jihad. What about McWorld might incite Jihadists to extremism?

2. Write an essay that resolves the contradiction between Jihad and McWorld. What changes would be necessary for the conflict to be terminated?

3. Refute Barber's Jihad vs. McWorld formulation. In what specific ways might he be wrong? What characterizations are flawed?

d. Tyler Cowen, "Trade between Cultures"

Tyler Cowen holds the Holbert C. Harris Chair of economics as a professor at George Mason University. He is the author of numerous books that treat a diverse range of topics in connection with economics. These include *Public Goods and Market Failures: A Critical Introduction* (1992), *Risk and Business Cycles: New and Old Austrian Perspectives* (1997), *In Praise of Consumer Culture* (2000), *What Price Fame?* (2000), *Markets and Cultural Voices: Liberty vs. Power in the Lives of Mexican Amate Painters* (2005), and *Discover Your Inner Economist* (2008). He currently writes the "Economic Scene" column for the *New York Times* and writes for such magazines as the *New Republic* and the *Wilson Quarterly*. Cowen is also general director of the Mercatus Center at George Mason University. He is co-author, with Alex Tabarrok, of the popular economics blog *Marginal Revolution*. Cowen received a BS from George Mason University and a PhD from Harvard University, both in economics.

The following essay, "Trade between Cultures," is drawn from Cowen's book *Creative Destruction: How Globalization Is Changing the World's Cultures* (2004). Cowen suggests that while global trade may tend toward cultural homogenization in some areas of society, some areas of society and most cultures in general become more heterogeneous. While far-flung cultures may become more alike, differences *within* these cultures actually increase.

As You Read: Think about the extent to which homogenization and/or heterogeneity have increased or decreased in your community over the past several years.

Trade between Cultures

Haitian music has a strong presence in French Guiana, Dominica, Martinique, Guadeloupe, and St. Lucia—the smaller Caribbean markets. Many Antillean musicians have resented the Haitian success, even though they derived many musical ideas from the Haitian style of compas (pronounced "comb-pa"). The founder of Kassav, the leading Antillean group in the funky style of zouk, stated: "It's this Haitian imperialism [i.e., the popularity of the groups] that we were rising against when we began Kassav." Governments responded with protective measures to limit the number of Haitian bands in the country. Ironically, Antillean zouk now has penetrated Haiti. Haitian musicians resent the foreign style, although like their Antillean counterparts they do not hesitate to draw on its musical innovations. Haiti's compas style was originally a modified version of Cuban dance music and Dominican merengue.[1]

---

1   On these episodes, see Guilbault (1993, chap. 5).

The Canadian government discouraged the American book-superstore Borders from entering the Canadian market, out of fear that it would not carry enough Canadian literature. Canadians subsidize their domestic cinema and mandate domestic musical content for a percentage of radio time, which leads to extra airplay for successful Canadian pop stars like Celine Dion and Barenaked Ladies. Americans take pride in the global success of their entertainment industry, but Canadian writer Margaret Atwood coined the phrase "the Great Star-Spangled Them" to express her opposition to NAFTA.

The French spend approximately $3 billion a year on cultural matters and employ twelve thousand cultural bureaucrats, trying to nourish and preserve their vision of a uniquely French culture.[2] They have led a world movement to insist that culture is exempt from free trade agreements. Along these lines, Spain, South Korea, and Brazil place binding domestic content requirements on their cinemas; France and Spain do the same for television. Until recently India did not allow the import of Coca-Cola.

Trade is an emotionally charged issue for several reasons, but most of all because it shapes our sense of cultural self. More than ever before, we are aware that not everyone likes how international trade and globalization are altering today's cultures. The terrorist attacks of September 11, 2001, on America were directed first at the World Trade Center, a noted icon of global commerce.

Harvard philosopher Robert Nozick, in his *Anarchy, State, and Utopia*, argued that market society offered a cultural utopia based on freedom of choice. He portrayed a hypothetical libertarian world where individuals would freely choose their lifestyles, their mores, and their culture, so long as they did not impinge on the rights of others to make the same choices. Such a vision has held great appeal for many, but it has skirted the empirical question of how much choice actually is available in the market, or would be available in a more libertarian society.

Numerous commentators, from across the traditional political spectrum, have argued that markets destroy culture and diversity. Benjamin Barber claimed that the modern world is caught between Jihad, a "bloody politics of identity," and McWorld, "a bloodless economics of profit," represented by the spread of McDonald's and American popular culture. John Gray, an English conservative, has argued that global free trade is ruining the world's polities, economies, and cultures. His book is entitled *False Dawn: The Delusions of Global Capitalism*. Jeremy Tunstall defined the "cultural imperialism thesis" as the view that "authentic, traditional and local culture in many parts of the world is being battered out of existence by the indiscriminate dumping of large quantities of slick commercial and media products, mainly from the United States." Fredric Jameson writes: "The standardization of world culture, with local popular or traditional forms driven out or dumbed down

---

2   For data on French expenditures, see Drozdiak (1993).

to make way for American television, American music, food, clothes and films, has been seen by many as the very heart of globalization."[3]

Alexis de Tocqueville, the nineteenth-century French author of *Democracy in America*, provided foundations for many modern critics of commercialism. Tocqueville is not typically considered an economic thinker, but in fact his book is permeated with a deep and original economics of culture; he provides the most serious nineteenth-century attempt to revise Adam Smith. He sought, for instance, to disprove the Scottish Enlightenment dictum that an increase in the size of the market leads to more diversity. For Tocqueville, market growth serves as a magnet, pulling creators towards mass production and away from serving niches. For this reason, Tocqueville portrayed America as producing a culture of the least common denominator, in contrast to the sophistication of European aristocracy. While Tocqueville's account of America was subtle and nuanced, and in many regards favorable, he believed that broader markets for cultural goods lowered their quality.

Given the recurring nature of such criticisms, we cannot help but wonder whether the market does in fact expand our positive liberties and increase the menu of choice. If not, the freedom to engage in marketplace exchange will stand in conflict with other notions of freedom, such as an individual's ability to choose or maintain a particular cultural identity. More generally, the question at stake is what kinds of freedom are possible in the modern world.

To pursue this issue, I ask some fundamental questions about culture in a market economy. Does trade in cultural products support the artistic diversity of the world, or destroy it? Will the future bring artistic quality and innovation, or a homogeneous culture of the least common denominator? What will happen to cultural creativity as freedom of economic choice extends across the globe?

Modern debates refer frequently to the buzzword of globalization. Commentators invest this term with many meanings, including the growth of world trade and investment, world government, international terrorism, imperialist conquest, IMF technocracy, the global arms trade, and the worldwide spread of infectious diseases. I make no attempt to evaluate globalization in all its manifestations, but rather I focus on the trade in cultural products across geographic space.

A typical American yuppie drinks French wine, listens to Beethoven on a Japanese audio system, uses the Internet to buy Persian textiles from a dealer in London, watches Hollywood movies funded by foreign capital and filmed by

---

3   See Barber (1995, p. 8), Tunstall (1977, p. 57) and Jameson (2000, p. 51). For related contemporary perspectives, see Tomlinson (1991), Robertson (1992), and Schiller (1992). Barnet and Cavanagh (1996) provide another clear statement of the typical charges leveled against cultural globalization. For a critique of Gray, see Klein (2000). The more general doctrine of primitivism found early expression in Rousseau's Noble Savage, and, going back farther in time, in the Greek view that historical change represents corruption and decay. Christian doctrine, especially the Garden of Eden and Man's Fall, provided inspiration for the doctrine that pure, original cultures are doomed to fall from grace. On the Christian roots of primitivism, see Boas (1948); on the history of the Noble Savage idea, see Fairchild (1961). On primitivism in classical antiquity, see Lovejoy and Boas (1965).

a European director, and vacations in Bali; an upper-middle-class Japanese may do much the same. A teenager in Bangkok may see Hollywood movies starring Arnold Schwarzenegger (an Austrian), study Japanese, and listen to new pop music from Hong Kong and China, in addition to the Latino singer Ricky Martin. Iraq's Saddam Hussein selected Frank Sinatra's "My Way" as the theme song for his fifty-fourth birthday.[4]

I focus on one particular aspect of culture, namely those creative products that stimulate and entertain us. More specifically, I treat music, literature, cinema, cuisine, and the visual arts as the relevant manifestations of culture. Given this field of inquiry, I focus on how trade shapes artistic creativity in the marketplace.

I leave aside broader social practices. I do not consider how globalization influences family norms, religion, or manners, except as they may affect creative industries. These social practices, while relevant for an overall assessment of globalization, are outside my chosen purview. I focus on markets, rather than on peoples or communities per se. I consider what kinds of freedom are available in the marketplace, rather than what kinds of freedom we have to remain outside the marketplace. I do not, for instance, examine whether we should attach intrinsic value to preventing the commodification of global creativity.

Instead I treat international commerce as a stage for examining an age-old question, dating back at least as far as Greek civilization: are market exchange and aesthetic quality allies or enemies? Furthermore our look at markets, and the resulting menu of choice, will help address other questions from classic antiquity. Was Herodotus pointing to a more general phenomenon when he ascribed the cultural vitality of the Greeks to their genius for synthesis? Was Plutarch correct in suggesting that the exile, and the corresponding sense of foreignness, is fundamentally creative in nature, rather than sterile? Along the lines of the Stoics, to what extent should our loyalties lie with the cosmopolitan, or to what extent should they lie with the local and the particular?

Our Conflicting Intuitions

We have strongly conflicting intuitions about the worldwide trade in cultural products. On the plus side, individuals are liberated from the *tyranny of place* more than ever before. Growing up in an out-of-the-way locale limits an individual's access to the world's treasures and opportunities less than ever before. This change represents one of the most significant increases in freedom in human history.

More specifically, the very foundations of the West (and other civilizations throughout history) are multicultural products, resulting from the international exchange of goods, services, and ideas. To varying degrees, Western cultures draw their philosophical heritage from the Greeks, their religions from the Middle East,

---

4 Micklethwait and Wooldridge (2000, p. 190).

their scientific base from the Chinese and Islamic worlds, and their core populations and languages from Europe.

If we consider the book, paper comes from the Chinese, the Western alphabet comes from the Phoenicians, the page numbers come from the Arabs and ultimately the Indians, and printing has a heritage through Gutenberg, a German, as well as through the Chinese and Koreans. The core manuscripts of antiquity were preserved by Islamic civilization and, to a lesser extent, by Irish monks. The period between 1800 and the First World War saw an unprecedented increase in internationalization. The West adopted the steamship, the railroad, and the motor car, all of which replaced travel by coach or slow ship. International trade, investment, and migration grew rapidly. The nineteenth century, by virtually all accounts, was a fantastically creative and fertile epoch. The exchange of cultural ideas across Europe and the Americas promoted diversity and quality, rather than turning everything into homogenized pap.[5] Conversely, the most prominent period of cultural decline in Western history coincides with a radical shrinking of trade frontiers. The so-called Dark Ages, which date roughly from the collapse of the Roman Empire in AD 422 to early medieval times in 1100, saw a massive contraction of interregional trade and investment. The Roman Empire had brought regular contact between the distant corners of Europe and the Mediterranean; the Roman network of roads was without historical parallel. After the fall of the empire, however, trade dried up, cities declined, and feudalism arose as nobles retreated to heavily armed country estates. During this same period, architecture, writing, reading, and the visual arts all declined drastically. The magnificent buildings of antiquity fell into disrepair, or were pillaged for their contents. Bronze statues were melted down for their metal, and many notable writings perished.

The rise of medieval society and the Renaissance was, in large part, a process of reglobalization, as the West increased its contacts with the Chinese and Islamic worlds. At the same time, trade fairs expanded, shipping lanes became more active, scientific ideas spread, and overland trade paths, many dormant since the time of the Romans, were reestablished.

These successes did not involve cultural exchange on equal terms. To put it bluntly, the notion of a cultural "level playing field" is a myth and will never be seen in practice. Never did the Greek city-states compete on an even basis. Christian and Graeco-Roman cultures were entrenched in Europe partly by fiat. British culture has had a significant head start in North America. The benefits of cultural exchange usually have come from dynamic settings in great imbalance, rather than from calm or smoothly working environments.

"Third World" and "indigenous" arts have blossomed on the uneven playing field of today's global economy. Most Third World cultures are fundamentally

---

5 As a percentage of the world economy, international trade grew from 3 to 33 percent; world trade, as a share of world output, did not return to its 1913 levels until the 1970s. See Waters (1995, p. 67) and Krugman (1996, p. 208).

hybrids—synthetic products of multiple global influences, including from the West. None of the common terms used to describe these cultures, whether it be "Third World," "indigenous," "original," or "underdeveloped," are in fact appropriate designations, given the synthetic nature of the creative arts.

To give one example, the sculpture of the Canadian Inuit was not practiced on a large scale until after World War II. Even the earlier, nineteenth-century carvings drew on sailors' scrimshaw art for inspiration. White artist James Houston, however, introduced soapstone carving to the Inuit in 1948. Since then the Inuit have created many first-rate works in the medium. The sale of stone-carved works in Western art markets, often for lucrative sums, also has allowed the Inuit to maintain many of their traditional ways of life. The Inuit have moved into printmaking as well, and with commercial and aesthetic success.[6]

Analogous stories are found around the world. The metal knife proved a boon to many Third World sculpting and carving traditions, including the totem poles of the Pacific Northwest and of Papua New Guinea. Acrylic and oil paints spread only with Western contact. South African Ndebele art uses beads as an essential material for the adornment of aprons, clothing, and textiles. These beads are not indigenous to Africa, but rather were imported from Czechoslovakia in the early nineteenth century. Mirrors, coral, cotton cloth, and paper—all central materials for "traditional" African arts—came from contact with Europeans. The twentieth-century flowering of Third World "folk arts," prominent throughout the world, has been driven largely by Western demands, materials, and technologies of production. Charlene Cerny and Suzanne Seriff have written of the "global scrap heap," referring to the use of discarded Western material technology in folk arts around the world.[7] World musics are healthier and more diverse than ever before.

Rather than being swamped by output from the multinational conglomerates, musicians around the world have adapted international influences towards their own ends. Most domestic musics have no trouble commanding loyal audiences at home. In India, domestically produced music comprises 96 percent of the market; in Egypt, 81 percent; and in Brazil, 73 percent. Even in a small country such as Ghana, domestically produced music is 71 percent of the market.[8] Most world music styles are of more recent origin than is commonly believed, even in supposedly "traditional" genres. The twentieth century brought waves of musical innovation to most cultures, especially the large, open ones. The musical centers of the Third World—Cairo, Lagos, Rio de Janeiro, pre-Castro Havana—have been

---

6 On scrimshaw art, see Furst and Furst (1982, p. 138); on the minor role of stone carving among the Inuit prior to Houston, see J.C.H. King (1986, pp. 88-89). Good general treatments are Swinton (1972) and Hessel (1998).

7 See Brunside (1997, p. 93), and Bascom (1976, p. 303). On the Ndebele, see Glassie (1989, p. 64). The artistic benefits of Western metal knives were widely recognized, including in such locales as Papua New Guinea, Melanesia, and New Zealand; see Weatherford (1994, pp. 250-51).

8 See Cowen and Crampton (2001), drawing on UNESCO data from World Culture Report 2000, table 5.

heterogeneous and cosmopolitan cities that welcomed new ideas and new technologies from abroad.

In all of these examples, the notable creators are active, searching artists, drawing on many sources to produce the sought-after aesthetic effect. These points do not denigrate non-Western artists or imply that they "owe it all to the West." It is the contrary emphasis on monoculture that insults, by portraying non-Western artists as unchanging and static craftworkers, unable to transcend their initial styles for synthetic improvements.

Cinema is one of the most problematic areas for globalized culture, as we will see in chapter 4 [not reprinted here], due largely to the export success of Hollywood. Nonetheless in the last twenty years Hong Kong, India, China, Denmark, Iran, and Taiwan, among other locales, have produced many high-quality and award-winning movies. African cinema remains an undiscovered gem for most viewers, and European cinema shows signs of commercial revitalization. Hollywood cinema itself has relied on international inspiration from the beginning, and should be considered as much a cosmopolitan product as an American one.

American books do not typically dominate fiction best-seller lists abroad. At any point in time American books typically account for no more than two or three of the top ten best-sellers, if even that many, in countries such as Germany, France, Italy, Israel, the Netherlands, and the United Kingdom. The Netherlands is a very small country, with fewer than ten million people, but most of its best-sellers are of Dutch origin. Many people still prefer to read books written originally in their native language, and about their native culture. Even in Canada, American books do not typically command half of the fiction best-seller lists.[9]

Nor are the most influential books, in the international arena, necessarily from today's richest countries. Arguably the most influential books in the world remain the Bible and the Koran, neither of which is a Western product in the narrow sense, though the form has been shaped by Western interpretations.

Western literature, as well as the bookstore and the modern printing press, typically has spurred native writers. Salman Rushdie of India, Gabriel Garcia Marquez of Colombia, Naguib Mahfouz of Egypt, and Pramoedya Toer of Indonesia, among others, are world-class writers, comparable to the best of Europe and the United States, if not better. These fictional traditions, now worldwide, drew directly on Western literary models and institutions.

Appropriately, Third World writers have been some of the strongest proponents of a cosmopolitan multiculturalism. Salman Rushdie describes his work as celebrating hybridity, impurity, and mongrelization. Ghanaian writer Kwame Anthony Appiah believes that cosmopolitanism complements "rootedness," rather than destroying it, and that new innovative forms are maintaining the diversity of

---

9 The magazine The Economist surveys international best-sellers on a periodic basis. Cowen and Crampton (2001) present one summary version of this information.

world culture. Rabindranath Tagore, Gandhi's foil earlier in the century, favored international trade and cooperation over national isolation or boycotts of foreign goods. He saw the genius of Indian society in synthesizing the cultures of the East and the West. Even the critics of globalization have, for the most part, been diverse products of a worldwide intellectual culture, strongly rooted in Western and classic Greek methods of analysis and argumentation.[10]

The Downside

Despite the triumphs of synthetic culture, we should not ignore the costs of cross-cultural exchange. Montesquieu wrote: "The history of commerce is that of communication among peoples. Its greatest events are formed by their various destructions and certain ebbs and flows of population and of devastations."[11]

Globalized culture illustrates Joseph Schumpeter's metaphor of capitalist production as a gale of "creative destruction." Cultural growth, like economic development, rarely is a steady advance on all fronts at once. While some sectors expand with extreme rapidity, others shrink and wither away.

It is hard to argue that Polynesian culture is more vital today than several hundred years ago, even though the Polynesians are wealthier in material terms. Materialism, alcohol, Western technologies, and Christianity (according to some) have damaged the Polynesian sense of cultural potency. In Tahiti many creative traditional arts have been neglected or abandoned as they lost status to Western goods or proved uneconomical. Polynesian culture has hardly disappeared, but it now limps along on the margins of Western achievement.

Some commentators have suggested that China opened Tibet to the outside world, not out of tolerance and magnanimity, but to destroy the native culture. Coca-Cola and Western tourists may succeed in doing what decades of coercive Communist intervention failed to achieve—weakening traditional Tibetan attachments to their rich brocade of history, rituals, temples, and Buddhist religion. The Himalayan kingdom of Bhutan charges tourists two hundred dollars a day in the hope of maintaining a protected sense of identity. The country has no traffic lights and no city with more than ten thousand inhabitants. Wild dogs roam the streets. Poverty and malnutrition are rife, but the country maintains intense forms of Buddhist mythology and art that are perishing elsewhere.[12]

---

10 On Rushdie, see Waldron (1996, pp. 105-9). Also see Appiah (1992, 1998). On Tagore, see Sinha (1962) and Dutta and Robinson (1995). On the history of cosmopolitan thought more generally, see Wagar (1963). Montesquieu (1965 [1748], p. 24) saw the genius of the Romans in their synthetic abilities: "The main reason for the Romans becoming masters of the world was that, having fought successively against all peoples, they always gave up their own practices as soon as they found better ones."

11 Montesquieu (1989 [1748], p. 357).

12 On Tibet, see Iyer (1989, p. 71).

Travel puts the downside of cross-cultural exchange right before our eyes. Even travelers of only moderate experience complain that their fellow countrymen have "spoiled" various locales or diminished their authenticity. Sophisticated travelers go to great lengths to seek out places that are otherwise under-touristed, precisely for their unique qualities. It is the underdeveloped Papua New Guinea, divided by treacherous mountain ranges, that contains more than a quarter of the world's languages.[13]

Just as the mobility of people can have a homogenizing effect, so can the mobility of goods. Movie producers know that action films are easiest to export to many different countries. Heroism, excitement, and violence do not vary so much across cultures. Comedies, with their nuances of dialogue and their culturally specific references, are the hardest to sell abroad. A global market in cinema therefore encourages action films more than it does sophisticated comedy. Comedies for the global market tend to emphasize physical slapstick rather than clever wordplay, which is hard to translate into other languages. Some very fine movies use action and slapstick comedy, but these trends have not elevated the quality of movies in all regards.

What Is to Come

Many writers address cross-cultural exchange from the perspectives of "critical theory." They draw upon a diverse set of approaches—including Marxism, structuralism, the Frankfurt School, and postmodernism—to provide a critique of capitalism and globalization. They view markets as promoting hegemony, alienation, and a dumbing down of taste. To varying degrees, Bourdieu, Gramsci, Habermas, and Canclini all explore different aspects of these traditions. These thinkers cannot be reduced to a single common denominator, as is appropriate for such diverse (and global) intellectual products. Nonetheless they share common sources, taken largely from Continental philosophy, share a skepticism about market-driven culture, and have been influenced by Marxian economics.

In contrast to these sources, I use a "gains from trade" model to understand cultural exchange. Individuals who engage in cross cultural exchange expect those transactions to make them better off, to enrich their cultural lives, and to increase their menu of choice. Just as trade typically makes countries richer in material terms, it tends to make them culturally richer as well. Any story about the problems of globalization—and several plausible candidates will arise—must explain why this basic gains-from-trade mechanism might backfire.[14]

---

13 See "Cultural Loss Seen as Languages Fade."

14 In this regard my analysis differs from some of the writers who have defended synthetic or cosmopolitan culture. A variety of writers in the social sciences, such as James Clifford, Frederick Buell, Ulf Hannerz, Arjun Appadurai, and Edward Said, have pointed out the hybrid and synthetic nature of culture, but they have not focused on how the economics of trade shape that culture.

Chapter 2 [not reprinted here] examines the gains-from-trade story in more detail, showing how wealth, technology, and cross-cultural exchange drive many cultural blossomings. The following three chapters [not reprinted here] then consider three mechanisms that may overturn the gains-from-trade argument. Trade affects societal ethos and worldview, geographically clusters production of some goods and services, and alters customer thoughtfulness and concern for quality, not always for the better. These three mechanisms provide linchpins of anti-market arguments and thus they receive special attention.

I translate criticisms of globalization into stories about how individual cultural choices, made in the context of imperfect markets, may lead to undesirable consequences. In each case I examine how trade might damage creativity, convert anti-globalization polemics into a more systematic argument, and then assess the validity of the charges by looking at the evidence. When choosing empirical examples, I pay special attention to areas where the critics of globalization have been most vocal, such as cinema and handwoven textiles.

I do not seek to promote any single definition of what "quality" in global culture might consist of. One virtue of a broad menu of choice is to economize on the need for unanimity of opinion, which is hard to achieve. When it comes to the actual examples of quality culture, however, I have followed two principles. First, I have focused on what the critics cite as the hard cases for the optimistic perspective, as mentioned above. Second, when citing successes I have picked artistic creations that command widespread critical and popular support. For instance, I refer to French cooking, Persian carpets, and reggae music as examples of general cultural successes, though without meaning to endorse each and every manifestation of these genres. I do not spend time defending such judgments in aesthetic terms, which I take as given. Instead I focus on the role of the market, and cross-cultural exchange, in promoting or discouraging the relevant creations.

At the end of the day the reader must ultimately take home his or her personal opinion about whether a particular example is one of rot or one of cultural blossoming. I do not expect many readers to agree that every cited success is in fact splendid, but I hope nonetheless that the overall picture—which emphasizes the diversity of the menu of choice—will be a persuasive one.[15]

A discussion of globalization must range far and wide across numerous topics. Given my background as an economist, I approach each topic differently than might a specialist in a particular area. I have studied the relevant scholarly literature in each case, but the core of my knowledge results from my diverse experiences as a cultural consumer, rather than from a single path of specialized study. In the language of chapter 5 [not reprinted here], the book will sample topics extensively

---

15 An earlier book of mine, Cowen (1998), discusses aesthetic issues in more depth; I refer the interested reader to this treatment, especially chapter 5. In the literature I have found Hume (1985 [1777]), Hennstein Smith (1988), Danto (1981), Savile (1982), and Mukarovsky (1970) to be especially enlightening.

rather than intensively, and should be judged as such. Specialization, while it has brought immense benefits to science and academic life, is by its nature ill-suited to illuminate the diverse production and consumption made possible by the market economy.

The results of this inquiry will suggest three primary lessons, to be developed in the following chapters:

The concept of cultural diversity has multiple and sometimes divergent meanings.

It is misleading to speak of diversity as a single concept, as societies exhibit many kinds of diversity. For instance, diversity *within* society refers to the richness of the menu of choice in that society. Many critics of globalization, however, focus on diversity *across* societies. This concept refers to whether each society offers the same menu, and whether societies are becoming more similar.

These two kinds of diversity often move in opposite directions. When one society trades a new artwork to another society, diversity within society goes up (consumers have greater choice), but diversity across the two societies goes down (the two societies become more alike). The question is not about more or less diversity per se, but rather what kind of diversity globalization will bring. Crosscultural exchange tends to favor diversity within society, but to disfavor diversity across societies.[16]

Note that diversity across societies is to some extent a collectivist concept. The metric compares one society to another, or one country to another, instead of comparing one individual to another, or instead of looking at the choices faced by an individual.

Critics of globalization commonly associate diversity with the notion of cultural differentiation across geographic space. In reality, individuals can pursue diverse paths without having their destinies determined by their place of origin; indeed this is central to the notion of freedom. But many proponents of diversity expect that differentiation should be visible to the naked eye, such as when we cross the border between the United States and Mexico. By comparing the collectives and the aggregates, and by emphasizing the dimension of geographic space, this standard begs the question as to which kind of diversity matters. Under an alternative notion of diversity, different regions may look more similar than in times past, but the individuals in those locales will have greater scope to pursue different paths for their lives, and will have a more diverse menu of choice for their cultural consumption.

Trade tends to increase *diversity over time* by accelerating the pace of change and bringing new cultural goods with each era or generation. If diversity is a

---

16 Weitzman (1992, 1993) develops an economic metric for diversity, but considers only differences across societies (or biological units), not the menu of choice within or the other concepts presented below.

value more generally, surely we have some grounds for believing that diversity-over-time is a value as well. Yet many defenders of diversity decry the passing of previous cultures and implicitly oppose diversity-over-time. In the last chapter [not reprinted here] I will examine why this might be the case.

Operative diversity—how effectively we can enjoy the diversity of the world—differs from *objective diversity*, or how much diversity is out there. In some ways the world was very diverse in 1450, but not in a way that most individuals could benefit from. Markets have subsequently disseminated the diverse products of the world very effectively, even when those same cross-cultural contacts have damaged indigenous creative environments.

Cultural homogenization and heterogenization are not alternatives or substitutes; rather, they tend to come together.

Market growth causes heterogenizing and homogenizing mechanisms to operate in tandem. Some parts of the market become more alike, while other parts of the market become more different. Mass culture and niche culture are complements, once we take the broader picture into account. Growing diversity brings us more of many different things, which includes more mass culture as well.

Product differentiation and niche markets rely on certain kinds of social homogeneity. Mass marketing, for instance, also creates the infrastructure to peddle niche products to smaller numbers of consumers. Magazine advertising, mail order, and the Internet allow recording companies to make a profit issuing CDs that sell only five hundred copies. Book superstores enable readers to stumble across the products of small presses. Most generally, partial homogenization often creates the conditions necessary for diversity to flower on the micro level. Claude Levi-Strauss noted, "Diversity is less a function of the isolation of groups than of the relationships which unite them."[17]

Food markets illustrate the connection between heterogenization and homogenization with special clarity. Chain restaurants take an increasing percentage of American and global restaurant sales, and in this regard the market brings greater homogeneity. At the same time, the growth in dining out has led to an expansion of food opportunities of all kinds, whether it be fast food, foie gras, or Thai mee krob. American suburbs and cities offer a wide variety of Asian, Latin, African, and European foods, as well as "fusion" cuisines. High and low food-culture have proven to be complements, not opposing forces. Paris and Hong Kong, both centers of haute cuisine, have the world's two busiest Pizza Hut outlets.[18]

---

17 Levi-Strauss (1976, p. 328). Late-nineteenth-century sociology was strongly concerned with processes of differentiation and homogenization; see the works of Pareto and Weber. Shils (1981) is one twentieth-century work in this tradition.

18 Pillsbury (1998, p. 183). On Pizza Hut, see *Harper's*, November 1994, p. 11. On the growth in global food diversity, through trade; see Sokolov (1991).

Finally, cross-cultural exchange, while it will alter and disrupt each society it touches, will support innovation and creative human energies.

Cross-cultural exchange brings value clashes that cannot be resolved scientifically, as I will stress in the last chapter [not reprinted here]. So no investigation, no matter how comprehensive, can provide a final evaluation of cultural globalization. The world as a whole has a broader menu of choice, but older synthetic cultures must give way to newer synthetic cultures. Countries will share more common products than before. Some regions, in return for receiving access to the world's cultural treasures, and the ability to market their products abroad, will lose their distinctiveness. Not everyone likes these basic facts.

These trade-offs aside, much of the skepticism about cross-cultural exchange has nothing to do with diversity per se. Most critics of contemporary culture dislike particular trends, often those associated with modernity or commercialism more generally. They use diversity as a code word for a more particularist agenda, often of an anti-commercial or anti-American nature. They care more about the particular form that diversity takes in their favored culture, rather than about diversity more generally, freedom of choice, or a broad menu of quality options.

In response to commonly pessimistic attitudes, I will outline a more optimistic and more cosmopolitan view of cross-cultural exchange. The "creative destruction" of the market is, in surprising ways, artistic in the most literal sense. It creates a plethora of innovative and high-quality creations in many different genres, styles, and media. Furthermore, the evidence strongly suggests that cross-cultural exchange expands the menu of choice, at least provided that trade and markets are allowed to flourish.[19]

Nonetheless, an informed cosmopolitanism must be of the cautious variety, rather than based on superficial pro-globalization slogans or cheerleading about the brotherhood of mankind. Throughout the book we will see that individuals are often more creative when they do not hold consistently cosmopolitan attitudes. A certain amount of cultural particularism and indeed provincialism, among both producers and consumers, can be good for the arts. The meliorative powers of globalization rely on underlying particularist and anti-liberal attitudes to some extent. Theoretically "correct" attitudes do not necessarily maximize creativity, suggesting that a cosmopolitan culture does best when cosmopolitanism itself is not fully believed or enshrined in social consciousness.

---

19 I am indebted to John Tomasi for some of the wording of this paragraph, without wishing to hold him responsible for its use.

References

Appiah, Kwame Anthony. 1992. *In My Father's House: Africa in the Philosophy of Culture*. New York: Oxford University Press.

Barber, Benjamin R. 1995. *Jihad vs. McWorld: Terrorism's Challenge to Democracy*. New York: Ballantine Books.

Barnet, Richard, and John Cavanagh. 1996. "Homogenization of Global Culture." In *The Case against the Global Economy, and for a Turn Toward the Local*. Edited by Jerry Mander and Edward Goldsmith, 71-77. San Francisco: Sierra Club.

Bascom, William. 1976. *Changing African Art*. Berkeley: University of California Press.

Boas, George. 1948. *Essays on Primitivism and Related Ideas in the Middle Ages*. Baltimore: Johns Hopkins Press.

Brunside, M. 1997. *Spirits of the Passage: The Transatlantic Slave Trade in the Seventeenth Century*. Edited by R. Robotham. New York: Simon and Schuster.

Cowen, Tyler, and Eric Crampton. 2001. "Uncommon Culture." *Foreign Policy* (July/August): 28-29.

"Cultural Loss Seen as Languages Fade." 1999. *New York Times*, 16 May, 12.

Danto, Arthur C. 1981. *The Transfiguration of the Commonplace: A Philosophy of Art*. Cambridge: Harvard University Press.

Drozdiak, William. 1993. "The City of Light, Sans Bright Ideas." *Washington Post*, 28 October, D1, D6.

Dutta, Krishna, and Andrew Robinson. 1995. *Rabindranath Tagore: The Myriad-Minded Man*. New York: St. Martin's Press.

Fairchild, Hoxie Neale. 1961. *The Noble Savage: A Study in Romantic Naturalism*. New York: Russell and Russell.

Furst, Peter T., and Jill L. Furst. 1982. *North American Indian Art*. New York: Artpress Books.

Glassie, Henry. 1989. *The Spirit of Folk Art: The Girard Collection at the Museum of International Folk Art*. New York: Harry N. Abrams.

Guilbault, Jocelyne. *Zouk: World Music in the West Indies*. Chicago: University of Chicago Press, 1993.

Herrnstein-Smith, Barbara. 1988. *Contingencies of Value: Alternative Perspectives for Critical Theory*. Cambridge: Harvard University Press.

Hessel, Ingo. 1998. *Inuit Art: An Introduction*. New York: Harry N. Abrams.

Hume, David. 1985 [1777]. *Dialogues Concerning Natural Religion*. New York: Macmillan.

Iyer, Pico. 1989. *Video Night in Kathmandu*. New York: Vintage Books.

Jameson, Fredric. 2000. "Globalization and Strategy." *New Left Review*, July/August, 49-68.

King, J.C.H. 1986. "Tradition in Native American Art." In *The Arts of the North American Indian*, edited by Edwin L. Wade, 65-92. New York: Hudson Hill Press.

Klein, Naomi. 2000. *No Space, No Jobs, No Logo: Taking Aim at the Brand Bullies*. New York: Picador USA.

Krugman, Paul R. 1996. *Pop Internationalism*. Cambridge, MA: MIT Press.

Levi-Strauss, Claude. 1976. *Structural Anthropology*. Vol. 2. New York: Basic Books.

Lovejoy, Arthur O. and Arthur Boas. 1965. *Primitivism and Related Ideas in Antiquity*. New York: Octagon Books.

Micklethwait, John, and Adrian Wooldridge. 2000. *Future Perfect: The Challenge and Hidden Promise of Globalization*. New York: Crown Publishers.

Montesquieu, Charles-Louis de Secondat Baron de La Brede. 1965 [1748]. *Considerations on the Causes of the Greatness of the Romans and Their Decline*. Ithaca: Cornell University Press.

——. 1989 [1748]. *The Spirit of the Laws*. Cambridge: Cambridge University Press.

Mukarovsky, Jan. 1970. *Aesthetic Function. Norm and Value as Social Facts*. Ann Arbor: University of Michigan Press, Michigan Slavic Contributions.

Pillsbury, Richard. 1998. *No Foreign Food: The American Diet in Time and Place*. Boulder, Colo.: Westview Press.

Robertson, Roland. 1992. *Globalization: Social Theory and Global Culture*. London: Sage Publications.

Savile, Anthony. 1982. *The Test of Time: An Essay in Philosophical Aesthetics*. Oxford: Clarendon Press.

Schiller, Herbert I. 1992. *Mass Communications and American Empire*. Boulder, Colo.: Westview Press.

Shils, Edward. 1981. *Tradition*. Chicago: University of Chicago Press.

Sinclair, R.K. 1988. *Democracy and Participation in Athens*. Cambridge: Cambridge University Press.

Sinha, Sasadhar. 1962. *Social Thinking of Rabindranath Tagore*. London: Asia Publishing Guide.

Sokolov, Raymond. 1991. *Why We Eat What We Eat*. New York: Simon and Schuster.

Swinton, George. 1972. *Sculpture of the Eskimo*. Greenwich, Conn.: New York Graphic Society.

Tomlinson, John. 1991. *Cultural Imperialism: A Critical Introduction*. Baltimore: Johns Hopkins University Press.

——. 1999. *Globalization and Culture*. Chicago: University of Chicago Press.

Tunstall, Jeremy. 1977. *Media Are American*. New York: Columbia University Press.

Wagar, W. Warren. 1963. *The City of Man: Prophecies of a World Civilization in Twentieth-Century Thought*. Boston: Houghton Mifflin Company.

Waldron, Jeremy, Jr. 1996. "Multiculturalism and Mélange." In *Public Education in a Multicultural Society: Policy, Theory, Critique*, edited by Robert K. Fullinwider, 90-118. Cambridge: Cambridge University Press.

Source: *Creative Destruction: How Globalization Is Changing the World's Cultures*. Princeton, NJ; Woodstock: Princeton UP, 2004. 1-18.

WHAT IT SAYS

1. What aspect of globalization is Cowen's primary focus?

2. What is Cowen's response to critics of cultural globalization? In what specific ways does he think these critics are mistaken?

3. What are some of the downsides of cross-cultural exchange, according to Cowen? What are the benefits?

4. What is the relationship between homogeneity and heterogeneity, in Cowen's view? What examples does he use to illustrate these trends?

5. What distinction does Cowen draw between "operative diversity" and "objective diversity"?

6. Despite his advocacy of cosmopolitanism, Cowen suggests that we should be cautious about it. Why?

HOW IT SAYS IT

1. What strategies does Cowen use to establish his credibility?

2. Cowen acknowledges the opposing viewpoints of such scholars as Robert Nozick, Benjamin Barber, and Alexis de Tocqueville. How does doing so help him advance his argument?

3. Cowen chronicles historical forms of cultural exchange. How do these references help him make his case?

WRITE ABOUT IT

1. Write an essay in which you explore your own experience with the products of global culture (e.g., world music, international cuisine, foreign film).

2. Write an essay that proposes specific, practical ways in which one might go about achieving Cowen's ideal of "informed cosmopolitanism."

e. Kwame Anthony Appiah, "Cosmopolitan Contamination"

Kwame Anthony Appiah is a professor of philosophy and law at New York University. Previously, he was Laurance S. Rockefeller University Professor of Philosophy at the University Center for Human Values at Princeton University. He is the author of numerous books, including, with Amy Gutmann, *Color Conscious: The Political Morality of Race* (1996); the *Dictionary of Global Culture*, co-edited with Henry Louis Gates, Jr. (1997); *Bu Me Bé: Proverbs of the Akan*, an annotated edition of 7,500 proverbs in Twi, the language of Asante, co-authored with his mother, Peggy Appiah (2003); *Thinking It Through*, an introduction to contemporary philosophy (2004); *The Ethics of Identity* (2006); *Experiments in Ethics* (2008); and *The Honor Code: How Moral Revolutions Happen* (2010). He is also the author of three novels and regularly reviews for the *New York Review of Books*. In November 2009, *Forbes Magazine* listed Appiah as one of the world's seven most powerful thinkers. Appiah holds BA, MA, and PhD degrees in philosophy, all from Cambridge University.

The following selection is drawn from Appiah's book *Cosmopolitanism: Ethics in a World of Strangers*, published in 2006. In this essay, Appiah argues against the idea of cultural purity, which he deems impossible in any case, and in favor of "cosmopolitan contamination," or cultural eclecticism. He sees such cultural heterogeneity as an age-old feature of civilization itself and not strictly a recent development of contemporary globalization.

As You Read: Consider Appiah's characterizations of globalization and compare them with your own ideas, as received from the media or other reading.

Cosmopolitan Contamination

People who complain about the homogeneity produced by globalization often fail to notice that globalization is, equally, a threat to homogeneity. You can see this as clearly in Kumasi as anywhere. The capital of Asante is accessible to you, whoever you are—emotionally, intellectually, and, of course, physically. It is integrated into the global markets. None of this makes it Western, or American, or British. It is still Kumasi. What it isn't, just because it's a city, is homogeneous. English, German, Chinese, Syrian, Lebanese, Burkinabe, Ivorian, Nigerian, Indian: I can find you families of each description. I can find you Asante people, whose ancestors have lived in this town for centuries, but also Hausa households that have been around for centuries, too. There are people there from all the regions, speaking all the scores of languages of Ghana as well. And while people in Kumasi come from a wider variety of places than they did a hundred or two hundred years ago, even then there were already people from all over the place coming and going. I don't know who was the first Asante to make the pilgrimage to Mecca, but his trip would have followed trade routes that are far older than the kingdom. Gold, salt, kola nuts, and, alas, slaves have connected my hometown to the world for a very long time. And trade means travelers. If by globalization you have in mind something new and recent, the ethnic eclecticism of Kumasi is not the result of it.

But if you go outside Kumasi, only a little way—twenty miles, say, in the right direction—and if you drive off the main road down one of the many potholed side roads of red laterite, you can arrive pretty soon in villages that are fairly homogeneous. The people have mostly been to Kumasi and seen the big, polyglot, diverse world of the city. Here, though, where they live, there is one everyday language (aside from the English in the government schools), a few Asante families, and an agrarian way of life that is based on some old crops, like yam, and some new ones, like cocoa, which arrived in the late nineteenth century as a commercial product for export. They may or may not have electricity (this close to Kumasi, they probably do). When people talk of the homogeneity produced by globalization, what they are talking about is this: the villagers will have radios; you will be able to get a discussion going about the World Cup in soccer, Muhammad Ali, Mike Tyson, and hip-hop; and you will probably be able to find a bottle of Guinness or Coca-Cola (as well as Star or Club, Ghana's own delicious lagers). Then again, the language on the radio won't be a world language, the soccer teams they know best will be Ghanaian, and what can you tell about someone's soul from the fact that she drinks Coca-Cola? These villages are connected with more places than they were a couple of centuries ago. Their homogeneity, though, is still the local kind.

In the era of globalization—in Asante as in New Jersey—people make pockets of homogeneity. Are all these pockets of homogeneity less distinctive than they were a century ago? Well, yes, but mostly in good ways. More of them have access to medicines that work. More of them have access to clean drinking water. More of them have schools. Where, as is still too common, they don't have these things, this is not something to celebrate but to deplore. And whatever loss of difference there has been, they are constantly inventing new forms of difference: new hairstyles, new slang, even, from time to time, new religions. No one could say that the world's villages are—or are about to become—anything like the same.

So why do people in these places sometimes feel that their identity is threatened? Because the world, their world, is changing, and some of them don't like it. The pull of the global economy—witness those cocoa trees whose chocolate is eaten all around the world—created some of the life they now live. If the economy changes—if cocoa prices collapse again as they did in the early 1990s—they may have to find new crops or new forms of livelihood. That is unsettling for some people (just as it is exciting for others). Missionaries came a while ago, so many of these villagers will be Christian, even if they also have kept some of the rites from earlier days. But new Pentecostal messengers are challenging the churches they know and condemning the old rites as idolatrous. Again, some like it; some don't.

Above all, relationships are changing. When my father was young, a man in a village would farm some land that a chief had granted him, and his abusua, his matriclan, (including his younger brothers) would work it with him. If extra hands were needed in the harvest season, he would pay the migrant workers who came from the north. When a new house needed building, he would organize it. He would also make sure his dependents were fed and clothed, the children educated, marriages and funerals arranged and paid for. He could expect to pass the farm and the responsibilities eventually to one of his nephews.

Nowadays, everything has changed. Cocoa prices have not kept pace with the cost of living. Gas prices have made the transportation of the crop more expensive. And there are new possibilities for the young in the towns, in other parts of the country, and in other parts of the world. Once, perhaps, you could have commanded your nephews and nieces to stay. Now they have the right to leave; in any case, you may not make enough to feed and clothe and educate them all. So the time of the successful farming family has gone; and those who were settled in that way of life are as sad to see it go as some of the American family farmers whose lands are being accumulated by giant agribusinesses. We can sympathize with them. But we cannot force their children to stay in the name of protecting their authentic culture; and we cannot afford to subsidize indefinitely thousands of distinct islands of homogeneity that no longer make economic sense.

Nor should we want to. Cosmopolitans think human variety matters because people are entitled to the options they need to shape their lives in partnership with others. What John Stuart Mill said more than a century ago in *On Liberty* about diversity within a society serves just as well as an argument for variety across the globe:

> If it were only that people have diversities of taste, that is reason enough for not attempting to shape them all after one model. But different persons also require different conditions for their spiritual development; and can no more exist healthily in the same moral, than all the variety of plants can exist in the same physical, atmosphere and climate. The same things which are helps to one person towards the cultivation of his higher nature, are hindrances to another.... Unless there is a corresponding diversity in their modes of life, they neither obtain their fair share of happiness, nor grow up to the mental, moral, and aesthetic stature of which their nature is capable.[1]

---

1   John Stuart Mill, "On Liberty," in *Essays on Politics and Society*, ed. John M. Robson, vol. 18 of *The Collected Works of John Stuart Mill* (Toronto: University of Toronto Press, 1977), p. 270.

If we want to preserve a wide range of human conditions because it allows free people the best chance to make their own lives, there is no place for the enforcement of diversity by trapping people within a kind of difference they long to escape. There simply is no decent way to sustain those communities of difference that will not survive without the free allegiance of their members.

Don't Ever Change

Even if you grant that people shouldn't be forced into sustaining authentic cultural practices, you might suppose that a cosmopolitan should side with those who are busy around the world "preserving culture" and resisting "cultural imperialism." But behind these slogans you often find some curious assumptions. Take "preserving culture." It's one thing to provide people with help to sustain arts they want to sustain. I am all for festivals of Welsh bards in Llandudno funded by the Welsh Arts Council, if there are people who want to recite and people who care to listen. I am delighted with the Ghana National Cultural Center in Kumasi, where you can go and learn traditional Akan dancing and drumming, especially since its classes are spirited and overflowing. Restore the deteriorating film stock of early Hollywood movies; continue the preservation of Old Norse and early Chinese and Ethiopian manuscripts; record, transcribe, and analyze the oral narratives of Malay and Maasai and Maori: all these are a valuable part of our human heritage. But preserving *culture*—in the sense of cultural artifacts, broadly conceived—is different from preserving *cultures*. And the preservers of cultures are busy trying to ensure that the Huli of Papua New Guinea or, for that matter, Sikhs in Toronto or Hmong in New Orleans keep their "authentic" ways. What makes a cultural expression authentic, though? Are we to stop the importation of baseball caps into Vietnam, so that the Zao will continue with their colorful red headdresses? Why not ask the Zao? Shouldn't the choice be theirs?

"They have no real choice," the cultural preservationists may say. "We have dumped cheap Western clothes into their markets; and they can no longer afford the silk they used to wear. If they had what they really wanted, they'd still be dressed traditionally." Notice that this is no longer an argument about authenticity. The claim is that they can't afford to do something that they'd really like to do, something that is expressive of an identity they care about and want to sustain. This is a genuine problem, one that afflicts people in many communities: they're too poor to live the life they want to lead. If that's true, it's an argument for trying to see whether we can help them get richer. But if they do get richer and they still run around in T-shirts, so much the worse, I say, for authenticity.

Not that this is likely to be a problem in the real world. People who can afford it mostly like to put on traditional garb from time to time. American boys wear tuxedos to proms. I was best man once at a Scottish wedding. The bridegroom wore a kilt, of course. (I wore a kente cloth. Andrew Oransay, who piped us up the aisle, whispered in my ear at one point, "Here we all are then, in our tribal gear.") In Kumasi, people who can afford them, love to put on their kente cloths, especially the most "traditional" ones, woven in colorful silk strips in the town of Bonwire, as they have been for a couple of centuries. (The prices have risen in part because demand outside Asante has risen. A fine kente for a man now costs more than the average Ghanaian earns in a year. Is that bad? Not for the people of Bonwire.) But trying to find some primordially authentic culture can be like peeling an onion. The textiles most people think of as traditional West African cloths are known as java prints, and arrived with the Javanese batiks sold, and often milled by, the Dutch. The traditional garb of Herera women derives from the attire of nine-teenth-century German missionaries, though it's still unmistakably Herera, not least because the fabrics they use have a distinctly un-Lutheran range of colors. And so with our kente cloth: the silk was always imported, traded by Europeans, produced in Asia. This tradition was once an innovation. Should we reject it for that reason as untraditional? How far back must one go? Should we condemn the young men and women of the University of Science and Technology, a few miles outside Kumasi, who wear European-style gowns for graduation, lined with kente strips (as they do, now, at Howard and Morehouse, too). Cultures are made of continuities and changes, and the identity of a society can survive through these changes, just as each individual survives the alterations of Jacques's "seven ages of man."

The Trouble with "Cultural Imperialism"

Cultural preservationists often make their case by invoking the evil of "cultural imperialism." And its victims aren't necessarily the formerly colonized "natives." In fact, the French have a penchant for talking of "cultural imperialism" to make the point that French people like to watch American movies and visit English-language sites on the Internet. (*Evidemment*, the American taste for French movies is something to be encouraged.) This is surely very odd. No army, no threat of sanctions, no political saber rattling, imposes Hollywood on the French.

There is a genuine issue here, I think, but it is not imperialism. France's movie industry requires government subsidy. Part of the reason, no doubt, is just that Americans have the advantage of speaking a language with many more speakers than France (though this can't be the whole explanation, since the British film industry seems to require subsidy, too). Still, whatever the reason, the French would like to have a significant number of films rooted deeply in French life, which they watch alongside all those American movies. Since the resulting films are often wonderful, in subsidizing them for themselves, they have also enriched the treasury of cosmopolitan cultural experience. So far, I think, so good.

What would justify genuine concern would be an attempt by the United States through the World Trade Organization, say, to have these culturally motivated subsidies banned. Even in the United States, most of us believe it is perfectly proper to subsidize programs on public television. We grant tax-exempt status to our opera and ballet companies; cities and states subsidize sports stadiums. It is an empirical question, not one to be settled by appeal to a free market ideology, how much of the public culture the citizens of a democratic nation want can be produced solely by the market.

But to concede this much is not to accept what the theorists of cultural imperialism want. In broad strokes, their underlying picture is this. There is a world system of capitalism. It has a center and a periphery. At the center—in Europe and the United States—is a set of multinational corporations. Some of these are in the media business. The products they sell around the world promote the interests of capitalism in general. They encourage consumption not just of films, television, and magazines but of the other non-media products of multinational capitalism. Herbert Schiller, a leading critic of "media/cultural imperialism" has claimed that it is "the imagery and cultural perspectives of the ruling sector in the center that shape and structure consciousness throughout the system at large."[2]

People who believe this story have been taking the pitches of magazine and television company executives selling advertising space for a description of reality. The evidence doesn't bear it out. As it happens, researchers actually went out into the world and explored the responses to the hit television series *Dallas* in Holland and among Israeli Arabs, Moroccan Jewish immigrants, kibbutzniks, and new Russian immigrants to Israel. They have examined the actual content of the television media—whose penetration of everyday life far exceeds that of film—in Australia, Brazil, Canada, India, and Mexico. They have looked at how American popular culture was taken up by the artists of Sophiatown, in South Africa. They have discussed *Days of Our Lives* and *The Bold and the Beautiful* with Zulu college students from traditional backgrounds.[3]

And they have found two things, which you might already have guessed. The first is that, if there is a local product—as there is in France, but also in Australia, Brazil, Canada, India, Mexico, and South Africa—many people prefer it, especially when it comes to television. For more than a decade in Ghana, the one program you could discuss with almost anyone was a local soap opera in Twi called Osofo Dadzie, a lighthearted program with a serious message, each episode, about the problems of contemporary everyday life. We know, do we not, how the Mexicans love their telenovelas? (Indeed, people know it even in Ghana, where they are

---

2   Quoted in Larry Strelitz, "Where the Global Meets the Local: Media Studies and the Myth of Cultural Homogenization," *Transnational Broadcasting Studies*, no. 6 (Spring/Summer 2001), http://www.tbsjournal.com/Archives/Spring01/strelitz.html.

3   Ien Ang, *Watching "Dallas": Soap Opera and the Melodramatic Imagination* (London: Methuen, 1985); Tamar Liebes and Elihu Katz, *The Export of Meaning: Cross-cultural Readings of Dallas* (New York: Oxford University Press, 1990); John Sinclair, Elizabeth Jacka, and Stuart Cunningham, eds., *New Patterns in Global Television: Peripheral Vision* (New York: Oxford University Press, 1996); Rob Nixon, *Homelands, Harlem and Hollywood: South African Culture and the World Beyond* (New York: Routledge, 1994); Strelitz, "Where the Global Meets the Local."

shown in crudely dubbed English versions, too.) The academic research confirms that people tend to prefer television programming that's close to their own culture.[4] (The Hollywood blockbuster has a special status around the world; but here, as American movie critics regularly complain, the nature of the product—heavy on the action sequences, light on clever badinage—is partly determined by what works in Bangkok and Berlin. From the point of view of the cultural-imperialism theorists, this is a case in which the empire has struck back.)

The second observation that the research supports is that how people respond to these American products depends on their existing cultural context. When the media scholar Larry Strelitz spoke to those students from KwaZulu-Natal, he found that they were anything but passive vessels. One of them, Sipho, reported both that he was a "very, very strong Zulu man" and that he had drawn lessons from watching the American soap opera *Days of Our Lives* "especially relation-ship-wise." It fortified his view that "if a guy can tell a woman that he loves her she should be able to do the same." What's more, after watching the show, Sipho "realized that I should be allowed to speak to my father. He should be my friend rather than just my father. ..." One doubts that that was the intended message of multinational capitalism's ruling sector.

But Sipho's response also confirmed what has been discovered over and over again. Cultural consumers are not dupes. They can resist. So he also said,

> In terms of our culture, a girl is expected to enter into relationships
> when she is about 20. In the Western culture, the girl can be exposed
> to a relationship as early as 15 or 16. That one we shouldn't adopt in our
> culture. Another thing we shouldn't adopt from the Western culture has to
> do with the way they treat elderly people. I wouldn't like my family to be
> sent into an old-age home.[5]

The "old-age homes" in American soap operas may be safe places, full of kindly people. That doesn't sell the idea to Sipho. Dutch viewers of *Dallas* saw not the pleasures of conspicuous consumption among the super-rich—the message that theorists of "cultural imperialism" find in every episode—but a reminder that money and power don't protect you from tragedy. Israeli Arabs saw a program that confirmed that women abused by their husbands should return to their fathers. Mexican telenovelas remind Ghanaian women that, where sex is at issue, men are not to be trusted. If the telenovelas tried to tell them otherwise, they wouldn't believe it.

---

4   See J.D. Straubhaar, "Beyond Media Imperialism: Asymmetrical Interdependence and Cultural Proximity," *Critical Studies in Mass Communications* 8 (1991): 39-59.

5   The quotes from the Zulu student Sipho are from Larry Strelitz, *Where the Global Meets the Local: South African Youth and Their Experience of the Global Media* (PhD Thesis, Rhodes University, 2003), pp. 137-41.

Talk of cultural imperialism structuring the consciousnesses of those in the periphery treats Sipho and people like him as tabulae rasae on which global capitalism's moving finger writes its message, leaving behind another homogenized consumer as it moves on. It is deeply condescending. And it isn't true.

In Praise of Contamination

Behind much of the grumbling about the cultural effects of globalization is an image of how the world used to be—an image that is both unrealistic and unappealing. Our guide to what is wrong here might as well be another African. Publius Terentius Afer, whom we know as Terence, was born a slave in Carthage in North Africa, and taken to Rome in the late second century AD. Before long, his plays were widely admired among the city's literary elite; witty, elegant works that are, with Plautus's earlier, less cultivated works, essentially all we have of Roman comedy. Terence's own mode of writing—his free incorporation of earlier Greek plays into a single Latin drama—was known to Roman litterateurs as "contamination." It's a suggestive term. When people speak for an ideal of cultural purity, sustaining the authentic culture of the Asante or the American family farm, I find myself drawn to *contamination* as the name for a counter-ideal. Terence had a notably firm grasp on the range of human variety: "So many men, so many opinions" was an observation of his. And it's in his comedy *The Self-Tormentor* that you'll find what has proved something like the golden rule of cosmopolitanism: *Homo sum: humani nil a me alienum puto.* "I am human: nothing human is alien to me." The context is illuminating. The play's main character, a busybody farmer named Chremes, is told by his overworked neighbor to mind his own affairs; the *homo sum* credo is his breezy rejoinder. It isn't meant to be an ordinance from on high; it's just the case for gossip.

Then again, gossip—the fascination people have for the small doings of *other* people—shares a taproot with literature. Certainly the ideal of contamination has no more eloquent exponent than Salman Rushdie, who has insisted that the novel that occasioned his fatwa "celebrates hybridity, impurity, intermingling, the transformation that comes of new and unexpected combinations of human beings, cultures, ideas, politics, movies, songs. It rejoices in mongrelization and fears the absolutism of the Pure. Melange, hotchpotch, a bit of this and a bit of that is how newness enters the world. It is the great possibility that mass migration gives the world, and I have tried to embrace it."[6] But it didn't take modern mass migration to create this great possibility. The early Cynics and Stoics took their contamination from the places they were born to the Greek cities where they taught. Many were strangers in those places; cosmopolitanism

---

6   Salman Rushdie, *Imaginary Homelands: Essays and Criticism, 1981-1991* (London: Granta Books, 1991), p. 394.

was invented by contaminators whose migrations were solitary. And the migrations that have contaminated the larger world were not all modern. Alexander's empire molded both the states and the sculpture of Egypt and North India; first the Mongols then the Mughals shaped great swaths of Asia; the Bantu migrations populated half the African continent. Islamic states stretch from Morocco to Indonesia; Christianity reached Africa, Europe, and Asia within a few centuries of the death of Jesus of Nazareth; Buddhism long ago migrated from India into much of East and Southeast Asia. Jews and people whose ancestors came from many parts of China have long lived in vast diasporas. The traders of the Silk Road changed the style of elite dress in Italy; someone brought Chinese pottery for burial in fifteenth-century Swahili graves. I have heard it said that the bagpipes started out in Egypt and came to Scotland with the Roman infantry. None of this is modern.

No doubt, there can be an easy and spurious utopianism of "mixture," as there is of "purity." And yet the larger human truth is on the side of Terence's contamination. We do not need, have never needed, settled community, a homogeneous system of values, in order to have a home. Cultural purity is an oxymoron. The odds are that, culturally speaking, you already live a cosmopolitan life, enriched by literature, art, and film that come from many places, and that contains influences from many more. And the marks of cosmopolitanism in that Asante village— soccer, Muhammad Ali, hip-hop—entered their lives, as they entered yours, not as work but as pleasure. There are some Western products and vendors that appeal to people in the rest of the world *because* they're seen as Western, as modern: McDonald's, Levis. But even here, cultural significance isn't just something that corporate headquarters gets to decree. People wear Levis on every continent. In some places they are informal wear; in others they're dressy. You can get Coca-Cola on every continent, too. In Kumasi you will get it at funerals. Not, in my experience, in the West of England, where hot milky Indian tea is favored. The point is that people in each place make their own uses even of the most famous global commodities.

A tenable cosmopolitanism tempers a respect for difference with a respect for actual human beings—and with a sentiment best captured in the credo, once comic, now commonplace, penned by that former slave from North Africa. Few remember what Chremes says next, but it's as important as the sentence everyone quotes: "Either I want to find out for myself or I want to advise you: think what you like. If you're right, I'll do what you do. If you're wrong, I'll set you straight."

Source: *Cosmopolitanism: Ethics in a World of Strangers*. New York: Norton, 2006. 101-13.

WHAT IT SAYS

1. Appiah opens his essay with a comparison of Kumasi, the capital city of the Asante region of Ghana, with a small village twenty miles outside of the city. What does this comparison show? What is the point Appiah means to get across with this comparison?

2. What are some of the positive aspects of homogenization as a result of globalization, according to Appiah?

3. Appiah refers to a group of people whom he calls "cosmopolitans." The term is not defined here. What can you infer about the meaning of this term, given the selection you have read? What is a cosmopolitan and what does a cosmopolitan have to do with globalization?

4. On page 419, Appiah quotes the nineteenth-century political philosopher John Stuart Mill. What is the point Appiah hopes to make by citing this passage?

5. What are Appiah's objections to the idea of "cultural imperialism"? What does the theory of cultural imperialism fail to account for, according to Appiah?

6. What does Appiah mean by the term "cultural contamination," and what are its virtues?

HOW IT SAYS IT

1. Look again at the quotation from John Stuart Mill that Appiah uses to make his case about individual choice in the context of cultural authenticity. What might be the strategy for using this quotation? How does it help Appiah make his case?

2. Who are the intended readers of Appiah's essay? How can you tell?

3. Think about how Appiah handles the various perspectives on globalization in his essay. How does his treatment of differing views work to advance his own perspective?

WRITE ABOUT IT

1. Appiah's essay may seem somewhat straightforward, yet summarizing it may prove to be more difficult than you might imagine. Write a short (one- to two-page) summary of Appiah's essay. What is its main thesis? What are the most important supporting points?

2. Interview a classmate or other acquaintance from a non-Western country and ask him or her about the effects of Western media and culture on life in his or her own home community. Consider asking about how particular television programs or movies are understood, and/or how various Western products are consumed. What do his or her responses suggest about the cultural effects of globalization on non-Western societies?

3. Appiah appears to be rather upbeat regarding the effects of globalization. Are you pessimistic or optimistic about the prospects of globalization? Write an essay in which you consider the effects of globalization on your own life, drawing on specific examples from both work and home life, or your involvement in both the production and consumption of globally marketed goods. Think about how globalization may affect you in ways you have not previously imagined.

f. Yechan Do, "The Benefits or Detriments of Globalization"

Yechan Do, from Eagleville, Pennsylvania, is an undergraduate student at New York University. She is majoring in economics and East Asian studies and expects to graduate in May 2016.

Yechan Do
Dr. Rectenwald
Writing 1
December 2, 2012

The Benefits or Detriments of Globalization

As a world made up of over six billion people from over two hundred countries and with the latest advances in technology and communication, it is not surprising that we are becoming more connected and culturally aware. This phenomenon is often referred to as "globalization" and arguably has affected every country in the world. Today, we can go through our lives wearing clothes made in Indonesia, buying produce grown in Puerto Rico, using technology from Korea, and eating food from India. Needless to say, we are more connected than we think and there is a definite change in the level of contact we have with each other. With hundreds of economies, cultures, traditions, and ideas presented and adopted, there is bound to be a reaction for or against these changes. On one end of the spectrum, there is believed to be a homogenization of cultures, or the diminishing of cultures, producing global sameness. On the other end, there is argued to be a heterogenization of cultures, or the creation of diversity within cultures. Though it is clear that we are a changing world made up of different peoples and cultures, it is still questionable whether or not globalization is to the benefit or detriment of human beings.

As one of the newest areas of study, globalization addresses issues regarding the increasingly dependent state of the world's cultures. Critics of globalization, including Benjamin Barber, argue that with an increasing emphasis on a commerce-driven environment, homogeneity will be the outcome. In an attempt to preserve their identities among the "onrushing economic, technological, and ecological forces," cultural and religious groups will then lash back against the homogenous world, causing serious and violent repercussions (Barber 33). Advocates of globalization including Tyler Cowen, Bryant Simon, and Anthony Appiah, on the other hand, rebuke this idea. Though all three authors agree that with increasing trade and cultural influence there is an inevitable change in the dynamics of a culture, they view these changes as a movement towards positive development and the product of a co-existence of both global and local influences.

It is apparent that world cultures are connecting and growing in a huge cross-cultural trade. However, what is less apparent is the reaction against this exchange and the overall negative ramifications. For Barber, globalization enforces not only homogeneity but also two antithetical forces, with each creating equally destructive states. In what he calls "McWorld," Barber depicts the scenario of a cosmopolitan and hyper-globalized future in which countries are "tied together by communications, information, entertainment, and commerce" (Barber 33). Because of these effects caused by globalization and the resulting homogeniza-tion caused by McWorld, we may soon live in a type of "monoculture" in which nations are clumped together to form one homogenous ball of integration and uniformity so as to create the best environment for commerce (Barber 33). In McWorld, it is evident that globalization does not promote the development of cultural awareness but instead, promotes a homogenous global market driven by profit, consumption, and consumerism.

As the antithesis and violent reaction against McWorld, Jihad consists of a tribal world in which cultures are pitted against each other in a fight against "every kind of interdependence, every kind of artificial social cooperation and mutuality: against technology, against pop culture, and against integrated markets" (Barber 32). Essentially, Jihad is the opposition to every thing and every movement that makes up McWorld. Threatened by change in a swiftly moving future, Jihad creates an equal but opposite response by firmly holding on to its national identity and rejecting the outside world. Though the former seems to be almost inviting, or at least far more appealing than warfare, Barber points out that it is no better than Jihad. In a way, McWorld is the stealthy imminent version of Jihad; it is work-ing its way into our lives through the guise of economics, material goods, and popular culture (Barber 36). Although the tension between McWorld and Jihad is disconcerting, what is more alarming is the idea that by working against each other, they actually move towards the same goal: a bleak undemocratic future. In a chain reaction, McWorld's insatiable avarice for profit and gains generates an equal but opposite response from Jihad for more division and war in the name of local preservation. In both situations, there is a loss of personal identity that is imperative in a democratic society.

Through Barber's interpretation of homogenized globalization and its result-ing forms of McWorld and Jihad, it is clear that there is more to globalization than the supposed increases in economic and cultural development; there is a serious consequence in the loss of civil liberty and public interest, giving rise to a post democratic state (Barber 34).

Though Barber explores the opposing forces of globalization through a possible homogenous effect, Appiah, Cowen, and Simon highlight the heterogenization, synergy, and positive developments created by cross-cultural interactions. To begin, all three authors understand that with the movement of ideas into a culture, there is bound to be a definite change. However, unlike Barber and his idea of homogeneity and the overall negative impact of globalization, Appiah and Cowen stress that there is no real threat to culture because culture is founded upon globalization itself. Appiah argues that though critics of globalization cite recent increasing levels of homogenization in non-western cultures around the world, these changes are necessary in the creation of culture and have in fact, been occurring for centuries. Adoption of other ethnic values, goods, and ideals is not a form of homogenization but rather a necessary uptake of ideas and values for "... cultures are made up of continuities *and* changes, and the identity of a society can survive through these changes ..." (Appiah 107). Similarly to Appiah's idea of a multi-layer culture, Cowen states that Western culture itself, a target for critics as the main promoter of homogenization, is actually the creation of "... multicultural products, resulting from international exchange of goods, services, and ideas" (Cowen 6).

Appiah and Cowen extend their argument to assert that globalization produces numerous progressive transformations. The most apparent is the movement of commerce and ideas. Contrast to McWorld and its materialism, commerce according to Appiah is based on improvement of developing countries. Through continuous international trade, more countries will have access to medicine, clean drinking water, and education (Appiah 103). Furthermore, Cowen cites the Renaissance as a product of the flourishing trade routes between the East and West. He states that through reglobalization in new contact with Asian and Islamic cultures after a time of diminished trade, "trade fairs expanded, shipping lanes became more active, and scientific ideas spread" (Cowen 7), resulting in the numerous advances that we know today. Globalization demonstrates another positive growth in the liberation from what Cowen calls the "tyranny of place" (Cowen 5). Today, because of the worldwide trade in cultural products, there is more freedom and access to different ideologies, opportunities, and communities and we are no longer subjected to one mode of life. Appiah reinforces this idea of the importance of exposure to human variety and quotes John Stuart Mill as explaining that, "the same things which are helps to one person towards the cultivation of his higher nature, are hindrances to another" (Appiah 104). Though we may be born into one culture and its predominant customs and traditions, that does not mean that we should be forced to accept them as our own. As Appiah puts it, "there is no place for the enforcement of diversity by trapping people within a kind of difference they long to escape." Through globalization, we are now transforming societies towards having the means to help people acquire basic needs and having the ability to explore and apply different meanings of truth to their lives.

In another interesting result of globalization, Simon and Cowen examine the relationship between the original local foundations and the incoming global influences. In Barber's viewpoint, the consumption created by international markets leads to a fierce reaction from traditionalists, resulting in destructive consequences.

However, according to Simon, there does not have to be a malignant upshot as a result of cross-cultural trade. In fact, Simon explains that the local and the global work together interdependently. With the increasing presence of global brands such as McDonald's or Starbucks, there is "a grassroots pushback, an assertion of the enduring value of particular places, tastes and traditions" (Simon 1). With regards to this relationship, it is in a way similar to Barber's Jihad versus McWorld: one force creates an opposing force. However, the similarity ends here. For Simon, the global and the local do not wage war against each other with the hopes of destroying the other. In a seemingly endless cycle, the local creates the global and the global reinforces the local with the result that cultural influence is successfully integrated while regional customs are still held in place. Using the omnipresent Starbucks as an example, it once started as a small coffee shop in Seattle. However, due to marketing and expansion, it soon grew to become the global corporation that it is today. Though the expansion demonstrates Starbucks's popularity among millions of people worldwide, that same expansion would be its drawback as consumers complained of its overbearing presence and destruction of resources. Soon enough, there was a demand for small mom-and-pop coffee shops (Simon 2). Cowen also addresses this idea of the interaction between local and outsides forces. Using ideas of heterogenization and homogenization in the market, he concludes that the presence of global brands allows local commodities to be introduced too. The homogenizing effect of global products works in tandem with local markets in that "mass culture and niche culture are complements ... with partial homogenization often creating the conditions necessary for diversity to flower on the micro level" (Cowen 16).

Based on the rising influence of global cultures, there has been much debate on the effects of their presence. It is overt that with the increasing economic and technological ties, there has been a substantial change in the way we live. We cannot go through our days without having been touched or influenced by another country's products, language, ideologies, and government. To some, this change is feared to lead to a culture driven by money and consumption and subsequently, harmful reactions against this newfound world. To others, globalization is a movement of dynamic mechanisms to be praised for its positive and progressive push towards a stable future. Though the outlook is still uncertain, the only thing that is clear is that our external cultural influences will not subside any time in the near future and will bring about even more changes, for better or for worse.

Works Cited

Appiah, Anthony. "Cosmopolitan Contamination." *Cosmopolitanism: ethics in a world of strangers.* New York: W.W. Norton & Co., 2006. 101-113. Print.

Barber, Benjamin R. "Introduction." *Jihad vs. McWorld.* New York: Times Books, 1995. 33-39. Print.

Cowen, Tyler. "Trade between Cultures." *Creative destruction*. Princeton, NJ: Princeton University Press, 2002. 1-18. Print.

Simon, Bryant. "Global Brands Contend with Appreciation for the Local." *YaleGlobal Online Magazine*. N.p., n.d. Web. 2 Dec. 2012. <http://yaleglobal. yale.edu/content/global-brands-contend-appreciation-local>.

Questions for Synthesis

1. Write an essay that explores the issue of cultural diversity and the impact of globalization on it. You might approach the task by considering common points discussed in the essays in this chapter, including homogenization and heterogeneity, forms of provincialism (including perhaps "Jihad"), or another issue running through the essays or in the Suggested Additional Resources.

   Be sure to pay attention to the details and nuances of the authors' positions. Your goal in this essay is not to argue for or against a particular position, but rather to faithfully represent the various positions taken by a group of writers on a common point or set of common points. You may wish to visualize the various positions by constructing a synthesis grid (see pp. 77–79) before you begin to write.

2. Write an essay in which you explore various positions on mass media and local or indigenous arts and entertainment, as expressed by the authors in this chapter. Consider works from the Suggested Additional Resources if necessary. What, according to the authors, has been the impact of globalization?

Questions for Contribution

1. Write an essay that takes a stance on globalization and global culture. Are the forces of "McDonaldization" overwhelming the cultures of the world, or do some authors exaggerate this scenario? Assuming that democracy is a good thing, which is a greater threat to it: "Jihad" or "McDonaldization"? Be sure to find evidence to support your positions. Use photos and other graphics to help make your case.

   You will likely need to conduct additional research to formulate a well-informed contribution to the discourse of global culture and globalization.

2. Write an essay that argues a way forward in order to overcome "McDonaldization." In other words, imagine and sketch out the path to the future that George Ritzer claims is possible if we are able to retain the benefits of McDonaldization while creating other, more creative and diverse cultural developments.

   Draw on the readings in this chapter as well as from the Suggested Additional Resources, but aim for a fresh, innovative approach to the topic.

CHAPTER 5 OUR TRANSHUMAN FUTURE?

INTRODUCTION

Suppose it were possible, through some sort of instantaneous genetic engineering, to change any aspect of your nature, so that you could have any combination of capacities that has ever been in the range of human possibility: you could have Michael Jordan's fade-away shot, Mozart's musicality, Groucho Marx's comic gifts, Proust's delicate way with language. Suppose you could put these together with any desires you wanted—homo- or hetero-, or a taste for Wagner or Eminem.... Suppose, further, that there were no careers or professions in this world because all material needs were met by intelligent machines. Far from being a Utopia, so it seems to me, this would be a kind of hell.

—Anthony Appiah, *The Ethics of Identity* (2005)

Man is not born free, but is everywhere in biological chains. People of the world, unite. You have nothing to lose but your biological chains!

We stand at a turning point in human evolution. We have cracked the genetic code; translated the Book of Life. We will soon possess the ability to become designers of our own evolution....

As humanism freed us from the chains of superstition, let transhumanism free us from our biological chains.

—Simon Young, *Designer Evolution: A Transhumanist Manifesto* (2006)

Contexts of Discussion

In this chapter, we introduce you to breathtaking prospects for the future, a future seen as arising from a combination of scientific, technological, and engineering efforts known as **Genetics, Nanotechnology, and Robotics (GNR)**. 433

Transhumanism, sometimes called **posthumanism**,[1] is a philosophy based on GNR that argues that human beings can transcend their limitations by harnessing the power of science and technology. Transhumanists desire an enhanced human nature and often refer to this enhanced humanity as "humanity+."

Some transhumanists, such as Simon Young, quoted above, believe that we can take over where evolution has left off to create a new and improved species—either ourselves, or a successor to ourselves. The claims and aims of transhumanism are radical in intent and vast in scope. Transhumanism likewise gives rise to controversy. You may find some of this material hard to believe, and other parts dense and difficult. But we cannot imagine that you will find it boring.

As many of its enthusiasts and critics suggest, what may be at stake in the field is the very definition of being human. For better or worse, the transhumanist challenge to the conventional notions of human existence is very much a hot topic and is being taken seriously by proponents and opponents alike. The potential changes to our lives would be both far-reaching and extremely personal. Promoters of transhumanism say that GNR technologies will produce drastic changes in our external worlds, while deeply penetrating our bodies and minds. Some of these developments will be relatively mundane, such as regular genetic check-ups to scan for "programming errors" that may be treated with gene therapy. Others may seem like science fiction.

Imagine a world full of "designer babies," born of **genetic screening** and custom **genetic engineering**. Imagine **nanorobots** cleaning up the environment, recreating a green planet, and reversing global warming. What would life be like if computers exceeded human intelligence and memory chips, installed in our brains, enhanced memory by a thousand-fold? How would you feel knowing that nanorobots were coursing through your bloodstream, killing pathogens, eliminating cancer cells, repairing genetic codes, and reversing aging? Could death become a thing of the past? If you could upload your personality into a computer, and thus "live forever," would you do it?

The scope of such research and conjecture is so great that the proposals offered by enthusiasts and often feared and loathed by critics will not be left to scientific and technological thinkers alone. The field also engages moral, social, political, economic, and philosophical debate. This introduction will take you on a short tour of GNR and its philosophical underpinnings, pointing out areas of research and conjecture, as well as the issues and stakeholders involved.

---

1   The terms transhumanism and posthumanism are sometimes used interchangeably. Where a distinction is drawn, transhumanism is usually regarded as a transitional state between a human and a post-human being. We use the term transhumanism throughout because it is the more common term.

Areas of Research and Conjecture

Philosophy is the investigation of questions regarding the nature of existence (ontology), proper behavior (ethics), and knowledge (epistemology). Transhumanism is a movement based on science and technology, but since transhumanism is also a philosophical field that examines the possibilities and ethics of technological change, the most able transhumanists are trained philosophers, as are transhumanism's most avid opponents.

In this chapter, we include an essay by philosopher Francis Fukuyama, who opposes transhumanism. In the Suggested Additional Resources at the end of this introduction, we also list the work of several philosophers, transhumanist and otherwise, who examine transhuman questions and problems.

Critical theory is the examination and critique of society and culture, drawing from both the social sciences and the humanities. The methodology of critical theory lends itself to an examination of transhumanism, as the work of Katherine Hayles demonstrates. We include an essay by Hayles in this chapter.

Genetics is the oldest field within GNR. Genetics is the study of genes, the codes for the production and reproduction of proteins (and the genes themselves) that make up the structures of all life forms. The study of genes has existed at least since Gregor Mendel worked with plant reproduction in the nineteenth century. James Watson and Francis Crick discovered the double helix structure of DNA in 1953, and in the 1990s the US Department of Energy and the National Institutes of Health undertook the Human Genome Project, with the goal of mapping the entire human gene sequence within 15 years. (Later, researchers from the UK, Japan, France, Germany, China, and other countries joined the project.) The complete mapping was finished by 2003, years ahead of schedule. This breakthrough opened enormous possibilities: Once genes for various traits are isolated, treating and even altering them become plausible.

The least controversial of these methods is **somatic gene therapy** (somatic cells form the body of a developed organism). Somatic gene therapy involves targeting the genes in the developed body in order to treat an inherited disease. Although some successes are recorded in animal trials, most experiments have met with little success. The major obstacle to overcome or work around is the need to target specific cells, out of trillions in the body, for genetic manipulation. Further, because gene therapy works on existing cells in a fully developed individual, such changes cannot be genetically transmitted to offspring.

Genetic screening is more controversial. A commonly used type of genetic screening involves **amniocentesis**, a process in which a sample of amniotic fluid, the liquid surrounding a fetus in the uterus, is removed and tested for genetically heritable traits. Amniocentesis has been used to inform parents of some obvious and discernible genetic diseases, such as Tay-Sachs disease, giving them the opportunity to abort the fetus before it matures, should a test prove positive.

This process brings up such controversies as the following:

- What constitutes a "viable" human being?
- Does one human being have the right to decide whether a fetus, however compromised, lives or dies?
- What is the cost-to-benefit outcome in such a scenario?

Health practitioners, social scientists, economists, philosophers, human rights activists, and others are divided on these issues.

Yet advanced genetic screening will go much further. When scientists provide parents access to the scanned genetic material of their embryos created by in vitro fertilization (IVF), parents may reduce or even eliminate the risks of many more genetic diseases and even "deficiencies" in their children before embryos are implanted in the uterus. This process, specifically known as **preimplantation genetic diagnosis (PGD)**, would allow parents to decide which if any of their viable embryos to implant in the womb of the mother. Genetic screening might also take place before conception, allowing potential mates to search for partners who hold the genetic credentials they desire in their children. This scenario is treated in the 1997 science fiction movie *Gattaca*, which portrays a once-futuristic scenario in which one's genetic makeup is expected to determine success or failure to such an extent that it becomes a self-fulfilling prophecy.

Genetic engineering takes the use of genetic knowledge even further. **Germline engineering** (another term for genetic engineering) has been undertaken for several years in agricultural biotechnology, as well as in a variety of animals. Genetically engineered foods are common in markets around the world. By adding or swapping genes in seeds, corporations have been able to increase crop yields, as well as profits. For example, Ciba Seeds (later Novartis Seeds) developed a pest-resistant breed of corn called Bt Corn by inserting into the corn's DNA a gene from a bacterium whose proteins are lethal to pests. Monsanto used genetic splicing to create the Terminator Seed—a seed that developed into a sterile adult plant—in order to control its patented intellectual property.

Such **genetically modified organisms (GMOs)** also include animals. Harvard University researchers used gene-splicing techniques to create a mouse susceptible to cancer in order to test treatments. The "oncomouse" (cancerous mouse) was created by injecting fertilized eggs, preferably single-celled, with a cancer-inducing gene. Unlike somatic therapies, genetic engineering works on the individual before the zygote develops. The changes in genetic material become part of the organism's reproductive system and are passed to the next generation. The ultimate prospect for genetic engineering may be designer babies. This term refers to offspring engineered to "inherit" desired traits and exclude undesired ones. Critics such as Francis Fukuyama use the term "designer babies" primarily to suggest that the process makes children into commodities. Despite technical difficulties, risks, and ethical dilemmas involved in this process, genetic engineers are undaunted.

Nanotechnology applies technology to the field of **nanoscience**, which is the study of the fundamental principles of molecules and structures of 1 to 100 nanometers in size. ("Nano-" is a prefix meaning one billionth. To get an idea of nanoscale, consider that a human hair is approximately 50,000 nanometers in diameter.) Nanotechnology involves using nanostructures in nanoscale devices to carry out useful applications. For example, a nanostructure could deliver nutrients to cells as needed or collect and eliminate waste from cells.

Some scientists say that nanotechnology may allow the reconstruction of materials usually found only in nature or through expensive and arduous processes. In his *Engines of Creation* (1986), for example, Eric Drexler describes a future world in which nanoscientists manipulate matter at the atomic level, solving human needs. Nanotechnology may also be used in environmental applications, such as eliminating chemical waste from streams and rivers, or carbon dioxide from the atmosphere. Nanotechnology theoretically includes **nanorobotics**, or robots of nanoscale programmed for particular functions.

Robotics is the study of intelligent machines, or machines with onboard computers. Isaac Asimov, whose *Robot Visions* is included in the Suggested Additional Resources at the end of this introduction, coined the term in a 1942 short story. Robotics includes mobile or stationary machines that may act autonomously or semi-autonomously in such roles as receptionist, soccer player, or truck driver. Robotics is also used in real-world applications in numerous domains. For example, with funding from the Defense Advanced Research Projects Agency (DARPA), robotics research has traditionally included military defense projects. Contemporary applications include robots that navigate battlefields and scan them for mines, and unmanned drones that, in 2012, undertook bombing missions in Afghanistan, Pakistan, and elsewhere.

Of course, robotic engineering also includes numerous non-military applications. Robots are regularly used on assembly lines, in shipping processes, transportation, and many other industrial tasks. Robotics has been used in domains as varied as space exploration, precision surgery, facial recognition (for possible terrorist identification), and the merging of human vision with ultrasound imaging, to name just a few.

Robotics also includes **artificial intelligence**, or "soft robots" that operate "invisibly" in computers and on the Internet. For a sense of the extensive plans and projects underway in robotics, visit the homepage of the Robotics Institute at Carnegie Mellon University (http://www.ri.cmu.edu/index.html). Some futurists insist that robotics will soon include merging biological and machine functions to enhance human abilities. For example, new research in prosthetics allows patients to train their brains to operate prosthetic hands. Further, **bionics** researchers are developing interfaces that will allow prosthetic limbs to *feel*.

Futurists also envision reverse-engineering the human brain to create human-like intelligence in robots, which would exceed human intelligence thanks to faster computational times and superior memory. The possibilities in robotics include the creation of a "species" that may surpass, and, some fear, eventually replace us. The point beyond which life will be forever transformed is known as the **Singularity**, a term coined by computer scientist and science-fiction writer Vernor Vinge. Those who anticipate and probably welcome the prospect of the Singularity are called **Singulartarians**, and they expect or seek a future world—not necessarily a utopia or a dystopia—in which the technological changes will make life a radically different affair. In his essay "The Six Epochs," included in this chapter, Ray Kurzweil outlines his vision for the Singularity.

With or without faith in a future Singularity, most in the field agree that genetics, nanotechnology, and robotics are heading toward a convergence of significant consequences. The ultimate objectives of GNR transhumanists vary according to the stakeholders in the field. We discuss some of the issues and stakeholders in the following section.

Issues and Stakeholders

Eugenics: Coined in 1883 by Charles Darwin's cousin, Francis Galton, *eugenic* means well-rooted or well-bred. Galton inaugurated eugenics in order to produce conditions conducive to breeding "higher" types or races, especially of human beings. Galton himself was a eugenicist who welcomed the prospects of controlling evolution through human selection of traits.

Eugenics has a dark past. It is usually associated with one of the most brutal pogroms of the twentieth century, the Jewish Holocaust committed by the Nazis under the leadership of Adolf Hitler. The Holocaust was part of a Nazi *lebensborn* or "life-spring" program that aimed to increase the number of blue-eyed, blond-haired people, whom the Nazis called Aryans. Beginning with forced sterilization of the "unfit," the *lebensborn* program eventually led to the concentration camps in which some six million people died. But eugenics programs were also conducted in the United States, where forced sterilizations were undertaken over several decades in 33 states. In North Carolina, for example, where a eugenics program lasted into the 1970s, the state's Eugenics Compensation Task Force is recommending compensation for the estimated 117 surviving victims, many of them African Americans.

The specter of eugenics haunts the fields of genetics and genetic engineering. Studies suggesting a genetic basis for intelligence, criminality, or other complex behaviors have often met with charges of racism or eugenicist intentions. Likewise, prospects or plans for genetic engineering to produce children of higher intelligence or better emotional dispositions are vulnerable to harsh criticism. The defenders of genetic engineering, however, argue that eugenics is not necessarily an evil practice. They try to dissociate new genetic engineering possibilities from any state-supported eugenics programs of the past. "Liberal eugenics," as it has been called, will be private, controlled by parents, and not mandated by the state. Liberal eugenics stresses individual, private choice rather than the fantasies of racial or other supremacists. Private or liberal eugenics, advocates argue, will help parents create children free of genetic disease and possessing the traits for greater success and happiness.

"Playing God": One of the most common charges against GNR advocates is that they are trying to "play God." Those against GNR say that altering the God-given constitution of human beings violates God's plan for humanity, which they see as the ultimate hubris. Hubris, or extreme arrogance, was the crime of Prometheus, the Titan in Greek mythology who stole fire from the Olympians. The Olympian sky god Zeus, enraged by Prometheus' impertinence, condemned him to a life of torture, chaining him to a rock where an eagle could feed on his liver daily. Similarly, in the book of Genesis, Adam and Eve are punished with banishment from the paradise of Eden and from the promise of eternal life for eating from the Tree of Knowledge.

A more recent story of hubris and punishment is that portrayed in the novel *Frankenstein* (1818) by Mary Shelley. For assembling human parts exhumed from graves and bringing his creature to life, Dr. Frankenstein suffers unremitting agony over the death of loved ones at the hands of his unnatural progeny. Even those without a particularly religious bent respond to GNR by denouncing the impulse to play God. They suggest that such attempts are doomed to failure or disaster. According to the law of unintended consequences, they say, complications we cannot predict will always arise. Yet the transhumanist Simon Young answers that nature has done a poor job on its own, imposing numerous design flaws and limitations upon human nature.

Human rights and dignity: Objections to potential GNR enhancements to human beings go beyond religious grounds. For example, Francis Fukuyama argues that our notion of individual rights depends on a stable human nature. When some human beings are enhanced by GNR technologies, Fukuyama insists, those who are "unenhanced" will lose societal value. Their human rights will erode as the enhanced argue for privileges based on their supposed superiority. The only reasonable solution, Fukuyama argues, is governmental policies that ensure against such possibilities. However, GNR proponents such as Simon Young believe that such sanctions would amount to using legislation to impose infirmity, disease, aging, and death.

The rich and the poor: Access to GNR technologies is also an issue. Won't the recipients of enhancements most likely be those with the most money? GNR used for transhumanist purposes, some critics argue, threatens to widen an already growing gap between rich and poor. Advocates claim that enhancements may reach the rich first, but as technology advances, costs will fall, opening access to everyone. For a precedent, they point to the principle widely known as **Moore's Law**, a maxim of computer scientist Gordon Moore, who predicted (with relative success) that computer-processing capabilities would double every two years, without an increase in price. Extending Moore's Law, inventor and futurist Ray Kurzweil argues that the performance of other GNR technologies improves at an exponential rate without increasing in price. Further, rather than increasing inequality, these technologies will benefit those otherwise condemned to poverty due to differences in ability shown to be based on genetic inheritance.

Human successors: A successor follows and often replaces its predecessor. In the evolutionary process, better-adapted varieties and species replace competing varieties and species. This process works in all living things, from bacteria to human beings. Even advocates admit that super-intelligent machines or robots, even those created by other, earlier machines, could eventually replace us as the dominant species. Such predictions are based on the explosive rate of technological development, as described by Kurzweil, Hans Moravec, and others. The movie *I-Robot*, based on the fiction of Isaac Asimov, illustrates this scenario. But even before such a dystopia could come to pass, human-computer interaction will be more than a matter of texting on iPhones. What about human-robot hybrids, often called cyborgs? Might these mid-term "species"—either people with robotic parts or robots with human elements—elbow unenhanced human beings out of existence?

Some say that while these and other such futures are possible, safeguards can be installed to avoid them. Humanists like Francis Fukuyama and technologists like Bill Joy say that we must know when to say "enough" and put the brakes on runaway technology. A belief in technological determinism, they say, may become a self-fulfilling prophecy and lead to a robot or cyborg takeover, but it is still avoidable.

As You Read

The readings that follow, we believe, represent some of the most important writing on transhumanism and GNR to date. As you read this chapter, consider the issues, the points of conflict or agreement, that you see among the arguments presented. You may want to visualize these points of connection and divergence using a synthesis grid (see pp. 77–79) and write about them in a synthesis paper. At the same time, you will likely ponder the probability of a particular idea coming to pass.

If you find yourself dismissing all of the ideas, imagine how unlikely our current technology would have seemed to people living 100 or even 50 years ago, and how many and how fast changes have come about. Then begin to decide where you stand on some or all developments and prospects:

- Do you believe that, while possible, such changes would be for the worse and should be prevented?
- Do you think that, while impossible, some of the changes would be positive?
- Or do you generally embrace and welcome GNR's prospects and transhumanism's goals, with certain caveats?
- How would you support your position and answer your potential critics?

Before you decide, read closely and critically, and remember that this chapter is only an introduction to this fascinating field. Also refer to the Suggested Additional Resources that follow.

Suggested Additional Resources

Business and Economics

Croll, Alistair. "The Business Singularity." *O'Reilly Radar*. 31 Jan. 2013. Web.
De Garis, Hugo. *The Artilect War: Cosmists vs. Terrans: A Bitter Controversy Concerning Whether Humanity Should Build Godlike Massively Intelligent Machines*. Palm Springs, CA: ETC Publications, 2005.
Duivestein, Sander. "Big Data, Changing Business Models and Singularity." *Sogeti VINT*. 12 July 2012. Web.

Fiction

Card, Orson S. *Ender's Game*. New York: Tor, 1991.
Dann, Jack, and Gardner R. Dozois. *Beyond Flesh*. New York: Ace Books, 2002.
Douglas, Ian. *Singularity*. New York: Harper Voyager, 2012.
Egan, Greg. *Diaspora: A Novel*. New York: HarperPrism, 1998.
McClelland, Mark. *Upload*. Self-published, 2012.
Reynolds, Alastair. *Revelation Space*. New York: Ace Books, 2001.
Stross, Charles. *Accelerando*. New York: Ace Books, 2005.
——. *Halting State*. New York: Ace Books, 2007.
Vinge, Vernor. *A Fire Upon the Deep*. New York: Tor, 1992.
Wright, John C. *The Golden Age: A Romance of the Far Future*. New York: Tor, 2002.

Film

Esoteria Transhumanism (2008)
Gattaca (1997)

Metropolis (1927)

The Singularity Is Near: A True Story about the Future (2010)

Transcendence (2014)

Transcendent Man (2009)

Genetics, Nanotechnology, and Robotics

Alexander, Brian. *Rapture: A Raucous Tour of Cloning, Transhumanism, and the New Era of Immortality*. New York: Basic Books, 2004.

Church, George M., and Edward Regis. *Regenesis: How Synthetic Biology Will Reinvent Nature and Ourselves*. New York: Basic Books, 2012.

Crandall, B.C. *Nanotechnology: Molecular Speculations on Global Abundance*. Cambridge, MA: MIT Press, 1997.

Dery, Mark. *Escape Velocity: Cyberculture at the End of the Century*. New York: Grove Press, 1996.

Dyson, George. *Darwin among the Machines: The Evolution of Global Intelligence*. Reading, MA: Perseus Books, 1998.

Echevarria, Antulio J. *Strategic Implications of Emerging Technologies*. Carlisle, PA: Strategic Studies Institute, US Army War College, 2009. Web.

Exploratorium Demonstration. YouTube. 28 Feb. 2006. Web.

Frenkel, James, and Vernor Vinge. *True Names by Vernor Vinge and the Opening of the Cyberspace Frontier*. New York: Tor, 2001.

Häyry, Matti. *Rationality and the Genetic Challenge: Making People Better?* Cambridge: Cambridge UP, 2010.

Horn, Thomas. *Forbidden Gates: How Genetics, Robotics, Artificial Intelligence, Synthetic Biology, Nanotechnology, and Human Enhancement Herald the Dawn of Techno-Dimensional Spiritual Warfare*. Crane, MO: Defender, 2010.

Johnston, John. *The Allure of Machinic Life: Cybernetics, Artificial Life, and the New AI*. Cambridge, MA: MIT Press, 2008.

Kurzweil, Ray. *The Age of Spiritual Machines: When Computers Exceed Human Intelligence*. New York: Penguin, 1999.

——. *The Six Epochs from The Singularity is Near*. YouTube. 07 Jun. 2009. Web.

——, Jay W. Richards, and George F. Gilder. *Are We Spiritual Machines?: Ray Kurzweil vs. the Critics of Strong AI*. Seattle: Discovery Institute Press, 2002.

Launius, Roger D., and Howard E. McCurdy. *Robots in Space: Technology, Evolution, and Interplanetary Travel*. Baltimore: Johns Hopkins UP, 2008.

Luppicini, Rocci. *Handbook of Research on Technoself: Identity in a Technological Society*. Hershey, PA: Information Science Reference, 2013. Web.

Maes, Pattie. *Designing Autonomous Agents: Theory and Practice from Biology to Engineering and Back*. Special issues of Robotics and Autonomous Systems. Cambridge, MA: MIT Press, 1990.

Mallouk, Thomas E., and Ayusman Sen. "Powering Nanorobots: Catalytic Engines Enable Tiny Swimmers to Harness Fuel from Their Environment and Overcome the Weird Physics of the Microscopic World." *Scientific American* May 2009: 72-77.

Mongillo, John F. *Nanotechnology 101*. Westport, CT: Greenwood, 2007.

Moravec, Hans. *Robot: Mere Machine to Transcendent Mind*. Oxford: Oxford UP, 2000.

Mulhall, Douglas. *Our Molecular Future: How Nanotechnology, Robotics, Genetics, and Artificial Intelligence Will Transform Our World*. New York: Prometheus, 2002. Web.

Naam, Ramez. *More than Human: Embracing the Promise of Biological Enhancement*. New York: Broadway Books, 2005.

National Nanotechnology Initiative Workshop, Mihail C. Roco, and William Sims Bainbridge. *Nanotechnology: Societal Implications*. Dordrecht, Netherlands: Springer, 2007.

Ratner, Mark A., and Daniel Ratner. *Nanotechnology: A Gentle Introduction to the Next Big Idea*. Upper Saddle River, NJ: Prentice Hall, 2003.

Journalism

Basulto, Dominic. "Artificial Intelligence Has an Amazing Future. Dystopian Movies Get It Wrong." *Washington Post* 16 May 2014. Web.

Dooling, Richard. *Rapture for the Geeks: When AI Outsmarts IQ*. New York: Harmony Books, 2008.

Garreau, Joel. *Radical Evolution: The Promise and Peril of Enhancing Our Minds, Our Bodies—and What It Means to Be Human*. New York: Doubleday, 2005.

Hawking, Stephen. "Transcendence Looks at the Implications of Artificial Intelligence—but Are We Taking AI Seriously Enough?" *The Independent* 1 May 2014. Web.

MacLeod, Ken. "Socialism and Transhumanism." *Aeon Magazine* 12 Nov. 2012. Web.

McKibben, Bill. *Enough Staying Human in an Engineered Age*. New York: Henry Holt: 2003.

Morgan, John. "Science Cult Ray Kurzweil's Vision of a 'Singularity' Has Attracted Some Followers, but Don't Expect It Anytime Soon." *Newsweek* 18 May 2009. Print.

History and Philosophy

Agar, Nicholas. *Humanity's End: Why We Should Reject Radical Enhancement*. Cambridge, MA: MIT Press, 2010.

——. *Liberal Eugenics: In Defence of Human Enhancement*. Malden, MA: Blackwell, 2004.

Allhoff, Fritz. *Nanoethics: The Ethical and Social Implications of Nanotechnology*. Hoboken, NJ: Wiley-Interscience, 2007.

Bentham, Harry J. "Response: The Singularity and Socialism by Michael Rectenwald at Insurgent Notes." *H+ Magazine* 17 Oct. 2013. Web.

Blake, Charlie, Claire Molloy, and Steven Shakespeare. *Beyond Human: From Animality to Transhumanism*. London: Continuum, 2012.

Bostrom, Nick. "A History of Transhumanist Thought." *Journal of Evolution and Technology* 14.1 (Apr. 2005). Web.

Chu, Ted. *Human Purpose and Transhuman Potential: A Cosmic Vision for Our Future Evolution*. San Rafael, CA: Origin Press, 2014.

Easton, Thomas A. *Taking Sides: Clashing Views in Science, Technology, and Society*. New York: McGraw Hill, 2012.

Ettinger, R.C.W. *Man into Superman: The Startling Potential of Human Evolution—and How to Be Part of It*. Palo Alto, CA: Ria UP, 2005.

Farrell, Joseph P., and S.D. de Hart. *Transhumanism: A Grimoire of Alchemical Agendas*. Port Townsend, WA: Feral House, 2012.

Finn, Rosenda. *All About Transhumanism (Concepts and Applications)*. New Delhi: World Technologies, 2012. Web.

Fukuyama, Francis. *Our Posthuman Future: Consequences of the Biotechnological Revolution*. New York: Picador, 2002.

Fuller, Steve. *Humanity 2.0: What It Means to Be Human Past, Present and Future*. Houndmills, UK: Palgrave Macmillan, 2011.

——. *Proactionary Imperative: A Foundation for Transhumanism*. Houndmills, UK: Palgrave Macmillan, 2014.

Hansell, Gregory R., William Grassie, Russell Blackford, Nick Bostrom, and Jean P. Dupuy. *H±: Transhumanism and Its Critics*. Philadelphia: Metanexus Institute, 2011.

Harees, Lukman. *Mirage of Dignity on the Highways of Human Progress: The Bystanders Perspective*. Bloomington, IN: AuthorHouse, 2012.

Hughes, James. *Citizen Cyborg: Why Democratic Societies Must Respond to the Redesigned Human of the Future*. Cambridge, MA: Westview, 2004.

——. "The Politics of Transhumanism and the Techno-Millennial Imagination, 1626-2030." *Zygon* 47.4 (2012): 757-76.

Lilley, Stephen. *Transhumanism and Society: The Social Debate over Human Enhancement*. Dordrecht: Springer, 2013. Web.

More, Max, and Natasha Vita-More. *The Transhumanist Reader: Classical and Contemporary Essays on the Science, Technology, and Philosophy of the Human Future*. New York: Wiley, 2013. Web.

Olsen, Jan-Kyrre B., Evan Selinger, and Søren Riis. *New Waves in Philosophy of Technology*. Basingstoke, UK: Palgrave Macmillan, 2009. Web.

Rectenwald, Michael. "The Singularity and Socialism." *Insurgent Notes* 5 Oct. 2013. Web.

Savulescu, Julian, and Nick Bostrom. *Human Enhancement*. Oxford: Oxford UP, 2009.

Schneider, Susan. *Science Fiction and Philosophy: From Time Travel to Superintelligence*. Chichester, UK: Wiley-Blackwell, 2009. Web.

Seidel, Asher. *Inhuman Thoughts: Philosophical Explorations of Posthumanity*. Lanham, MD: Lexington Books, 2008.

Tirosh-Samuelson, Hava, and Kenneth L. Mossman. *Building Better Humans: Refocusing the Debate on Transhumanism*. Frankfurt: Peter Lang, 2012. Web.

Transhumanist Declaration. Prod. Humanity+. Mar. 2009. Web.

Young, Simon. *Designer Evolution: A Transhumanist Manifesto*. Amherst, NY: Prometheus, 2006.

Religious Studies

Cole-Turner, Ronald. *Transhumanism and Transcendence: Christian Hope in an Age of Technological Enhancement*. Washington, DC: Georgetown UP, 2011.

Colson, Charles W., and Nigel M. de S. Cameron. *Human Dignity in the Biotech Century: A Christian Vision for Public Policy*. Downers Grove, IL: InterVarsity Press, 2004.

Geraci, Robert M. *Apocalyptic AI: Visions of Heaven in Robotics, Artificial Intelligence, and Virtual Reality*. New York: Oxford UP, 2010.

Murphy, Nancey C., and Christopher C. Knight. *Human Identity at the Intersection of Science, Technology and Religion*. Farnham, UK: Ashgate, 2010.

Waters, Brent. *From Human to Posthuman: Christian Theology and Technology in a Postmodern World*. Aldershot, UK: Ashgate, 2006.

Social, Cultural, and Literary Studies

Clarke, Bruce. *Posthuman Metamorphosis: Narrative and Systems*. New York: Fordham UP, 2008.

Downey, Gary Lee, and Joseph Dumit. *Cyborgs & Citadels: Anthropological Interventions in Emerging Sciences and Technologies*. School of American Research Advanced Seminar Series. Santa Fe, NM: School of American Research Press, 1997.

Haraway, Donna. "A Manifesto for Cyborgs: Science, Technology and Socialist Feminism in the 1980s." *Reading Digital Culture*. Ed. David Trend. Malden, MA: Blackwell, 2001. 28-37.

——. *Modest_Witness@Second_Millennium.FemaleMan_Meets_OncoMouse: Feminism and Technoscience*. New York: Routledge, 1997.

Heil, Reinhard. *Tensions and Convergences: Technological and Aesthetic Transformations of Society*. Bielefeld: Transcript, 2007.

Leaver, Tama. *Artificial Culture: Identity, Technology and Bodies*. New York: Routledge, 2012.

Raulerson, Joshua. *Singularities: Technoculture, Transhumanism, and Science Fiction in the Twenty-First Century*. Liverpool: Liverpool UP, 2013.

Robertson, George. *FutureNatural: Nature, Science, Culture*. Futures: New Perspectives for Cultural Analysis. London: Routledge, 1996.

Schneider, Susan. *Science Fiction and Philosophy: From Time Travel to Superintelligence*. Chichester, UK: Wiley-Blackwell, 2009. Web.

a. Francis Fukuyama, "Transhumanism"

Francis Fukuyama, an American philosopher, has written widely on political and economic development. He is best known for his ground-breaking and controversial book *The End of History and the Last Man* (1992), in which he claims that we have reached the end-point of historical change, or at least the end of major, worldwide ideological differences. With the fall of right-wing dictatorship in Germany and left-wing dictatorship in the former Soviet Union, Fukuyama argues, capitalist liberal democracy has become the sole surviving system—the last man standing, so to speak.

Fukuyama received his BA from Cornell University in classics, and his PhD from Harvard University in political science. He is Bernard L. Schwartz Professor of International Political Economy at the Paul H. Nitze School of Advanced International Studies (SAIS) at Johns Hopkins University, and director of SAIS's International Development Program. He is also chairman of the editorial board of the magazine *The American Interest*. His book *The End of History and the Last Man* has appeared in more than twenty foreign editions. It made bestseller lists in the United States, France, Japan, and Chile, and has been awarded a *Los Angeles Times* Book Critics Award. Fukuyama also has published *Trust: The Social Virtues and the Creation of Prosperity* (1995), *The Great Disruption: Human Nature and the Reconstitution of Social Order* (1999), *Our Posthuman Future: Consequences of the Biotechnology Revolution* (2002), *State-Building: Governance and World Order in the 21st Century*, (2004), and *America at the Crossroads: Democracy, Power, and the Neoconservative Legacy* (2006).

In the following essay, Fukuyama summarizes the position he takes on transhumanism in his book *Our Posthuman Future*. He argues that our notion of a stable human nature is essential for guaranteeing equality and individual rights. When some human beings are enhanced, he claims, the dignity and rights of the unenhanced are endangered. The biotechnology revolution must therefore be kept in check by means of government policies and scientific protocols.

As You Read: What is your initial response to the idea of transhumanism? Do you share Fukuyama's attitude toward it?

Transhumanism

For the last several decades, a strange liberation movement has grown within the developed world. Its crusaders aim much higher than civil rights campaigners, feminists, or gay-rights advocates. They want nothing less than to liberate the human race from its biological constraints. As "transhumanists" see it, humans must wrest their biological destiny from evolution's blind process of random variation and adaptation and move to the next stage as a species.

It is tempting to dismiss transhumanists as some sort of odd cult, nothing more than science fiction taken too seriously: Witness their over-the-top websites and recent press releases ("Cyborg Thinkers to Address Humanity's Future," proclaims one). The plans of some transhumanists to freeze themselves cryogenically in hopes of being revived in a future age seem only to confirm the movement's place on the intellectual fringe.

But is the fundamental tenet of transhumanism—that we will someday use biotechnology to make ourselves stronger, smarter, less prone to violence, and longer-lived—really so outlandish? Transhumanism of a sort is implicit in much of the research agenda of contemporary biomedicine. The new procedures and technologies emerging from research laboratories and hospitals—whether mood-altering drugs, substances to boost muscle mass or selectively erase memory, prenatal genetic screening, or gene therapy—can as easily be used to "enhance" the species as to ease or ameliorate illness.

Although the rapid advances in biotechnology often leave us vaguely uncomfortable, the intellectual or moral threat they represent is not always easy to identify. The human race, after all, is a pretty sorry mess, with our stubborn diseases, physical limitations, and short lives. Throw in humanity's jealousies, violence, and constant anxieties, and the transhumanist project begins to look downright reasonable. If it were technologically possible, why wouldn't we want to transcend our current species? The seeming reasonableness of the project, particularly when considered in small increments, is part of its danger. Society is unlikely to fall suddenly under the spell of the transhumanist worldview. But it is very possible that we will nibble at biotechnology's tempting offerings without realizing that they come at a frightful moral cost.

The first victim of transhumanism might be equality. The US Declaration of Independence says that "all men are created equal," and the most serious political fights in the history of the United States have been over who qualifies as fully human. Women and blacks did not make the cut in 1776 when Thomas Jefferson penned the declaration. Slowly and painfully, advanced societies have realized that simply being human entitles a person to political and legal equality. In effect, we have drawn a red line around the human being and said that it is sacrosanct.

Underlying this idea of the equality of rights is the belief that we all possess a human essence that dwarfs manifest differences in skin color, beauty, and even intelligence. This essence, and the view that individuals therefore have inherent value, is at the heart of political liberalism. But modifying that essence is the core of the transhumanist project. If we start transforming ourselves into something superior, what rights will these enhanced creatures claim, and what rights will they possess when compared to those left behind? If some move ahead, can anyone afford not to follow? These questions are troubling enough within rich, developed societies. Add in the implications for citizens of the world's poorest countries—for whom biotechnology's marvels likely will be out of reach—and the threat to the idea of equality becomes even more menacing.

Transhumanism's advocates think they understand what constitutes a good human being, and they are happy to leave behind the limited, mortal, natural beings they see around them in favor of something better. But do they really comprehend ultimate human goods? For all our obvious faults, we humans are miraculously complex products of a long evolutionary process—products whose whole is much more than the sum of our parts. Our good characteristics are intimately connected to our bad ones: If we weren't violent and aggressive, we wouldn't be able to defend ourselves; if we didn't have feelings of exclusivity, we wouldn't be loyal to those close to us; if we never felt jealousy, we would also never feel love. Even our mortality plays a critical function in allowing our species as a whole to survive and adapt (and transhumanists are just about the last group I'd like to see live forever). Modifying any one of our key characteristics inevitably entails modifying a complex, inter-linked package of traits, and we will never be able to anticipate the ultimate outcome.

Nobody knows what technological possibilities will emerge for human self-modification. But we can already see the stirrings of Promethean desires in how we prescribe drugs to alter the behavior and personalities of our children. The environmental movement has taught us humility and respect for the integrity of nonhuman nature. We need a similar humility concerning our human nature. If we do not develop it soon, we may unwittingly invite the transhumanists to deface humanity with their genetic bulldozers and psychotropic shopping malls.

Source: *Foreign Policy* 1 Sept. 2004: n.p. Web. http://www.foreignpolicy.com/articles/2004/09/01/transhumanism.

WHAT IT SAYS

1. What advances in science and technology already point to a transhumanist future, as Fukuyama sees it?

2. Why are the promises held out by transhumanists so tempting? How might we fall under their sway?

3. From Fukuyama's point of view, we shouldn't tinker with human nature. Why not? What values are at risk? What else is at stake?

4. What does Fukuyama conclude regarding the attitude we should take toward human nature and transhumanism?

HOW IT SAYS IT

1. What seems to guide Fukuyama's word choice when he refers to transhumanists in this essay? What is his tone when referring to them? What effect might he be trying to achieve by describing transhumanism as "a strange liberation movement," and transhumanists as "some sort of odd cult"?

2. Fukuyama's argument relies on a basic definition of human nature. He writes:

> For all our obvious faults, we humans are miraculously complex products of a long evolutionary process—products whose whole is much more than the sum of our parts. Our good characteristics are intimately connected to our bad ones: If we weren't violent and aggressive, we wouldn't be able to defend ourselves; if we didn't have feelings of exclusivity, we wouldn't be loyal to those close to us; if we never felt jealousy, we would also never feel love. Even our mortality plays a critical function in allowing our species as a whole to survive and adapt.

Why does Fukuyama emphasize the complexities and apparent contradictions in human nature? How does this line of reasoning support his argument? What kind of an appeal is this?

3. Point to Fukuyama's use of pathos in this essay. How does his use of this form of appeal help to advance his argument?

WRITE ABOUT IT

1. Write a short essay in which you explore your own responses to the promises (or threats) posed by transhumanism and the technologies that may make a transhuman future possible. What do you see as the prospects for a transhuman future? How do you feel about these prospects? How does transhumanism either accord or conflict with your values?

2. Write an essay in which you defend transhumanism from Fukuyama's charges. Be sure to counter his main points and to add a few of your own.

3. Find a representation of the transhuman future in science fiction (movies or books). Write an essay that describes how transhumanism is treated in the piece. What is the argument of the movie or book? How does it compare with Fukuyama's argument?

b. Ronald Bailey, "Transhumanism: The Most Dangerous Idea? Why Striving to Be More than Human Is Human"

Ronald Bailey is an award-winning science correspondent for *Reason* magazine and Reason.com, where he writes a weekly science and technology column. In 2006, the editors of *Nature Biotechnology* listed Bailey as one of the personalities who have made the "most significant contributions" to biotechnology in the last ten years. Prior to joining *Reason* in 1997, Bailey produced several weekly national public television series, including *Think Tank* and *TechnoPolitics*, as well as several documentaries for PBS television and ABC News. In 1993, he was the Warren T. Brookes Fellow in environmental journalism at the Competitive Enterprise Institute. His articles and reviews have appeared in the *New York Times*, the *Wall Street Journal*, the *Washington Post*, and many other publications.

His article "The Battle for Your Brain," which delves into the ethical and political conflicts over new brain-enhancement technologies, won a 2004 Southern California Journalism Award. He is the author of the book *Liberation Biology: The Moral and Scientific Case for the Biotech Revolution* (2005), and his work was featured in *The Best American Science and Nature Writing* in 2004. Bailey earned a BA from the University of Virginia in philosophy and economics.

In the following essay, Bailey directly refutes Fukuyama's "Transhumanism" article, included above. He argues that all of human history has involved an effort to supersede human limitations. According to Bailey, Fukuyama's notion of a stable human nature is both mistaken and unnecessary for guaranteeing human rights.

As You Read: What thoughts and feelings did you have about transhumanism before you read this article? How, if at all, have your thoughts and feelings about it changed? Are you convinced by Bailey's argument?

Transhumanism: The Most Dangerous Idea? Why Striving to Be More than Human Is Human

"What ideas, if embraced, would pose the greatest threat to the welfare of humanity?" That question was posed to eight prominent policy intellectuals by the editors of *Foreign Policy* in its September/October issue.... One of the eight savants consulted was Francis Fukuyama, professor of international political economy at Johns

Hopkins School of Advanced International Studies, author of *Our Posthuman Future: Consequences of the Biotechnology Revolution*, and a member of the President's Council on Bioethics. His choice for the world's most dangerous idea? Transhumanism.

In his *Foreign Policy* article, Fukuyama identifies transhumanism as "a strange liberation movement" that wants "nothing less than to liberate the human race from its biological constraints." Sounds ominous, no? But wait a minute, isn't human history (and prehistory) all about liberating more and more people from their biological constraints? After all, it's not as though most of us still live in our species' "natural state" as Pleistocene hunter-gatherers.

Human liberation from our biological constraints began when an ancestor first sharpened a stick and used it to kill an animal for food. Further liberation from biological constraints followed with fire, the wheel, domesticating animals, agriculture, metallurgy, city building, textiles, information storage by means of writing, the internal combustion engine, electric power generation, antibiotics, vaccines, transplants, and contraception. In a sense, *the* goal toward which humanity has been striving for millennia has been to liberate ourselves from more and more of our ancestors' biological constraints.

What is a human capacity anyway? Biologist Richard Dawkins has propounded the notion of an extended phenotype. Genes not only mold the bodies of organisms but also shape their behaviors. Some of those behaviors result in the creation of inanimate objects that help organisms to survive and reproduce, such as beaver dams and bird nests.

Our ancestors had no wings; now we fly. Our ancient forebears could not hear one another over 1,000 miles; now we phone. And our Stone Age progenitors averaged 25 years of life; now we live 75. Thanks to our knack for technological innovation, humanity has by far the largest extended phenotype of all creatures on planet Earth. Nothing could be more natural to human beings than striving to liberate ourselves from biological constraints.

But Fukuyama would undoubtedly respond that Pleistocene hunter-gatherers are still recognizably human, no different in their innate capacities than people living today. What transhumanists seek is very different. They want to go beyond current innate human capacities. They want to change human bodies and brains.

Of course, humans have been deliberately changing their bodies through athletic training and their brains through schooling. Nevertheless, Fukuyama has a point. Can one be so transformed by technology as to be no longer human? "Our good characteristics are intimately connected to our bad ones: If we weren't violent and aggressive, we wouldn't be able to defend ourselves; if we didn't have feelings of exclusivity, we wouldn't be loyal to those close to us; if we never felt jealousy, we would also never feel love," asserts Fukuyama. He seems to be arguing that to be a human being one must possess all of the emotional capacities characteristic of our species. If biotechnological manipulations removed our ability to feel emotions like anger, hate, or violence, we would in some sense not be human beings any more.

Let's say that future genetic engineers discover a gene for suicidal depression, and learn how to suppress the gene, or adjust it. Would fixing it make subsequent generations non-human beings? After all, most people today do not fall into suicidal depressions, and those happy people are no less human than, say, Sylvia Plath.

Depression can already be fixed for many people by means of Prozac or Paxil. Surely, taking serotonin re-uptake inhibitors does not make people other or less than human. Sufferers of depression will tell you that the drugs restore them to their true selves. It seems unreasonable to claim that in order to qualify as human beings, we all must have the capacity to succumb to berserker rage or religious ecstasy.

"The first victim of transhumanism might be equality," writes Fukuyama. "If we start transforming ourselves into something superior, what rights will these enhanced creatures claim, and what rights will they possess when compared to those left behind?" Fukuyama seems to be entertaining an X-Men-like fantasy in which enhanced posthumans seek to destroy unenhanced naturals. But where Fukuyama is a bit coy, left-leaning bioethicists George Annas, Lori Andrews, and Rosario Isasi are brutally blunt:

> The new species, or "posthuman," will likely view the old "normal" humans as inferior, even savages, and fit for slavery or slaughter. The normals, on the other hand, may see the posthumans as a threat and if they can, may engage in a preemptive strike by killing the posthumans before they themselves are killed or enslaved by them. It is ultimately this predictable potential for genocide that makes species-altering experiments potential weapons of mass destruction, and makes the unaccountable genetic engineer a potential bioterrorist.

Let's take their over-the-top scenario down a notch or two. The enhancements that are likely to be available in the relatively near term to people now living will be pharmacological—pills and shots to increase strength, lighten moods, and improve memory. Consequently, such interventions could be distributed to nearly everybody who wanted them. Later in this century, when safe genetic engineering becomes possible, it will enable parents to give their children beneficial genes for improved health and intelligence that other children already get naturally. Thus, safe genetic engineering in the long run is more likely to ameliorate than to exacerbate human inequality.

In any case, political equality has never rested on the facts of human biology. In prior centuries, when humans were all "naturals," tyranny, slavery, and purdah were common social and political arrangements. In fact, political liberalism is already the answer to Fukuyama's question about human and posthuman rights. In liberal societies the law is meant to apply equally to all, no matter how rich or poor, powerful or powerless, brilliant or stupid, enhanced or unenhanced.

The crowning achievement of the Enlightenment is the principle of tolerance, of putting up with people who look differently, talk differently, worship differently, and live differently than we do. In the future, our descendants may not all be natural homo sapiens, but they will still be moral beings who can be held accountable for their actions. There is no reason to think that the same liberal political and moral principles that apply to diverse human beings today wouldn't apply to relations among future humans and posthumans.

But what if enhanced posthumans took the Nietzschean superman option? What if they really did see unenhanced people "as inferior, even savages, and fit for slavery or slaughter"?

Let's face it, plenty of unenhanced humans have been quite capable of believing that millions of their fellow unenhanced humans were inferiors who needed to be eradicated. However, as liberal political institutions have spread and strengthened, they have increasingly restrained technologically superior groups from automatically wiping out less advanced peoples (which was usual throughout most of history). I suspect that this dynamic will continue in the future as biotechnology, nanotechnology, and computational technologies progressively increase people's capabilities and widen their choices.

In his famous book *The End of History and the Last Man*, Fukuyama declared that we are witnessing "the end point of mankind's ideological evolution and the universalization of Western liberal democracy as the final form of human government." Fair enough. But for Fukuyama, the end of history is a "sad time" because "daring, courage, imagination, and idealism will be replaced by economic calculation." Also, he claims, "in the post-historical period there will be neither art nor philosophy, just the perpetual caretaking of the museum of human history." How ironic that Fukuyama now spends his time demonizing transhumanism, a nascent philosophical and political movement that epitomizes the most daring, courageous, imaginative, and idealistic aspirations of humanity.

"The environmental movement has taught us humility and respect for the integrity of nonhuman nature. We need a similar humility concerning our human nature. If we do not develop it soon, we may unwittingly invite the transhumanists to deface humanity with their genetic bulldozers and psychotropic shopping malls," concludes Fukuyama. I say, bring on those genetic bulldozers and psychotropic shopping malls that help people to live healthier, smarter, and happier lives.

I have my own nomination for an "idea [that], if embraced, would pose the greatest threat to the welfare of humanity": Banning technological progress in the name of "humility."

Source: *Reason* 25 Aug. 2004: n.p. Web. http://reason.com/archives/2004/08/25/transhumanism-the-most-dangero.

WHAT IT SAYS

1. How might we define human history and prehistory, according to Bailey, and how is this definition relevant to the debate about transhumanism?

2. Bailey refers to the notion of an extended phenotype introduced by biologist Richard Dawkins. What is an extended phenotype? How does this notion relate to transhumanism?

3. How does Bailey counter Fukuyama's point that to be a human being, one must possess the full range of human capacities, including the ones that we consider undesirable? What kinds of genetic traits might be eliminated or suppressed without risking human nature, according to Bailey?

4. How does Bailey refute Fukuyama's charge that transhumanism threatens equality and human rights? On what, according to Bailey, do human rights depend? Why won't transhumanism endanger these rights?

5. Some opponents of transhumanism suggest that enhanced human beings would consider themselves superior and proceed to wipe out the unenhanced. What is Bailey's retort to this claim?

6. What does Bailey claim is the world's most dangerous idea?

HOW IT SAYS IT

1. Bailey makes clear from the outset that he will engage the ideas on transhumanism held by Fukuyama. How does he signal his disagreement with Fukuyama? What words suggest that he will challenge Fukuyama's views?

2. Bailey writes that liberation from human constraints began when

   an ancestor first sharpened a stick and used it to kill an animal for food. Further liberation from biological constraints followed with fire, the wheel, domesticating animals, agriculture, metallurgy, city building, textiles, information storage by means of writing, the internal combustion engine, electric power generation, antibiotics, vaccines, transplants, and contraception.

   How do these examples of human innovation help Bailey's case? Why does he begin with such rudimentary technologies as a sharpened stick and the development of fire?

3. Characterize the audience for Bailey's article. What kinds of readers follow Reason.com? What is their attitude toward science and technology likely to be?

WRITE ABOUT IT

1. Imagine that you are Francis Fukuyama and have just read Bailey's essay. Write a rebuttal of Bailey's counterargument. Make sure you defend your original argument and counter Bailey's most damaging points.

2. Write an essay in which you describe a transhuman future that is different from that suggested by both Fukuyama and Bailey. Will human beings still exist, as such? What enhancements will be common? What will become of morality, equality, and human rights? Base your essay on the technological possibilities you have read about so far.

3. Write an essay about the state of technology today and how it relates to transhumanism. Are we already living in a transhuman period? Be specific about particular technological and scientific developments.

c. Ray Kurzweil, "The Six Epochs"

Ray Kurzweil is an inventor, entrepreneur, author, and leading futurist. He is most widely recognized for devising the law of accelerating returns. According to this law, the rate of evolution and technological advancements increases exponentially, and technological innovation is viewed as a continuation of biological evolution. Kurzweil argues that an exponential increase in technological advance will soon lead to the Singularity, a new stage or epoch when human life will be forever changed.

Kurzweil earned a BS in computer science from the Massachusetts Institute of Technology (1970), but he began his career as a prize-winning inventor as a teenager. While he was still in high school, Kurzweil created a computer program that was adopted by IBM. He has spent the better part of his life inventing and theorizing about the future of technology. He was the principal developer of the first commercial optical character recognition (OCR) software, the first flat-bed scanner, the first text-to-speech synthesizer, the first music synthesizer capable of reproducing the sounds of the grand piano and other instruments, and the first commercial large-vocabulary speech-recognition software.

Kurzweil's work in futurism has earned him the titles "the restless genius" (the *Wall Street Journal*) and "the ultimate thinking machine" (*Forbes Magazine*). He is the author of several books, including *The Age of Intelligent Machines* (1990), *The Age of Spiritual Machines: When Computers Exceed Human Intelligence* (2000), and *The Singularity Is Near: When Humans Transcend Biology* (2005). In 2002, he was inducted into the National Hall of Fame, established by the US Patent Office. He received the $500,000 Lemelson-MIT Prize, the nation's largest award in invention and innovation. He also received the 1999 National Medal of Technology, the nation's highest honor in technology, from President Clinton. He has served as chancellor and trustee of Singularity University in Silicon Valley, California, which was founded in 2008 as an interdisciplinary institution supported by Google, Canon, and others. Its aim is to prepare leaders for the challenges and opportunities posed by what founders and funders see as the coming Singularity. In 2012, Ray Kurzweil was appointed Director of Engineering at Google, heading up a team developing machine intelligence and natural language understanding.

In "The Six Epochs," Kurzweil lays out the main argument of his book *The Singularity Is Near*, from which the excerpt is taken. In a series of graphs and explanations, Kurzweil hopes to show that evolution has been very rapidly accelerating since the beginning of the universe itself. This trend will likely continue, he says. If it does, the Singularity will arrive very soon—by the mid-twenty-first century at the latest. At this point, technological innovation will take over from biological evolution, with a host of astounding results.

As You Read: Kurzweil makes sweeping statements accompanied by graphs and charts. Pay attention to the charts as carriers of meaning. Then, on a separate piece of paper, translate the message conveyed by one or more graphs into your own words. Take note of unfamiliar concepts and terms and define them for yourself. Try to summarize Kurzweil's argument in one or two paragraphs.

The Six Epochs

First we build the tools, then they build us.
—Marshall McLuhan

The future ain't what it used to be.
—Yogi Berra

Evolution is a process of creating patterns of increasing order. The emphasis in this section is on the concept of patterns. I believe that it's the evolution of patterns that constitutes the ultimate story of our world. Evolution works through indirection: each stage or epoch uses the information-processing methods of the previous epoch to create the next. I conceptualize the history of evolution—both biological and technological—as occurring in six epochs. As we will discuss, the Singularity will begin with Epoch Five and will spread from Earth to the rest of the universe in Epoch Six.

Epoch One: Physics and Chemistry. We can trace our origins to a state that represents information in its basic structures: patterns of matter and energy. Recent theories of quantum gravity hold that time and space are broken down into discrete quanta, essentially fragments of information. There is controversy as to whether matter and energy are ultimately digital or analog in nature, but regardless of the resolution of this issue, we do know that atomic structures store and represent discrete information.

A few hundred thousand years after the Big Bang, atoms began to form, as electrons became trapped in orbits around nuclei consisting of protons and neutrons. The electrical structure of atoms made them "sticky." Chemistry was born a few million years later as atoms came together to create relatively stable structures called molecules. Of all the elements, carbon proved to be the most versatile; it's able to form bonds in four directions (versus one to three for most other elements), giving rise to complicated, information-rich, three-dimensional structures.

The rules of our universe and the balance of the physical constants that govern the interaction of basic forces are so exquisitely, delicately, and exactly appropriate for the codification and evolution of information (resulting in increasing complexity) that one wonders how such an extraordinarily unlikely situation came about. Where some see a divine hand, others see our own hands—namely, the anthropic principle, which holds that only in a universe that allowed our own evolution would we be here to ask such questions. Recent theories of physics concerning multiple universes speculate that new universes are created on a regular basis, each with its own unique rules, but that most of these either die out quickly or else continue without the evolution of any interesting patterns (such as Earth-based biology has created) because their rules do not support the evolution of increasingly complex forms.[1] It's hard to imagine how we could test these theories of evolution applied to early cosmology, but it's clear that the physical laws of our universe are precisely what they need to be to allow for the evolution of increasing levels of order and complexity.[2]

Epoch Two: Biology and DNA. In the second epoch, starting several billion years ago, carbon-based compounds became more and more intricate until complex aggregations of molecules formed self-replicating mechanisms, and life originated. Ultimately, biological systems evolved a precise digital mechanism (DNA) to store information describing a larger society of molecules. This molecule and its supporting machinery of codons and ribosomes enabled a record to be kept of the evolutionary experiments of this second epoch.

Epoch Three: Brains. Each epoch continues the evolution of information through a paradigm shift to a further level of "indirection." (That is, evolution uses the results of one epoch to create the next.) For example, in the third epoch, DNA-guided evolution produced organisms that could detect information with their own sensory organs and process and store that information in their own brains and nervous systems. These were made possible by second-epoch mechanisms (DNA and epigenetic information of proteins and RNA fragments that control gene expression), which (indirectly) enabled and defined third-epoch information-processing mechanisms (the brains and nervous systems of organisms). The third epoch started with the ability of early animals to recognize patterns, which still accounts for the vast majority of the activity in our brains. Ultimately, our own species evolved the ability to create abstract mental models of the world we experience and to contemplate the rational implications of these models. We have the ability to redesign the world in our own minds and to put these ideas into action.

---

1 According to some cosmological theories, there were multiple big bangs, not one, leading to multiple universes (parallel multiverses or "bubbles"). Different physical constants and forces apply in the different bubbles; conditions in some (or at least one) of these bubbles support carbon-based life. See Max Tegmark, "Parallel Universes," *Scientific American* (May 2003): 41-53; Martin Rees, "Exploring Our Universe and Others," *Scientific American* (December 1999): 78-83; Andrei Linde, "The Self-Reproducing Inflationary Universe," *Scientific American* (November 1994): 48-55.

2 The "many worlds" or multiverse theory as an interpretation of quantum mechanics was developed to solve a problem presented by quantum mechanics and then has been combined with the anthropic principle.

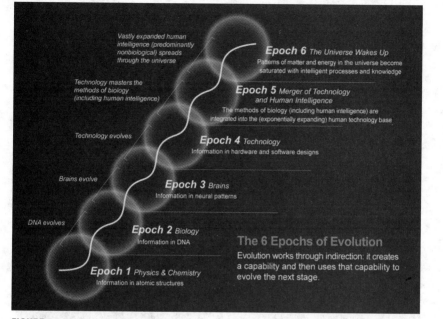

FIGURE 5.1. Six Epochs of Evolution

Epoch Four: Technology. Combining the endowment of rational and abstract thought with our opposable thumb, our species ushered in the fourth epoch and the next level of indirection: the evolution of human-created technology. This started out with simple mechanisms and developed into elaborate automata (automated mechanical machines). Ultimately, with sophisticated computational and communication devices, technology was itself capable of sensing, storing, and evaluating elaborate patterns of information. To compare the rate of progress of the biological evolution of intelligence to that of technological evolution, consider that the most advanced mammals have added about one cubic inch of brain matter every hundred thousand years, whereas we are roughly doubling the computational capacity of computers every year. Of course, neither brain size nor computer capacity is the sole determinant of intelligence, but they do represent enabling factors.

If we place key milestones of both biological evolution and human technological development on a single graph plotting both the x-axis (number of years ago) and the y-axis (the paradigm-shift time) on logarithmic scales, we find a reasonably straight line (continual acceleration), with biological evolution leading directly to human-directed development.[3]

3　With a "linear" plot (where all graph divisions are equal), it would be impossible to visualize all of the data (such as billions of years) in a limited space (such as a page of this book). A logarithmic ("log") plot solves that by plotting the order of magnitude of the values rather than the actual values, allowing you to see a wider range of data.

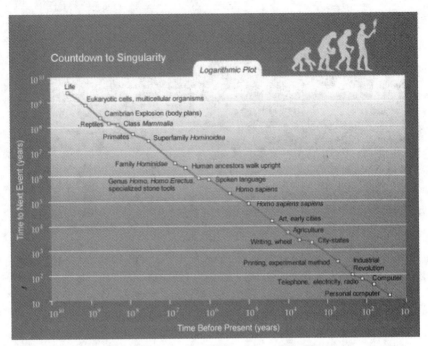

FIGURE 5.2. Countdown to Singularity: logarithmic plot

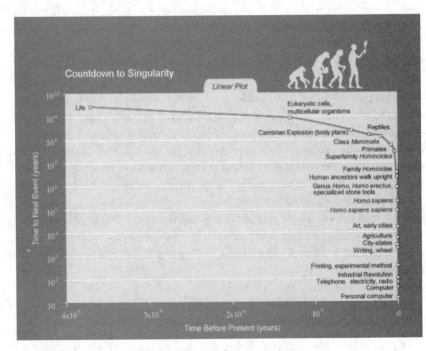

FIGURE 5.3. Countdown to Singularity: linear plot

The above figures reflect my view of key developments in biological and technological history. Note, however, that the straight line, demonstrating the continual acceleration of evolution, does not depend on my particular selection of events. Many observers and reference books have compiled lists of important events in biological and technological evolution, each of which has its own idiosyncrasies. Despite the diversity of approaches, however, if we combine lists from a variety of sources (for example, the Encyclopaedia Britannica, the American Museum of Natural History, Carl Sagan's "cosmic calendar," and others), we observe the same obvious smooth acceleration. The following plot combines fifteen different lists of key events.[4] Since different thinkers assign different dates to the same event, and different lists include similar or overlapping events selected according to different criteria, we see an expected "thickening" of the trend line due to the "noisiness" (statistical variance) of this data. The overall trend, however, is very clear.

Physicist and complexity theorist Theodore Modis analyzed these lists and determined twenty-eight clusters of events (which he called canonical milestones) by combining identical, similar, and/or related events from the different lists.[5] This process essentially removes the "noise" (for example, the variability of dates between lists) from the lists, revealing again the same progression (see Figure 5.2).

The attributes that are growing exponentially in these charts are order and complexity. This acceleration matches our commonsense observations. A billion years ago, not much happened over the course of even one million years. But a quarter-million years ago epochal events such as the evolution of our species occurred in time frames of just one hundred thousand years. In technology, if we go back fifty thousand years, not much happened over a one-thousand-year period. But in the recent past, we see new paradigms, such as the World Wide Web, progress from inception to mass adoption (meaning that they are used by a quarter of the population in advanced countries) within only a decade.

Epoch Five: The Merger of Human Technology with Human Intelligence.
Looking ahead several decades, the Singularity will begin with the fifth epoch. It will result from the merger of the vast knowledge embedded in our own brains with the vastly greater capacity, speed, and knowledge-sharing ability of our

---

4   Theodore Modis, professor at DUXX, Graduate School in Business Leadership in Monterrey, Mexico, attempted to develop a "precise mathematical law that governs the evolution of change and complexity in the Universe."

5   Modis notes that errors can arise from variations in the size of lists and from variations in dates assigned to events (see T. Modis, "The Limits of Complexity and Change," *The Futurist* [May-June 2003], http://ourworld.compuserve.com/homepages/tmodis/Futurist.pdf). So he used clusters of dates to define his canonical milestones. A milestone represents an average, with known errors assumed to be the standard deviation. For events without multiple sources, he "arbitrarily assign[ed] the average error as error." Modis also points out other sources of error—cases where precise dates are unknown or where there is the possibility of inappropriate assumption of equal importance for each data point—which are not caught in the standard deviation. Note that Modis's date of 54.6 million years ago for the dinosaur extinction is not far enough back.

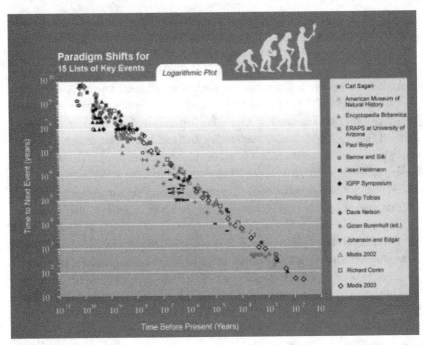

FIGURE 5.4. Paradigm Shifts

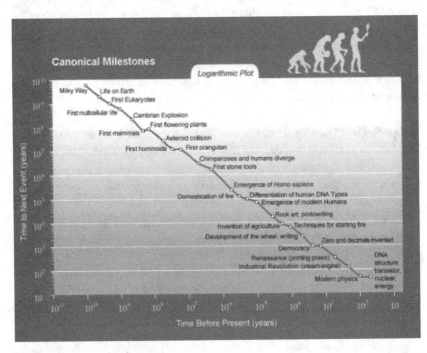

FIGURE 5.5. Canonical Milestones

technology. The fifth epoch will enable our human-machine civilization to transcend the human brain's limitations of a mere hundred trillion extremely slow connections.[6]

The Singularity will allow us to overcome age-old human problems and vastly amplify human creativity. We will preserve and enhance the intelligence that evolution has bestowed on us while overcoming the profound limitations of biological evolution. But the Singularity will also amplify the ability to act on our destructive inclinations, so its full story has not yet been written.

Epoch Six: The Universe Wakes Up. In the aftermath of the Singularity, intelligence, derived from its biological origins in human brains and its technological origins in human ingenuity, will begin to saturate the matter and energy in its midst. It will achieve this by reorganizing matter and energy to provide an optimal level of computation to spread out from its origin on Earth.

We currently understand the speed of light as a bounding factor on the transfer of information. Circumventing this limit has to be regarded as highly speculative, but there are hints that this constraint may be able to be superseded. If there are even subtle deviations, we will ultimately harness this superluminal ability. Whether our civilization infuses the rest of the universe with its creativity and intelligence quickly or slowly depends on its immutability. In any event the "dumb" matter and mechanisms of the universe will be transformed into exquisitely sublime forms of intelligence, which will constitute the sixth epoch in the evolution of patterns of information.

This is the ultimate destiny of the Singularity and of the universe.

The Singularity Is Near

You know, things are going to be really different! ... No, no, I mean really different!
—Mark Miller (computer scientist) to Eric Drexler, around 1986

What are the consequences of this event? When greater-than-human intelligence drives progress, that progress will be much more rapid. In fact, there seems no reason why progress itself would not involve the creation of still more intelligent entities—on a still-shorter time scale. The best analogy that I see is with the evolutionary past: Animals can adapt to problems and make inventions, but often no faster than natural selection can do its work—the world acts as its own simulator in the case of natural

---

6 Typical interneuronal reset times are on the order of five milliseconds, which allows for two hundred digital-controlled analog transactions per second. Even accounting for multiple nonlinearities in neuronal information processing, this is on the order of a million times slower than contemporary electronic circuits, which can switch in less than one nanosecond.

selection. We humans have the ability to internalize the world and conduct "what if's" in our heads; we can solve many problems thousands of times faster than natural selection. Now, by creating the means to execute those simulations at much higher speeds, we are entering a regime as radically different from our human past as we humans are from the lower animals. From the human point of view, this change will be a throwing away of all the previous rules, perhaps in the blink of an eye, an exponential runaway beyond any hope of control.

—Vernor Vinge, "The Technological Singularity," 1993

Let an ultraintelligent machine be defined as a machine that can far surpass all the intellectual activities of any man however clever. Since the design of machines is one of these intellectual activities, an ultraintelligent machine could design even better machines; there would then unquestionably be an "intelligence explosion," and the intelligence of man would be left far behind. Thus the first ultraintelligent machine is the last invention that man need ever make.

—Irving John Good, "Speculations Concerning the First Ultraintelligent Machine," 1965

A Mathematical Singularity *Linear Plot*

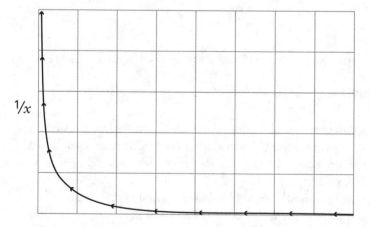

A mathematical singularity: As x approaches zero (from right to left). $^1/x$ *(or y) approaches infinity.*

FIGURE 5.6. A Mathematical Singularity

To put the concept of Singularity into further perspective, let's explore the history of the word itself. "Singularity" is an English word meaning a unique event with, well, singular implications. The word was adopted by mathematicians to denote a value that transcends any finite limitation, such as the explosion of magnitude that results when dividing a constant by a number that gets closer and closer to zero. Consider, for example, the simple function $y = 1/x$. As the value of x approaches zero, the value of the function (y) explodes to larger and larger values.

Such a mathematical function never actually achieves an infinite value, since dividing by zero is mathematically "undefined" (impossible to calculate). But the value of y exceeds any possible finite limit (approaches infinity) as the divisor x approaches zero.

The next field to adopt the word was astrophysics. If a massive star undergoes a supernova explosion, its remnant eventually collapses to the point of apparently zero volume and infinite density, and a "singularity" is created at its center. Because light was thought to be unable to escape the star after it reached this infinite density,[7] it was called a black hole.[8] It constitutes a rupture in the fabric of space and time.

One theory speculates that the universe itself began with such a Singularity.[9] Interestingly, however, the event horizon (surface) of a black hole is of J finite size, and gravitational force is only theoretically infinite at the zero-size center of the black hole. At any location that could actually be measured, the forces are finite, although extremely large.

The first reference to the Singularity as an event capable of rupturing the fabric of human history is John von Neumann's statement quoted above. In the 1960s, I. J. Good wrote of an "intelligence explosion" resulting from intelligent machines' designing their next generation without human intervention. Vernor Vinge, a mathematician and computer scientist at San Diego State University, wrote about

---

7   Stephen Hawking declared at a scientific conference in Dublin on July 21, 2004, that he had been wrong in a controversial assertion he made thirty years ago about black holes. He had said information about what had been swallowed by a black hole could never be retrieved from it. This would have been a violation of quantum theory, which says that information is preserved. "I'm sorry to disappoint science fiction fans, but if information is preserved there is no possibility of using black holes to travel to other universes," he said. "If you jump into a black hole, your mass energy will be returned to our universe, but in a mangled form, which contains the information about what you were like, but in an unrecognizable state." See Dennis Overbye, "About Those Fearsome Black Holes? Never Mind," *New York Times*, July 22, 2004.

8   An event horizon is the outer boundary, or perimeter, of a spherical region surrounding the singularity (the black hole's center, characterized by infinite density and pressure). Inside the event horizon, the effects of gravity are so strong that not even light can escape, although there is radiation emerging from the surface owing to quantum effects that cause particle-antiparticle pairs to form, with one of the pair being pulled into the black hole and the other being emitted as radiation (so-called Hawking radiation). This is the reason why these regions are called "black holes," a term invented by Professor John Wheeler.

9   Joel Smoller and Blake Temple, "Shock-Wave Cosmology Inside a Black Hole," *Proceedings of the National Academy of Sciences* 100.20 (September 30, 2003): 11216-18.

466 ACADEMIC WRITING, REAL WORLD TOPICS

a rapidly approaching "technological singularity" in an article for Omni magazine in 1983 and in a science-fiction novel, *Marooned in Realtime*, in 1986.[10]

My 1989 book, *The Age of Intelligent Machines*, presented a future headed inevitably toward machines greatly exceeding human intelligence in the first half of the twenty-first century.[11] Hans Moravec's 1988 book *Mind Children* came to a similar conclusion by analyzing the progression of robotics.[12] In 1993 Vinge presented a paper to a NASA-organized symposium that described the Singularity as an impending event resulting primarily from the advent of "entities with greater than human intelligence," which Vinge saw as the harbinger of a runaway phenomenon.[13] My 1999 book, *The Age of Spiritual Machines: When Computers Exceed Human Intelligence*, described the increasingly intimate connection between our biological intelligence and the artificial intelligence we are creating.[14] Hans Moravec's book *Robot: Mere Machine to Transcendent Mind*, also published in 1999, described the robots of the 2040s as our "evolutionary heirs," machines that will "grow from us, learn our skills, and share our goals and values, ... children of our minds."[15] Australian scholar Damien Broderick's 1997 and 2001 books, both titled *The Spike*, analyzed the pervasive impact of the extreme phase of technology acceleration anticipated within several decades.[16] In an extensive series of writings, John Smart has described the Singularity as the inevitable result of what he calls "MEST" (matter, energy, space, and time) compression.[17]

From my perspective, the Singularity has many faces. It represents the nearly vertical phase of exponential growth that occurs when the rate is so extreme that technology appears to be expanding at infinite speed. Of course, from a mathematical perspective, there is no discontinuity, no rupture, and the growth rates remain finite, although extraordinarily large. But from our currently limited framework, this imminent event appears to be an acute and abrupt break in the continuity of progress. I emphasize the word "currently" because one of the salient implications

---

10 Vernor Vinge, "First Word," *Omni* (January 1983): 10.

11 Ray Kurzweil, *The Age of Intelligent Machines* (Cambridge, Mass.: MIT Press, 1989).

12 Hans Moravec, *Mind Children: The Future of Robot and Human Intelligence* (Cambridge, Mass.: Harvard University Press, 1988).

13 Vernor Vinge, "The Coming Technological Singularity: How to Survive in the Post-Human Era," VISION-21 Symposium, sponsored by the NASA Lewis Research Center and the Ohio Aerospace Institute, March 1993. The text is available at http://machineslikeus.com/news/coming-technological-singularity-how-survive-post-human-era.

14 Ray Kurzweil, *The Age of Spiritual Machines: When Computers Exceed Human Intelligence* (New York: Viking, 1999).

15 Hans Moravec, *Robot: Mere Machine to Transcendent Mind* (New York: Oxford University Press, 1999).

16 Damien Broderick, two works: *The Spike: Accelerating into the Unimaginable Future* (Sydney, Australia: Reed Books, 1997) and *The Spike: How Our Lives Are Being Transformed by Rapidly Advancing Technologies*, rev. ed. (New York: Tor/Forge, 2001).

17 One of John Smart's overviews, "What Is the Singularity," can be found at http://www.kurzweilai.net/what-is-the-singularity; for a collection of John Smart's writings on technology acceleration, the Singularity, and related issues, see http://www.singularitywatch.com and http://www.Accelerating.org.

of the Singularity will be a change in the nature of our ability to understand. We will become vastly smarter as we merge with our technology.

Can the pace of technological progress continue to speed up indefinitely? Isn't there a point at which humans are unable to think fast enough to keep up? For unenhanced humans, clearly so. But what would 1,000 scientists, each 1,000 times more intelligent than human scientists today, and each operating 1,000 times faster than contemporary humans (because the information processing in their primarily nonbiological brains is faster) accomplish? One chronological year would be like a millennium for them.[18] What would they come up with?

Well, for one thing, they would come up with technology to become even more intelligent (because their intelligence is no longer of fixed capacity). They would change their own thought processes to enable them to think even faster. When scientists become a million times more intelligent and operate a million times faster, an hour would result in a century of progress (in today's terms).

The Singularity involves the following principles:

- The rate of paradigm shift (technical innovation) is accelerating, right now doubling every decade.
- The power (price-performance, speed, capacity, and bandwidth) of information technologies is growing exponentially at an even faster pace, now doubling about every year. This principle applies to a wide range of measures, including the amount of human knowledge.
- For information technologies, there is a second level of exponential growth: that is, exponential growth in the rate of exponential growth (the exponent). The reason: as a technology becomes more cost effective, more resources are deployed toward its advancement, so the rate of exponential growth increases over time. For example, the computer industry in the 1940s consisted of a handful of now historically important projects. Today total revenue in the computer industry is more than one trillion dollars, so research and development budgets are comparably higher.
- Human brain scanning is one of these exponentially improving technologies. The temporal and spatial resolution and bandwidth of brain scanning are doubling each year. We are just now obtaining the tools sufficient to begin serious reverse engineering (decoding) of the human brain's principles of operation. We already have impressive models and simulations of a couple dozen of the brain's several hundred

---

18 An emulation of the human brain running on an electronic system would run much faster than our biological brains. Although human brains benefit from massive parallelism (on the order of one hundred trillion interneuronal connections, all potentially operating simultaneously), the reset time of the connections is extremely slow compared to contemporary electronics.

regions. Within two decades, we will have a detailed understanding of how all the regions of the human brain work.

- We will have the requisite hardware to emulate human intelligence with supercomputers by the end of this decade and with personal-computer-size devices by the end of the following decade. We will have effective software models of human intelligence by the mid-2020s.

- With both the hardware and software needed to fully emulate human intelligence, we can expect computers to pass the Turing test, indicating intelligence indistinguishable from that of biological humans, by the end of the 2020s.[19]

- When they achieve this level of development, computers will be able to combine the traditional strengths of human intelligence with the strengths of machine intelligence.

- The traditional strengths of human intelligence include a formidable ability to recognize patterns. The massively parallel and self-organizing nature of the human brain is an ideal architecture for recognizing patterns that are based on subtle, invariant properties. Humans are also capable of learning new knowledge by applying insights and inferring principles from experience, including information gathered through language. A key capability of human intelligence is the ability to create mental models of reality and to conduct mental "what-if" experiments by varying aspects of these models.

- The traditional strengths of machine intelligence include the ability to remember billions of facts precisely and recall them instantly.

- Another advantage of nonbiological intelligence is that once a skill is mastered by a machine, it can be performed repeatedly at high speed, at optimal accuracy, and without tiring.

- Perhaps most important, machines can share their knowledge at extremely high speed, compared to the very slow speed of human knowledge-sharing through language.

- Nonbiological intelligence will be able to download skills and knowledge from other machines, eventually also from humans.

---

19 In a 1950 paper published in *Mind: A Quarterly Review of Psychology and Philosophy*, the computer theoretician Alan Turing posed the famous questions "Can a machine think? If a computer could think, how could we tell?" The answer to the second question is the Turing test. As the test is currently defined, an expert committee interrogates a remote correspondent on a wide range of topics such as love, current events, mathematics, philosophy, and the correspondent's personal history to determine whether the correspondent is a computer or a human. The Turing test is intended as a measure of human intelligence; failure to pass the test does not imply a lack of intelligence. Turing's original article can be found at http://www.abelard.org/turpap/turpap.htm; see also the *Stanford Encyclopedia of Philosophy*, http://plato.stanford.edu/entries/turing-test, for a discussion of the test.

There is no set of tricks or algorithms that would allow a machine to pass a properly designed Turing test without actually possessing intelligence at a fully human level. Also see Ray Kurzweil, "A Wager on the Turing Test: Why I Think I Will Win," http://www.KurzweilAI.net/turingwin.

- Machines will process and switch signals at close to the speed of light (about three hundred million meters per second), compared to about one hundred meters per second for the electrochemical signals used in biological mammalian brains.[20] This speed ratio is at least three million to one.

- Machines will have access via the Internet to all the knowledge of our human-machine civilization and will be able to master all of this knowledge.

- Machines can pool their resources, intelligence, and memories. Two machines—or one million machines—can join together to become one and then become separate again. Multiple machines can do both at the same time: become one and separate simultaneously. Humans call this falling in love, but our biological ability to do this is fleeting and unreliable.

- The combination of these traditional strengths (the pattern-recognition ability of biological human intelligence and the speed, memory capacity and accuracy, and knowledge and skill-sharing abilities of nonbiological intelligence) will be formidable.

- Machine intelligence will have complete freedom of design and architecture (that is, they won't be constrained by biological limitations, such as the slow switching speed of our interneuronal connections or a fixed skull size) as well as consistent performance at all times.

- Once nonbiological intelligence combines the traditional strengths of both humans and machines, the nonbiological portion of our civilization's intelligence will then continue to benefit from the double exponential growth of machine price-performance, speed, and capacity.

- Once machines achieve the ability to design and engineer technology as humans do, only at far higher speeds and capacities, they will have access to their own designs (source code) and the ability to manipulate them. Humans are now accomplishing something similar through biotechnology (changing the genetic and other information processes underlying our biology), but in a much slower and far more limited way than what machines will be able to achieve by modifying their own programs.

- Biology has inherent limitations. For example, every living organism must be built from proteins that are folded from one-dimensional strings of amino acids. Protein-based mechanisms are lacking in strength and speed. We will be able to reengineer all of the organs and systems in our biological bodies and brains to be vastly more capable.

---

20 See John H. Byrne, "Propagation of the Action Potential," *Neuroscience Online*, https://oac22.hsc.uth. tmc.edu/courses/nba/s1/i3-1.html: "The propagation velocity of the action potentials in nerves can vary from 100 meters per second (580 miles per hour) to less than a tenth of a meter per second (0.6 miles per hour)."

Also see Kenneth R. Koehler, "The Action Potential," http://www.rwc.uc.edu/koehler/ biophys/4d.html.

- Human intelligence does have a certain amount of plasticity (ability to change its structure), more so than had previously been understood. But the architecture of the human brain is nonetheless profoundly limited. For example, there is room for only about one hundred trillion interneuronal connections in each of our skulls. A key genetic change that allowed for the greater cognitive ability of humans compared to that of our primate ancestors was the development of a larger cerebral cortex as well as the development of increased volume of gray-matter tissue in certain regions of the brain. This change occurred, however, on the very slow timescale of biological evolution and still involves an inherent limit to the brain's capacity. Machines will be able to reformulate their own designs and augment their own capacities without limit. By using nanotechnology-based designs, their capabilities will be far greater than biological brains without increased size or energy consumption.

- Machines will also benefit from using very fast three-dimensional molecular circuits. Today's electronic circuits are more than one million times faster than the electrochemical switching used in mammalian brains. Tomorrow's molecular circuits will be based on devices such as nanotubes, which are tiny cylinders of carbon atoms that measure about ten atoms across and are five hundred times smaller than today's silicon-based transistors. Since the signals have less distance to travel, they will also be able to operate at terahertz (trillions of operations per second) speeds compared to the few gigahertz (billions of operations per second) speeds of current chips.

- The rate of technological change will not be limited to human mental speeds. Machine intelligence will improve its own abilities in a feedback cycle that unaided human intelligence will not be able to follow.

- This cycle of machine intelligence's iteratively improving its own design will become faster and faster. This is in fact exactly what is predicted by the formula for continued acceleration of the rate of paradigm shift. One of the objections that has been raised to the continuation of the acceleration of paradigm shift is that it ultimately becomes much too fast for humans to follow, and so therefore, it's argued, it cannot happen. However, the shift from biological to nonbiological intelligence will enable the trend to continue.

- Along with the accelerating improvement cycle of nonbiological intelligence, nanotechnology will enable the manipulation of physical reality at the molecular level.

- Nanotechnology will enable the design of nanobots: robots designed at the molecular level, measured in microns (millionths of a meter), such as "respirocytes" (mechanical red-blood cells).[21] Nanobots will have myriad roles within the human body, including reversing human aging (to the extent that this task will not already have been completed through biotechnology, such as genetic engineering).

- Nanobots will interact with biological neurons to vastly extend human experience by creating virtual reality from within the nervous system.

- Billions of nanobots in the capillaries of the brain will also vastly extend human intelligence.

- Once nonbiological intelligence gets a foothold in the human brain (this has already started with computerized neural implants), the machine intelligence in our brains will grow exponentially (as it has been doing all along), at least doubling in power each year. In contrast, biological intelligence is effectively of fixed capacity. Thus, the nonbiological portion of our intelligence will ultimately predominate.

- Nanobots will also enhance the environment by reversing pollution from earlier industrialization.

- Nanobots called foglets that can manipulate image and sound waves will bring the morphing qualities of virtual reality to the real world.[22]

- The human ability to understand and respond appropriately to emotion (so-called emotional intelligence) is one of the forms of human intelligence that will be understood and mastered by future machine intelligence. Some of our emotional responses are tuned to optimize our intelligence in the context of our limited and frail biological bodies. Future machine intelligence will also have "bodies" (for example, virtual bodies in virtual reality, or projections in real reality using foglets) in order to interact with the world, but these nanoengineered bodies will be far more capable and durable than biological human bodies. Thus, some of the "emotional" responses of future machine

---

21　Robert A. Freitas Jr., "Exploratory Design in Medical Nanotechnology: A Mechanical Artificial Red Cell," *Artificial Cells, Blood Substitutes, and Immobil. Biotech.* 26 (1998): 411-30; http://www.foresight. org/Nanomedicine/Respirocytes.html; see also the Nanomedicine Art Gallery images (http://www. foresight.org/Nanomedicine/Gallery/Species/Respirocytes.html) and award-winning animation (http://www.phleschbubble.com/album/beyondhuman/respirocyte01.htm) of the respirocytes.

22　Foglets are the conception of the nanotechnology pioneer and Rutgers professor J. Storrs Hall. Here is a snippet of his description: "Nanotechnology is based on the concept of tiny, self-replicating robots. The Utility Fog is a very simple extension of the idea: Suppose, instead of building the object you want atom by atom, the tiny robots [foglets] linked their arms together to form a solid mass in the shape of the object you wanted?

Then, when you got tired of that avant-garde coffee table, the robots could simply shift around a little and you'd have an elegant Queen Anne piece instead." J. Storrs Hall, "What I Want to Be When I Grow Up, Is a Cloud," *Extropy*, Quarters 3 and 4, 1994. Published on KurzweilAI.net July 6, 2001: http://www.KurzweilAI.net/foglets. See also J. Storrs Hall, "Utility Fog: The Stuff That Dreams Are Made Of," in *Nanotechnology: Molecular Speculations on Global Abundance*, B.C. Crandall, ed. (Cambridge, Mass.: MIT Press, 1996). Published on KurzweilAI.net July 5, 2001: http://www. KurzweilAI.net/utilityfog.

intelligence will be redesigned to reflect their vastly enhanced physical capabilities.[23]

- As virtual reality from within the nervous system becomes competitive with real reality in terms of resolution and believability, our experiences will increasingly take place in virtual environments.

- In virtual reality, we can be a different person both physically and emotionally. In fact, other people (such as your romantic partner) will be able to select a different body for you than you might select for yourself (and vice versa).

- The law of accelerating returns will continue until nonbiological intelligence comes close to "saturating" the matter and energy in our vicinity of the universe with our human-machine intelligence. By saturating, I mean utilizing the matter and energy patterns for computation to an optimal degree, based on our understanding of the physics of computation. As we approach this limit, the intelligence of our civilization will continue its expansion in capability by spreading outward toward the rest of the universe. The speed of this expansion will quickly achieve the maximum speed at which information can travel.

- Ultimately, the entire universe will become saturated with our intelligence. This is the destiny of the universe. We will determine our own fate rather than have it determined by the current "dumb," simple, machine-like forces that rule celestial mechanics.

- The length of time it will take the universe to become intelligent to this extent depends on whether or not the speed of light is an immutable limit. There are indications of possible subtle exceptions (or circumventions) to this limit, which, if they exist, the vast intelligence of our civilization at this future time will be able to exploit.

This, then, is the Singularity. Some would say that we cannot comprehend it, at least with our current level of understanding. For that reason, we cannot look past its event horizon and make complete sense of what lies beyond. This is one reason we call this transformation the Singularity.

I have personally found it difficult, although not impossible, to look beyond this event horizon, even after having thought about its implications for several decades. Still, my view is that, despite our profound limitations of thought, we do have sufficient powers of abstraction to make meaningful statements about the nature of life after the Singularity. Most important, the intelligence that will emerge will continue to represent the human civilization, which is already a human-machine civilization. In other words, future machines will be human, even

---

23 Sherry Turkle, ed., "Evocative Objects: Things We Think With," forthcoming.

if they are not biological. This will be the next step in evolution, the next high-level paradigm shift, the next level of indirection. Most of the intelligence of our civilization will ultimately be nonbiological. By the end of this century, it will be trillions of trillions of times more powerful than human intelligence. However, to address often-expressed concerns, this does not imply the end of biological intelligence, even if it is thrown from its perch of evolutionary superiority. Even the nonbiological forms will be derived from biological design. Our civilization will remain human—indeed, in many ways it will be more exemplary of what we regard as human than it is today, although our understanding of the term will move beyond its biological origins.

Many observers have expressed alarm at the emergence of forms of nonbiological intelligence superior to human intelligence. The potential to augment our own intelligence through intimate connection with other thinking substrates does not necessarily alleviate the concern, as some people have expressed the wish to remain "unenhanced" while at the same time keeping their place at the top of the intellectual food chain. From the perspective of biological humanity, these superhuman intelligences will appear to be our devoted servants, satisfying our needs and desires. But fulfilling the wishes of a revered biological legacy will occupy only a trivial portion of the intellectual power that the Singularity will bring.

Source: *The Singularity Is Near: When Humans Transcend Biology*. New York: Viking, 2005. 14-31.

WHAT IT SAYS

1. What is the meaning of the term "the Singularity"? What does Kurzweil mean by the term in this context? How does his use of the term differ from earlier usages?

2. In this excerpt, Kurzweil writes about evolution and technological innovation. What is the relationship between the two? How are they connected?

3. Kurzweil's argument is based on "the law of accelerating returns," which he defined in an article by the same name in 2001. What does the theory mean? How does it apply to the Singularity that Kurzweil envisions?

4. Toward the end of this excerpt, Kurzweil writes that "the 'dumb' matter and mechanisms of the universe will be transformed into exquisitely sublime forms of intelligence, which will constitute the sixth epoch in the evolution of patterns of information. This is the ultimate destiny of the Singularity and of the universe" (463). What does he mean by this statement? What will the universe be like after being transformed as such?

HOW IT SAYS IT

1. Kurzweil uses six graphs to illustrate his ideas. How do these graphs work to support his argument? What do you think is the importance of the figures on page 462, which plot "Paradigm Shifts for 15 Lists of Key Events" and "Canonical Milestones based on clusters of events from thirteen lists," respectively? Why are these graphs necessary for Kurzweil's argument?

2. Kurzweil divides his version of the Singularity into six epochs. Discuss how this approach works to advance his argument. How does this progression work to support the claims that Kurzweil makes about the Singularity?

3. Kurzweil makes a general statement about evolution on page 457: "each stage or epoch uses the information-processing methods of the previous epoch to create the next." What is the effect of discussing all of evolution in terms of information-processing? How does this advance his argument?

4. From pages 467 to 472, Kurzweil lists in bulleted points the principles that the Singularity involves. What is the effect of using a bulleted list to make these points? How does this usage advance his argument?

WRITE ABOUT IT

1. Think about the possible weaknesses in Kurzweil's argument. How might he be wrong? How else might his evidence be interpreted? Write an essay in which you refute Kurzweil's argument about the Singularity and/or its imminence.

2. On pages 457 to 458, Kurzweil writes the following rather lofty and puzzling remarks about the improbability of our universe:

> The rules of our universe and the balance of the physical constants that govern the interaction of basic forces are so exquisitely, delicately, and exactly appropriate for the codification and evolution of information (resulting in increasing complexity) that one wonders how such an extraordinarily unlikely situation came about. Where some see a divine hand, others see our own hands—namely, the anthropic principle, which holds that only in a universe that allowed our own evolution would we be here to ask such questions. Recent theories of physics concerning multiple universes speculate that new universes are created on a regular basis, each with its own unique rules, but that most of these either die out quickly or else continue without the evolution of any interesting patterns (such as Earth-based biology has created) because their rules do not support the evolution of increasingly complex forms. It's hard to imagine how we could test these theories of evolution applied to early cosmology, but it's clear that the physical laws of our universe are precisely what they need to be to allow for the evolution of increasing levels of order and complexity.

Write an informal essay in which you explore the possible implications of what Kurzweil is saying in this passage. Assuming that Kurzweil is correct, what does it mean to say that our universe, with its "codification and evolution of information ... is extraordinarily unlikely"? Kurzweil points to possibilities for explanation: a divine hand or "the anthropic principle." What is the difference between the two, and what does this difference imply about the appearance of our universe? What other explanations might be implied or left unstated? Why? Kurzweil suggests that "new universes are created on a regular basis ... but that most of these either die out quickly or else continue without the evolution of any interesting patterns...." What are the plausible interpretations of the idea that apparently only one universe (ours) exists that evolved complex patterns of information, such as those that support life? Kurzweil further remarks that "the physical laws of our universe are precisely what they need to be to allow for evolution...." Again, what might one conclude about the implications of this observation?

d. Bill Joy, "Why the Future Doesn't Need Us"

Bill Joy is a computer scientist. In 1982, he co-founded Sun Microsystems with Vinod Khosla, Scott McNealy, Andy Bechtolsheim, and Vaughan Pratt. He was Sun's chief scientist until 2003 and was also a critical developer of the operating system BSD UNIX, SPARC microprocessors, and the Java programming language.

Joy received his BS in electrical engineering from the University of Michigan, and his MS and PhD in electrical engineering from UC Berkeley. He worked for the Computer Systems Research Group as a graduate student, where he helped develop BSD UNIX, the basis of Apple's Mac OS X and other important software. The Association for Computing Machinery awarded him a Grace Murry Hopper Award in 1986 for his work on the Berkeley UNIX operating system. Since leaving Sun Microsystems in 2003, Joy has devoted himself to addressing pandemic disease and biological weapons. He is a limited partner in KPCB, a venture-capital firm investing in high-technology enterprises.

The essay below, for which Joy is widely known, expresses his concerns about where modern technology will lead us. Joy's fear is that intelligent robots will replace human beings, or at least that they could come to dominate us intellectually and socially. He says that positive and negative uses of GNR technologies are impossible to regulate; therefore, we should give up these technologies altogether. Some critics have called Joy's stance Luddite, meaning that he is philosophically opposed to technology across the board. However, Joy is not a technophobe but rather believes that we must take care to consider the negative social implications of new technologies instead of racing ahead heedlessly.

As You Read: Consider what Joy considers the ideal world to be, as it pertains to technology. In what ways does Joy's ideal correspond to your own?

Why the Future Doesn't Need Us

Our most powerful 21st-century technologies—robotics, genetic engineering, and nanotech—are threatening to make humans an endangered species.

From the moment I became involved in the creation of new technologies, their ethical dimensions have concerned me, but it was only in the autumn of 1998 that I became anxiously aware of how great are the dangers facing us in the 21st century. I can date the onset of my unease to the day I met Ray Kurzweil, the deservedly famous inventor of the first reading machine for the blind and many other amazing things.

Ray and I were both speakers at George Gilder's Telecosm conference, and I encountered him by chance in the bar of the hotel after both our sessions were over. I was sitting with John Searle, a Berkeley philosopher who studies consciousness. While we were talking, Ray approached and a conversation began, the subject of which haunts me to this day.

I had missed Ray's talk and the subsequent panel that Ray and John had been on, and they now picked right up where they'd left off, with Ray saying that the rate of improvement of technology was going to accelerate and that we were going to become robots or fuse with robots or something like that, and John countering that this couldn't happen, because the robots couldn't be conscious.

While I had heard such talk before, I had always felt sentient robots were in the realm of science fiction. But now, from someone I respected, I was hearing a strong argument that they were a near-term possibility. I was taken aback, especially given Ray's proven ability to imagine and create the future. I already knew that new technologies like genetic engineering and nanotechnology were giving us the power to remake the world, but a realistic and imminent scenario for intelligent robots surprised me.

It's easy to get jaded about such breakthroughs. We hear in the news almost every day of some kind of technological or scientific advance. Yet this was no ordinary prediction. In the hotel bar, Ray gave me a partial preprint of his then-forthcoming book *The Age of Spiritual Machines*, which outlined a utopia he foresaw—one in which humans gained near immortality by becoming one with robotic technology. On reading it, my sense of unease only intensified; I felt sure he had to be understating the dangers, understating the probability of a bad outcome along this path.

I found myself most troubled by a passage detailing a *dys*topian scenario:

THE NEW LUDDITE CHALLENGE

First let us postulate that the computer scientists succeed in developing intelligent machines that can do all things better than human beings can do them. In that case presumably all work will be done by vast, highly organized systems of machines and no human effort will be necessary. Either of two cases might occur. The machines might be permitted to make all of their own decisions without human oversight, or else human control over the machines might be retained.

If the machines are permitted to make all their own decisions, we can't make any conjectures as to the results, because it is impossible to guess how such machines might behave. We only point out that the fate of the human race would be at the mercy of the machines. It might be argued that the human race would never be foolish enough to hand over all the power to the machines. But we are suggesting neither that the human race would voluntarily turn power over to the machines nor that the machines would willfully seize power. What we do suggest is that the human race might easily permit itself to drift into a position of such dependence on the machines that it would have no practical choice but to accept all of the machines' decisions. As society and the problems that face it become more and more complex and machines become more and more intelligent, people will let machines make more of their decisions for them, simply because machine-made decisions will bring better results than man-made ones. Eventually a stage may be reached at which the decisions necessary to keep the system running will be so complex that human beings will be incapable of making them intelligently. At that stage the machines will be in effective control. People won't be able to just turn the machines off, because they will be so dependent on them that turning them off would amount to suicide.

On the other hand it is possible that human control over the machines may be retained. In that case the average man may have control over certain private machines of his own, such as his car or his personal computer, but control over large systems of machines will be in the hands of a tiny elite—just as it is today, but with two differences. Due to improved techniques the elite will have greater control over the masses; and because human work will no longer be necessary the masses will be superfluous, a useless burden on the system. If the elite is ruthless they may simply decide to exterminate the mass of humanity. If they are humane they may use propaganda or other psychological or biological techniques to reduce the birth rate until the mass of humanity becomes extinct, leaving the world to the elite. Or, if the elite consists of soft-hearted liberals, they may decide to play the role of good shepherds to the rest of the human race. They will see to it that everyone's physical needs are satisfied, that all children are raised under psychologically hygienic conditions, that everyone has a wholesome hobby to keep him busy, and that anyone who may become dissatisfied undergoes "treatment" to cure his "problem." Of course, life will be so purposeless that people will have to be biologically or psychologically engineered either to remove their need for the power process or make them "sublimate" their drive for power into some harmless hobby. These engineered human beings may be happy in such a society, but they will most certainly not be free. They will have been reduced to the status of domestic animals.[1]

---

1   The passage Kurzweil quotes is from Kaczynski's Unabomber Manifesto, which was published jointly, under duress, by *The New York Times* and *The Washington Post* to attempt to bring his campaign of terror to an end. I agree with David Gelernter, who said about their decision:
   "It was a tough call for the newspapers. To say yes would be giving in to terrorism, and for all they knew he was lying anyway. On the other hand, to say yes might stop the killing. There was also a chance that someone would read the tract and get a hunch about the author; and that is exactly what happened. The suspect's brother read it, and it rang a bell.
   "I would have told them not to publish. I'm glad they didn't ask me. I guess." (*Drawing Life: Surviving the Unabomber.* Free Press, 1997: 120.)

In the book, you don't discover until you turn the page that the author of this passage is Theodore Kaczynski—the Unabomber. I am no apologist for Kaczynski. His bombs killed three people during a 17-year terror campaign and wounded many others. One of his bombs gravely injured my friend David Gelernter, one of the most brilliant and visionary computer scientists of our time. Like many of my colleagues, I felt that I could easily have been the Unabomber's next target.

Kaczynski's actions were murderous and, in my view, criminally insane. He is clearly a Luddite, but simply saying this does not dismiss his argument; as difficult as it is for me to acknowledge, I saw some merit in the reasoning in this single passage. I felt compelled to confront it.

Kaczynski's dystopian vision describes unintended consequences, a well-known problem with the design and use of technology, and one that is clearly related to Murphy's law—"Anything that can go wrong, will." (Actually, this is Finagle's law, which in itself shows that Finagle was right.) Our overuse of antibiotics has led to what may be the biggest such problem so far: the emergence of antibiotic-resistant and much more dangerous bacteria.

Similar things happened when attempts to eliminate malarial mosquitoes using DDT caused them to acquire DDT resistance; malarial parasites likewise acquired multi-drug-resistant genes.[2]

The cause of many such surprises seems clear: The systems involved are complex, involving interaction among and feedback between many parts. Any changes to such a system will cascade in ways that are difficult to predict; this is especially true when human actions are involved.

I started showing friends the Kaczynski quote from *The Age of Spiritual Machines*; I would hand them Kurzweil's book, let them read the quote, and then watch their reaction as they discovered who had written it. At around the same time, I found Hans Moravec's book *Robot: Mere Machine to Transcendent Mind*. Moravec is one of the leaders in robotics research, and was a founder of the world's largest robotics research program, at Carnegie Mellon University. *Robot* gave me more material to try out on my friends—material surprisingly supportive of Kaczynski's argument. For example:

The Short Run (Early 2000s)

Biological species almost never survive encounters with superior competitors. Ten million years ago, South and North America were separated by a sunken Panama isthmus. South America, like Australia today, was populated by marsupial mammals, including pouched equivalents of rats, deer, and tigers. When the isthmus connecting

2   Garrett, Laurie. *The Coming Plague: Newly Emerging Diseases in a World Out of Balance*. Penguin, 1994: 47-52, 414, 419, 452.

North and South America rose, it took only a few thousand years for the northern placental species, with slightly more effective metabolisms and reproductive and nervous systems, to displace and eliminate almost all the southern marsupials.

In a completely free marketplace, superior robots would surely affect humans as North American placentals affected South American marsupials (and as humans have affected countless species). Robotic industries would compete vigorously among themselves for matter, energy, and space, incidentally driving their price beyond human reach. Unable to afford the necessities of life, biological humans would be squeezed out of existence.

There is probably some breathing room, because we do not live in a completely free marketplace. Government coerces nonmarket behavior, especially by collecting taxes.

Judiciously applied, governmental coercion could support human populations in high style on the fruits of robot labor, perhaps for a long while.

A textbook dystopia—and Moravec is just getting wound up. He goes on to discuss how our main job in the 21st century will be "ensuring continued cooperation from the robot industries" by passing laws decreeing that they be "nice,"[3] and to describe how seriously dangerous a human can be "once transformed into an unbounded superintelligent robot." Moravec's view is that the robots will eventually succeed us—that humans clearly face extinction.

I decided it was time to talk to my friend Danny Hillis. Danny became famous as the cofounder of Thinking Machines Corporation, which built a very powerful parallel supercomputer. Despite my current job title of Chief Scientist at Sun Microsystems, I am more a computer architect than a scientist, and I respect Danny's knowledge of the information and physical sciences more than that of any other single person I know. Danny is also a highly regarded futurist who thinks long-term—four years ago he started the Long Now Foundation, which is building a clock designed to last 10,000 years, in an attempt to draw attention to the pitifully short attention span of our society.[4]

So I flew to Los Angeles for the express purpose of having dinner with Danny and his wife, Pati. I went through my now-familiar routine, trotting out the ideas and passages that I found so disturbing. Danny's answer—directed specifically

---

3   Isaac Asimov described what became the most famous view of ethical rules for robot behavior in his book *I, Robot* in 1950, in his Three Laws of Robotics: 1. A robot may not injure a human being, or, through inaction, allow a human being to come to harm. 2. A robot must obey the orders given it by human beings, except where such orders would conflict with the First Law. 3. A robot must protect its own existence, as long as such protection does not conflict with the First or Second Law.

4   See "Test of Time," *Wired* 8.03, page 78.

at Kurzweil's scenario of humans merging with robots—came swiftly, and quite surprised me. He said, simply, that the changes would come gradually, and that we would get used to them.

But I guess I wasn't totally surprised. I had seen a quote from Danny in Kurzweil's book in which he said, "I'm as fond of my body as anyone, but if I can be 200 with a body of silicon, I'll take it." It seemed that he was at peace with this process and its attendant risks, while I was not.

While talking and thinking about Kurzweil, Kaczynski, and Moravec, I suddenly remembered a novel I had read almost 20 years ago—*The White Plague*, by Frank Herbert—in which a molecular biologist is driven insane by the senseless murder of his family. To seek revenge he constructs and disseminates a new and highly contagious plague that kills widely but selectively. (We're lucky Kaczynski was a mathematician, not a molecular biologist.) I was also reminded of the Borg of *Star Trek*, a hive of partly biological, partly robotic creatures with a strong destructive streak. Borg-like disasters are a staple of science fiction, so why hadn't I been more concerned about such robotic dystopias earlier? Why weren't other people more concerned about these nightmarish scenarios?

Part of the answer certainly lies in our attitude toward the new—in our bias toward instant familiarity and unquestioning acceptance. Accustomed to living with almost routine scientific breakthroughs, we have yet to come to terms with the fact that the most compelling 21st-century technologies—robotics, genetic engineering, and nanotechnology—pose a different threat than the technologies that have come before. Specifically, robots, engineered organisms, and nanobots share a dangerous amplifying factor: They can self-replicate. A bomb is blown up only once—but one bot can become many, and quickly get out of control.

Much of my work over the past 25 years has been on computer networking, where the sending and receiving of messages creates the opportunity for out-of-control replication. But while replication in a computer or a computer network can be a nuisance, at worst it disables a machine or takes down a network or network service.

Uncontrolled self-replication in these newer technologies runs a much greater risk: a risk of substantial damage in the physical world.

Each of these technologies also offers untold promise: The vision of near immortality that Kurzweil sees in his robot dreams drives us forward; genetic engineering may soon provide treatments, if not outright cures, for most diseases; and nanotechnology and nanomedicine can address yet more ills. Together they could significantly extend our average life span and improve the quality of our lives. Yet, with each of these technologies, a sequence of small, individually sensible advances leads to an accumulation of great power and, concomitantly, great danger.

What was different in the 20th century? Certainly, the technologies underlying the weapons of mass destruction (WMD)—nuclear, biological, and chemical (NBC)—were powerful, and the weapons an enormous threat. But building nuclear weapons required, at least for a time, access to both rare—indeed, effectively unavailable—raw materials and highly protected information; biological and chemical weapons programs also tended to require large-scale activities.

The 21st-century technologies—genetics, nanotechnology, and robotics (GNR)—are so powerful that they can spawn whole new classes of accidents and abuses. Most dangerously, for the first time, these accidents and abuses are widely within the reach of individuals or small groups. They will not require large facilities or rare raw materials. Knowledge alone will enable the use of them.

Thus we have the possibility not just of weapons of mass destruction but of knowledge-enabled mass destruction (KMD), this destructiveness hugely amplified by the power of self-replication.

I think it is no exaggeration to say we are on the cusp of the further perfection of extreme evil, an evil whose possibility spreads well beyond that which weapons of mass destruction bequeathed to the nation-states, on to a surprising and terrible empowerment of extreme individuals.

Nothing about the way I got involved with computers suggested to me that I was going to be facing these kinds of issues.

My life has been driven by a deep need to ask questions and find answers. When I was 3, I was already reading, so my father took me to the elementary school, where I sat on the principal's lap and read him a story. I started school early, later skipped a grade, and escaped into books—I was incredibly motivated to learn. I asked lots of questions, often driving adults to distraction.

As a teenager I was very interested in science and technology. I wanted to be a ham radio operator but didn't have the money to buy the equipment. Ham radio was the Internet of its time: very addictive, and quite solitary.

Money issues aside, my mother put her foot down—I was not to be a ham; I was antisocial enough already.

I may not have had many close friends, but I was awash in ideas. By high school, I had discovered the great science fiction writers. I remember especially Heinlein's *Have Spacesuit Will Travel* and Asimov's *I, Robot*, with its Three Laws of Robotics. I was enchanted by the descriptions of space travel, and wanted to have a telescope to look at the stars; since I had no money to buy or make one, I checked books on telescope-making out of the library and read about making them instead. I soared in my imagination.

Thursday nights my parents went bowling, and we kids stayed home alone. It was the night of Gene Roddenberry's original *Star Trek*, and the program made a big impression on me. I came to accept its notion that humans had a future in space, Western-style, with big heroes and adventures. Roddenberry's vision of the centuries to come was one with strong moral values, embodied in codes like the Prime Directive: to not interfere in the development of less technologically advanced civilizations. This had an incredible appeal to me; ethical humans, not robots, dominated this future, and I took Roddenberry's dream as part of my own.

I excelled in mathematics in high school, and when I went to the University of Michigan as an undergraduate engineering student I took the advanced curriculum of the mathematics majors. Solving math problems was an exciting challenge, but when I discovered computers I found something much more interesting: a machine into which you could put a program that attempted to solve a problem, after which the machine quickly checked the solution. The computer had a clear notion of correct and incorrect, true and false. Were my ideas correct? The machine could tell me. This was very seductive.

I was lucky enough to get a job programming early supercomputers and discovered the amazing power of large machines to numerically simulate advanced designs. When I went to graduate school at UC Berkeley in the mid-1970s, I started staying up late, often all night, inventing new worlds inside the machines. Solving problems. Writing the code that argued so strongly to be written.

In *The Agony and the Ecstasy*, Irving Stone's biographical novel of Michelangelo, Stone described vividly how Michelangelo released the statues from the stone, "breaking the marble spell," carving from the images in his mind.[5] In my most ecstatic moments, the software in the computer emerged in the same way. Once I had imagined it in my mind I felt that it was already there in the machine, waiting to be released. Staying up all night seemed a small price to pay to free it—to give the ideas concrete form.

After a few years at Berkeley I started to send out some of the software I had written—an instructional Pascal system, Unix utilities, and a text editor called vi (which is still, to my surprise, widely used more than 20 years later)—to others who had similar small PDP-11 and VAX minicomputers.

These adventures in software eventually turned into the Berkeley version of the Unix operating system, which became a personal "success disaster"—so many people wanted it that I never finished my PhD. Instead I got a job working for Darpa putting Berkeley Unix on the Internet and fixing it to be reliable and to run large research applications well. This was all great fun and very rewarding. And, frankly, I saw no robots here, or anywhere near.

---

5 Michelangelo wrote a sonnet that begins:
   Non ha l' ottimo artista alcun concetto
   Ch' un marmo solo in sè non circonscriva
   Col suo soverchio; e solo a quello arriva
   La man che ubbidisce all' intelleto.
Stone translates this as:
   The best of artists hath no thought to show which the rough
   stone in its superfluous shell doth not include; to break the
   marble spell
   is all the hand that serves the brain can do.
Stone describes the process: "He was not working from his drawings or clay models; they had all been put away. He was carving from the images in his mind. His eyes and hands knew where every line, curve, mass must emerge, and at what depth in the heart of the stone to create the low relief." (*The Agony and the Ecstasy*. Doubleday, 1961: 6, 144.)

Still, by the early 1980s, I was drowning. The Unix releases were very successful, and my little project of one soon had money and some staff, but the problem at Berkeley was always office space rather than money—there wasn't room for the help the project needed, so when the other founders of Sun Microsystems showed up I jumped at the chance to join them. At Sun, the long hours continued into the early days of workstations and personal computers, and I have enjoyed participating in the creation of advanced microprocessor technologies and Internet technologies such as Java and Jini.

From all this, I trust it is clear that I am not a Luddite. I have always, rather, had a strong belief in the value of the scientific search for truth and in the ability of great engineering to bring material progress. The Industrial Revolution has immeasurably improved everyone's life over the last couple hundred years, and I always expected my career to involve the building of worthwhile solutions to real problems, one problem at a time.

I have not been disappointed. My work has had more impact than I had ever hoped for and has been more widely used than I could have reasonably expected. I have spent the last 20 years still trying to figure out how to make computers as reliable as I want them to be (they are not nearly there yet) and how to make them simple to use (a goal that has met with even less relative success). Despite some progress, the problems that remain seem even more daunting.

But while I was aware of the moral dilemmas surrounding technology's consequences in fields like weapons research, I did not expect that I would confront such issues in my own field, or at least not so soon.

Perhaps it is always hard to see the bigger impact while you are in the vortex of a change. Failing to understand the consequences of our inventions while we are in the rapture of discovery and innovation seems to be a common fault of scientists and technologists; we have long been driven by the overarching desire to know that is the nature of science's quest, not stopping to notice that the progress to newer and more powerful technologies can take on a life of its own.

I have long realized that the big advances in information technology come not from the work of computer scientists, computer architects, or electrical engineers, but from that of physical scientists. The physicists Stephen Wolfram and Brosl Hasslacher introduced me, in the early 1980s, to chaos theory and nonlinear systems. In the 1990s, I learned about complex systems from conversations with Danny Hillis, the biologist Stuart Kauffman, the Nobel-laureate physicist Murray Gell-Mann, and others. Most recently, Hasslacher and the electrical engineer and device physicist Mark Reed have been giving me insight into the incredible possibilities of molecular electronics.

In my own work, as co-designer of three microprocessor architectures—SPARC, picoJava, and MAJC—and as the designer of several implementations thereof, I've been afforded a deep and firsthand acquaintance with Moore's law. For decades, Moore's law has correctly predicted the exponential rate of improvement of semiconductor technology. Until last year I believed that the rate of advances predicted by Moore's law might continue only until roughly 2010, when some physical limits would begin to be reached. It was not obvious to me that a new technology would arrive in time to keep performance advancing smoothly.

But because of the recent rapid and radical progress in molecular electronics—where individual atoms and molecules replace lithographically drawn transistors—and related nanoscale technologies, we should be able to meet or exceed the Moore's law rate of progress for another 30 years. By 2030, we are likely to be able to build machines, in quantity, a million times as powerful as the personal computers of today—sufficient to implement the dreams of Kurzweil and Moravec.

As this enormous computing power is combined with the manipulative advances of the physical sciences and the new, deep understandings in genetics, enormous transformative power is being unleashed. These combinations open up the opportunity to completely redesign the world, for better or worse: The replicating and evolving processes that have been confined to the natural world are about to become realms of human endeavor.

In designing software and microprocessors, I have never had the feeling that I was designing an intelligent machine. The software and hardware is so fragile and the capabilities of the machine to "think" so clearly absent that, even as a possibility, this has always seemed very far in the future.

But now, with the prospect of human-level computing power in about 30 years, a new idea suggests itself: that I may be working to create tools which will enable the construction of the technology that may replace our species. How do I feel about this? Very uncomfortable. Having struggled my entire career to build reliable software systems, it seems to me more than likely that this future will not work out as well as some people may imagine. My personal experience suggests we tend to overestimate our design abilities.

Given the incredible power of these new technologies, shouldn't we be asking how we can best coexist with them? And if our own extinction is a likely, or even possible, outcome of our technological development, shouldn't we proceed with great caution?

The dream of robotics is, first, that intelligent machines can do our work for us, allowing us lives of leisure, restoring us to Eden. Yet in his history of such ideas, *Darwin Among the Machines*, George Dyson warns: "In the game of life and evolution there are three players at the table: human beings, nature, and machines. I am firmly on the side of nature. But nature, I suspect, is on the side of the machines." As we have seen, Moravec agrees, believing we may well not survive the encounter with the superior robot species.

How soon could such an intelligent robot be built? The coming advances in computing power seem to make it possible by 2030. And once an intelligent robot exists, it is only a small step to a robot species—to an intelligent robot that can make evolved copies of itself.

A second dream of robotics is that we will gradually replace ourselves with our robotic technology, achieving near immortality by downloading our consciousnesses; it is this process that Danny Hillis thinks we will gradually get used to and that Ray Kurzweil elegantly details in *The Age of Spiritual Machines*.[6]

But if we are downloaded into our technology, what are the chances that we will thereafter be ourselves or even human? It seems to me far more likely that a robotic existence would not be like a human one in any sense that we understand, that the robots would in no sense be our children, that on this path our humanity may well be lost.

Genetic engineering promises to revolutionize agriculture by increasing crop yields while reducing the use of pesticides; to create tens of thousands of novel species of bacteria, plants, viruses, and animals; to replace reproduction, or supplement it, with cloning; to create cures for many diseases, increasing our life span and our quality of life; and much, much more. We now know with certainty that these profound changes in the biological sciences are imminent and will challenge all our notions of what life is.

Technologies such as human cloning have in particular raised our awareness of the profound ethical and moral issues we face. If, for example, we were to reengineer ourselves into several separate and unequal species using the power of genetic engineering, then we would threaten the notion of equality that is the very cornerstone of our democracy.

Given the incredible power of genetic engineering, it's no surprise that there are significant safety issues in its use. My friend Amory Lovins recently cowrote, along with Hunter Lovins, an editorial that provides an ecological view of some of these dangers. Among their concerns: that "the new botany aligns the development of plants with their economic, not evolutionary, success."[7] Amory's long career has been focused on energy and resource efficiency by taking a whole-system view of human-made systems; such a whole-system view often finds simple, smart solutions to otherwise seemingly difficult problems, and is usefully applied here as well.

After reading the Lovins' editorial, I saw an op-ed by Gregg Easterbrook in *The New York Times* (November 19, 1999) about genetically engineered crops, under the headline: "Food for the Future: Someday, rice will have built-in vitamin A. Unless the Luddites win."

Are Amory and Hunter Lovins Luddites? Certainly not. I believe we all would agree that golden rice, with its built-in vitamin A, is probably a good thing, if developed with proper care and respect for the likely dangers in moving genes across species boundaries.

Awareness of the dangers inherent in genetic engineering is beginning to grow, as reflected in the Lovins' editorial. The general public is aware of, and uneasy

---

6   We are beginning to see intimations of this in the implantation of computer devices into the human body, as illustrated on the cover of *Wired* 8.02.

7   See "A Tale of Two Botanies," page 247.

about, genetically modified foods, and seems to be rejecting the notion that such foods should be permitted to be unlabeled.

But genetic engineering technology is already very far along. As the Lovins note, the USDA has already approved about 50 genetically engineered crops for unlimited release; more than half of the world's soybeans and a third of its corn now contain genes spliced in from other forms of life.

While there are many important issues here, my own major concern with genetic engineering is narrower: that it gives the power—whether militarily, accidentally, or in a deliberate terrorist act—to create a White Plague.

The many wonders of nanotechnology were first imagined by the Nobel-laureate physicist Richard Feynman in a speech he gave in 1959, subsequently published under the title "There's Plenty of Room at the Bottom." The book that made a big impression on me, in the mid-'80s, was Eric Drexler's *Engines of Creation*, in which he described beautifully how manipulation of matter at the atomic level could create a utopian future of abundance, where just about everything could be made cheaply, and almost any imaginable disease or physical problem could be solved using nanotechnology and artificial intelligences.

A subsequent book, *Unbounding the Future: The Nanotechnology Revolution*, which Drexler cowrote, imagines some of the changes that might take place in a world where we had molecular-level "assemblers." Assemblers could make possible incredibly low-cost solar power, cures for cancer and the common cold by augmentation of the human immune system, essentially complete cleanup of the environment, incredibly inexpensive pocket supercomputers—in fact, any product would be manufacturable by assemblers at a cost no greater than that of wood—spaceflight more accessible than transoceanic travel today, and restoration of extinct species.

I remember feeling good about nanotechnology after reading *Engines of Creation*. As a technologist, it gave me a sense of calm—that is, nanotechnology showed us that incredible progress was possible, and indeed perhaps inevitable. If nanotechnology was our future, then I didn't feel pressed to solve so many problems in the present. I would get to Drexler's utopian future in due time; I might as well enjoy life more in the here and now. It didn't make sense, given his vision, to stay up all night, all the time.

Drexler's vision also led to a lot of good fun. I would occasionally get to describe the wonders of nanotechnology to others who had not heard of it. After teasing them with all the things Drexler described I would give a homework assignment of my own: "Use nanotechnology to create a vampire; for extra credit create an antidote."

With these wonders came clear dangers, of which I was acutely aware. As I said at a nanotechnology conference in 1989, "We can't simply do our science and not worry about these ethical issues."[8] But my subsequent conversations with

---

8 First Foresight Conference on Nanotechnology in October 1989, a talk titled "The Future of Computation." Published in Crandall, B.C. and James Lewis, editors. *Nanotechnology: Research and Perspectives*. MIT Press, 1992: 269. See also www.foresight.org/Conferences/MNT01/Nano1.html.

physicists convinced me that nanotechnology might not even work—or, at least, it wouldn't work anytime soon.

Shortly thereafter I moved to Colorado, to a skunk works I had set up, and the focus of my work shifted to software for the Internet, specifically on ideas that became Java and Jini.

Then, last summer, Brosl Hasslacher told me that nanoscale molecular electronics was now practical. This was *new* news, at least to me, and I think to many people—and it radically changed my opinion about nanotechnology. It sent me back to *Engines of Creation*. Rereading Drexler's work after more than 10 years, I was dismayed to realize how little I had remembered of its lengthy section called "Dangers and Hopes," including a discussion of how nanotechnologies can become "engines of destruction." Indeed, in my rereading of this cautionary material today, I am struck by how naive some of Drexler's safeguard proposals seem, and how much greater I judge the dangers to be now than even he seemed to then. (Having anticipated and described many technical and political problems with nanotechnology, Drexler started the Foresight Institute in the late 1980s "to help prepare society for anticipated advanced technologies"—most important, nanotechnology.)

The enabling breakthrough to assemblers seems quite likely within the next 20 years. Molecular electronics—the new subfield of nanotechnology where individual molecules are circuit elements—should mature quickly and become enormously lucrative within this decade, causing a large incremental investment in all nanotechnologies.

Unfortunately, as with nuclear technology, it is far easier to create destructive uses for nanotechnology than constructive ones. Nanotechnology has clear military and terrorist uses, and you need not be suicidal to release a massively destructive nanotechnological device—such devices can be built to be selectively destructive, affecting, for example, only a certain geographical area or a group of people who are genetically distinct.

An immediate consequence of the Faustian bargain in obtaining the great power of nanotechnology is that we run a grave risk—the risk that we might destroy the biosphere on which all life depends.

As Drexler explained:

> "Plants" with "leaves" no more efficient than today's solar cells could out-compete real plants, crowding the biosphere with an inedible foliage. Tough omnivorous "bacteria" could out-compete real bacteria: They could spread like blowing pollen, replicate swiftly, and reduce the biosphere to dust in a matter of days. Dangerous replicators could easily be too tough, small, and rapidly spreading to stop—at least if we make no preparation. We have trouble enough controlling viruses and fruit flies.
>
> Among the cognoscenti of nanotechnology, this threat has become known as the "gray goo problem." Though masses of uncontrolled

replicators need not be gray or gooey, the term "gray goo" emphasizes that replicators able to obliterate life might be less inspiring than a single species of crabgrass. They might be superior in an evolutionary sense, but this need not make them valuable.

The gray goo threat makes one thing perfectly clear: We cannot afford certain kinds of accidents with replicating assemblers.

Gray goo would surely be a depressing ending to our human adventure on Earth, far worse than mere fire or ice, and one that could stem from a simple laboratory accident.[9] Oops.

It is most of all the power of destructive self-replication in genetics, nanotechnology, and robotics (GNR) that should give us pause. Self-replication is the modus operandi of genetic engineering, which uses the machinery of the cell to replicate its designs, and the prime danger underlying gray goo in nanotechnology. Stories of run-amok robots like the Borg, replicating or mutating to escape from the ethical constraints imposed on them by their creators, are well established in our science fiction books and movies. It is even possible that self-replication may be more fundamental than we thought, and hence harder—or even impossible—to control. A recent article by Stuart Kauffman in *Nature* titled "Self-Replication: Even Peptides Do It" discusses the discovery that a 32-amino-acid peptide can "autocatalyse its own synthesis." We don't know how widespread this ability is, but Kauffman notes that it may hint at "a route to self-reproducing molecular systems on a basis far wider than Watson-Crick base-pairing."[10]

In truth, we have had in hand for years clear warnings of the dangers inherent in widespread knowledge of GNR technologies—of the possibility of knowledge alone enabling mass destruction. But these warnings haven't been widely publicized; the public discussions have been clearly inadequate. There is no profit in publicizing the dangers.

The nuclear, biological, and chemical (NBC) technologies used in 20th-century weapons of mass destruction were and are largely military, developed in government laboratories. In sharp contrast, the 21st-century GNR technologies have clear commercial uses and are being developed almost exclusively by corporate enterprises. In this age of triumphant commercialism, technology—with science as its handmaiden—is delivering a series of almost magical inventions that are the most phenomenally lucrative ever seen. We are aggressively pursuing the promises of these new technologies within the now-unchallenged system of global capitalism and its manifold financial incentives and competitive pressures.

---

9   In his 1963 novel *Cat's Cradle*, Kurt Vonnegut imagined a gray-goo-like accident where a form of ice called ice-nine, which becomes solid at a much higher temperature, freezes the oceans.

10 Kauffman, Stuart. "Self-Replication: Even Peptides Do It." Nature, 382, August 8, 1996: 496. See www.santafe.edu/sfi/People/kauffman/sak-peptides.html.

This is the first moment in the history of our planet when any species, by its own voluntary actions, has become a danger to itself—as well as to vast numbers of others.

It might be a familiar progression, transpiring on many worlds—a planet, newly formed, placidly revolves around its star; life slowly forms; a kaleidoscopic procession of creatures evolves; intelligence emerges which, at least up to a point, confers enormous survival value; and then technology is invented. It dawns on them that there are such things as laws of Nature, that these laws can be revealed by experiment, and that knowledge of these laws can be made both to save and to take lives, both on unprecedented scales. Science, they recognize, grants immense powers. In a flash, they create world-altering contrivances. Some planetary civilizations see their way through, place limits on what may and what must not be done, and safely pass through the time of perils. Others, not so lucky or so prudent, perish.

That is Carl Sagan, writing in 1994, in *Pale Blue Dot*, a book describing his vision of the human future in space. I am only now realizing how deep his insight was, and how sorely I miss, and will miss, his voice. For all its eloquence, Sagan's contribution was not least that of simple common sense—an attribute that, along with humility, many of the leading advocates of the 21st-century technologies seem to lack.

I remember from my childhood that my grandmother was strongly against the overuse of antibiotics. She had worked since before the First World War as a nurse and had a commonsense attitude that taking antibiotics, unless they were absolutely necessary, was bad for you.

It is not that she was an enemy of progress. She saw much progress in an almost 70-year nursing career; my grandfather, a diabetic, benefited greatly from the improved treatments that became available in his lifetime. But she, like many levelheaded people, would probably think it greatly arrogant for us, now, to be designing a robotic "replacement species," when we obviously have so much trouble making relatively simple things work, and so much trouble managing—or even understanding—ourselves.

I realize now that she had an awareness of the nature of the order of life, and of the necessity of living with and respecting that order. With this respect comes a necessary humility that we, with our early-21st-century chutzpah, lack at our peril. The commonsense view, grounded in this respect, is often right, in advance of the scientific evidence. The clear fragility and inefficiencies of the human-made systems we have built should give us all pause; the fragility of the systems I have worked on certainly humbles me.

We should have learned a lesson from the making of the first atomic bomb and the resulting arms race. We didn't do well then, and the parallels to our current situation are troubling [...]

In our time, how much danger do we face, not just from nuclear weapons, but from all of these technologies? How high are the extinction risks?

The philosopher John Leslie has studied this question and concluded that the risk of human extinction is at least 30 percent,[11] while Ray Kurzweil believes we have "a better than even chance of making it through," with the caveat that he has "always been accused of being an optimist." Not only are these estimates not encouraging, but they do not include the probability of many horrid outcomes that lie short of extinction.

Faced with such assessments, some serious people are already suggesting that we simply move beyond Earth as quickly as possible. We would colonize the galaxy using von Neumann probes, which hop from star system to star system, replicating as they go. This step will almost certainly be necessary 5 billion years from now (or sooner if our solar system is disastrously impacted by the impending collision of our galaxy with the Andromeda galaxy within the next 3 billion years), but if we take Kurzweil and Moravec at their word it might be necessary by the middle of this century.

What are the moral implications here? If we must move beyond Earth this quickly in order for the species to survive, who accepts the responsibility for the fate of those (most of us, after all) who are left behind? And even if we scatter to the stars, isn't it likely that we may take our problems with us or find, later, that they have followed us? The fate of our species on Earth and our fate in the galaxy seem inextricably linked.

Another idea is to erect a series of shields to defend against each of the dangerous technologies. The Strategic Defense Initiative, proposed by the Reagan administration, was an attempt to design such a shield against the threat of a nuclear attack from the Soviet Union. But as Arthur C. Clarke, who was privy to discussions about the project, observed: "Though it might be possible, at vast expense, to construct local defense systems that would 'only' let through a few percent of ballistic missiles, the much touted idea of a national umbrella was nonsense. Luis Alvarez, perhaps the greatest experimental physicist of this century, remarked to me that the advocates of such schemes were 'very bright guys with no common sense.'"

Clarke continued: "Looking into my often cloudy crystal ball, I suspect that a total defense might indeed be possible in a century or so. But the technology involved would produce, as a by-product, weapons so terrible that no one would bother with anything as primitive as ballistic missiles."[12]

In *Engines of Creation*, Eric Drexler proposed that we build an active nanotechnological shield—a form of immune system for the biosphere—to defend against

11 This estimate is in Leslie's book *The End of the World: The Science and Ethics of Human Extinction*, where he notes that the probability of extinction is substantially higher if we accept Brandon Carter's Doomsday Argument, which is, briefly, that "we ought to have some reluctance to believe that we are very exceptionally early, for instance in the earliest 0.001 percent, among all humans who will ever have lived. This would be some reason for thinking that humankind will not survive for many more centuries, let alone colonize the galaxy. Carter's doomsday argument doesn't generate any risk estimates just by itself. It is an argument for *revising* the estimates which we generate when we consider various possible dangers." (Routledge, 1996: 1, 3, 145.)

12 Clarke, Arthur C. "Presidents, Experts, and Asteroids." *Science*, June 5, 1998. Reprinted as "Science and Society" in *Greetings, Carbon-Based Bipeds! Collected Essays, 1934-1998*. St. Martin's Press, 1999: 526.

dangerous replicators of all kinds that might escape from laboratories or otherwise be maliciously created. But the shield he proposed would itself be extremely dangerous—nothing could prevent it from developing autoimmune problems and attacking the biosphere itself.[13]

Similar difficulties apply to the construction of shields against robotics and genetic engineering. These technologies are too powerful to be shielded against in the time frame of interest; even if it were possible to implement defensive shields, the side effects of their development would be at least as dangerous as the technologies we are trying to protect against.

These possibilities are all thus either undesirable or unachievable or both. The only realistic alternative I see is relinquishment: to limit development of the technologies that are too dangerous, by limiting our pursuit of certain kinds of knowledge.

Yes, I know, knowledge is good, as is the search for new truths. We have been seeking knowledge since ancient times. Aristotle opened his *Metaphysics* with the simple statement: "All men by nature desire to know." We have, as a bedrock value in our society, long agreed on the value of open access to information, and recognize the problems that arise with attempts to restrict access to and development of knowledge. In recent times, we have come to revere scientific knowledge.

But despite the strong historical precedents, if open access to and unlimited development of knowledge henceforth puts us all in clear danger of extinction, then common sense demands that we reexamine even these basic, long-held beliefs.

It was Nietzsche who warned us, at the end of the 19th century, not only that God is dead but that "faith in science, which after all exists undeniably, cannot owe its origin to a calculus of utility; it must have originated *in spite of* the fact that the disutility and dangerousness of the 'will to truth,' of 'truth at any price' is proved to it constantly." It is this further danger that we now fully face—the consequences of our truth-seeking. The truth that science seeks can certainly be considered a dangerous substitute for God if it is likely to lead to our extinction.

If we could agree, as a species, what we wanted, where we were headed, and why, then we would make our future much less dangerous—then we might understand what we can and should relinquish. Otherwise, we can easily imagine an arms race developing over GNR technologies, as it did with the NBC technologies in the 20th century. This is perhaps the greatest risk, for once such a race begins, it's very hard to end it. This time—unlike during the Manhattan Project—we aren't in a war, facing an implacable enemy that is threatening our civilization; we are driven, instead, by our habits, our desires, our economic system, and our competitive need to know.

---

13 And, as David Forrest suggests in his paper "Regulating Nanotechnology Development," available at www.foresight.org/NanoRev/Forrest1989.html, "If we used strict liability as an alternative to regulation it would be impossible for any developer to internalize the cost of the risk (destruction of the biosphere), so theoretically the activity of developing nanotechnology should never be undertaken." Forrest's analysis leaves us with only government regulation to protect us—not a comforting thought.

I believe that we all wish our course could be determined by our collective values, ethics, and morals. If we had gained more collective wisdom over the past few thousand years, then a dialogue to this end would be more practical, and the incredible powers we are about to unleash would not be nearly so troubling.

One would think we might be driven to such a dialogue by our instinct for self-preservation. Individuals clearly have this desire, yet as a species our behavior seems to be not in our favor. In dealing with the nuclear threat, we often spoke dishonestly to ourselves and to each other, thereby greatly increasing the risks. Whether this was politically motivated, or because we chose not to think ahead, or because when faced with such grave threats we acted irrationally out of fear, I do not know, but it does not bode well.

The new Pandora's boxes of genetics, nanotechnology, and robotics are almost open, yet we seem hardly to have noticed. Ideas can't be put back in a box; unlike uranium or plutonium, they don't need to be mined and refined, and they can be freely copied. Once they are out, they are out. Churchill remarked, in a famous left-handed compliment, that the American people and their leaders "invariably do the right thing, after they have examined every other alternative." In this case, however, we must act more presciently, as to do the right thing only at last may be to lose the chance to do it at all [...]

It is now more than a year since my first encounter with Ray Kurzweil and John Searle. I see around me cause for hope in the voices for caution and relinquishment and in those people I have discovered who are as concerned as I am about our current predicament. I feel, too, a deepened sense of personal responsibility—not for the work I have already done, but for the work that I might yet do, at the confluence of the sciences.

But many other people who know about the dangers still seem strangely silent. When pressed, they trot out the "this is nothing new" riposte—as if awareness of what could happen is response enough. They tell me, There are universities filled with bioethicists who study this stuff all day long. They say, All this has been written about before, and by experts. They complain, Your worries and your arguments are already old hat.

I don't know where these people hide their fear. As an architect of complex systems I enter this arena as a generalist. But should this diminish my concerns? I am aware of how much has been written about, talked about, and lectured about so authoritatively. But does this mean it has reached people? Does this mean we can discount the dangers before us?

Knowing is not a rationale for not acting. Can we doubt that knowledge has become a weapon we wield against ourselves?

The experiences of the atomic scientists clearly show the need to take personal responsibility, the danger that things will move too fast, and the way in which a process can take on a life of its own. We can, as they did, create insurmountable problems in almost no time flat. We must do more thinking up front if we are not to be similarly surprised and shocked by the consequences of our inventions.

My continuing professional work is on improving the reliability of software. Software is a tool, and as a toolbuilder I must struggle with the uses to which the tools I make are put. I have always believed that making software more reliable, given its many uses, will make the world a safer and better place; if I were to come to believe the opposite, then I would be morally obligated to stop this work. I can now imagine such a day may come.

This all leaves me not angry but at least a bit melancholic. Henceforth, for me, progress will be somewhat bittersweet.

Do you remember the beautiful penultimate scene in *Manhattan* where Woody Allen is lying on his couch and talking into a tape recorder? He is writing a short story about people who are creating unnecessary, neurotic problems for themselves, because it keeps them from dealing with more unsolvable, terrifying problems about the universe.

He leads himself to the question, "Why is life worth living?" and to consider what makes it worthwhile for him: Groucho Marx, Willie Mays, the second movement of the Jupiter Symphony, Louis Armstrong's recording of "Potato Head Blues," Swedish movies, Flaubert's *Sentimental Education*, Marlon Brando, Frank Sinatra, the apples and pears by Cézanne, the crabs at Sam Wo's, and, finally, the showstopper: his love Tracy's face.

Each of us has our precious things, and as we care for them we locate the essence of our humanity. In the end, it is because of our great capacity for caring that I remain optimistic we will confront the dangerous issues now before us.

My immediate hope is to participate in a much larger discussion of the issues raised here, with people from many different backgrounds, in settings not predisposed to fear or favor technology for its own sake.

As a start, I have twice raised many of these issues at events sponsored by the Aspen Institute and have separately proposed that the American Academy of Arts and Sciences take them up as an extension of its work with the Pugwash Conferences. (These have been held since 1957 to discuss arms control, especially of nuclear weapons, and to formulate workable policies.)

It's unfortunate that the Pugwash meetings started only well after the nuclear genie was out of the bottle—roughly 15 years too late. We are also getting a belated start on seriously addressing the issues around 21st-century technologies—the prevention of knowledge-enabled mass destruction—and further delay seems unacceptable.

So I'm still searching; there are many more things to learn. Whether we are to succeed or fail, to survive or fall victim to these technologies, is not yet decided. I'm up late again—it's almost 6 am. I'm trying to imagine some better answers, to break the spell and free them from the stone.

Source: *Wired* 8.04 (April 2000): 238-46. Web. http://www.wired.com/wired/archive/8.04/joy_pr.html.

WHAT IT SAYS

1. What dangers might arise from runaway technology, according to Bill Joy?

2. While troubled by and disdainful of the actions of Theodore Kaczynski (the Unabomber), Joy also finds his views somewhat valid. How can this be? In what sense does he agree with Kaczynski? In what sense does he oppose Kaczynski?

3. What is a "Luddite"? What would a Luddite think about the technological changes that Joy discusses?

4. Near the end of his essay, Joy refers to a scene from the Woody Allen movie *Manhattan*. This allusion to popular culture might reassure his audience that he is, in some sense, "with it." Aside from this reassurance, what is the point of this illustration?

HOW IT SAYS IT

1. Joy presents himself as an important player in the development of computer technology. How does this self-presentation work to persuade his audience to adopt his position?

2. Why is it important to Joy's argument that he establishes himself as a "non-Luddite"? Is he successful in persuading you that he is *not* anti-technology?

3. Discuss how Joy uses narration, description, and exposition to advance his argument.

4. Joy's essay was first published in *Wired*, a non-peer-reviewed magazine about the impact of technology on culture, the economy, and politics. In what ways can you tell that Joy is writing for *Wired* and not an academic journal?

5. Joy cites numerous authors to make his point about the dangers of GNR. Discuss how he draws on one or more of these authors to help make his argument. What use does he make of Carl Sagan, for example? Nietzsche? How does citing a scientist like Sagan function differently than citing a philosopher like Nietzsche?

WRITE ABOUT IT

1. Joy's essay is rather drawn out and complicated in organization. Write a summary of the essay, picking out the most important points and connecting them in a way that makes the argument easier to follow. Look for a means of organization that combines or puts together like parts that may be scattered throughout the original essay. Clearly and succinctly present Joy's argument, including all the major points that Joy makes and the most important sources that he draws from.

2. Write an essay in which you argue against some aspect, or the entirety, of Joy's essay. You may disagree with possibilities that he envisions, or with the impact he attributes to these possibilities. Be sure to address specific points that Joy makes and to provide solid reasoning to rebut them.

e. N. Katherine Hayles, "Prologue," *How We Became Posthuman: Virtual Bodies in Cybernetics, Literature and Informatics*

N. Katherine Hayles is a postmodern literary critic, most notable for her contribution to the fields of literature and science, electronic literature, and American literature. She is a professor and the director of graduate studies in the Program in Literature at Duke University. Hayles has taught at UCLA, the University of Iowa, the University of Missouri-Rolla, the California Institute of Technology, and Dartmouth College. She was faculty director of the Electronic Literature Organization from 2001-2006.

Hayles is a prolific author. Her many books include *The Cosmic Web: Scientific Field Models and Literary Strategies in the Twentieth Century* (1984), *Chaos Bound: Orderly Disorder in Contemporary Literature and Science* (1990), *How We Became Posthuman: Virtual Bodies in Cybernetics, Literature and Informatics* (1999), *Writing Machines* (2002), *My Mother Was a Computer: Digital Subjects and Literary Texts* (2005), *Electronic Literature: New Horizons for the Literary* (2008), and *How We Think: Digital Media and Contemporary Technogenesis* (2012). She has also edited several anthologies, including *Chaos and Order: Complex Dynamics in Literature and Science* (1991), and *Nanoculture: Implications of the New Technoscience* (2004).

Hayles has received numerous awards, including the Susanne Langer Award for Outstanding Scholarship (*Writing Machines*, 2002) and the René Wellek Prize for the best book in literary theory (*How We Became Posthuman*, 1998-1999). Hayles received a PhD in English Literature from the University of Rochester, an MA in English Literature from Michigan State University, an MS in Chemistry from California Institute of Technology, and a BS in Chemistry from Rochester Institute of Technology.

In the following essay, the prologue to *How We Became Posthuman*, Hayles considers the "Turing test" invented by the famous computer scientist Alan Turing, and the biography of Turing by Andrew Hodges. Hayles views the Turing test as "the inaugural moment of the computer age," and the moment at which the posthuman was born. The essay hints at what she means by the posthuman: the moment when intelligence and rationality are seen as disembodied and locatable in machines.

As You Read: Hayles's writing is dense in places. Consider annotating it, adding whatever notes may help you make sense of this difficult piece.

Prologue to How We Became Posthuman

You are alone in the room, except for two computer terminals flickering in the dim light. You use the terminals to communicate with two entities in another room, whom you cannot see. Relying solely on their responses to your questions, you must decide which is the man, which the woman. Or, in another version of the famous "imitation game" proposed by Alan Turing in his classic 1950 paper "Computer Machinery and Intelligence," you use the responses to decide which is the human, which the machine.[1] One of the entities wants to help you guess correctly. His/her/its best strategy, Turing suggested, may be to answer your questions truthfully. The other entity wants to mislead you. He/she/it will try to reproduce through the words that appear on your terminal the characteristics of the other entity. Your job is to pose questions that can distinguish verbal performance from embodied reality. If you cannot tell the intelligent machine from the intelligent human, your failure proves, Turing argued, that machines can think.

Here, at the inaugural moment of the computer age, the erasure of embodiment is performed so that "intelligence" becomes a property of the formal manipulation of symbols rather than enaction in the human lifeworld. The Turing test was to set the agenda for artificial intelligence for the next three decades. In the push to achieve machines that can think, researchers performed again and again the erasure of embodiment at the heart of the Turing test. All that mattered was the formal generation and manipulation of informational patterns. Aiding this process was a definition of information, formalized by Claude Shannon and Norbert Wiener, that conceptualized information as an entity distinct from the substrates carrying it.

From this formulation, it was a small step to think of information as a kind of bodiless fluid that could flow between different substrates without loss of meaning or form. Writing nearly four decades after Turing, Hans Moravec proposed that human identity is essentially an informational pattern rather than an embodied enaction. The proposition can be demonstrated, he suggested, by downloading human consciousness into a computer, and he imagined a scenario designed to show that this was in principle possible. The Moravec test, if I may call it that, is the logical successor to the Turing test. Whereas the Turing test was designed to show that machines can perform the thinking previously considered to be an exclusive capacity of the human mind, the Moravec test was designed to show that machines can become the repository of human consciousness—that machines can, for all practical purposes, become human beings. You are the cyborg, and the cyborg is you.

---

1   Alan M. Turing, "Computing Machinery and Intelligence," *Mind* 54 (1950): 433-57.

In the progression from Turing to Moravec, the part of the Turing test that historically has been foregrounded is the distinction between thinking human and thinking machine. Often forgotten is the first example Turing offered of distinguishing between a man and a woman. If your failure to distinguish correctly between human and machine proves that machines can think, what does it prove if you fail to distinguish woman from man? Why does gender appear in this primal scene of humans meeting their evolutionary successors, intelligent machines? What do gendered bodies have to do with the erasure of embodiment and the subsequent merging of machine and human intelligence in the figure of the cyborg?

In his thoughtful and perceptive intellectual biography of Turing, Andrew Hodges suggests that Turing's predilection was always to deal with the world as if it were a formal puzzle.[2] To a remarkable extent, Hodges says, Turing was blind to the distinction between saying and doing. Turing fundamentally did not understand that "questions involving sex, society, politics or secrets would demonstrate how what it was possible for people to *say* might be limited not by puzzle-solving intelligence but by the restrictions on what might be *done*" (pp. 423-24). In a fine insight, Hodges suggests that "the discrete state machine, communicating by teleprinter alone, was like an ideal for [Turing's] own life, in which he would be left alone in a room of his own, to deal with the outside world solely by rational argument. It was the embodiment of a perfect J.S. Mill liberal, concentrating upon the free will and free speech of the individual" (p. 425). Turing's later embroilment with the police and court system over the question of his homosexuality played out, in a different key, the assumptions embodied in the Turing test. His conviction and the court-ordered hormone treatments for his homosexuality tragically demonstrated the importance of *doing* over *saying* in the coercive order of a homophobic society with the power to enforce its will upon the bodies of its citizens.

The perceptiveness of Hodges's biography notwithstanding, he gives a strange interpretation of Turing's inclusion of gender in the imitation game. Gender, according to Hodges, "was in fact a red herring, and one of the few passages of the paper that was not expressed with perfect lucidity. The whole point of this game was that a successful imitation of a woman's responses by a man would *not* prove anything. Gender depended on facts which were *not* reducible to sequences of symbols" (p. 415). In the paper itself, however, nowhere does Turing suggest that gender is meant as a counterexample; instead, he makes the two cases rhetorically parallel, indicating through symmetry, if nothing else, that the gender and the human/machine examples are meant to prove the same thing. Is this simply bad writing, as Hodges argues, an inability to express an intended opposition

---

2   Andrew Hodges, *Alan Turing: The Enigma of Intelligence* (London: Unwin, 1985), pp. 415-25. I am indebted to Carol Wald for her insights into the relation between gender and artificial intelligence, the subject of her dissertation, and to her other writings on this question. I also owe her thanks for pointing out to me that Andrew Hodges dismisses Turing's use of gender as a logical flaw in his analysis of the Turing text.

between the construction of gender and the construction of thought? Or, on the contrary, does the writing express a parallelism too explosive and subversive for Hodges to acknowledge?

If so, now we have two mysteries instead of one. Why does Turing include gender, and why does Hodges want to read this inclusion as indicating that, so far as gender is concerned, verbal performance cannot be equated with embodied reality? One way to frame these mysteries is to see them as attempts to transgress and reinforce the boundaries of the subject, respectively. By including gender, Turing implied that renegotiating the boundary between human and machine would involve more than transforming the question of "who can think" into "what can think." It would also necessarily bring into question other characteristics of the liberal subject, for it made the crucial move of distinguishing between the enacted body, present in the flesh on one side of the computer screen, and the represented body, produced through the verbal and semiotic markers constituting it in an electronic environment. This construction necessarily makes the subject into a cyborg, for the enacted and represented bodies are brought into conjunction through the technology that connects them. If you distinguish correctly which is the man and which the woman, you in effect reunite the enacted and the represented bodies into a single gender identity. The very existence of the test, however, implies that you may also make the wrong choice. Thus the test functions to create the possibility of a disjunction between the enacted and the represented bodies, regardless which choice you make. What the Turing test "proves" is that the overlay between the enacted and the represented bodies is no longer a natural inevitability but a contingent production, mediated by a technology that has become so entwined with the production of identity that it can no longer meaningfully be separated from the human subject. To pose the question of "what can think" inevitably also changes, in a reverse feedback loop, the terms of "who can think."

On this view, Hodges's reading of the gender test as nonsignifying with respect to identity can be seen as an attempt to safeguard the boundaries of the subject from precisely this kind of transformation, to insist that the existence of thinking machines will not necessarily affect what being human means. That Hodges's reading is a misreading indicates he is willing to practice violence upon the text to wrench meaning away from the direction toward which the Turing test points, back to safer ground where embodiment secures the univocality of gender. I think he is wrong about embodiment's securing the univocality of gender and wrong about its securing human identity, but right about the importance of putting embodiment back into the picture. What embodiment secures is not the distinction between male and female or between humans who can think and machines which cannot. Rather, embodiment makes clear that thought is a much broader cognitive function depending for its specificities on the embodied form enacting it. This realization, with all its exfoliating implications, is so broad in its effects and so deep in its consequences that it is transforming the liberal subject, regarded as the model of the human since the Enlightenment, into the posthuman.

Think of the Turing test as a magic trick. Like all good magic tricks, the test relies on getting you to accept at an early stage assumptions that will determine how you interpret what you see later. The important intervention comes not when you try to determine which is the man, the woman, or the machine. Rather, the important intervention comes much earlier, when the test puts you into a cybernetic circuit that splices your will, desire, and perception into a distributed cognitive system in which represented bodies are joined with enacted bodies through mutating and flexible machine interfaces. As you gaze at the flickering signifiers scrolling down the computer screens, no matter what identifications you assign to the embodied entities that you cannot see, you have already become posthuman.

Source: *How We Became Posthuman: Virtual Bodies in Cybernetics, Literature, and Informatics.* Chicago: University of Chicago, 1999. xi-xiv.

WHAT IT SAYS

1. What is the "Turing test" (originally the "imitation game") and what is it meant to determine?

2. How did Moravec define "human identity"?

3. What is the difference between the "Turing test" and the hypothetical "Moravec test," as described by Hayles?

4. Describe Turing's ideal human being—as presented by Hayles from Hodges's biography.

5. As Hayles reads it, why did Turing imagine a parallel experiment with a man and a woman in one test, and a machine and a man in another? What was Turing trying to demonstrate with the two parallel experiments, according to Hayles? What would making the wrong choice in distinguishing between the man and the woman suggest? What is Hayles's problem with Hodges's interpretation of this aspect of "the imitation game"?

6. What does Hodges's misreading of the "imitation game" suggest about his (probably subconscious) intentions? What was he attempting to do, according to Hayles? Why?

7. Hayles asks us to consider the Turing test as a magic trick. How does a magic trick work, according to Hayles? What is the magic of the Turing test? What conditions set up the illusion? When during the test is the magic conducted?

HOW IT SAYS IT

1. Hayles begins by asking the reader to imagine that he or she is about to take the Turing test. How does her use of second person ("*You* are alone in the room, except for two computer terminals flickering in the dim light ...) work to introduce the text? What does the second-person address accomplish and how is it related to Hayles's argument in the prologue (and book)?

2. Hayles first compliments Hodges for his biography of Turing but goes on to criticize his reading of the Turing test. Why do you suppose she is complimentary on the one hand, when she will be critical on the other? What is the point of her initial concession of praise?

3. Who are the intended readers of Hayles's text? What are their backgrounds? How can you tell? What interest might they have in reading this book?

WRITE ABOUT IT

1. Write a brief description of the Turing test, updating it for the digital age. How might the test be conducted today? What kinds of computers and programs might be involved? Finally, how likely is it that a computer or robot could pass the test today? Search the Web or see the Suggested Additional Resources for information about artificial intelligence.

2. Hayles's prologue is dense and difficult in parts. Write a short summary of the piece for a general audience.

3. Write an essay in which you explore your own view of intelligence. What is intelligence? What are its conditions? Can it be extracted from the body and deposited in machines, as some authors contend, or is it possible only as part of the body? Explain your position in connection with what Hayles has written in this prologue.

f. Jeremy Maitin-Shepard, "Science, Technology, and Morality"

Jeremy Maitin-Shepard was born and raised in the Boston area, where he attended the Commonwealth School, an independent liberal arts high school. He studied computer science at Carnegie Mellon University, graduating with a Bachelor of Science degree in 2008. He is currently a doctoral student in the Electrical Engineering and Computer Sciences department at the University of California, Berkeley, where he has researched topics in robotics, computer vision, machine learning and cryptography, and is working on algorithms for reconstructing neural circuits from microscopy data. He is also an avid rock climber.

Science, Technology, and Morality

Jeremy Maitin-Shepard
Michael Rectenwald
76-101 D
December 10, 2004

Recent advances in biology and psychology have provided dramatic new insights into the understanding of biological processes, specifically the operation of human and animal brains, and have allowed explanation of human behavior and psychological conditions in terms of environmental and genetic factors; at the same time, technological advances, particularly in biotechnology and artificial intelligence, raise the possibility for genetically engineered humans, animals, and hybrid organisms, direct interfacing between brains and machines, and development of machines capable of highly intelligent, sophisticated and human-like behavior. These advances, in blurring the distinction between humans, animals, and machines, and in suggesting biological causes for individual ability and behavior, pose problems with common conceptions of morality and personal responsibility, which depend on such distinctions and on uncertainty regarding the causes for individual ability. Specifically, consideration of these possibilities exposes the common classification of humans, animals, and other objects for differential treatment as largely arbitrary.

Ethical controversy over technological innovations is nothing new; military technology, life-support systems, birth control and abortion technology, and neurosurgical procedures have always spawned such controversy. But these recent advances do more than create ethical controversy; they expose fundamental problems with common moral theory. Regarding brain-related biotechnology and genetic engineering, although ethical responses to specific technologies and procedures vary widely, there is general consensus that certain applications of these technologies are clearly unethical, and that society must place certain limits on the use of such technology. Although 'unethical' situations can be avoided by effective prohibition of such uses, prohibition does not resolve the problems such possibilities pose to the foundation of moral theory. In the case of artificial intelligence, because the technology in question is not generally believed to be unethical, some philosophers simply deny that human-like behavior will ever be achieved, while others attempt to distinguish in some way between human behavior and the behavior that could possibly be achieved through 'artificial intelligence'; detailed analysis, however, shows flaws in such arguments that artificial intelligence poses no challenges to the bases of moral theory. Specific examples of recent developments and future possibilities in genetic engineering of humans, artificial intelligence, and the interfacing between brains and machines show that such advances pose unique challenges to moral theory.

The theoretical possibilities for genetically engineering humans and animals are nearly limitless. The relevant forms of genetic engineering include so-called gene therapy, or insertion of genes into somatic, namely non-reproductive, cells of existing humans or animals, and so-called germ line manipulation, which involves either prenatal selection of embryos based on their genetics or insertion of genes into embryos or the reproductive cells of existing humans or animals; of particular note regarding germ line manipulation is that any changes made affect all of the descendants of the human or animal.[4, 5]

The extent to which a particular instance of genetic engineering is controversial depends largely on the type of genes affected. Changes involving insertion of specific genes in order to prevent or reduce the risk of specific diseases are less controversial compared to the more controversial insertion of genes for the purpose of improving fitness of various sorts, or for the purpose of affecting behavioral traits or physical traits. (Although behavior may be substantially affected by the environment, there is good reason to believe it is at least partially controllable through genetic manipulation.) Far more controversial possibilities exist, however, such as insertion of animal genes into human cells or insertion of human genes into animal cells. The effect of this, to produce a human-animal hybrid organism, could possibly also be achieved by adding human stem cells to animal embryos or adding animal stem cells to human embryos. Even more controversial is the possibility of designing new proteins for specific purposes, and inserting into human or animal cells the DNA sequence to produce the protein, and thereby allow humans to function in ways that neither humans nor animals have functioned before.

Many of the challenges posed by the possibilities of genetic engineering to common or traditional morality are readily apparent. In the case of human children with a selected or 'designed' genome, depending on the extent and precision of the selection or design, the children could easily be viewed as inferior to their designers, as is argued by the organization Human Genetics Alert.[3, p. 7] Furthermore, depending on the extent to which behavior of the children is predictably controlled, it could well be reasonable to morally hold the designers partially responsible for the actions of the children, even after such children become adults. Assuming that no 'abnormal' genes are inserted, the children would 'objectively' be no different biologically from other people, which would imply that, according to common moral theory, they should not receive differential treatment, and specifically they should be considered no less autonomous than other people; in this way, common moral theory proves to be incoherent in this case.

Genetic engineering also poses problems with common moral theory to the extent that there is an association made between merit and ability; evidence of such an association can be seen, among other things, in the favorable connotations of meritocracy. It seems contrary to general belief that a person who uses genetic engineering to enhance certain of his abilities should consequently be considered to have greater merit, particularly since such enhancements would surely be more available to those with more money. At the same time, however, education seems to be commonly associated with merit, even though better education is available to those with more money. More fundamentally than merit, however, common conceptions of morality place humans in a class of their own, in so far as they claim humans have certain inalienable rights, while claiming that all other things, including machines and animals, have few or no rights. If a group of humans were genetically engineered with various enhancements, such that they become superior in ability to ordinary humans, and also diverge from ordinary humans to the point that they cannot reproduce with humans, it would be reasonable to say that these individuals are not humans, and yet it would also seem unreasonable to deny them the same rights as humans, particularly since they have superior abilities; in this way, classifying individuals for differential treatment, upon which common conceptions of morality depend, proves problematic. Richard Hayes, former assistant political director and national director of volunteer development for the Sierra Club, comes close to this point in stating that "[d]evelopment and use of these technologies would irrevocably change the nature of human life and human society. It would destabilize human biological identity and function."[2] In fact, though, a stronger point can be made: that the mere possibility of the development and use of these technologies is sufficient for exposing incoherences in common morality and its associated conception of a "human biological identity."

The concept of artificial intelligence similarly challenges conventional moral theory. The field of artificial intelligence covers a broad range of topics, unified only in that they all relate to developing algorithms for producing intelligent and useful behavior. Of particular interest, however, is the so-called Turing Test, proposed

by Alan Turing in an article *Computing machinery and intelligence*[8]; he proposes
the test as a suitable alternative to the question, which he argues is meaningless,
of whether machines can think; the purpose of the test is to determine whether a
particular algorithm can reliably imitate a human in a natural language dialogue;
more specifically, an algorithm passes the test if a human interrogator is unable
to reliably distinguish between responses given by an actual human and responses
given by the algorithm. As the field of artificial intelligence has matured over the
past fifty years, and researchers have realized the need to develop specialized
approaches to specific problems, the usefulness of the Turing test as a practical
benchmark has come into question. Nonetheless, the test is of great significance
in suggesting the theoretical possibility of a machine indistinguishable through
verbal communication with a human, and in this way presenting certain philosophical questions. Clearly, it would be inconsistent with common moral theory to
give any sort of rights to a machine, but a machine capable of passing the Turing
test could, by definition, argue as convincingly as any human that it should receive
the same rights as humans for the same reasons that members of previously
oppressed groups have argued that all humans should receive the same rights.

A common rationale given for distinguishing between human and machine
intelligence is that machines lack 'consciousness,' which humans, it is stated,
surely have. This claim is in fact considered in Turing's original article; essentially, because a precise definition of consciousness cannot be given, the claim
boils down to nothing; there is no reason to assume other humans are intelligent
or conscious except by communicating with them, and since a machine passing
the Turing test is indistinguishable from a human in verbal communications,
consciousness of such a machine could just as well be inferred. John R. Searle
argues, however, that such a response is unsatisfactory: he argues that human
consciousness is rooted in the biological nature of the human brain.[6] Although
Searle's claim can be dismissed as arbitrary and unfounded, recent developments
in brain-machine interfaces allow for a much stronger response.

There has been substantial development recently in brain-machine interfaces, which depend on usefully associating the electrical activity in the brain
with higher-level mental processes. Electrical signals in the brain can be moni-
tored using electrodes either placed outside the skull or implanted inside the skull;
through a calibration procedure, the readings of these signals can be correlated
to some degree with certain slightly higher-level mental processes and states;
devices have been developed that allow humans to learn to control a computer
cursor through such an interface; under a more refined system, sophisticated
brain control of computers might be possible. Communication in the opposite
direction is also possible. By sending small electrical impulses to specific regions
of the brain, specific sensations can be induced. The recent success in 'remotely
controlling' rats using a brain-machine interface is of particular note. Electrodes
were implanted into the brains of rats such that electrical signals could be used

to separately give the rat a rewarding sensation, simulate stimulation of the left whisker, and simulate stimulation of the right whisker. A training procedure was designed such that the rats would learn that simulated stimulations of the left or right whisker would be followed by the rewarding sensation if the appropriate movements were made. The rats were thus trained to behave in certain ways based on the electrical signals, and in this way they could be remotely controlled.[7]

More recently, an advance in far more sophisticated brain-machine interaction was made. 25,000 brains cells taken from a rat were cultured in a petri dish. Over a short period of time, the cells formed neural connections. Electrodes at the bottom of the dish allowed the network of neurons to interact electrically with a computer. By connecting the network of neurons to a flight simulator, and providing certain feedback signals, the network of neurons was made to learn in only a short amount of time to interact with the flight simulator such that the plane achieved the desired behavior.[1] Thus, the neurons acted as a living computer. Although the task to which the living neural network was applied in this particular experiment was of limited complexity, it is straightforward to see that a larger number of brain cells could be used to achieve more sophisticated tasks. In particular, if an algorithm for passing the Turing test were developed, such a living neural network could be trained to execute it, which would invalidate Searle's claim; common conceptions are morality can at best give ambiguous answers regarding the sort of treatment a biological computer capable of passing the Turing test should receive, particularly if human brain cells were used. Furthermore, in so far as such devices could be used on fully developed human brains, they raise the possibility of some sort of human-computer hybrid, which similar to human-animal hybrids, is highly problematic for moral theories.

Ultimately, the theoretical possibilities suggested by recent technological and scientific advances challenge the bases on which moral theory classify the group of things or individuals that should receive certain 'rights'. Classifications based on biological similarity to humans prove problematic in considering the possibilities of genetic engineering; such classifications inevitably exclude genetically engineered humans that it would seem should intuitively receive the same 'rights' as ordinary humans. Classifications based on intelligence of behavior alone, however, are problematic for several reasons; they exclude humans with certain mental disabilities, while theoretically including machines capable of passing the Turing test. Even classifications based on some combination of biological and behavioral criteria, such as the criteria given by Searle, prove problematic when the possible applications of brain-machine interface are considered. Given these problems with common existing moral bases, the only coherent basis for a moral theory may be essentially an economic one, specifically a theory that dictates treatment based solely on expected benefit to the society; even this definition leaves open the question of coherently defining the relevant group to consider as the society.

References

[1] Carolyn Gramling. UF scientists: "brain" in a dish acts as autopilot, living computer. *University of Florida News*, October 2004. URL: http://www.napa.ufl.edu/2004news/braindish.htm.

[2] Richard Hayes. The quiet campaign for genetically engineered humans. *Earth Island Journal*, 16(1), Spring 2001. URL: http://www.earthisland.org/eijournal/new_ articles.cfm?articleID=98&journalID=44.

[3] David King. Why should i be concerned about human genetics? Briefing, Human Genetics Alert, March 2002. URL: http://www.hgalert.org/briefings/briefing1. PDF.

[4] Rachel Massey. Engineering humans, part 1. *Rachel's Environment & Health News*, 720, March 2001. URL: http://online.sfsu.edu/~rone/GEessays/engineerhumans.html.

[5] Rachel Massey. Engineering humans, part 2. *Rachel's Environment & Health News*, 721, March 2001. URL: http://online.sfsu.edu/~rone/GEessays/engineerhumans.html.

[6] John R. Searle. Minds, brains, and programs. *The Behavioral and Brain Sciences*, 3, 1980.

[7] Sanjiv K. Talwar, Shaohua Xu, Emerson S. Hawley, Shennan A. Weiss, Karen A. Moxon, and John K. Chapin. Behavioural neuroscience: Rat navigation guided by remote control. *Nature*, 417:37-38, May 2002. URL: http://www.nature.com/cgi-taf/DynaPage.taf?file=/nature/journal/v417/n6884/full/417037a_fs.html.

[8] A. M. Turing. Computing machinery and intelligence. *Mind*, 59(236):433, October 1950.

Questions for Synthesis

1. A central controversy in the field of transhumanism is the ability and/or desirability of computers or robots to replicate or exceed human intelligence. Synthesize various views on the issue through a guided tour of the essays in this chapter. Do not suggest a solution to this issue; your goal in this essay is to give your reader a proper understanding of the problem as seen by various writers in the field.

2. What do the writers in this chapter predict will happen in the twenty-first century? To what extent have their predictions already come to pass? Give specific examples from your own experience with technology and from other essays you've read. You may want to do further research using materials from the Suggested Additional Resources at the end of the introduction to the chapter.

Questions for Contribution

1. Write an essay in which you explore short- and long-term possibilities for the use of GNR technologies. Will they lead to a transhuman future? Or is this a far-fetched idea of some wild enthusiasts and fearful opponents? This paper will require additional research into the technologies involved, as well as your own deductions about the consequences such technologies may produce.

2. The transhumanist movement poses challenges to conventional moral belief systems. Re-read the essays in this chapter, and find other arguments in the Suggested Additional Resources or through your own research.

    Write an essay that argues for a particular moral position regarding transhumanism and GNR. How should we approach the transhuman future from a moral standpoint? Your contribution to the field will not stand alone. Imagine every author in this chapter—and other authors that you draw from in your research—critiquing your position.

    Your job is to consider the relevant positions taken by others and to forge your own argument in connection with them. Make sure that you fairly represent the arguments of others. As you advance your claims, take relevant opposing arguments into account and answer potential critics.

CHAPTER 6 SURVIVING ECONOMIC CRISIS AND THE FUTURE

INTRODUCTION

Contexts of Discussion

In fall 2008, financial institutions in the United States and subsequently the world economy suffered a massive shock from which many claim it had not yet fully recovered by early 2014. As you will see, scholars and pundits disagree about the ultimate causes, the severity, and the ultimate prospects for emerging from the "financial crisis," as it came to be called. Some economists and other writers suggest that we live in the worst economic conditions since the Great Depression of the 1930s, a severe worldwide economic depression that also originated in the United States. According to many economists and pundits, we will feel the effects of this crisis for some time. Others argue that the crisis will not be solved without drastic change.

How did this crisis come about, and what can be done about it? This chapter focuses on the economic crisis and the way forward proposed by various thinkers.

Almost all experts agree that the housing asset bubble, primarily in the United States, was the immediate cause of the financial crisis. The US housing bubble was caused by the rising demand for and value of housing. These increases in demand, which fueled the rising prices, were based at least partly on the easing of credit standards and the growing availability of loans for home purchases (mortgages). In other words, banks loaned money to people who previously might not have qualified, and they offered borrowers low interest rates and other incentives. As you might expect, hundreds of thousands of people bought houses with these loans. Soon, the housing market became infested with these mortgage loans, known as "subprime" loans. Not only were houses over-valued, but also many of the loans were doomed to failure.

Furthermore, in addition to direct lending and mortgage holding, the bubble also included very complicated and often obscure financial instruments and trading schemes, including:

- the packing and selling of bundled mortgages,
- the buying and selling of insurance against bundled mortgages, and
- a kind of betting on the failure of bundled mortgage assets.

These mortgage-backed assets or securities infiltrated financial markets around the world.

As housing values declined, many homeowners found their homes "under water," i.e., they owed more money on their homes than their homes were worth. Many of the borrowers had adjustable rate mortgages (ARMs), which meant that the bank could increase the interest rate on their loans. As the ARM rates increased, borrowers owed more on their loans each month and eventually found that they could no longer afford to pay their mortgages. As a result, droves of buyers defaulted on their loans; by the third quarter of 2009, close to a million buyers had defaulted and faced foreclosure.

Given that mortgage-backed assets had spread so extensively and involved so many financial players worldwide, the defaults affected banks and other financiers around the world. The results on a global scale were disastrous:

- stock values declined sharply;
- credit began to dry up;
- hiring freezes and layoffs resulted;
- spending decreased;
- the international economy was in peril;
- many financial institutions teetered on the brink of failure, while others failed completely.

On September 24, 2008, President George W. Bush announced to US television audiences that without dramatic government intervention in the form of an economic rescue plan directed at banks and other lending institutions, the situation would likely become much worse:

The market is not functioning properly. There has been a widespread loss of confidence, and major sectors of America's financial system are at risk of shutting down. The government's top economic experts warn that, without immediate action by Congress, America could slip into a financial panic and a distressing scenario would unfold. More banks could fail, including some in your community. The stock market would drop even more, which would reduce the value of your retirement account. The value of your home could plummet. Foreclosures would rise dramatically. And if you own a business or a farm, you would find it harder and more expensive to get credit. More businesses would close their doors, and millions of Americans could lose their jobs.

The president, along with leading Republicans and Democrats, including then-presidential candidate Barack Obama, supported a plan to rescue the financial sector and thus, it was hoped, the entire US and international economy, from imminent disaster. A bill was introduced to enact the Trouble Asset Relief Program (TARP), a government bailout of the financial sector in the amount of $700 billion. TARP was signed into law under President Bush and enacted under presidents Bush and Obama. It was followed by further bailouts under President Obama, including the Public-Private Investment Program (PPIP), the FDIC Temporary Liquidity Guarantees (TLG), the Targeted Investment Program (TIP), and the Term Asset-Backed Securities Lending Facility (TALF). These packages, drawn from the US Treasury, amounted to almost $3 trillion. Obama also signed into law a stimulus package, a series of federal governmental spending initiatives aimed at "jump-starting" the economy. Increased federal spending, it was hoped, would inject demand into the economy and spur growth. European countries implemented similar bailout and stimulus measures.

The financial crisis provoked numerous commentaries and prognoses. Some even said that the current economic system—capitalism—had failed. These comments came from unusual sources, including business-oriented publications such as the *Financial Times*, Great Britain's equivalent of the *Wall Street Journal*.

As of this writing, the American economy was slowly recovering from what several analysts refer to as a depression. Indeed, Richard A. Posner, whose essay is included in this chapter, insists that the term "depression" best describes contemporary economic woes, at least as late as 2009. In 2009, unemployment hit a high of 10 per cent; by 2014 it was as low as 5.8 per cent. These unemployment numbers do not include those who have given up hunting for jobs or have settled for reduced hours and wages. When these people are included, the unemployment rate may be as high as 14.5 per cent, according to one government measurement.

Unemployment in the European Union (EU) remains steady at 11 per cent; official rates were as high as 24.1 per cent in Spain in March 2012. The most alarming statistic may be unemployment among the young (ages 15-24), which reached 20 per cent in Europe and 19.1 per cent in the United States by April 2010, and by April 2012 was 22.4 per cent and 16.4 per cent, respectively. Greece and Spain posted staggering youth unemployment rates: more than 50 per cent in April 2012. Civil unrest has been felt in European countries, most notably in Greece, as austerity measures—cuts in jobs, wages, benefits, and social services—have been imposed on the population. In the United States, housing starts, which are one indicator of how healthy the economy is, plunged 33 per cent between 2007 and 2008. Between September 2013 and September 2014, however, housing starts had increased 17.8 per cent.

Meanwhile, the institutions that threatened the economic system in 2008 now thrive. Goldman Sachs, for example, a company that received $10 billion from the US Treasury, earned $3.19 billion in profits between July and September of 2009. This was nearly the most it had made in any three-month period, a record it set in the second quarter of the same year, with earnings of $3.44 billion.

Explanations for the causes of the financial and economic crisis and solutions for the future health of the economy often clash. Many economists and commentators, especially the followers of the reformer John Maynard Keynes, argue that the financial and economic crisis was caused by government's failure to properly monitor and regulate the economy. In Keynesian economics, government plays a key role in the free market economy: it stimulates the economy by creating jobs during recessions, and when people are earning money, they buy goods. This trade keeps the economy afloat. A Keynesian government also must monitor and regulate key financial institutions.

For contemporary neo-Keynesian reformers, the deregulation that began during the Reagan administration in the 1980s was the main culprit in the financial and economic crisis of 2008 and beyond. According to this view, governmental agencies are to blame for removing or relaxing regulations and/or for failing to keep pace with novel, complex, and hard-to-monitor financial instruments, such as credit default swaps (CDS) and derivatives. Neo-Keynesians recommend increased or improved regulation or such measures as a government agency that oversees the entire financial system. For neo-Keynesians such as Paul Krugman of the *New York Times*, the economic crisis of 2008 amounted to a bittersweet vindication of Keynesian economic theory. This chapter includes an essay by Judge Richard A. Posner, a recent convert to neo-Keynesianism from the famous neo-classical Chicago School of economics.

Other reform-oriented authors point to a number of measures that could have been taken to prevent the financial crisis. Some fault monetary policy for the financial meltdown. According to this view, the federal treasury failed to adjust interest rates properly so as to discourage reckless lending and borrowing. Had interest rates been raised at the appropriate time, making loans more expensive and thus harder to get, the housing bubble would not have developed to the size that it did. This view is represented by John B. Taylor in his article "The Financial Crisis and the Policy Responses: An Empirical Analysis of What Went Wrong," listed in the Suggested Additional Resources at the end of this introduction.

Others fault both the market and government players for failure first to avoid and then to respond to signs of trouble. At least three factors created a "perfect storm":

- deregulation
- lack of financial transparency, and
- insufficient disclosure of financial risks.

According to this perspective, regulation, access to information about new financial instruments, and full disclosure of new risks are necessary. This view is taken by Richard Zeckhauser of the Harvard Kennedy School of Business, in his essay "Causes of the Financial Crisis: Many Responsible Parties," listed in Suggested Additional Resources.

On the other hand, neo-classical economists, whose perspective is based on the *laissez-faire* approach to economics, argue that government regulation is not the solution; it's the *problem*. This approach was first elaborated in the late eighteenth century by Adam Smith and David Ricardo. *Laissez-faire* economists like Smith and Ricardo, as well as some politicians and pundits, blame governmental regulation and non-market incentives for tampering with the natural workings of the economy.

In connection with the current crisis, the American Enterprise Institute fellow Peter J. Wallison blames the government for compelling banks and other lenders to make risky loans in order to meet government-mandated mortgage quotas for low-income and minority home buyers. If not for these risky loans, Wallison says, a housing asset bubble might have burst, but it would not have led to the bust that resulted in 2008. Wallison's essay, "Not a Failure of Capitalism—A Failure of Government," is included in this chapter.

So far, we have mentioned two kinds of responses: reformist and *laissez-faire*. But a third, more radical, position also exists. According to socialism, the financial crisis of 2008 may mark a crisis of the capitalist system itself. The crisis, in this view, was not a result of the actions or inactions of the government, or even of the misbehavior of institutions or individuals; it was the inevitable consequence of capitalism, a system based on inherent flaws and contradictions. According to this view, the crisis resulted not from regulation or deregulation but from the inherent and incessant demand for profits.

In the United States, this demand resulted in the steady decline of real wages for workers beginning in the 1970s. To compensate for reduced wages, workers borrowed more and went into debt. This debt put their main asset—their homes—at risk. US corporations and banks, facing increasing competition from Asia, Germany, and elsewhere, loaned with interest what they had once paid in wages. Thus, in the hunt for easy profits, they engaged in competitive financial specula-tion. Such speculation, with its inherent risks, commanded a greater and greater percentage of the economy, largely because it was more profitable than produc-ing tangible goods, and eventually this bubble of speculation collapsed. Socialists say that the only solution to repeated economic shocks and the current economic crisis is to replace the system with an economy in which human need rather than profit is the basis of production and distribution. The socialist perspective is repre-sented in this chapter by Stephen Resnick and Richard Wolff, Marxist economists at the University of Massachusetts Amherst.

Two other perspectives must also be introduced. Feminist economists have long noted how both reformist and classical economics devalue women's labor. They consider how gender roles and inequities contribute to and are reflected in economic systems. In this chapter, an essay, "Why Did the Bankers Behave So Badly?" by Anne Sibert, professor and head of the School of Economics, Mathematics and Statistics at Birkbeck College in London, argues that the gender composi-tion of investment firms, among other factors, helped cause the economic crisis.

Finally, according to the green economic perspective, economic prosperity and sustainability demand the immediate greening of major sectors of the economy. According to Achim Steiner, executive director of the United Nations Environment Programme (UNEP), a green economy is compatible with both state-run and market-driven systems. But importantly, neither of these economic systems will work without major green initiatives to avert or mitigate environmental damage and potential environmental and economic catastrophe (see http://sites. broadviewpress.com/realworldtopics). The green perspective is represented by the Foreword and Introduction to the UNEP policy paper "Towards a Green Economy: Pathways to Sustainable Development and Poverty Eradication," published in 2011.

As this overview suggests, various thinkers are diagnosing the financial and economic crisis and making recommendations for the future. Below, we discuss some of the areas of research and conjecture as well as the serious issues at stake.

Areas of Research and Conjecture

Economics is the study of the production, distribution, and use of valued resources, as well as the stimulants to their creation. Economists are obviously interested in economic declines such as the 2008 financial crisis. This chapter includes essays by the neo-classical economist Peter J. Wallison, the Marxist economists Stephen Resnick and Richard Wolff, and the feminist economist Anne Sibert.

Modern economic systems are intertwined with government; public policy regarding economic matters is often signed into law. Likewise, **law and public policy** scholars study the economy, in particular the impact of law and policy on economic matters, and vice versa. Richard Posner is a circuit court judge whose expertise has been the application of economic models to the study of law. After the 2008 crisis, he turned his attention to the economy at large. An essay from his book *A Failure of Capitalism: The Crisis of '08 and the Descent into Depression*, is included in this chapter.

Political science is the study of governmental systems and practices, political processes and parties, and the relations between citizens and their governments. Political science has a vested interest in economic matters. In fact, the earliest study of economics was called political economy, and one of the most important works in this area was Adam Smith's *The Wealth of Nations* (1776). The title of this work makes clear that economics and political science have a long-standing connection. Today, political scientists continue to take an interest in economic matters because economic wealth is one of the most important measures of social and political well-being. Economic production and distribution involve politics in the broadest sense. The nineteenth-century philosopher and economic theorist Karl Marx argued that the most advantaged economic class always dominates political systems. Under capitalism, this class is the capitalist class, which owns the means of production. We include several works by political scientists in the Suggested Additional Resources at the end of this introduction.

Environmental science is an interdisciplinary field that examines the relationship between living and non-living systems, in particular the impact of human activity on these systems. Given that the economy depends on environmental resources, many environmental scientists study economic issues, in particular the impact of economic activity on the environment, and vice versa. Environmental science is represented in this chapter by the UNEP policy paper "Towards a Green Economy: Pathways to Sustainable Development and Poverty Eradication," published in 2011.

Issues and Stakeholders

Financial failures, bailouts, and bonuses: The financial crisis resulted in the failure of banks and other financial institutions, including that of Lehman Brothers, the largest bankruptcy filing in United States history, with the company holding more than $600 billion in assets. Companies such as Lehman Brothers were "allowed" to fail, while others, deemed "too large to fail," were bailed out by the federal government. Those bailed out included Goldman Sachs, Wells Fargo, American International Group (AIG), Bank of America, and Morgan Stanley, among many others. Today, some of the rescued companies are posting record profits.

Why were some firms rescued while others were left to fail? This question has been variously answered. Some believe that those institutions that were deemed "too large to fail" had to be bailed out to preserve the entire financial system. Others believe that some firms benefited from political favoritism. The firms that received bailouts had ties to pivotal players in the federal government. For example, Henry Merritt Paulson, Jr. was Treasury secretary during the bailouts under President George W. Bush. He had previously served as chairman and chief executive officer of Goldman Sachs. Some argue that this connection explains why Goldman Sachs was saved while Lehman Brothers, for example, was not.

The bailouts also raised some more fundamental issues. Free market economists, politicians, and pundits argue that the federal government should have no role in saving insolvent companies from bankruptcy. They claim that

- companies who had performed poorly deserved to fail;
- failure is the market's way of dealing with inefficiency and incompetence, clearing the way for deserving competitors; and
- government intervention in such matters amounts to "socialism" (although it is not socialism as defined by socialists themselves).

Likewise, a cadre of Republican politicians in Congress voted against TARP and other bailout provisions. Moderates argued that without such provisions, the entire US economy faced collapse. Many on the political left also opposed the bailouts. They argued that

- the bailouts represented the largest transfer of public wealth into private coffers in US history;
- the public, already negatively affected by job losses, home foreclosures, credit freezes, and other tribulations, should not have had to foot the bill for failed financial giants; and
- the bailouts were a form of corporate welfare paid for by the mass of working people.

As unpopular as the bailouts have been among a majority of Americans, the bonuses received by executives at companies who received bailouts are perhaps more unpopular. All told, the top 17 banks that received bailouts later handed out $1.6 billion in bonuses to executives. Two examples will suffice to illustrate this:

- Goldman Sachs received a bailout of $10 billion. Its executives received record bonuses in 2009.
- Citibank received a $45-billion bailout as well as guarantees on another $306 billion in risky loans. Executive pay increased by 50 per cent in 2009. Andrew J. Hall, the head of a small but profitable Citigroup subsidiary, received a $100-million bonus less than a year after the bailout.

News of such executive compensation caused a public furor. Many in the media, however, said that such compensation was necessary to attract the highest-caliber talent, and that legal contracts cannot be broken.

Facing political fallout over bonuses, President Obama scolded companies for serving mega-bonuses to executives while millions of Americans suffered the effects of economic disaster. Nevertheless, no legal measures were taken to deter bailed-out companies from delivering bonuses to their executives. Such bonuses remain controversial. Free-market analysts and some reformers defend them, while critics say they display arrogant disregard for the broader public.

Debt and foreclosures: Financial institutions and consumers were left holding a bag of debts when the crisis hit. As housing prices fell and high interest rates kicked in for those with adjustable rate mortgages (ARMs), a record number of Americans defaulted on their mortgages while banks and other financial companies foreclosed on their homes. We address the question of responsibility in a later subsection. For now we simply ask what might have been done to prevent this disaster for both financial institutions and their financial customers.

Could the relief funds have been directed at the consumer, so that homeowners facing default and foreclosure could pay their mortgages and keep their homes, while banks and other financiers received monthly or lump-sum payments from borrowers? Could a moratorium on foreclosures have been enforced? While the effects of this disaster on homeowners are now mostly irreversible, it still is worth asking whether bailouts were the only way to keep the financial system afloat. Defaults and foreclosures, while slowing, continue. And bailouts of the financial markets have not, as was promised, significantly improved the availability of credit for consumers.

Joblessness and unemployment benefits: As the crisis developed, job layoffs and cutbacks mushroomed. Each month, hundreds of thousands in the United States alone lost their jobs. The rate of unemployment leapt from around 5 per cent in the summer of 2008 to 10.1 per cent in the winter of 2009; by 2014, as mentioned above, it was just under 6 per cent. It remained at 11 per cent in the EU in April 2012. In the United States, unemployment benefits were extended several times, but legislation to extend them again for the nearly 2.5 million people who had been unemployed for the previous six months languished in Congress before finally passing in 2010. Those unemployed for 99 weeks or more remained ineligible.

Internationally, unemployment has remained a significant problem since the 2008 financial crisis. These questions remain:

- How and when will pre-crisis employment rates be restored?
- Or will employment rates remain at present levels for the foreseeable future?
- If so, what does this mean for the majority of workers?
- What does it suggest about expected standards of living for consumers?
- *Economic responsibility*: Who is responsible for the financial meltdown that became apparent in the fall of 2008?
    - The consumers of home mortgages who bought homes that they could not afford under terms that they failed to sufficiently examine?
    - The lenders who initiated bad loans that hamstrung their borrowers with ARMs and other subprime mortgages?
    - The government whose regulators failed to protect consumers and stockholders?
    - All of the above?

Neo-Keynesians generally blame the government for failing to properly oversee and regulate financial transactions. Other reformers blame the federal treasury for failing to adjust interest rates in a timely fashion. Neo-classical economists, meanwhile, suggest that the government, combined with the personal irresponsibility of consumers, should bear the brunt of the blame. And, for their part, socialists blame the capitalist system as a whole, while claiming that the banking and finance industry, the group that has benefitted the most from the crisis, bears responsibility for its consequences.

As You Read

The 2008 financial crisis (and its economic aftermath) is a significant historical event that may continue to have long-lasting effects.

- Consider the explanations of the crisis provided by the essayists we present here.
- Consider a common point or set of common points that each writer addresses. You may want to represent these views using a synthesis grid (pp. 78–79).
- You may want to or be required to do additional reading or viewing. The Suggested Additional Resources at the end of this introduction is a good place to start.
- Add any new views to your synthesis grid.
- After you plot the various positions on a common point or set of common points, consider which explanations are most compelling:
  - How well does the writer explain the crisis in general?
  - How well does a particular writer explain a particular aspect of the crisis?
  - What other explanations or perspectives are possible?

When you have created a synthesis grid and considered these questions, you will be well on your way to writing a contribution paper on the economic crisis and the way forward. This task could provide important insights as you prepare for your own financial future.

Suggested Additional Resources

Anthropology and Geography

Smith, Neil. "Toxic Capitalism." *New Political Economy* 14.3 (2009): 407-12.

Business, Economics, and Finance

Acharya, Viral V., and Matthew Richardson. *Restoring Financial Stability: How to Repair a Failed System*. Hoboken, NJ: John Wiley & Sons, 2009.

Attali, Jacques. *After the Crisis: How Did This Happen?* Portland, OR: Eska Publishing, 2010.

Ayres, Jeffrey M.K., and Laura Macdonald. *North America in Question: Regional Integration in an Era of Economic Turbulence*. Toronto: U of Toronto P, 2012.

Bayoumi, Tamim A., and Trung Bui. *Apocalypse Then: The Evolution of the North Atlantic Economy and the Global Crisis*. Washington, DC: International Monetary Fund, 2011. Web.

Bergeijk, Peter A.G., Arjan Haan, and Rolph Hoeven. *The Financial Crisis and Developing Countries: A Global Multidisciplinary Perspective*. Cheltenham, UK: Edward Elgar, 2011.

Birch, Kean, and Vlad Mykhnenko. *The Rise and Fall of Neoliberalism: The Collapse of an Economic Order?* London: Zed Books, 2010. Web.

Chinn, Menzie D., and Jeffry A. Frieden. *Lost Decades: The Making of America's Debt Crisis and the Long Recovery.* New York: Norton, 2011.

Deaton, Angus. *The Financial Crisis and the Well-Being of Americans.* Cambridge, MA: National Bureau of Economic Research, 2011. Web.

Dufresne, Todd, and Clara Sacchetti. *The Economy as Cultural System: Theory, Capitalism, Crisis.* New York: Continuum, 2013.

Evanoff, Douglas Darrell, Philipp Hartmann, George G. Kaufman, International Banking and Finance Conference, and Federal Reserve Bank of Chicago. *The First Credit Market Turmoil of the 21st Century.* Proc. of The First Credit Market Turmoil of the 21st Century. Singapore; Hackensack, NJ: World Scientific, 2009.

Fu, Xiaolan. *China's Role in Global Economic Recovery.* Abingdon, UK: Routledge, 2012.

Garnaut, Ross, and David Llewellyn-Smith. *The Great Crash of 2008.* Carlton, Australia: Melbourne U, 2009.

Griffith-Jones, Stephany, Jose Antonio Ocampo, and Joseph E. Stiglitz. *Time for a Visible Hand: Lessons from the 2008 World Financial Crisis.* Oxford and New York: Oxford UP, 2010.

Hodgson, Geoffrey M. "The Great Crash of 2008 and the Reform of Economics." *Cambridge Journal of Economics* 33.6 (2009): 1205-21.

Iley, Richard A., and Mervyn Lewis. *Global Finance after the Crisis: The United States, China and the New World Order.* Cheltenham, UK: Edward Elgar Pub, 2013. Web.

International Monetary Fund. *Containing Systemic Risks and Restoring Financial Soundness.* Washington, DC: International Monetary Fund, 2008.

——. *Fiscal Implications of the Global Economic and Financial Crisis.* Washington, DC: International Monetary Fund, 2009. Internet resource.

——. *Global Financial Stability Report, October 2010.* Washington, DC: International Monetary Fund, 2010.

——. *Navigating the Financial Challenges Ahead.* Washington, DC: International Monetary Fund, 2009.

Isaac, Guy. *The Benefits of the New Economy: Resolving the Global Economic Crisis through Mutual Guarantee.* Toronto and New York: Bnei Baruch/Laitman Kabbalah Publishers, 2012. Web.

Ivry, Bob. *The Seven Sins of Wall Street: Big Banks, Their Washington Lackeys, and the Next Financial Crisis.* New York: PublicAffairs, 2014.

Justin, Yifu L., and Doemeland Doerte. *Beyond Keynesianism: Global Infrastructure Investments in Times of Crisis.* Washington, DC: The World Bank, 2012. Web.

Kattel, Rainer. "Financial and Economic Crisis in Eastern Europe." *Journal of Post Keynesian Economics* 33.1 (2010): 41-59.

Keeley, Brian, and Patrick Love. *From Crisis to Recovery: The Causes, Course and Consequences of the Great Recession*. Paris: OECD, 2010.

Lin, Carol Y.-Y. *National Intellectual Capital and the Financial Crisis in Greece, Italy, Portugal, and Spain*. New York: Springer, 2013. Web.

Liodakes, G. *Totalitarian Capitalism and Beyond*. Farnham, UK; Burlington, VT: Ashgate, 2010.

Rothstein, Jesse. *The Labor Market Four Years into the Crisis: Assessing Structural Explanations*. Cambridge, MA: National Bureau of Economic Research, 2012. Web.

Savona, Paolo, John J. Kirton, and Chiara Oldani. *Global Financial Crisis: Global Impact and Solutions*. Burlington, VT: Ashgate, 2011. Web.

Schiller, Dan. *Digital Depression: Information Technology and Economic Crisis*. Champaign: U of Illinois P, 2014.

Schweizer, Peter. *Architects of Ruin: How Big Government Liberals Wrecked the Global Economy—and How They Will Do It Again if No One Stops Them*. New York: HarperCollins, 2009.

Solow, Robert M. *Rethinking the Financial Crisis*. New York: Russell Sage, 2012.

Soros, George. *The Crash of 2008 and What It Means: The New Paradigm for Financial Markets*. Oxford and New York: PublicAffairs, 2009.

Stelzer, Irwin. *The New Capitalism*. Hudson Institute. Oct. 2008. Web.

Stuckler, David, and Sanjay Basu. *The Body Economic: Why Austerity Kills: Recessions, Budget Battles, and the Politics of Life and Death*. New York: Basic Books, 2013. Web.

Sun, William, Jim Stewart, and David Pollard. *Reframing Corporate Social Responsibility: Lessons from the Global Financial Crisis*. Bingley, UK: Emerald, 2010. Web.

West, G.P., and Robert Whaples. *Economic Crisis in Retrospect: Explanations by Great Economists*. Cheltenham, UK: Edward Elgar, 2013. Web.

Wolff, Richard D. *Capitalism Hits the Fan: The Global Economic Meltdown and What to Do about It*. Northampton, MA: Olive Branch, 2010.

Zeckhauser, Richard. "Causes of the Financial Crisis: Many Responsible Parties." Harvard Kennedy School Faculty Research Working Paper Series RWP10-016, April 2010.

Economic History

Allen, Larry. *The Global Economic Crisis: A Chronology*. London: Reaktion Books, 2013. Web.

Education

Organisation for Economic Co-operation and Development. "What Is the Impact of the Economic Crisis on Public Education Spending?" OECD, 2013. Web.

Ethics (Philosophy)

Dobos, Ned, Christian Barry, and Thomas Pogge. *Global Financial Crisis: The Ethical Issues*. Basingstoke, UK: Palgrave Macmillan, 2011.

Law and Economics

Posner, Richard A. *The Crisis of Capitalist Democracy*. Cambridge, MA: Harvard UP, 2010.

Political Science

Hart, Paul T., and Karen Tindall. *Framing the Global Economic Downturn: Crisis Rhetoric and the Politics of Recessions*. Acton, Australia: ANU E, 2009.

Helleiner, Eric, Stefano Pagliari, and Hubert Zimmermann. *Global Finance in Crisis: The Politics of International Regulatory Change*. London and New York: Routledge, 2010.

Streeck, Wolfgang. "Has Capitalism Seen Its Day?" Blog post. *Public Seminar*. 9 May 2014. Web.

Sociology

Gallie, Duncan. *Economic Crisis, Quality of Work, and Social Integration: The European Experience*. Oxford: Oxford UP, 2013.

Sociology of Economics

Knorr-Cetina, Karin D. *The Sociology of Financial Markets*. Proc. of The Sociology of Financial Markets. Oxford: Oxford UP, 2006.

MacKenzie, Donald A. *An Engine, Not a Camera: How Financial Models Shape Markets*. Cambridge, MA: MIT Press, 2006.

a. Anne Sibert, "Why Did the Bankers Behave So Badly?"

Anne Sibert is a professor of economics at Birkbeck College, University of London. Her research interests include central bank design, public finance, the economic and political aspects of economic and monetary union in Europe, and the political economy of structural reform.

She is a member of the Monetary Policy Committee of the Central Bank of Iceland and a fellow of several economic institutes, including the Centre for Economic Policy Research, the CESifo Research Network, the Kiel Institute for World Economy, and the European Economic Association. Additionally, Sibert is a member of the Panel of Economic and Monetary Experts for the Committee for Economic and Monetary Affairs of the European Parliament. She is a founding contributor to VOX, an online policy portal established by the Centre for Economic Policy Research for the publication of "research-based policy analysis and commentary from leading economists."

Sibert is the author of numerous refereed journal articles, invited papers, and book reviews, as well as numerous policy papers and speeches. She earned a PhD in economics from Carnegie Mellon University in 1982.

In this article, published by VOX, Sibert argues that bankers who participated in the risk-taking culture of the male-dominated banking industry are largely to blame for the 2008 financial crisis.

As You Read: Consider your own experience: Are men less risk-averse (more likely to take risks) than women? Sibert provides some evidence to support this claim, but doesn't provide any explanations. What might be a plausible explanation for such gender differences, if they do exist?

Why Did the Bankers Behave So Badly?

Greedy bankers are getting most of the blame for the current financial crisis. This column explains that bankers did behave badly for mainly three reasons. They committed cognitive errors involving biases towards their own prior beliefs; too many male bankers high on testosterone took too much risk, and a flawed compensation structure rewarded perceived short-term competency rather than long-run results.

Many people share the blame for the current financial crisis; politicians, supervisors, regulators and even imprudent households and businesses. One group, however, has been judged to be especially guilty; the employees in the financial services sector. In response to their perceived greed and bad judgment, the US House of

Representatives passed a bill that would effectively confiscate the 2008 bonuses of employees of financial firms receiving significant bailout assistance. In the UK, vandals smashed the windows and trashed the Mercedes of the former head of the Royal Bank of Scotland, while protestors tried to take over a London branch of the bank. In Iceland, financiers have wisely fled the country.

The populist outrage may be excessive, but it is hard to deny that certain aspects of these employees' conduct were undesirable. Bankers imprudently counted on a continuation of the US housing boom long after most economists predicted its demise; they were overly sanguine about sustainable leverage ratios; managers of insurance companies and pension funds failed to exercise sufficient caution when they purchased collateralised debt obligations and asset-backed securities that they did not understand or know the value of. Since few would characterise the bankers and other employees of financial firms as an unintelligent group, it is interesting to ask why they behaved in such an egregious fashion; I advance three theories.

Humans Are Prone to Cognitive Errors

The first explanation is that humans are prone to cognitive errors involving biases towards their own prior beliefs. A vast empirical psychology literature documents that people fail to put sufficient weight on evidence that contradicts their initial hypotheses, that they are overconfident in their own ideas and have a tendency to avoid searching for evidence that would disprove their own theories. Psychologists attribute these cognitive errors, collectively known as *confirmation bias*, to several factors. These include emotional reasons, such as embarrassment, stubbornness and hope, and cultural reasons, such as superstition and tradition. There may also be physiological explanations; the evolutionary development of the human brain may have facilitated the ability to use heuristics which provide good judgements rapidly, but which can also lead to systematic biases. In addition, recent research supports the theory that the human brain arrives at outcomes—such as confirming one's own beliefs—that promote positive and minimise negative emotional responses.

Sexism and the City

UK Labour cabinet member Hazel Blears suggests a second reason, commenting that, "Maybe if we had some more women in the boardrooms, we [might] not have seen as much risk-taking behaviour" (Sullivan and Jordan 2009). Indeed, the financial services industry—one in which lap dancing is apparently considered appropriate corporate entertainment (UK Equality and Human Rights Commission)—is overwhelmingly male dominated. Women hold only 17% of the corporate directorships and 2.5% of the CEO positions in the finance and insurance industries in the US (Sullivan and Jordan 2009). In Iceland—home to a particularly spectacular collapse—it is said that there was just one senior woman banker, and that she quit in 2006 (Lewis 2009). If men are especially prone to being insufficiently risk averse and overly confident, then this male dominance may have contributed to the financial crisis.

There is a substantial economics literature on the effect of gender on attitudes toward risk and most of it appears to support the idea that men are less risk averse than women in their financial decision making.[1] There is also a sizable literature documenting that men tend to be more overconfident than women. Barber and Odean (2001) find that men are substantially more overconfident than women in financial markets. In general, overconfidence is not found to be related to ability (see Lundeberg et al [1994]) and that success is more likely to increase overconfidence in men than in women (see, for example, Beyer [1990]). Thus, if confidence helps produce successful outcomes, there is more likely to be a strong feedback loop in confidence in men than in women.

In a fascinating and innovative study, Coates and Herbert (2008) advance the notion that steroid feedback loops may help explain why male bankers behave irrationally when caught up in bubbles. These authors took samples of testosterone levels of 17 male traders on a typical London trading floor (which had 260 traders, only four of whom were female). They found that testosterone was significantly higher on days when traders made more than their daily one-month average profit and that higher levels of testosterone also led to greater profitability—presumably because of greater confidence and risk taking. The authors hypothesise that if raised testosterone were to persist for several weeks the elevated appetite for risk taking might have important behavioural consequences and that there might be cognitive implications as well; testosterone, they say, has receptors throughout the areas of the brain that neuro-economic research has identified as contributing to irrational financial decisions.

If—as the research may suggest—men are less risk averse than women, then a work group composed primarily of men (or primarily of women) may be a particularly bad idea. A vast psychology literature documents the phenomenon that group deliberation tends to result in an average opinion that is more extreme than the average original position of group members. If a group is composed of overly cautious individuals, it will be even more cautious than its average member; if it is composed of individuals who are overly tolerant of risk, it will be even less risk averse than its average member (Buchanan and Huczynski 1997).

Bonuses Distort Behaviour

In a recent paper, Hamid Sabourian and I advance a third reason for the behaviour of bankers; a flawed compensation structure that rewards perceived short-term competency, rather than good long-run results causes bankers to distort their

---

1   See, for example, Jianakoplas and Bernasek (1998), Bernasek and Shwiff (2001), Holt and Laury (2002) and Eckel and Grossman (2002). Schubert et al (1999) is a rare exception. The differences between men and women may, of course, be due to nurturing rather than nature.

behaviour in an attempt to increase their perceived ability (Sabourian and Sibert 2009). We suppose that a banker's choices are unobservable. Bankers differ in their ability to make the correct decision and this ability is known only to themselves. In the long run, it can be determined whether the action chosen is the best one or not and the banker would rather make the correct decision than the wrong one. However, in the short run, the banker's bonus depends upon how competent he is perceived to be.

In the first variant of our model, we suppose that a banker chooses an action and is then confronted with publicly observable conflicting information.

He then chooses whether or not to change his course of action. If he is especially competent, then he knows that his original choice is probably still the best and does not change it. If he is less competent, the conflicting information tells him that his choice is probably not the best. We show that, for a range of banker competencies, even if the banker realises that his original choice is not likely to be the best, he does not change it. Instead, in the interest of receiving a higher bonus, he mimics an especially competent banker and continues with his original decision.

In the second variant of the model, the banker chooses an action. There is no publicly observed information in this case. Instead, the banker is asked how likely he thinks it is that his decision is the best. We think of this as a proxy for how strongly the banker sells his views to his employer or customers. In the long run, if the banker's decision is wrong, he bears a cost that is increasing in his stated confidence. Even though it can be costly to claim to be correct with high probability and there is no intrinsic benefit from being overly optimistic, if bankers who are perceived to be especially competent receive high enough bonuses, then all bankers will imitate the most competent and oversell their decision.

In the third variant of the model, the banker chooses an action and is then given the opportunity to acquire additional information, at a cost, which, if his initial choice is incorrect, might confirm that it is incorrect. The banker could then abandon his original choice. Highly competent bankers are unlikely to devote resources to questioning their decision as they are unlikely to be wrong. Thus, less competent bankers attempt to increase their bonuses by masquerading as more competent ones; they do not search out additional information either.

References

Barber, Brad M., and Terrance Odean. "Boys Will Be Boys: Gender, Overconfidence and Common Stock Investment," *Quarterly Journal of Economics* 66, 2001, 261-292.

Bernasek, Alexandra, and Stephanie Shwiff. "Gender, Risk and Retirement," *Journal of Economic Issues* 35, 2001, 345-356.

Beyer, Sylvia. "Gender Differences in the Accuracy of Self-Evaluations of Performance," *Journal of Personality and Social Psychology* 59, 1990, 960-970.

Buchanan, David, and Andrzej Huczynski. *Organizational Behaviour*. London, Prentice-Hall, 1997.

Coates, J.M., and J. Herbert. "Endogenous Steroids and Financial Risk Taking on a London Trading Floor," *Proceedings of the National Academy of Sciences* 105, 2008, 6167-6172.

Eckel, Catherine C., and Philip J. Grossman. "Sex Differences and Statistical Stereotyping in Attitudes toward Financial Risk," *Evolution and Human Behaviour* 23, 2002, 281-295.

Holt, Charles A., and Susan K. Laury. "Risk Aversion and Incentive Effects," *American Economic Review* 92, 2002, 1644-1655.

Jianakoplas, Nancy A., and Alexandra Bernasek. "Are Women more Risk Averse?" *Economic Inquiry* 36, 1998, 620-630.

Lewis, Michael. "Wall Street on Tundra," *Vanity Fair* Apr. 2009.

Lundeberg, Mary A., Paul W. Fox, and Judith Punccohar. "Highly Confident but Wrong: Gender Differences and Similarities in Confidence Judgements," *Journal of Educational Psychology* 86, 1994, 114-121.

Sabourian, Hamid, and Anne Sibert. "Banker Compensation and Confirmation Bias," CEPR Working Paper no. 7263, Apr. 2008.

Schubert, Renate, Martin Brown, Matthias Gyster, and Hans Wolfgang Brachinger. "Financial Decision Making: Are Women Really more Risk Averse?" *American Economic Review* 89, 1999, 381-385.

Sullivan, Kevin, and Mary Jordan. "In Banking Crisis, Guys Get the Blame: More Women Needed in Top Jobs, Critics Say," *Washington Post Foreign Service* 11 Feb. 2009.

Source: *Vox* 18 May 2009. Web. http://www.voxeu.org/article/why-did-bankers-behave-so-badly.

WHAT IT SAYS

1. Sibert asserts in paragraph two that bankers "were overly sanguine about sustainable leverage ratios" in the lead-up to the financial meltdown. What does she mean by this? What are sustainable leverage ratios?

2. What does Sibert mean when she suggests that human beings are prone to cognitive error? In what direction does cognitive error usually tend, according to Sibert and her sources? What is "confirmation bias"?

3. What are "steroid feedback loops" and how do they affect behavior, according to Sibert and her sources?

4. What is a "feedback loop in confidence"?

5. Sibert discusses studies on gender and confidence and then a study on testosterone on the trading floor. What is the implied relationship between these two types of studies?

6. How do bonuses negatively affect banking performance, according to Sibert?

HOW IT SAYS IT

1. Describe the tone and diction of Sibert's essay. How are these related to her argument? For example, how does her header "Sexism and the City" work to advance her claims? What is the function of using this reference to a popular sitcom?

2. What type of article is this? Is it a formal academic paper, a blog post, or something in between? How can you tell?

3. Note Sibert's use of sources in this short article. How does her reference to studies help to support her claims?

4. What is Sibert's intended readership? How can you tell?

WRITE ABOUT IT

1. Write an essay in which you assert a different viewpoint than Sibert's. Provide the reasons you disagree with her premises regarding the causes of the risky behavior of bankers. Give other explanations for such risky speculation. Support your claims with evidence and reasoning.

2. Write an essay in which you consider other reasons behind the financial meltdown, perhaps in which bankers themselves play a less significant role.

3. Write an essay in which you apply Sibert's reasoning to careers other than banking as a way of imagining whether the three reasons for bankers' bad behavior might apply to these fields. For example, Sibert cites a study that concludes, "higher levels of testosterone" may drive men to "greater confidence and risk-taking." Apply that theory outside of the financial sector.

   - Would "higher levels of testosterone" benefit a surgeon who is performing a risky operation, for example?
   - Would a male leader always be a better choice than a female leader at the negotiation table?
   - Do cognitive errors and bonuses apply to these fields?
   - How might bonuses affect outcomes, either negatively or for the better?

   Or write an essay in which you argue against Sibert's reasoning entirely, drawing on other research and applying it to the field(s) you choose to discuss.

b. Richard A. Posner, "The Depression and Its Proximate Causes"

Richard A. Posner is a sitting judge on the United States Court of Appeals for the Seventh Circuit, an appointee of President Ronald Reagan. He served as a law clerk to Justice William Brennan on the United States Supreme Court following law school, and worked for Commissioner Phillip Elman at the Federal Trade Commission from 1963 to 1965. He became an associate professor at Stanford Law School in 1968 and began teaching at the University of Chicago School of Law in 1969, where he remained until 1981 when he was appointed to the US Court of Appeals for the Seventh Circuit. He served as Chief Judge of that court from 1993 to 2000.

Posner is the author of more than 300 articles and 30 books. His books include *Economic Analysis of Law* (1972), *The Economics of Justice* (1981), *Overcoming Law* (1995), *Natural Monopoly and Its Regulation* (1999), *Law, Pragmatism and Democracy* (2003), and *How Judges Think* (2008). He earned undergraduate and law degrees from Yale, and honorary degrees from Harvard, Syracuse, and Georgetown.

In this essay, excerpted from his book *A Failure of Capitalism: The Crisis of '08 and the Descent into Depression* (2009), Posner explains economic depressions and lays out his case that the crisis of 2008 should be so labeled. He then explains the reasons for the depression, and the measures that could have been taken to avoid it.

As You Read: What images come to mind when you think about an economic depression? Compare these images with the descriptions of depression given in Posner's essay.

The Depression and Its Proximate Causes

A sequence of dramatic events has culminated in the present economic emergency; low interest rates, a housing bubble, the collapse of the bubble, the collapse of the banking system, frenzied efforts at resuscitation, a drop in output and employment, signs of deflation, an ambitious program of recovery. I need to trace the sequence and explain how each stage developed out of the preceding one. This chapter opens with a brief sketch of the basic economics of depression and of fighting depression and then turns to the particulars of this depression.

Suppose some shock to the economy—say a sudden fall in the value of people's houses and securities—reduces the value of personal savings and induces people to spend less so they can rebuild their savings. The demand for goods and services will therefore fall. Before the shock, both demand and supply were both X; now the demand is X-Y. How will suppliers respond? If—a critical assumption—all prices, including the price of labor (wages), are completely flexible, suppliers, including suppliers of labor—workers—will reduce their prices in an effort to retain as many buyers as possible. With consumers saving more because they are buying less, and at lower prices, interest rates—earnings on savings—will fall because there will be a savings glut. The lower interest rates will induce borrowing and with more borrowing and lower prices, spending will soon find its way back to where it was before the shock. One reason this will happen is that not all consumers are work-ers, and those who are not, and those whose incomes are therefore unimpaired, will buy more goods and services as prices fall.

The flaw in this classical economic theory of the self-correcting business cycle is that not all prices are flexible; wages especially are not. This is not primarily because of union-negotiated or other employment contracts. Few private-sector employers in the United States are unionized, and a few non-unionized workers have a wage guaranteed by contract. But even when wages are flexible, employ-ers generally prefer, when demand for their products drops, laying off workers to reducing wages. Think of all the financial executives who have been laid off even while bonuses—often amounting to half the executive's pay—were being cut, sometimes to zero.

There are several reasons that employers prefer layoffs to cutting wages. (1) Layoffs reduce over-head expenses. (2) By picking the least productive workers to lay off, an employer can increase the productivity of its workforce. (3) Workers may respond to a reduction in their wages by working less hard, or, conversely, may work harder if they think that by doing so they may reduce the likelihood that *they* will be laid off. (4) When the wages of all workers in a plant or office are cut, all are unhappy, with layoff, the unhappy workers are off the premises.

If wages fall far enough, many workers will lay themselves off, finding better uses of their time (such as getting more schooling) than working for a pittance—and they may be workers whom the employer would have preferred to retain.

The reason for employers' preference for layoffs are attenuated when instead of a worker's wage being cut, he is reduced from full-time to part-time status. He is still part of the team; and he may be able to assuage his distress at his lower wage by adding another part-time job and thus restoring his full income. So reduc-tion from full-time to part-time employment are more common than wage cuts. Similarly, a reduction in bonus is less demoralizing than a cut in salary. There is less of an expectation of receiving a bonus than of continuing to receive one's base salary, and so there is less disappointment when the bonus is cut.

When, in order to reduce output from X to X-Y in my example and thus restore equilibrium, producers and other sellers of goods and services, such as retailers, begin laying off workers, demand is likely to sink even further; that is, Y will be a larger number. Unemployment reduces the incomes of the formerly employed and creates uncertainty about economic prospects—the uncertainty of the unemployed about whether and when they will find comparable employment, the uncertainty of the still-employed about whether they will retain their jobs. Workers who are laid off spend less money because they have less to spend, and those not laid off fear they may be next and so begin to save more of their income. The less savings, especially safe savings, people have, the more they will reduce their personal consumption expenditures in order to increase their savings, and therefore the more output will fall. Interest rates will fall too, but many people will be afraid to borrow (which would increase economic activity by giving them more money to spend). So spending will not increase significantly even though low interest rates reduce the cost of consumption; people will want to have precautionary savings because of the risk their incomes will continue to decline.

Still, the downward spiral is unlikely to become uncontrollable even without radical government intervention unless the shocks that started the economy on the path to depression either were extremely severe or, because of widespread over-indebtedness, created default cascades that reduced banks' capital to a point at which they could no longer lend money in quantity. For then consumers who wanted to borrow to maintain their level of consumption could not do so, and their inability would accelerate the fall in demand for goods and services. Commercial activity would fall dramatically; it depends vitally on credit, in part just because costs of production and distribution are almost always incurred before revenues are received.

With demand continuing to fall, sellers lay off more workers, which exerts still more downward pressure on demand. They also reduce prices in an effort to avoid losing all their customers and be stuck with unsalable inventory. As prices fall, consumers may start hoarding their money in the expectation that prices will keep falling. And they will not borrow at all. For with prices expected to keep falling, they would be paying back their loans in dollars with greater purchasing power because the same number of dollars will buy more goods and services. That is deflation—money is worth more—as distinct from inflation in which money is worth less because more money is chasing the same quantity of goods and services.

With demand continuing to fall, bankruptcies soar, layoffs increase, incomes fall, prices fall further, and so there are more bankruptcies, etc.—the downward spiral continues. Adverse feedback loops—"vicious cycles" in an older vocabulary—are a formula for catastrophe; other examples are pandemics and global warming.

Irving Fisher, writing in the depths of the Great Depression, said, that a depression was "something like the 'capsizing' of a ship, which under ordinary conditions, is always near stable equilibrium but which, after being tipped beyond a certain angle, has no longer the tendency to return to equilibrium, but, instead, a tendency to depart further from it."

So it is not really the initial shock to a robust system that is the main culprit in a depression; it is vulnerability of the process by which the system adjusts to a shock. This makes the adequacy of the institutional response to that vulnerability critical.

One institutional response to a deflationary spiral is for the Federal Reserve to increase the supply of money, so that a given number of dollars doesn't buy more goods than it used to. The Federal Reserve creates money in various ways. The most common one, but not the most intuitive, is by altering the federal funds rate; I discuss this later. Another way is by buying federal securities, such as T bills (T for Treasury), from banks. The cash the banks receive from the sale is available to them to lend, and loan proceeds, deposited in the borrower's bank account, increase the number of dollars available to be spent. Fearing deflation, the Federal Reserve has been expanding the money supply in the current crisis, but with limited success. Because banks are on the edge, or even over the edge, of being insolvent, they are fearful of making risky loans, as most loans in a depression are. So they have put more and more of their capital into short-term securities issued by the federal government—securities that, being backed by the full faith and credit of the United States, are safe.

The effect of competition to buy these securities has been to bid down the interest rate on them virtually to zero. Short-term federal securities that pay no interest are the equivalent of cash. When banks want to hold cash or its equivalent rather than lend it, the action of the Federal Reserve in buying cash-equivalent securities does nothing to increase the money supply. So the Fed is now buying other debt, and from other financial firms as well as from banks—debt that has a positive interest rate, the hope being that if the Federal Reserve buys the debt for cash the seller will lend out the cash in order to replace the interest income that it had been receiving on the debt. But this program has not yet had a great deal of success either. If people and firms are extremely nervous about what the future holds for them, low interest rates will not induce them to borrow.

If monetary policy does not succeed in equating demand to supply by closing the gap between demand of X-Y and supply of X, maybe government spending can do the trick. The government can buy Y worth of goods and services, thus replacing private with public demand, or it can reduce taxes by Y (or give people after-tax income in some other form, such as increased unemployment benefits), so that people have more money to spend, or it can do some of both. Whichever course it follows, it will be engaged in deficit spending. The buying part of the program, like the tax cuts, can be financed only by borrowing (or by the Federal Reserve's creating money to pay for the program) and not by taxing, for if financed by taxation it would not increase aggregate demand; it would inject money into the economy with one hand and remove it with the other. (It was always obvious that the government could reduce unemployment by hiring people, what makes it a device for fighting a depression is doing so without financing the program by means of taxes.) At this writing [February 2009], Congress is on the verge of enacting a massive deficit-spending program involving public spending on infrastructure improvement and other public-works-type projects, plus tax cuts and other subsidies. [The American Recovery and Reinvestment Act of 2009 in the amount of $787 billion was signed by President Obama on February 17, 2009.]

Such is the anatomy of depression, and of recovery from depression. But there are different types of depression or recession and we must distinguish among them. In the least interesting and usually the least serious, some unanticipated shock, external to the ordinary workings of the market, disrupts the market equilibrium. The oil-price surges of the early and then the late 1970s, and the terrorist attacks of September 11, 2001 (which deepened a recession that had begun earlier that year), are illustrative. The second type, illustrated by the recession of the early 1980s, in which unemployment exceeded 10 percent for part of 1982, is the induced recession. The Federal Reserve broke what was becoming a chronic high rate of inflation by a steep increase in interest rates. In neither type of recession is anyone at fault, and the second was beneficial to the long-term health of the economy.

The third and most dangerous type of recession/depression is caused by the bursting of an investment bubble. It is depression from within, as it were, and is illustrated by both the depressions of the 1930s and the current one, though by other depressions and recessions as well, including the global recession of the early 1990s. A bubble is a steep rise in the value of some class of assets that cannot be explained by a change in any of the economic fundamentals that determine value, such as increased demand due to growth in population or to improvements in product quality. But often a bubble is generated by a *belief* that turns out to be mistaken that fundamentals *are* changing—that a market, or maybe the entire economy, is entering a new era of growth, for example because of technological advances. Indeed that is probably the main cause of bubbles.

A Stock market developed in the 1920s, powered by a plausible optimism (the years 1924 to 1929 were ones of unprecedented economic growth) and enabled by the willingness of banks to lend on very generous terms to people who wanted to play the stock market. You had to put up only 10 percent of the purchase price of the stock; the bank would lend the rest. That was risky lending, since stock price could and did decline by more than 10 percent, and explains why the bursting of the stock market bubble in 1929 precipitated widespread bank insolvencies. New profit opportunities and low interest rates had led to overindebtedness, an investment bubble, a freezing of credit when the bubble burst because the sudden and steep fall in asset prices caused a cascade of defaults, a rapid decline in consumption because people could not borrow, and finally deflation. Overindebtedness leading to deflation was the core of Irving Fisher's theory of the Great Depression, and there is concern that history may be repeating itself.

The *severity* of the 1930s depression may have been due to the Federal Reserve's failure to expand the supply of money in order to prevent deflation, a failure connected to our adherence to the gold standard: a country that allows its currency to be exchanged for a fixed amount of gold on demand cannot increase its money supply without increasing its gold reserves, which is difficult to do. The United States went off the gold standard in 1933, and there was an immediate economic upturn. Yet the depression persisted until the United States began rearming in earnest shortly before it entered World War II; its persistence may have been due to the Roosevelt Administration's premature abandonment of deficit spending, employed at the outset of the Administration along with the abandonment of the gold standard with apparent success in arresting the economic downturn.

There was a smaller bubble, in stocks of dot-com, telecommunications, and other high-tech companies, in the late 1990s. But its bursting had only a modest adverse effect on the economy as a whole, as did the sharp drop in the stock market triggered by the terrorist attacks of September 11, 2001.

The current economic emergency is similarly the outgrowth of the bursting of an investment bubble. The bubble started in housing but eventually engulfed the financial industry. Low interest rates, aggressive and imaginative marketing of home mortgages, auto loans, and credit cards, diminishing regulation of the banking industry, and perhaps the rise of a speculative culture—an increased appetite for risk, illustrated by a decline in the traditional equity premium (the margin by which the average return on an investment in stocks exceeds that of an investment in bonds, which are less risky than stocks)—spurred speculative lending, especially on residential real estate, which is bought mainly with debt. As in 1929, the eventual bursting of the bubble endangered the solvency of other banks and other financial institutions. Residential-mortgage debt is huge ($11 trillion by the end of 2006), and many defaults were expected as a result of the bubble's collapse. The financial system had too much risk in its capital structure to take these defaults in stride. The resulting credit crisis—a drastic reduction in borrowing and lending, indeed a virtual cessation of credit transactions, for long enough to disrupt the credit economy—precipitated a general economic downturn. The downturn depressed stock prices, which exacerbated the downturn by making people feel poorer; for when they feel poorer, even before they become poorer, they spend less, as a precaution.

As the downturn deepened, bank solvency received a second shock: the default rate on bank loans secured by assets other than residential real estate rose because many borrowers were in financial straits. It is expected to rise further. The financial industry is beginning to resemble an onion: one peels successive layers of debt and wonders whether there is any solid core at all. [There have been no failures or bailouts of large financial services firms since February 2009; however, failures of small banks continue.]

How severe is the economic downturn, and how much worse is it likely to get? If one looks only at statistics for 2008 (as we are still in the first quarter of 2009), the situation does not look too terrible: an unemployment rate of 7.2 percent and a gross domestic product (the market value of the nation's total output of goods and services) that in the last three months of 2008 was 3.8 below the level in the corresponding period the previous year. [Comparable figures for July of 2009 are an unemployment rate of 9.4 percent and second quarter gross domestic product decrease of 1.0 percent from the second quarter of 2008.] But these snapshots of the economy are incomplete; there is also an $8 trillion decline in the value of traded stocks since 2007 to be reckoned with, together with an estimated $2 trillion of losses by American banks. The snapshots are also misleading. At the beginning of 2008, the unemployment rate was below 5 percent, and few observers think it has plateaued at 7.2 percent. And when discouraged workers and workers involuntarily working part-time rather than full-time are added to the "officially" unemployed, we discover the percentage of underutilized workers increased from 8.7 percent in December 2007 to 13.5 percent a year later, implying a significant drop in income available to buy goods and services. [As of July 2009 underutilized workers were 16.3 percent.] The 3.8 percent decline in gross domestic product is also misleading because the figure is likely to grow and because it would have been 5.1 percent had production for inventory been excluded. The buildup of inventory was the unintended result of an unanticipated fall in demand. Carrying charges for inventories are considerable, and the built-up likely inventories are likely to be liquidated at very steep discounts, which by pulling down the price level will increase the danger of a deflation. Until they are liquidated, moreover, production will be depressed, since sales from inventory are substitutes for sales of newly produced goods. [From January 2009 to July 2009 prices rose by 2.0 percent while inventories decreased by $103.7 billion.]

The distinguished macroeconomist Robert Lucas estimates that in 2008 the gross domestic product was 4.1 percent below where it would have been in an average year (that is 4.1 percent below the long-term trend line of gross domestic product, which is upward), and that if one may judge from consensus forecasts of economic activity it will be 8.3 percent below the trend for 2009. That is nothing to write home about if your benchmark is 1933 (34 percent [below the potential output]), but it is greater than in any year since the end of the Great Depression. [As of March 2009, the Congressional Budget Office estimates the GDP gap— difference between potential output and actual output—will be about 7.4 percent below potential output for 2009 and 6.3 percent below potential output for 2010.] Another ominous sign is that almost every economic estimate of the economic situation has later been revised downward, which feeds pessimism both directly and by revealing that financial experts have an imperfect grasp of the situation; if they don't know what's happening, they're unlikely to be able to provide much guidance to arresting the downward spiral of the economy.

Personal consumption expenditures and consumer prices are falling significantly, which is uncharacteristic of mere recessions and is worrisome because deflation can greatly darken the economic picture. The consumer price index (seasonally adjusted) stopped rising in September 2008 and then fell 1.0 percent in October, 1.7 percent in November , and 0.7 percent in December. [Comparable data for January through July 2009 are: January 0.3, February 0.4, March -0.1, April 0.0, May 0.1, June 0.7, July 0.0.] Another symptom of deflation is that many employers are cutting wages as well as laying off workers. [From the fourth quarter 2007 to second quarter 2009, the index of seasonally adjusted wages and salaries of all civilian workers did not decrease in any quarter-to-quarter comparison workers index; so while some employers may have reduced wages, overall wages and salaries did not decrease.] This is an unusual response to economic adversity but makes sense in a deflation, when the purchasing power of money increases because prices are falling. For then a reduction in nominal wages need not mean a reduction in purchasing power (real wages). Indeed, unless nominal wages are cut in a deflation workers will be receiving higher wages in real terms—and for an employer to pay his workers more in an economic downturn would be anomalous.

What is important is not the price declines for the last three months of 2008 as such but whether they will engender expectations of further declines. If so, the result is likely to be hoarding of cash on a large scale, which would dry up economic activity. If one averages the declines in the consumer price index for the last three months of 2008 and projects them out for a year, the result is a more than 12 percent decline in consumer prices. That would be catastrophic. I am not predicting such a decline; I make no forecasts. [Using the above data, for January through July 2009, consumer prices for all of 2009 will increase by 1.1 percent.] But only deflation anxiety can explain the extraordinary efforts that the Federal Reserve has been making to increase the supply of money. The fact that the entire world has been caught up in our financial crisis is a further danger sign, because it foreshadows an economically disruptive reduction in foreign trade. [Based on the more recent trends of consumer prices and wage rates, by Posner's definition a depression has not materialized, although that was not evident at the time (early 2009) he was writing.]

Still another portent is that it is a financial crisis rather than some other shock that is convulsing the economy. A similar financial crisis ushered in the deflationary stage of the Great Depression. The reason a financial crisis is such a downer is that the usual means by which the Federal Reserve pulls the economy out of a recession is by expanding the supply of money so that interest rates fall, which stimulates borrowing and hence, because most borrowing is for spending, whether for consumption or production, economic output [increases]. But the Federal Reserve does its money creation through the banks, and if the banks have solvency problems that make them reluctant to lend, the Fed's efforts to expand the money supply are impeded.

To understand the central role of banks' problems in our economic plight, we need to understand the contemporary meaning of "bank" and how that meaning was produced by the movement to deregulate the financial industry. The genus of bank of which "bank" is one of the species is "financial intermediaries"—firms that borrow money and then lend (or otherwise invest, but my focus will be on lending) the borrowed money. The difference between the cost of the borrowed money to the firm [(bank)] and the price it charges when it lends out the money that it has borrowed covers the firm's [(bank's)] other costs and profit. There are many different types of financial intermediary—commercial banks, trust companies, home-loan banks, ("thrifts"), custodian banks, investment banks and other security broker-dealers, money market funds, other mutual funds, hedge funds, private equity funds, insurance companies, credit unions, and mortgage lenders (in the 1940s and 1950s my father had a successful business of making second-mortgage loans on commercial properties). But today the regulatory barriers separating the different types of financial intermediary have eroded to the point where, for most of my purposes in this book, all financial intermediaries can be regarded as "banks," even when different types of bank are combined in one enterprise—and that has become common too.

There isn't that much difference anymore even between a commercial bank and a hedge fund. Not that there is no difference. Commercial banks tend, paradoxically, to have riskier capital structures than hedge funds, in part because they have less equity capital and make longer-term loans and in part because some of their capital (demand deposits—the money in checking accounts) is federally insured. Commercial banks differ from all other financial intermediaries in only a few ways that remain important. The most important is their role, which I will be touching on from time to time, in expanding and contracting the supply of money in the US economy.

We need to consider why—the answer is not obvious—the bursting of a housing bubble should cause banks to go broke. Long-term lending secured by mortgages on residential real estate has traditionally been a low-risk business activity. If the homeowner defaulted, the lender would (in effect) seize and sell the house. If real estate prices had fallen, the house might not be worth the unpaid principal of the mortgage, but this risk was minimized by the unwillingness of mortgagees (the lenders—the borrowers are mortgagors) to lend the entire purchase price of a house, or its entire market value if the house had been acquired earlier. The mortgagee would usually require the mortgagor to make a 20 percent down payment on the purchase, so that the mortgagee would be safe as long as the house did not lose more than 20 percent of its value.

Even then the loan might be pretty safe, because banks refused to make mortgage loans to people who would be likely, because of inadequate income, heavy debts, or other serious underwriting risks, to default on a loan. Discipline in lending was reinforced by state usury laws that are now largely pre-empted by federal law as a result of the deregulation movement. By limiting the interest rate that an individual could be charged, usury laws discouraged the making of risky loans because the lender is forbidden to charge an interest rate high enough to compensate him for a high risk that the borrower will default.

We should consider why a lender would *want* to make a risky loan. The basis reason is the greater the risk, the higher the interest rate, to compensate the lender for the possibility that the borrower will default and as a result the lender will not be repaid unless there is an adequate collateral for the loan or the loan has been guaranteed by someone of substance. If the lender is able somehow to reduce or offset the risk, or just is lucky, or doesn't worry about the risk because it is likely to materialize, if at all, beyond his planning horizon, the risky loan will be more profitable than a safe loan would be. But before deregulation, banks would get into serious trouble with their regulators if they made risky loans, or at least enough risky loans to create a nontrivial risk of bankruptcy.

So there was safe lending, by banks, and risky lending by other financial inter-mediaries. [Other financial intermediaries were not and many currently are not regulated.] One thing that made banks safe was that they were forbidden to pay interest on demand deposits, traditionally their major source of capital. Another was that they were required to hold a portion of their deposits in the form of cash or an account with a federal reserve bank. These assets constituted the bank's "reserves" and did not pay interest. They were riskless and so reduced the over-all riskiness of the bank's asset portfolio. But then business depositors took to practicing "sweeps"—moving the money in their bank accounts into investment funds until they need to pay it to pay bills, at which point they moved it back. And money market funds arose to provide people with checkable accounts, just like bank accounts (though uninsured)—except that they paid interest. Banks responded by supplementing deposits as a source of bank capital with loans from other sources, on which they had to pay interest—and hence had to lend their capital out at a higher interest rate than they were paying for the capital furnished by their depositors. This required them to make riskier loans. The deregulatory strategy of allowing nonbank financial intermediaries to provide services virtu-ally indistinguishable from those of banks, such as the interest-bearing checkable accounts offered by money market funds, led inexorably to a complementary deregulatory strategy of freeing banks from restrictions that handicapped them in competing with unregulated (or very lightly regulated) financial intermediar-ies—nonbank banks, in effect.

As regulatory and customary restrictions on risky lending by banks eroded, banks became willing to make "subprime" mortgage loans—a euphemism for mortgage loans to people at high risk of defaulting. (Some of these loans are what are called NINJA loans—no income, no job, no assets, meaning that the borrower does not have to undergo a credit check in advance of the loan's being approved.) Such people tend not to have enough money to make a substantial down payment on a home—so suppose lenders are willing to lend them 100 percent of the purchase price. Many of the borrowers may even have trouble making monthly interest payments—so suppose the loan agreement makes the interest rate vary with the market rate of interest; the borrower pays a low inter-est rate now but the lender can raise it later if the market interest rate rises. The required monthly payment may even be set below the interest rate—may even be zero for the first two years of the loan—because the borrower cannot afford more. So instead of the mortgage sinking month by month because the borrower is paying interest and repaying principal, the mortgage grows because the unpaid interest gets added to the principal.

In risky mortgage lending, the lender (more precisely, whoever ends up bearing the risk of a default by the borrower) is more like a partner in a real estate business than like a secured lender. For suppose the value of the property drops, even slightly, before much of the loan has been repaid (and in the early years of the typical mortgage loan, very little of the principal is repaid because the monthly payments on a mortgage are a fixed amount and the interest component dominates at the outset when none of the principal has been repaid). The owner will find himself owing more on the house than it is worth. He may therefore decide to abandon it to the lender. If he had bought the house as a speculation, he may abandon it if its value simply fails to increase. He may *have* to do that, if he was counting on an increase in its value to enable him to refinance the mortgage at a lower interest rate because his equity in the house would be greater [if its value had increased possibly allowing him to qualify for a lower interest rate].

Risky mortgage lending can be *extremely* risky from the lender's standpoint, because a single default can wipe out the earnings on several good mortgage loans. Suppose that after expenses of foreclosure and brokerage and the like the lender will recover only 60 percent of his loan if the owner defaults. That 40 percent loss could well exceed the annual interest earned on seven or eight mortgage loans of the same size on other houses.

So subprime lenders, and anyone else who had an interest in a subprime mortgage loan, were skating on thin ice. When it broke—because it turned out that they were lending into a housing bubble that would burst long before the mortgages were repaid—many of them were rendered insolvent because of the huge volume of risky mortgage loans. As many as 40 percent of the $3 trillion in mortgage loans made in the United States in 2006 may have been subprime or otherwise of high risk, such as "Alt-A" mortgages, where the borrower has a decent credit rating but there is some other serious risk factor.

As pointed out in a prescient article by the finance theorist Raghuram Rajan in 2005, the attractiveness of risky lending or other risky investing is enhanced by the asymmetrical response of most investors to the good and bad results of an investment strategy. A strategy that produces good results attracts new investments, and the investment fund grows. If the fund (a trust fund administered by a bank, for example) does poorly, it will lose investors, but generally at a slower rate than it gains them when it does well.

Investors tend to stay with a poor performer for a time, either out of inattention or because they are hoping that its performance will improve; whatever attracted them to the fund in the first place may feed that hope.

And because of economies of scale in financial management, the profit margin of an investment fund increases as the fund grows. In a rising market, the fund can grow rapidly—attracting new investors because it is earning high returns while at the same time reducing its average costs—by increasing leverage. "Leverage" is the ratio of debt to equity (borrowed to owned assets) in a firm's capital structure. Because debt is a prescribed sum owed to a creditor regardless of how well or how badly the debtor does, the higher the ratio of debt to equity, the more money a financial firm will make in a rising market—its revenues will rise, but not its costs.

As Rajan has pointed out, banks and other financial companies have little incentive, in deciding how much risk to take, to worry about small probabilities of disaster. By definition, low-probability events occur rarely, and if they occur at all it is unlikely to be in the immediate future. Until disaster does occur, the risk-iness of the firm's investment strategy, although it may be the cause of the firm's high return, will be invisible to most investors and so it will look as if the firm is generating a high return with low risk. The higher the return on an investment is relative to risk, the more attractive the investment is to a risk-adverse investor, and so the better the performance of the financial manager seems.

That is one reason the private sector cannot be expected to adopt measures, such as forbearing to engage in highly risky lending, that might prevent a depression, and thus why preventing depressions has to be a government responsibility. Even though the financial industry has more information bearing on the likelihood of a depression than the government does, it has little incentive to analyze that information. A depression is too remote an event to influence business behavior. Given discounting to present value[—determination of the current value of a future event—]and the fact that by virtue of the principle of limited liability the creditors of a bankrupt corporation cannot go after the personal assets of the corporation's [(bank's)] owners or managers, events that are catastrophic to a corporation if they occur but are highly unlikely to occur, and therefore if they do occur are likely to in the distant future, will not influence a corporation's [(bank's)] behavior. A bankruptcy is not the end of the world for a company's executives, or even for its shareholders if they have a diversified portfolio of stocks and other assets. But a cascade of bank bankruptcies can be a disaster for a nation.

The more leveraged a bank's (or other financial company's) capital structure is, the greater the risk of insolvency [and hence bankruptcy]. Whether bank insolvencies, even if they precipitate a stock market crash, will trigger a depression thus depends on how widespread the insolvencies are, how deep the decline in the stock market is, and—of critical, but until the depression was upon us of neglected, importance—how much savings people have.

The balance between consumption and savings is critical to depression analysis. The higher the savings rate, the less likely it is that a difficulty in borrowing, caused by bank insolvencies, and a loss of wealth, caused by a decline in the stock market, will result in a steep reduction in the demand for goods and services.

People will dip into their savings to maintain something close to their habitual level of consumption.

To understand the interplay of the depression-inducing factors I have been discussing, we now need to consider the fundamentals of borrowing and lending, and in particular their relation to consumption and savings. A person who borrows money in order to buy things (a house, a car, etc.) is increasing his present consumption at the expense of his future consumption, because he will have to pay back the loan eventually. The firm that borrows money in order to produce things (build a house for example) is increasing its present production, though most short-term business borrowing is necessitated simply by the fact that production (cost) normally precedes sale (revenue), and businesses borrow to bridge the gap between expenditure and receipt. Either way, borrowing increases current economic activity. The lower interest rates are, the more borrowing there is and therefore the more buying and selling. When rates are low, you want to be a borrower, not a lender (that is, not a saver). Interest rates were very low in the early 2000s. That was a critical factor in the credit binge that has brought the economy low. A credit binge in the 1920s is widely believed to have been a precipitant of the Great Depression.

A consumer who lends, say by placing some of his money in a money market fund, is reducing his present consumption in order to increase his future consumption; he is saving for the future. Savings are the source of money for lending to other consumers, the ones who want to consume more today. Because borrowing and lending—credit transactions—increase present economic activity, a sudden sharp decline in borrowing and lending reduces that activity—reduces both consumption and production—and can trigger a vicious cycle that produces a high rate of unemployment of both human and capital[(—production—)]resources.

That is the principle justification for ex ante regulation of the finance industries. (A subordinate justification is that since the government insures demand deposits, it wants to make sure that banks don't take excessive risks with that money.) By "ex ante" regulation I mean regulating behavior before anything bad happens. Speed limits are a form of ex ante regulation; liability for injuring someone in an automobile accident is a form of ex poste regulation. The latter form of regulation is cheaper because it comes into play only in the relatively rare instances in which a mishap occurs. But it operates on the principle of deterrence—the threat of liability is assumed to make people more careful—and deterrence is rarely perfect. So when the consequences of a single accident can be catastrophic, the emphasis shifts from deterrence to prevention. That is the case concerning mishaps in the finance industry. As we are experiencing, such mishaps can cause economic disaster. Ex ante regulation failed in this instance.

Personal savings might be expected to act as a brake on the vicious cycle that I have been describing, thus reducing the vicious cycle. If people cannot sustain their current level of consumption by continued borrowing, because the credit market has seized up, they can reallocate some of their savings to consumption—that is, shift consumption from future to present. But in the years leading up to the current depression, the personal savings rate of Americans has plummeted. From 10 percent in 1980 it dropped into negative territory in 2005 (meaning people were spending more than they were earning and thus were dissaving) and then fluctuated in a narrow band around zero percent until the financial crisis began inducing people to save more of their income—in December 2008 the personal savings rate rose to 3.6 percent. The drop was natural because, as I said, the lower interest rates are, the more advantageous it is to borrow rather than to save.

The economic significance of the decline in the personal savings rate was marked by the fact that the market value of people's savings concentrated as those savings were not only in houses, but also in common stocks held in brokerage accounts, profit-sharing and retirement accounts, health savings plans, college savings plans, was rising because house and stock prices were rising, the first vertiginously. But it is important to distinguish between the market value of a person's savings and the composition of the portfolio of assets that constitutes his savings. If the portfolio is risky because it is dominated by risky assets, the market value of the portfolio, and thus of the person's savings, may fall unexpectedly, just like the market value of banks whose asset portfolios had high risk. Even if the market value does not fall a great deal, the expectation created by hard times that it will fall more may cause people to sell their assets (thus causing further declines in the market values of those assets) and invest the proceeds in safe assets, or shift some of their income from consumption to savings.

Many people don't have much in the way of savings, risky or safe. They tend to be heavily dependent on credit to finance their consumption, and so when credit dries up they have to cut their personal consumption expenditures drastically.

When a person's wealth increases, he can use the increment to consume more or to invest[—save—]more, or both; probably he will use at least some of it to invest more. As the value of a person's house or of his stock portfolio rises, he is likely to buy more stock and more house (maybe a bigger house, or a second home, or improvements to his home). Those are the assets he is familiar with, and as they are doing well, they seem a good investment. The additional investment pushes up the price of stocks and houses, and hence the measured wealth of people who own such assets. Adjusted for risk, however, personal savings will be shrinking along with the savings rate, not growing; more precisely, precautionary (rainy-day) savings will be shrinking. Thus despite the increase in measured personal wealth in the early 2000s, debt service (interest) as a percentage of personal income rose sharply, though the rise was partly offset by the deductibility of mortgage interest from federal income tax because so much savings was in the form of home-owner-ship. People's savings were at once smaller relative to their personal consumption expenditures and riskier, and both are reasons that an economic shock would cause a sharp reduction in those expenditures.

When stock prices and especially housing prices plummeted after their steep ascent fueled by cheap credit (as they had to do eventually because they had been driven up not by fundamental economic changes but by expectations that turned out to be mistaken), the market value of personal savings, concentrated in those risky assets, plummeted too. The inadequacy of people's savings was thus exposed; and when savings are inadequate, people who lose their jobs, or cannot sell the houses they can no longer afford, cannot or dare not reallocate savings to consumption. Instead, consumption falls steeply. Some people use money they would otherwise have spent on consumption to rebuild their savings, in order to cope with the uncertainty of their economic future—and indeed, as I have noted, the personal savings rate has soared. [The percentage personal savings is of personal income in current dollars rose from the fourth quarter of 2007 to the second quarter of 2009; 2007 IV 1.5%, 2008 I 1.2 %, 2008 II 3.4 %, 2008 III 2.2%, 2008 IV 3.8%, 2009 I 4.0%, 2009 II 5.2%.] Other people, whose incomes have already fallen, reduce their consumption because they do not have enough savings to enable them to maintain their standard of living even if they reallocate all their savings to consumption.

There is a parallel between the behavior of banks and the behavior of consumers, with safe personal savings corresponding to banks' reserves (cash or an account with a federal reserve bank, which is the equivalent of cash) and other safe assets. When savings/safe assets decline to a dangerous level, consumers buy less and banks lend less.

As consumption falls, output falls, precipitating layoffs that further reduce consumption, creating the vicious cycle dramatized by the virtual collapse of the American-owned automobile industry—already in perilous straits because of dwindling demand for gas guzzlers—as people decided to postpone the purchase of new cars. Cheap credit and risky lending had created a kind of automobile bubble—not an increase in the price of automobiles, of course, because the supply of automobiles is much more elastic than that of housing, but rather an increase in the number of automobiles produced, as more people bought second and even third cars and replaced their cars more frequently. US auto sales rose sharply in the early 2000s—a rise inexplicable in terms of fundamental factors—to 17 million 2005, falling to little more than 13 million in 2008 and expected to be even lower in 2009.

With the economy's output dropping, and therefore corporate profits as well, with no end of the decline in sight and a growing aversion to owning risky assets, it is no surprise that the stock market has plummeted too. Another cause is the need for cash by firms and individuals whose income has declined. The market decline has made people reduce their spending because they are poorer and face greater uncertainty. If they do not need to use their entire reduced income for consumption, the reduction in spending will increase their savings, and what is saved does not contribute to the demand for goods and services.

The timing of the financial crisis, moreover, could not have been worse. It struck during a presidential campaign and deepened during a presidential transition. The lame-duck president seemed uninterested in and uninformed about economic matters and was unable to project an image of leadership and instead spent his final months in office in frequent trips abroad and in legacy-polishing while the domestic economy melted away. Economic officials and private business leaders alike displayed slow uptake and stumbling responses to the financial crisis, undermining confidence in the nation's economic management. And the crisis accelerated during the Christmas shopping season, which normally accounts for 30 to 50 percent of annual retail sales of most goods and services other than food, drugs, and utilities. The buying binge that had been financed by a reduction in safe savings (because savings had been used to buy risky assets like houses and stock) and by heavy borrowing left American consumers awash in consumer durables, and this made it easy for them to postpone buying when the housing bubble burst. Consumer durables are more durable than they used to be, moreover, so that replacement—for example of cars—can be deferred without hardship longer than used to be possible.

Furthermore, for many Americans, shopping has a recreational aspect, and tastes in recreation can change rapidly. One of the extraordinary aspects of the current economic situation is that buying luxury items has become unfashionable. Many people who can afford to buy such items despite the depression are not doing so.

But wait—since savings are the source of lending, how could a decline in the personal savings rate have coincided with excessive borrowing for personal consumption? Heavy borrowing should increase interest rates, which should in turn reduce the demand for credit. But the Federal Reserve, in reaction to a recession triggered by the collapse, which began in March 2000, of a bubble in dot-com stocks, had used its control over the supply of money to push interest rates way down in order to encourage consumption and production. It kept them down for five years. And the emergence of a global capital surplus kept them low even when the Federal Reserve raised them in 2006. With personal savings by Americans a diminishing source of funds for lending, the slack was taken up by foreign owners of capital, including sovereign (government) loan funds of nations such as China and the major oil-producing countries of the Middle East that exported much more than they imported and as a result had large dollar surpluses that they were eager to invest.

China's role in setting the stage for the current crises has received a good deal of criticism. The criticism is that by depreciating its currency relative to the dollar, China made its products very cheap to businesses and consumers in the United States and US products very expensive to Chinese businesses and consumers. The story is more complicated. Chinese incomes are very low; few Chinese can afford our goods. And China is not the only major country that exports more to the United States than it imports from us and reinvests its surplus dollars in this country. Japan and Germany are others—German state banks were big buyers of mortgages-backed securities originated by American banks.

When domestic demand is weak, moreover, as in China, encouraging exports is a way of achieving fuller employment of productive resources. We are in that position today. Our domestic demand is weak. Would that we could offset that weakness with brisk exporting. We cannot because—in another frightening resemblance to the Great Depression—we are in a *global* depression, which has reduced the demand for our exports.

Throughout the early 2000s, we were flooded with foreign capital. Our chronic trade deficit swelled. We were living on credit. That is a precarious state for a nation, as it is for an individual. But it is a delicious state for lenders, and therefore banks. One might think that low interest rates would hurt as well as help lenders, since competition would limit how much banks could charge for loans. But the banking industry can make more money by borrowing at 2 percent and lending at 6 percent than by borrowing at 6 percent and lending at 10 percent, because the lower the interest rate paid by borrowers, the greater the demand for loans.

It would be a mistake, however, to think that because the world was awash in money, the Federal Reserve had lost control over interest rates—that countries that had large dollar balances that they choose to invest in the United States were to blame for our low interest rates. Had the Federal Reserve feared inflation in 2000, it would have used its control over US Banks to raise interest rates. It was able to raise those rates in 2006 notwithstanding the continued influx of foreign capital.

Source: *A Failure of Capitalism: The Crisis of '08 and the Descent into Depression*. Cambridge, MA: Harvard UP, 2009. 1-40.

WHAT IT SAYS

1. How, according to Posner, do economic downturns spiral into depressions? How do economies recover from depression?

2. How does the "current" economic crisis differ from other kinds of economic downturns? What causes crises like that of 2008?

3. What are the "proximate causes" of the economic depression, according to Posner? What factors indicate that the economic downturn is a depression and how do they make matters worse?

4. What is deflation and why is it a real danger, according to Posner? What are the causes and effects of deflation? Why is deflation harder to combat during a financial crisis?

5. What was the role of financial intermediaries other than banks—what Posner calls "nonbank banks"—in the financial crisis? How did these nonbank banks affect the behavior of traditional banks?

6. Why is government regulation of banking and other financial intermediaries necessary, according to Posner? Why can't banks and other financial institutions be relied upon to regulate themselves?

HOW IT SAYS IT

1. What is the significance of Posner's repeated reference to the Great Depression of the 1930s? How does this repeated reference help to advance his argument?

2. Posner spends a good deal of time discussing "the anatomy of depression." What does this "anatomy" lesson do for him? How does it connect to his main argument?

3. As we state in the introduction to this essay, Posner is a circuit court judge and a legal scholar. Where and how does Posner's legal training come into play in this essay? Point to specific words and phrases that seem legalistic or that are drawn from legal reasoning.

WRITE ABOUT IT

1. Posner's essay is rather long and drawn out. Write a summary (see pp. 77–79) of Posner's essay that briefly explains the essay, making clear what the main argument is and how the specific points support that argument. What is the essay's main line of argument? Be sure to find the most important parts and explain how they fit together to make Posner's case.

2. Write an essay that provides a different explanation for the crisis that Posner discusses. Provide alternative causes for the effects that Posner discusses. Account for most of the major points that Posner makes. Be sure that you have Posner's argument clear in your mind before you begin.

c. Peter J. Wallison, "Not a Failure of Capitalism — A Failure of Government"

Peter J. Wallison holds the Arthur F. Burns Chair in Financial Market Studies and is co-director of the American Enterprise Institute's (AEI) program on financial market deregulation. Prior to joining AEI, he practiced banking, corporate, and financial law at Gibson, Dunn & Crutcher in Washington and New York. Wallison has also held several governmental posts. In the early to mid-1980s, he was general counsel of the United States Treasury Department, where he helped to develop the Reagan administration's proposals for deregulating the financial services industry. During 1986 and 1987, he served as Reagan's White House counsel.

Wallison is the author of several books, including *Back from the Brink* (1990), *The GAAP Gap: Corporate Disclosure in the Internet Age* (2000), *Ronald Reagan: The Power of Conviction and the Success of His Presidency* (2002), and *Competitive Equity: A Better Way to Organize Mutual Funds* (2007). He is the editor of *Optional Federal Chartering and Regulation of Insurance Companies* (2000) and *Serving Two Masters, Yet Out of Control: Fannie Mae and Freddie Mac* (2001). He is a frequent contributor to the op-ed pages of the *New York Times*, the *Wall Street Journal*, and the *Financial Times*. He received an undergraduate degree from Harvard College and a law degree from Harvard Law School.

In this essay, Wallison proposes to dismantle the arguments of those who suggest that the financial and economic crisis was the result of deregulation. He takes particular aim at the arguments of Richard Posner.

As You Read: What do the terms "regulation" and "deregulation" mean to you? What does Wallison do to confirm or change your mind about these terms?

Not a Failure of Capitalism—A Failure of Government

Since the beginning of the turmoil in the financial markets that is now commonly referred to as the "financial crisis," many voices have asserted that this is a "crisis of capitalism." These are not merely the voices of socialist groups, who could be expected to see this event as a vindication of their views;[1] government officials also

---

1   Barry Grey, "The Wall Street Crisis and the Failure of American Capitalism," World Socialist Website (16 September 2008): www.wsws.org/articles/2008/sep2008/lehm-s16.shtml.

joined the chorus,[2] as did many commentators on financial matters. As Samuel Brittan observed early in the mortgage meltdown that ultimately became the financial crisis, "Any failures on the financial side are sure to bring the opponents of capitalism out of their burrows. Pundits who until recently conceded that 'capitalism is the only game in town' are now rejoicing at what they hope is the longed-for death agony of the system."[3] Billionaire investor George Soros, who had been arguing at least since 1997 that the capitalist system was "coming apart at the seams," finally found vindication, telling a group in New York in February 2009, according to a Bloomberg News summary, that "the current economic upheaval has its roots in the financial deregulation of the 1980s and signals the end of a free-market model that has since dominated capitalist countries."[4] In 2009, the debate over the responsibility of capitalism for the current crisis rose to such significance that the *Financial Times* ran a gloomy series on the future of capitalism.[5]

An examination of these contributions shows that, with the exception of the socialist view, the critics are not actually recommending the abandonment of a market system but only the imposition of stronger forms of government control over markets through greater regulation and supervision. Much of the rhetoric about crises or failures of capitalism either posits a straw man—an unfettered laissez-faire capitalism that does not exist in the United States, or for that matter anywhere else—or suggests that excessive deregulation has allowed banks to take excessive risks. It has certainly not been the policy of the US government to allow financial markets to "regulate themselves," as some have claimed, although safety and soundness regulation—the supervision of the financial health of institutions—has been limited at the federal level to banks and to two government-sponsored enterprises (GSEs), Fannie Mae and Freddie Mac. Such regulation is logical because commercial banks are backed by the government through deposit insurance, a lender of last resort facility offered by the Federal Reserve, and a Federal Reserve payment system to which only banks have access. The GSEs, although not explicitly backed by the government, were seen in the markets as performing a government mission and, hence, as being government backed. Once any kind of financial institution is seen as being backed by the government, market discipline is severely impaired, and—to protect itself against losses—the government must impose some kind of safety and soundness regime.

---

2   Chris Giles and Jean Eaglesham, "Another Country?" *Financial Times* (20 April 2009), quoting President Nicolas Sarkozy of France after the G-20 meeting in April 2009 that the world had "turned the page" on the dominant model of Anglo-Saxon capitalism; see also "Global Crisis 'Failure of Extreme Capitalism': Australian PM," Breitbart.com (15 October 2008): www.breitbart.com/article.php?id=081015113127.9uzhf7lf&show_article=1.

3   Samuel Brittan, "The Financial Crises of Capitalism," *Financial Times* (8 May 2008).

4   Walid el-Gabry, "Soros Says Crisis Signals End of a Free-Market Model (Update 2)," Bloomberg.com (23 February 2009): www.bloomberg.com/apps/news?pid=newsarchive&sid=aI1pruXkjros.

5   www.ft.com/indepth/capitalism-future.

Other major participants in financial markets—securities firms and insurance companies—are not backed by the government and are thus subject to a far less intrusive regulatory regime than banks are, but they nevertheless function within a complex web of regulation on business conduct and consumer protection. The condition of the banking industry today, far from offering evidence that regulation has been lacking, is actually a demonstration of the failure of regulation and its inability to prevent risk taking. Because this is not the first time that regulation has failed to prevent a major banking crisis, it makes more sense to question whether intrusive and extensive financial regulation and supervision is a sensible policy rather than to propose its extension to other areas of the financial sector.

What most critics of the current system do not seem to recognize is that the regulation of banks has been very stringent, particularly in the United States. As I will show, the commercial banks that have gotten themselves into trouble did so *despite* strong regulation. This is an uncomfortable fact—maybe what some would call an "inconvenient truth"—for those in the Obama administration and elsewhere who are advocating not only more regulation but also extending it to the rest of the financial system.

The critics seem to have been led into error by a faulty kind of inductive logic. It begins with the assumption that capitalism, if left unchecked by regulation, will produce instability. Thus, when instability appears—as it certainly has in the current financial crisis—it must be the result of a failure to adequately regulate financial markets. With this logical underpinning, critics almost uniformly make no effort to describe the "deregulation" that they are certain must have occurred. They may name a statute, such as the Gramm-Leach-Bliley Act of 1999, but they never explain how that law led to the current financial crisis, or any part of it. And because they assume their worldview is correct almost by definition, they also assume that the evidence is there to support it and that actual evidence does not need to be collected or critically examined. A more logical—and less ideological—approach would be to look for the causes of instability first and to propose an appropriate remedy after the causes have been established. As I will argue later, if that had been done by the critics in this case, their indictment would not have extended to capitalism, or even the lack of regulation, but to government intervention in the housing finance system in the United States.

Did Deregulation or Nonregulation Cause the Financial Crisis?

A good example of the faulty approach to the causes of the financial crisis is the recent book *A Failure of Capitalism* by Judge Richard Posner. Certainly the most surprising member of the group that sees deregulation as the cause of the crisis, Judge Posner is a highly respected and prolific writer of articles and books as well as legal opinions. Because of his reputation as a leader of the judiciary and an advocate of using economic analysis to address legal questions, his position has attracted a lot of attention from the media, with reviews and articles in the *New York Times*, *New York Review of Books*, and the *Atlantic Monthly*. But like so many other critics, Judge Posner merely asserts that deregulation is the cause of the financial crisis; he never cites the laws he is blaming. Where he describes deregulation without citing actual laws, he gets it wrong in material respects. Moreover, and perhaps more important, he never successfully connects the "deregulation" he identifies with the causes of the crisis in any way that makes sense either as economics or logic.

An example is what seems to be the central argument in the book—that "deregulation" permitted other financial firms, particularly money market mutual funds, to compete with banks, requiring banks to pay more for their money and, in turn, seek and obtain deregulatory action that allowed them to take greater risks in their lending. Here is the argument in his words:

> One thing that made banks safe was that they were forbidden to pay interest on demand deposits, traditionally their major source of capital ... [M]oney market funds arose to provide people with checkable accounts, just like bank accounts (although uninsured)—except that they paid interest.... The deregulatory strategy of allowing nonbank financial intermediaries to provide services virtually indistinguishable from those of banks, such as interest-bearing checkable accounts offered by money market funds, led inexorably to a complementary deregulatory strategy of freeing banks from the restrictions that handicapped them in competing with unregulated (or very lightly regulated) financial intermediaries—nonbank banks, in effect.
>
> As regulatory and customary restrictions on risky lending by banks eroded, banks became willing to make "subprime" mortgage loans—a euphemism for mortgage loans at high risk of defaulting.[6] (pp. 22-23)

There are many errors in this argument, and it is hard to know where to begin. First, money market funds were not the result of any kind of "deregulation." They were a product spawned by the mutual fund industry to take advantage of an ill-founded rate regulation on banks—the cap on bank interest rates that had been imposed by government regulation many years before. During the inflationary period of the late 1970s and early 1980s, interest rates in the money markets rose far above the 5 percent cap on bank interest allowed by a Fed-imposed limitation known as Regulation Q. As a result, funds flowed out of banks and into other instruments, such as Treasury bills and commercial paper. These instruments were sold in large principal amounts and were thus not suitable for retail investors.

---

6   Richard A. Posner, *A Failure of Capitalism: The Crisis of '08 and the Descent into Depression* (Cambridge, MA: Harvard University Press, 2009).

Money market funds were an innovation that enabled retail investors and small businesses to participate directly in the safety and stability of investing in government securities and high-quality commercial paper by purchasing shares of a money market fund, which, in turn, bought and held these safe money market instruments. Prior to the advent of money market funds, bank deposits were the safest instruments for the retail investment because they were government insured. If bank interest rates had not been capped by government action, money market funds might never have developed. So, government *regulation* of bank deposit rates, not deregulation, was the initial cause of the competition banks encountered from money market funds.

Second, there is no evidence whatsoever that the higher costs of competing with money market funds caused banks to take greater risks in their lending, such as by purchasing subprime mortgages. For one thing, the threat from money market funds began in the late 1970s and accelerated in the 1980s until Regulation Q was abolished. Subprime lending did not begin in any size until more than 10 years later, in the mid-1990s, and did not become a major feature of the mortgage market until the early 2000s. The connection that Judge Posner draws between bank competition and bank risky lending on mortgages is simply wrong.

In addition, the idea that paying a market rate for funds might weaken banks, or require them to take more risks, harks back to the discredited idea—popular during the New Deal—that "excessive competition" is bad because it can be "ruinous" to competitors. The *benefit* of resources to flow to the competition comes from the fact that it is ruinous to the less-effective competitors, forcing more-effective ones. The focus on the health of individual firms, rather than on the benefits of competition itself for consumers and the health of the economy generally, is one of the mistakes most commonly made when discussing economics.

Glass-Steagall "Repeal." Another favorite target of the critics who are searching for deregulation in the US financial system is the so-called repeal of the Glass-Steagall Act of 1933 by the Gramm-Leach-Bliley Act of 1999. For example, Kaufman writes:

> If you're looking for a major cause of the current banking meltdown, you need seek no farther than the 1999 repeal of the Glass-Steagall Act.... According to Wikipedia, many economists "have criticized the repeal of the Glass-Steagall Act as contributing to the 2007 subprime mortgage financial crisis. The repeal enabled commercial lenders such as Citigroup, the largest US bank by assets, to under-write and trade instruments such as mortgage-backed securities and collateralized debt obligations and establish so-called structured investment vehicles, or SIVs, that bought those securities."[7]

---

7   William Kaufman, "Shattering the Glass-Steagall Act," *Counterpunch* (19 September 2008): www.counterpunch.org/kaufman09192008.html. See also Nigel Lawson, "Capitalism Needs a Revived Glass-Steagall," *Financial Times* (15 March 2009).

Wikipedia got it wrong. The portions of the 1933 Glass-Steagall Act relevant to this discussion consist of four small sections of text that did two things—prohibited commercial banks from (1) owning or dealing in securities or (2) being *affiliated* with firms that engage in underwriting or dealing in securities (i.e., investment banks). The Gramm-Leach-Bliley Act of 1999 (GLBA) repealed the affiliation restrictions of Glass-Steagall but left the restrictions on banks' securities activities intact. Thus, before the repeal, commercial banks could not underwrite or deal in securities, and the same rules applied to them after repeal. The only difference was that, after repeal, they were able to affiliate through subsidiaries and holding companies with firms engaged in underwriting and dealing in securities. In other words, the GLBA made no changes in what commercial banks themselves were permitted to do in the securities field. They remained forbidden to deal in or underwrite securities, including mortgage-backed securities or the other instruments mentioned in the Wikipedia entry.

But what about the affiliation repeal? Could it reasonably be argued that the affiliations now permitted between commercial banks and investment banks somehow caused commercial banks to take more risks or to behave less like banks? This is highly unlikely. Although all of the banks that got into trouble in the current financial crisis had securities affiliates, they got into financial difficulties because they made imprudent decisions as *banks*, not because of the activities of their securities affiliates. Citibank, Bank of America, Wachovia, IndyMac Federal Bank, Wells Fargo, and the rest weakened themselves by purchasing securities backed by mortgages and other assets that banks are allowed to hold as investments (but not to deal in or underwrite). Under banking rules, both before and after the repeal of the affiliation restrictions in Glass-Steagall, banks were permitted to hold asset-backed securities if the underlying assets, such as mortgages and credit card receivables, were assets that banks were generally permitted to hold.[8] In other words, the claim that the GLBA, by repealing Glass-Steagall's affiliation provisions, enabled banks to invest differently from how they could before the GLBA is wrong.

Similarly, none of the investment banks got into trouble because of the affiliations with banks that were permitted after the GLBA. Although all of them had small banks or S&Ls (savings and loan associations) as subsidiaries, the parent companies—Bear Stearns, Lehman Brothers, Merrill Lynch, Morgan Stanley, and Goldman Sachs—were completely independent of control by banks or bank holding companies and also got into trouble by making the same imprudent investments they were allowed to make before the GLBA was passed. In other words, the repeal of Glass-Steagall's affiliation provisions had no effect on these investment banks and was not responsible for the losses they suffered by holding mortgage-backed and other risky securities as assets.

---

8   See Title 12, Code of Federal Regulations, Part 1, Sections 1.1-1.3.

"Deregulation" of Credit Default Swaps. One final argument concerning deregulation is the claim that deregulation or a mania for free markets caused the Clinton administration and the US Congress to deregulate credit default swaps (CDS). The episode is complicated, but it is not an example of deregulation because CDS had *never* been regulated. In 1999, the chair of the US Commodity Futures Trading Commission (CFTC) asserted that CDS were subject to regulation by the CFTC. Because the assertion raised questions about the continued legality of trading in these derivatives, the Clinton administration (including Robert Rubin and Lawrence Summers at the US Department of the Treasury and Arthur Levitt at the US Securities and Exchange Commission) sought legislation that would permanently bar the CFTC from regulating these swap transactions, thus removing any doubt as to the legality of the unregulated CDS market.

The role of credit default swaps in the financial crisis has been as exaggerated as the role of the Glass-Steagall "repeal." Once again, the complexities of the matter have eluded the media, which have simply reported what they were told by people who were themselves speculating about the effect of CDS. There is no evidence that CDS caused any serious losses to any individual firm or the market as a whole after Lehman Brothers failed, and there is no evidence that American International Group (AIG) had to be bailed out because its CDS liabilities would have damaged the market or caused a systemic breakdown.

Many of the media stories about AIG have focused on AIG's Financial Products subsidiary and the obligations that this entity assumed through CDS. However, it is highly questionable whether there would have been a significant market reaction if AIG had been allowed to default on its CDS obligations in September 2008. CDS are guarantee contracts that pay off when an issuer of a security defaults. If a CDS issuer fails, it is much the same as when a homeowner's insurance company goes out of business before there has been a fire or other loss to the home. In that case, the homeowner must go out and find another insurance company, but he has not lost anything except the premium he has paid. If AIG had been allowed to default, there would have been little if any near-term loss to the parties that had bought protection; they would simply have been required to go back into the CDS market and buy new protection. CDS contracts normally require a party like AIG that has sold protection (i.e., agreed to reimburse a counterparty's loss) to post collateral as assurance to its counterparties that it can meet its obligations when they come due. The premiums for the new protection might have been more expensive than what they were paying AIG, but even if that were true, many of AIG's counterparties had received collateral from AIG that could have been sold to defray the cost of the new protection.[9]

---

9   A full description of the operation of credit default swaps appears in Peter J. Wallison, "Everything You Wanted to Know about Credit Default Swaps—But Were Never Told," *Financial Services Outlook* (December 2008): www.aei.org/publication29158.

This analysis is consistent with the publicly known facts about AIG. In mid-March, the names of some of the counterparties that AIG had protected with CDS became public. The largest of these counterparties was Goldman Sachs. AIG's obligation to Goldman was reported as $12.9 billion; the others named were Merrill Lynch ($6.8 billion), Bank of America ($5.2 billion), Citigroup ($2.3 billion), and Wachovia ($1.5 billion). Recall that the loss of CDS coverage—the obligation in this case—is not an actual cash loss or anything like it; it is only the loss of a guarantee against a possible future default on a debt that is held by a protected party. For institutions of this size, with the exception of Goldman, the loss of AIG's CDS protection would not have been a problem, even if they had in fact already suffered losses on the underlying obligations that AIG was protecting. Moreover, when questioned about what it would have lost if AIG had defaulted, Goldman said its losses would have been "negligible." This claim is entirely plausible. Goldman's spokesman cited both the collateral it had received from AIG under the CDS contracts and the fact that it had hedged its AIG risk by buying protection from third parties against the possibility of AIG's default.[10] Also, as noted earlier, Goldman only suffered the loss of its CDS *coverage*, not a loss on the underlying debt the CDS was supposed to cover. If Goldman, the largest counterparty in AIG's list, would not have suffered substantial losses, then AIG's default on its CDS contracts would have had no serious consequences in the market.

Inadequate Regulatory Authority. Finally, after considering all the allegations about the relationship between deregulation and the financial crisis, it is necessary to consider whether the problem is one of insufficient regulatory authority, rather than deregulation. The problem might not be that regulatory authority was taken away from the regulators by deregulation but simply that it was never given to them at all. That argument, however, is not supported by the facts. Since 1991, the regulators of all insured banks have had plenty of authority to crack down on bank risk taking. Their authority was significantly *strengthened* immediately after the S&L debacle, when much of the S&L industry collapsed and almost 1,600 commercial banks were closed by the FDIC. At that point, Congress adopted the Federal Deposit Insurance Corporation Improvement Act of 1991 (FDICIA), a reform measure developed by the first Bush administration. FDICIA was a very tough regulatory law. Among other things, it provided for prompt corrective action (PCA) by supervisors when a bank's capital position began to erode. As that happened, PCA required regulators to take increasingly stringent actions to control the bank's activities and to close the bank entirely if they believed that it would become insolvent in the future. The law also provided for personal fines of up to $1 million a day on bank directors and officers who violated bank regulations. FDICIA was so tough that Alan Greenspan, then the chair of the Federal

---

10 Steven Malanga, "Obsessive Housing Disorder," *City Journal* (Spring 2009): www.city-journal.org/printable.php?id=4376.

Reserve, complained that it was too tough on banks. He might have been on to something. Now, 18 years later, we are in the midst of the worst banking crisis since the Great Depression.

Thus, none of the explanations for the financial crisis that blame capitalism or deregulation, or Glass-Steagall, or any one of a number of other alleged deficiencies in the regulatory regime applicable to banks, has any validity. The banking system is in very bad shape today, as is the world's economy, but none of the explanations usually advanced by commentators, and reported in the media, can be plausibly shown to be a cause of the financial crisis.

If Deregulation or Nonregulation Did Not Cause the Financial Crisis, What Did?

Many analyses of the current crisis have pointed to the existence of a massive housing bubble that—according to the Case-Shiller Index—began to deflate in mid-2006. There is no question that the deflation of any large asset bubble will cause a downturn in the US economy. Before the collapse of the housing bubble, a similar asset bubble in internet-related equities (known as the dot-com or tech bubble) caused a huge stock market decline and a recession when it deflated in 2001. Asset bubbles of various kinds are not unusual or unexpected, but they do not always cause worldwide financial crises. The key question is why the housing bubble that began to deflate in 2006 or 2007 had this effect.

It is a widely held, although by no means universally accepted, view that a principal cause of the Great Depression was government policy—particularly the actions of the Federal Reserve in tightening rather than loosening the money supply and credit as a major recession took hold. It is my view that US government policy is again responsible for the current financial crisis. An explanation begins with some numbers that are not well known—even now. There are 25 million subprime and other nonprime mortgages currently outstanding in the United States, with an unpaid principal balance of more than $4 trillion. Subprime mortgages are loans made to people with blemished credit and low scores on the measures that are used to estimate credit quality. Other nonprime mortgages, which I will call Alt-A in this article, are considered poor quality because of the characteristics of the loans themselves and not the borrowers. Alt-A loans have adjustable rates, no or low down payments, and negative amortization or were made to people who did not have to state their income or to people whose income or jobs were not verified. Many of these borrowers were not intending to live in the homes they were buying but were investing or speculating in housing.

Twenty-five million subprime and Alt-A loans amount to almost 45 percent of all single-family mortgages in the United States. These poor quality mortgages are defaulting at unprecedented rates. As these mortgages decline in value, so does the capital and the financial condition of every bank and financial institution that is holding them. These include not only US banks and financial institutions but also banks and other financial institutions around the world that invested in these mortgages, usually through mortgage-backed securities (MBS). More than any other cause, the sharp decline in the value of these mortgages accounts for the worldwide financial collapse we are now experiencing.

Financial institutions invested in these mortgages because they believed from historical evidence that Americans always pay their mortgages. This was certainly true when almost all mortgages were prime—made to people with jobs and substantial down payments and at fixed interest rates for 30 years. Even in the worst downturns, foreclosure rates rarely reached 4 percent. However, some projections of foreclosure rates for the subprime and Alt-A loans in the current downturn run as high as 30 percent—a completely unprecedented phenomenon, exceeding even the Great Depression.

The boom in subprime and Alt-A mortgages is something entirely new. These instruments always existed but were a small part of the total mortgage pool because of their high-risk characteristics. It was possible to have a profitable business as a subprime mortgage lender, but it was necessary to obtain a substantial risk premium to compensate for the high rate of foreclosure and loss. However, as outlined later, beginning in the early 1990s and continuing until 2007, government policy artificially inflated the value of subprime and Alt-A loans, reducing the necessary risk premium and leaving the holders of these mortgages with serious losses as they began to default.

The government policies that ultimately caused these developments have a long history. Since the beginning of the 20th century, the United States has had a policy of fostering homeownership. This policy caused regular economic downturns as the government attempted by various means to make it easier for Americans to buy homes. As reported by Steven Malanga, the first major campaign along these lines was initiated by Herbert Hoover, who was alarmed by a decline in homeownership revealed by the 1920 census.[11] Hoover began a campaign to increase homeownership, and Congress cooperated in 1927 by freeing banks to make more mortgage loans. Homeownership rates did indeed improve, rising from about 46 percent when Hoover began his program to almost 48 percent in 1930, but the number of defaults rose substantially during the ensuing depression. After World War II, there was another effort to increase homeownership, but Malanga observes:

> As homeownership grew, political pressure to allow riskier loans increased.... Under pressure to keep meeting housing demand, the government began loosening its mortgage-lending standards [on FHA and VA loans]—cutting the size of required down payments, approving loans

---

11 Letter, dated 20 January 2009, in possession of author.

with higher ratios of payments to income, and extending the terms of mortgages. (pp. 3-4)

The failure rate on these government-backed mortgages spiked, but Malanga notes, "the foreclosure rate of conventional mortgages barely increased, since many traditional lenders had maintained stricter underwriting standards, which had proved a good predictor of loan quality over the years" (p. 4).

The differences between government policy and private-lending policies began to change in 1977, with the adoption of the Community Reinvestment Act (CRA), which gave regulators the right to deny bank applications for expansion if an applicant had failed to lend sufficiently in minority neighborhoods. As Malanga reported, the most significant denial came in 1979, when the Greater New York Savings Bank was denied the opportunity to open a branch on the Upper East Side of Manhattan because it had not lent enough in its Brooklyn home market. In the early 1990s, the Clinton administration revised the regulations under CRA so that banks were required to make the loans, not just show good faith efforts to find borrowers in underserved communities. That was a turning point. Although the government had previously taken the risks of making weak loans, now—through CRA—the government was requiring private banks to take risks they had previously eschewed.

Many of the communities that CRA was intended to benefit contained borrowers who had blemished credit or no money for down payments or who did not have steady jobs or incomes. That did not excuse banks from making mortgage loans to these borrowers. They were directed to use "flexible underwriting standards." The bank regulators were supposed to enforce these rules. In effect, the regulators were required to suspend their normal attention to prudent lending. Loans they formerly would have criticized, they now had to consider good loans. In a letter sent to shareholders, the chairman of a local bank in Colorado described the difficulties of dealing with the regulators about CRA (the name of the bank has been withheld for obvious reasons):

> Under the umbrella of the Community Reinvestment Act (CRA), a tremendous amount of pressure was put on banks by the regulatory authorities to make loans, especially mortgage loans, to low income borrowers and neighborhoods. The regulators were very heavy handed regarding this issue. I will not dwell on it here but they required [our bank] to change its mortgage lending practices to meet certain CRA goals, even though we argued the changes were risky and imprudent.[12]

---

12 A single pool of "collateral" (a group of mortgages) can be used to create tranches that differ in risk because they have different priority claims on the cash flows from the mortgages, much like senior and junior debt of a corporation, with an equity residual at the "bottom." Basically, all asset-backed (including mortgage-backed) securities' structures incorporate this design.

In the end, CRA did not produce enough weak loans to create a financial crisis, but it began the process of degrading the quality of mortgages to make them affordable for borrowers who had previously not been able to meet normal lending standards in the prime market. The flexible underwriting standards that the government wanted the banks to use really meant lowering down payments and not insisting on income, a steady job, or unblemished credit. The low-quality mortgages that were required by CRA—and approved by bank regulators—gradually spread to the rest of the mortgage market. By 2006, almost half of all mortgages made in the United States were subprime or Alt-A.

The vehicles for creating this astonishing growth of low-quality loans were two companies that were also subject—like regulated banks—to direct control by Congress: Fannie Mae and Freddie Mac. Being GSEs, Fannie and Freddie were—until they were taken over in September 2008 because they were insolvent—shareholder-owned entities that were chartered by Congress to perform a specific government mission. Initially, this mission was to maintain a liquid secondary market in residential mortgages, but their mission was expanded in 1992 to include promoting affordable housing. This obligation was backed up by regulatory authority that Congress granted to the US Department of Housing and Urban Development (HUD). HUD's affordable housing regulations, implementing the new affordable housing mission of the two GSEs, were to be very important elements in the growth of subprime and other low-quality mortgages.

The importance of the GSEs sprang from their ability to access substantial and low-cost funding because of their perceived connection to the US government. There were many reasons for this perception, but the fact that they were chartered by Congress to perform a government mission was probably the most important. Their government backing enabled them to raise funds cheaply—paying only a little more than the US Treasury itself—and in virtually unlimited amounts. In addition, their capital requirements were set by statute at a very low level, so they were able to operate at leverage of 60:1. These advantages enabled them to dominate the mortgage finance market; by 2003, they were buying about 57 percent of all mortgages made that year and 79 percent of all the loans that fell within their lending limits.

HUD's requirements that Fannie and Freddie promote affordable housing were gradually escalated over the years. Initially, in the early 1990s, 30 percent of the mortgages that Fannie and Freddie purchased from banks and other originators had to be loans made to low- and moderate-income (LMI) borrowers. By 2005, about 55 percent had to be LMI and 25 percent had to be to low- or very low-income borrowers. The real work in reducing the quality of mortgage loans was, therefore, done by Fannie and Freddie, operating under the lash of HUD's affordable housing regulations.

By the time they were taken over by the government in September 2008, Fannie and Freddie were responsible for the credit risk on approximately $5.3 trillion in mortgages that they either held in portfolio or had guaranteed through MBS. Thus, when Fannie and Freddie started to reduce the quality of the loans they would buy from banks and others, it had a real impact on what kinds of loans the market produced. Their initial steps were modest, and the subprime and Alt-A loans they bought were generally of high quality within that group. But by 1998, Fannie was offering a mortgage with a 3 percent down payment, and by 2001, a mortgage with no down payment at all. During the 2000-03 period, when unusually low interest rates drove huge numbers of refinancings, Fannie and Freddie bought about $1.3 trillion of subprime and Alt-A loans and securities, amounting to about 25 percent of their total purchases in those years. Many of these would be prepaid or refinanced in later years because they were made to buyers who could not, or had no intention to, pay the cost of these loans when interest rates rose. As long as housing prices were rising, it was possible for home buyers to prepay their mortgages by selling the home for more than the principal amount of the loan, or in cases where they received a low "teaser" rate, to refinance into another short-term loan at a low rate before the loan reset to a higher market-based rate.

But in 2004, both GSEs started on what can only be called a binge. Over the period from late 2004 to 2007, when interest rates had risen again and refinancings were not driving volume, they purchased about $1.7 trillion in subprime and Alt-A loans—about 50 percent of their total purchases during a period when originations and refinancings were substantially lower than in the earlier period. At the time they were taken over by the government, the remnants of their earlier purchases amounted to $1.6 trillion in mortgages and securities—about 10 million loans and 34 percent of their single-family portfolio.

As a result primarily of Fannie's and Freddie's purchases, homeownership rates rose. From the 1960s until about 1995, the rate in the United States had remained at about 64 percent, but after that year, it began to rise. By 2000, it had risen to 67.3 percent, and to a high point of 69.2 percent in 2004. So, the policy of increasing homeownership did work, but the unintended consequences were disastrous. Fannie's and Freddie's own losses will probably cost the taxpayers about $400 billion, perhaps more. But the other costs—the current financial crisis—are far worse.

Fannie's and Freddie's Role in the Financial Crisis

The connection between the GSEs' purchases and the current crisis is important to understand. Fannie's and Freddie's funding advantages allowed them to drive all private-sector competition to the edges of the housing finance market. This meant that Wall Street commercial and investment banks were relegated to buying and securitizing two kinds of mortgages—*jumbos*, which exceeded the size Fannie and Freddie were permitted by law to buy, and *junk*, which until the early 2000s, Fannie and Freddie would not buy in substantial amounts. For this reason, the subprime and Alt-A market was relatively small; the secondary market in these loans was carried on by commercial and investment banks, which would buy mortgages from the originators, package them into pools, and sell MBS backed by the payments of principal and interest on the mortgages in the pool. The pools were structured to create "tranches," or classes of securities with the same collateral but different levels of risk. The lowest-risk tranche was typically rated AAA by the rating agencies; other tranches bore other ratings (sometimes also as high as AAA); and the highest-risk tranche was a small equity piece at the bottom of the structure.

This market was growing until 2003, when in the midst of a huge refinancing boom Fannie and Freddie started buying large amounts of the AAA tranches of the pools—known as "private label"—that Wall Street was creating. These purchases doubled in 2003 to $82 billion and doubled again in 2004 to $180 billion. In 2004, probably because they thought it was more efficient than paying Wall Street's fees for intermediation, they decided to buy large amounts of subprime and Alt-A loans directly from originators. Their chairmen—Franklin Raines of Fannie and Richard Syron of Freddie—went to meetings of mortgage bankers and other orig-inators and asked for the mortgages of people with blemished credit. These loans were of substantial assistance to Fannie and Freddie in reaching HUD's increas-ingly ambitious affordable housing goals.

When someone with virtually unlimited funds asks for something as easy to deliver as subprime and Alt-A mortgages, the result is just as easy to predict: There was a huge frenzy at the originator level to produce the subprime and Alt-A loans that would then be sold to the GSEs or to the Wall Street investment banks and to commercial banks. In 2005, the GSEs began to buy large quantities of subprime and Alt-A loans directly from mortgage bankers and other firms, such as Countrywide Financial, that specialized in originating subprime and Alt-A loans. Meanwhile, they continued to buy AAA rated tranches of mortgage-backed secu-rities from Wall Street—more than $500 billion of them between 2005 and 2007.

The GSEs' purchases—driven by their need to meet HUD's increasingly tough affordable housing regulations—affected the market for subprime and Alt-A loans in three ways. First, by increasing competition for these loans, the GSEs' purchases drove down the risk premiums that subprime loans usually carried, putting more potential buyers with blemished credit in a position to qualify for mortgages. Second, the competition between the GSEs and Wall Street drove the numbers of subprime and Alt-A loans still higher. And finally, the quality of these loans increasingly declined; the competitors were scraping the bottom of the potential borrower barrel. During this period, conventional prime loans (including jumbo loans) declined from 69 percent of all mortgages in 2003 to 36 percent at the end of 2006, and subprime and Alt-A loans increased from 20 percent of all origina-tions to 46 percent. In 2006, almost half of all mortgages made in the United States were subprime and Alt-A loans. The GSEs were responsible for buying 39 percent of 2006 originations of subprime and Alt-A loans. In the end, including the loans underlying the AAA rated tranches that they bought from Wall Street, Fannie and Freddie held or guaranteed 34 percent of all subprime mortgages and 60 percent of all the Alt-A loans that were outstanding on 30 June 2008.

Although many have argued that it was Wall Street that led the subprime boom, that claim is disproven by the total number of subprime and Alt-A mortgages that Fannie and Freddie ultimately became responsible for. As subprime and Alt-A loans became a larger and larger proportion of all mortgages in the United States, it was the purchases by Fannie and Freddie that drove this growth. The conventional wisdom—that they were trying to compete for market share with Wall Street—seems contradicted by the fact that Fannie and Freddie ultimately acquired nearly as many of these mortgages as the rest of the market combined. The more plausible way to look at the issue is that Fannie and Freddie were, by and large, the creators of the subprime and Alt-A boom and that they did this for political reasons (discussed later) and *not* for the economic reasons that would motivate a Wall Street firm. They first stimulated the development of the Wall Street acquisition and distribution system by purchasing huge amounts of AAA rated private label tranches. Then, in late 2004, they began to buy these junk loans in ever larger amounts themselves, competing for product with Wall Street.

The GSEs' binge on subprime and Alt-A loans was obviously a disastrous business policy; it eventually destroyed two companies that had solid gold franchises. But it was also responsible for turning what would have been a troubling housing-bubble deflation into a worldwide financial crisis. Although US taxpayers will have to bear the losses that Fannie and Freddie will realize from their purchases of subprime and Alt-A loans, banks and other financial intermediaries in the United States and around the world will suffer equally large losses because of the MBS—based in part on subprime and Alt-A loans—that they purchased from Wall Street banks and securities firms. Although these are not the direct responsibility of Fannie and Freddie, the GSEs bear indirect responsibility for stimulating the explosive growth in junk mortgage loans beginning in 2004.

Why It Happened

The pressures that drove Fannie and Freddie to buy junk mortgages are complex. Most commentators point to their desire to take market share from Wall Street, but as noted earlier, this is highly implausible. Fannie and Freddie had funding at such low cost that they had no serious competition for any assets they were allowed to buy. Once Fannie and Freddie began to enter the market for subprime and Alt-A loans, it was just a matter of time before the Wall Street banks and securities firms would lose substantial portions of their market. Only an *expansion* of the market—the growth in subprime and Alt-A loans—would enable them to maintain a profitable business. So, the real question for policymakers is why Fannie and Freddie entered this market with such force beginning in late 2004.

One answer, of course, is HUD's affordable housing regulations. It is clear that the regulations were influential in determining what securities Fannie and Freddie purchased; subprime and Alt-A loans were both "goal rich" in terms of complying with the increasingly tight requirements for promoting "affordable" housing. We do not know the nature of any conversations that might have been held between the GSEs and the officials at HUD who oversaw the development of these regulations. But we do know from internal e-mail messages at Freddie and memoranda that were prepared at Fannie that both companies were well aware of the risks they were taking. It is difficult to believe that if the sole reason for taking those risks was to meet HUD's regulatory requirements, these risks could not have been brought to HUD's attention. In addition, many in the subprime housing business argue that there were plenty of high-quality subprime loans available in the market, but the GSEs did not look for them.

The most likely answer is that Fannie and Freddie were trying to retain support in Congress that would prevent new and tougher regulation. In 2003 and 2004, both companies had accounting scandals; they were found to have been manipulating their financial reports—to smooth earnings in Freddie's case and to hide massive hedging losses in Fannie's. At the time, there was a Republican Congress and a hostile Republican administration, raising the possibility that Congress might adopt legislation authorizing tough new regulation. Indeed, legislation of this kind passed the Senate Banking Committee in 2005 but never received a vote on the Senate floor. Alan Greenspan—who was highly regarded on Capitol Hill—was warning in virtually every appearance before Congress that the GSEs could cause a financial meltdown if they were not curbed, and economists at the Fed had recently done a study that showed the GSEs were not even successful in reducing interest rates for middle-class home buyers—the central justification they always claimed for their existence.

Under these circumstances, it is likely that Fannie and Freddie hoped to curry favor with their supporters in Congress by showing that they could boost home-ownership rates, especially in low-income communities. If that was their strategy, it worked; there was no new legislation that curbed their activities until July 2008. But by then, it was too late.

Conclusion

Explanations for the current financial crisis range widely: Some see it as a crisis or failure of capitalism; others see it as a case of excessive deregulation or just not enough regulation. Still others cite the Fed's failure to raise interest rates quickly enough after the economy began to recover from the dot-com collapse. There is no question that a housing bubble grew in the first seven years of the 21st century and then abruptly collapsed. But housing and other asset bubbles have deflated rapidly before without such dire consequences. The reason that this housing-price deflation created what is essentially a worldwide financial crisis is that the mortgages produced in the United States, beginning early in the 2000s and accelerating until 2007, were of much lower quality than had ever been true in the past. Not only were borrowers of lower credit quality, but also the loans themselves were not backed by the down payments or other equity that encouraged borrowers to continue making mortgage payments after housing values fell below the principal amount of the mortgage. Thus, the most plausible explanation for the extraordinary losses associated with the collapse of this bubble is the unprecedented growth of subprime and Alt-A mortgages in the United States. At the height of the housing bubble, in 2006, almost half of all mortgages originated in the United States were subprime or Alt-A. When these mortgages began to default, it was at unprecedented rates, weakening the financial condition of banks and other financial intermediaries around the world.

The growth of the market in subprime and Alt-A loans can be directly attributed to the policies of the US government. For much of the 20th century, the government attempted to foster homeownership in the United States. In most cases, the government took the risks associated with this policy. But beginning in the 1990s, Congress and the administration began to require that private enterprises—insured banks and the GSEs Fannie Mae and Freddie Mac—take on the risks of lending to potential home buyers who did not have the credit records or resources to meet their obligations. In this process, the usual mortgage standards that prevailed in the private housing finance market were eroded, and the housing bubble was gradually engorged with poor-quality mortgages. Without this factor—the element of government policy—the collapse of the great housing bubble of the early 21st century would not have been nearly as calamitous.

Source: American Enterprise Institute. 2 Dec. 2009. Web. http://www.aei.org/papers/economics/fiscal-policy/not-a-failure-of-capitalism--a-failure-of-government/.

WHAT IT SAYS

1. Wallison opens his essay by discussing the responses to the financial crisis of other "pundits." What have these pundits said about the crisis? What have they said about the "failure of capitalism"?

2. To which "critics of the system" does Wallison direct his argument? How can you tell? What are the causes of the crisis, according to these critics?

3. What caused the financial crisis, according to Wallison? How does his explanation differ from those of other critics? According to Wallison, what has been the role of government in the crisis? What should it be?

4. What are the "errors" that Wallison finds in the argument of Judge Richard Posner as shown in the passage from Posner that Wallison cites? Explain the corrections that Wallison makes to Posner's claims.

5. What is Wallison's point regarding "the so-called repeal of the Glass-Steagall Act of 1933" and the "'Deregulation' of Credit Default Swaps"?

HOW IT SAYS IT

1. How does Wallison treat his opponents, those whose views he criticizes? In particular, what is his attitude toward Richard Posner? Point to specific words and phrases that reveal his attitude.

2. How does Wallison's treatment of Posner's argument help him to advance his own? What opportunities does Posner's passage provide for Wallison?

3. Describe the overall organization of Wallison's essay. How do subsections and subheadings help to organize and advance his claims?

WRITE ABOUT IT

1. Using Wallison's premises and terms consistent with his analysis, write an essay that makes recommendations for avoiding another severe economic crisis like the one that occurred in 2008.

2. Explain the financial crisis in a way that opposes the explanations given by Wallison. Be sure to account for some of the factors that Wallison points to. What doesn't Wallison take into consideration? Where does his explanation go wrong? Explain why your interpretation of events is better than his.

d. Stephen Resnick and Richard Wolff, "The Economic Crisis: A Marxian Interpretation"

Stephen Resnick (1938-2013) was a professor emeritus of economics at the University of Massachussetts, Amherst. Over the last 25 years of his career, in collaboration with his colleague Richard Wolff, Resnick developed a Marxian approach to political economy that retains the class analysis of classical Marxism yet rejects the economic determinism—the idea that all human decision-making boils down to economics—often found in other economic theories, as well as in Marxism itself.

In 1988, Resnick was a founder, with Wolff and others, of the Association of Economic and Social Analysis (AESA) and its quarterly journal *Rethinking Marxism*. In addition to books and articles co-authored with Wolff, Resnick was the author, with Thomas Birnberg, of *Colonial Development: An Econometric Study* (1975). He also co-edited numerous anthologies with Wolff and others. Resnick received a BS from the University of Pennsylvania and a PhD from the Massachusetts Institute of Technology.

Richard D. Wolff is professor emeritus of economics at the University of Massachusetts, Amherst, where he taught economics from 1973 to 2008. He is currently a visiting professor in the graduate program in international affairs at New School University, New York City. Wolff earned a BA in history from Harvard College, an MA in economics from Stanford University, an MA in history from Yale University, and a PhD in economics from Yale University. In addition to books co-authored with Resnick (mentioned below), Wolff is also the author of *Capitalism Hits the Fan: The Global Economic Meltdown and What to Do About It* (2009), and *Democracy at Work: A Cure for Capitalism* (2012), among others.

Wolff and Resnick have co-authored numerous books and articles. Their books include *Knowledge and Class: A Critique of Political Economy* (1987), *Economics: Marxism vs. Neoclassical* (1987), *Bringing It All Back Home: Class, Gender, and Power in the Modern Household* (also with Harriet Fraad, 1994), *Class Theory and History: Capitalism and Communism in the USSR* (2002), *Challenging Capitalism* (2012), *Contending Economic Theories: Neoclassical, Keynesian, and Marxian* (2012).

In this essay, originally published in *Rethinking Marxism* in 2010, Resnick and Wolff argue that the economic crisis of 2008 resulted, at least in part, from the class structure of capitalism, in particular the intensified exploitation of workers over several decades, and the increasing debt load that they carried to compensate for real wage stagnation.

As You Read: Consider what you've heard about "socialism" or "Marxism" in the media or from family and friends. How does your impression of socialism compare with what you encounter in Resnick and Wolff's essay? How does their explanation of the crisis square with your own experiences of the economic situation over the past several years?

The Economic Crisis: A Marxian Interpretation

Like most capitalist crises, today's challenges economists, journalists, and politicians to explain and to overcome it. The post-1930s struggles between neoclassical and Keynesian economics are rejoined. We show that both proved inadequate to preventing crises and served rather to enable and justify (as "solutions" for crises) what were merely oscillations between two forms of capitalism differentiated according to greater or lesser state economic interventions. Our Marxian economic analysis here proceeds differently. We demonstrate how concrete aspects of US economic history (especially real wage, productivity, and personal indebtedness trends) culminated in this deep and enduring crisis. We offer both a class-based critique of and an alternative to neoclassical and Keynesian analyses, including an alternative solution to capitalist crises.

Key Words: Capitalist Crisis, Exploitation, Keynesian Economics, Neoclassical Economics, Marxian Economics

Two different and contending mainstream theories have explained capitalism's repeated crises over the last century. Each time each theory proposed correspondingly different solutions. Today's crisis is no exception. One theory—called, after one of its founders, "Keynesian economics"—claims that unregulated private markets inevitably yield price movements that react back on the decisions of businesses, workers, and consumers to produce out-of-control price spirals. These periodically push the economy into inflations, recessions, or even depressions. Without intervention from outside, capitalism's private economy may remain depressed or inflated long enough to threaten capitalism itself. Keynesian—or now more generally "macro"—economics identifies the key private economy mechanisms that produce cyclical crises. These range from market imperfections arising from agents' unequal and/or unfair access to information to a plethora of noneconomic causes typically grouped together as "animal spirits."[1] Political

---

1   Perhaps Joseph Stiglitz is the most important and best-known macroeconomist arguing that unfettered markets yield cyclical crises. The animal spirits argument first appeared in Keynes (1964, 161); it refers to how the expected yield of business investment in relation to its cost is "determined by the uncontrollable and disobedient psychology of the business world" (317). Everything and anything shapes "business psychology," hence the central causal role of "animal spirits" in governing capitalist investment behavior and why it fluctuates. This kind of argument is nicely summarized and extended to today's economic world in Akerlof and Shiller (2009).

fear combines with macroeconomics to organize and enact state interventions aimed at counteracting the unwanted extremes of capitalism's inherent instability. "Regulate, regulate" is the Keynesian prophets' mantra.

The other mainstream theory is associated with Adam Smith, the classical "founder of modern economics" who first celebrated the private capitalist economy (free markets plus private property) as uniquely enabling society to produce the maximum wealth it is capable of. In its evolved form, it has come to be known as "neoclassical" or, more generally, microeconomics. Neoclassical economics continues the project of showing how and why an economy of privately owned means of production and free, competitive markets yields the best ("optimum") of all possible economic outcomes. When, occasionally, a nonoptimal outcome occurs, it likely follows from some market "imperfection" that is, from the neoclassical perspective, probably the result of some perhaps well-intentioned but fundamentally misguided state intervention. The best solution then is to let private markets and private enterprises heal themselves via their internal mechanisms. Neoclassical economists typically denounce Keynesian-inspired state interventions, including their incessant market regulations as inevitably yielding regulators' mistakes, politically manipulated markets, and the resulting inefficiencies including inflation, stagnation, and stagflation. State officials cannot replace, let alone improve upon, the market mechanism that accommodates the infinity of different demands and supplies, communicates the infinity of information far more efficiently than any state could, and generates the incentives leading individual buyers and sellers to correct whatever excesses appear. "Deregulate, deregulate" is the neoclassical economists' mantra.

As today's global capitalist crisis unfolds, Keynesian state interventions are everywhere on the rise after more than thirty years of marginalization. Since the 1970s, neoclassical economists had effectively reversed and suppressed such interventions in a global movement called "neoliberalism." They were reacting against the domination of Keynesians and Keynesian macroeconomics in the aftermath of the Great Depression of the 1930s. The neoclassical economists had always attacked the Keynesian state interventions associated with Franklin Delano Roosevelt's New Deal for seriously constraining and distorting the economy's growth and thereby promoting social conflict (sometimes dubbed "class war"). They sought to reinstitute Smith's grand vision of a growing capitalism: private and competitive markets lifting the real incomes of both labor and capital and thereby avoiding the "class conflicts" associated with insufficient growth.

In the 1970s, neoclassical economics displaced Keynesian economics globally. Market deregulation and privatization became the official and prevailing principles of business, politics, journalism, and academia. Neoclassical economics became once again, as it had been before the Great Depression, the modern economics. Its other—Keynesian economics—was banished as a relic of earlier misunderstandings of how economies "really" worked. The dominance of neoclassical microeconomics went so far as to spawn a generation of "new" Keynesians who reformulated their paradigm as an extension/application of neoclassical economics. Unrepentant Keynesians who refused to become "new" in this way found their professional advances blocked and their careers often ended. Such extreme intolerance of differences between neoclassical and Keynesian economics in the realms of theory, academic discipline, and professional careers replicated the ways both of them had jointly suppressed Marxian economics since the late 1940s.

From the 1970s onward, deregulation of markets yielded, at first, the changed incentives, prices, and growth the neoclassicists had promised. As the years passed however, the economy also exhibited the market swings, uneven income and wealth developments, and eventual economic bubbles in stock markets, real estate, and finance darkly predicted by Keynesian critics. Then the new millennium opened with a stock market crash followed a few years later by a real estate collapse, a liquidity crisis, and now a deep recession threatening to slide into a depression of major proportions. Neoclassical economists are in retreat and the Keynesians are emerging out of their banishment. Paradoxically, the latter find allies (business leaders whose survival suddenly depends on government largesse) among some stalwart former defenders of the market system.

The Keynesian message remains what it always was: the state must save capitalism from itself. It has become, again, today's wisdom. Faced with the current crisis, fewer neoclassical economists still advocate what has become yesterday's wisdom: markets yield prosperity and growth and occasionally heal problems without much, if any, need of state intervention.

However, we have not lost confidence in the ability of neoclassical economics to reemerge again someday to reaffirm their old program of deregulation of markets. Our confidence in their restorative powers rests on the continuation of a capitalism that will give rise to future economic problems and crises, including those fostered by the very Keynesian regulations instituted today. Neoclassical economics had reemerged before in the 1970s when it undid many of the Keynesian interventions that had aimed to overcome the Great Depression of the 1930s and prevent future depressions. We see little compelling evidence not to expect yet another future neoclassical revival if today's crisis results in no more than a Keynesian response.

Indeed, the repeated oscillations between the two theories and their associate policy prescriptions emerge also from a fundamental perspective both sides share. They largely agree that the market system is the best of all known mechanisms to allocate resources efficiently. Many would add that markets also allocate resources equitably. They claim that fully competitive markets enable those who contribute to wealth production to receive rewards (incomes) exactly equal to the size of their contribution. Where the two sides differ is in how to insulate and protect the market system from the criticisms and movements for state economic interventions that flow from citizens who suffer from the economy's recurring recessions and inflations. Against the criticism and movement, one side argues to "leave the market alone so that it can find its way to a new, efficient, and just solution." "No," says the other. "We need state intervention to help guide the market's search for a new and efficient solution." Capitalism—defined as private enterprise and free markets—remains the optimum system for both sides in terms of wealth creation and social welfare.

Both sides thus share a profound conservatism vis-à-vis capitalism, despite holding radically different views on the need for state intervention. The oscillation between them serves their shared conservatism. It prevents crises in capitalism from becoming crises of capitalism, when the system itself is placed in question. It does this by shaping and containing the public debate provoked by crisis-caused social suffering. When serious crises hit a deregulated capitalism, the two sides debate whether the solution is regulation or letting the system heal itself. When serious crises hit a regulated capitalism, the two sides debate whether the solution is deregulation or more or different regulation. This effectively keeps from public debate any serious consideration of an alternative solution to capitalism's recurring crises: namely, transition to an economic system other than and different from capitalism.

A Marxian Analysis

An alternative to both neoclassical and Keynesian explanations and solutions for capitalist crises emanates from the Marxian tradition. Its explanation stresses neither what Keynesians focus on (destabilizing maneuvers by self-seeking individual consumers, producers, merchants, and banks facing an inherently uncertain economy and/or possessing asymmetrical information in regard to markets) nor what neoclassicists pinpoint (market-destabilizing concentrations of private power by market participants and/or public power by the state). Rather, Marxian theory pursues the connections between capitalism's crises and its distinctive class structure (its particular juxtaposition of capitalists appropriating and distributing the surpluses workers produce). We propose to show these connections in the rest of this paper. On that basis, Marxian theory reaches very different conclusions from those of the neoclassical and Keynesian economists. Briefly, durable solutions to capitalist crises require, in the Marxian view, transition to a different class structure. That is because capitalism's class structure has so systematically and repeatedly contributed to crises in both the regulated and deregulated forms of capitalism. That is why Marxian theory does not share the fundamental conservatism of both neoclassical and Keynesian economics vis-à-vis capitalism.

Exploitation and US History

Not surprisingly, our Marxian explanation connects the current capitalist crisis in the United States to exploited workers and exploiting capitalists.[2] The failure of US capitalism in 2008-09 has deep class roots in the previous 120 years. From the early 1890s to the late 1970s, two key trends emerged in industry. In one, the real wage of workers in manufacturing rose by about 1.8 percent per year and, in the other, workers' productivity in manufacturing steadily rose at an even higher rate amounting to 2.3 percent per year.[3] Roughly interpreting these two trends in terms of Marxian value theory, we conclude that the rate of surplus value in the United States—the growth of real output per industrial worker relative to the real remuneration per industrial worker—rose steadily for almost ninety years. In Marx's language, that century saw US capitalism deliver a surplus to its capitalists that rose faster than the real wages of workers. Workers were ever more exploited (the excess of the value added by their labor over the value paid for their labor power), but they were also ever better paid. We doubt any other capitalism, then or ever, delivered such results for so long. It drew tens of millions of immigrants and propelled the United States into its global superpower position.

That century was a sustained success for US capitalism. Capitalists' steadily rising surpluses were distributed effectively to expand and enhance the conditions for their class exploitation. Such distributions thereby yielded an ever growing surplus to fund further distributions in the cumulative growth of US capitalism to global hegemony. The diversity of capitalists' different surplus distributions illustrates the socially transformative scope of US capitalist development. Sizeable portions of the surplus went for capital accumulation (machines, factories, infra-structure, etc.) that directly expanded workers' outputs (and hence expanded surpluses). Newly expanded means of production often embodied new technol-ogies that raised labor productivity, lowered unit values of consumer goods, and hence raised the rate of exploitation. Surplus devoted to cover research and devel-opment expenses created a flood of new industries and their new commodities embodying ever more surpluses. The uses of surpluses to fund growing corporate bureaucracies (investing in the "intangible asset" of management) enabled them to extract increased surpluses from their workers.[4] The portion of the surplus

---

2   To avoid ambiguity about what we mean by "connect," we do not aim to reduce capitalist crises to an underlying class cause. We reject essentialist explanation of all kinds, Marxian or non-Marxian. Rather, we wish to add class as one of many contributing and interacting causes of economic crisis; in this we are mindful of the exclusion of class from most other analyses of the crisis.

3   These are average annual growth rates calculated from the data described in the note on sources. The growth of real wages and productivity is calculated from 1890 to 1978.

4   The term "intangible asset" is taken from Teece, Pisano, and Shuen (1997, 521). The authors present a view of the importance of corporate management—in our Marxian terms, a subsumed class of corporate managers—in shaping (overdetermining) the present and future profitability (surplus value) of enterprises.

paid to merchants (usually in the form of discounts on capitalist commodities sold to them) was less than what capitalists had had to pay their own sales staffs. Effectively economizing on the costs of selling, and thereby generating a major wholesale and retail trade system, capitalists had that much more surplus to distribute elsewhere. The portion of their appropriated surpluses that industrial capitalists paid to banks as interest gave them access to the savings of others used for additional productive investment, research and development, and expanded and improved corporate bureaucracies and thus more surplus. Likewise, surplus paid out as dividends to share owners enabled capitalist corporations to tap yet another source of money for investment by selling such shares publicly. Finally, the portion of capitalists' surplus paid as taxes enabled and pressured federal, state, and local governments to provide the infrastructure (laws, road systems, education, health services, the military, new research and its yield of new products and technology, and so on) that lowered capitalists' costs and facilitated rising surplus production.

The genius of US capitalism before the 1970s consisted in the combination of rising real wages, surpluses rising faster, and surplus distributions that reacted back to reinforce the pattern of rising wages and faster-rising surpluses. The possibility of such a capitalism was articulated in Marx's *Capital*, as were the contradictions. In volume 1, Marx identifies, locates, and analyzes workers' production of the surplus value appropriated by their capitalist employers. In volumes 2 and 3, Marx elaborates capitalists' distribution of the surplus value they have appropriated to secure the conditions of their positions atop a growing capitalist system. Although repeatedly punctuated by crises, the century of US capitalism ending in the 1970s exemplified the self-expansion possible if and when sufficient surpluses were appropriated (the argument of volume 1) and effectively distributed (the argument of volumes 2 and 3). However, Marxian theory also stresses the contradictions in every system. Capitalism's particular contradictions were also illustrated in US history as the system's success coexisted with its failure. The other side of the workers' rising real wages was deepening exploitation. The ever louder nationalist celebration of a merely formal democracy and equality thus coexisted with—and served ideologically to obscure—an ever widening real divide between a growing mass of exploited workers and an ever more concentrated elite of multinational corporate capitalists and their various "hangers on."

Yet few among the surplus producers and fewer still among those who lived off surplus distributions acknowledged the social costs and miseries arising from the relative disparity growing across US history. Most public debate missed the connections between capitalist exploitation and social problems such as urban decay, corruption, crime, family disintegration, personal and civic alienation, and wars. The notion of poverty as linked to capitalists' refusal to employ workers (because of their profit considerations, cyclical crises, etc.) was widely repressed in favor of blame-the-victim alternatives (for example, unemployed workers lacked requisite qualifications or preferred leisure to paid work). The recurring capitalist crises themselves were rarely connected to capitalist exploitation and its underlying class structure; rather, they were caused by the "greed" of a few "bad apples," inappropriate government action or criminal misbehavior, animal spirits haunting individual and group decisions, or unintended consequences arising from market imperfections. Because of the neglected connection of the capitalist class structure to economic crises, we focus here on that connection to the current crisis.

Rising Exploitation with Rising Real Wages

From the last decade of the nineteenth century to the last third of the twentieth century, rising workers' real wages allowed rising consumption levels. Over those decades, new meanings came to be deeply attached to workers consuming more goods and services. Personal consumption became the standard by which workers measured personal success in life: their own and almost everyone else's. More consumption, quantitative and/or qualitative, was equated with more pleasure derived therefrom. Career choices and marriages were undertaken with a growing focus on their prospects for rising consumption. Parents defined their suitability as such in terms of enabling their children to consume more and hence live better lives. Education promised better-paying jobs and higher levels of consumption. What you consume merged into what you are.

Perhaps no great surprise should arise then at the origin, explosive growth, and central place of advertising in American life. Its social function was and is to persuade individuals to buy as much as possible of what advertisers' clients sell. Advertising accelerated transformation of the simple acts of buying and consuming into essential strategies for achieving the American dream. Show others who you really are by consuming accordingly. Fool others by cleverly buying and consuming cheap imitations of more costly goods and services. Faced with widespread social acceptance of consumption as the key standard of personal success and achievement, dissenting religious leaders, politicians, writers, and others have sometimes reacted with critical denunciations of "materialism." Their recurring reactions are another index of the social power, influence, and celebration of consumption in the United States, henceforth referred to as consumerism.

Consumerism stands in a special relationship to US workers' lack of awareness of their class exploitation. Consumerism conceptualized rising wages and consumption levels as the full and appropriate compensation for workers' wage labor. By stressing that capitalism recognized and rewarded workers appropriately, even generously, consumerism effectively displaced Marxian concepts of workers' exploitation. Indeed, the very term "exploited" was redefined to mean that minority of workers temporarily and perhaps unfairly denied the wages and consumption standards capitalism normally delivered to all workers. Consumerism affirmed that rising consumption proved that (1) capitalism could and would "deliver the goods," and (2) high and rising individual consumption levels in capitalist societ-ies reflected their superiority to any socialist alternative. Of course, consumerism alone did not suppress Marxian explanations; government repression and procap-italist ideological campaigns waged by business, religious, and other groups also contributed. So, too, did the relentless association of personal liberties with private enterprise and free markets against oppressive government intrusion associated (when not simply equated) with socialism. However, consumerism helped lever-age US capitalism's successful growth from 1890 to 1970 into a profound mass disinclination to confront class exploitation, its social costs, or its root in the capi-talist class structure, as argued in Marxian explanations.

Rising Exploitation with Constant Real Wages

Starting in the late 1970s and continuing thereafter, real wages of industrial workers in the United States stopped rising. This was a profound change from the record of the previous ninety years. While manufacturing productivity continued to rise (at a rate of 3.26 percent per year from 1978 to 2007), real wages paid workers in manufacturing remained more or less constant and even fell a bit from then to today (declining slightly at a rate of -0.37 per year between 1978 and 2007). We present these two series in Figure 6.1, based on the data sources described below. Employers kept getting more and more output per worker (the productivity line),

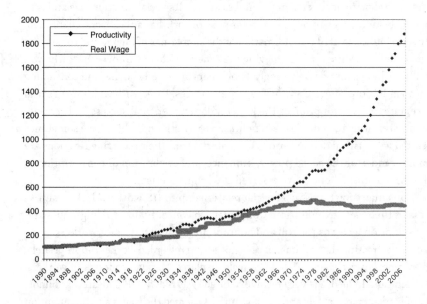

FIGURE 6.1. Indexes of Output and Real Wages per Hour, Manufacturing, 1890-2007. Index 1890 =100.

but no longer had to pay the workers more (the real wage line). Workers no longer shared in productivity gains; the latter thus raised surpluses even faster than before. In Marxian terms, the rate of exploitation (the ratio of surplus value to the value of labor power) rose steadily to possibly unprecedented heights. The social divide between producers and appropriators of the surplus surged as well. Most important, the end of rising real wages closed an era. The impact on the United States cannot be overstated; a capitalism that had come to define, celebrate, and defend itself by reference to rising consumption enabled by rising wages for its workers could no longer do so. The impact was all the greater because no public debate about the meaning and implications of the change occurred. Workers experienced and reacted to the change as a personal and individual matter rather than as a sweeping social change.

The post-1970s explosion of surplus value production transformed US capitalism. Wealth poured into capitalists' accounts as they appropriated ever more surpluses from workers who no longer needed to be paid rising real wages. Since most capitalist enterprise in the United States is corporate, the results were a stunning expansion of corporate wealth, power, and influence over all of society. Corporate boards of directors distributed most of the exploding surpluses partly to themselves (as skyrocketing top managerial salaries, stock options, and bonuses) and partly to lower-level managers (as their remuneration and operating budgets), bankers (interest and fees), merchants (discounted wholesale and retail prices), share owners (dividends), and owners of land and technology (rents). These groups prospered while the vast mass of workers found life increasingly difficult, as we explore below.

Why Real Wages Stopped Rising

By the late 1970s, a severe problem confronted US capitalists: they were appropriating ever larger surpluses, but new demands for distributions of those surpluses were rising even faster. Corporate managers demanded more of the surplus to undertake capital accumulation and improved technologies to compete more effectively with foreign competition. The special period after World War II, when no serious competitors confronted US capitalists, had ended. Western European and Japanese capitalists had rebuilt their industrial capacities with an effective eye to outcompete the dominant Americans.[5] At the same time, government officials demanded huge distributions of the surplus, chiefly in the form of corporate taxes, not only to finance the continued postwar dominance of America, but also to fund a host of social programs directed at the increasingly restive poor, the newly rediscovered "other America." Labor unions continued to

---

5   In Marxian terms, US industrial enterprises (in steel, autos, rubber products, and electronics) were losing superprofits to foreign competitors. This reduced available supplies of surpluses to capitalists in these industries while surplus demands rose.

use their state-sanctioned monopoly power to press for ever more of the surplus to go back to workers in the form of higher wages and health and pension benefits. Corporations took the lead in devising strategies to cope with the disjunction between appropriated surplus and distributional demands upon it.

By the end of the decade, a new president was elected who identified the state and unions as special interest groups that threatened all Americans. With compliant legislators and public opinion makers, he attacked unions, reduced chiefly corporate taxes and individual taxes on the rich, and deregulated. Ronald Reagan's new policy conformed to the neoclassicist strategy of eliminating the concentrations of power in society believed to thwart the otherwise smooth operation of an unfettered market system. With reduced tax collections, the state could do less (especially in terms of public employment) and/or became ever more dependent on buyers of government debt (chiefly corporations and the rich). Unions lost what legal and moral support the state once provided. Their eroded bargaining power undercut workers' abilities to win rising real wages and eventually benefits, too. The combination of flat real wages, reduced corporate taxes, and deregulated markets provided many capitalists with a "solution" to the immediate pressures on their surpluses. Neoclassical theory warranted these policies as good economics.

In Marxian terms, Reagan's policies enabled capitalists (1) to hire more labor power and make it more productive without raising wages and (2) to secure the state's services to business for lower tax payments. More surplus value was thereby produced and more was freed (by lower corporate tax obligations) to be redirected to expand capital accumulation, research and development budgets, and the costly shift of production facilities outside the United States where wages and other costs were far lower. A substantial and sustained entry of women into the labor force, partly a result of the long struggle of women to gain more control over their lives and partly due to the need to supplement pinched family incomes, only added to the downward pressure on real wages. Computerization of most workplaces across the country, starting in the 1970s, also changed the supply and demand conditions in labor markets to the detriment of real wages. Massive immigration in search of jobs and the American dream, actively abetted and abused by countless employers, likewise operated to undermine real wage increases. In these multiple ways, US capitalists sought to compete more successfully on the increasingly contested terrain of the emerging world economy. However, this preferred solution for capitalists produced new problems for US workers and the state. Capitalists' responses to their gains, together with workers' and the state's responses to their losses, eventually converged to become US capitalism's gravest crisis since the 1930s.

Workers' Response to the End of Rising Real Wages

The end of rising real wages confronted workers' families with a deep crisis. Would they forgo rising consumption since they lacked the rising wages to afford it? Given the significance of rising consumption and consumerism in US history, workers' answer proved to be a resounding no. Rising consumption was the realization of personal hopes, the sign of social success, the return on education, and the promise to one's children that one *had* to keep. With rising wages no longer available (nor any organized, social response by unions or social movements that had been seriously weakened since the 1960s), workers and their families responded individually.

First of all, in reaction to stagnating real hourly wages, workers' households sent more of their members to do more hours of labor. Husbands took second and even third jobs and/or worked additional hours at first jobs, teenagers took jobs after school, retirees returned to part- or full-time work, and most important, millions of housewives and mothers entered the labor markets. While these responses helped raise additional family income, the increased supply of labor further undermined any chance for real wages to resume rising, which reinforced the exodus of labor from households.

Increased paid labor by more members of workers' households imposed enormous personal costs and thereby social costs. Women increasingly held two full-time jobs, one outside and one inside households. Housework and childcare remained largely women's obligations even when they performed full-time paid labor. The added stress of this double shift altered and strained household relationships. The divorce rate rose as did signs of alienation (drug dependency and intrafamily abuse). The added costs of women's wage labor (in childcare, women's work clothes, transportation, purchased meals, cleaning expenses, drugs, counseling services, etc.) largely negated the net contribution that paid labor could make to resuming a trend toward rising consumption. Thus, another source of funds for that purpose had to be tapped.

That source was household debt. The Federal Reserve records a total household debt in 1975 of $734 billion. By 2006, it had risen to $12.817 trillion. This thirty-year debt explosion, mostly based on mortgages (what collateral workers possess, if any, is the home), had no precedent. Workers largely stopped saving and millions took on debt levels at or above what they could reasonably expect to sustain. Native-born and immigrants were determined to aim at the American dream no matter the risks and costs; so had the nation's history prepared them. By the new millennium, US workers were exhausted by their long labor hours, emotionally stressed by the disintegration of families and households, and extremely anxious about unprecedented debt levels.

In Marxian terms, the combination of roughly constant real wages with rising labor productivity in the production of wage goods meant that the value of labor power fell. More and more of the total value added by US workers took the form of surplus value appropriated by capitalist employers. What the mass of workers no longer got comprised the unprecedented gains of the relatively small group of surplus-appropriating capitalists and those favored by their enlarged distributions of those gains.

The Capitalists' Responses

The other side of the post-1970s squeezing of the American worker has been the expansion of the American capitalist. Over the last thirty years, the rate of exploitation outperformed its historic upward trend. As suggested by the widening gap between the productivity and real wage lines in our chart, it literally took off. Indeed, the remarkable shift in income distribution over these decades, favoring the very top income earners in the United States, reflects this rise in exploitation (Saez 2009).[6] Capitalists were drowning in fast-growing revenue inflows initially deposited (chiefly by the corporations who account for most sales) in banks and other financial institutions. From there, corporate boards of directors allocated the net (after replenishing used-up inputs and paying "nonsupervisory" employees) revenues in increasingly spectacular forms.

They enlarged the budgets, salaries, and bonuses of top corporate managers to produce a new "gilded" age for them. Their gaudy celebration of personal wealth became the object of media adulation that cultivated mass envy. This pattern replicated at the end of the twentieth century what John D. Rockefeller et al. had arranged at the end of the previous century. One difference was that then they were called "captains of industry" by some, but also "robber barons" by many others. Today, the softer "new corporate super-rich" seems to prevail; we now live, after all, in a postideological time.

Especially since the 1970s, corporate boards of directors have also spent lavishly on computerization, on research and development, and on moving production facilities abroad: all to advance their competitive positions in the world economy.[7] They generously lubricated politicians to reinforce many of the conditions that generated the exploding revenue inflows. Likewise, enlarged payments of dividends to share owners, rents to owners of land and technology, fees to merchants, interest and other fees to banks, and fees to armies of high-priced specialists and consultants (lawyers, advertisers, public relations firms, and so on) became the norm.

Exploding wealth concentrated in relatively few hands led to very rapid growth in enterprises specializing in managing such wealth: investment banks, hedge funds, and so on. Wealth management slid seamlessly into speculation, as happened in

---

6   It is worth quoting in some detail the findings for the changing US income distribution from 1917 to 2007: "The overall pattern of the top decile share over the century is U-shaped. The share of the top decile is around 45 percent from the mid-1920s to 1940. It declines substantially to just above 32.5 percent in four years during World War II and stays fairly stable around 33 percent until the 1970s ... After decades of stability in the post-war period, the top decile share has increased dramatically over the last twenty-five years and has now regained its pre-war level. Indeed, the top decile in 2007 is equal to 49.7 percent, a level higher than any other year since 1917 and even surpasses 1928, the peak of the stock market bubble in the 'roaring' twenties" (Saez 2009, 2). Income is measured as the sum of all market incomes, including realized capital gains and gross of income taxes. "Top decile" refers to families with an income of more than $109,600.

7   That is, in Marxian terms, not only to arrest the drain of surpluses to foreign competitors but also to go on the offensive and gain superprofits from them.

past run-ups to capitalist crises. Thus, financial enterprises competed ever more intensely for deposits from the surplus-appropriating capitalists and those they favored with surplus distributions. To this end they "found" and often created new financial instruments ("special investment vehicles," "collateralized debt obligations," "credit default swaps," and so on) that would yield better returns. They went ever further—in terms of geography (drawing deposits globally and investing globally), legality (skirting around financial regulations and expanding unregulated financial activities), and prudence (making ever riskier investments). So long as the flood of surplus into the financial sector continued, that sector grew much faster than any other part of the US economy. It fattened fast from the huge fees and commissions it drew from handling and circulating that flood. A generation of college graduates forsook other careers for quick wealth on Wall Street or elsewhere "in finance."

Contradiction and Crisis

Marxian theory focuses on contradiction. Thus, it centers attention on the nexus connecting, on the one hand, workers squeezed by the end of rising real wages, and, on the other, capitalists raking in the resulting explosion of surplus value. That nexus was debt. The financial industry in the United States invented and proliferated the requisite mechanisms. They enabled capitalists with rising surpluses to lend a good portion of them to workers. The latter borrowed chiefly because they had no other way to realize the American dream once real wages stopped rising, and secondarily because countless reassurances were made that borrowing was safe, appropriate, and itself very American. The workers' demand for credit was an effect of rising exploitation in the United States over the last thirty years. Bankers were flush with the deposits of expanded surplus value from that rising exploitation. Competition among them drove all to seek newer, more profitable outlets for loans. Whereas in earlier centuries bankers had lent to needy feudal lords and kings, now they lent to workers whose real wages stopped rising and to a government that cut taxes. To charge that borrowing workers were stupid or irresponsible, or that bank and other lenders were particularly devious or greedy, substitutes moral denunciations for social analysis. Our Marxian approach aims instead to understand how and why the economic, political, and cultural (including various moral failings as well) conditions of capitalism generated the contradictory post-1970s development that culminated in its second global collapse in seventy-five years.

Key to the debt nexus between workers and capitalists was debt securitization. Because the only collateral workers could ever offer were their homes, mortgages soared after the 1970s and with them securities comprised of/backed by bundles of mortgages. Across the country, banks and bank agents ("mortgage brokers") pushed mortgages and quickly resold them to the bundlers/securitizers who then resold them to "investors" (including those with the mushrooming surplus value-based incomes). Because mortgage originators earned their fees and immediately resold mortgages, they had every incentive not to ascertain whether the borrowing families could reasonably afford such mortgages. Given the intense competition in the financial industry, corruption inevitably bloomed. It eventually sparked the larger financial crisis when default rates on the least affordable ("subprime") mortgages undermined the values of securities into which such mortgages had been bundled. Of course, once the subprime mortgage securities market collapsed, the crisis spread to the rest of the mortgage-backed securities market and the credit markets more broadly and, from there, to all the other interconnected markets. Since capitalist markets interconnect different parts of the economy, transmitting change in one part to all others, they, too, contributed to the system's current crisis.

Capitalists could and did exult after the 1970s as the system accumulated income and wealth for them on an unprecedented scale. They had, although without acknowledging the fact, substituted rising loans to their workers in place of the rising real wages their workers had enjoyed for the previous century. This was little short of a capitalist fantasy come true. They preferred to believe instead that the efficiency-driven mechanisms of private enterprise and free markets accounted for their good fortune, "benefited everyone," and thereby proved private, unregulated capitalism's superiority to any conceivable alternative system. While the good times for capitalists rolled, the worlds of politics, media, and academia affirmed such beliefs only too eagerly. The ideas that the end of rising real wages was the hard reality that dissolved the magic, and that the capitalists' gains were the workers' losses, were unacceptable and therefore generally ignored. Only when the resulting mass worker exhaustion, stress, and debt collapsed the system did that "other side" of capitalist euphoria—that contradiction that Marxian analysis had earlier found and elaborated—begin to become more generally visible.

A Marxian Solution

If, as we would argue, a steadily rising rate of exploitation propelled workers first into debt and from there to default, one solution (or part of a solution) would logically follow: eliminate class exploitation. The Marxian policy of pursuing such a solution would sharply distinguish it from today's Keynesian or yesterday's neoclassical policies. A Marxian approach of the sort we recommend would not aim to reform capitalism by either increasing or decreasing state economic intervention, by regulating or deregulating credit and perhaps other markets. Instead, we would aim to eliminate capitalism in the precise sense of fundamentally changing the class structure in production. That, for us, is the key change which could be achieved together with more or less state intervention or regulation as people might prefer.

The change we advocate would put workers inside each industrial enterprise in the position of first receivers of the surplus value they produced in that enterprise. That would, of course, also position them as the first distributors of that received surplus value. The surplus-producing workers would become in effect their own board of directors, displacing traditional corporate boards chosen by and responsible to major shareholders. This is what we mean by eliminating the capitalist class structure. It could be a major first step in a new kind of class democratization of the economy generally and of each productive enterprise.[8] In addition to this move, all employees in each enterprise might be given equal roles in deciding what, where, and how to produce and how to distribute the enterprise's surpluses. Subsequent steps would entail enlarging economic democracy by including those residential communities interdependent with each enterprise. Workers and residents would share democratic power over the products and surpluses produced in and distributed by each enterprise. Changing the class structure in this way will not eliminate contradictions or even crises arising in an economy. But postcapitalist crises will be different, will be understood differently, and will be responded to in different ways. And these differences matter. First of all, crises will be less likely to emerge, as the current one did, from a rising rate of surplus appropriation, since workers who are their own board of directors would be far less likely to impose or permit such a rising rate. What crises did arise would be responded to much more humanely and equitably precisely because of the extension of a new kind of class democracy entailed by eliminating capitalist class structures. The costs and pains of crisis response would be equitably shared in principle, since that principle is embedded in and follows directly from the postcapitalist class structure. The grotesque capitalist disparities of today—when foreclosure and unemployment stagger millions while others suffer neither, when some collapsing industries receive massive government bailouts and others are left to die, when some municipalities and states continue to provide basic public services and others do not—would far less likely occur on the basis of a post-capitalist class structure. There is another key difference to consider. Roosevelt's New Deal imposed a mass of regulations upon capitalism with the explicit intention of ending the Great Depression and preventing another such depression in the future. The regulations taxed and otherwise constrained the ways and means for capitalists to pursue their goals. However, those regulations always stopped short of changing the capitalist class structure. The regulations always left in place the corporate

---

8   Still another and different step might involve surplus producers—wherever located—put into the position of first appropriators and distributors of surpluses wherever produced. In other words, instead of surplus production and appropriation occurring in one space—the individual enterprise—they may occur in different spaces. In more centralized arrangements, surplus labor appropriation could be aggregated across various or all surplus-producing units. In the latter arrangements, the collectivity of workers who produce the surpluses would be the first appropriators and distributors of surpluses aggregated across these operating units. We have worked out the social conditions for these various forms of appropriation and distribution in our *Class Theory and History* (Resnick and Wolff 2002, 16-20).

boards of directors running most of the US capitalist economy. Those boards had every incentive—given their responsibilities to shareholders and their own self-interests—to evade, weaken, or undo the New Deal regulations. Moreover, as the first receivers of the surpluses produced inside each enterprise, they also had the resources to evade, weaken, or undo the New Deal regulations. As we know from US history, corporate America responded to their incentives and utilized their resources to undo the New Deal, especially after the 1970s, under the regimes of Reagan, Bush I, Clinton, and Bush II. In a postcapitalist class structure of the sort sketched above, it would be far less likely for enterprise boards to want or to be able to similarly undermine future anticrisis reforms.

A Concluding Parable

Perhaps we might conclude with a parallel parable. For a long time, when crises occurred inside southern US slavery and caused great suffering among the slaves, many demanded government intervention to alleviate that suffering. Governmental responses sometimes entailed greater and sometimes lesser regulations of slavery. After repeated crises, a growing group realized that oscillations between more and less regulation of slavery did not work to prevent crises. They began to move toward the position of those who had already come to oppose slavery on moral, ethical, and other grounds. That is, they began *to see the best solution to slavery's repeated crises in the abolition of slavery itself*. Today, after repeated capitalist crises followed by alternating government regulation, deregulation, and reregulation, it is perhaps time for the victims of capitalist crises to move toward the position of those who have come to oppose capitalism on moral, ethical, and other grounds. That is, the time has come to acknowledge and debate whether *the best solution to capitalist crises might not be the abolition of capitalism itself.*

Note on Data Sources

We are indebted to statistical research by Jason Ricciuti-Borenstein in utilizing and interpreting the data sources below, as indicated.

Sources of Hourly Wage Data

A. Historical Statistics of the United States (HSUS), Series D 765-778, "Average Hours and Average Earnings in Manufacturing," 1890 to 1926
B. HSUS, Series D 845-876, "Average Days in Operation per Year, Average Daily Hours, and Annual and Hourly Earnings, in Manufacturing," 1889 to 1914
C. HSUS, Series D 830-844, "Earnings and Hours of Production Workers in 25 Manufacturing Industries," 1914 to 1948

D. HSUS, Series D 802-810, "Earnings and Hours of Production Workers in Manufacturing," 1909 to 1970

E. U.S. Bureau of Labor Statistics, Current Employment Statistics, "Average Hourly Earnings of Production and Non-supervisory Workers in Manufacturing," 1939 to 2007, http://www.bls.gov/ces/

Sources for the Consumer Price Index

F. HSUS, Series D 735-738, "Average Annual and Daily Earnings of Nonfarm Employees," 1860 to 1900

G. HSUS, Series D 722-727, "Average Annual Earnings of Employees," 1900 to 1970

H. U.S. Bureau of Labor Statistics, http://www.bls.gov/cpi/

The series was constructed first by converting the various hourly wage series into real values of 2007 dollars. Second, in years for which multiple entries of the hourly wage existed, an average was taken such that:

- 1890-1914: average of sources A and B
- 1914-1919: B was the only source
- 1920-1938: average of sources C and D
- 1939-1948: average of sources C, D and E
- 1949-1970: average of sources D and E
- 1970-2007: E was the only source

Next, this hourly real wage series was converted into an index, in which 100 was set equal to the real hourly wage for 1890.

Sources for Productivity Data

A. Historical Statistics of the United States, Series D 683-688, "Indexes of Employee Output," 1869 to 1969

B. U.S. Bureau of Labor Statistics, "Industry analytical ratios for manufacturing, all persons," http://www.bls.gov/lpc/
   - Superseded historical SIC measures for manufacturing, durable manufacturing, and nondurable manufacturing sectors, 1949-2003; ftp://ftp.bls.gov/pub/special.requests/opt/lpr/histmfgsic.zip

C. U.S. Bureau of Labor Statistics, Series Id PRS30006092, http://www.bls.gov/lpc/, 1987 to 2007

The above data sources provide the annual percentage change in the quantity of output per hour for the manufacturing sector. The index was constructed as follows:

- 1890 to 1949, from source A
- 1949 to 1987, from source B
- 1987 to 2007, from source C

Year 1890 was set equal to 100.

Source for Household Debt Data

Board of Governors of the Federal Reserve System, "Federal Reserve Statistical Release, Z.1, Flow of Funds Accounts of the United States," http://federalreserve.gov/releases/z1/; table D2, Borrowing by Sector, and table D3, Debt Outstanding by Sector

References

Akerloff, G. A., and R. J. Shiller. 2009. *Animal spirits*. Princeton, N.J.: Princeton University Press.

Keynes, J. M. 1964. *The general theory of employment, interest, and money*. New York: Harcourt Brace Jovanovich.

Resnick, S., and R. Wolff. 2002. *Class theory and history*. New York: Routledge.

Saez, E. 2009. Striking it richer: The evolution of top incomes in the United States (update with 2007 estimates). http://elsa.berkeley.edu/~saez (accessed August 2009).

Teece, D., G. Pisano, and A. Shuen. 1997. Dynamic capabilities and strategic management. *Strategic Management Journal* 18 (7): 509-33.

Source: *Rethinking Marxism: A Journal of Economics, Culture & Society* 22.2 (2010): 170-86; 2 Apr. 2010. Web. http://www.tandfonline.com/doi/abs/10.1080/08935691003625182.

WHAT IT SAYS

1. What is the message of Keynesian economics? What is the message of neoclassical economics? Why has Keynesian economics currently regained the upper hand in its long-standing feud with neoclassical economics? Why might neoclassical economics reemerge, according to Resnick and Wolff?

2. Resnick and Wolff argue that both Keynesian and neoclassical economics share a "conservatism." What is the nature of this conservatism? What does the continuous feud between Keynesian and neoclassical economics prevent from happening, according to Resnick and Wolff? What is the relationship between this feud in economics and the perspective that Resnick and Wolff represent?

3. What two major trends emerged in US industry from 1890 to 1970? How do the authors interpret these trends using Marxian analysis?

4. How have the defenders of the capitalist system explained such persistent problems as "urban decay, corruption, crime, family disintegration, personal and civic alienation, and wars," according to the authors? What explanation do the authors hint at?

5. Of the two major trends that the authors discuss, which changed after 1970? What factors contributed to the change?

6. What is the relationship between consumption and "the American dream," as the authors see it?

7. What is the relationship among the changing wage trend after 1970, consumption, debt, and the crisis of 2008?

8. What is the Marxian solution to the problems that the authors address? Why would a Marxian economy overcome or at least minimize future crises, according to the authors?

HOW IT SAYS IT

1. Describe the tone and diction of the essay. How do these features help to shape the argument being made? Why do you suppose the authors adopt this tone?

2. The authors use one figure in the essay. What does it show? How does it help to advance the authors' argument?

3. What is the intended audience for this essay? How can you tell?

WRITE ABOUT IT

1. Resnick and Wolff's essay is fairly long and combines several points. Write a summary (see pp. 73–76) of the essay that briefly explains the main argument, the parts of the argument, and how they fit together.

2. Write an essay in which you defend the capitalist system from Resnick and Wolff's attack. How might you counter their arguments? How else might you explain the crises they point to? What is wrong with their solution? What does the capitalist system provide that a Marxian one wouldn't, for example? Be sure to account for the phenomena that Resnick and Wolff mention and to counter their specific points.

3. Write an essay in which you develop a new economic perspective that is different from the three perspectives described in this essay. What would this other economic perspective look like? How might it account for economic crises and the 2008 crisis in particular?

e. UNEP, "Foreword" and "Introduction" to *Towards a Green Economy: Pathways to Sustainable Development and Poverty Eradication*

The United Nations Environment Programme (UNEP) is an international institution (a program, rather than an agency, of the UN) that coordinates United Nations environmental activities. UNEP assists developing countries in implementing environmentally sound policies and practices. The institution was founded as a result of the United Nations Conference on the Human Environment in June 1972. UNEP is headquartered in the Gigiri neighborhood of Nairobi, Kenya, with six regional and several national offices.

Towards a Green Economy: Pathways to Sustainable Development and Poverty Eradication, from which this chapter's excerpts are taken, is a 631-page report. The report asserts that despite fatigue induced by the 2008 financial crisis, increasing evidence suggests that a way forward is possible—but only if a new economic paradigm is quickly and fully adopted, one in which material wealth is not produced at the expense of environmental catastrophes, dwindling biodiversity, and vast disparities in social wealth and well-being. The report cites current global problems, such as food security and the lack of fresh water, amidst an exploding world population. The authors state that although the causes of the world's crises vary, at base, the common feature of the crises is the "gross misallocation of capital."

As You Read: What comes to mind when you think of a "green economy"? Have the authors changed your mind about the meaning of the term or its importance? Do you think that the world is anywhere near achieving it?

Foreword

Nearly 20 years after the Earth Summit, nations are again on the Road to Rio, but in a world very different and very changed from that of 1992.

Then we were just glimpsing some of the challenges emerging across the planet from climate change and the loss of species to desertification and land degradation.

Today many of those seemingly far off concerns are becoming a reality with sobering implications for not only achieving the UN's Millennium Development Goals, but challenging the very opportunity for close to seven billion people—rising to nine billion by 2050—to be able to thrive, let alone survive.

Rio 1992 did not fail the world—far from it. It provided the vision and important pieces of the multilateral machinery to achieve a sustainable future.

But this will only be possible if the environmental and social pillars of sustainable development are given equal footing with the economic one: where the often invisible engines of sustainability, from forests to freshwaters, are also given equal if not greater weight in development and economic planning.

Towards a Green Economy is among UNEP's key contributions to the Rio+20 process and the overall goal of addressing poverty and delivering a sustainable 21st century.

The report makes a compelling economic and social case for investing two per cent of global GDP in greening ten central sectors of the economy in order to shift development and unleash public and private capital flows onto a low-carbon, resource-efficient path.

Such a transition can catalyse economic activity of at least a comparable size to business as usual, but with a reduced risk of the crises and shocks increasingly inherent in the existing model.

New ideas are by their very nature disruptive, but far less disruptive than a world running low on drinking water and productive land, set against the backdrop of climate change, extreme weather events and rising natural resource scarcities.

A green economy does not favour one political perspective over another. It is relevant to all economies, be they state or more market-led. Neither is it a replacement for sustainable development. Rather, it is a way of realizing that development at the national, regional and global levels and in ways that resonate with and amplify the implementation of Agenda 21.

A transition to a green economy is already underway, a point underscored in the report and a growing wealth of companion studies by international organizations, countries, corporations and civil society. But the challenge is clearly to build on this momentum.

Rio+20 offers a real opportunity to scale-up and embed these "green shoots." In doing so, this report offers not only a roadmap to Rio but beyond 2012, where a far more intelligent management of the natural and human capital of this planet finally shapes the wealth creation and direction of this world.

Introduction

From Crisis to Opportunity

The last two years have seen the idea of a "green economy" float out of its specialist moorings in environmental economics and into the mainstream of policy discourse. It is found increasingly in the words of heads of state and finance ministers, in the text of G20 communiqués, and discussed in the context of sustainable development and poverty eradication.[1]

This recent traction for a green economy concept has no doubt been aided by widespread disillusionment with our prevailing economic paradigm, a sense of fatigue emanating from the many concurrent crises and market failures experienced during the very first decade of the new millennium, including especially the financial and economic crisis of 2008. But at the same time, we have seen increasing evidence of a way forward, a new economic paradigm—one in which material wealth is not delivered perforce at the expense of growing environmental risks, ecological scarcities and social disparities.

Mounting evidence also suggests that transitioning to a green economy has sound economic and social justification. There is a strong case emerging for a redoubling of efforts by both governments as well as the private sector to engage in such an economic transformation. For governments, this would include leveling the playing field for greener products by phasing out antiquated subsidies, reforming policies and providing new incentives, strengthening market infrastructure and market-based mechanisms, redirecting public investment, and greening public procurement. For the private sector, this would involve understanding and sizing the true opportunity represented by green economy transitions across a number of key sectors, and responding to policy reforms and price signals through higher levels of financing and investment.

We argue in UNEP's forthcoming Green Economy Report, and in this extracted Synthesis for Policy Makers, that the rewards of greening the world's economies are tangible and considerable, that the means are at hand for both governments and the private sector, and that the time to engage the challenge is now.

An Era of Capital Misallocation

Several concurrent crises have either sprung up or accelerated during the last decade: crises in climate, biodiversity, fuel, food, water, and of late in the financial system and the economy as a whole. Accelerating climate-changing emissions indicate a mounting threat of runaway climate change, with potentially disastrous human consequences. The fuel price shock of 2008, and a related flare up in food and commodity prices, both indicate structural weaknesses and risks which remain unresolved. Rising demand, forecast by the International Energy Agency (IEA) and others, suggests an ongoing dependence on oil and other fossil fuels and much higher energy prices as the world economy struggles to recover and grow.

As regards to food security, we are seeing neither widespread understanding of the nature of the problem, nor globally collaborative solutions for how we shall feed

---

1   The "Rio+20" agenda has adopted "green economy" as a key theme in the context of sustainable development and poverty eradication.

a population of 9 billion by 2050. Freshwater scarcity is already a global problem, and forecasts suggest a growing gap[2] by 2030 between annual freshwater demand and renewable supply. The outlook for improved sanitation still looks bleak for over 2.6 billion people; 884 million people still lack access to clean drinking water.[3]

Collectively, these crises are severely impacting our ability to sustain prosperity worldwide and to achieve the Millennium Development Goals (MDGs) for reducing extreme poverty. They are compounding persistent social problems from job losses, socio-economic insecurity and poverty, and threatening social stability.

Although the causes of these crises vary, at a fundamental level they all share a common feature: the gross misallocation of capital. During the last two decades, much capital was poured into property, fossil fuels and structured financial assets with embedded derivatives, but relatively little in comparison was invested in renewable energy, energy efficiency, public transportation, sustainable agriculture, ecosystem and biodiversity protection, and land and water conservation. Indeed, most economic development and growth strategies encouraged rapid accumulation of physical, financial and human capital, but at the expense of excessive depletion and degradation of natural capital, which includes our endowment of natural resources and ecosystems. By depleting the world's stock of natural wealth—often irreversibly—this pattern of development and growth has had detrimental impacts on the well-being of current generations and presents tremendous risks and challenges for future generations. The recent multiple crises are symptomatic of this pattern.

Existing policies and market incentives have contributed to this problem of capital misallocation because they allow businesses to run up significant social and environmental externalities, largely unaccounted for and unchecked. "Unfettered markets are not meant to solve social problems"[4] so there is a need for better public policies, including pricing and regulatory measures, to change the perverse market incentives that drive this capital misallocation and ignore social and environmental externalities. Increasingly too, the role of appropriate regulations, policies and public investments as enablers for bringing about changes in the pattern of private investment is being recognized and demonstrated through success stories from around the world, especially in developing countries.[5]

2   *Charting Our Water Future: Economic Frameworks to Inform Decision Making.* Munich: 2030 Water Resources Group. McKinsey and Company (2009), p. iv.

3   *Progress on Sanitation and Drinking Water: 2010 Update.* WHO/UNICEF Joint Monitoring Programme for Water Supply and Sanitation. World Health Organization and UNICEF (2010), pp. 6-7.

4   Yunus, Muhammad and Karl Weber. *Creating a World without Poverty: Social Business and the Future of Capitalism.* Public Affairs (2007), p. 5.

5   *Green Economy Developing Countries Success Stories.* United Nations Environment Programme (2010), p. 6.

What Is a Green Economy?

UNEP defines a green economy as one that results in *improved human well-being and social equity, while significantly reducing environmental risks and ecological scarcities.* In its simplest expression, a green economy can be thought of as one which is low carbon, resource efficient and socially inclusive. In a green economy, growth in income and employment should be driven by public and private investments that reduce carbon emissions and pollution, enhance energy and resource efficiency, and prevent the loss of biodiversity and ecosystem services. These investments need to be catalysed and supported by targeted public expenditure, policy reforms and regulation changes. The development path should maintain, enhance and, where necessary, rebuild natural capital as a critical economic asset and as a source of public benefits, especially for poor people whose livelihoods and security depend on nature.

The concept of a "green economy" does not *replace* sustainable development, but there is now a growing recognition that achieving sustainability rests almost entirely on getting the economy right. Decades of creating new wealth through a "brown economy" model have not substantially addressed social marginalization and resource depletion, and we are still far from delivering to the Millennium Development Goals. Sustainability is still a vital long-term goal, but we must work on greening the economy to get us there.

To make the transition to a green economy, specific enabling conditions will be required. These enabling conditions consist of the backdrop of national regulations, policies, subsidies and incentives, and international market and legal infrastructure and trade and aid protocols. At present, enabling conditions are heavily weighted towards, and encourage, the prevailing brown economy, which, inter alia, depends excessively on fossil fuel energy.

For example, price and production subsidies for fossil fuels collectively exceeded US$650 billion in 2008,[6] and this high level of subsidization can adversely affect transition to the use of renewable energies. In contrast, enabling conditions for a green economy can pave the way for the success of public and private investment in greening the world's economies. At a national level, examples of such enabling conditions are: changes to fiscal policy, reform and reduction of environmentally harmful subsidies; employing new market-based instruments; targeting public investments to "green" key sectors; greening public procurement; and improving environmental rules and regulations as well as their enforcement. At an international level, there are also opportunities to add to market infrastructure, improve trade and aid flows, and foster greater international cooperation.

---

6 *Analysis of the Scope of Energy Subsidies and Suggestions for the G20 Initiative.* IEA, OPEC, OECD, and World Bank joint report prepared for submission to the G20 Summit Meeting, Toronto (Canada), 26-27 June 2010, p. 4.

UNEP's Green Economy Report, entitled *Towards a Green Economy*, aims to debunk several myths and misconceptions about the economics of "greening" the global economy, and provides timely and practical guidance to policy makers on what reforms they need to unlock the productive and employment potential of a green economy.

Perhaps the most widespread myth is that there is an inescapable trade-off between environmental sustainability and economic progress. There is now substantial evidence that the "greening" of economies neither inhibits wealth creation nor employment opportunities, and that there are many green sectors which show significant opportunities for investment and related growth in wealth and jobs. A caveat, however, is that there is a need to establish new enabling conditions to promote the transition to a green economy, and this is where urgent action is required of policy makers around the world.

A second myth is that a green economy is a luxury only wealthy countries can afford, or worse, a developed-world imposition to restrain development and perpetuate poverty in developing countries. Contrary to this perception, we find there are a plethora of examples of greening transitions taking place in various sectors in the developing world, which deserve to be emulated and replicated elsewhere. *Towards a Green Economy* brings some of these examples to light and highlights their scope for wider application.

UNEP's work on the green economy raised the visibility of this concept in 2008, particularly through our call for a Global Green New Deal (GGND). The GGND recommended a package of public investments and complementary policy and pricing reforms aimed at kick-starting a transition to a green economy while reinvigorating economies and jobs and addressing persistent poverty.[7] Designed as a timely and appropriate policy response to the economic crisis, the GGND proposal was an early output from the United Nations'Green Economy Initiative. This initiative, coordinated by UNEP, was one of the nine Joint Crisis Initiatives undertaken by the Secretary-General of the UN and his Chief Executives Board in response to the 2008 economic and financial crisis.

Towards a Green Economy—the main output of the Green Economy Initiative—demonstrates that the greening of economies is not generally a drag on growth but rather a new engine of growth; that it is a net generator of decent jobs, and that it is also a vital strategy for the elimination of persistent poverty. The report also seeks to motivate policy makers to create the enabling conditions for increased investments in a transition to a green economy in three ways.

Firstly, it makes an economic case for shifting investment, both public and private, to transform key sectors that are critical to green the global economy. It

---

7   See Barbier, E.B. *A Global Green New Deal: Rethinking the Economic Recovery*. Cambridge University Press and UNEP (2010), Cambridge, UK.

illustrates through examples how added employment through green jobs offsets job losses in the process of transitioning to a green economy.

Secondly, it shows how a green economy can reduce persistent poverty across a range of important sectors—agriculture, forestry, freshwater, fisheries and energy. Sustainable forestry and ecologically friendly farming methods help conserve soil fertility and water resources in general, and especially for subsistence farming, upon which depend the livelihoods of almost 1.3 billion people.[8]

Lastly, it provides guidance on policies to achieve this shift: by reducing or eliminating environmentally harmful or perverse subsidies, by addressing market failures created by externalities or imperfect information, through market-based incentives, through appropriate regulatory framework and green public procurement, and through stimulating investment.

How Far Are We from a Green Economy?

Over the last quarter of a century, the world economy has quadrupled, benefiting hundreds of millions of people.[9] In contrast, however, 60% of the world's major ecosystem goods and services that underpin livelihoods have been degraded or used unsustainably.[10] Indeed, this is because the economic growth of recent decades has been accomplished mainly through drawing down natural resources, without allowing stocks to regenerate, and through allowing widespread ecosystem degradation and loss.

For instance, today only 20% of commercial fish stocks, mostly of low priced species, are underexploited, 52% are fully exploited with no further room for expansion, about 20% are overexploited and 8% are depleted.[11] Water is becoming scarce and water stress is projected to increase with water supply satisfying only 60% of world demand in 20 years;[12] agriculture saw increasing yields primarily due to the use of chemical fertilizers,[13] which have reduced soil quality[14] and failed to curb the growing trend of deforestation—remaining at 13 million hectares of forest per year in 1990-2005.[15] Ecological scarcities are therefore seriously

---

8   *Green Jobs: Towards Decent Work in a Sustainable, Low-carbon World.* UNEP, ILO, IOE, ITUC. United Nations Environment Programme (2008), p. 11.

9   *World Economic Outlook Database,* IMF: Washington D.C. (September 2006), Available at: http://www.imf.org/external/pubs/ft/weo/2006/02/data/download.aspx.

10   *Ecosystem and Human Well-being: Synthesis. Millennium Ecosystem Assessment* (2005). p. 1.

11   *State of World Fisheries and Aquaculture 2008.* UN Food and Agricultural Organization (2009), p. 30.

12   *Charting Our Water Future: Economic Frameworks to Inform Decision Making.* Munich: 2030 Water Resources Group. McKinsey and Company (2009), p. 7.

13   FAOSTAT, 2009.

14   Müller, Adrian, and Joan S. Davis. *Reducing Global Warming: The Potential of Organic Agriculture.* Rodale Institute and FiBL (2009), p. 1.

15   *Global Forest Resources Assessment 2010: Main Report.* Rome. UN Food and Agriculture Organization (2010), p. xiii.

affecting the entire gamut of economic sectors, which are the bedrock of human food supply (fisheries, agriculture, freshwater, forestry) and a critical source of livelihoods for the poor. And ecological scarcity and social inequity are definitional signatures of an economy which is very far from being "green."

Meanwhile, for the first time in history, more than half of the world population lives in urban areas. Cities now account for 75% of energy consumption[16] and 75% of carbon emissions.[17] Rising and related problems of congestion, pollution, and poorly provisioned services affect the productivity and health of all, but fall particularly hard on the urban poor. With approximately 50% of the global population now living in emerging economies[18] that are rapidly urbanizing and will experience rising income and purchasing power over the next years—and a tremendous expansion in urban infrastructure—the need for smart city planning is paramount.

The transition to a green economy will vary considerably between nations, as it depends on the specifics of each country's natural and human capital and on its relative level of development. As demonstrated graphically below, there are many opportunities for all countries in such a transition (see Box 6.1). Some countries have attained high levels of human development, but often at the expense of their natural resource base, the quality of their environment, and high GHG emissions. The challenge for these countries is to reduce their per capita ecological footprint without impairing their quality of life. Other countries still maintain relatively low per capita ecological footprints, but need to deliver improved levels of services and material well-being to their citizens. Their challenge is to do this without drastically increasing their ecological footprints. As the diagram below illustrates, one of these two challenges affects almost every nation, and globally, we are very far from being a green economy.

How to Measure Progress towards a Green Economy

We cannot hope to *manage* what we do not even *measure*. Therefore, we argue that notwithstanding the complexity of an overall transition to a green economy, we must identify and use appropriate indicators at both a macroeconomic level and a sectoral level.

Conventional economic indicators, such as GDP, provide a distorted lens for economic performance particularly since such measures fail to reflect the extent to which production and consumption activities may be drawing down natural

---

16 *Cities and Climate Change Initiative Launch and Conference Report*. UN Habitat (March 2009), p. 8.

17 *Clinton Foundation Annual Report 2009*. Clinton Foundation (2010), p. 33. For a critique of these figures, see Satterthwaite, D. (2008), "Cities' contribution to global warming: notes on the allocation of greenhouse gas emissions," *Environment and Urbanization*, Vol. 20, No 2. pp. 539-549.

18 In 2009, Brazil, China, India, Indonesia, Mexico, Russia and South Africa accounted for 3.2 billion people or nearly half of the world population. Source: World Bank, World Development Indicators, 2010.

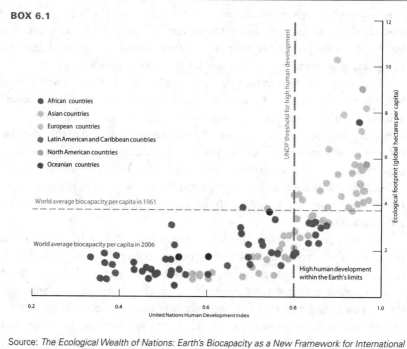

BOX 6.1

Source: *The Ecological Wealth of Nations: Earth's Biocapacity as a New Framework for International Cooperation.* Global Footprint Network (2010), p. 13; *Human Development Index data from Human Development Report 2009—Overcoming Barriers: Human Mobility and Development.* UNDP (2009).

capital. By either depleting natural resources, or degrading the ability of ecosystems to deliver economic benefits, in terms of provisioning, regulating or cultural services, economic activity is often based on the depreciation of natural capital.

Ideally, changes in stocks of natural capital would be evaluated in monetary terms and incorporated into the national accounts, as is being pursued in the ongoing development of the System of Environmental and Economic Accounting (SEEA) by the UN Statistical Division, and the adjusted net national savings methods of the World Bank.[19] The wider use of such measures would provide a truer indication of the real level and viability of growth in income and employment. Green Accounting or Inclusive Wealth Accounting are available frameworks which we expect will be adopted by a few nations[20] initially and pave the way for measuring a green economy transition at the macroeconomic plane.

---

19 *Where Is the Wealth of Nations? Measuring Capital for the 21st Century.* World Bank: Washington, D.C. (2006), p. 123.

20 World Bank, together with UNEP and other partners, have recently (at Nagoya, CBD COP-10, October 2009) announced a global project on "Ecosystem Valuation and Wealth Accounting" which will enable a group of developing and developed nations to test this framework and evolve a set of pilot national accounts that are better able to reflect and measure sustainability concerns.

In this report, we explored through a macroeconomic model[21] the impacts of investments in greening the economy as against investments in "business as usual"—measuring results not only in terms of traditional GDP but also impacts on employment, resource intensity, emissions and ecological impact. We estimated, based on several studies, that the annual financing demand to green the global economy was in the range of US $1.05-2.59 trillion. To place this demand in perspective, it is less than one-tenth of the total global investment per year (as measured by global Gross Capital Formation). Taking an annual level of US $1.3 trillion (i.e., 2% of global GDP) as a target reallocation from "brown" investment to "green" investment, our macroeconomic model suggests that over time, investing in a green economy enhances long-run economic performance and can increase total global wealth. Significantly, it does so while enhancing stocks of renewable resources, reducing environmental risks, and rebuilding our capacity to generate future prosperity.

Towards a Green Economy

Our report, *Towards a Green Economy*, focuses on 10 key economic sectors because we see these sectors as driving the defining trends of the transition to a green economy, including increasing human well-being and social equity, and reducing environmental risks and ecological scarcities. Across many of these sectors, we have found that greening the economy can generate consistent and positive outcomes for increased wealth, growth in economic output, decent employment, and reduced poverty. These cross-cutting observations are summarized as our "key findings" in the next section.

We have also found several sector-specific investment opportunities and policy reforms to be of global importance as they appear replicable and scalable in our goal to transition to a green economy. These are largely in renewable energy and resource efficiency. Resource efficiency is a theme that has many dimensions as it cuts across energy efficiency in manufacture and habitation, materials efficiency in manufacture, and better waste management.

Finally, to transition successfully to a green economy the importance of adequate and favourable enabling conditions cannot be overemphasized. The latter includes appropriate domestic fiscal measures and policy reforms, international collaboration through trade, aid, market infrastructure, and capacity-building support. These are described and addressed, along with steps necessary to mobilize finance for a green economy transition, in the final sections of this *Synthesis for Policy Makers* [not reprinted here].

Source: *Towards a Green Economy: Pathways to Sustainable Development and Poverty Eradication: A Synthesis for Policy Makers*. Nairobi, Kenya: United Nations Environment Programme, 2011. Web. http://www.unep.org/greeneconomy/.

---

21 "T-21" model used in chapter on Enabling Conditions for a Green Economy.

WHAT IT SAYS

1. The authors state that although the causes of the world's crises vary, the common feature of such crises is "the gross misallocation of capital." What does "the gross misallocation of capital" mean? Explain how it contributes to the world's crises, according to the report.

2. What is the difference between a "green economy" and a "brown economy"?

3. What is GDP? How, according to UNEP, does GDP contribute to a "distorted lens" regarding economic performance?

4. The UNEP report cites "G20 communiqués." What is the G20? What role does the G20 have in developing and defining global economic policies?

5. What is "sustainability"? How can it be attained, according to the foreword and introduction?

HOW IT SAYS IT

1. Describe the tone and diction of the UNEP "Green Economy" foreword and introduction. How are these related to UNEP's argument?

2. The excerpt you read was issued by an international institution, UNEP. How does the international status of the organization contribute to the report's reputability or ethos?

3. Note UNEP's use of statistics and sources in the introduction. How do such statistics and sourcing help to support UNEP's claims?

4. What is the report's intended readership? How can you tell?

WRITE ABOUT IT

1. Write an essay in which you assert a viewpoint that is different from UNEP's. For example, consider whether a "green planet" should be a primary international goal. What other objective(s) might be more important? Support your claims with evidence and reasoning.

2. Form a "green economy committee" consisting of yourself and other classmates. In a series of tweets to the committee, compile a set of green economy practices that can be implemented in your school's community. Meet to discuss this list, and then, based on the tweets and discussion, draft a multimedia proposal to the community leadership in which you explain how your community should take steps toward implementing a "green economy" locally.

3. Write an essay in which you argue that a particular nation either has or has not begun taking steps toward a green economy. Support your argument with evidence and reasoning.

Questions for Synthesis

1. Write an essay that explores the various perspectives on the financial and economic crisis taken by the authors in this chapter. What, according to the authors, were the causes of the crisis? What do the authors recommend to solve the crisis?

   Your goal in this essay is not to argue for or against a particular position, but rather to faithfully represent the possibilities suggested by this group of writers. Pay attention to the common points that all or most of the authors address.

   You may wish to organize your paper according to these common points and represent all of the authors' views on each of the points. You may wish to visualize the various positions by constructing a synthesis grid (see pp. 77–79) before you begin to write.

2. Write an essay that explores the ideal economic future as envisioned by four authors: three from this chapter, and one author included in the Suggested Additional Resources.

   - What kinds of economies do the authors envision?
   - In what ways, if any, are the ideal economies of some (or all) of the authors alike?
   - What would be the role of government in the economy for each of the authors?
   - How should each of the economies be regulated, if at all?
   - What is the role of banks and other financial institutions?
   - What would happen to the stock market and other forms of speculation in each of the models?
   - How can depressions be avoided, according to each of the perspectives?

   Your goal in this essay is not to argue for or against a particular ideal model, but to represent the possibilities as suggested by your four authors.

Questions for Contribution

1. Argue for or against one of the perspectives represented in this chapter, or included in the Suggested Additional Resources. Be sure that you treat the particular aspects of the economy that the author addresses.

2. Write an essay in which you argue for a particular change to be made to the current economic system.

   - Be specific about the change you propose.
   - Tell why the change is necessary and exactly how it will improve economic conditions.
   - Make sure to take into account how all of the affected parties and other economic theorists might respond to your proposed change.
   - Refute your critics in advance by responding to potential objections.

CHAPTER 7 ASSESSING ARMED GLOBAL CONFLICT

INTRODUCTION

Contexts of Discussion

Because war has been waged across the ages and around the world, we might take it for granted that human beings are inherently warlike. After all, animals from chimpanzees to ants are known to engage in intra-species violence. The idea of human beings as warriors has pervaded anthropological, political, and historical studies of war for centuries.

The first written histories are histories of war. Revered scholars such as philosopher Thomas Hobbes, chemist and Nobel laureate Richard E. Smalley, and military scholar Carl Von Clausewitz, author of the seminal book *On War*, have argued that war is universal and inevitable in human society. Human beings, they say, are genetically predisposed to war. Recent scholars have challenged this view, arguing that nomadic societies did not wage war and that societal acts of domination began to occur only with the introduction of agriculture and the beginning of stationary, hierarchically based societies. Still others accept the evolutionary premises of human behavior but argue that some modern societies may live in peace for centuries. This leads them to conclude that while human beings may not have an *instinct* for violence, we possess a genetic endowment for violence, which we use only under certain circumstances. Indeed, according to experimental psychologist Steven Pinker, violence has declined over the centuries thanks to the socializing factors of government, literacy, commerce, and the advance of reason. These factors encourage us to curb our violent impulses, empathize with others, and employ reason to solve problems. His 2012 essay "Why the World Is More Peaceful" is included in this chapter.

Whatever one's stance, it's a curious question: What possible evolutionary purpose might this apparently self-destructive and species-destructive practice serve? What do recent wars and acts of terrorism tell us about human society's progress—or regression—in preventing violence?

We use the term "armed conflict" here to mean both war and terrorism, terms whose meanings shift depending on one's perspective. For example, a government entity might label opposing groups "terrorists," while the so-called terrorists might refer to themselves as "warriors," defending and promoting human rights, religious traditions, economic self-determination, or geographical territory. "War" generally refers to a conflict in which large organized groups fight for domination. "Terrorism," on the other hand, may be defined as an element of an asymmetrical conflict—one in which a small, relatively powerless group opposes a large, powerful state. Again, the less-powerful group might protest economic inequities or discriminatory ideological or religious policies, or might wish to assert power over the more powerful group. Because of its relative weakness, the second group may resort to violent, unpredictable acts that inspire terror or fear in the government and the larger populace. Their tactics will likely be secretive and will not conform to the conventions of regular war.

In the academic community, the scholars who study armed conflicts and terrorism have traditionally been historians and political scientists. In addition, many non-military universities have separate departments devoted to the study of peace, war, and military science. However, interest in armed global conflicts and terrorism has expanded across the university curriculum to include researchers in departments of public health, sociology, psychology, criminal justice, legal studies, international studies, economics, anthropology, cultural studies, music, and life sciences. Their proposals for ending armed conflict range from methods for improving the efficacy of torture to preventing or dissipating conflict through music therapy. This chapter introduces you to views on armed conflict held by contemporary scholars in psychology, public health, medicine, literature, technology and international relations, and Arab and Islamic studies.

Articles in the chapter focus on issues related to contemporary warfare, particularly the wars in Iraq and Afghanistan. An artist and professor of Arab and Islamic studies considers photographs taken at Abu Ghraib prison in Iraq, alongside the work of an Iraqi painter, and contemplates stereotypes of Arabs and Arab society. A public health researcher, a medical doctor, and professors of endocrinology and nutrition present their study of the health effects on Iranian children of the Iran-Iraq war. An English professor writes about the necessity of stories about war. A Harvard undergraduate warns us of the immediate dangers of cyber-infiltrations into the militaries of the United States and other nations. And a psychologist, taking a broader approach, argues that human society has become less violent over the centuries—and explains why.

More articles on armed conflict and terrorism from a diversity of academic disciplines are listed in the Suggested Additional Resources following this introduction.

Areas of Research and Conjecture

History, as the study of past events or important figures from the past, is often a way to help us understand the present. Military historians focus on historical conflicts, sometimes applying that knowledge to contemporary conflicts. A military historian might uncover a previously unknown facet of an armed conflict; research a key figure in one of these conflicts; present a perspective on how that conflict or that figure exemplifies a larger idea about human nature, armed conflict, political motivation or strategy; or examine the sociopolitical context in which the conflict occurred. Military historians also are likely to apply the lessons of one war to another. Such historians usually specialize in a specific kind of war (for example, guerilla warfare) or a specific period or conflict, and focus on a specific country. Some, however, take a much broader view, examining human behavior in armed conflicts over time.

Recently, military scholars have compared the war in Afghanistan to the Vietnam War. War-specific military history studies have included works on the global War on Terror, property confiscation during the American Civil War, and religion and the Cold War. Recent personality or group-based books and articles include works on mercenary soldiers, US General David Petraeus, and Native Americans in the US military. An essay by military historian Azar Gat, who claims that war is an evolution-based predisposition, though not an instinct, as some have claimed, is listed in the Suggested Additional Resources.

Political science is the study of governmental systems and practices, political processes and parties, and interactions between citizens and their governments. Political scientists thus focus on the political causes and consequences of armed conflict. Like military historians, they may consider historical or ongoing conflicts. On the subject of war, political scientists ask such questions as these:

- What was it about the current regime in a given country that incited a populist uprising?
- What factors might motivate a given administration to declare war on a country that was posing no direct harm to its citizens, or on a country in which a small group of militants was thought to reside?
- What political alliances and tensions between and within countries allowed disputes to escalate into armed conflict?

Recent research in political science and war is wide-ranging and includes studies of such topics as war and political participation in Uganda, war and state-building in medieval Japan, predictions of war duration, financial and military factors that make a country prone to civil war, and an examination of the idea that democracies do not wage war against each other. Included in the Suggested Additional Resources for this chapter is an essay by political scientist Clement Fatovic, who applies philosopher John Locke's views on extra-legality to US policies in the War on Terror.

Public health researchers conduct studies in epidemiology (the study of epidemic illness and disease) as it relates to armed conflict. Recent public health research has focused on the risk of heart disease among those who have engaged in military combat, vaccination rates and the spread of disease among soldiers, as well as rates of sexually transmitted disease among soldiers. Other medical researchers have recently studied health professionals conducting surgeries with limited resources and supplies, craniofacial surgery in response to war injuries, and the use and development of artificial limbs as a result of war injuries. Life scientists might also take an evolutionary view of armed conflict and conduct research on genetic links to aggression and war.

Ecologists and environmental scientists study the effect of armed conflict on the natural environment and the means for preventing or limiting its damages. During the Vietnam War, for example, a chemical known as Agent Orange was sprayed across vast areas in Vietnam to kill foliage hiding enemy forces. This chemical proved devastating to the environment, of course, but also increased cancer rates in people exposed to it. Research conducted by chemists, toxicologists, ecologists, and botanists have helped to document the effects of this chemical; their findings were used in a number of lawsuits undertaken by those who claimed their lives or health were endangered by the chemical.

Included in this chapter is a study, by three public health researchers and a physician, of the health effects of the Iran-Iraq War (1980-88; also known as the First Persian Gulf War) on children. Using such measurements of health as blood pressure, heart rate, and height and weight, the researchers studied a group of Iranian children born during that war, comparing these measurements with those of children born after the war.

Sociology is the study of human behavior within groups and within society at large. Sociologists study social organization and trends and develop theories for understanding them. Sociology has long focused on the causes and effects of armed conflict, and on how a society as a whole responds to armed conflict. A sociologist working in this area might ask the following questions: What are the effects of war on the victors and the vanquished both during and after armed conflicts? What effects are specific to actual combat, and what effects continue decades after war? Recent studies have looked at the effects of forced migration, causes for rebellion in ethnic groups and other social minorities, social constructs of refugee communities, and the sociological effects of civil war. The Suggested Additional Resources section for this chapter includes a recent study of war and violence by Croatian political sociologist Siniša Malešević.

Psychology is the study of the mental processes and behavior of individuals. Recent psychological research focusing on war and terrorism has included studies on reducing the effects of post-traumatic stress disorder (PTSD), therapies to ease the negative emotional effects of war on children and other civilians, and ways to detect simulated PTSD. An essay in this chapter by well-known psychologist Steven Pinker aims to prove, contrary to popular belief, that global violence has *decreased* over the centuries. This 2012 essay continues the argument Pinker details in his book *The Better Angels of Our Nature: Why Violence Has Declined* (2011).

In regard to armed conflict, scholars of **criminal justice and law** consider such questions as the following:

- What kinds of laws should govern armed conflict and the conduct of individual armies and soldiers?
- Are international standards viable, given the variety of governments, ideologies, and issues involved, particularly in civil war?
- How might one define a war criminal?
- How should they be tried and punished, and by whom?
- Is torture ethical?
- Under what circumstances should torture be legalized?
- What legal standards govern—or should govern—policies on war and terrorism?

Recent legal research has considered the role of international humanitarian law in war, the preservation of and access to Iraqi records and archives, and the definition and prosecution of war crime in Pakistan. Included in the Suggested Additional Resources is an article by Harvard law professor Jack Goldsmith, who compares the policies of the Bush and Obama administrations in the War on Terror.

International relations, or **international studies**, is a broad academic and public policy field that includes the study of foreign affairs and global issues among states. The field plays a large role in the study of armed conflict, in terms of both international war policy and ways to negotiate and maintain peace among countries. Recently, international studies scholars have studied the problems associated with state-building during postwar peace operations; civil war durations and outcomes; how democracies limit the human costs of war; and war, economic, and political development in the contemporary international system. This chapter includes an editorial first published in the *Harvard International Review* that warns about the potential hazards of cybercrime on the militaries of America and other countries.

Economics is the study of the production, distribution, and use of valued resources, as well as what stimulates their creation. Economists concerned with armed conflict study the monetary motivations and effects of war and terrorism, in terms of both the military costs and the overall effect on the economies of countries at war. Listed in the Suggested Additional Resources are articles on post-conflict economic reconstruction, the economics of civil war, and trade disruption as a result of war.

Anthropology is the study of human origins and physical development (physical anthropology) and human diversity (cultural anthropology). Cultural anthropologists might study the practice of armed conflict in a given society or within a given group of people, while physical anthropologists concern themselves with war as a human behavior, and the possible cultural and genetic origins of that behavior. Recent anthropological research has included studies on conducting field research during an active war (in this case, in Afghanistan), the neglect of anthropology during the Second World War, and the ethics of military anthropology (embedding anthropologists with troops) in Afghanistan and Iraq. *Beyond War: The Human Potential for Peace*, a book by anthropologist Douglas P. Fry, claims that war is not natural human behavior but is a product of agricultural society; it is listed in the Suggested Additional Resources.

An **education** scholar focusing on armed conflict might study the effect of armed conflict on schooling quality, conflict-related interruptions in education, and changes in educational ideologies and systems based on the outcomes of conflict. For instance, countries in the midst of war might discontinue their schools for safety reasons, or because school buildings have been destroyed. Even during peacetime or truce, countries destroyed by war may struggle to keep citizens fed, let alone be able to afford education. Recent research in education and armed conflict has centered on how educational institutions support and oppose wartime efforts, how to reach educational objectives in countries affected by conflict, and how to educate children on conflict and peace worldwide. In the Suggested Additional Resources, we include articles on the effects of recent conflicts on education, and on how soldiers adapt to the classroom after participating in a war.

Though war is not a typical concern for **music** theorists and practitioners, music scholars do occasionally consider armed conflict. Recent research on war and armed conflict includes a study of music played by American soldiers during the Iraq War, compositions by Aaron Copland during the Great Depression and World War II, music therapy for victims of armed conflict, and music produced for wartime documentary films. Articles on these topics are included in the Suggested Additional Resources. Their very presence indicates the pervasive nature of war and its causes and effects in human society.

Issues and Stakeholders

Increased armed conflicts worldwide: By late 2014, numerous violent conflicts had intensified worldwide, despite a period of low-bloodshed government takeovers during the Arab Spring in the Middle East and Africa:

- The United States had begun limited military involvement in the civil war in Syria to support the Free Syria Army against the military jihadist group Islamic States in Iraq and Syria, or ISIS. In reaction to the violence in Syria, some 600,000 Syrian refugees flooded Jordan between 2011 and 2014, in addition to some two million Palestinian refugees, causing political instability and a drain on Jordan's economy and natural resources.

- As sectarian violence continued in Iraq, the United States also authorized air strikes against ISIS in the northern part of that country. In 2013 alone, more than 8,000 Iraqis were killed due to sectarian violence, according to a United Nations report.
- Terrorist-led violence in Yemen, Somalia, and Kenya, as al-Qaeda and al-Qaeda-affiliated al-Shabab intensified their expansion into the Arab Peninsula and North Africa.
- Violence escalated in the Israel-Palestine conflict.
- In Ukraine, what began as a civil conflict escalated into an international crisis when the Ukraine government, the European Union, and NATO accused Russia of military support of Ukrainian separatists.
- The Korean peninsula became a high-risk area after North Korea, ignoring UN resolutions, continued to develop nuclear weapons and long-range missiles.
- In North America, the United States continues to be on high alert for cyberattacks against its infrastructure and financial institutions; recent cyberattacks are reported to have originated in China and Iran. In Mexico, drug-related violence has led to some 60,000 deaths since 2006. Mexican citizens have begun to blame the government for its failure to control the drug cartels.

The University of Maryland's Center for International Development and Conflict Management (CIDCM), which compiles periodic reports, assesses the risk of political instability in countries across the globe in its report, *Peace and Conflict 2014* (see Suggested Additional Resources).

Since 2001, the war in Afghanistan involved the United States, the United Kingdom, Australia, and the Afghan United Front as Operation Enduring Freedom. The United States and the United Kingdom officially withdrew their troops from Afghanistan in late 2014, handing over operations to the Afghan military.

The Iraq War, in which the United States, the United Kingdom, and other countries invaded Iraq in 2003, based on Iraq's alleged possession of weapons of mass destruction, officially ended in 2011. However, the bloody sectarian violence continues. The global War on Terror, of which the invasion of Afghanistan and the Iraq War are presumably a part, pits worldwide governments against all terrorists.

Defining terrorists and terrorism: What is a terrorist? Would you know a terrorist if you saw one? When Americans envision a terrorist, they might picture a Saudi Arabian al-Qaeda member. The attacks on the World Trade Center in New

York City and the Pentagon in Washington, DC, on September 11, 2001, undertaken by al-Qaeda, killed nearly 3,000 people. In an article listed in the Suggested
Additional Resources, writing professor and journalist Christopher Thornton
recalls his acquaintance with the men who would later destroy the World Trade
Center, citing it as a warning against making snap judgments about the face of
terror. Indeed, the contemporary face of terror is multinational and multiethnic.

Since the September 11 attacks, terrorist acts perpetrated by a number of
groups have occurred around the world: in the Russian province of Chechnya; in
Istanbul, Turkey; in Madrid; in Beslan, Russia; in London; in Delhi and Mumbai,
India; in Kampala, Uganda; in Greece; and across Iran. Terrorist violence increased
steadily between 2007 and 2013, with a significant jump (43 per cent) between 2012
and 2013, according to US State Department figures. Terrorist-related violence
caused the most deaths in Iraq, Pakistan, and Afghanistan in 2013. In 2014, the
US Department of State urged US citizens to "maintain a high level of vigilance"
against terrorist attacks, particularly in response to its military action against ISIS.

Academics often respond to worldwide violence with reports such as the one
mentioned above; scholars of international relations, political science, anthropology and sociology also work to find solutions that might affect public policy.
As discussed below, many advocate non-violent methods while others contend a
show of force is the only way to end terrorism.

Responses to terrorism: One topic that has been of particular interest to scholars in the last decade is the phenomenon of military terrorism: how can we guard
ourselves against it, especially without sacrificing our human freedoms? How
should we treat people accused of terrorism? Escalating attacks by the Syrian
army against civilians and rebels since the uprising began in 2011 have provoked
global outrage; although some United Nations members advocate military intervention, Russia, China, Cuba, and Iran oppose intervention.

What is the difference between aggressive civil disobedience and terrorism? A
recent book by Robert Imre et al., listed in the Suggested Additional Resources,
gives a useful overview of key issues related to contemporary terrorism. These
issues include the relative efficacy of torture and counterterrorism, torture and
natural law versus actual law, the socio-politics of terror, and the politics of religious violence. In their introduction, the authors note the remarkable lack of
consensus about what motivates terrorists, what constitutes acts of terrorism,
and what needs to be done about terrorism. Amy Lifland examines the possibility of cyberterrorism in an editorial included in this chapter.

Ethics of torture: One of the major issues related to armed conflict is the definition of torture and the ethics of its application. Some legal scholars, sociologists,
and psychologists call torture any practice that inflicts severe mental or physical suffering on another, while others maintain that only inflicting great pain
is torture. And scholars are divided over whether torture is an ethical practice.

Utilitarians argue that torture is acceptable if it results in information that saves lives. Idealists side with eighteenth-century philosopher Immanuel Kant, who believed that human beings should never treat people as mere means to an end, no matter what the circumstances. One contemporary debate regarding torture concerns the ethics of various forms of interrogation, and whether they constitute torture. American interrogation of prisoners using a technique called waterboarding, or simulated drowning, brought this issue to the public attention recently. Some, including many in the US military and the George W. Bush administration, claimed that waterboarding was torture, which was outlawed by the Geneva Convention. Others claimed that waterboarding did not constitute torture but was instead a useful method for extracting valuable information from suspected terrorists. Still others claimed that waterboarding was indeed torture, but that it served the greater good, providing information useful for national security. Recent articles by philosopher David Sussman and by Jessica Wolfendale represent two sides of this many-faceted debate, and are listed in the Suggested Additional Resources.

Counterterrorism: This is a major issue for academics, especially with respect to the roles of the United States, post-industrial Western democracies, and the United Nations in the global War on Terror. The war was launched as an international security measure in 2001, soon after the September 11 attacks. It remains unclear how many subsequent attacks the resultant measures have prevented.

The sustained campaign against terrorism has aroused much debate in several quarters, particularly among academics, security analysts, and rights advocates. Arguments tend to focus on measures such as the internment center for purported terrorists at Guantanamo, Cuba, the use of military tribunals to secretly try accused non-military, and the denial of travel visas to foreign scholars and others on watchlists. Additionally, the second invasion and subsequent occupation of Iraq in 2003 gave rise to speculation that the West has motives other than decreasing the terrorist threat—such as securing Western oil interests.

Moreover, human-rights advocates, including professors of philosophy, political science, international relations, and other fields, have charged that post-9/11 security measures have severely curtailed civil liberties around the world. By contrast, others have found that the measures implemented to prevent terrorism have *not* resulted in appreciable increase in violations of the human rights of citizens or accused terrorists. This latter group contends that internal political conflict is a much stronger indicator of security rights violations than the efforts at counterterrorism.

Many scholars have also studied the economic and political effects of the ramping up of national security measures. What does this ballooning of counterterrorism and security activities mean for American citizens? What similar efforts have other countries made in recent years, and to what avail? These are the questions that engage academics studying the nature and results of counterterrorism and national security measures around the world.

Military intervention as a response to human-rights violations: One issue of interest to both policymakers and academics is how to protect citizens whose rights have been violated. Should another country intervene with military force? Does it help? Is it legal? Is it ethical? Who decides when and under what circumstances intervention is appropriate?

A 2002 report by the International Council on Human Rights Policy discussed some of the dilemmas that arise when armed force is proposed to protect civilians. Recent military interventions by United Nations security forces designed to protect civilians in Somalia and Kosovo were not successful. On the other hand, some say that UN military force could have saved the lives of hundreds of thousands of Tutsi civilians attacked by the Hutu majority. However, the UN lent only a peacekeeping contingent, authorizing military intervention too late. Similarly, when hundreds of thousands of ethnic Albanians were killed or expelled from the former Republic of Yugoslavia, the UN sent only relief supplies for three years.

Many groups say that military intervention is not helpful or appropriate, and that economic and other sanctions against the country involved are the best way to prevent or ameliorate human-rights violations. Still others suggest that while human-rights violations are abhorrent, military intervention is not the solution; these scholars would advocate diplomacy and trade sanctions as more effective and humane options.

Trade sanctions in response to illegal armament: In 2010, South Korea and the United States initiated trade sanctions on North Korea, putting a strain on the latter's fragile economy. South Korea was responding to the sinking of one of its warships, for which it blamed North Korea. The United States was motivated to sanction North Korea in order to help end the proliferation of North Korea's nuclear weapons programs. Some economists believe that trade and financial sanctions could cause famine in North Korea.

In another case, the European Union (EU) debated imposing stricter trade sanctions against Iran to deter its nuclear arms program. These sanctions would include banning investment in Iran's oil and gas industry and further restricting shipping and finance between EU members and Iran. Such economic pressure, although much of it affects privately held companies, might put political pressure on the Iranian government and encourage them to dismantle their nuclear program—if indeed they have a military nuclear program.

Although many economists believe these sanctions are the best solution, some political scientists, military historians, and other scholars argue that they disproportionately punish citizens already short of food and other necessities.

Ethics/viability of military draft: The United States has not had a military draft since the end of the Vietnam War in 1973. Its military is staffed by full-time volunteer soldiers and National Guard soldiers; the latter have been called to active service in increasing numbers since the Iraq War began in 2003. Although there is little political or public support for a draft, military analysts believe it might be necessary, according to a 2007 Congressional Budget Office report. First, the US military might need more troops to accomplish its missions. Second, military personnel and their families are shouldering hardships on behalf of the United States that are not shared by the rest of the population. And third, the military is disproportionately staffed by the underclass, creating an unfair burden on this group to the benefit of the wealthy.

Enforced disarmament: Under what circumstances does a country have the authority, legal and/or ethical, to forcibly disarm another? Forcible disarmament was common in ancient wars; the stronger or victorious army considered it a humane alternative to continued violence or subjugation. From that perspective, a democratic country is most likely to choose disarmament over its alternatives. After the Gulf War, for example, the United Nations adopted a policy of forced disarmament in Iraq. But is this an effective method for a lasting peace? Does it cause antagonism to build in the vanquished country to the point of instigating further violence? Also, is it legal, ethical, or even possible to disarm a government without going to war? These are the questions that surround enforced disarmament today. Philip Towle, in his book *Enforced Disarmament: From the Napoleonic Campaigns to the Gulf War*, considers this issue in depth; the book is listed in the Suggested Additional Resources at the end of this introduction.

As You Read

Consider the ways in which global conflicts have affected your life and the lives of those around you. Chances are you know someone who is or has been in the military. Perhaps you know someone with relatives in a war-torn country. How does this personal connection to war affect your attitude to it? Think about how you react when you read about armed conflict or are deciding whether to vote for a politician who supports or does not support a particular armed conflict.

Suggested Additional Resources

Anthropology, Psychology, and Sociology

Fry, Douglas P. *Beyond War: The Human Potential for Peace*. New York: Oxford UP, 2007.
Houghton, David Patrick. *Political Psychology: Situations, Individuals and Cases*. New York: Routledge, 2008.
Kelly, Raymond C. *Warless Societies and the Origin of War*. Ann Arbor: U of Michigan P, 2000.

Lucas, George R. *Anthropologists in Arms: The Ethics of Military Anthropology.* Lanham, MD: AltaMira Press, 2009.

Malešević, Siniša. *The Sociology of War and Violence.* New York: Cambridge UP, 2010.

Omidian, Patricia A. "Living and Working in a War Zone: An Applied Anthropologist in Afghanistan." *Practicing Anthropology* 31.2 (Spring 2009): 4-11. Web.

Solomon, Z., R. Dekel, and Gadi Zerach. "Posttraumatic Stress Disorder and Marital Adjustment: The Mediating Role of Forgiveness." *Family Process* 48.4 (Dec 2009): 546-58. Web.

Arts and Humanities

Clifford, Hubert. *British Film Music.* Cambridge: Cambridge UP, 2010. Print.

Grant, M.J., Rebecca Möllemann, Ingvill Morlandstö, Simone Christine Münz, and Cornelia Nuxoll. "Music and Conflict: Interdisciplinary Perspectives." *Interdisciplinary Science Reviews* 35.2 (June 2010): 183-98. Web.

Hell and Back Again. Dir. Danfung Dennis. Docurama Films, 2011. Film.

Pieslak, Jonathan. *Sound Targets: American Soldiers and Music in the Iraq War.* Bloomington: Indiana UP, 2009.

Restrepo. Dirs. Tim Hetherington and Sebastian Junger. Outpost Films, 2010. Film.

Taylor, Steve. "The Psychology of War: Why Do Human Beings Find It So Difficult to Live in Peace?" *Psychology Today* 5 March 2014. Web.

Thornton, Christopher. "Faces of Terror." *Sewanee Review* 118.2 (Spring 2010): 199-209. Web.

Economics

Collier, Paul, Anke Hoeffler, and Dominic Rohner. "Beyond Greed and Grievance: Feasibility and Civil War." *Oxford Economic Papers* 61.1 (2009): 1-27. Web.

del Castillo, Graciana. *Rebuilding War-Torn States: The Challenge of Post-Conflict Economic Reconstruction.* New York: Oxford UP, 2008.

Glick, Reuven, and Alan M. Taylor. "Trade Disruption and the Economic Impact of War." *The Review of Economics and Statistics* 92.1 (Feb 2010): 102-27. Web.

Education

Blair, Elizabeth E., Rebecca B. Miller, and Mara Casey Tieken, eds. *Education and War.* Cambridge, MA: Harvard Education Press, 2009.

Cohen, Michael David. *Reconstructing the Campus: Higher Education and the American Civil War*. Charlottesville: U of Virginia P, 2012.

Hulsey, Timothy L. "From the Battleground to the Classroom." *Phi Kappa Phi Forum* 90.2 (Summer 2010): 25 Web.

Law and Ethics

Evangelista, Matthew. *Law, Ethics, and the War on Terror*. Cambridge: Polity Press, 2008.

Solis, Gary D. *The Law of Armed Conflict: International Humanitarian Law in War*. Cambridge: Cambridge UP, 2010.

Wolfendale, Jessica. "The Myth of 'Torture Lite.'" *Ethics & International Affairs* 23.1 (2009): 47-61. Web.

Life Sciences

Embrey, Ellen P., Robert Clerman, Mark F. Gentilman, Fred Cecere, and William Klenke. "Community-Based Medical Disaster Planning: A Role for the Department of Defense and the Military Health System." *Military Medicine* 175.5 (May 2010): 298-300. Web.

Feczer, Diana, and Pamela Bjorklund. "Forever Changed: Posttraumatic Stress Disorder in Female Military Veterans: A Case Report. *Perspectives in Psychiatric Care* 45.4 (Oct 2009): 278-91. Web.

Gariti, Katherine O., Leila Joisa Sadeghi, D. Sowmya, and William C. Holmes. "Veterans' Distress Related to Participation in a Study about Detainee Abuse." *Military Medicine* 174.11 (Nov 2009): 1149-54. Web.

Military History and Political Science

Barua, Pradeep. *The Military Effectiveness of Post-Colonial States*. Boston: Brill, 2013.

Center for International Development and Conflict Management. *Peace and Conflict 2014*. College Park: University of Maryland, 2014. Web.

Clausewitz, Carl. *On War*. Princeton, NJ: Princeton UP, 1976.

Codevilla, Angelo. *War: Ends and Means*. Dulles, VA: Potomac Books, 2006.

Coffman, Edward M. *The Embattled Past: Reflections on Military History*. Lexington: The UP of Kentucky, 2013.

Fatovic, Clement. "Settled Law in Unsettling Times: A Lockean View of the War on Terror." *The Good Society* 18.2 (Autumn 2009): 14-19.

Gat, Azar. "So Why Do People Fight? Evolutionary Theory and the Causes of War." *European Journal of International Relations* 15 (Dec. 2009): 571-99. Web.

Goldsmith, Jack. *Power and Constraint: The Accountable Presidency after 9/11.*
    New York: Norton, 2012.

Harvey, James A. III. "Logistics and Analysis in the Science of War." *Army*
    Sustainment 44.3 (2012): n.p. Web.

Imre, Robert, T. Brian Mooney, and Benjamin Clarke. *Responding to Terrorism:*
    Political, Philosophical and Legal Perspectives. Burlington, VT: Ashgate,
    2008.

Johnson, Dominic D.P., and Dominic Tierney. *Failing to Win: Perceptions of*
    Victory and Defeat in International Politics. Cambridge, MA: Harvard
    University Press, 2006.

Lindley-French, Julian, and Yves Boyer, eds. *The Oxford Handbook of War.* New
    York: Oxford UP, 2012.

Paige, Glenn D. *Nonkilling Global Political Science.* Honolulu: Center for Global
    Nonkilling, 2009.

Paris, Roland, and Timothy D. Sisk, eds. *The Dilemmas of Statebuilding:*
    Confronting the Contradictions of Postwar Peace Operations. New York:
    Routledge, 2009.

Seividge, Maria J. "Religion, Greed, and the Insanity of War." *Political Theology*
    10.4 (Oct. 2009): 721-45. Web.

Theis, Cameron G., and David Sobek. "War, Economic Development, and
    Political Development in the Contemporary International System."
    International Studies Quarterly 54.1 (2010): 267-87. Web.

Towle, Philip. *Enforced Disarmament: From the Napoleonic Campaigns to the Gulf*
    War. Oxford: Clarendon Press, 1997.

a. Amy Lifland, "Cyberwar: The Future of Conflict"

Amy Lifland is a senior associate for corporate strategy at Capital One in Washington, DC. She wrote this piece as an undergraduate student at Harvard University and a staff writer for the *Harvard International Review*. Lifland is also the author of "Starvation and the Sahel" (*Harvard International Review* July 7, 2012). This article, originally published in the *Harvard International Review*, emphasizes the immediate and widespread nature of the threat of cybercrime, both in America and across the globe. Lifland is particularly concerned with the possible dangers to worldwide military operations.

Lifland's article is short, of-the-moment, and opinionated. Though it was published in an academic journal, it was published as an editorial, not as an academic study. Thus, though it presents a brief, one-sided view characteristic of a commentary, it also presents facts and examples to back up its claims, as required for academic argument.

As You Read: Think about any experiences you have had in which the information on your computer, tablet, or phone has been compromised. Is cybercrime common, in your experience? Does Lifland's claim that cybercrime could jeopardize global security seem alarmist to you? Or does it seem realistic? What points can you think of that Lifland's short piece does not consider? What points might someone raise to refute her claims?

Cyberwar: The Future of Conflict

In the past six months, hackers have infiltrated the websites and internal servers of the United States Senate, the CIA, numerous other state and federal agencies, private corporations, and individuals. The onslaught seems unstoppable, and the FBI and other US law enforcement agencies struggle to identify and arrest the hackers responsible for the attacks. Many hackers are after money, concentrating on identity theft and other frauds that have allowed them to steal tens of millions of dollars, primarily from small businesses in the United States. More ominous, however, is the recent trend of attempted and successful cyber-infiltrations into government agencies, the military, and the email accounts of government officials and other individuals with high security clearances, in the United States as well as other nations.

At the same time that attacks are being launched against the United States, the United States has come much closer to launching its own cyber attacks. In early 2011, before leading conventional military strikes against Gaddafi's regime in Libya, the United States considered, and ultimately rejected, initiating a cyber attack against Libya's air-defense system, hoping to cripple its ability to act against the upcoming airstrikes. Although the United States rejected the plan, that it was even considered is strong evidence of the importance that the Obama administration has placed on cybersecurity, as it has become increasingly pressing for both homeland security and offensive military tactics.

Since taking office, Obama has taken unprecedented steps to develop a coherent United States policy on the issues surrounding cyberspace, particularly those relating to defense. The Obama administration was the first to appoint a Director of Cybersecurity and has released several publications detailing its cyberstrategy, starting with the *Cyberspace Policy Review* and the *International Strategy for Cyberspace*, in the first years of Obama's presidency. Published in July 2011, the *Department of Defense Strategy for Operating in Cyberspace*, as the title implies, outlined how the Pentagon, which is in charge of all military domains, would approach cybersecurity issues. The Obama administration has also pushed Congress to draft and pass comprehensive cybersecurity legislation, a move which has received bipartisan support. One factor that greatly complicates the issue of cyberdefense, however, is that cyber attacks are not solely made against the government or other public networks, but rather against private companies. There is debate amongst experts about how much the government should be involved in ensuring private companies are adequately protected against cyber attacks.

The United States is also an active participant in international conversations about cybersecurity, where there is much less consensus about appropriate rules and norms. Broadly speaking, there are two different approaches to cybersecurity that countries tend to take. The first, which is exemplified by the policies of the United States and the United Kingdom, want to be able to crack down on cybercrime without inhibiting the free flow of information between and within countries. The second, primarily promoted by Russia and China, is concerned with limiting the flow of information across borders. Russian and Chinese leaders are concerned that free information could make their societies less stable. While the Obama administration has stated that it would support the creation of an international treaty on cyberspace, it seems unlikely that agreement could be reached on any such treaty in the near future, given the divergent views on the most pressing issues of cyberspace.

Another important issue on which there is no international consensus is whether a cyber attack should be recognized as a use of force against another nation and what the appropriate response to such intrusions should be. The target of an attack is important when determining whether it constitutes an act of war against a nation. In the United States, the President's Commission on Critical Infrastructure Protection identified five sectors, Information and Communications, Physical Distribution, Energy, Banking, and Finance, which are so critical to

American economic and national security that a cyber attack against them would constitute an act of war and therefore justify the use of force in response. Clearly, the recommendations of this commission are not binding, and certainly do not apply to countries besides the United States, but they are an illuminating example of considerations that must be made regarding cyber attacks. One goal of an international cyberspace treaty would be to outline what types of cyber attacks constitute an act of force and therefore legitimize a retaliatory act of force.

Another reason that it is so difficult to develop domestic and international legislation around cybersecurity issues is that it is often hard to pinpoint exactly who the perpetrators of a cyber attack are and therefore how to respond to them. Even though Google was able to trace a successful campaign to infiltrate the email accounts of thousands of people in the United States to China, including some high ranking government officials, there was no clear next course of action for the United States. The Chinese government quickly denied any involvement, a claim the United States and Google had no way of proving definitively. Because the attacks were purported to be perpetrated by non-state actors, the United States could not take any direct action against the Chinese government, and instead pursued a law-enforcement program, attempting to identify and arrest the hackers within the confines of normal diplomatic rules, its usual and only course of action in such cases.

The United States clearly has a long way to go in solidifying its own policies regarding cybersecurity, and even more time will be required before any kind of international consensus on these issues can be reached. The aborted cyber attack on Libya demonstrates how legal concerns about cybersecurity have yet to be resolved. One of the main reasons that the Libyan attack did not take place was that military officials were not convinced that the United States had the technology to launch an attack on such short notice and insure that it would be contained to the air-defense system without spilling over into other networks. Experts also feared that the United States launching its first full-scale cyber attack against another state would establish a precedent for Russia, China, or other nations to initiate similar campaigns, which would undoubtedly derail progress in establishing international cybersecurity norms. Furthermore, it was also questioned whether the attack needed to be authorized by Congress under the War Powers Resolution, depending on whether it qualified as using forces to initiate "hostilities." While the technological impediments to a cyber attack like the one against Libya will undoubtedly be resolved in the near future, the other legal issues face questions that must eventually be resolved through domestic and international legislation.

Source: *Harvard International Review* Spring (2012): 7-8.

WHAT IT SAYS

1. Lifland begins by describing what crime? What was the purpose of the crime? What was the victims' response to the crime?

2. What trend is even "more ominous" than the crime Lifland first describes? Who are the victims of this trend?

3. What similar crime did the United States military consider launching? What was the result? According to Lifland, what is the significance of this plan?

4. What has the Obama administration done to counter cybercrime? What issue complicates these measures?

5. What two types of cybersecurity approaches do countries generally take? In what way do these divergent approaches complicate global cybersecurity? What other factors complicate passage of an international cyberspace treaty?

6. What types of cyberattack does the United States consider grounds for retaliation?

7. What factors prevented the United States from launching a cyberattack on Libya, according to Lifland?

HOW IT SAYS IT

1. How does Lifland begin her essay? What are the benefits and drawbacks of beginning the essay in this way? How does she end her essay? What is the effect of this kind of ending?

2. Whom does Lifland seem to address in this essay? What does she do to tailor her essay to this audience?

3. What rhetorical devices does Lifland use to make her argument? Discuss the effectiveness of these devices.

WRITE ABOUT IT

1. Imagine that you are the director of the team tasked with preparing a policy for fighting cybercrime in the United States. Prepare a proposal to present to the president and his cabinet that acknowledges the issues involved and argues that your plan is the best way to fight cybercrime.

2. Consider the issues involved in creating an international treaty on cybersecurity. Then draft a treaty that sets out standards that countries across the globe are likely to sign. Use Lifland's essay as a resource, as well as sample international treaties and any other material that will help you create a treaty that is likely to be ratified and enforced.

3. Write a response to Lifland's essay that disputes the urgency of a national and an international policy on cybercrime. If you wish, write this piece as a speech to be delivered before a Congressional committee or other governing body. Or produce it as a video that lawmakers will watch online. Illustrate your data with graphs, charts, and photographs.

b. Thomas G. Bowie, Jr., "Memory and Meaning: The Need for Narrative: Reflections on the Symposium 'Twentieth Century Warfare and American Memory'"

Thomas G. Bowie, Jr. directs the honors program at Regis University in Denver, Colorado. He has written extensively on war literature, first as an associate editor for the journal *War, Literature, and the Arts* in the 1990s, and then as its managing editor from 1999 to 2002. His writing includes interviews with and essays about such writers as Tim O'Brien, Bill Ehrhart, Philip Caputo, Edmund Blunden, and Robert Graves.

Before coming to Regis University in 2004, Bowie spent 28 years in the US Air Force. Bowie holds a BS in humanities from the US Air Force Academy, an MA in strategic studies from Air War College, an MA in English from the University of Denver, and a PhD in English from Brown University.

The article below is an introduction to a 2009 symposium on war and literature held at Regis University. Bowie introduces and briefly discusses the presentations of five authors, and adds examples of his own. In this sense, Bowie's piece is an excellent example of synthesis (see pp. 77–79). Here, Bowie contemplates the role of stories in human existence and then narrows his scope to the purpose of war literature. Human beings may well have "a primal need for narrative," Bowie writes. And this need is especially sharp when people attempt to create meaning from "the shifting and chaotic phantasmagoria of wartime memories."

As You Read: Contemplate the role of stories and storytelling in your everyday life. How many stories do you think you hear every day? How many do you tell? Does Bowie's interpretation of the special role of war stories make sense to you?

Memory and Meaning: The Need for Narrative: Reflections on the Symposium "Twentieth Century Warfare and American Memory"

"We tell ourselves stories in order to live" claims Joan Didion, a modern American writer who has thought lots about stories. "We look for the sermon in the suicide, for the social or moral lesson in the murder of five," she continues. "We interpret what we see, select the most workable of the multiple choices. We live entirely, especially if we are writers, by the imposition of a narrative line upon disparate images, by the 'ideas' with which we have learned to freeze the shifting phantasmagoria which is our actual experience" (*White Album*, 11). We tell ourselves stories in order to live, especially, I might add, if we are veterans of modern warfare, living by imposing a narrative line upon the shifting and chaotic phantasmagoria of wartime memories. In some fashion, we all select the most workable option to make sense of our world with stories. We all cherish the stories that help organize and order our world. We all seek the stories that give it meaning. But that search for meaning is especially important to veterans of modern conflict, to men and women who so often struggle with memory in the hope of finding meaning, and through meaning, to find hope.

Let me be clear at the outset: I believe that memory and meaning are often negotiated in the arena of narrative. As another American writer, Reynolds Price, a former professor at Duke University, puts it:

> A need to tell and hear stories is essential to the species *Homo Sapiens*— second in necessity apparently after nourishment and before love and shelter. Millions survive without love or home, almost none in silence; the opposite of silence leads quickly to narrative, and the sound of story is the dominant sound of our lives, from the small accounts of our days' events to the vast incommunicable constructs of psychopaths. (qtd. in Gregory, 35)

Man—and woman—the storytelling animal. Second only to physical sustenance is our hunger for stories, the dominant sound of our lives. The symposium at Regis University last fall focused deliberately on a special brand of stories, the "soldiers' tale" as Samuel Hynes would have it. We joined together those who study war stories for a living and those who bear witness to modern war as they tell their tales, as they share their stories. Just where do the experiences a man or woman encounters during wartime intersect with the stories he or she subsequently tells about them? Does a primal need for narrative, as Reynolds Price suggests, provoke these stories? If so, where might the memories of experience intersect most fully with a corresponding quest for meaning? To what extent is every narrative something made, something formed—something, for example, with a beginning and an ending; something that has a completeness because of its narrative shape; something, finally, that exceeds the gritty details of actual experience (those details that are so often beyond comprehension in the actual moment of experience, yet the very essence that insistently begs for this comprehension nonetheless) in its essential cry for meaning? Samuel Hynes in *The Soldiers' Tale* spends much time thinking his way through these complex intersections. Here is how he begins to pin down the essence of war narratives early in *The Soldiers' Tale*:

If war narratives aren't travel writing, aren't autobiography, aren't history, what are they? *Stories*, first of all: responses to that primal need we all have to tell and hear individual experiences, and so to understand our own lives and imagine the lives of others. Stories answer the question that we ask of any experience, whether our own or somebody else's: What happened? What was it like? How did it feel? The soldier asks those questions of his war life and answers them in the telling of his story, and so discovers its meaning and gets his war straight in his mind. We, his readers, ask those questions too: they are our motive for reading. (16)

Hynes raises a number of key points in this quotation, ones that I want to dwell on briefly because they will help illuminate some of the papers that follow from the symposium. Why are stories, especially personal narratives, so important to our understanding of conflict? Hynes suggests, in part, because they begin to answer the most basic questions we ask of any experience, something I too believe. In addressing these questions, a personal narrative invites memory to coalesce into meaning, inviting both the storyteller and his or her audience to "get the war straight" in our minds. Yet as we do so, ever more urgent questions begin to interrogate the narrative we are forming. After all, how do we know what war means? By the way, *what does war mean*? *How* does war mean? *Why* does war mean what it means? *Whose stories* have the power to give war such meaning, and *which stories* lead us to the greatest clarity about how and why war means? Put differently, how do you tell a true war story and why are such stories vitally important to us, as readers or hearers, even as they help the teller discover the meaning of his or her own war experience?

These are among the questions various participants in the symposium Twentieth Century Warfare and American Memory took up, each from his or her own perspective. In the papers assembled here, each author approaches his slice of the truth cautiously, contingently, probing the details of lived experience in the hope of locating a locus of meaning within it. In his reflection titled "War Memories, Archives, and *Friendship*," Daryl Palmer blends a reading of Willa Cather's novel of World War I, *One of Ours*, with a "reading" of the personal archive of his father's World War II memorabilia. Suggesting that Cather is one of our "great American writers because she is our preeminent novelist of memory," Palmer goes on to explain how a "readerly experience of attachment has everything to do with memory"—with how we remember, what we remember, and ultimately with what such rememberings in the guise of stories come to mean. "Does anyone, male or female, ever really tell another person's stories of war?" Professor Palmer asks. "Or are we always telling our own story?" Although he intentionally leaves this an open question, it is in the telling of *his* own story, reading in the personal archives of his father's war, that he ultimately locates a true war story that invests his experience with meaning.

Yet whatever limits we face in telling another's story, in order to comprehend the complex legacy of modern wars, in order to approach—however tentatively—the truths stories about them seek to articulate, we must try. Today we are embroiled in what Dexter Filkins calls the Forever War in Iraq and Afghanistan, wars that often seem to defy meaning, wars whose human costs will weigh upon us for decades to come. So it seems especially important to tell all the stories about these wars that we possibly can because the legacy of modern conflict is a lasting one, one that endures at the individual level for a lifetime. Ed Wood, in his powerful meditation, "Memory and Myth: What Was World War II Really Like?" reminds us that various myths associated with this war have "led us to deny the reality of World War II, to conveniently forget what happened to a whole generation of young men in combat, to civilians killed and wounded, to cities destroyed, to millions of refugees without homes." Wood tells his own story briefly as he recounts the larger tragic story of the Army Specialized Training Program, a program that subjected marginally trained replacement soldiers during late 1944 and early 1945 to a brutal casualty rate in the European Theater of Operations. Probing the "mythical nature of memory," Wood argues that our belief in key myths associated with World War II has made it difficult, perhaps almost impossible, for us to remember what World War II was really like.

And remembering what war—any war—was really like is a theme that punctuated virtually every presentation during the symposium. Terry Rizzuti, a marine during the Vietnam War, desperately wants us to understand the importance of stories in that remembering. In his case, trying to tell a true war story consumed his life for almost 25 years as he wrote and rewrote the novel that seeks to invest his experience with appropriate meaning (*The Second Tour*, 2008). In modern conflict, Rizzuti suggests, things go wrong and then you live with the consequences—consequences where the human spirit is tried and sometimes broken. The story of consequences, then, both individual and collective, becomes Rizzuti's theme as he explores the life-long impact of PTSD, or the therapeutic perspective associated with writing, or the way in which such writing might open doors for readers to rarely discussed subjects such as veterans rejecting veterans. As Rizzuti explores these issues, he focuses on the "tricky" nature of memory, and on the way the "necessary imaginings" associated with daily life on patrol—or with telling "whoppers to keep that beer flowing" in the enlisted men's club—constantly shape his consciousness of real events, constantly contextualize the memories that provide the concrete details his narratives are always rooted in. Most tellingly, the longer Rizzuti works with these fraught dimensions of memory, the more convinced he becomes that "psychological blurring can bring historical blurring, not only for an individual but perhaps also for a nation that experiences war year after year after year." In his own way, Rizzuti is engaging the same question of myth that interests Wood, the same question that animates the inquiry addressed above about what, how, and why war comes to mean what it does—both for individuals and for a nation.

These questions also provide a central locus for many of the narratives collected in the archives of the Regis Center for the Study of War Experience over the past fifteen years. An interdisciplinary enterprise whose archive contains hundreds of hours of video-recorded testimonies of war veterans and thousands of items of personal war effects, the Center's archive is a sizeable repository of war memories and an important location of primary source research materials. The entire collection is catalogued and the Center operates as a professional working archive open to students, scholars, and the public. The Center's Director, Dan Clayton, narrates some of the history of the Center in his essay "Remembering World War Two at Regis University," even as he notes the way in which his memories and those of his father—a World War II veteran who traveled with Patton's Third Army in their drive across France and Germany, 1944-45—intersect with the many stories collected in the archives, refining, among other things, his understanding of the myth of the "good war" and the "Greatest Generation." For example, Clayton notes that "for a long time, the World War Two in our heads did not include memories of African-Americans fighting the war both at home and abroad, Japanese-American citizens held in our version of concentration camps, or women in the Armed Services." Echoing the comments of Wood and Rizzuti, Clayton questions the consequences of presenting "a highly sanitized and romanticized narrative" of the Good War "which effectively removed its horrors from our collective memory." Given the force of such a seductive myth of World War Two, Clayton focused an entire panel during the symposium on how WWII *should be* remembered. Orchestrating a conversation between literary critics, historians, best-selling authors, and veterans of the air war in Europe, the ground war in the Pacific, and the home front, Clayton reminds us that "memory is a slippery process, and the task of using memories as evidence of actual experience is complicated by all the ambiguities associated with them." And yet, even with the challenges memory poses, negotiating the meaning of these experiences through narrative remains a vital enterprise. Given the urgency associated with such telling, then, Clayton suggests "if we seek to elicit a bigger 'truth' from these stories, perhaps the best we can do—and we try to do this at Regis—is to keep both sides of the dichotomy in our consciousness. WWII needed to be fought, but that doesn't make it 'good' in all respects. Like all wars, WWII had its fair share of sadistic, brutal, and insane behavior, but it was also filled with acts of extraordinary courage, honor, and heroism." As Hynes reminds us, "collectively these narratives contribute, by a shifting process that is gradual and probably not conscious, to the emerging, evolving story of their wars, a story that is neither history nor memory, but myth—a compound war-story that gives meaning and coherence to the incoherences of war-in-its-details" ("Personal Narratives and Commemoration," 220).

The necessity to locate such meaning and coherence, and the astonishing costs of living within coherence, provides the framework for Ron Langer's insightful essay "Combat Trauma, Memory, and the World War II Veteran." Langer's work as a psychotherapist with the VA brought him into contact with many WWII veterans whose PTSD appeared or reappeared after a long period of dormancy in mid-life. Speculating on the phenomena of "delayed-onset PTSD" Langer suggests that the large blocks of unscheduled time most retirees encounter often leads to introspection, which can lead to self-deprecating thoughts and excessive regret for past actions. "A satisfying life must have meaning," Langer argues, "and unfortunately for many of us that meaning is tied up in our work. A life without meaning leaves plenty of room for PTSD." Through his work with hundreds of veterans, Langer is able to offer a unique perspective on the relationship between memory and meaning. "Remarkably," Langer observes, "memories and dreams of the war remain vivid, even more than 65 years later. However, the vividness and subjective sense of their immutability does not necessarily prove their accuracy, since they are necessarily mediated by language and meaning." And it is this process of mediation that all of these essays engage from various perspectives.

Given this enormously complex intersection between memory and meaning, and given the essential role narrative plays in negotiating the two, it is tempting to simply say that each experience is unique, as is each teller, so in the end we can't ever *tell* a true war story (in both senses of *tell*: a veteran can't really share the full truth of his or her experience in a telling any more than any reader or listener can *tell* or discern its truth value). But deconstructing the power of narrative into such meaningless relativity also has grave consequences, and in Clayton's words we must do "the best we can do" to locate whatever elusive truths lurk behind these tellings. Marshall Gregory, an authority on narrative, argues that "the vicarious experiences of narrative create the potential for real and significant effects—ethical, emotional, intellectual, political, and so on— in readers' lives" (36-37). In brief, Gregory argues that stories are built from concrete details, which allows them to actively engage a reader's imagination, which then provokes vicarious experiences in readers that educate and connect us, thus giving narratives—giving stories—a power that has real and significant effects, a power that actually can change the world. Little wonder, then, that we have needed narrative from the dawn of human history. As we more fully consider the way in which American war experience is remembered, as we chart the many ways such experience is mapped and narrated, as we continually probe the vital intersection between memory and meaning, we discover the ways in which these powerful stories have actually formed who we are today. In short, the stories that have formed us, and those that we form, because they are firmly rooted in often overpowering and incomprehensible details, yet also energized with an imaginative force that connects us, draw us into vicarious participation with them. Most importantly, this vicarious participation located at the intersection of memory and meaning gives these narratives the power to continually shape our world.

Although each of the following essays makes this point in its own unique way, I'd like to illustrate it with a brief concrete example from a personal narrative of conflict. This narrative comes from a B-17 bombardier who also served as a gunner defending the Flying Fortress on its way to and from the battle ... a bombardier very special to my family because the diary I'm quoting from belonged to my wife's father, Bobby Metcalf.

Bobby Metcalf trained in B-17s much of 1942 and deployed for Europe on Jan 20th, 1943. On Feb 8th the crew delivered the B-17 they had flown to South America, to North Africa, to Spain, and finally to England, where they began training for combat at Bovington on Feb 10th. After 10 days of "school" their "very green crew" was assigned to the 364th Sq of the 305th Bomb Group. "Contrary to our former beliefs," Bobby confides, "the Fortresses are going down. We now start sweating out 25 raids! At that time it's US bound! No doubt the future will prove very interesting with FW-190's and flak playing the leading roles!" As you listen to Bobby's account of the next six months, note how his image of war—the "war in his head" as Sam Hynes would put it—is slowly reshaped by the actual experience of combat. The sense that this experience is just an extension of boyhood school lessons and that all the actors involved are merely playing roles in some larger drama quickly gives way to a less coherent narrative for his overwhelming experiences, yet one that nonetheless invites us to join it vicariously, and in so doing, to help its author discover what it all means. Here is the account from his diary:

2-25-43 Our first raid, and Sam and I didn't get to go ... today was my first day of waiting for the boys to come back. Bobby, Tim, and Ham returned safely, but still no news of Wally and Swede. We still have hopes. Lakey, Wells, and Moberly came back all shot to hell. They were plenty lucky.

2-27-43 Another raid today. Bobby, Tim, Ham and John safe. Still no news of Wally and Swede! No news is good news, but they were shot up pretty bad ...

3-8-43 Haven't had time to write here lately. I was on a raid to Lorient, France on Saturday.... We really blew it to hell. My bombs blew up two bridges and perhaps two trains. Not much enemy action. Two 17s went down. Sam got a telegram today that Pat is going to have a baby in Sept. Bobby is now a 1st LT. Ham got a hun today on his fifth raid. Nice. Rose got one a couple of days ago—I guess Wally and Swede have gone West as there is still no word of them. Art Spatz was seriously injured today by "Jerry." I sure hope he will be OK ...

And so goes the narrative, slightly less connected than a fully realized story might be, because it is written one entry at a time. Nonetheless, the concrete details, the invitations to join Bobby Metcalf in his hopes for lost comrades, his joy at success against the "jerries or huns" and his sorrow at the loss of his friends all resonate with the narrative elements I highlighted above. On March 18th, Bobby records his "biggest and luckiest day so far. We raided Vegasack, Germany. It was the farthest we have ever penetrated into Germany. Met very stiff fighters and flak. We also set a new record for accuracy! The target was demolished. We only lost two bombers, one 17 and one 24. Our new navigator is OK only he can't handle a machine gun yet. But he'll learn!"

A month into combat and the individual chronicle of names—those who fly, those who die—has given way to "only" losing 2 planes. And the novice of last month has become the seasoned veteran ready to critique and teach his new navigator. Given the loss rate during the combined bomber offensive over Germany—for example, later that year, on Aug. 17, the targets were Schweinfurt and Regensburg, deep inside Germany; 60 of the 376 bombers were shot down, the AAF's most disastrous air battle to date. On Sep. 6, the target was Stuttgart; 45 of the 262 attacking bombers were lost; dozens more were so damaged that repair was impractical—perhaps the change in the tone and detail of Bobby's story makes more sense.

3-31-43 brings the following account: Wow what a day! We raided installations and shipping west of Rotterdam, Holland. We were under a very heavy fighter attack by the "yellow nose"—God what pilots! They're unequaled. They peeled off in squadrons. My right nose gun ran away, but still got in some good shots. Ash was knocked down and had his crew bail out and he crash landed on the English coast. So far all but one reported OK. We had a mid-air collision in the 303rd. Ten killed.... We were lucky beyond words. I thought our number was up today!"

4-4-43 As I write this it's still hard to realize that I'm alive. We raided Paris today. The bombing was the best ever recorded. The complete target area was demolished. I saw the Eiffel Tower and Arc de Triumph very plainly. When we left the target area, the flak started and then the fighters. There were between 75 and 100 of the hottest apples Jerry's got. They choose our squadron and then started head-on attacks that seemed to last an eternity. On the first attack a .30 cal explosive burst a few feet in front of me, blowing off my sights. I had to shoot by tracer after that. I used up all my ammunition on the first ten fighters, and had to transfer ammunition three more times. They were coming by in droves, while we fired like men possessed. I got my tracers on one and pumped at least 70 rounds into him. He was on fire and passed just under my nose and exploded just behind our tail. The one just behind him tried to ram us head on. I was looking him square in the face. I think he may have been dead. Bobby and Sam pulled up just in time and he passed about ten feet under us. I may have got two more and I know I hit at least six but it's hard to tell unless you see them break up or in flames. They ended up by getting our entire second element. Jonesey went down. He was one of the greatest. His cockpit blew up and he spun in. There were four chutes seen. Our squadron alone definitely destroyed 30 with as many more probables. I'll never understand why we came back. I still can't believe it! I said every prayer I ever knew and some new ones too! ... But what a sight with "Dry" all shot to hell on our left wing, fighters screaming towards us, fighters blowing up and spinning in, forts going down, chutes blossoming, all hell breaking loose. I've never been so proud of anything in my life as I am of my crew ... [one with a wound in his knee, one with a punctured lung— "God what guts he showed"—only 14 rounds of ammo left out of 2200 when they landed ...] there were thousands of shells with our name on them but it just wasn't our time. What we went through yesterday could never be put into words, it is something beyond comprehension ...

There are dozens of other days like this one in the missions ahead. By the time his crew gets 13 combat missions to their credit, Bobby is leading the group, and when planes break and leave formation, he even leads the wing on occasion. He records these as the "most important days in my life" even as he searches for what all this must mean. In August they attack the heart of the Ruhr valley, Gelsenkirchen, and then on Aug 17th go to Schweinfurt ... "probably the greatest air battle in history" Bobby records, a "mad melee of planes all over the sky." "Our left wing was pretty well torn up by cannon fire, also our left stabilizer and rudder. Once again, I can't see how we were spared." On September 7th Bobby finishes his 25th mission and sets sail for the US: "boy it's a wonderful feeling to be finished."

Amazement at surviving punctuates Bobby's diary, mission after mission, loss after loss. Pride too, at being the best bombardier in his group, at earning the honor of leading. Beyond the calculus of war—how many bombers and friends lost, how many "jerrys" shot down, how many bombs on target, how many missions accomplished and how many left to go—Bobby seems uncertain of how best to make sense of this overwhelming experience. Like so many other soldiers, sailors, airmen, and marines, he turns to the limited narrative of his diary, faithfully recording his own personal account of his moment in history. At the end of his opening chapter of *Soldiers' Tale*, Sam Hynes comes back to the elements of personal narrative one last time, contrasting them with the imaginary wars any of us might greet battle with, the romantic notions that turn war into fictions, into "shapely untruths." In contrast, he maintains, "personal narratives are not like that: they subvert the expectations of romance. They work at a level below the big words and brave sentiments, down on the surface of the earth where men fight. They don't glorify war, or aestheticize it, or make it literary or heroic; they speak in their own voices, in their own plain language" (30). As I hope you have heard in Bobby's story, these narrative voices ring loud and clear with the individual personalities of the teller. They stand in awe at things like heroism, bravery, guts, but that's not really why they fight. And finally, that's not really why they share their stories either. Although their experiences often seem beyond human comprehension, as Bobby Metcalf writes, they still need to share their stories with us, across wars, across time, across even the great divide of death.

In describing these stories for you, I have oversimplified them in an attempt to help you understand what it means to be in the presence of a soldiers' tale. Doing so, I join a long tradition of writers and critics who try to help us understand the powerful complexity of these narratives. In closing, consider the words of a writer who deals frequently with the literature of the Vietnam War, Donald Anderson: "These stories are more complex than I have described them. They are about memory and love and resentment and loss and disbelief and defiance and humiliation and earnestness and blame and shame and blood and sacrifice and courage and sorrow. These are stories that, even if set in a past, seem to be written in an urgent and immortal present. Such stories are about what we must live with after any fought war, soldier or no. They identify us, these stories. *They are about us.*" (*Aftermath*, xxxi). Not only are these personal narratives vitally important to the men and women who tell them, but they are equally important to us. They do indeed identify us; they are about us. In the final story of his collection *The Things They Carried*, Tim O'Brien makes this claim: "This too is true: stories can save us." Need I add that, in their quest to wrest meaning from memory, I believe our need for narrative comes down finally to the quest for such redemption? We identify with these powerful stories, in the end, because they can ... *and must* ... save us.

Works Cited

Anderson, Donald. *Aftermath: An Anthology of Post-Vietnam Fiction*. New York: Henry Holt, 1995.

Didion, Joan. *The White Album*. New York: Farrar, Straus and Giroux, 1990.

Gregory, Marshall. "The Sound of Story: Narrative, Memory, and Selfhood." *Narrative* 3.1: 33-56.

Hynes, Samuel. "Personal Narratives and Commemoration." In *War and Remembrance in the Twentieth Century*. Ed. By Jay Winter and Emmanuel Sivan. Cambridge: Cambridge UP, 1999. pp. 205-220.

Hynes, Samuel. *The Soldiers' Tale: Bearing Witness to Modern War*. New York: Penguin, 1997.

Metcalf, Robert D. Unpublished diary from World War Two experience.

Source: *War, Literature & the Arts: An International Journal of the Humanities* (2009): 22-33.

WHAT IT SAYS

1. According to Bowie, why is Joan Didion's statement "We tell each other stories in order to live" especially true for veterans of war?

2. Why are war stories important, according to Hynes and Bowie? What do these stories accomplish for the storyteller and his or her audience?

3. What arguments do symposium speakers Palmer, Wood, Rizzuti, Clayton, and Langer make about the importance or impact of war stories? What common threads do you notice among the stories?

4. What does Bowie mean when he says that war stories "have actually formed who we are today"?

5. How does Bobby Metcalf's journal illustrate Bowie's point that war stories have formed who we are today?

HOW IT SAYS IT

1. How do quotations of writers other than the symposium speakers help Bowie construct his argument?

2. How does Bowie use ethos to appeal and persuade his reader?

3. What other rhetorical devices (besides ethos) does Bowie use to make his argument? Discuss the effectiveness of these devices.

WRITE ABOUT IT

1. Reflect on first-hand war stories you have heard, war movies you have seen, and/or books about war you have read. Write an essay that discusses the ways in which these narratives support or contradict Bowie's claims.

2. Read the first chapter of either Joan Didion's *White Album* or Samuel Hynes's *The Soldiers' Tale*. Based on your reading, construct an argument that differs from or contradicts the position Bowie takes on narrative in his essay.

3. Imagine that Regis University is in financial trouble and that administrators are deciding whether to pull funding from the Regis Center for the Study of War Experience in order to save money. Write a paper, speech, or make a video that argues for or against funding the Center and designed to be presented at a forum on this issue. Base your argument on Bowie's paper, as well as on any other relevant sources.

c. Steven Pinker, "Why the World Is More Peaceful"

Steven Pinker is an experimental psychologist and one of the world's leading experts on language and the mind. Pinker has been a strong, scholarly, and public proponent of the idea that language is an instinct rather than an entirely learned behavior. He is also well known for supporting the perspective of evolutionary psychology in general.

Pinker earned a bachelor's degree in experimental psychology at McGill University and a doctorate at Harvard in 1979. Currently he is Harvard College Professor and the Johnstone Family Professor in the department of psychology. He is the author of many books. Those directed at more general audiences include *The Language Instinct* (1994), *How the Mind Works* (1997), *Words and Rules: The Ingredients of Language* (1999), *The Blank Slate: The Modern Denial of Human Nature* (2002), and *The Stuff of Thought: Language as a Window into Human Nature* (2007).

In his recent book *The Better Angels of Our Nature: Why Violence Has Declined* (2011), Pinker argues that, over the centuries, violence has declined across the globe. He claims that the markers of civilization—government, literacy, and commerce—have encouraged us to curb our violent impulses, empathize with others, and employ reason to solve problems. This article, published in 2012 in the journal *Current History*, continues this argument. The phrase "the better angels of our nature" is an allusion to Abraham Lincoln's 1861 inaugural address, in which Lincoln expressed hope that, rather than split apart, Americans would follow "the better angels of our nature" and preserve the Union.

As You Read: Think of times when your first instinct was to fight or act aggressively, but your "better angel" took over. What factors do you think caused this switch in your behavior? In what ways do they align—or not align—with Pinker's more general claims about changes in human response to problems?

Why the World Is More Peaceful

Believe it or not—and most people do not—violence has declined historically, and we may be living today in the most peaceable era in our species's existence. This decline in violence has certainly not been smooth, nor is it guaranteed to continue. But it is an unmistakable and empirically demonstrable development.

No aspect of life is untouched by humans' retreat from violence. Daily existence is very different if you always have to worry about being abducted, raped, or killed. And it is hard to develop sophisticated arts, learning, or commerce if the institutions that support them are looted and burned as quickly as they are built.

The historical trajectory of violence affects not only how life is lived but how it is understood. What could be more fundamental to our sense of meaning and purpose than a conception of whether the strivings of the human race over long stretches of time have left us better or worse off? How, in particular, are we to make sense of modernity—of the erosion of family, tribe, tradition, and religion by the forces of individualism, cosmopolitanism, reason, and science? So much depends on how we understand the legacy of this transition: whether we see our world as a nightmare of crime, terrorism, genocide, and war, or as a period that, by the standards of history, is blessed by unprecedented levels of peaceful coexistence.

The question of whether the arithmetic sign of trends in violence is positive or negative also bears on our conception of human nature. Although theories of human nature rooted in biology are often associated with fatalism about violence, and the theory that the mind is a blank slate is associated with progress, in my view it is the other way around. How are we to understand the natural state of life when our species first emerged and the processes of history began? The belief that violence has increased suggests that the world we made has contaminated us, perhaps irretrievably. The belief that it has decreased suggests that we started off nasty and that the artifices of civilization have moved us in a noble direction, one in which we can hope to continue.

Rising Standards

The very idea that violence has gone down over the course of history invites incredulity. The human mind tends to estimate the probability of an event from the ease with which it can recall examples—and scenes of carnage in contemporary media are ubiquitous.

Also, a large swath of our intellectual culture is loath to admit that there could be anything good about civilization, modernity, and Western society. Yet perhaps the main cause of the illusion of ever-present violence springs from one of the forces that drove violence down in the first place. The decline of violent behavior has been paralleled by a decline in attitudes that tolerate or glorify violence, and often the attitudes are in the lead. By the standards of the mass atrocities of human history, the lethal injection of a murderer in Texas, or an occasional hate crime in which a member of an ethnic minority is intimidated by hooligans, is pretty mild stuff. But from a contemporary vantage point, we see them as signs of how low our behavior can sink, not of how high our standards have risen.

In fact, violence has diminished on many scales—in the family, in the neighborhood, between tribes and other armed factions, and among major nations and states. One can imagine a historical narrative in which different practices went in different directions: Slavery stayed abolished, for example, but parents decided to bring back savage beatings of their children; or states became increasingly humane to their citizens but more likely to wage war on one another. That has not happened. Most practices have moved in the less violent direction—too many to be a coincidence. Indeed, now is a good time in history to be a potential victim.

Pointing Peaceward

The many developments that make up the human retreat from violence can be grouped into six major trends. The first, which took place on the scale of millennia, was the transition from the anarchy of the hunting, gathering, and horticultural societies in which our species spent most of its evolutionary history, to the first agricultural civilizations beginning around five thousand years ago. With that change came a reduction in the chronic raiding and feuding that characterized life in a state of nature. According to evidence from forensic archeology and ethnographic vital statistics, the change helped produce a more or less fivefold decrease in rates of violent death.

The second transition spanned more than half a millennium and is best documented in Europe. Between the late Middle Ages and the twentieth century, European countries saw a tenfold-to-fiftyfold decline in their rates of homicide. In his classic book *The Civilizing Process*, the sociologist Norbert Elias attributed this surprising decline to the consolidation of a patchwork of feudal territories into large kingdoms with centralized authority and an infrastructure of commerce.

The third transition unfolded on the scale of centuries and took off around the time of the Age of Reason and the European Enlightenment in the seventeenth and eighteenth centuries. This "humanitarian revolution" saw the first organized movements to abolish socially sanctioned forms of violence such as absolute despotism, slavery, dueling, judicial torture, superstitious killing, sadistic punishment, and cruelty to animals, together with the first stirrings of systematic pacifism.

The fourth major transition took place after the end of World War II. The two-thirds of a century since then have witnessed a historically unprecedented development: The great powers, and developed states in general, have stopped waging war on one another. Historians have called this blessed state of affairs the "long peace."

The fifth trend is also about armed combat but is more tenuous. Though it may be hard for news readers to believe, since the end of the cold war in 1989, organized conflicts of all kinds—civil wars, genocides, repression by autocratic governments, and terrorist attacks—have declined throughout the world.

Finally, the postwar era, symbolically inaugurated by the Universal Declaration of Human Rights in 1948, has seen a growing revulsion against aggression on smaller scales, including violence against ethnic minorities, women, children, homosexuals, and animals. These spinoffs from the concept of human rights—civil rights, women's rights, children's rights, gay rights, and animal rights—were asserted in a cascade of movements from the late 1950s to the present day.

To be sure, some developments have gone the other way: the destructiveness of European wars through World War II (overshadowing the decrease in wars' frequency, until both destructiveness and frequency declined in tandem), the heyday of genocidal dictators in the middle decades of the twentieth century, the rise of crime in the 1960s, and the bulge of civil wars in the developing world following decolonization. Yet every one of these developments has been systematically reversed, and from where we sit on the time line, most trends point peaceward.

Calming Effects

Human nature has always contained a capacity for violence, whether driven by predation, dominance, revenge, sadism, or ideology. But it also contains psychological faculties that inhibit violence, such as self-control, empathy, reason, and the moral sense—what Abraham Lincoln called the better angels of our nature. What has changed that has allowed our better angels to prevail?

The first pacifying force appears to be the leviathan, a state and judiciary with a monopoly on the legitimate use of force. By penalizing aggression, a state can defuse the temptation of exploitative attack, inhibit the impulse for revenge, and circumvent the self-serving biases that make all parties believe they are on the side of the angels. When bands, tribes, and chiefdoms came under the control of the first states, violent feuding and raids diminished dramatically. As fiefs coalesced into kingdoms and sovereign states, the consolidation of law enforcement sharply reduced homicide rates.

Pockets of anarchy that lay beyond the reach of government—the peripheral and mountainous backwaters of Europe, for example, and the frontiers of the American South and West—retained their violent cultures of honor. The same is true of pockets of anarchy in the socioeconomic landscape, such as lower classes that are deprived of consistent law enforcement and purveyors of contraband who cannot avail themselves of it. Inadequate or inept governance turns out to be among the biggest risk factors for civil war, and perhaps the principal asset that distinguishes violence-torn developing countries from the more peaceful developed world.

Importantly, the leviathan and rule of law do not rely on force alone. Thanks to the generalized effects of self-control that have been demonstrated in the psychology lab, refraining from aggression can become a habit, so civilized parties will inhibit their temptation to aggress even when the leviathan's back is turned. And occasionally the soft power of influential third parties or the threat of shaming and ostracism can have the same effect as police or armies.

This soft power is crucial in the international arena, where world government has always been a fantasy, but in which judgments by third parties, intermittently backed by sanctions or symbolic displays of force, can go a long way. The lowered risk of war when countries belong to international organizations or host international peacekeepers are two quantifiable examples of the pacifying effects of unarmed or lightly armed third parties.

A second factor contributing to the historical decline of violence is commerce, a positive-sum game in which everybody can win. As technological progress allows the exchange of goods and ideas over longer distances and among larger groups of trading partners, other people become more valuable alive than dead, and they are less likely to become targets of demonization and dehumanization.

The idea that an exchange of benefits can turn zero-sum warfare into mutual profit was one of the key ideas of the Enlightenment, and it was revived in modern biology as an explanation of how cooperation among nonrelatives evolved. Although commerce does not eliminate the disaster of being defeated in an attack, it reduces the adversary's incentive to attack (since he benefits from peaceful exchange too) and helps to take that worry off the table. And once people are enticed into voluntary exchange, they are encouraged to take each other's perspectives to clinch the best deal ("the customer is always right"), which in turn may lead them to respectful consideration of each other's interests, if not necessarily to warmth.

Beginning in the late Middle Ages, expanding kingdoms not only penalized plunder and nationalized justice but also supported an infrastructure of exchange, including money and the enforcement of contracts. This infrastructure—together with technological advances such as in roads and clocks, and the removal of taboos on interest, innovation, and competition—made commerce more attractive. As a result, merchants, craftsmen, and bureaucrats displaced knightly warriors, and violent death rates plunged.

Among larger entities such as cities and states, commerce was enhanced by ocean-going ships, new financial institutions, and a decline in mercantilist policies. These developments have been credited in part with the eighteenth-century domestication of warring imperial powers such as Sweden, Denmark, the Netherlands, and Spain into commercial states that made less trouble.

Two centuries later the transformation of China and Vietnam from authoritarian communist into authoritarian capitalist states was accompanied by a decreased willingness to indulge in the all-out ideological conflict that in preceding decades had made both countries the deadliest places on earth. In other parts of the world as well, the tilting of values away from national glory and toward making money may have taken the wind out of the sails of cantankerous revanchist movements.

Careful statistical studies have demonstrated that countries that trade with each other are less likely to cross swords, holding all else constant, and countries that are more open to the world economy are less likely to host genocides and civil wars. Pulling in the other direction, governments that base their nations' wealth on digging oil, minerals, and diamonds out of the ground rather than adding value to it via commerce and trade are more likely to fall into civil wars.

The Female Factor

A third force promoting the species's retreat from violence has been feminization—that is, a growing respect among cultures for the interests and values of women. Since violence is largely a male pastime, societies that empower women tend to move away from the glorification of violence and are less likely to breed dangerous subcultures of rootless young men.

From the time they are boys, males play more violently than females, fantasize more about violence, consume more violent entertainment, commit the lion's share of violent crimes, take more delight in punishment and revenge, take more foolish risks in aggressive attacks, vote for more warlike policies and leaders, and plan and carry out almost all the wars and genocides.

Female-friendly values may be expected to reduce violence because of the psychological legacy of the basic biological difference between the sexes, namely that males have more of an incentive to compete for sexual access to females, while females have more of an incentive to stay away from risks that would make their children orphans. Zero-sum competition, whether it takes the form of the contests for women in tribal and knightly societies or the contests for honor, status, dominance, and glory in modern ones, is more a man's obsession than a woman's.

Societies in which women get a better deal, both traditional and modern, tend to be societies that have less organized violence. This is obvious enough in tribes and chiefdoms that literally went to war to abduct women or avenge past abductions. But it can also be statistically verified among contemporary countries in the contrast between the low levels of political and judicial violence in the über-feminist democracies of Western Europe and the high levels in the genital-cutting, adulteress-stoning, burqa-cladding sharia states of Islamic Africa and Asia.

Feminization need not consist of women literally wielding more power in decisions on whether to go to war. It can also consist in a society moving away from a culture of manly honor, with its approval of violent retaliation for insults, toughening of boys through physical punishment, and veneration of martial glory.

Rates of violence correlate with an abundance of young males within population groups. At least two large studies have suggested that countries with a larger proportion of young men are more likely to fight interstate and civil wars. In the developing world, sclerotic economies cannot nimbly put a youth bulge to work. As a result, many unemployed or underemployed men with nothing to lose may find work and meaning in militias, warlord gangs, or terrorist cells.

But demographic trends are not immutable. A mass of evidence suggests that when women are given access to contraception and the freedom to marry on their own terms, they have fewer offspring than when the men of their societies force them to be baby factories. This means their countries' populations will be less distended by a thick slab of youth at the bottom with a greater tendency toward violence.

Women's empowerment often must proceed in the teeth of opposition from traditional men who want to preserve their control over female reproduction, and from religious institutions that oppose contraception and abortion. But worldwide polling data show that even in the most benighted countries there is considerable pent-up demand for such empowerment, and many international organizations are committed to hurrying it along. These are hopeful signs for further reductions in violence around the world.

Heart and Head

Fourth, forces of cosmopolitanism—such as literacy, mobility, and mass media—can prompt people to take the perspective of people unlike themselves and to expand their circle of sympathy to embrace them. Living in a more cosmopolitan society, one that puts us in contact with a diverse sample of other people and invites us to take their points of view, changes our emotional response to their well-being. A perfect fusion of the interests of every living human is an unattainable nirvana. But smaller increments in the valuation of other people's interests—say, a susceptibility to pangs of guilt when thinking about enslaving, torturing, or annihilating others—can shift the likelihood of aggressing against them.

Beginning in the seventeenth century, with technological advances in publishing and transportation, more people read books, including fiction that led them to inhabit the minds of other people, and satire that led them to question their society's norms. Vivid depictions of the suffering wrought by slavery, sadistic punishments, war, and cruelty to children and animals preceded the reforms that outlawed or reduced those practices. Chronology does not prove causation, but studies showing that hearing or reading a first-person narrative can enhance people's sympathy for the narrator at least make causation plausible.

Literacy, urbanization, mobility, and access to mass media continued their rise in the nineteenth and twentieth centuries, and in the second half of the twentieth century a global village began to emerge that made people even more aware of others unlike themselves. Just as the spread of reading helped kindle the humanitarian revolution of the eighteenth century, the global village and the electronic revolution may have aided the postwar long peace and the rights revolutions of the twentieth century. A number of studies have shown statistical links between the cosmopolitan mixing of peoples and the endorsement of humanistic values.

Finally, reason—the intensifying application of knowledge and rationality to human affairs—can force people to recognize the futility of cycles of violence, to ramp down the privileging of their own interests over others', and to reframe violence as a problem to be solved rather than a contest to be won. Whereas the expanding circle of sympathy involves occupying another person's vantage point and imagining his or her emotions as if they were one's own, the power of reason involves ascending to an Olympian, superrational vantage point—the perspective of eternity, the view from nowhere—and considering one's own interests and another person's as equivalent.

As humans honed the institutions of knowledge and reason, and purged superstitions and inconsistencies from their systems of belief, certain conclusions were bound to follow, just as when one masters the laws of arithmetic certain sums and products are bound to follow. And in many cases the conclusions are ones that led people to commit fewer acts of violence.

At various times in history superstitious killings, such as in human sacrifice, witch hunts, blood libels, inquisitions, and ethnic scapegoating, fell away as the factual assumptions on which they rested crumbled under the scrutiny of a more intellectually sophisticated populace. Carefully reasoned briefs against slavery, despotism, torture, religious persecution, cruelty to animals, harshness to children, violence against women, frivolous wars, and the persecution of homosexuals were not just hot air but entered into the decisions of the institutions and people who attended to the arguments and implemented reforms.

Of course it is not always easy to distinguish empathy from reason, the heart from the head. But the limited reach of empathy, with its affinity for people like us and people close to us, suggests that empathy needs the universalizing boost of reason to bring about changes in policies and norms that actually reduce violence in the world.

These changes include not just legal prohibitions on acts of violence but institutions that are engineered to reduce the temptations of violence. Among these wonkish contraptions are democratic government; reconciliation movements in the developing world; nonviolent resistance movements; international peacekeeping operations; and tactics of containment, sanctions, and wary engagement designed to give national leaders more options than just the game of chicken that led to the First World War or the appeasement that led to the Second.

A broader effect of the historically cumulative application of reason, albeit one with many stalls, reversals, and holdouts, is the movement away from tribalism, authority, and purity in moral systems and toward humanism, classical liberalism, autonomy, and human rights. A humanistic value system, which privileges human flourishing as the ultimate good, is a product of reason because it can be justified: It can be mutually agreed on by any community of thinkers who value their own interests and are engaged in reasoned negotiation, whereas communal and authoritarian values are parochial to a tribe or hierarchy.

When cosmopolitan currents bring diverse people into discussion, when freedom of speech allows the discussion to go where it pleases, and when history's failed experiments are held up to the light, the evidence suggests that value systems evolve in the direction of liberal humanism. We have seen this in the recent decline of totalitarian ideologies and the genocides and wars they ignited. We have seen this in the contagion of the rights revolutions, when the indefensibility of oppressing racial minorities was generalized to the oppression of women, children, homosexuals, and animals. We have seen this as well in the way that these revolutions eventually swept up the conservatives who first opposed them.

The exception that proves the rule is the insular societies that are starved of ideas from the rest of the world and muzzled by governmental and clerical repression of the press. They are also the societies that most stubbornly resist humanism and cling to their tribal, authoritarian, and religious ideologies. But even these societies may not be able to withstand forever the liberalizing currents of the new global electronic cosmopolitanism.

Modern Gifts

The decline of violence may be the most significant and least appreciated development in the history of our species. Its implications touch the core of our beliefs and values. Hanging in the balance are conceptions of a fall from innocence, of the moral authority of religious scripture and hierarchy, of the innate wickedness or benevolence of human nature, of the forces that drive history, and of the moral valuation of nature, community, tradition, emotion, reason, and science.

Lamentations of a fall from Eden have a long history in intellectual life, and a loathing of modernity is one of the great constants of contemporary social criticism. But empirical acquaintance with how premodern people lived in fact should not invite envy. Our recent ancestors were infested with lice and parasites and lived above cellars heaped with their own feces. Food was bland, monotonous, and intermittent. Health care consisted of the doctor's saw and the dentist's pliers. Both sexes labored from sunrise to sundown, whereupon they were plunged into darkness.

And it was not just mundane physical comforts that our ancestors did without. It was also the higher and nobler things in life, such as knowledge, beauty, and human connection. Until recently most people never traveled more than a few miles from their place of birth. Everyone was ignorant of the vastness of the cosmos, the prehistory of civilization, the genealogy of living things, the genetic code, the microscopic world, and the constituents of matter and life. Musical recordings, affordable books, instant news of the world, reproductions of great art, and filmed dramas were inconceivable, let alone available in a tool that can fit in a shirt pocket. When children emigrated, their parents might never see them again, or hear their voices, or meet their grandchildren. And then there are modernity's gifts of life itself: the additional decades of existence, the mothers who live to see their newborns, the children who survive their first years on earth.

Even with all these reasons why no romantic would really step into a time machine, the nostalgic have always been able to pull out one moral card: the profusion of modern violence. At least, they say, our ancestors did not have to worry about muggings, school shootings, terrorist attacks, holocausts, world wars, killing fields, napalm, gulags, and nuclear annihilation. Surely no Boeing 747, no antibiotic, no iPod is worth the suffering that modern societies can wreak.

And here is where unsentimental history and statistical literacy can change our view of modernity. For they show that nostalgia for a peaceable past is the biggest delusion of all. We now know that native peoples, whose lives are so romanticized in today's children's books, had rates of death from warfare that were greater than those of our world wars. The romantic visions of medieval Europe omit the exquisitely crafted instruments of torture and are innocent of the thirtyfold greater risk of murder in those times.

The centuries for which people are nostalgic were times in which the wife of an adulterer could have her nose cut off, a seven-year-old could be hanged for stealing a petticoat, a prisoner's family could be charged for easement of irons, a witch could be sawed in half, and a sailor could be flogged to a pulp. The moral commonplaces of our age, such as that slavery, war, and torture are wrong, would have been seen as saccharine sentimentality, and our notion of universal human rights almost incoherent. Genocide and war crimes were absent from the historical record only because no one at the time thought they were a big deal.

From the vantage point of almost seven decades after the world wars and genocides of the first half of the twentieth century, we see that they were not harbingers of worse to come, nor a new normal to which the world would grow inured, but a local high from which the world would bumpily descend. And the ideologies behind these horrors were not woven into modernity but were atavisms that ended up in the dustbin of history.

The forces of individualism, cosmopolitanism, reason, and science have not, of course, pushed steadily in one direction; nor will they ever bring about a utopia or end the frictions and hurts that come with being human. But on top of all the benefits that modernity has brought us in health, experience, and knowledge, we can add its role in the reduction of violence.

The Work Ahead

As a scientist, I must be skeptical of any mystical force or cosmic destiny that carries us ever upward. Declines of violence are a product of social, cultural, and material conditions. If the conditions persist, violence will remain low or decline even further; if they do not, it will not. Still, as one becomes aware of the retreat from violence, the world begins to look different: The past seems less innocent, the present less sinister.

The shift is not toward complacency. We enjoy the peace we find today because people in past generations were appalled by the violence in their time and worked to reduce it, and so we should work to reduce the violence that remains in our time. Indeed, it is a recognition of the decline of violence that best affirms that such efforts are worthwhile.

Source: *Current History* (January 2012): 34-39.

WHAT IT SAYS

1. What does Pinker mean by the term "modernity"? Why is one's conception of modernity important, according to Pinker?

2. What is Pinker's conception of human nature? What does he think of the idea of human beings as a "blank slate"?

3. Why does Pinker say that lethal injection and hate crimes are "pretty mild stuff"? And why does he believe that "now is a good time in history to be a potential victim"?

4. What six major trends in human history have contributed to the decline in violence? List and briefly explain each trend.

5. Explain what is meant by the terms below, and how each works to reduce violence:

   - the leviathan
   - soft power
   - commerce
   - feminization
   - cosmopolitanism
   - reason

6. What was life like for pre-modern people, according to Pinker?

7. How should people react to the news that our lives are less violent today, according to Pinker?

HOW IT SAYS IT

1. What kinds of evidence does Pinker produce to support his argument?

2. How does Pinker employ Lincoln's quotation about "the better angels of our nature" to promote his argument? How does this work as an effective rhetorical move?

3. How does Pinker acknowledge opposing arguments? What phrases does he use to introduce them? How do these acknowledgments work to strengthen his argument?

WRITE ABOUT IT

1. Create a synthesis grid that includes all the evidence (historical facts, studies) Pinker mentions. Before you begin, review the section on synthesis grids in the Guide to academic writing (pp. 77–79).

2. Write an essay that considers Pinker's evidence and argues against his conclusions.

3. Bring in recent global events and ongoing situations that seem to disprove Pinker's thesis. Also consider historical events, and acknowledge indisputable points that Pinker makes.

4. Pinker ends his argument by suggesting that "we should work together to reduce the violence that remains in our time." Propose practical measures that your local, state, or national government can implement to reduce violence. Also consider a role for non-governmental organizations, schools, and community groups.

d. Safdar Ahmed, "'Father of No One's Son': Abu Ghraib and Torture in the Art of Ayad Alkadhi"

Safdar Ahmed is an artist and academic who teaches in the department of Arabic and Islamic studies at the University of Sydney, Australia. His research focuses on Islamic thought in the modern Arab world and northern India, contemporary Islamic liberalism and feminism, Islam within Orientalist and modern Western discourses, and classical and modern Islamic art, among other areas. Ahmed is co-founder, with Omid Tofighian, of the Refugee Art Project. In his YouTube video "The Refugee Art Project" (2012), Ahmed gives a guided tour of artworks in an exhibition of works by refugees and asylum seekers, and explains how artistic expression improves their lives.

Ahmed received a BFA degree from the National Art School in Sydney, and his BA and PhD degrees from the University of Sydney.

This article considers photographs taken at Abu Ghraib Prison in Iraq, in conjunction with the work of the Iraqi painter Ayad Alkadhi. Abu Ghraib was a notorious site of torture in the Iraq war. Ayad Alkadhi is an Iraqi painter whose recent paintings focus on the Iraq war and incorporate references to the Abu Ghraib photographs. As Ahmed points out, the Abu Ghraib images are important not only for what they depict but also because they were made available to the public. Ahmed's art historical approach is unusual for academic studies of war, which more commonly take historical, sociological, anthropological, or philosophical/theological approaches.

Ahmed draws on his knowledge of Arab culture to raise insights into Western stereotypes of Arabs and Arab society. Then he digs deeper: While he uses the Abu Ghraib photographs and paintings as examples, his concerns extend to broader issues, including stereotyping, empathy, the power of language, and the nature of art.

As You Read: Perhaps you have already seen some of the photographs that Ahmed discusses. If so, what was your reaction when you first saw them? In any case, what is your reaction now? In what ways do Alkadhi's paintings affect your reaction to the original photographs, if at all? If you were to create a visual response to the photographs, what would it look like?

"Father of No One's Son": Abu Ghraib and Torture in the Art of Ayad Alkadhi

Introduction: Torture and "The Arab Mind"

An indelible image of the American war in Iraq is that of a male figure standing on a small C-ration box, draped in a makeshift poncho, with a sandbag placed over his head and electrical wires attached to his fingers and toes. Reportedly, he was told he would be executed if he lowered his arms or fell from the box. There are other images of prisoners enduring various stages of 'interrogation,' in which they are coerced to masturbate, perform oral sex with one another and other acts of sexual rape and humiliation. Some show prisoners bound in painful positions, being terrorised by dogs or piled up in a human pyramid, their buttocks and anuses exposed. One shows a man who died under torture with visible wounds to his face and an ice pack cellophaned to his chest. Then there are the practices which lawyers for the United States' Justice Department under the Bush administration designated as not legally constituting torture. These include such 'enhanced interrogation measures' as keeping suspects awake for eleven days continuously, slamming them into walls, stripping them naked, waterboarding them hundreds of times, putting them into cramped boxes and tying them into stress positions for hours at a time. To add to this are photographs from Abu Ghraib which we know exist but which the Obama administration has refused to make public on the grounds that they may incite anti-American sentiment in such places as Iraq and Afghanistan. These are reported to show further atrocities against detainees,

FIGURE 7.1. Unknown Iraqi prisoner at Abu Ghraib, 2003

including the rape, abuse and murder of men, women and children by American soldiers. The horror of such news is confirmed by the International Committee of the Red Cross's estimate that seventy to ninety per cent of those held at Abu Ghraib had been arrested by mistake and had no connection to terrorism. In what follows, I will relate the meaning of the photographs from Abu Ghraib to the work of the Iraqi painter, Ayad Alkadhi.

The importance of the Abu Ghraib photographs can be attributed not only to what they depict but to the fact that we are able to see them at all. Since the Gulf War of 1991, the Western coverage of war has been meticulously controlled by, and merged into, the American military establishment. Thus our visual memory of Operation Desert Storm, as of the invasion of Iraq in 2003, compared more to the experience of watching a video game than of witnessing a war. Instead of seeing the carnage wrought by American "smart bombs" on the ground, audiences were given the vision of airborne missiles, planes and drones whose pixelated footage of exploding targets provided an abstract simulacrum of war. Troubled by such unreal and contrived coverage, the French philosopher Jean Baudrillard famously pronounced that the 1991 Gulf War "did not take place," which is to say that from media representations of the event one would never know how it happened, or if it even conformed to a normative definition of war.[1] In this context, the unexpected and unauthorised release of photographs depicting tortured prisoners disturbed the formulaic style of the commercial media and brought audiences closer to the reality of the Iraq war than they had hitherto been.

The image of Private Lynndie England, cigarette in mouth, giving a thumbs-up sign and pointing in mock satisfaction at the genitals of a naked, hooded male detainee who had been ordered to masturbate himself, implicates the role of photography in the torture of Iraqi prisoners. In this context, the camera was not an innocent bystander to the events taking place but played an integral part in the practice of sexual torture and humiliation. Moreover, the photograph was intended as a keepsake. It was a memento of Private England's wartime service to be distributed and shared amongst colleagues and friends. In this sense the image was to be viewed in a context that was continuous with the circumstances in which it was made. As a document of the war, the photograph is important for informing us of the attitudes which American soldiers held towards their prisoners and, by extension, towards the people and culture of Iraq.

Concerning the sexual humiliation shown in the Abu Ghraib photographs (and similar acts of torture that occurred in United States bases in Afghanistan and Guantanamo Bay), there is a strong argument to say that it had its origins not in the improvised cruelty of a few "bad apples" (as the Bush administration had argued) but was shared amongst the upper and lower echelons of the American

---

1   Jean Baudrillard, *The Gulf War Did Not Take Place*, Paul Patton, trans, Power Publications, Sydney, 2000.

FIGURE 7.2. Private Lynndie England posing with Iraqi prisoners at Abu Ghraib, 2003

military establishment. Whilst methods of sexual humiliation and rape are a common feature of war, in this case they conform to stereotypes surrounding Arab society which recur in the historical and anthropological scholarship that the Bush administration chose for its understanding of the Muslim Middle East.

One such notion is that Arab culture is overwhelmingly controlled by notions of sexual jealousy, honour and shame, for which an important source (first reported by the investigative journalist, Seymour Hersh) is the work of the cultural anthropologist, Raphael Patai (1910-1996).[2] An understudy to such Orientalist historians as Ignaz Goldziher and Carl Brockelmann, Patai sought to identify "modal personality structures" which are so commonly shared amongst a community as to define that people's "national character." Thus, he constructed scholarly-sounding generalisations about an entire people (in this case "the Arabs") based on a limited and selective use of anthropological data.[3]

In *The Arab Mind*, Patai underscores the importance of sexual shame and honour for the psychological make-up of the Arab male. He does this by arguing that the sexually repressive nature of Arab society corresponds to a "syndrome" of sexual frustration and aggression amongst its men. Because Arab masculinity is inherently aggressive, it valorises the act of sexual penetration: either of women or of other men. Therefore: "it is felt degrading for a man to play the role of the female" in the homosexual act, which represents a form of emasculation. Likewise is it "shameful" to engage in masturbation, which suggests an "inability to perform the

---

2   Seymour Hersh, 'The Gray Zone: How a Secret Pentagon Program Came to Abu Ghraib,' *The New Yorker*, 25 May 2004.

3   Raphael Patai, *The Arab Mind* (revised edition), Hatherleigh Press, New York, 2002, pp. 18-19.

active sex act" with another.[4] In this context, one might better understand why male prisoners were coerced to masturbate and perform homosexual acts before the camera, amongst mocking female and male soldiers. Whilst Patai's scholarship does not advocate policies of torture, it does supply a reductive and simplistic psychological profile of the Arab "personality" without which the American sex-torture at Abu Ghraib would not have occurred in the way that it did.[5]

The connection between Orientalist scholarship and the torture that occurred at Abu Ghraib is stronger than the argument which attributes blame only to the prevalence of commercialised pornography and the exhibitionist culture of internet networking sites. For although pornography and the culture of social networking influenced the way the photographs were made and distributed, they do not provide an accurate description of what the images in fact depict. This is because the function of pornography is to act as tableaux for the socially mediated (and often phallocentric) projection of erotic intimacy, fantasy and desire. It is a very different thing to coerce prisoners to enact pornographic scenarios for the purpose of shaming and humiliating them. In forcing naked detainees to simulate the guards' conception of a gay orgy, or a sexual bondage and sadism session (amongst other acts of violence) the latter were attempting to inflict psychological and psychical harm upon their prisoners—near or to the point of death.

Another theme, which the Bush administration derived from Orientalist scholarship, asserts that Arab culture most clearly respects the language of force. Or, as Bernard Lewis (a Professor of Near Eastern Studies at Princeton University) put it: "if the one with the power does not exhaust his ability to bring about ... victory, his conduct is interpreted [amongst Arabs] as cowardice."[6] Because anti-Americanism in the Middle East is partly inspired by the United States' support for harsh dictatorships across the region, Lewis advocated "regime change" in Iraq and has recommended the bombing of Iran as a step towards the introduction of democracy in these countries.[7] As an informal adviser to the Bush Administration in the build-up to the invasion of Iraq, Lewis shared the neoconservative view that it is possible to wage pre-emptive war in order to make peace. "Either we bring them freedom," he counselled with reference to Iran in an article written in 2006,

---

4   Ibid. p. 135.

5   In a foreword to the most recent reprint of Patai's book, Colonel Norvell B. De Atkine, an instructor in Middle East Studies at the John F. Kennedy Special Warfare School, advocates its usefulness for instructing military personnel on the cultural mores of the Middle East. Moreover, a US army interrogator at Abu Ghraib from 2001 to 2005, Tony Lagouranis, describes the direct influence of Patai's ethnography on the culture of abuse that developed towards Iraqi prisoners amongst US military personnel. See Norvell B. De Atkine, "Foreword," in ibid., pp. x-xvii; and Tony Lagouranis et al., *Fear Up Harsh: An Army Interrogator's Dark Journey through Iraq*, UAL Caliber, New York, 2007.

6   Bernard Lewis, interview, http://aish.com.jw/me/48891177.html; accessed 20 January 2010.

7   Bernard Lewis, "Does Iran Have Something in Store?," http://www.opinionjournal.com; accessed 20 January 2010.

"or they destroy us."[8] This misguided sentiment (of a threat which must be pre-emptively combated) played an important role in mustering popular opinion in the United States in support of the invasion of Iraq in 2002.

Photography and the Ambivalent Image of War

Whilst war photography is an important source for our understanding and memory of modern conflicts, the images from Abu Ghraib tell a partial story. This is because photography cannot complete our understanding of the event depicted in it. To put it another way, photography isolates an event, lifting it out of the time and context in which it arose. As John Berger points out: "the issue of the war which has caused that moment is effectively depoliticised. The picture becomes evidence of the general human condition. It accuses nobody and everybody."[9] For this reason, images of war must exist within an understanding of their contextual importance if they are to have any meaning for the larger issues over which such wars are fought in the first place. If media images of the Vietnam War catalysed a peace movement in the United States during the 1970s, they were only able to do so by fitting within a narrative, and popular sentiment, which was then growing amongst sections of American society. As Susan Sontag observes: "photographs cannot create a moral position, but they can reinforce one—and can help build a nascent one."[10]

Of the photographs at Abu Ghraib, the American administration has invited us to see them as an isolated exception to what is routinely presented as a war fought somehow on behalf of the people of Iraq. In the immediate aftermath of the scandal, this was achieved through an obsessive focus upon the immorality, and subsequent prosecution, of individual perpetrators, which distracted attention from the broader motives underlying the policy of torture (including the need to extract information from Iraqi prisoners and recruit them as informers). Moreover, the Bush administration seemed less concerned with what the scandal said about the United States' occupation of Iraq than its potential impact on support for the war. In this context, President Bush apologised for the suffering of prisoners at Abu Ghraib whilst complaining, in the same breath, that "people seeing these pictures didn't understand the true nature and heart of America."[11] From this perspective, the images of Iraqi torture victims are an aberration. They do not reflect the war that generated them, but are an accidental and insignificant by-product of it.

---

8   Bernard Lewis, "Bring Them Freedom, Or They Destroy Us," http://www.realclearpolitics.com/articles/2006/09/bring_them_freedom_or_they_ des.html; accessed 20 January 2010.

9   John Berger. *About Looking*. New York: Vintage, 1991, p. 44.

10 Susan Sontag. *On Photography*. London: Penguin, 2008, p. 17.

11 Quoted in Bruce Tucker et al., "Lynndie England, Abu Ghraib, and the New Imperialism," *Canadian Review of American Studies* vol. 38, no. 1, 2008, p. 86.

Furthermore, the treatment of these images in the commercial media did little to disturb those who planned and prosecuted the war. Because the social and political identity of Western news organisations (and their viewing public) conditions the way information is categorised and filtered, the imagery from Abu Ghraib was placed within a hierarchy that prioritises Western over non-Western suffering as a cause for moral concern. This was seen, for instance, in the reluctance of American news organisations, and of other news associations sympathetic to the war, to label the activities within Abu Ghraib as "torture." Instead, they opted for the inaccurate and weaker euphemism of "abuse."[12]

From this framing of the event, a rift occurs: between the fact of what is portrayed in the images at Abu Ghraib and how they are presented to us. On the surface, they depict the obvious pain of individuals under torture. But our shock can quickly disappear if strangeness and cultural unfamiliarity are imputed to the prisoners, making them unworthy of our empathy. This returns us to my previous point. Namely, that images of human suffering do not affect us (as evidence of a universal "human condition") if we cannot contextualise and understand the position of the victim.

Reinterpreting Abu Ghraib

I will now look at how the images from Abu Ghraib have been reinterpreted in the work of the Iraqi painter, Ayad Alkadhi. In particular, Alkadhi's work alludes to the potential role of art or, more specifically of the *artistic imagination*, to deconstruct the misconceptions that surround the Iraq war. One of the purposes of art is to filter the world through an interior or imaginary lens, thus enabling us to explore—or represent anew—the thoughts, concepts, values and feelings which make up the human condition. Art can shine a new light on familiar subjects, by taking us out of ourselves, and return us to the world with a deeper and more complex understanding of it than we had before. In this sense, art may challenge received doctrine and take us beyond the superficial and often selective fact gathering of the media news cycle. This can be achieved in many ways: as a formal-aesthetic exercise and/or through the manipulation of images and themes which circulate in our social, cultural and political life. This is not to claim that art is in itself free of political and ideological attachments. Rather, it is only by dint of its role as a cultural mediator that art may contribute to a re-evaluation of received doctrines and assumptions.

Ayad Alkadhi is an Iraqi painter whose recent works address the invasion of Iraq, the destruction of Baghdad, the suffering of Iraq's civilian population and the despair of its refugees. Born in 1972, he experienced childhood under the regime

---

12 Timothy M. Jones et al., "Torture in the Eye of the Beholder," *Political Communication* vol. 26, no. 3, 2009, pp. 278-295.

FIGURE 7.3. Price of a Barrel, 2007 – 2008, acrylic, charcoal, pencil on newspaper on canvas, 121.9 x 91.4 cm, collection of the artist, photo: Ayad Alkadhi

of Saddam Hussein before leaving Iraq, as a young man, after the 1991 Gulf War. Since then he has lived in Jordan, New Zealand, and finally the United States, where he currently resides.

Alkadhi's series of three paintings, "Father of No One's Son" (2007-2008), use the Abu Ghraib photographs as their starting point, though they are not confined to them. In "Price of a Barrel" we see the upper body of a shrouded figure with arms outstretched before a spattered background of white paint upon Arabic newspapers. The figure recalls the shape and appearance of the hooded prisoner at Abu Ghraib who stood upon the box with wires protruding from his fingers. Only now, a face emerges from the hood, which is that of the artist, implicating the viewer in the scene depicted. The image of a cross overlaying Arabic text glows in the figure's torso and behind his head are the words "Price of a Barrel," underlined by a gash of red paint which colours his eyes. Alkadhi's works have a strong graphic quality. The terse strength of his draughtsmanship is complemented by looser areas, in which wet paint is allowed to drip over, and run down, the surface of the canvas.

FIGURE 7.4. Bloody Red Freedom, 2007 – 2008, acrylic, charcoal, pencil on newspaper on canvas, 182.9 x 60.7 cm, private collection, photo: Ayad Alkadhi

On one level, the painting acts as a political statement: decrying a war fought less for human rights or political freedom in Iraq than to grasp control over its oil fields. The other two paintings in the series (with the equally derisive titles of "Bloody Red Freedom" and "Cross to Bare") make a similar point. But beyond this, all three paintings allude to particular cultural, religious and nationalist symbols which give them a deeper historical context and interest.

The presence of calligraphic text, for instance, invokes the cultural heritage of traditional Arabic literature. At first glance, this use of script echoes the work of modernist painters in Iraq, such as Madiha Omar (1908-2005) and Shakir Hassan al-Said (1925-2004), who, from the 1940s on, married elements of calligraphic writing with the styles and techniques of European modernism. Referred to as *hurufiyya* (which roughly translates as letterism), this movement fused elements of modernist painting with Middle Eastern art's strong focus on the visual, oral and semantic beauty of the Arabic language. As the grandson of a professor of Arabic literature, and as one who grew up in the presence of literary and calligraphic manuscripts, Alkadhi claims a personal connection to this heritage. Yet unlike the modernists of the last century, who were committed to exploring new ways of seeing and thinking about art, Alkadhi's works centre on established themes. In formal terms, Alkadhi's combination of Arabic script and Western-style figuration does not attempt a new cultural synthesis, as it did for his modernist forebears. Rather, the combination of Arab and Western elements locates Alkadhi in a space *amongst and between* different cultures and visual traditions, in this sense reflecting his experience as a member of the Iraqi diaspora.

Furthermore, Alkadhi's use of Arabic script evokes a comparison between the putatively stable culture and identity of Iraq on one hand, and the recent history of its unstable present on the other. If the delicate and learned curvatures of calligraphic text once conveyed something of the semantic power of traditional Arabic poetry or the sacred language of the Quran, Alkadhi employs it (sometimes legibly, sometimes not) to depict the traumatic experience of the postcolonial Arab

FIGURE 7.5. Cross to Bare, 2007 – 2008, acrylic, charcoal, pencil on newspaper on canvas, 121.9 x 91.4 cm, private collection, photo: Ayad Alkadhi

state. In some instances, text acts to chain or shackle the subject, whilst in others, a scrawled graffiti embodies the agentive voice (and sole means of expression) of those imprisoned. Language can either oppress or liberate, and where English script appears it does so in order to underscore or signpost the predicament of the victim. All such uses of text accord with Alkadhi's description of himself as a "storyteller," albeit one committed to a less than conventional narrative.[13]

As a feature of this counter-narrative, Alkadhi's decision to paint over a surface of Arabic newspapers recalls the inadequacy of the public discourse surrounding the Iraq war. Obvious examples of this include the commercial media's reluctance to question the United States' accusation that Iraq was harbouring "weapons of mass destruction" and its failure to provide adequate reportage of the deaths amongst Iraq's civilian population commensurable with our knowledge of the losses experienced by Western troops. To portray Iraq as a human story, rather

---

13 Personal communication with the artist.

than merely an issue of foreign policy or international security, is to reject the objectifying and cliché-ridden language of the commercial media which is most people's only source of knowledge about the war.

One cannot mistake the colour and symbolism of Iraq's national flag in the "Father of No One's Son" paintings. Though, for Alkadhi, the presence of the flag is an oblique reference, evoking nostalgia and memory for the time of his child-hood, it also suggests the trajectory of Iraq's recent political history. For instance, the three green stars of the Iraqi Ba'ath party, which once symbolised that party's will to unify Iraq with the neighbouring countries of Egypt and Syria, now forms an accusation against what the American administration has termed a "Ba'athist insurgency," arbitrarily imposed over the prisoner's body. Such references are intended not to evoke familiar pan-Arabist or nationalist sentiments but to point out the fate of those who are in part the victims of these.

Another allusion to the victimisation of Iraq's people is seen in Alkadhi's appro-priation of the crucifixion image. Notably, this points to the iconography that nationalism and religion seem to share. For if invocations to self-sacrifice and martyrdom in the name of a higher cause are familiar to Christian and Muslim traditions in the Middle East, they are no less familiar to the secular national-ist ideologies that anticolonial intellectuals took from Europe in order to free their countries from colonial rule in the modern period. Modern states, under the conditions of war, have glorified and institutionalised the theme of sacrifice. In this regard nationalism constitutes a "political theology" whose conflicts have aestheticised, and transcendentalised, the deaths of those civilians and soldiers it calls its own. This is not to suppose that secular political theories have their true origins in religious theology or vice versa, but to underscore the historical characteristics they share. Whilst Alkadhi's tortured body resembles the broken figure of Christ, there is no resurrection: no providential or otherworldly end for the victim of one's own nationalism or of foreign imperialism.

If Alkadhi is not alone in comparing the tortured prisoners of Abu Ghraib to the mortified body of Christ, others have dwelt more on their external visual similarities than on the meaning of such themes in the context of war.[14] On a personal note, the artist recalls seeing an Iraqi woman, and mother of one of those tortured in the photographs, on Arab television. Describing her reaction to the photographs of her tortured son, she compared her helplessness to that which the Virgin Mary must have felt watching Christ undergo the torment of crucifix-ion.[15] The cross is employed not for devotional purposes but to deepen the emotive context of a modern scene of punishment. In this way, the figure in "Price of a

---

14 For comparisons between the torture photographs of Abu Ghraib and Christian iconography, see Dora Apel, "Torture Culture: Lynching Photographs and the Images of Abu Ghraib," *Art Journal* no. 2, 2005, pp. 91-92.

15 Personal communication with the artist.

Barrel" is purposefully mimetic of the "Christ-like" appearance, so often attributed to the hooded prisoner in Abu Ghraib.

I will conclude this article by restating the need to resist the discursive misconceptions that surround the Iraq war. For, as I have argued, one must understand the circumstances of another's suffering before one can enter it into the imaginative categories of universal human experience. In the case of Iraq, prejudice prevents this. The problem occurs when one's first-order level of empathy (in which one relates directly to the experiences of pain and loss endured by others) is usurped by a second-order antipathy (which is spurred by one's slanted perception of a foreign culture—in this case, the "Arab mind"). It is no exaggeration to say that the ethnographic racism embraced by members of the Bush administration and that persists today presents a challenge to our faculty of imagination and empathy. If those who authorised the torture of Iraqi prisoners are right, then their actions should not be labelled as torture, but seen rather as a set of culture-specific procedures used to prod already irrational, dangerous and sexually aggressive Arab men.

The only way to counter this is to show that such arguments are based on unsustainable generalisations concerning Arabs and Islam. By alluding to aspects of Arab culture and history, Alkadhi refuses the ideological biases that would objectify and so minimise the suffering of Iraq's war victims. Whilst I do not suggest that Alkadhi's paintings give us the tools to develop empathy (for empathy is much more complicated than that), he nonetheless clears a space with which to address its relevant themes.

Source: *Third Text* 25.3 (2011): 325-34.

WHAT IT SAYS

1. What three categories of images or knowledge does Ahmed describe in his opening paragraph? How are these categories related, and what relation do they have to the purpose of Ahmed's essay?

2. In what way are images of the Gulf War different from images of the Iraq War? What effect do these two kinds of images have on viewers?

3. What does Ahmed mean by the claim that "the camera was not an innocent bystander" to torture during the Iraq War?

4. In what ways did the Allied soldiers' torture and humiliation of Iraqi captives reveal Western stereotypes of Arab culture, according to Ahmed?

5. What "misguided sentiment" about Arab culture encouraged US leaders to advocate forced regime change in Iraq? What are the origins of these stereotypes?

6. Why does Ahmed claim that the photographs taken of naked captives in sexually suggestive situations were *not* pornographic? What is required for an image to be pornographic, according to Ahmed?

7. What point does Ahmed make about the importance of context in images of war? Why were photographs of tortured Iraqi prisoners presented out of context, and what was the result, according to Ahmed?

8. What does Ahmed mean when he says that art is a "cultural mediator"? In what ways do the paintings of Ayad Alkadhi perform the role of cultural mediation?

HOW IT SAYS IT

1. What is the effect of Ahmed's graphic opening paragraphs? How do these paragraphs help to set up what is to follow?

2. How does Ahmed's description of Alkadhi's paintings, especially in the context of Iraqi art, work to advance his argument?

3. Ahmed does not hide his antipathy to the political and ethical decisions the Bush administration made in launching and carrying out the Iraq war. How does this use of pathos work to advance his argument?

WRITE ABOUT IT

1. Ahmed makes a number of claims in this essay, both specific and general. Working from a list of these claims, write an essay that assesses the ways in which these claims work together—or work at odds with each other—to advance Ahmed's argument.

2. Write an essay that considers the work of a Western artist who focuses on images of war. Compare this artwork with that of Alkadhi, especially in terms of expressions of political or cultural belief.

3. Compose an essay, a short slideshow, or a video documentary on the effects on public opinion of wartime photographs. Consider Ahmed's essay, as well as other relevant essays and images.

e. Azra Ramezankhani, Yadollah Mehrabi, Parvin Mirmiran, and Fereidoun Azizi, "Comparison of Anthropometric and Biochemical Indices of Adolescents Born During and After the Iran-Iraq War; Tehran Lipid and Glucose Study"

Azra Ramezankhani is a public health researcher affiliated with the Obesity Research Center of the Research Institute of Endocrine Sciences at Shaheed Beheshti University of Medical Sciences in Tehran, Iran. His co-authors also are affiliated with the university. **Yadollah Mehrabi** works in the department of epidemiology in the School of Public Health. **Parvin Mirmiran** is an assistant professor of nutrition in the Food Sciences and Obesity Research Center at the Research Institute for Endocrine Sciences. **Fereidoun Azizi** is a medical doctor in the Endocrine Research Center at the Research Institute for Endocrine Sciences.

In this brief lab report, Ramezankhani et al. describe their findings regarding the health effects of the Iran-Iraq war on Iranian children. The study looks at anthropometric indices—that is, data related to human measurement. The researchers measured height, weight, serum lipids (fat and cholesterol in the blood), fasting blood sugar (FBS), systolic and diastolic blood pressure, and body mass index (BMI) of the study's subjects.

This report provides a good example of the IMRAD format (see p. 87) common in the physical and social sciences. In this example, the abstract contains a helpful abbreviation of each section.

AS YOU READ: Unless you have a background in health sciences, you may have a hard time understanding the methods and data of this study. Don't worry about it.

Focus on the introduction and conclusion, which are well written and explain the background for and significance of the study.

- Do the study's conclusions surprise you? How?
- In what ways might this study's results be a significant addition to medical knowledge?
- To what practical uses could the results be applied?
- How might this new information change a country's military policies?

Comparison of Anthropometric and Biochemical Indices of Adolescents Born During and After the Iran-Iraq War; Tehran Lipid and Glucose Study

Abstract

Background: A country's developmental progress and overall changes in socio-economic structure are reflected in the outcome of secular trend studies on physical growth of children. The aim of this study was to compare anthropometric and biochemical indices of adolescent boys and girls born during and after the Iran-Iraq war.

Methods: Adolescents, aged 11-18 years, were selected from the TLGS cohort and divided into two groups. In the first group, adolescents born during the war and in the second group adolescents born after the war were included. Height, weight, serum lipids, FBS, systolic and diastolic blood pressure, and BMI were compared amongst adolescents of the same ages between the two groups.

Results: Mean weight and height increased at the ages of 12, 13, 14, and 17 years in boys of the post-war group. The mean weight of girls in the post-war group increased at the ages of 11, 13, and 14 years. Between 11-14 years, the means for total and LDL cholesterol, and between the ages of 15-18 years FBS, total cholesterol and LDL cholesterol decreased in boys of the post-war group. For girls between the ages of 11-14, FBS, total cholesterol, TG and LDL cholesterol, and between the ages of 15-18 years, FBS, total cholesterol and LDL cholesterol decreased in the post-war group. Systolic and diastolic blood pressure decreased at all ages in both groups.

Conclusion: This study showed that some anthropometric indices such as height and weight increased in boys who were born after the war; but in girls, the mean weight in the age groups increased. Systolic and diastolic blood pressure, and some lipid profiles decreased in boys and girls of the post-war group.

Keywords: anthropometric indices, biochemical indices, war

Introduction

Studies on the physical attributes in child and adult populations clearly point to long-term (e.g., secular) changes.[1] Secular changes are due to the interaction of genetic and environmental factors. This interaction is manifested at a specific time as a function of different living conditions in various social groups, as well as on a long-term basis under the influence of gradual changes in living conditions.[1,2] A country's developmental progress and overall changes in socio-economic structure are reflected in the outcome of secular trend studies on physical growth, development, and rate of maturation in children.[3] Wars are man-made disasters with a recognized direct impact on enhancing the spread of disease, which have been shown to be related to several somatic disorders, as well as to a wide range of psychiatric disorders such as depression and anxiety.[4] Research on the status of children during war shows that in comparison to the whole population, children are the most jeopardized group. Children's war experiences include the following: death of a parent or close family members, separation from parents, bombardment and shelling, physical injuries, and handicaps as well as extreme poverty and deprivation. War events can have both short and long-term effects. The short term stress/traumatic effects of war events on children are intrapersonal repetitions of the experience, fears and insecurities, emotional changes, confusion, and disorientation. The long-term stress/traumatic effects of war events on children may exist even for several years after the war has ended. Long-term war effects can be characterized by deviations in child development, changes in personality and identity, school failure, poor physical health, a pessimistic view of the future, etc.[5] Despite some studies about the Iran-Iraq war, there is no research regarding the physical growth of adolescents born during the war years, which is the purpose for conducting this study, e.g., to compare anthropometric and biochemical indices of adolescent boys and girls born during and after this war.

Materials and Methods

The current study was conducted within the framework of the Tehran Lipid and Glucose Study (TLGS). We selected 3816 persons aged between 11 and 18 years, and divided them into two groups. The first group included 2540 boys and girls born during the war years (from September 22, 1980 until August 20, 1988). The second group included 1276 boys and girls born after the war (after August 20, 1988). The first group (war group), were investigated between 1998-2002 while the second group of adolescents (after war group) were studied between 2005-2008. Subjects were interviewed privately, face to face, by trained interviewers using questionnaires. Blood pressure was measured by a qualified physician using a standard mercury sphygmomanometer. Additional information regarding age, sex, education, marital status, and employment history was obtained with questionnaires. Weight and height were measured according to standard protocol and body mass index (BMI) was calculated.[6,7] Blood samples were drawn from all subjects between 7:00 and 9:00 a.m. after 12-14 hr of overnight fasting and all blood lipid analyses were done at the TLGS research laboratory on the day of blood collection, using the Selectra 2

Auto-analyzer (Vital Scientific, Spankeren, Netherlands). Fasting blood sugar (FBS) was measured on the day of blood collection by the enzymatic colorimetric method using glucose oxidase. Serum total cholesterol and triglyceride concentration were measured by commercially available enzymatic reagents (Pars Azmoon, Iran) adapted to the Selectra Auto-analyzer. HDL cholesterol was measured after precipitation of the apolipoprotein B-containing lipoproteins with phosphotungstic acid. LDL cholesterol was calculated according to the method of Friedewald et al.[8] and it was not calculated when the serum concentration of triacylglycerol was >400 mg/dL. All samples were analyzed only when internal quality control met the acceptable criteria. Inter- and intra-assay CVs were 2% and 0.5% for total cholesterol, 16% and 0.6% for triacylglycerol, and 2.2% and 2.2% for glucose, respectively. In the TLGS cohort study, for reducing the time effect of the cohort in data gathering and to avoid changing methods and instruments during the years of study, a data quality program was performed to ensure the accuracy of the interview, instruments such as weight scales, the measurement method, laboratory facilities and data entry, etc. This program, as a protocol, has been described elsewhere.[9,10]

STATISTICAL METHODS

Means of anthropometric indices were calculated in each age group and differences were compared between the two groups. Bonferroni correction was used for multiple comparisons. Because of the large amount of data, we have presented the data in three age groups: 13, 15, and 17 years (Table 7.1) and data related to ages 11, 12, 14, 16, 18 have been presented in the text. Mean of serum lipids (total cholesterol, triglycerides, LDL cholesterol, HDL cholesterol, fasting blood sugar, as well as systolic and diastolic blood pressure) were compared between the two groups for ages 11-14 and 15-18 years, and separately for boys and girls. We used SPSS software (version 16; SPSS Inc., Chicago IL) for all statistical analyses. P values less than 0.01 were considered statistically significant.

Results

The war group included 2540 individuals, (1,340 girls, 1,200 boys) and the post-war group consisted of 1,276 persons (662 girls, 614 boys). Anthropometric indices of each age group in girls and boys are as follows:

ANTHROPOMETRIC INDICES

Age group 11 years: In girls of the post-war group, the average weight increased 5.74 kg ($P<0.01$), and BMI increased 2.2 kg/m^2 compared to girls of the war group who were of the same age ($P<0.001$). In boys of the post-war group, waist circumference increased 5.7 cm ($P<0.001$) compared to same age boys of the war group.

TABLE 7.1. Mean±SD for Anthropometric Indices in the Two Groups

Variables	Age 13			Age 15			Age 17		
	War group	After war group	P	War group	After war group	P	War group	After war group	P
Boys (n)	161	101		161	94		152	65	
Height (cm)	156.3±8.7	159.1±7.9	0.01	168.5±7.8	170.7±6.8	0.023	173.3±6.3	175.4±5.6	0.022
Weight (kg)	48.3±12.2	54.1±12.4	0.001	59.9±14.8	64.5±16.1	0.022	67.1±14.2	72.6±14.4	0.009
Waist circumference (cm)	67.6±10.4	76.4±11.5	0.001	72.5±12.3	80.2±14.1	0.001	76.05±11.2	82.8±11.3	0.001
BMI (kg/m²)	19.6±4.1	21.3±4.1	0.002	21.1±4.8	22.2±5.4	0.068	22.3±4.4	23.6±4.4	0.046
Hip circumference (cm)	81.7±8.9	86.2±8.5	0.001	88.8±10	92.8±9.8	0.002	92.4±8.5	96.5±8.5	0.001
Wrist circumference (cm)	15.8±1.2	16.15±1.19	0.014	16.6±1.1	16.9±1.1	0.028	17.1±0.9	17.2±0.9	0.237
Girls (n)	187	80		184	102		180	64	
Height (cm)	156.4±6.1	156.1±5.9	0.718	159.4±6.1	158.0±5.5	0.058	159.49±5.8	160.7±5.8	0.155
Weight (kg)	49.3±10	53.2±10.8	0.005	55.2±9.6	56±9.9	0.482	56.2±11.1	56.8±9.4	0.678
Waist circumference (cm)	70.2±8.7	71.6±9.2	0.214	71.9±7.8	70.4±8.6	0.139	73.1±8.78	69.88±8.8	0.016
BMI (kg/m²)	20.1±3.7	21.8±4.2	0.001	21.7±3.6	22.5±4	0.102	22.1±4.2	22.1±3.8	0.967
Hip circumference (cm)	89.8±8.2	92.2±8.4	0.029	94.9±7.6	94.7±7.3	0.772	96.5±8.1	95.7±7	0.465
Wrist circumference (cm)	15.1±0.8	14.9±0.9	0.282	15.2±0.8	14.9±0.8	0.004	15.2±0.9	14.7±0.8	0.001

BMI= body mass index

TABLE 7.2. Mean±SD for Blood Pressure, Blood Sugar and Serum Lipids in the Two Groups

Variables	Ages 11-14			Ages 15-18		
	War group	After war group	P	War group	After war group	P
Boys (n)	601	328		569	269	
Fasting blood sugar (mg/dL)	90.4±14.9	89.6±7.1	0.340	88.9±7.5	86.9±6.8	0.001
Total cholesterol (mg/dL)	166±31.7	155.3±29.2	0.001	160.6±32.3	145.9±29.4	0.001
Triglyceride (mg/dL)	103.9±59.5	103.5±57.9	0.924	114.9±69.3	103.5±59.4	0.021
HDL cholesterol (mg/dL)	44.4±10.5	44.5±10.3	0.918	40.2±9.2	40±7.7	0.663
LDL cholesterol (mg/dL)	100.4±27.9	89.4±24.6	0.001	97.6±26.8	85.3±25.1	0.001
Systolic blood pressure (mm Hg)	103.9±11.6	100.9±12	0.001	110.7±12.1	107±10.9	0.001
Diastolic blood pressure (mm Hg)	69.5±9.1	64.2±9.7	0.001	72.7±8.6	69.6±9.4	0.001
Girls (n)	624	335		694	322	
Fasting blood sugar (mg/dL)	89.1±7.9	87.7±6.5	0.004	85.9±7.5	84±7.2	0.001
Total cholesterol (mg/dL)	169.4±29.7	157.7±30.7	0.001	169.3±30.9	153.2±29.5	0.001
Triglyceride (mg/dL)	121.4±61.9	107.8±55.3	0.001	101.5±47.7	93.5±46.2	0.012
HDL cholesterol (mg/dL)	42±9.8	43.2±10.1	0.069	43.9±10.2	44.9±9.9	0.156
LDL cholesterol (mg/dL)	103±26.5	92.3±24.7	0.001	104.8±27.1	89.9±25.9	0.001
Systolic blood pressure (mm Hg)	102.4±10.9	97.3±11.3	0.001	106.5±10.6	98.6±11.4	0.001
Diastolic blood pressure (mm Hg)	70±9.5	63.9±9.4	0.001	72.9±8.4	65.4±9.3	0.001

Age group 12 years: At the age of 12 years, the differences in anthropometric indices were not statistically significant between girls of both groups while all anthropometric indices increased in boys of the post-war group. The most important of these indices were height (4.51 cm), weight (7.81 kg), waist circumference (10.36 cm), BMI (2.23 kg/m^2) and hip circumference (6.29 cm), $P < 0.001$.

Age group 14 years: In girls of the post-war group, weight increased 6.6 kg ($P < 0.01$), waist circumference increased 3.5 cm ($P < 0.01$), BMI increased 2.2 kg/m^2 ($P < 0.001$) and hip circumference increased 3.4 cm ($P < 0.01$) compared to girls of the war group. In boys of the post-war group, height increased 4.5 cm, weight increased 11.2 kg, waist circumference increased 12.8 cm, BMI increased 2.92 kg/m^2 and hip circumference increased 7.7 cm compared to boys of the war group ($P < 0.001$).

Age group 16 years: Waist circumference increased 5.54 cm in boys of the post-war group ($P < 0.001$).

Age group 18 years: There were no significant indices in this age group.

The maximum height and weight increments were observed in boys of the post-war group at the ages of 12 and 14 years (4.5 cm for height and 7.8-11.2 kg for weight). Anthropometric indices at the age of 13, 15 and 17 are shown in Table 7.1.

Biochemical indices: The results of blood pressure and biochemical indices in the two age groups (11-14) and (15-18) are shown in Table 7.2.

Discussion

This study showed that anthropometric indices of boys in the post-war group increased in all age groups, although the number of significant indices in all age groups was not equal. Anthropometric indices only increased in girls of the post-war group for ages 11, 13, and 14 years. Blood pressure and most biochemical indices decreased significantly in both girls and boys in the post-war group compared to the war group.

There are several studies showing that during the last century children of the same age have experienced a progressive rise in mean body height and weight. The phenomenon is termed secular trend or growth acceleration.[11,12] Variations in adolescent growth are ascribed to the improvement of environmental conditions, socioeconomic conditions of the family, nutritional status, standards of health care and care provided by parents, both strongly associated with the parents' educational level. [11,13] In an overview based on a literature review and new data from three cohorts, it has been determined that genetic predisposition is a major determinant of height, in addition to early life environment, which also has an important impact. Plausible non-genetic determinants of height include nutrition, illness, socioeconomic status, and psychosocial stress.[14]

In this study, we cannot determine with certainty the cause of the differences between the two groups. There are many confounding factors in this regard, which were not studied, for example: lifestyle, level of access to food, economic status of families, parental education level, and age of menarche in girls. In addition, data pertaining to subjects before the war was not available. There are some possible factors that appear to cause these differences. The subjects in both groups were assessed at different times and in the six year interval between the two assessments, many national health programs have been initiated,[15] many factors may have changed, which possibly influence anthropometric and biochemical indices. Another factor may be related to the natural secular trend in physical growth. In a study it has been shown that in 2001, 18-year-old males attained a mean height of 180.1 cm, which is 12 cm greater than the mean height of 18-year-old men in 1895. The mean height of 18-year-old women in 2001 was 167.2 cm, an increase of 10 cm over the mean height in 1895.[13] In our study there were no significant height differences between girls in the two groups. In an overview it has been shown that growth in males is more sensitive to changes in living conditions than females.[14] Another study has shown a diminishing secular increase in female stature whereas height in men has continued to rise in a stepwise fashion.[16] In the present study, the duration between both groups studied was 3 to 10 years; therefore, it seems that the observed height rise in this study is greater than the normal trend of physical growth during these years. Another possible factor that can be noted is the circumstances of war. The Iran-Iraq imposed war, a war between the Republic of Iraq and the Islamic Republic of Iran, lasted from September 22, 1980 until August 20, 1988. This war, one of the disasters of the twentieth century, was the longest war in the world after the Vietnam War.[17] Some studies have shown the effects of war on physical growth in children born during the war that was ascribed to war-induced degradation in economic conditions.[11,18,19] Also, in a study it has been shown that blood pressure was higher in males born during the war;[20] other studies have shown that psychosocial stress caused by war is an important risk factor for the increase in blood sugar during the years following a war in addition to the incidence of diabetes.[21-24]

Future longitudinal studies that control for confounding factors and assessment of more variables can more accurately determine the causes of these differences.

In conclusion, this study has shown that most anthropometric indices such as height and weight increased in boys who were born after the war; whereas in girls, the mean weight in the three age groups increased. Systolic and diastolic blood pressure, as well as some lipid profiles decreased in both boys and girls who were born after the war years.

Acknowledgments

This study was funded by the Research Institute of Endocrine Sciences, Shaheed Beheshti University of Medical Sciences, Tehran, Iran. The authors express their appreciation to the participants of the Tehran Lipid and Glucose Study and would like to acknowledge the assistance given by Ms. N. Shiva for language editing of the manuscript.

References

1. Vignerová J, Brabec M, Bláha P. Two centuries of growth among Czech children and youth. *Econ Hum Biol.* 2006; 4: 237-252.

2. Vignerová J, Humemíkova L, Brabec M, Riedlová J, Bláha P. Long-term changes in body weight, BMI, and adiposity rebound among children and adolescents in the Czech republic. *Econ Hum Biol.* 2007; 5: 409-425.

3. Dasgupta P, Saha R, Nube M. Changes in body size, shape, and nutritional status of middle-class Bengali boys of Kolkata, India, 1982-2002. *Econ Hum Biol.* 2008; 6: 75-94.

4. Engel Dr. Rickets in Germany: a study of the effects of war on children. *Lancet.* 1920; 195: 88-190.

5. Farhood L, Zurayk H, Chaya M, Saadeh F, Meshefedjian G, Sidani T. The impact of war on the physical and mental health of the family: the Lebanese experience. *Soc* Sci *Med.* 1993; 36: 1555-1567.

6. Brajsa-Zganec A. The long-term effects of war experiences on children's depression in the Republic of Croatia.*Child Abuse Negi.* 2005; 29: 31-43.

7. Azizi F, Rahmani M, Mohammad M, Emami H, Mirmiran P, Hajipour R. Introducing the objectives, implementation methods and structure of Tehran Lipid and Glucose [In Farsi]. *Iran J Endocrinol Metabol.* 2000; 2: 77-86.

8. Azizi F, Rahmani M, Emami H, Madjid M. Tehran lipid and glucose study: rationale and design. *CVD Prevention.* 2000; 3: 242-247.

9. Friedewald WT, Levy RI, Fredrickson OS. Estimation of the concentration of low-density lipoprotein cholesterol in plasma, without use of the preparative ultracentrifuge. *Clin Chem.* 1 972; 18: 499-502.

10. Azizi F, Ghanbarian A, Momenan AA, Hadaegh F, Mirmiran P, Hedayati M, et al. The Tehran Lipid and Glucose Study Group. Prevention of non-communicable disease in a population in nutrition transition: Tehran Lipid and Glucose Study phase II. *Trials.* 2009; 10: 5.

11. Azizi F, Rahmani M, Emami H, Mirmiran P, Hajipour R, Madjid M, et al. Cardiovascular risk factors in an Iranian urban population: Tehran Lipid and Glucose Study. *Soz Praventiv Med.* 2002; 47: 408-426.

12. Jakić M, Jakić M. Secular growth trend in urban children enrolling primary school in the war time. *Acta Med Croatica.* 2006; 60: 195-199.

13. Cole TJ. The secular trend in human physical growth: a biological view. *Am J Epidemiol.* 2003; 1: 161-168.

14. Vignerová J, Brabec M, Bláha P. Two centuries of growth among Czech children and youth. *Econ Hum Biol.* 2006; 4: 237-252.

15. Batty GD, Shipley MJ, Gunnell D, Huxley R, Kivimaki M, Woodward M, et al. Height, wealth, and health: an overview with new data from three longitudinal studies. *Econ Hum Biol.* 2009; 7: 137-152.

16. Rafati M, Ghotbi M, Ahmad Nia H. Principle of disease prevention and surveillance. In: *Surveillance Systems of Non-Communicable Diseases* [In Farsi]. 1st ed. Tehran: Sepid Barg Bagh Ketab; 2008.

17. Cavelaars AE, Kunst AE, Geurts JJ, Crialesi R, Grotvedt L, Helmert U, et al. Persistent variations in average height between countries and between socio-economic groups: an overview of 10 European countries. *Ann Hum Biol.* 2000; 27: 407-421.

18. Abrahamian E. *A History of Modern Iran.* New York: Cambridge University Press; 2008.

19. Jakić M, Jakić M. Influence of the war events on body weight and height in children enrolling the first grade of elementary school. *Lijec Vjesn.* 2005; 127: 211-214.

20. Yoo JH. Deletion polymorphism in the gene for angiotensin-converting enzyme is associated with essential hypertension in men born during the Pacific War. *Mech Ageing Dev.* 2005; 126: 899-905.

21. Nonogaki K. New insights into sympathetic regulation of glucose and fat metabolism. *Diabetologia.* 2000; 43: 533-549.

22. Diabetes Epidemiology Research International. Preventing insulin dependent diabetes mellitus: the environmental challenge. *BMJ.* 1987; 295: 479-481.

23. Kumar D, Gemayel NS, Deapen D. North-American twins with IDDM. Genetic, etiological, and clinical significance of disease concordance according to age, zygosity, and the interval after diagnosis in first twin. *Diabetes.* 1993; 42: 1351-1363.

24. Dahlquist G. The aetiology of type I diabetes: an epidemiological perspective. *Acta Paediatr Suppl.* 1998; 425: 5-10.

Source: *Archives of Iranian Medicine* 14.1 (2011): 27-31.

WHAT IT SAYS

1. What effects does war have on public health, according to previous studies?

2. In what sense are children "the most jeopardized group" in wartime, according to Ramezankhani et al.? Discuss both short- and long-term effects of war on children.

3. How does the purpose of this study differ from other studies on the effects of war on health?

4. What was the purpose of the "data quality program" in this study?

5. Overall, what differences in weight, height, and blood pressure between the pre-Iran-Iraq War study group and the postwar group did this study show? Consult the narrative as well as Tables 7.1 and 7.2.

6. What factors prevent the authors from stating with certainty the causes for the observed differences in weight, height, and blood pressure between the two groups?

HOW IT SAYS IT

1. How does the structure of this study's abstract differ from that of abstracts more commonly used in the physical sciences? What purpose does this unusual structure serve?

2. How do Tables 7.1 and 7.2 work to support the conclusions of Ramezankhani et al.?

3. What is the effect of the acknowledgment by the authors that they cannot state with certainty that the war caused the health differences they noted, and that further study is needed?

WRITE ABOUT IT

1. Based on the findings in this study and perhaps other sources, write a public-health policy paper designed to protect children living in a country at war.

2. Write a grant proposal for a follow-up study to Ramezankhani et al. This does not need to be the follow-up that the authors suggest, but it should follow from their research. You may first need to research the organizations that fund such studies, and the protocols for the content and structure of grant proposals of this kind.

3. Write and produce a short documentary on the effects of war on public health in general, or on children's health in particular. Use existing video footage and photographs exclusively, or add your own images, interviews, etc., to existing footage.

Questions for Synthesis

1. Write an essay that explores the views expressed by the authors in this chapter on the human impulse toward war and conflict. Be especially aware of contradictions and confluences among the various arguments.

   - How do the various authors explain the human impulses toward—and/or away from—conflict and war?
   - How do these impulses play out in practice, according to the authors?
   - On what specific points do the authors agree and disagree?

   Remember that this is a synthesis essay, not a contribution. Your goal is to faithfully represent the positions of these writers, not to argue your position. You may wish to construct a synthesis grid (see pp. 77–79) to begin writing.

2. Write an essay that explores proposals the authors in this chapter make for managing the inevitable conflicts that arise within and between peoples and nations. Contrast the ideals of the authors (which they may only imply rather than explicitly state) with what really goes on in the world. What factors prevent the ideal from becoming reality, according to these authors?

   Write this essay as a synthesis of the authors' views, not as a contribution.

Questions for Contribution

1. Write an essay that presents a plan—one that is both effective and humane—for dealing with global terrorism and with individual terrorists. Consider ways in which your plan will acknowledge and accommodate diverse cultures, beliefs, and governmental systems. Include in your plan a series of steps necessary to arrive at your proposed goal.

   You may wish to present your plan as a videotaped presentation that is posted online, or as a speech delivered live before your class.

   Illustrate your points with slides, photographs, and video and audio clips, so that your presentation involves more than just a "talking head." For support and examples, draw on the sources included in this chapter, the Suggested Additional Resources, and on recent news events. Be sure to acknowledge and address views contrary to your own.

2. Write an essay that argues for a global policy on war and conflict, and that proposes specific protocols for implementing and enforcing these policies. You might wish to write your piece as a presentation to the United Nations, or another international body. Structure your essay or presentation so that a non-expert can easily follow it.

   For support, draw on the sources in this chapter, the Suggested Additional Resources, and, if applicable, your own experience.

abstract (in writing): a brief summary of a scientific or other study and its findings. In the **IMRAD format**, an abstract is generally followed by the **introduction**.

Academic Bill of Rights: a document created and distributed by Students for Academic Freedom, a public advocacy group whose mission is to "end the political abuse of the university and to restore integrity to the academic mission as a disinterested pursuit of knowledge." The Bill's eight principles call for an academic environment free from political or religious discrimination. The group's detractors say the SAF promotes a specific conservative agenda and thus is not bipartisan, as it claims.

academic freedom: the relative freedom of a teacher to study and discuss controversial issues or beliefs without being penalized by administrators or others in power.

alternating comparison (also **point-by-point** or **subject-by-subject**): a comparison structure in which the writer discusses one element or feature that is common to both subjects, and then moves on to discuss another element or feature common to both subjects, and so on. This structure is useful with lengthy, complex subjects.

al-Qaeda: an Islamic jihadist movement originally led by Osama bin Laden with the goal of replacing non-Muslim governments or countries with Islamic fundamentalist regimes.

AMA (citation style): a format for documenting sources in a research paper or analysis that has been adopted by the American Medical Association. Generally used in medical journals.

American studies: an interdisciplinary field dealing with the study of the United States and including scholarship in history, literature, the arts, contemporary and urban life, media, and other aspects of US culture and society.

amniocentesis: a process in which a sample of amniotic fluid, the liquid surrounding a fetus in the uterus, is removed and tested for genetically heritable traits.

analysis (in writing): a writing strategy that involves examining the content and structure of another writer's argument, as well as any "holes" in the argument. Analysis is also used to assess a problem or issue itself, ideally leading to a contribution to the existing academic conversation on a given topic.

annotation (also **glossing**): to make notes within or in the margins of an article or book. Used to clarify, explain, or comment on the text.

anthropogenic causes (of global warming): climate change believed to be linked to the activities of human beings (i.e., through **greenhouse gases**).

anthropology: the study of human origins and physical development (physical anthropology) and human cultural diversity (cultural anthropology).

AP (citation style): a format for citing sources in a research paper or analysis that has been adopted by the Associated Press. Used in journalism and journalism research.

APA (citation style): a format for citing sources in a research paper or analysis that has been adopted by the American Psychological Association. Used in the social sciences and sometimes in the physical sciences.

argument: a position or stance taken in a piece of writing or a speech, usually involving several claims backed up by reasons based on logical thinking and data.

artificial intelligence (AI): the simulation of human (or greater) intelligence in machines and the development and study of such intelligence.

ASA (citation style): a format for citing sources in a research paper or analysis that has been adopted by the American Sociological Association. Used in sociology and related disciplines.

asset bubble: inflation of a particular class of assets, such as real estate or commodities. Asset bubbles generally occur when a rush to purchase such assets heightens investor demand for a particular class of assets.

attitude (in writing): an aspect of **writing style** that describes the manner in which the writer approaches a **topic** (for example, casual, skeptical, ironic, or formal).

autoethnography: a genre of writing and research that connects the personal to the cultural, placing the self within a social context.

bathos: an insincerely emotional approach to a topic; sentimentality. Intended to sway the reader, this approach has the counter-effect of eroding the writer's credibility.

behavioral psychology: a specialization within the field of psychology that focuses on observable human behaviors, including the effects of conditioning, reinforcement, and punishment on the individual.

biodiversity: variety among and within plant and animal species in a given environment, generally considered an asset. Some experts on global warming warn that biodiversity is in danger as the planet warms.

biological determinism: a form of determinism based on biological characteristics, especially genetic factors. The term suggests that biology determines outcomes, especially forms of behavior. One form of biological determinism is **genetic determinism**. The terms biological determinism and genetic determinism are often used pejoratively by critics to refer to explanations of behavior that do not account for social and other environmental factors.

biological potentiality: the belief or theory that genes or biology do not determine specific behaviors but rather make a wide range of behaviors possible.

biology: the study of living things. Biology consists of two main branches: **botany** is the study of plant life; **zoology** is the study of animal life. Microbiology is the study of microorganisms, which may be either plants or animals, or neither.

bionics: the study and reproduction of biological organs and functions using various technologies, including electronics, engineering, robotics, and other fields.

botany: the study of plant life. Botany is divided into several subspecialties.

bundled mortgages: a usually large number of home **mortgages** that are packaged and sold to banks and other financial firms. Extensive buying and selling of subpar bundled home mortgages and the widespread failure of such loans has been cited as a major cause of the 2008 financial crisis.

business and marketing: an academic field concerned with designing and evaluating processes and practices by which businesses can be organized, including those for creating and maintaining markets for their goods.

canon / literary canon: the books or other works considered indispensible to an educated person of a particular culture. The term derives from the biblical canon, the collection of books accepted as the official Bible, but is now applied to a broader cultural heritage. In the Western cultural tradition, the canon includes the works of ancient Greece and Rome, as well as the works of major authors in modern languages. The traditional English literary canon includes the works of Chaucer, Spenser, Shakespeare, Milton, and others; this has been contested by some literary scholars, however, and expanded to include work by women, non-Westerners, and others.

capitalism: the economic system of production and exchange that is based on the private ownership of property and industry. Capitalism is the economic system of the United States and most of the world. The global economy is a capitalist economy.

CBE (citation style): an earlier name for **CSE**.

Chicago style (of citation): see **CMS**.

citizenship: the behavior or character of an individual, based on how he or she carries out the obligations and functions of a citizen, or member of a specific society.

claim (in writing): a single stance or position statement used as part of a **thesis** in an essay.

climate: the weather conditions characteristic of an area or region, as expressed in terms of median temperatures, humidity, and rainfall. May also refer to the social and political attitudes and conditions that characterize a region or group.

climatology: the academic study of **climate**.

CMS (citation style): a format for citing sources in a research paper or analysis that has been adopted by the *Chicago Manual of Style*. Used in the social sciences and the humanities.

CMS author-date style: a documentation option from the *Chicago Manual of Style*. Uses the author and date of the reference work in the text, and detailed documentation at the end of a scholarly paper.

CMS notes and bibliography style: a documentation option from the *Chicago Manual of Style*. Uses endnotes or footnotes in the text, and detailed documentation at the end of a scholarly paper.

cognition: an individual's ability to perceive, understand, learn, reason, judge, and imagine.

cognitive science: the field of science concerned with **cognition** based on the study of the parts and properties of the brain. The field of cognitive science draws from psychology, philosophy, neuroscience, computer science, and linguistics.

comparison: a structural option for an academic essay that focuses on similarities and differences between two (or more) topics, or arguments.

computer science: the study of computing and computation, including computer hardware and software components and their interactions. The body of knowledge comprising computer science includes theories for understanding computing systems, methods for the design of computer languages, and tools for the use of computer languages.

conclusion: the final paragraph or paragraphs of an essay. The conclusion should not merely reiterate the introduction; rather, it should sum up the findings of a study, suggest areas of further study, or discuss the implications of the study's findings or claims to the larger field. In the latter instance, the conclusion expresses the ways in which the essay contributes to its field.

contribution: in academic terms, an addition to current knowledge or theory—the academic "conversation"—on a given subject. Every academic paper should make a contribution to its field by producing new data or a new theory that contradicts or refines earlier research, proposing a new stance on an issue fraught with controversy, or filling in a "hole" in existing writing on a given topic.

convergence, convergence theory (media convergence): a prevailing theory in the study of digital media which holds that the phenomenon of digital media cannot be adequately understood in terms of a **digital revolution** wherein digital media replace all other forms of media. According to convergence theory, digital media "converge" with older media, digital media products converge with each other, and media producers converge in the production of new and changed media forms.

corporate domination (of media): the control of media outlets and forms by large corporations. The term is used **pejoratively** to describe the impossibility of alternative points of view or ideological positions reaching a mass audience.

The notion of corporate domination of the media has recently been challenged by the notion of **participatory culture**, made possible by digital media forms.

counterargument(s): **arguments** that oppose the author's in a given scholarly article or book. A creditable claim must take into account and address counter-arguments, either to acknowledge their validity in certain circumstances or to refute them.

counterterrorism: any of a number of measures undertaken (usually by a govern-ment) to respond to acts of terrorism, or to prevent acts of terrorism from occurring. These measures include tightened national security, armed missions to capture or kill suspected terrorists, and interrogation and torture of suspected terrorists.

credit default swaps (CDS): a credit **derivative** or a type of insurance agree-ment between buyer and seller in which the buyer pays a lump sum deposit and a premium at periodic intervals in exchange for insurance against loss on the value of a loan in the event that a third party defaults. Credit default swaps were among the main immediate causes of the financial crisis of 2008, as many mort-gages defaulted and lenders lost the value of their investments. Also affected by mortgage defaults, many insurers were unable to deliver on their promise to pay in cases of default. Credit default swaps are sold "across the counter"—directly between buyers and sellers—not on traditional trading platforms such as the US Stock Exchange.

creolization (see also **hybridization**): a theory of globalization suggesting that complex processes of cultural borrowing and lending occur when cultures inter-act. The term derives from the root word "creole," which referred to a person of mixed African and French and/or Spanish ancestry but is no longer considered acceptable usage.

critical theory: the examination and critique of society and culture, drawing from knowledge and methods across the social sciences and humanities. The methods and approaches of critical theory were initially derived from schools of thought associated with **Marxism**, in particular the neo-Marxist body of thought associ-ated with the **Frankfurt School of Critical Theory**. Critical theory now includes other approaches, including psychoanalysis and **psychoanalytic theory**, **femi-nism**, **deconstruction**, **postcolonial theory**, and others.

CSE (citation style): a format for citing sources in a research paper or analy-sis that has been adopted by the Council of Science Editors. Used in the physical sciences.

cultural imperialism: the cultural domination of one group over others. Cultural imperialism works subtly to undermine the cultures into which the dominant culture is imported. It has been associated with the dominance of Western, especially American, culture throughout the world.

cultural studies: an interdisciplinary field drawing chiefly from **critical theory** and other methods to study cultural phenomena. According to some theorists, cultural studies deals with contemporary culture; others maintain that historical phenomena are part of its purview.

cybersphere: the realm where digital participants meet to produce, consume, and exchange digital texts, including images, sound, video, and other digital artifacts. The **Internet** is the largest but not the only component of the cybersphere.

deconstruction (also deconstructionism): a theory of criticism introduced by the French philosopher Jacques Derrida that analyzes the underlying contradictions in texts and aims to uncover the inherent instability of the language upon which important concepts are based.

default (in finance): failure to pay on a loan according to the terms agreed upon by the lender and borrower in a signed document, usually a promissory note. In the case of **mortgage** loans, defaulting generally results in **foreclosure**.

democratization: the process of moving toward a democratic society. In terms of the **Information Age**, access to the **Internet** and other parts of the **cybersphere** is considered instrumental (and sometimes necessary) for democratization to occur.

derivatives (in economics): financial instruments whose value is derived from the price of underlying assets. Derivatives trading figured significantly in the 2008 financial crisis.

developmental psychology: the scientific study of the changes that occur in human beings as they develop emotionally and cognitively. Developmental psychologists may focus on any level of development and change, from infancy to old age; they consider human development within social, cultural, and/or socioeconomic contexts.

diction: word choice in a given piece of writing. Diction affects the **tone** or **attitude** of the piece and can give hints as to the author's intended audience.

digital divide: the gap between those with access to digital media (such as the **Internet**) and those with limited or no access. Those with limited or no access are thought to be disadvantaged economically and otherwise.

digital generation: digital natives, or those for whom digital technologies already existed when they were born. The digital generation is often considered more adept than non-natives at using digital technologies such as the **Internet**, the iPod, and multimedia mobile phones.

digital humanities: an interdisciplinary humanities field aimed at developing publishing, teaching, and research methodologies derived from computing. **Digitalization** made possible an array of computational tools with the potential to radically change reading, publishing, and research. These tools include data mining of vast data sets (for example, periodicals from the nineteenth century), textual analysis and text classification, and the curating of online publications.

digital native: see **digital generation**.

digital revolution thesis: the thesis that the change from analog mechanical and electronic technology to digital technology that has taken place since about 1980 involves a dramatic overthrow of earlier media, genres, and habits. The digital revolution thesis has recently been contrasted with **convergence** or **convergence theory**.

digitalization (also digitization): the conversion of images, music, texts, and video to digital form based on code reducible to patterns of zeros and ones.

dot.com bubble: an **asset bubble** that developed during the developmental stages of the **Internet** involving the stocks of Internet-based companies. The bubble reached its peak in March of 2000 and subsequently burst, with asset values declining rapidly as numerous Internet-based firms became bankrupt and investors lost money.

dystopia: an imagined place or future that is mostly negative or nightmarish. Generally the opposite of a utopia.

ecology: a subfield of zoology that considers the effects of organisms, including human beings, on their environments. The ecology of a specific environment also can refer to its flora, fauna, air quality, and climate, and the ways in which these elements interact.

economics: the study of the production, distribution, and use of valued resources, as well as the stimulants to their creation.

education: the acquisition of knowledge and skills and the development and study of methods and theories for imparting them.

educational technology: a relatively new interdisciplinary field that involves the study of learning with the use of appropriate technologies. The field incorporates theories of learning and thus is not strictly the study of technological devices.

empirical evidence: evidence based on observation and experimentation.

endnotes: numbered notes at the end of the paper that correspond to superscripted numbers in the text. Like footnotes, these notes may give reference information or may add extra information or explain a word or phrase in the context of the essay.

Enlightenment: the philosophical, intellectual, and cultural movement of the seventeenth and eighteenth centuries, emphasizing reason, logic, criticism, and freedom of thought over dogma, blind faith, and superstition. The reactions to the Enlightenment's emphasis on rationality have included the movements of Romanticism and **Postmodernism**.

environmental science: an interdisciplinary field that examines the relationship between living and non-living systems, in particular the impact of human activity on these systems.

epistemology: a branch of philosophy that investigates human knowledge—its origin, nature, methods, and limits.

essay: an academic paper written by students and experts in the field that presents a unique thesis and that results in a **contribution** to a given field.

essay body: the part of the essay between the introduction and conclusion that presents evidence or argument supporting a claim, illustrations, examples, and any other information relevant to and supportive of the essay's **thesis**.

essentialism (in critical theory): the belief that people or groups have an unchangeable essence or a set of stable, necessary properties. The term is often used **pejoratively** by critics who suggest that essentialism serves to support dominant and often oppressive categorizations. Compare to **existentialism** and **social constructionism**.

ethics: a system of moral principles held by a culture or individual. Also, a branch of philosophy that deals with human values, specifically beliefs of right and wrong that manifest in how human beings conduct, or should conduct, themselves.

ethos: a kind of appeal designed to persuade the reader by establishing the writer as credible because he or she is of sound ethical character, is sane and reasonable, and is worthy of respect based on his or her education and experience in the field. The idea is that a reader who finds a writer credible will find the writer's claim credible.

eugenics: the endeavor to produce conditions conducive to the selective breeding of "higher" or more fit types or races of human beings. The term was coined in 1883 by Charles Darwin's cousin, Francis Galton, and means well-rooted or well-bred.

evidence: information meant to support an essay's argument. Evidence can vary in type from lab or study results, to the research and opinions of experts in the field, to personal experience.

evolution debate (or origin debate): a dispute between creationists and evolutionists about the origins of the universe and humanity, with cultural, political, educational, and theological implications. Creationists tend to be religious thinkers who contend that God created the Earth and human beings (and, as some biblical literalists maintain, in seven days), as described in the Bible. Evolutionists, backed by scientific consensus, maintain that human beings developed from organic predecessors, over millions of years.

evolutionary psychology (see also **sociobiology**): the attempt to explain behavior and psychological traits in terms of evolutionary adaptation based on the process of natural selection occurring over millions of years.

exercise physiology: the study of the body's responses to a wide range of physical exercise conditions.

existentialism: the postwar philosophical movement credited primarily to the French philosopher Jean-Paul Sartre and based on the belief that human beings are free to determine their own beings and the course of their lives. The basic principle of existentialism is that existence precedes essence. Compare to **essentialism**.

exposition (also **expository prose**): a kind of writing that illuminates or explains a topic or idea with facts, examples, definitions, and instructions. The tone of exposition is objective; ideally, the information or explanations are verifiable and not subject to interpretation.

fair use / fair use doctrine: provisions in the US copyright law (a part of **intellectual property** law) for the use of copyrighted materials for particular purposes and to a limited extent. Four factors are considered when determining whether the use of a copyrighted work constitutes fair use. A full explanation is found at http://www.copyright.gov/fls/fl102.html.

feminism: a movement started in the mid-nineteenth century with the women's suffrage movement, aimed at establishing equal rights and access for women, and which now includes a diverse set of approaches to culture, society, and gender or sexual politics.

footnotes: numbered notes found at the bottom of the page corresponding to superscripted numbers in the text. Like endnotes, these notes may give reference information or may add extra information or explain a word or phrase in the context of the essay.

foreclosure: the legal proceedings initiated by a lender to repossess the collateral for a loan that is in default. **Mortgage** foreclosures constituted a major precipitating factor of the 2008 financial crisis, as hundreds of thousands of home loans went into default.

Frankfurt School of critical theory: the neo-**Marxist** school of thought centered on the Institute of Social Research founded in Frankfurt, Germany. The thinkers in this school attempted to apply Marxist theory to such cultural, social, and political trends as mass media, the rise of fascism, the world wars, and the state of communism in the Soviet Union. Their work formed the basis of **media studies** and **critical theory**. Because of their increasing pessimism regarding the role of the working class in history and their negative attitude toward science and the Enlightenment, the Frankfurt School thinkers were not orthodox Marxists.

free will: the purported ability of conscious agents to make choices from among a variety of possibilities. Free will is precluded if **determinist** explanations for behavior are correct.

free writing: a pre-writing strategy that involves writing continuously, usually on a given topic, for a short time and without censoring oneself. The idea is that such writing helps writers get their ideas on screen or on paper without the pressure of having to "get it right" early in the writing process.

game studies or **gaming theory**: an interdisciplinary field that focuses on game design, players, and the roles of both in society and culture. "Games" most commonly refers to video and computer games.

gender studies: the interdisciplinary study of gender as a social category linked with other social categories, such as race and sexuality. Gender studies is associated with forms of **feminism**, particularly feminism that rejects **essentialist** notions of gender. Gender studies is thus informed by **social constructivism**.

genetic determinism: a form of **determinism** based on biology, in particular genetic inheritance.

genetic engineering (see also **germ-line engineering**): the technology for altering the genetic material of organisms using splicing and other techniques. Genetic engineering can alter the genetic material prior to the development of the organism, thus allowing organisms to pass the changes along to the offspring. Genetic engineering has been used on microorganisms, crops, and mammals such as mice. Its application, especially to human genetic material, is controversial.

genetic screening: a technique for analyzing the genetic makeup of individuals. The scanning of the genetic material of human embryos created by **in vitro fertilization** is called **pre-implantation genetic diagnosis (PGD)**, a controversial procedure often used for selecting potential offspring.

genetically modified organisms (GMOs): organisms whose genetic material has been altered using **genetic engineering**. Genetically modified organisms include food crops, microorganisms, and mice, among others. GMOs are very controversial among environmentalists and others opposed to genetically modified foods.

genetics: the study of inheritance and variation in organisms based on the action of genes.

genetics, nanotechnology, and robotics (GNR): a combination of scientific, technological, and engineering efforts involving these three fields and thought to be essential for the philosophical movements known as **transhumanism** and **Singulartarianism**.

Geneva Conventions: four treaties and three protocols that set international standards for the humanitarian treatment of prisoners of war, the wounded, and all those located near a war zone. Geneva Convention typically refers to the most recent treaty (1949), now ratified by 194 countries.

germ-line engineering (see also **genetic engineering**): **genetic engineering** prior to the development of an organism. This process enables organisms to pass the changes along to subsequent generations.

global culture: the cultural results of and responses to **globalization**. The notion of a global culture suggests that the processes of globalization change cultures worldwide.

global studies: a relatively new interdisciplinary field that incorporates **sociology**, **political science**, **international relations**, **environmental science**, **economics**, and others to address the issues associated with **globalization**.

global warming: an increase in the average temperature of the earth's atmosphere, particularly those increases linked to human activity (known as **anthropogenic causes**).

globalization: the increasingly interconnected and interdependent nature of communication systems, economies, cultures, and politics of contemporary societies on a global scale.

glossing (see also **annotation**): a way of taking notes on a piece of writing in order to better understand and remember its main points. Glossing can take many forms, but it generally consists of making marginal notes (by hand or on the computer) that very briefly summarize the thesis and main points, point out how ideas connect to each other and/or to another text, and summarize important or striking quotations—all information that you might want to return to when you write a response essay.

green economy: an economy that significantly reduces environmental and ecological degradation while also including more people in the benefits of economic activity.

greenhouse effect: a process by which heat from the Earth's surface is absorbed by **greenhouse gases** in the atmosphere and emitted back toward the surface. This re-radiation causes an increase in the Earth's surface temperature.

greenhouse gases: gases in a planet's atmosphere that absorb and then emit heat from a planet's surface, causing the **greenhouse effect**. These gases include methane, carbon dioxide, nitrous oxide, ozone, and water vapor.

heterogenization: a theory of **globalization** suggesting that interactions among diverse cultures increase the cultural heterogeneity or difference within each culture. Compare to **homogenization**.

heuristic: a teaching and learning method encouraging experimentation and evaluation of possible answers, responses, and solutions.

homogenization: a theory of **globalization** suggesting that the interaction between diverse cultures results in the creation of cultural sameness between cultures. According to homogenization theory, Western culture generally prevails over the indigenous cultures of non-Western societies. Compare to **heterogenization**.

Human-computer interaction (HCI): the study of human beings as they interact with computer technology. The field is an amalgam of several disciplines, including **anthropology**, **computer science**, **psychology**, **sociology**, and even **literary studies**. HCI researchers undertake quantitative studies of user response to software interfaces. HCI research also includes qualitative or descriptive studies of users' responses to less quantifiable aspects of computing experience, such as the level of enjoyment experienced by computer users.

hybridization, of culture (see also **creolization**): a theory of **globalization** suggesting that the interaction between cultures often results in mixing and sharing of each other's characteristics, rather than the domination of one culture (usually non-Western) by another (usually Western) culture.

IMRAD: an acronym for an essay structure used in the physical sciences; stands for Introduction, Materials and Methods, Results, and Discussion/Conclusion. Sub-headings in a physical sciences paper generally indicate these divisions.

indigenous: native to or characteristic of a specific geographical area.

Information Age: the current stage in societal development that emerged at the end of the twentieth century. It was made possible by **digitalization** and is marked by the increased production, transmission, and consumption of, and reliance on, information. Many consider information to be altering social, economic, and even political relations and conditions.

information and communication technologies (ICTs): the interconnected tools and technologies of the **infosphere** or **cybersphere**.

infosphere (see also **cybersphere**): the electronic space for the production, distribution, and consumption of information (data), including the **Internet** and other digital sites and services.

instructional technology: the study of the uses of various technological devices for teaching and learning.

intellectual property: the intangible products of creativity—including literature, music, artwork, photographs, movies, computer software, inventions, and medicines. Intellectual property is protected by intellectual property law, which includes copyright, patent, trademark, and publicity rights.

Internet: the global computing network, including the connected databases of the **World Wide Web** and the infrastructural components necessary for their access and interaction.

in-text citation: a method for citing a source within the text of an essay. Usually paired with a more complete reference on a works-cited list at the end of a paper. In-text citation formats vary according to the citation style used.

in vitro fertilization: a process in which a human embryo is "conceived" in the laboratory using the mother's ova (eggs) and the father's sperm. If fertilization is successful, the embryo is then placed in the womb of the mother or a surrogate mother to develop.

issue: in the academic community, a **topic** of concern within or across a field or fields. Scholars generally have a variety of perspectives on a given issue; this variety generates the academic conversation.

Keynesian economics: the economic theory following the principles of John Maynard Keynes, characterized by a belief in active government intervention in economic matters.

Kyoto Protocol: a treaty that limits **greenhouse gas** emissions in an effort to slow **global warming**. While the United States signed the treaty in 1998, the federal government has not ratified it.

law: the body of rules that make up the civil and criminal governance of a society; also, the field that studies those rules.

legal studies: an interdisciplinary field that examines the meanings, values, practices, and institutions of **law** and legality.

literary studies: the study and interpretation of **literature** (poetry, fiction, drama, and creative non-fiction).

literary theory: the large body of ideas and methods used to reveal possible meanings of literature and other texts.

literature: a written record of creative expression, e.g., poetry, fiction, drama, and creative non-fiction.

logos: a type of logical appeal that uses logical reasoning and **empirical evidence** to support a claim and persuade the reader.

ludology: a term recently proposed by game theorist Gonzalo Frasca to refer to the academic study of game and play activities.

mapping: a survey or forecasting of the points of argument an academic essay will address. The mapping section outlines, in complete sentences, the way in which the author will discuss the issue or problem.

Marxism: a theory and method for the study of and intervention into socioeconomic and political situations. It develops a materialist interpretation of history, emphasizing class conflict as the motor of historical development and change. Marxism calls for a working-class (proletarian) revolution to bring about a socialist (and eventually communist) society.

materials and methods: in a physical sciences article or lab report, this section describes how the experiment was conducted, a discussion that helps establish the validity of the results.

media: the means and content of large-scale publication and electronic transmission.

media revolution: a drastic change in existing media conditions. The theory of media revolution has been used to understand the introduction of the printing press and, more recently, the advent of digital media.

media studies: the study of mass media, in particular printed media, film, radio, television, and Web-based media.

medical science: a general term for the applied science of disease diagnosis, treatment, and prevention. The field includes health science, biomedical research, medical technology, and psychotherapy, among others.

meteorology: the academic study of atmospheric phenomena, including weather and **climate**.

mimesis: imitation or mimicry; a term used in zoology and biology to describe animal behavior, such as adaptive coloring. Also used in literary theory and philosophy to explain a reproduction of human thought patterns or "real life" in fiction and poetry. For Aristotle, true art was mimetic in that it involved the imitation and perfection of nature.

MLA (citation format): a format for documenting sources in a research paper or analysis that has been adopted by the Modern Language Association; used in literature, foreign languages, and other humanities disciplines.

Moore's Law: a maxim of computer scientist Gordon Moore, who predicted (with relative success) that computer processing capabilities double every two years, without an increase in price.

mortgage: an agreement between a lender and a borrower wherein the borrower secures a loan by transferring interest in a property to a lender. Home mortgage **defaults** were among the chief immediate factors giving rise to the financial crisis of 2008.

mortgage-backed security: a type of asset-backed security that is secured by a **mortgage** or collection of mortgages.

multiculturalism: the doctrine that cultural diversity is valuable to **pluralistic** society and that people from different cultures can coexist peacefully and in mutual appreciation. In education, multiculturalists work to introduce the histories and cultures of minority and non-Western groups into the curriculum.

nanorobots: microscopic machines measured on the scale of nanometers that some believe will be able to perform tasks at the atomic and cellular levels with precision and reproducibility. Nanorobots may be applied in the fields of **medical science**, **environmental science**, molecular manufacturing, electronics, and others. It is thought that nanorobots will have the ability to self-replicate.

nanoscience: the study of the fundamental principles of molecules and structures of 1 to 100 nanometers in size.

nanotechnology: the study of controlling matter on a scale of nanometers.

narrative: a sequence or structure of events created in written or oral works; a story. The term is also used to describe a **rhetorical** strategy in which the writer tells a story in order to advance his or her argument.

narrative perspective: the position from which a storyteller or essay writer tells a story or makes a statement. Includes first-person perspective (I said, I saw, I thought) and third-person **omniscient** perspective (she said, he thought, she saw, it was).

narratology: the academic study of the structure of a **narrative**, or story, in comparison with other narratives. Literary theorists have long used narratology to examine **literature**.

natural selection: the process by which traits that are more beneficial for the survival of an organism are preserved and passed down to the next generation. Natural selection is the mechanism of evolutionary change identified by Charles Darwin in *On the Origin of Species* (1859).

neurobiology: the area of study concerned with the anatomy and physiology of the nervous system.

neurology: the branch of biology that deals with the nervous system. The field's contributions to **cognitive science** are particularly important for understanding the brain.

omniscient voice: literally, the all-knowing voice; a **narrative** style that uses the third person **perspective** and in which the narrator has access to the words, actions, and thoughts of all the characters. A limited omniscient narrator has access to the words and actions of all the characters, but to the thoughts of only one or a few.

ontology: the study of the nature of existence or being; a branch of **philosophy**.

opinion: an appeal based on the writer's beliefs, values, and judgments rather than on data and more "objective" means of support.

organization (in writing): the structure of an essay; varies by academic division.

pablum: trite, naive, bland, or simplistic ideas.

parenthetical notation: an in-text citation style in which reference information (usually the publication's author and date) appears in parenthesis. Complete information on the publication appears in the reference list at the end of the essay.

participatory culture: a term suggesting that audiences of media actively participate in the making of media products, a phenomenon made possible by the introduction of digital media. Participatory culture is opposed to the characterization, inaugurated by the **Frankfurt School of critical theory**, of media audiences as passive, hapless consumers of mass culture.

pathos: a type of appeal that uses emotion to support a claim and persuade the reader.

pedagogy: the theories, beliefs, policies, and discourses related to education and teaching.

peer-reviewed: read and deemed worthy of publication by a group of scholars in a field that is the same or similar to that of the author. Articles in scholarly journals are generally reviewed anonymously by the author's peers.

pejorative: having a negative implication or meaning. A phrase can be said to be used pejoratively.

perception: the body's process of identifying, organizing, and interpreting information gathered from the senses.

perspective: see **narrative perspective**.

philosophy: the investigation of questions regarding being (**ontology**), proper behavior (**ethics**), and knowledge (**epistemology**).

physical therapy: a practice concerned with helping injured and disabled people to improve their bodies' mobility and reduce their pain through evaluation and physical intervention.

pluralism: the theory that a political body, philosophy, or culture can only be understood or considered complete when it consists of or includes more than one perspective, group, or substance.

point-by-point comparison, subject-by-subject comparison: see **alternating**.

political science: the study of governmental systems and practices, political processes and parties, and the relations between citizens and their governments.

postcolonial theory: an interdisciplinary approach of **postmodern theory** that studies and responds to the political, economic, and cultural legacies of colonialism.

posthumanism, posthumanist (also **transhumanism, transhumanist**): a philosophy that argues for the transcendence of human limitations by harnessing the power of science and technology to advantage. It is often based on the technologies available through **genetics, nanotechnology, and robotics (GNR)**, and **artificial intelligence**.

postmodernism: an artistic and intellectual trend of the late twentieth and early twenty-first centuries characterized by emphasis on the historical and local distinctiveness of experience, the supposed failure of comprehensive explanatory modes ("master narratives") such as **Marxism**, the juxtaposition of different, fragmented cultures and time periods in contemporary life, and an ironic attitude. Postmodernism has generally been a reaction to the rationalism of the **Enlightenment**.

preimplantation genetic diagnosis (PGD): procedures of scanning the genetic material of embryos created by **in vitro fertilization** for detecting genetic disorders and/or other genetic characteristics prior to the implantation of embryos in the womb.

Protestant Reformation: a major sixteenth-century European movement aimed initially at reforming the beliefs and practices of the Roman Catholic Church but which resulted in a major division of the Christian world into Catholicism and Protestantism.

pseudoscience: a belief, practice, or theory that appears scientific but lacks the rigorous methodology and testing procedures of legitimate science. Many theories considered scientific at the time are later viewed as pseudoscience.

psychoanalytic theory: a mode of analysis based on the model of the personality developed primarily in the work of Sigmund Freud and applied to many realms, including **literary studies**, **feminist** studies, and **gender studies**, among others. According to Freud, the personality is a complex of drives, the most important being the sex drive, as well as the mechanisms for inhibiting drives for the development of the well-adjusted (though generally unfulfilled) individual.

psychology: the study of the mental processes and behavior of individuals.

public policy: a guide to action taken by a local, state, national, or international governing branch, consistent with the laws and customs of the area it affects. Also an academic field that focuses on the ways in which governing bodies create guides to action, critiques both the guides and actions resulting from them, and researches ways to create guides that create effective and beneficial governmental organization and action.

qualifier(s): language added to a statement that specifies its limits.

racism: a belief in the intrinsic superiority of one race over another and the systematic means by which such a belief is institutionalized.

reasons (supporting a claim): the data, examples or logical analysis that back up a claim. A **thesis** is a **claim** with **reasons**.

rebuttal: a counterargument that challenges the validity of an argument.

research protocol: the organizing rules and guidelines of a particular study, or the rules and guidelines customary in studies of a certain kind.

reservation: in academic **essays**, a way of qualifying a thesis so that it allows for specific exceptions. A reservation holds the thesis to be true, but only when a condition is met or a factor is absent.

results: in social science and physical science, the data produced in a study. In a social science or physical science article, the Results section describes the data, which is also often presented in graphs and charts.

rhetorical, rhetoric: the methods a writer uses to persuade the reader of his or her argument. The elements of rhetoric include **ethos**, **pathos**, and **logos**.

robotics: a field concerned with the design and study of robots, or computerized machines. The field draws from many disciplines, including **computer science**, electrical and mechanical engineering, orthopedics, and **human-computer interaction (HCI)**, among others. Robotics consists of both software and hardware design and study.

second person (perspective): a narrative approach employing the second person (you), thereby directly addressing the reader. Epistolary novels (novels composed of letters) are written in the second person. The author of a scholarly article also might employ the second person as a way of engaging the reader or encouraging the reader's complicity.

secular: of or about the world as separate from religion, the spirit, or the sacred. Generally used to describe a political or social system or an educational institution not tied to religion or religious beliefs.

secularism: a political or social philosophy that avoids religion or faith-based practice. Also, the idea that civic activity should be carried out without regard to or intrusion from religion.

semantics: the study of the meaning of words, or the system by which words produce meaning.

sexism: the belief that one sex or gender is superior to another, and the systematic means by which this belief is institutionalized.

Singularity: coined in connection with technology by computer scientist and science fiction writer Vernor Vinge to mean the point beyond which life will be forever transformed by technology. The Singularity generally means that a greater than human intelligence will have been created using the tools of **GNR** and **artificial intelligence**.

Singulartarians: those who believe in and/or seek to hasten the emergence of the **Singularity**.

social agents: individuals thought capable of making choices and impacting their surroundings.

social construct: an object, belief, or identity thought to be the product of historically and socially contingent rather than natural or universal processes.

social constructionism (also **social constructivism**): the theory of social and cultural existence holding that social objects, beliefs, and identities are products of historically and socially contingent rather than natural or universal processes.

social environmentalism: the theory that human beings are the products of their social environments (nurture), more so than their inherent makeup (nature). A strict social environmentalism suggests that since beliefs are also the products of the social environment, a person cannot be held responsible for them.

social learning theory: developed by psychologist Albert Bandura in the mid-twentieth century, the theory that social behavior (the ways in which we act and interact with others) is learned primarily by observing and imitating the actions of others, and by being rewarded or punished for these actions.

socialism: the economic and political system based on the common ownership and control of the means of production and cooperative management for the distribution of resources.

sociobiology: the theory that social behavior can be explained in terms of evolutionary adaptation and survivability. Behavioral traits of species are seen as the results of **natural selection**.

sociology: the study of human behavior within groups and within society at large. Sociologists study social organization and trends and develop theories for understanding them.

somatic gene therapy: a genetic engineering technique or process that involves targeting the genes in the developed body in order to treat an inherited disease.

status quo: a Latin term literally meaning "the state in which," generally signifying the present or existing state of affairs, especially in connection with social and political conditions.

stimulus package: a roughly $800-billion bundle of spending measures initiated by President Barack Obama and approved by Congress in February 2009. The spending was designed to quickly jumpstart economic growth and save 900,000 to 2.3 million jobs.

summary: writing that restates and explains other writing (or movies, stage plays, etc.) in more concise and often clearer terms.

sustainability: in broad terms, the capacity to endure. From an environmental perspective, assuring sustainability requires the long-term, responsible maintenance of land, water, and air quality. **Ecologists** use the term to refer to the ways in which a biological system, such as a wetland or forest, thrives over time.

syntax: the structure or arrangement of words involved in meaning making, or the study of such structure or arrangement.

synthesis: as a writing practice, an assemblage of the views, perspectives or theories of a number of sources as a way of clarifying each element and seeing how each works in concert with or in opposition to the others.

synthesis grid: a graphic method for visualizing the **synthesis** of a number of writers/positions in a single unit, presenting the arguments made by a number of authors in a format that is easier to consult. A synthesis grid is generally arranged in a tabular format.

textual evidence: in academic writing, evidence gleaned from another text that is used to support a thesis or claim.

theology: the study of religious beliefs and the investigation of claims about the being and nature of God and God's relationship to and significance for human beings.

thesis: the central **argument** of an academic paper. Usually contains a number of claims that are supported by evidence, or **reasons**. All elements of a paper should work to support the thesis.

thesis statement: a short announcement of the point or **thesis** that a paper or speech will demonstrate.

third person (perspective): a narrative point of view that uses the third person (he, she, it) to discuss a subject or tell a story; it allows the writer to achieve a distance from the subject that may make the writer appear less involved in the **argument** or **narrative** and thus more reliable than a writer using the first person.

tone (in writing): a mood or attitude the writer takes toward his or her subject or audience. Tone also can be created by characters within a short story or novel.

topic: in academic writing, an area of discussion, or what a discussion is about.

trade: the exchange of commercial goods.

trade sanctions: the refusal to engage in trade, or limitations placed upon trade with another country; a strategy used by one government against another to censure that government for policies that the sanctioning country deems illegal, immoral, or destructive to citizens or the environment.

traditionalism: the strict adherence to tradition in cultural and/or religious matters.

transhumanism (also **posthumanism**): a philosophy based on the technologies of **genetics, nanotechnology, and robotics (GNR)**, and **artificial intelligence** that argues for the transcendence of human limitations by harnessing the power of science and technology to advantage. Transhumanism is also used to denote a philosophical field that examines the possibilities and ethics of such dramatic technological change as represented by GNR and artificial intelligence.

Web 2.0: a combination of Web technologies that allows for and encourages Web users to engage in a greater degree of interactive participation and interaction on the **World Wide Web**, as opposed to the technologies used for browsing information.

World Wide Web: an **Internet**-based system for the production, distribution, and consumption of information between distributed users and their servers by means of a client, browser, or other mode of access. The World Wide Web supports text, graphics, sound, video, and multimedia. With the inception of **Web 2.0**

technologies, the Web involves a greater degree of active participation, interoperability, and interaction between users than had been previously possible.

writing style: the particular manner of addressing a topic and argument that characterizes a given writer. Style may include **tone**, **diction**, figures of speech, **narrative perspective**, and numerous other elements.

zoology: the study of animal life. Zoology is divided into several subspecialties.

PERMISSIONS ACKNOWLEDGMENTS

Ahmed, Safdar. "'Father of No One's Son': Abu Ghraib and Torture in the Art of Ayad Alkadhi," from *Third Text* 25.3 (2011): 325-34. Reprinted by permission of the publisher, Taylor & Francis Ltd., http://www.tandfonline.com.

Appiah, Kwame Anthony. "Cosmopolitan Contamination," from *Cosmopolitanism: Ethics in a World of Strangers*. Copyright © 2006 by Kwame Anthony Appiah. Used by permission of W.W. Norton & Company, Inc.

Bailey, Ronald. "Transhumanism: The Most Dangerous Idea? Why Striving to Be More than Human Is Human," from *Reason*, 25 August 2004. Reprinted with the permission of *Reason Magazine* and Reason.com.

Barber, Benjamin R. "Jihad vs. McWorld." Originally published in *The Atlantic* 269 (3 March 1992): 53-65. Reprinted with the permission of Benjamin R. Barber.

Blythe, Mark, and Paul Cairns. "Critical Methods and User Generated Content: The iPhone on YouTube." *Proceedings of the 27th International Conference on Human Factors in Computing Systems*. Copyright © 2009, Association for Computing Machinery, Inc. Reprinted by permission. http://dl.acm.org/citation.cfm?id=1518923.

Bowie, Thomas G., Jr. "Memory and Meaning: The Need for Narrative: Reflections on the Symposium," from *War, Literature & the Arts: An International Journal of the Humanities* (2009): 22-33.

Burgess, Stephen R., Steven Paul Stermer, and Melinda C.R. Burgess. "Video Game Playing and Academic Performance in College Students." *College Student Journal* 46.2 (2012): 376-87. Reprinted with the permission of *College Student Journal*.

Carr, Nicholas. "Is Google Making Us Stupid?" *The Atlantic Magazine*, July-August 2008. Copyright © 2008, The Atlantic Media Company, as first published in *The Atlantic Magazine*. All rights reserved. Distributed by Tribune Content Agency, LLC.

Cowen, Tyler. "Trade between Cultures," from *Creative Destruction: How Globalization Is Changing the World's Cultures*. Copyright © 2002, Princeton University Press. Reprinted by permission of Princeton University Press.

Davidson, Cathy N. "I'll Count—You Take Care of the Gorilla," (Introduction) from *Now You See It: How the Brain Science of Attention Will Transform the Way We Live, Work, and Learn*, by Cathy N. Davidson. Copyright © 2011 by Cathy N. Davidson. Used by permission of Viking Penguin, a division of Penguin Group (USA) LLC.

Do, Yechan. "The Benefits or Detriments of Globalization." Reprinted with the permission of Yechan Do.

Farmer, Lesley S. "Are Girls Game? How School Libraries Can Provide Gender Equity in E-Gaming," from *Knowledge Quest* 40.1 (2011): 16-17. Reprinted with the permission of Dr. Lesley S. Farmer.

Ferguson, C.J. "A Further Plea for Caution Against Medical Professionals Overstating Video Game Violence Effects," from *Mayo Clinic Proceedings* 86.8 (2011): 820-21. Reprinted with permission from Elsevier.

Freie, John F., and Susan M. Behuniak. "Paulo Freire and ICTs: Liberatory Education Theory in a Digital Age," from *The International Journal of Technology, Knowledge and Society* 3.4 (2007): 53-61. Reprinted with the permission of Common Ground Publishing.

Friedman, Thomas L. "Come the Revolution," from *The New York Times*, 15 May 2012; copyright © 2012, The New York Times Company. All rights reserved. Used by permission and protected by the Copyright Laws of the United States. The printing, copying, redistribution, or retransmission of this Content without express written permission is prohibited.

INDEX

from the publisher

A name never says it all, but the word "broadview" expresses a good deal of the philosophy behind our company. We are open to a broad range of academic approaches and political viewpoints. We pay attention to the broad impact book publishing and book printing has in the wider world; we began using recycled stock more than a decade ago, and for some years now we have used 100% recycled paper for most titles. As a Canadian-based company we naturally publish a number of titles with a Canadian emphasis, but our publishing program overall is internationally oriented and broad-ranging. Our individual titles often appeal to a broad readership too; many are of interest as much to general readers as to academics and students.

Founded in 1985, Broadview remains a fully independent company owned by its shareholders—not an imprint or subsidiary of a larger multinational.

If you would like to find out more about Broadview and about the books we publish, please visit us at **www.broadviewpress.com**. And if you'd like to place an order through the site, we'd like to show our appreciation by extending a special discount to you: by entering the code below you will receive a 20% discount on purchases made through the Broadview website.

Discount code: **broadview20%**

Thank you for choosing Broadview.

Please note: this offer applies only to sales of bound books within the United States or Canada.

The interior of this book is printed on 30% recycled paper.